Computers and Information Processing

CONCEPTS AND APPLICATIONS

SIXTH EDITION

Computers and Information Processing

CONCEPTS AND APPLICATIONS

SIXTH EDITION

Steven L. Mandell
BOWLING GREEN STATE UNIVERSITY

WEST PUBLISHING COMPANY
ST. PAUL ◼ NEW YORK ◼ LOS ANGELES ◼ SAN FRANCISCO

Copy Editor: Ben Shriver
Illustrations: Randy Miyake
Composition: Parkwood Composition Service, Inc.
Cover Art: James Russell, courtesy Unisys Corporation
(Cover art is the design theme of the Unisys brochure ''OSI Options for You.'' Creative
director: Anne McCuen. Designer: Shannon Terry. Airbrush artist: James Russell.)

Photo credits appear following the Index.

WEST'S COMMITMENT TO THE ENVIRONMENT

In 1906, West Publishing Company began recycling materials left over from the production of
books. This began a tradition of efficient and responsible use of resources. Today, up to 95
percent of our legal books and 70 percent of our college texts are printed on recycled, acid-free
stock. West also recycles nearly 22 million pounds of scrap paper annually—the equivalent of
181,717 trees. Since the 1960s, West has devised ways to capture and recycle waste inks,
solvents, oils, and vapors created in the printing process. We also recycle plastics of all kinds,
wood, glass, corrugated cardboard, and batteries and have eliminated the use of Styrofoam book
packaging. We at West are proud of the longevity and the scope of our commitment to the
environment.

99 98 97 96 95 94 93 92   8 7 6 5 4 3 2 1

Library of Congress Cataloging-in-Publication Data

Mandell, Steven L.
    Computers and information processing, concepts and applications / Steven L. Mandell. —
6th ed.
        p.   cm.
    Includes index.
    ISBN 0-314-92964-9
    1. Electronic data processing.   2. Electronic digital computers.
I. Title
QA76.M27472   1992
004—dc20   91-44540
                                                   CIP

Contents

CHAPTER 3

Introduction to Information Systems   55

Hardware   81

Input and Output   107

CHAPTER 6

Storage Devices **133**

File Organization and Data Base Design   159   CHAPTER 7

Microcomputers   187   CHAPTER 8

CHAPTER 9	**Telecommunications and Networks**	**221**

CHAPTER 10	**System Software**	**251**

Software Development   **273**   CHAPTER 11

System Analysis and Design   355   CHAPTER 14

CHAPTER 15

Management Information Systems and Decision Support Systems 389

CHAPTER 16

The Impact of Computers on People and Organizations 411

Computer Security, Crime, Ethics, and the Law   435

CHAPTER 18

Computers in Our Lives: Today and Tomorrow

461

APPENDIX A

IBM PC and MS-DOS Operating System Commands

489

APPENDIX B

Macintosh Conventions and Commands

494

Application Software Supplement   A-1

Preface

COMPUTERS & INFORMATION PROCESSING, Sixth Edition marks an exciting departure from its earlier versions. Because of the fast changing market environment, a wide variety of courses exist. These courses differ in their emphasis on traditional topics, microcomputers, hands-on application software coverage, and programming. Because of this diversity in course offerings, a major attempt has been made to ensure that the Sixth Edition is sufficiently flexible to accommodate almost any course within this broad spectrum.

Toward this end, the book is offered in two versions:

■ A version with an expanded BASIC supplement.
■ A version which is language free.

Additionally, free supplemental manuals are available for Q-Basic and for Macintosh BASIC.

To provide even further flexibility, four separate application software manuals are available to accompany the text. These manuals provide hands-on experience for the following application software packages:

■ Word Perfect 5.1, Lotus 2.2, dBASE IV, VP Expert
■ Microsoft Works for the IBM
■ Microsoft Works for the Macintosh
■ PC Type, PC File, PC Calc

The revision work associated with the Sixth Edition has been challenging to say the least. Major developments and advances in information systems have occurred so rapidly that providing current examples is more difficult than ever before. Feedback from instructors using the text continued to provide an excellent source of ideas for making improvements. When it comes to improving content, nothing can replace the actual classroom testing of material. While prior editions of this text have been highly successful, a great deal of care went into updating and refining the latest edition. The result is a Sixth Edition textbook vastly improved in structure and substance.

New Features

Readers familiar with the fifth edition of the text will notice several changes incorporated into the Sixth Edition:

■ Updated and revised application software supplement. An entirely new section has been added which covers graphical user interface software in general and, more specifically, applications that are run under Windows 3.0.
■ New Articles and Highlights.
■ New and updated corporate applications.
■ Expanded coverage of business systems.
■ Reorganized and improved coverage of computer hardware.
■ Increased coverage of portable microcomputers.

- Increased coverage of microcomputer operating systems (including two new appendices).
- Increased coverage of Local Area Networks (LANs).
- Expanded chapter on programming with emphasis on program structure.
- Coverage of Arrays and Sorting has been included in the BASIC supplement.
- Updated coverage on the impact of computers in our society.

Chapter Structure

The most inspiring lectures on computers that I have had the good fortune to attend were presented by Rear Admiral Grace Hopper (Ret.), a leader in the development of early computers. In analyzing her material, which always seemed so interesting, it became apparent to me that she permitted no new concept to remain abstract. Rather, she described actual examples encouraging the listener to visualize their applications. Following Admiral Hopper's example, each chapter in this book is followed by an *Application* that shows how a corporation implements the concepts presented.

Several other important features are included within each chapter. The introductory section serves a dual purpose: as a transition between chapters and a preview of material. An *Article* with high interest appeal draws the student into the chapter. *Highlights* containing interesting computer applications or controversial topics are interspersed throughout the chapter to maintain reader interest. *Concept Summaries* enable students to review quickly the important key topics covered in the text. Chapter summary points, key terms, and review questions are also provided. A comprehensive glossary and index are placed at the end of the text.

Throughout the development of this book the emphasis has been on orienting material to students and assisting students in the learning process. Important concepts are never avoided regardless of their complexity. Many books on information processing emphasize one or two aspects of the subject—either informational relationships or computer capabilities. This book attempts to balance and blend both subjects.

Support Materials for the Instructor

The **Instructor's Manual** by Steven L. Mandell includes answers to review questions, discussion points, exercises and problems, a classroom administration section, enrichment lectures, complete testbank and additional Applications.

Westest 2.0—a computerized testing program for IBM PCs and compatible microcomputers or for the Macintosh.

Transparency acetates. Two and four-color acetates are available to qualified adopters.

Support Materials for the Student

In addition to the supplemental applications software and BASIC manuals, there is a **Student Study Guide** written by the author which includes a summary, review of key terms and definitions, and various self-testing formats for review of each chapter.

Acknowledgements

It is appropriate at this point to thank the following people who reviewed the book or provided invaluable comments based on their experience using the Fifth Edition of *Computers and Information Processing*.

Robert A. Barrett
Indiana University-Purdue at Fort Wayne

Alfred G. Borth
San Antonio College

Stephen Brown
Gannon University

Al Campbell, Jr.
Golden West College

Mary Curtis
Louisana State University

Vernon Griffin
Austin Community College

Sharon Hill
Prince George's Community College

John Konvalina
University of Nebraska at Omaha

Diane Krebs
Valparaiso University

James R. Walters
Pikes Peak Community College

Donald J. Weinshank
Michigan State University

Judy Yaeger
Western Michigan University

Of the individuals listed, above, I would like to give special recognition to Professor Donald J. Weinshank and the students of Computer Science 115 at Michigan State University for their suggestions.

In addition, the student feedback from this course had a significant impact on the new edition.

Many individuals and companies have been involved in the development of the material for this book. The corporations whose Applications appear in this book have provided invaluable assistance. Many professionals provided the assistance required for completion of a text of this magnitude: Russ Thompson and Sarah Basinger on chapter development; Meredith Flynn on the application manuals; Sue Baumann on the BASIC Supplement and instructor material; and Sally Oates on the manuscript preparation.

The design of the book is a tribute to the many talents of Ann Rudrud. Jan Lamar carefully guided the text through the development process. And, one final acknowledgment goes to my publisher and valued friend, Clyde Perlee, Jr., for his encouragement and ideas.

Steven L. Mandell

Computers and Information Processing

CONCEPTS AND APPLICATIONS

SIXTH EDITION

CHAPTER 1

Introduction to Information Processing

ARTICLE

EDS Speeds Chicago Parking Ticket Collection

Ellis Booker, *Computerworld*

CHICAGO—This city's backlogged parking ticket collection system, described by its own administrators as the worst in the nation, is being towed into the next century.

Electronic Data Systems Corp. (EDS), which began handling the data processing side of the ticket operation . . . as part of a five-year, $40 million contract, is also revamping the troubled computerized system, adding such state-of-the-art components as radio-frequency data terminals for crews in the city's "Denver boot" patrol trucks and equipping enforcement personnel with hand-held computers and portable printers.

However, the new system's most unique element will be an imaging subsystem that will permit on-line access to the 12,000 to 15,000 parking violations the city issues each day.

"Chicago's [parking system] is about the worst of any big city," city parking administrator Inge Fryklund said. She added that she has high hopes for the imaging portion of the system—the first of its kind in the country.

Chicago had plenty of incentive to try to leapfrog other cities. Its parking system reportedly has a backlog of hundreds of thousands of overdue tickets; $50 million worth of fines go uncollected each year.

The total cost of the old system, including the keypunch and trafficking personnel, was $13 million. "We'll be paying $8 million annually to EDS instead of $13 million," Fryklund said.

Chicago residents may also appreciate the swift justice the new system promises. Instead of the whopping six-month lag time between when a ticket is issued and when it is keypunched into the computer system, the EDS contract stipulates that tickets must be entered into the image database within three days.

To make that possible and to automate other functions of the new system, Chicago will shift to a new parking ticket form containing machine-readable codes. . . . The codes will enable the new system to generate detailed management reports showing city officials where tickets are being written, where parking meters are breaking down and which hydrants are attracting the most cars.

Until now, ticket information has been entered (or sometimes not entered) on 1957-vintage keypunch terminals—part of an old punch card system that was later converted to a batch tape system.

The image database, which will also contain correspondence from citizens, will be accessed from 14

Sun Microsystems, Inc. workstations at City Hall, the existing traffic court building and three remote locations around Chicago.

EDS replaces Computil Corp., a Clifton, N.J.-based service bureau that provided information systems services for the old system.

"The employees who were in data processing are being recycled into information processing clerks for the [ticket] hearing centers," said Michael McGowan, deputy director of revenue in charge of planning for the city of Chicago. McGowan said that no IS layoffs were caused by the outsourcing deal with EDS. "As a matter of fact, we're asking for a few more people," he said.

Next year, Chicago expects to issue about 4.5 million parking violations.

■ INTRODUCTION

CPU, RAM, ROM, hard copy, hard disk, modem, LAN, data base, laser printer, desktop publishing, bits, bytes: these are all terms that pertain to the ever-changing technology of computers. Computers are changing our language, our habits, our environment and, in general, our lives. No longer are computer experts the only people who interact with computers on a daily basis. In our current world nearly all of our lives are indirectly or directly affected by computers each and every day. For example:

■ You get cash after the bank is closed by using the (computer-based) automatic teller machine (ATM).

■ A scanner reads the coded price tags of your purchases at a department store to speed your shopping.

■ Your daily newspaper is transmitted via satellite to a printing facility thousands of miles away where it is printed using computer-controlled printing presses.

■ Your late model car contains a computer chip that controls such things as the fuel mixture, emissions, and anti-lock braking system.

■ While you are on vacation a pharmacist at a drug store you've never visited before consults a data base in order to fill your needed prescription.

Countless other examples of how computers affect our daily lives can be cited. This text, however, will focus primarily on how computer technology has impacted information processing in business. We will examine the past and present computer and information processing technologies and also speculate on what the future might hold in this dynamic area. This chapter will begin by presenting an overview of computers and information processing and then discussing the various classifications of computers. The chapter concludes with a brief overview of some of the more popular ways computer and information technology are currently being used.

■ COMPUTERS AND INFORMATION PROCESSING

Yesterday's **computers** were tools for scientists, mathematicians, and engineers. When computers became commercially available, only the largest businesses acquired them, often simply for the prestige of owning one. Today, many businesses and organizations own computers although they may have different types of computers and use them for many different purposes.

Two terms which are probably the most used in relation to computers are hardware and software. **Hardware,** the tangible parts of a computer, ranges from equipment that fills a large room to computers that fit on your lap. Hardware also includes **peripheral devices** that can be attached to the computer, such as a printer or a storage device. **Software** consists of the instructions given to the computer that enable it to do things, such as finding the best spot to drill for oil, or playing a competitive game of bridge. These computer instructions are also called **programs.**

Both hardware and software play a critical role in information processing; without them, information processing as we know it today would not be possible. The following section introduces information processing and provides the foundation for study of the remainder of this text.

■ INFORMATION PROCESSING: AN OVERVIEW

Many people use the terms **data processing** and **information processing** interchangeably, yet the two have a subtle difference in meaning. Data processing refers to the steps involved in collecting, manipulating, and distributing data to achieve certain goals. Data processing can be performed manually or electronically. Using computers for data processing is called **electronic data processing (EDP).** The term *data processing* historically has been used to mean EDP.

The objective of all data processing, whether manual or electronic, is the conversion of data into information that can be used in making decisions. The term *information processing,* then, includes all the steps involved in converting data into information: Thus it includes data processing as well as the process of converting data into information.

What is the difference between data and information? **Data** refers to raw facts collected from various sources, but not organized or defined in a meaningful way. Data cannot be used to make meaningful decisions. For example, a bank manager may have very little use for a daily list of the amounts of all checks and deposits from the branch offices. But once data is organized, it can provide useful information—perhaps in the form of a summary report giving the dollar value and total number of deposits and withdrawals at each branch. **Information,** then, is processed data that increases understanding and helps people make intelligent decisions (see Figure 1–1). To be useful, information must be accurate, timely, complete, concise, relevant, and in a form easily understood by the user. It must be delivered to the right person at the right time. If information fails to meet any of these requirements, it fails to meet the needs of those who must use it and is of little value.

Data Organization

Data must be organized before it can be processed effectively. For that reason, data items are placed in the following groups:

1. *Bit.* Data is represented by on and off states of the computer's electronic circuitry (see the section on Analog and Digital Computers that follows.) The symbols that represent on and off are the binary digits 0 and 1. Each 0 or 1 is called a **bit,** short for **bi**nary dig**it.** The bit is the smallest unit of data a computer can process.

2. *Character.* There are obviously more letters and numbers than two, but the computer only recognizes 0 and 1. Therefore, combinations of bits (0s and 1s) are used to represent **characters**—letters, digits, and special symbols such as %, #, or $. In the student name Kevin Miller, the characters are the letters, K, e, v, i, n, M, i, l, l, e, r, and one space. A fixed combination of adjacent bits that represents a character is called a **byte.** In our example, eight bits are used to represent a character. It just so happens that many computers are designed to accept eight-bit bytes.

3. *Field.* A university maintains specific data about its students, such as home address, social security number, major, courses, GPA, and so on. Each of these categories is called a **field.** A field is a collection of related characters that conveys a unit of information. Note that the size of a field depends upon the information placed in the field. For example, the field for names would need to be larger than the field for GPA (see Figure 1–2).

4. *Record.* A collection of fields that relate to a single unit is a **record.** A student record might consist of fields for student name, social security number, address, GPA, and major.

FIGURE 1–1

The Data Processing Flow

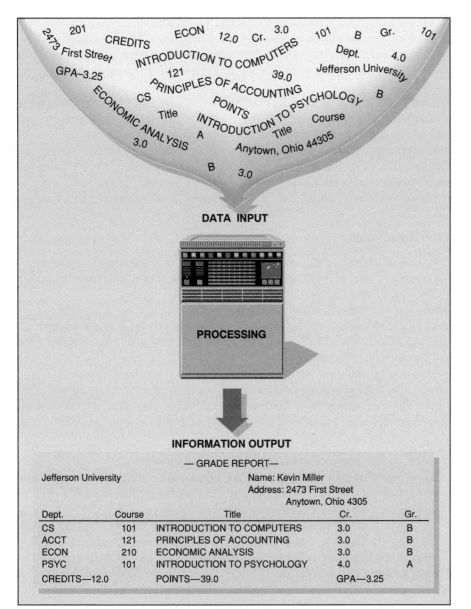

DATA INPUT

PROCESSING

INFORMATION OUTPUT

— GRADE REPORT —

Jefferson University

Name: Kevin Miller
Address: 2473 First Street
Anytown, Ohio 4305

Dept.	Course	Title	Cr.	Gr.
CS	101	INTRODUCTION TO COMPUTERS	3.0	B
ACCT	121	PRINCIPLES OF ACCOUNTING	3.0	B
ECON	210	ECONOMIC ANALYSIS	3.0	B
PSYC	101	INTRODUCTION TO PSYCHOLOGY	4.0	A
CREDITS—12.0		POINTS—39.0	GPA—3.25	

FIGURE 1–2

Organization of a Data Base

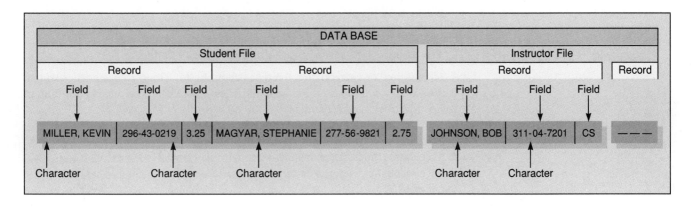

5. *File.* A grouping of related records is a **file.** All the student records for a university would constitute the university's student file. Many times different offices of a university will have their own separate files stored on the computer. For example, the housing office may have a set of files and the registration office may have a different set of files.

6. *Data base.* If each office in a university has its own set of files, the same piece of data may be stored in more than one place. For example, both the housing and registration offices would need a student's name and social security number. In order to eliminate this redundancy, a data base system can be used. A **data base** consolidates various independent files into one integrated unit. All users who need the information can access this one main file. In the above example both the registrar and the bursar would access the same student file to obtain a student's address and telephone number.

The Data Flow

In order to change data into information, data must be manipulated, or processed. All processing follows the same basic flow: input, processing, and output. Each step is described in detail below.

INPUT. Input is the process of capturing data and putting it in a form that the computer can "understand." Input includes both the data that is to be manipulated and the software to do that.

Data can be input into a computer by typing on a keyboard, using a scanning device such as the counter-mounted scanners found in grocery stores, speaking into a microphone connected to the computer, or running a magnetic tape or disk. Such devices are described in greater detail in Chapters 4 and 5.

Input involves three steps:

■ Collecting the raw data and assembling it at one location.
■ Verifying, or checking, the accuracy and completeness of data (facts). This step is very important since most computer errors are caused by human error.
■ Coding the data into a machine-readable form for processing.

PROCESSING. Once the data has been input, it is processed. **Processing** occurs in the part of the computer called the **central processing unit (CPU),** examined in Chapter 4. The CPU includes the circuitry needed for performing arithmetic and logical operations and **memory.** Memory is the internal area of the computer that holds programs and data used in immediate processing.

Once an instruction or data element is stored at a particular location in memory, it stays there until new data or instructions are written on top of it. This means the same data can be **accessed** repeatedly during processing, or the same instructions can be used repeatedly to process many different pieces of data.

Processing entails several types of manipulations (see Figure 1–3):

■ Classifying, or categorizing, the data according to certain characteristics so that it is meaningful to the user. For example, course data can be grouped according to student, instructor, or department.
■ Sorting, or arranging, the data alphabetically or numerically. A student file may be sorted by social security number or by last name.
■ Calculating the data arithmetically or logically. Examples include calculating students' grade point averages and testing to see if a student is eligible to be placed on the dean's list.

FIGURE 1–3

Processing Functions

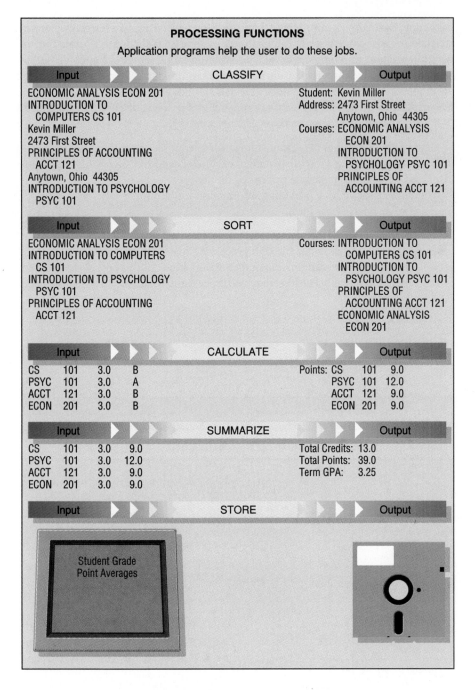

Summarizing data; that is, reducing it to concise, usable forms. All grades for all students in all classes can be summarized by grade point averages, naming those students who earn a place on the dean's list.

Storing, or retaining, data on storage media such as magnetic disks, tapes, or microfilm for later retrieval and processing.

OUTPUT. After data has been processed according to some or all of the steps above, information can be distributed to users. There are two types of **output:** soft copy and hard copy. **Soft copy** is information that is seen on a televisionlike screen or monitor attached to most computers. It is temporary; as soon as the monitor is turned off or new information is required, the old information vanishes. **Hard copy** is output printed in a tangible form such as on paper or microfilm. It can be read without using the computer and can be conveniently carried around, written on, or passed to other readers. Hardware that produces hard copy includes printers, discussed in Chapter 5.

The output phase of data flow consists of three steps:

■ Retrieving, or pulling, data from storage for use by the decision maker.

■ Converting data into a form that humans can understand and use (words or pictures displayed on a computer screen or printed on paper).

■ Communicating, that is providing information to the proper users at the proper time and in an appropriate form.

Information processing is monitored and evaluated in a step called **feedback.** Over time, the information provided through processing may lose its effectiveness. Feedback is the process of evaluating the output and making adjustments to the input or to the processing steps to ensure that the processing continues to result in good information.

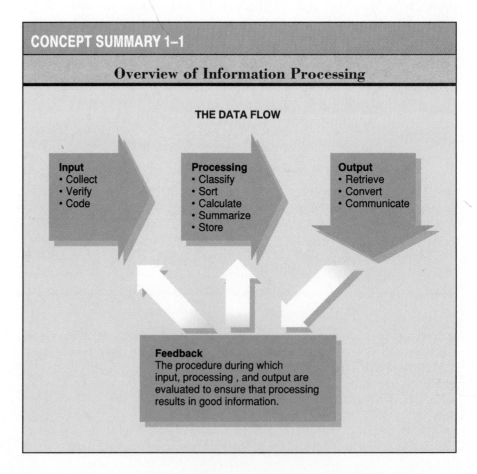

CONCEPT SUMMARY 1–1

Overview of Information Processing

THE DATA FLOW

Input
• Collect
• Verify
• Code

Processing
• Classify
• Sort
• Calculate
• Summarize
• Store

Output
• Retrieve
• Convert
• Communicate

Feedback
The procedure during which input, processing , and output are evaluated to ensure that processing results in good information.

Why Computers?

Within the limits of its circuits, a computer can perform three basic functions:

1. Arithmetic operations (addition, subtraction, multiplication, division).
2. Logical comparisons of values (greater than, less than, equal to).
3. Storage and retrieval operations.

If the three functions named above are all computers can do, then why have these machines become so widely used? Computers are useful because they are very fast, their circuits are reliable, and they can store vast amounts of data. In other words, computers are used because of their speed, accuracy, and storage capabilities.

SPEED. The speed of a computer is controlled by a number of physical factors. First, the switching speed of its electronic components, such as switching the state from on to off or switching the direction the current travels, affects the speed of the computer. A second factor is the distances that electric currents must travel within the circuits. By packing circuits closer together and increasing the switching speed, engineers have been able to increase the speed of computers vastly. Other factors that affect computer speeds are the **programming language** (that is, type of code) used in writing programs (see Chapter 12), the amount of data a computer can handle at one time, and the amount of data and instructions readily available in the computer's memory.

Modern computers can perform millions of instructions per second. This is why computer speeds are sometimes discussed in terms of millions of instructions per second (or MIPS). Their speed is fast reaching the physical limitation of the speed of light, 186,000 miles per second. Computer speed is also measured in terms of nanoseconds and other small units (see Figure 1–4). Today's processors can perform from 35 million to 150 million instructions per second.

ACCURACY. The accuracy of a computer refers to the inherent reliability of its electronic components. The same type of current passed through the same circuits yields the same results each time. We take advantage of this aspect of circuitry every time we switch on an electric device. When we turn on a light switch a light comes on, not a radio or a fan. The computer is reliable for the same reason—its circuitry is reliable. A computer can run for hours, days, and weeks at a time, giving accurate results for millions of activities. Of course, if the data or programs submitted to the computer are faulty, the computer will not produce correct results. The output will be useless and meaningless, illustrating the human error involved. This concept is called garbage in—garbage out (GIGO) and is fundamental in understanding computer "mistakes."

FIGURE 1–4

Divisions of a Second

Unit	Symbol	Fractions of a Second	
Millisecond	ms	one-thousandth	(1/1,000)
Microsecond	μs	one-millionth	(1/1,000,000)
Nanosecond	ns	one-billionth	(1/1,000,000,000)
Picosecond	ps	one-trillionth	(1/1,000,000,000,000)

FIGURE 1–5

Tape Storage

STORAGE. Besides being very fast and reliable, computers can store large amounts of data. Some data is held in memory for use during immediate operations. The amount of data held in memory varies among computers. Some small computers hold as few as 16,000 characters, whereas large computers can hold billions of characters. Data can also be recorded on magnetic disks and tapes (see Figure 1–5); this **storage** makes a computer's "memory" almost limitless. Storage holds data that is not immediately needed by the computer.

The ability of the computer to store, retrieve, and process data—all without human intervention—separates it from a simple calculator and gives it its power and appeal to humans. So while humans can perform the same functions as the computer, the difference is that the computer can reliably execute millions of instructions in a second and store the results in an almost unlimited memory.

CONCEPT SUMMARY 1–2

Computer Functions

■ The computer performs three functions: arithmetic operations, comparison operations, and storage and retrieval operations.

■ A computer's appeal is based on its speed, accuracy, and memory.

■ A computer's internal memory is called memory and media used to hold data outside the computer constitute storage. Storage makes the computer's memory almost limitless.

◼ COMPUTER CLASSIFICATIONS

Computers can be categorized in a number of ways. In general, computers fall into one of two categories—analog or digital. Digital computers, then, are normally cat-

Will Cars of the Future Drive Themselves?

Look out, Richard Petty! BMW is currently testing a computer system designed to take over the driving of a car if it detects that the car is being driven improperly. The Heading Control system being developed by BMW reacts to pictures sent to it by a camera mounted behind the car's rearview mirror. The computer system connected to the camera looks at pictures of the road ahead to determine how the driver is doing. The system checks the driver's performance by recognizing the center stripe and the edge line on the right-hand side of the road. The system is also capable of determining the weather conditions in which the car is being driven. If the driver gets too close to either the center stripe or the right shoulder, or if the car is not being driven properly given the current weather conditions, the computer will activate a small electric motor attached to the car's steering system. The electric motor will attempt to adjust for the driver's actions; however, the system can be overridden easily by the driver so no one will be taken on a nightmare ride by a malfunctioning computer.

Future versions of the Heading Control system will be able to recognize the difference between broken and solid lines. This will allow the system to determine if the driver is trying to cross a solid center line to pass. However, engineers at BMW believe that it will be up to five years before the system is built into cars sold to the general public. They are betting that the system will be extremely popular with drivers once they get used to it.

This and other computerized automotive systems currently in use and under development will, undoubtedly, make automobile travel much safer in the future. It's doubtful that Heading Control will increase your chances of driving a winner at Daytona, though, we admit.

egorized according to size, capability, price range, and speed of operation. However, it is becoming increasingly difficult to distinguish among the different classifications of computers. Today, smaller computers have increasingly larger memories and are able to connect to a greater number of peripheral devices such as printers and storage devices. In addition, the speed of smaller computers has increased dramatically since their introduction. The four common categories of digital computers are microcomputers, minicomputers, mainframes, and supercomputers. Before discussing these types, though, let us consider the most basic distinction of all.

Analog vs. Digital Computers

Computers are divided into two main types, analog computers and digital computers. **Analog computers** measure change in continuous physical or electrical states, such as pressure, temperature, voltage, length, volume, or shaft rotations. A speedometer is an example of an analog device. The computer measures the rotations of the driveshaft and then uses a pointer to indicate the speed of the car.

Unlike analog computers, **digital computers** count. In a digital computer, data is represented by discrete ''on'' and ''off'' (conducting/nonconducting or yes/no) states of the computer's electronic circuitry. Numbers, letters, and symbols are represented by a code based on the binary number system, a number system consisting of two digits, 1 and 0. This number system is well suited to represent the on/off states of electric current. The digital computer must convert all data to binary form. The computers discussed in this book are digital computers.

FIGURE 1–6

The Apple Macintosh IIsi
Microcomputer

Microcomputers

Once technology had advanced to the point where many circuits could be etched
onto a single silicon chip, the **microprocessor** was developed. A microprocessor is
a chip that contains the portions of the CPU that control the computer and perform
arithmetic and logic operations. It may also contain some memory. The microprocessor became the foundation for the **microcomputer,** also called the personal
computer.

Microcomputers are the most popular type of computer today. The demand for
microcomputers continues to increase. Even the stock market crash of October 1987,
did not have an adverse effect on the sales of microcomputers. In addition, the sale
of microcomputer software is greatly increasing.

The prefix *micro* applies more to size and cost than to capability. They may fit
on a desktop or in a briefcase (see Figure 1–6). Some microcomputers designed for
home use cost as little as $100, while microcomputers for professional use may cost
over $10,000. Yet current microcomputers are very powerful for their size. Micro-
computers cannot perform as many complex functions as today's large computers,
and they have much smaller memories; however, technology continues to give them
more speed and memory at decreasing costs.

Most microcomputers are single-user systems. As such they must be easy to
operate. One important aspect of microcomputer design involves the development
of user-friendly hardware and software; that is, equipment that is easy to learn and
easy to use. The concern for user friendliness has overflowed into the development
of other computers, too.

Microcomputers are available in computer stores, office supply stores, and department stores. In some cases, they are sold much as an appliance, like a television
or a videocassette recorder. Microcomputers often use **packaged software,** that is,
standardized software for solving a wide range of problems, but many users like the
challenge of developing their own and many businesses and custom-developed software. Chapter 8 provides a detailed discussion of microcomputers.

FIGURE 1–7

The DEC Microvax Minicomputer System
The VAX 4000 Family of Minicomputer Systems, from Digital Equipment Corporation

Minicomputers

Minicomputers were developed in the 1960s for doing specialized tasks. They were smaller, less powerful, and less expensive than the large computers available at the time. As they became increasingly sophisticated, their capabilities, memory size, and overall performance have overlapped those of mainframes. The more powerful minicomputers are called *superminis.*

Minicomputers are easier to install and operate than mainframe computers. They take up less floor space than mainframes; they may fit on a desk or they may be as large as a file cabinet (see Figure 1–7). They require few special environmental conditions. Minicomputers can be plugged into standard electrical outlets and often do not require facilities such as air conditioning and special platforms. Prices for minicomputers range from a few thousand dollars to two or three hundred thousand dollars.

Minicomputers are used for multiuser applications, numerical control of machine tools, industrial automation, and word processing. They are also used in conjunction with communication facilities for sharing data and peripherals or serving a geographically dispersed organization. Like microcomputers, they also can use packaged software.

A minicomputer system can easily be enlarged to meet the needs of a growing organization since it can be implemented in a modular fashion. For example, a hospital may install one minicomputer in its out-patient department for record keeping and another in the pharmacy or laboratory. As additional minicomputers are installed, they can be connected to existing ones to share common data.

In the late 1970s and early 1980s, the minicomputer industry grew at a rate of 35 to 40 percent annually. Today, the market for minicomputers is weakening. The increased capabilities and improved software of microcomputers has led to the increased use of micros in traditional minicomputer markets. Many companies now link microcomputers with mainframes or existing minicomputers to hold down equipment

FIGURE 1–8

The Unisys A-19 Mainframe
Computer System

investment costs and still meet processing needs. This practice, however, creates new security problems for many corporations.

Manufacturers of minicomputers include Digital Equipment Corporation (DEC), Hewlett-Packard, Data General, Honeywell, General Automation, Unisys, Texas Instruments, Wang Laboratories, Prime Computer Inc., and IBM.

Mainframes

During the 1960s, the term *mainframe* was synonymous with CPU. Today the word refers simply to a category of computers between the supercomputer and the minicomputer.

Mainframes operate at very high speeds and support main input and output devices that also operate at very high speeds. They can be subdivided into small, medium, and large systems. Most mainframes are manufactured as "families" of computers. A family consists of several mainframe models varying in size and power. An organization can purchase or lease a small system and, if processing needs expand, upgrade to a medium or large system. Purchase prices range from $200,000 to several million dollars for a large mainframe with peripherals. Mainframes are used chiefly by large businesses, hospitals, universities, and banks with large data processing needs (see Figure 1–8).

A mainframe requires special installation and maintenance procedures. It creates a fair amount of heat, so it requires a cooling system. A mainframe cannot be plugged into a standard electrical outlet; it needs special electrical wiring. It may rest on special platforms so that wires and cables can be housed beneath it. Furthermore, a mainframe runs day and night and provides access to a large amount of data. Because this access needs to be controlled, users must implement some type of security system. All these factors add to the cost of using a mainframe.

Mainframe computers are sold or leased and can include support from the vendor. The vendor can invest considerable time and money in helping a customer select and install a mainframe. Once the system is installed, the vendor spends additional effort

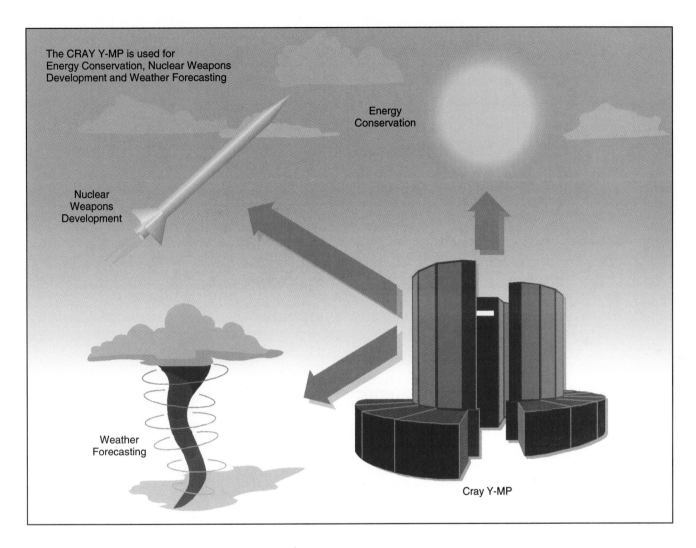

The CRAY Y-MP is used for
Energy Conservation, Nuclear Weapons
Development and Weather Forecasting

Energy
Conservation

Nuclear
Weapons
Development

Weather
Forecasting

Cray Y-MP

training the customer's employees from top executives to clerical workers to use the
system, servicing and repairing the mainframe, and solving questions and problems
that arise periodically. Major mainframe manufacturers are IBM, Unisys, Honeywell,
and National Cash Register (NCR).

Supercomputers

Supercomputers are the largest, fastest, and most expensive computers made (see
Figure 1–9). Some supercomputers have as many as eight central processing units.
Manufacturers of supercomputers claim they will soon produce supercomputers that
can execute more than one billion instructions per second. The computers are so fast
that their chips must be surrounded by a liquid coolant to prevent melting. As for
price, the newest supercomputers cost as much as $20 million.

Supercomputers are used for figuring lengthy and complex calculations. Scientists
use them in weather forecasting, oil exploration, energy conservation, seismology,
nuclear reactor safety analysis, and cryptography. In addition, supercomputers are
used for simulations in nuclear energy research and for stress tests in automotive and
aircraft design.

FIGURE 1–9

The Cray Y-MP Supercomputer
System

Most organizations have no need for supercomputers, nor can they justify the large cost of the hardware and software. Software development for supercomputers is much more complex and expensive because the design of the machines is so different from the design of less powerful computers. Still, the demand for supercomputers is increasing. In 1980, there were only 21 supercomputers in the world. Today, hundreds of supercomputers are busy crunching numbers, and the appetite for them seems insatiable. Even universities are beginning to install supercomputers for their extensive research projects.

Research in supercomputer development has become a heated race between the United States and Japan. Whoever develops and commercializes the technology that improves supercomputers will have the competitive edge in all computer-related industries—an important consideration for both economics and national defense. Companies developing supercomputers include Cray Research, Fujitsu, ETA Systems, Inc., and Evans and Sutherland. Scientific Computer Systems Corporation and Supertek Computers, Inc., are producing what they call mini supercomputers. These manufacturers hope to capture the market for products between regular supercomputers and mainframes.

CONCEPT SUMMARY 1–3

Factors to Consider in Buying a Computer System

	Micro-Computer	Mini-Computer	Mainframe	Super-Computer
Cost	$100 to $10,000	A few thousand to two or three hundred thousand dollars	$200,000 to several million dollars	Several million dollars
Other facts	Can fit on desk or lap. Many applications. Can be linked to mainframes or minicomputers. Newer computers and software are user-friendly.	Fits in small space. Uses standard electrical outlets. Often needs no air conditioning. Expandable in modular fashion. Micros rapidly approaching minicomputer capabilities.	Additional costs: platforms, security, wiring, air conditioning. Vendor support. Easily upgraded to next size in family.	Largest, fastest computer. Good for complex, lengthy calculations. Hard to justify costs. Software development complex.

◼ USING COMPUTERS IN TODAY'S SOCIETY

Early computers were tools used by scientists, mathematicians, and engineers. Because of their initial cost and the costs associated with maintaining them, these computers were economically feasible for only very large corporations. Today's computers are quite different. As a result of their cost, small computers are accessible to nearly every member of our society. Because computers are so available to so many different kinds of people, they touch our lives, indirectly or directly, in countless ways. The remainder of the chapter provides a glimpse of just a few of the ways computers are used today.

Computers in Business

Hardly a day goes by when we do not make a computer-controlled business transaction. Each time we visit the bank, use a credit card, pay a bill, or buy groceries, a computer lurks behind the scene, recording each transaction. Computers can process data in a fraction of the time it would take to perform the same jobs manually. They reduce the paperwork involved in these transactions and also reduce costs.

Computers in business provide many services. Airlines, travel agencies, and hotels use extensive networks of computer equipment for scheduling reservations. The computers in branches of a business across the country from one another can be connected by communication lines. Businesses use computers for sharing data, preparing documents, sending messages, and performing clerical duties. Since computers can work very fast, handle large amounts of data, and provide results exactly when needed, they are almost indispensable in areas of business such as banking, construction and manufacturing, and sales.

BANKING. In banking, a huge number of documents related to transactions must be processed daily. Some of the types of documents that must be processed by a bank include personal and business checks, deposit and withdrawal slips, credit card slips, and stock purchase and sales tickets. The balances of all accounts affected by these documents must be kept up to date. Computers and their related technologies are used extensively by the banking industry to do all this work.

The majority of banks today also offer automated services such as direct deposit of payroll checks, automatic payment of bills, electronic funds transfer, home banking using a personal computer, and 24-hour access to accounts through automatic teller machines (ATMs). These services are all a direct result of computer technology and its impact on the banking industry. One of the significant impacts that computer technology has had in the banking industry is in the efficient processing of checks. Check-digitizing equipment has helped the banking industry process 50 to 100 billion checks annually at 20 to 30 percent greater efficiency than in the past (see Figure 1–10).

FIGURE 1–10

A Unisys Check Digitizing Scanner

FIGURE 1–11

An electrical test system checks the on-board computers and wiring of the Buick Reatta in a GM assembly plant.

FIGURE 1–12

A Computerized Numerical Control Machining Center
The Sabre 1250 uses 21 different tools to sculpt metal by milling, drilling, tapping, and boring and is capable of accuracies as high as 1/10,000".

CONSTRUCTION. In construction, computers have also had a significant impact. Computer-aided design has dramatically improved the way in which buildings and other structures are designed. Architectural and engineering firms are now using computers to produce detailed building designs, of interiors as well as exteriors. In some cases, the computer-aided design system is capable of creating an animated, visual ''walk'' through a proposed building design in order to provide a client with a vivid picture of its future interior.

MANUFACTURING. In manufacturing, computers have greatly improved productivity. Computer-controlled robots are used extensively in the auto industry during the manufacturing of a car (see Figure 1–11). Engineers use computers not only to draw plans for products and to design machines to build the products, but to design machines to build the machines that build the products. During the manufacturing process, computers are used in controlling the operation of the machinery (see Figure 1–12). Computers are also used to test prototypes of products, whether car seats, lenses in sunglasses, sport shoes, or practically any product you can name. Major computer manufacturers even use computers to design and build better computers.

SALES. Computers have provided a competitive advantage to those companies whose sales forces use them effectively. Some insurance companies have chosen to provide small portable computers to their agents. This allows the agent to take the computer into a potential client's home and provide quick and accurate rate proposals as well as offer tangible financial planning services (see Figure 1–13).

A shirt company has elected to give portable computers to the members of its sales force. The machines speed order processing and reduce costly errors in the ordering process. Formerly, the sales-person had to manually write orders dealing with 42,000 shirt designs including color and size selections. Mistakes in orders were common and costly. Now with the automated system on the portable computer, the salesperson only needs to select choices from lists displayed on the computer screen.

FIGURE 1–13

A Compaq LTE/286 Laptop
Microcomputer

Once orders are entered into the system, they are transmitted to company headquarters by the salesperson's computer and loaded onto the company's mainframe computer for processing.

In addition to the specific business applications discussed, computers have had a dramatic affect on typical functions performed in nearly all businesses. Almost every office function—typing, filing, communications, all of it—can be automated. The term applied to the integration of computer and communication technology with traditional office procedures is **office automation.** Among the specific applications in office automation are word processing, information retrieval, electronic mail including facsimiles and voice mail, teleconferencing, and telecommuting. Office automation will be discussed in greater detail in Chapter 16.

Computers in Arts and Entertainment

Computer technology has been employed in almost all areas of arts and entertainment. In music, the technology has allowed single instruments to synthesize (or simulate) any number of other instruments. For example, the Roland E-20 Intelligent Synthesizer (see Figure 1–14) is capable of producing sounds like telephones ringing, trumpets, base drums, and even a guitar.

FIGURE 1–14

The Roland E-30 Intelligent
Synthesizer

Automated Rent-A-Car

National Car Rental System, Inc. and Budget Rent-A-Car are now using ATM-like machines to rent cars to customers. National Car Rental has chosen to place these automated car rental booths mostly in airports, where customers can get frustrated waiting in long lines simply to sign a prearranged car rental contract. Budget is installing its automated rental booths at shopping malls throughout the United States and Canada.

The Smart Key system used by National Car Rental provides the customer with an up-to-the-minute list of cars available at the user's location. The customer is provided with this list by simply inserting a National credit card into the car rental machine. Once the car is selected, the system prints a receipt providing the details of the transaction and passes out a set of keys for the car. The customer can then pro-

ceed directly to the parking spot, get the car, and drive off.

The Smart Key II system is slightly different from the original Smart Key systems in that it does not give the user the keys to the car at the same time it gives out the transaction receipt. Once the user has the receipt, he or she goes to the lot where the car is parked, gets in, and drives to a check-out booth. (The cars are parked in secure lots where the keys can be left in the ignition.) The only time the user must come in contact with another human being is upon leaving the parking lot at the airport. At that time an attendant verifies that the receipt and the car taken by the renter are in agreement.

The Budget Rent-A-Car system allows a customer to connect to a central reservation desk through a telephone at an automated rental booth. The customer inserts a credit card into a magnetic stripe reader

and a contract is printed out. A reservation clerk at the central desk provides directions on how to complete the contract. The clerk then verifies that the contract has been signed and that the renter has a valid driver's license by looking at a video monitor connected to both the rental booth and the central reservation desk. Once the contract and driver's license have been verified, a carousel at the booth hands out the appropriate set of keys. The average time required to complete a rental transaction using the Budget system is five minutes.

With the success of ATM machines in the banking industry, it is likely that we'll see more and more types of businesses taking advantage of ATM-like technologies in the near future.

In photography, computers are being used to touch up photographs, to restore old photographs, and in some cases even to create photographs. Many experts believe, however, that the ability to alter and create photographs may lead to ethical problems.

In making feature films, computers have been used for a number of years to produce extremely realistic special effects. The *Star Wars* trilogy, for example, relied heavily on computer-generated special effects. Computer-generated animation is also making its mark in the entertainment industry. *Jetsons: The Movie* and *Who Framed Roger Rabbit?* are feature films that have relied on computer technology to produce success at the box office.

Computers in Education

Computers have, over the years, gained wider acceptance as an educational tool. Today, computers are used not only for learning about computers but are used to aid in teaching other subjects as well. They have proven to be an extremely effective teaching tool.

Computer-based training (or CBT) is one of the more popular ways of using the computer in education. Applications of this technology range from teaching six year

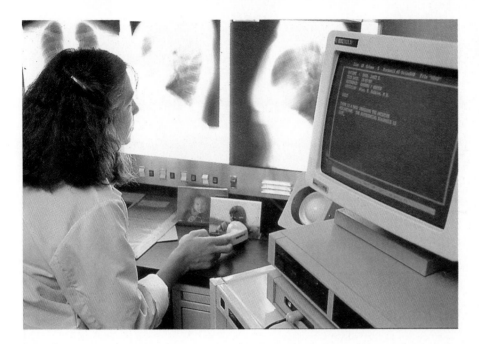

FIGURE 1–15

A Kurzweil Voice RAD system for use by physicians

old students basic math skills to providing in-depth instruction on sophisticated computer programming languages. In most cases, the student uses the computer to interact with a special software employed to teach the particular subject matter.

The ultimate in the use of computers in education is referred to as multimedia. Multimedia essentially combines text, audio and video, and graphics to create an integrated educational system. An example of such a system might be a multimedia presentation on how to assemble a personal computer. A text could be provided to the student, offering a detailed explanation of how to assemble the computer. In addition, a video (including audio) demonstrating the process would be part of the curriculum. The multimedia package might also include a CBT module to interactively test the student and provide additional instruction as needed. The video and CBT portions of the instruction would be computer based while the text would serve as a reference for the student.

Computers in Medicine

Computers have also had a tremendous impact on the field of medicine. One area especially where computers have made a significant difference is in producing physician reports. One hospital uses a system that employs voice-recognition units (see Figure 1–15) and a data base of descriptive paragraphs to aid doctors in producing a report for each patient examined. The system matches key words or phrases spoken by the doctor to the descriptive paragraphs stored in the data base. When the doctor finishes speaking, a one- or two-page report is generated from the descriptive paragraphs selected. This allows the doctor to produce the report in one to two minutes, as compared to the much longer time required to hand write a report of that length.

Computer technology is also being used in hospitals to closely monitor the critically ill. Monitoring devices attached to the patients in an intensive care unit, for example, are electronically monitored and allow nurses to more effectively track the status of patients (see Figure 1–16). Bedside portable computers are also being used by nurses

FIGURE 1–16

ICU Monitoring Devices

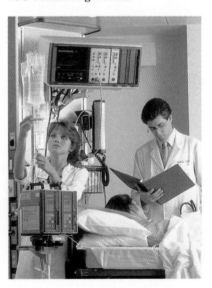

FIGURE 1–17

A Typical Emergency 9-1-1 System

to record patients' vital signs. This system eliminates a large amount of the paperwork a nurse normally has to fill out and allows a nurse to have more time for patient care.

Computers in Government

The federal government is the largest user of computers in the United States. This fact is not surprising considering the many government agencies that collect, process, and store information about the population. Typical examples are taking the U.S. census every ten years, processing the millions of income tax returns received each year, maintaining the large data bases in the Library of Congress and Federal Bureau of Investigation, and managing the welfare and social security systems.

Local governmental agencies are also using computers to improve their services. In Chicago, a new computerized parking ticket system will be saving $5 million dollars per year (including the cost of the new system) in comparison to the cost of the old system. Many communities have also implemented emergency 9-1-1 systems to provide better responses to emergencies (see Figure 1–17).

▢ SUMMARY POINTS

■ Electronic data processing, often simply called data processing, involves the use of computers in collecting, manipulating, and distributing data to achieve goals. The terms *hardware* and *software* describe the physical components of a computer and the instructions or programs used in electronic data processing.

■ Data refers to unorganized, raw facts, whereas information is data that has been organized and processed so that it can be used in making intelligent decisions.

■ For effective data processing, data is organized in meaningful units. The units, from smallest to largest, are bit, character (or byte), field, record, file, and data base.

- Converting data into information follows this pattern: input, processing, output.
- Input involves collecting, verifying, and coding data.
- Processing involves classifying, sorting, calculating, summarizing, and storing data.
- Information retrieved and converted so that it can be communicated to the user in an intelligible form is output.
- The computer performs three functions: arithmetic operations, logic comparisons, and storage and retrieval operations.
- The computer's appeal is based on its speed, accuracy, and memory.
- Analog computers measure the change in continuous physical and electric states, while digital computers count data in the form of yes/no, on/off, conducting/non-conducting states of electronic circuitry. The digital computer must convert all data to binary form, which is based on the binary number system of two digits, 0 and 1.
- The area inside the computer where data and instructions are stored during processing is called memory. Media used to hold data outside the computer constitute storage. Storage makes the computer's memory almost limitless.
- Computers are categorized by size, capability, price range, and speed of operation. The four classifications are supercomputer, mainframe, minicomputer, and microcomputer.
- Advances in technology have blurred the distinctions between the classifications of computers, to the point where some minicomputers have capabilities as great as mainframes and some microcomputers have capabilities as great as minicomputers.
- Many companies are linking microcomputers to existing systems so as to increase capabilities yet hold down costs.
- Current computer technology allows the banking industry to process extremely large amounts of documents in a more efficient fashion than in previous years.
- Computers allow banks to provide such services as direct deposit payroll, automatic payment of bills, electronic funds transfer, home banking, and 24-hour ATMs.
- Computers are helping architects to design buildings and even to simulate what the proposed interior of the building will look like.
- Computers are used in the auto industry to improve quality and to increase efficiency.
- Portable computers are being used efficiently in selling services and products to customers.
- Computers used to perform every-day business functions such as typing, filing, and communications comprise what is known as office automation.
- Computers have had a dramatic impact in the area of musical instrument sound synthesis.
- Special effects in feature films have been greatly enhanced through the use of computers.
- Computer-based training (CBT) and multimedia have become important instructional tools used by educators.
- Voice recognition units in combination with a data base of descriptive paragraphs act to automatically prepare emergency room reports for doctors.

❏ TERMS FOR REVIEW

accessed, p. 6

analog computers, p. 11

bit (binary digit), p. 4

byte, p. 4

central processing unit (CPU), p. 6

characters, p. 4

■ REVIEW QUESTIONS

1. How does data differ from information? Give examples of both data and information.

2. What is the objective of data processing? What is the objective of electronic data processing (EDP)?

3. What is hardware? What is software?

4. How does a file differ from a data base? What type of data element is a file composed of?

5. What steps comprise the data flow?

6. Why is processing an important part of the data flow? In what part of the computer does processing take place?

7. What is hard copy? What is soft copy? What data processing step produces hard and soft copy?

8. What operations are computers capable of performing? Give a brief explanation of each of these operations.

9. How do analog computers differ from digital computers? Why do you feel digital computers are used for electronic data processing instead of analog computers?

10. When categorizing digital computers according to size, capability, price, and speed, what categories are most commonly used? Why has it become increasingly difficult to fit a particular computer into a category?

APPLICATION

Texas Instruments

Texas Instruments began in 1930 as Geophysical Service—later known as Geophysical Service Inc. (GSI)—to provide geophysical exploration services to the petroleum industry. During World War II, GSI manufactured electronic equipment for the U.S. Navy. In 1946, GSI formally added electronic systems manufacturing to its operations. In 1951, the company adopted its current name, Texas Instruments Incorporated (TI), and the following year entered the semiconductor business—the most significant event in its history.

TI's position as a world leader in electronics is founded on a long tradition of transforming technological ideas into useful products and services. TI "firsts" include the commercial pocket radio, the commercial silicon transistor, the integrated circuit, the terrain-following airborne radar, the hand-held calculator, the single chip microcomputer, and the single-chip artificial intelligence microprocessor or LISP chip. These and other innovations give TI a technological base that spans materials, components, systems, and software.

TI'S BUSINESSES
TI has its headquarters in Dallas, Texas. It has manufacturing operations in more than 50 facilities in 18 countries and sales offices and service centers throughout the world. TI has annual revenues of approximately $6.5 billion and employs more than 60,000 people. Semiconductors are TI's principal business, as well as the technological foundation for the rest of the company.

The company's business mix is well balanced between components—principally semiconductors—and electronic systems. Defense electronics is TI's largest electronic systems business, currently representing about one-third of TI's billings. TI also manufactures semiconductors for military use as well as for a wide variety of other uses, including automotive systems and instrumentation for medical and industrial markets. The company is one of the world market leaders in the computer-aided software engineering (CASE) market. Its integrated CASE product, the Information Engineering Facility™ (IEF™) is used by over 500 corporations and institutions worldwide. IEF™ is a set of software tools which allows programmers to automatically generate error-free code for large information systems. The company also manufactures business computer systems and peripherals such as printers, notebook computers, and portable computer terminals. TI's materials and controls business is based on the technology of bonding two or more dissimilar metals together. Discs made from these metals are used to sense and control temperature, pressure, and electrical current in many products. The consumer products business is concentrated on calculators and electronic educational products for developing skills in spelling, math, reading, and music.

TI'S TECHNOLOGIES AND NETWORKS
Each business of TI is built upon a technological base and worldwide support. Because of its global operations, TI uses a high degree of computer-aided manufacturing (CAM) and computer-aided software engineering in the manufacturing, business, planning, and financial application areas. Some of the functions encompassed in these large information and manufacturing systems are factory scheduling; inventory management, tracking, and valuation; order processing and quotation; product availability; demand forecasting; cost management; and financial reporting.

TI's network enables customers in Europe and Asia to design their products at technical centers a continent away.

Since 1969, TI has been using the concept of electronic data interchange (EDI) to facilitate its operations. EDI helps TI integrate its customers and systems by electronically exchanging the documents normally used for conducting business. The documents (or transaction sets) follow industry standard formats. They are used for placing orders, forecasting, transportation tracking through advance shipping notices, invoicing, remittance, test data for quality control, and receiving. TI has found that EDI has

APPLICATION
Texas Instruments

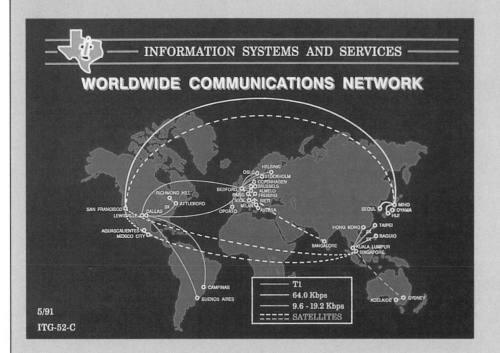

improved the accuracy and quality of data because the system eliminates the rekeying of data often needed when paper documents are used. EDI has also reduced costs and has improved the cycle time from order to delivery. The company is currently using EDI with over 1,000 other companies.

To conduct all of its operations efficiently, Texas Instruments has implemented one of the most sophisticated private computer networks in the world to support corporate communication and control. The integrated network includes 75,169 workstation/terminals, 3,300 minicomputers, and 22 large mainframe computers. The mainframe computers alone handle about 5 million daily requests for information through regional hubs in Singapore, Bedford (U.K.), Dallas, and Miho (Japan).

One of TI's most innovative and strategic uses of the network is connecting the 15 advanced software develop-

ment and semiconductor design facilities located in strategic markets. This network enables customers in Europe and Asia to design their products at technical centers a continent away. Software is distributed worldwide on more than 300 computers linked in about 35 local area networks. Therefore the same software development tools can be used in any design centers in the world.

DISCUSSION POINTS
1. Relate TI's contributions to technology to the concept of information processing.
2. How has TI dealt with the input stage of data processing?
3. Discuss how TI's operations demonstrate the speed, accuracy, and storage capabilities of computers.

CHAPTER 2

The Evolution of Computers

Micro Chip Patent Rewrites History

Maura J. Harrington, *Computerworld*

A California engineer staked claim last week to inventing the single-chip microcomputer. But although a patent granted in July was first claimed in 1970 and predates all other microcomputer patents, the stir it made in Silicon Valley is unlikely to be felt soon—if ever—by computer users, observers said.

Gilbert Hyatt claimed that the impact of his patent is broad and covers anything that includes a CPU and an input/output device.

However, analysts and patent lawyers agreed that the short-term impact on end users is virtually nil and that red tape in the U.S. Patent Office and court system could tie up the case for years before anything comes of Hyatt's 20-year-old invention.

Hyatt indicated that he would be attempting to gain royalty payments from semiconductor vendors that he said infringe on his patent. "I don't think there's going to be litigation with any other vendors regarding this patent, because the patent is very broad and very strong, and we're ready to go into negotiations with a major electronics corporation on a joint venture for this," he said.

Hyatt received a patent numbered 4,942,516 on July 17, 1990, for his "computer on a chip"—a microcomputer having a CPU, operand memory and read-only memory on one integrated circuit chip. The claim was filed in December 1970 for work dating back to 1968.

"If the patent was valid and infringed and asserted, it could affect all microprocessors made or developed since the patent was filed," said attorney Gary Hecker, a partner at Los Angeles-based Hecker & Harriman who specializes in patent protection cases of computer hardware and software.

Though he is not directly involved in the Hyatt case, Hecker said that because of the complexity of the case, it is unlikely that end users or chip vendors will be affected by the patent in the near future.

"This was an extraordinary, lengthy and exhausted patent process," Hecker said. "Typically, a filing process would be from two to five years, not 20. So the interpretation, scope and validity of those claims can't be assessed until this lengthy file can be examined, which I guess will begin fairly soon and last up to several years."

However, analyst Andrew Seybold in Santa Clara, Calif., and publisher of "The Outlook On Professional Computing," said that even if Hyatt were to receive modest royalties from chip manufacturers, that "would make him a very wealthy man."

While Hyatt said he will have minimal trouble in collecting what he feels are moderate and fair royalties, some analysts disagreed. "Pennies per chip has virtually no impact on the end user, but if I were any of these companies, I'd look at this carefully, and if I thought it was unfair—no matter how small the fee— I'd pursue legal action," Seybold said.

Microcomputer chip manufacturers, most of whom admitted to being taken by surprise by Hyatt's patent award, reacted with caution, saying their lawyers were studying the patents.

■ INTRODUCTION

Although the computer is a relatively recent innovation, its development rests on centuries of research, thought, and discovery. Advances in information-processing technology are responses to the growing need to find better, faster, cheaper, and more reliable methods of handling data. The search for better ways to store and process data is not new. Data-processing equipment has gone through generations of change and improvement. An understanding of the evolution of data processing is especially helpful in understanding the capabilities and limitations of modern computers.

This chapter presents a discussion of significant people and events that led to the development of the modern computer. Each of the four computer generations is described. Additionally, an overview of the computer industry, including both the hardware and software industries, is presented. The chapter concludes with a discussion of the revolution in computing that has been wrought by the microcomputer.

■ THE TECHNOLOGY RACE

True electronic computers entered the technological revolution less than fifty years ago. They can be traced through a long line of calculating and recording methods that began with tying knots in pieces of rope to keep track of livestock and carving marks on clay or stone tablets to record transactions.

Later, the **abacus,** a device made of beads strung on wires, was used for adding and subtracting (see Figure 2–1). The abacus, along with hand calculations, was adequate for computation until the early 1600s when John Napier designed a portable multiplication tool called **Napier's Bones,** or Napier's rods. The user slid the ivory rods up to figure multiplication and division problems. Napier's idea led to the invention of the slide rule in the mid-1600s.

These tools were anything but automatic. As business became more complicated and tax systems expanded, people needed faster, more accurate aids for computation and record-keeping. The idea for the first mechanical calculating machine grew out

FIGURE 2–1

The Abacus
The abacus is still used by some Chinese as the primary calculating device. It is also a popular desk accessory and educational toy.

FIGURE 2–2

Blaise Pascal and the Pascaline
The Pascaline worked very well for addition, but subtraction was performed by a roundabout adding method.

of the many tedious hours a father and his son spent preparing tax reports. Once this machine was introduced, the way was opened for more complex machines as inventors built upon each succeeding development. The race for automation was on.

Early Developments

In the mid-1600s, Blaise Pascal, a mathematician and philosopher, and his father, a tax official, were compiling tax reports for the French government in Paris. As they agonized over the columns of figures, Pascal decided to build a machine that would do the job much faster and more accurately. His machine, the **Pascaline,** could add and subtract (see Figure 2–2). The Pascaline functioned by a series of eight rotating gears, much as an odometer keeps track of a car's mileage. But the market for the Pascaline never grew. Clerks and accountants would not use it. They were afraid it might replace them on their jobs and thought it could be rigged, like a scale or a roulette wheel.

About fifty years later, in 1694, the German mathematician Gottfried Wilhelm von Leibniz designed the **Stepped Reckoner** that could add, subtract, multiply, divide, and figure square roots. Although the machine did not become widely used, almost every mechanical calculator built during the next 150 years was based on its design.

The first signs of automation benefited France's weaving industry when Joseph-Marie Jacquard built a loom controlled by punched cards. Heavy paper cards linked in a series passed over a set of rods on the loom. The pattern of holes in the cards determined which rods were engaged, thereby adjusting the color and pattern of the product (see Figure 2–3). Prior to Jacquard's invention, a loom operator adjusted the loom settings by hand before each glide of the shuttle, a tedious and time-consuming job.

Jacquard's loom emphasized three concepts important in computer theory. One was that information could be coded on **punched cards.** A second key concept was that cards could be linked to provide a series of instructions—essentially a program—allowing a machine to do its work without human intervention. Finally, the loom illustrated that programs could automate jobs.

The first person to use these concepts in a computing machine was Charles Babbage, a professor at Cambridge University in England. As a mathematician, Babbage needed an accurate method for computing and printing tables of the properties of numbers (squares, square roots, logarithms, and so on). A model of his first machine worked well, but the technology of the day was too primitive for manufacturing parts precise enough to build a full-sized version (see Figure 2–4).

Later, Babbage envisioned a new machine, the **analytical engine,** for performing any calculation according to instructions coded on cards. The idea for this steam-powered machine was amazingly similar to the design of computers. It had four parts: a "mill" for calculating, a "store" for holding instructions and intermediate and final results, an "operator" or system for carrying out instructions, and a device for "reading" and "writing" data on punched cards. Although Babbage died before he could construct the machine, his son built a workable model based on Babbage's notes and drawings. Because of the ideas he introduced, Babbage is known as the "father of computers."

Punched cards played an important role in the next advance toward automatic machines. Dr. Herman Hollerith, a statistician, was commissioned by the U.S. Census Bureau to develop a faster method of tabulating census data. His machine read and compiled data from punched cards. These cards were the forerunners of the standard computer card. Thanks to Hollerith's invention, the time needed to process the census data was reduced from seven and a half years in 1880 to two and a half years in 1890, despite an increase of thirteen million people in the intervening decade (see Figure 2–5).

Encouraged by his success, Hollerith formed the Tabulating Machine Company in 1896 to supply equipment to census takers in western Europe and Canada. In 1911, Hollerith sold his company, which later combined with twelve others to form the Computing-Tabulating-Recording Company (CTR).

FIGURE 2–3

The Jacquard Loom
Although other weavers had already designed looms that used punched cards, Jacquard refined the idea and he has received credit for the invention.

FIGURE 2–4

**Charles Babbage
and the Difference Engine**
Even very slight flaws in the brass and pewter rods and gears designed for a larger version of the difference engine threw the machine out of whack and invalidated results.

FIGURE 2–5

**Herman Hollerith
and the Tabulating Machine**
*Hollerith's code fit a grid of twelve
rows and eighty columns on his cards.
Once data was punched onto the cards,
a tabulator read the cards as they
passed over tiny brushes. Each time a
brush found a hole, it completed an
electrical circuit and caused special
counting dials to increment the data.
The cards were then sorted into 24
compartments by the sorting component
of the machine.*

In 1924, Thomas J. Watson, Sr. became president of CTR and changed the name to International Business Machines Corporation (IBM). The IBM machines made extensive use of punched cards. After Congress set up the social security system in 1935, Watson won for IBM the contract to provide machines needed for this massive accounting and payment distribution system. The U.S. Census Bureau also bought IBM equipment.

During the late 1920s and early 1930s, **accounting machines** evolved that could perform many record-keeping and accounting functions. Although they handled the U.S. business data-processing load well into the 1950s, they did little more than manipulate vast quantities of punched cards. These machines were limited in speed, size, and versatility.

World War II also had an impact on the development of computers. Cryptologists on the Allied side were determined to build a computer that would decipher the codes developed by the German machine, Enigma. The Allies smuggled Richard Lewinski, a Jewish factory worker, out of Poland because he had made parts for the Enigma. He designed a mockup of the German machine for the Allies. Two Englishmen, Dilwyn Knox and Alan Turing, used this model to build the **Bletchley Park computer,** which successfully deciphered the German codes.

A major advance toward modern computing came in 1944 when Howard Aiken's team at Harvard University designed a machine called the **Mark I.** This machine, the first automatic calculator, consisted of seventy-eight accounting machines controlled by punched paper tapes. The U.S. Navy used the Mark I for designing weapons and calculating trajectories until the end of World War II.

Regardless of its role in computer history, the Mark I was outdated before it was finished. Only two years after work on it was begun, John Mauchly and J. Presper Eckert, Jr. introduced an electronic computer for large-scale, general use at the University of Pennsylvania Moore School of Engineering. This machine was called the **ENIAC,** short for **Electronic Numerical Integrator and Calculator** (see Figure

FIGURE 2–6

The ENIAC
The ENIAC's first job was calculating the feasibility of a proposed design for the hydrogen bomb. The computer was also used for studying weather and cosmic rays.

2–6). It represented the shift from mechanical/electromechanical devices that used wheels, gears, and relays for computing to devices that depended upon electronic parts such as vacuum tubes and circuitry for operations.

The ENIAC was a huge machine; its 18,000 vacuum tubes took up a space eight feet high and eighty feet long. It weighed thirty tons and gobbled 174,000 watts of power. It could multiply two ten-digit numbers in three-thousandths of a second, compared with the three seconds required by the Mark I. At the time, the ENIAC seemed so fast the scientists predicted that seven computers like it could handle all the calculations the world would ever need.

The first electronic computer built in the United States is often thought to be the ENIAC. However, a recent lawsuit on the patent of the concepts of the ENIAC brought to light the name of John V. Atanasoff. Atanasoff was a graduate student at the University of Wisconsin in the late 1920s when he became fascinated with the idea of an electronic digital computer. Later, while a professor of physics at Iowa State College, he and a graduate student began to build the Atanasoff-Berry Computer (ABC). However, the two men were unable to complete their work because of their involvement in World War II.

Many of Atanasoff's concepts are evident in early computers such as the ENIAC. These concepts include data being represented in digital form; switches that are electronic, not mechanical; memory separated from processing; and the use of rules of logic and binary numbers.

The ENIAC had two major problems, however. First, the failure rate of the vacuum tubes was very high. Research showed that it was often the new tubes that failed, so Richard Clippinger developed a method for curing the tubes. New tubes were burned for about six hours, after which weak tubes would be isolated and discarded.

FIGURE 2–7

John von Neumann and the EDVAC
As it turned out, two groups of people were working simultaneously on a stored-program computer. Scientists at Cambridge University in England were building the EDSAC (Electronic Delay Storage Automatic Computer). The EDSAC received the title of first stored-program computer, although it was completed only a few months before the EDVAC.

A second problem with ENIAC was that operating instructions had to be fed into it manually by setting switches and connecting wires on control panels called plugboards. This was a tedious, time-consuming, and error-prone task. In the mid-1940s, the mathematician John von Neumann proposed a way to overcome this difficulty. The solution involved the **stored-program concept,** the idea of storing both instructions and data in the computer's memory. Although Eckert and Mauchly actually conceived of the stored-program concept long before von Neumann, they had not outlined a plan for its use.

Von Neumann's principles spurred the development of the first stored-program computer in the United States, the **EDVAC (Electronic Discrete Variable Automatic Computer).** The EDVAC's stored instructions decreased the number of manual operations needed in computer processing. This development marked the beginning of the modern computer era and the information society (see Figure 2–7). Subsequent refinements of the computer concept have focused on speed, size, and cost.

First Generation: 1951–1958

Improvements in computer capabilities are grouped in generations based upon the electronic technology available at the time. The first generation of computers—based upon the designs of the ENIAC and EDVAC—began with the sale of the first commercial electronic computer. This machine, called the **UNIVAC I,** was developed by Mauchly and Eckert, who had approached Remington Rand for financing (see Figure 2–8). Remington Rand (later Sperry Corporation) bought Mauchly and Eckert's company and propelled itself into the computer age with a product that was years ahead of the machines produced by competitors. In 1951, the first UNIVAC I replaced IBM equipment at the U.S. Census Bureau. Another UNIVAC was installed at General Electric's Appliance Park in Louisville, Kentucky. For the first time, business firms saw the possibilities of computer data processing.

FIGURE 2–8

The UNIVAC I
The most popular business uses for the UNIVACs were payroll and billing.

The UNIVAC I and other **first-generation computers** were huge, costly to buy, expensive to power, and often unreliable. They were slow compared to today's computers, and their memory capacity was limited. They depended upon the first-generation technology of **vacuum tubes** for internal operations. The masses of vacuum tubes took up a lot of space and generated considerable heat, requiring an air-conditioned environment. Vacuum tubes could switch on and off thousands of times per second, but one tube would fail about every fifteen minutes. Too much time was wasted hunting for the burned-out tubes (see Figure 2–9).

FIGURE 2–9

Racks of Vacuum Tubes
Vacuum tubes were used in the architecture of first-generation computers.

Punched cards were used to enter data into the machines. Memory consisted of **magnetic drums,** cylinders coated with magnetizable material. A drum rotated at high speeds while a device was poised just above it either to write on the drum by magnetizing small spots or to read from it by detecting spots already magnetized. Then results of processing were punched on blank cards.

Early first-generation computers were given instructions coded in **machine language,** that is, a code that designates the electrical states in the computer as combinations of 0s and 1s. Preparing the program or instructions was extremely tedious and errors were common. In order to overcome the difficulty, symbolic languages were developed. **Symbolic languages** use mnemonic symbols to represent instructions. For example, ADD would stand for addition. These symbols were easier for people to use than the strings of 0s and 1s of binary code, but the computer had to translate each symbol into machine language. A special set of language-translator programs was developed for this job. Rear Admiral Grace Murray Hopper of the U.S. Navy worked with a team that developed the first of these programs.

In the early 1950s, the public was not yet aware of the amazing computing machines. This changed with the 1952 presidential election. After analyzing only 5 percent of the tallied vote, a UNIVAC I computer predicted that Dwight David Eisenhower would defeat Adlai E. Stevenson. CBS doubted the accuracy of the prediction and did not release the information to the public until the election results were confirmed by actually counting the votes. The electronic prediction became the first in a burgeoning trend that has culminated in today's controversy about predicting election results from East Coast tallies before polls are closed on the West Coast.

Business acceptance of computers grew quickly. In 1953, Remington Rand and IBM led the infant industry, having placed a grand total of nine installations. But by the late 1950s, IBM alone had leased one thousand of its first-generation computers.

Second Generation: 1959–1964

Four hardware advances led to the **second-generation computers** of the early 1960s: the transistor, magnetic core memory, magnetic tapes, and magnetic disks. **Transistors** replaced the vacuum tubes of first-generation machines. A transistor is a small component made of solid material that acts like a vacuum tube in controlling the flow of electric current (see Figure 2–10). Using transistors in computers resulted in smaller, faster, and more reliable machines that used less electricity and generated much less heat than the first-generation computers.

Just as transistors replaced vacuum tubes as primary electronic components, **magnetic cores** replaced magnetic drums as memory units. Magnetic cores consisted of tiny rings of magnetic material strung on fine wires. Each magnetic core was placed at the intersection of a vertical and horizontal wire. To turn on a core, half the electricity needed was run through each wire. Thus, only at the intersection of specific wires would a core become charged. In this way, groups of cores stored instructions and data (see Figure 2–11). The development of magnetic cores resulted from the U.S. Navy's need for a more advanced, reliable high-speed flight trainer. Known as Whirlwind I, the navy project was one of the most innovative and influential projects in the history of the computer. Because of the high speed with which instructions and data could be located and retrieved using magnetic cores (a few millionths of a second), the Whirlwind allowed the real-time processing necessary in flight simulation. (Real time describes the ability of the computer to provide output fast enough to control the outcome of an activity.) The development led to other real-time functions such as air traffic control, factory management, and battle simulations.

FIGURE 2–10

Transistors

Transistors were mounted close together and connected with tiny, flat wires on small cards called circuit boards.

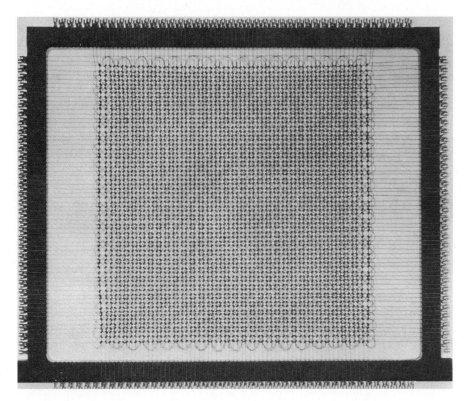

FIGURE 2–11

A Frame of Magnetic Cores
An assembled core unit looked much like a window screen.

This new type of memory was supplemented by storage on magnetic tapes and disks. During World War II, the Germans used huge, heavy steel tapes for sound recording. Plastic magnetic tapes eventually replaced the metal tapes, and later were tried for recording computer output. Output was recorded in the form of magnetized spots on the tape's surface. Another by-product of sound recording, the platter, led to the introduction of the magnetic disk. Much as a record is ''accessed'' on a jukebox, magnetic disks allowed direct access to data, contributing to the development of real-time activities such as making airline reservations. Disks and tapes greatly increased the speed of processing and enlarged storage capacities, and they soon replaced punched cards (see Figure 2–12).

FIGURE 2–12

A Second-Generation Computer System
This IBM 7070 system relied heavily on magnetic tape storage and required many tape drives to read from and write to the tapes.

During this period, more sophisticated, English-like computer languages such as COBOL and FORTRAN were commonly used.

Third Generation: 1965–1970

At the same time that transistors were replacing vacuum tubes, Jack S. Kilby of Texas Instruments and Robert Noyce at Fairchild Semiconductor were separately developing the **integrated circuit (IC).** Using separate methods, they discovered that the components of electronic circuits would be placed together—or integrated—onto small chips. Soon a single silicon chip less than one-eighth inch square could hold sixty-four complete circuits. This seems crude to us since today's chips may contain as many circuits as five hundred thousand transistors.

The chips marked the beginning of **third-generation computers,** computers that used less power, cost less, and were smaller and much more reliable than previous machines. Although computers became smaller, their internal memories increased due to the placement of memory on chips (see Figure 2–13).

A major third-generation innovation resulted when IBM realized that its company was turning out too many incompatible products. The company responded to the problem by designing the System/360 computers, which offered both scientific and business applications and introduced the family concept of computers. The first series consisted of six computers designed to run the same programs and use the same input, output, and storage equipment. Each computer offered a different memory capacity. For the first time, a company could buy a computer and feel that its investment in programs and peripheral equipment would not be wasted when the time came to move to a machine with a larger memory. Other manufacturers followed IBM's lead, and before long, more than 25,000 similar computer systems were installed in the United States.

FIGURE 2–13

A Third-Generation Minicomputer
The development of minicomputers allowed many small businesses to acquire computer power since the costs were much less than the costs of mainframes.

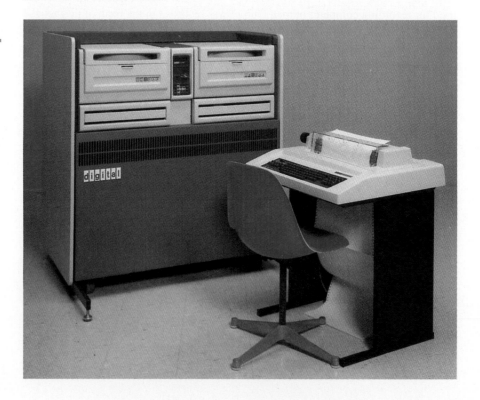

Other developments in this period included minicomputers. Although these machines had many of the same capabilities as large computers, they were much smaller, had less storage space, and cost less. Use of remote terminals also became common. **Remote terminals** are computer terminals that are located some distance away from a main computer and linked to it through cables such as telephone lines.

The software industry also began to emerge in the 1960s. Programs to perform payroll, billings, and other business tasks became available at fairly low costs. Yet software was rarely free of ''bugs,'' or errors. The computer industry experienced growing pains as the software industry lagged behind advances in hardware technology. The rapid advancements in hardware meant that old programs had to be rewritten to suit the circuitry of the new machines, and programmers skilled enough to do this were scarce. Software problems led to a glut of computer-error horror stories: a $200,000 water bill or $80,000 worth of duplicate welfare checks.

Fourth Generation: 1971–Today

Although the dividing lines between the first three generations of computers are clearly-marked by major technological advances, historians are not so clear about when the fourth generation began. They do agree that in **fourth-generation computers** the use of magnetic cores had been discontinued, replaced by memory on silicon chips.

Engineers continued to cram more circuits onto a single chip. The technique by which this was accomplished was called **large-scale integration (LSI),** which characterized fourth-generation computers (see Figure 2–14). LSI put thousands of electronic components on a single silicon chip for faster processing (the shorter the route electricity has to travel, the sooner it gets there). At this time, the functions that could be performed on a chip were permanently fixed during the production process.

Ted Hoff, an engineer at Intel Corporation, introduced an idea that resulted in a single, programmable unit—the microprocessor, or ''computer on a chip.'' He packed the arithmetic and logic circuitry needed for computations onto one microprocessor chip that could be made to act like any kind of calculator or computer desired. Other functions, such as input, output, and memory, were placed on separate chips. The development of the microprocessor led to a boom in computer manufacturing that gave computing power to homes and schools in the form of microcomputers.

As microcomputers became more popular, many companies began producing software that could be run on the smaller machines. Most early programs were games. Later, instructional programs began to appear. One important software development was the first electronic spreadsheet for microcomputers, VisiCalc, introduced in 1979. VisiCalc vastly increased the possibilities for using microcomputers in the business world. Today, a wide variety of software exists for microcomputer applications in business, school, and personal use.

Very-large-scale integration (VLSI) has virtually replaced large-scale integration. In VLSI, thousands of electronic components can be placed on a single silicon chip. This further miniaturization of integrated circuits offers even greater improvements in price, performance, and size of computers (see Figure 2–15). A single microprocessor based on VLSI is more powerful than a room full of 1950s computer circuitry.

Trends in miniaturization led, ironically, to the development of the largest and most powerful computers, the supercomputers. By reducing the size of circuitry and changing the design of the chips, companies that manufacture supercomputers were able to create computers powerful enough and with memories large enough to handle

FIGURE 2–14

First-, Second-, Third-, and Fourth-Generation Components
Vacuum tubes gave way to transistors and transistors gave way to chips in the effort to reduce the size of computer components. Fourth-generation computers were the first to use large-scale integration (LSI).

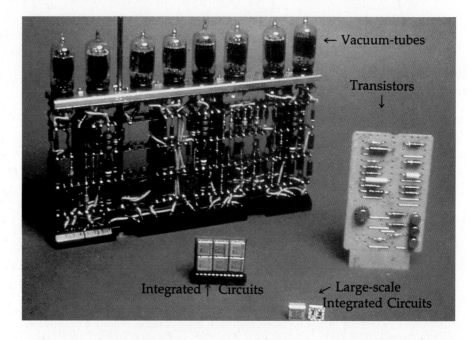

FIGURE 2–15

A 16-Bit Microprocessor
This microprocessor was designed on the principles of very-large-scale integration (VLSI).

40

CHAPTER 2: THE EVOLUTION OF COMPUTERS

the complex calculations required in aircraft design, weather forecasting, nuclear research, and energy conservation. In fact, the main processing unit of some super-computers is so densely packed with miniaturized electronic components that, like the early mainframe computers, it needs to be cooled and so is submerged in a special liquid coolant bath that disperses the tremendous heat generated during processing.

When will the fifth-generation begin? Unlike most computer processing today that mainly performs arithmetic operations, the next generation of computers will imitate human thinking and perform logically (i.e., will display **artificial intelligence**). In addition, experts predict that users will be able to easily communicate with these computers simply by using their native languages (e.g., English). Computer capabilities have improved drastically in the past forty-five years and there are a number of technological innovations on the horizon that could start a new computer generation. It will most likely be up to the historians of the future, however, to look back and identify one significant technological advance that thrust us into the fifth computer generation.

CONCEPT SUMMARY 2–1

The Technology Race: Generations of Computer Development

Period	Characteristics
First Generation 1951–1958	Vacuum tubes for internal operations. Magnetic drums for memory. Limited memory. Heat and maintenance problems. Punched cards for input and output. Slow input, processing, and output. Low-level symbolic languages for programming.
Second Generation 1959–1964	Transistors for internal operations. Magnetic cores for memory. Increased memory capacity. Magnetic tapes and disks for storage. Reductions in size and heat generation. Increase in processing speed and reliability. Increased use of high-level languages.
Third Generation 1965–1970	Integrated circuits on silicon chips for internal operations. Increased memory capacity. Compatible systems. Introduction of minicomputers. Emergence of software industry. Reduction in size and cost. Increase in speed and reliability. Operating systems on storage media.
Fourth Generation 1971–Today	Large-scale integration for internal operations. Development of the microprocessor. Introduction of microcomputers and supercomputers. Greater versatility in software. Introduction of very-large-scale integration. Increase in speed, power, and storage capacity.

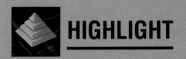
Don't Count Silicon Out

For years, researchers have been trying to find a compound other than silicon that will allow computer circuits to switch on and off at even faster speeds. Recent experiments have concentrated on such compounds as gallium arsenide and indium arsenide, for example. However, researchers at IBM now claim to have developed new silicon-based circuits that can switch on and off at a rate of 75 billion times per second. This is up to a thousand times faster than the switching speed of today's computer circuits.

By continuing to use silicon-based computer circuitry, the manufacturing processes used to build computer chips will not require a major overhaul. Manufacturing chips

out of compounds other than silicon would require computer chip manufacturers to develop completely new manufacturing techniques. The circuits being researched by IBM are not entirely made out of silicon, however. The chips contain just a trace of germanium. Germanium was used in the 1960s to produce very fast integrated circuits. Its use in the development of future computer circuits will enhance the processing speeds of computers, eliminate the need for new manufacturing techniques, and add only one step to the manufacturing process.

Even though new silicon-based computer circuits could switch on and off at a rate of 75 billion times per second, that's not so fast. New

gallium-based computer circuits are capable of switching on and off at a rate of 250 billion times per second. The manufacturing process required to build these circuits, however, calls for completely new computer circuit manufacturing techniques. To date, these new techniques have proven to be considerably less efficient—and therefore more costly—than the current silicon-based manufacturing techniques. Who knows, though, as manufacturing techniques for compounds other than silicon improve, the processing speed of tomorrow's computers may exceed today's standards by one, two, or even three thousand times.

◘ THE COMPUTER INDUSTRY

Computers have become powerful machines that have played a significant role in our country's growth and economic development in the last forty-five years. In the process, computer manufacturing and marketing have become big business. In this section we will examine briefly the hardware and software industries and vendor maintenance and support.

The Hardware Industry

The hardware industry encompasses manufacturers of computer equipment, including makers of the different sizes of computer systems and makers of peripheral devices such as monitors, disk drives, communications equipment, and printers.

There are many hardware manufacturers in existence today, but the number of manufacturers of large computer systems is fairly limited, primarily due to the huge capital investment required to produce large systems. The leading manufacturer of large computer systems is IBM (see Figure 2–16). Unisys, NCR, Control Data, and Honeywell are all major competitors in the large-system market. Some of these companies, such as IBM and Honeywell, also compete in the production of mini-computer systems against Digital Equipment Corporation, Hewlett-Packard, Data

FIGURE 2–16

General, and Wang Laboratories, among others. In the last few years some Japanese companies have begun to manufacture large computers, creating more competition in the international market. The leading Japanese manufacturers are Toshiba, Fujitsu, and Hitachi.

There are far fewer supercomputers built than any other type of computer. Cray Research and Control Data are the leading manufacturers of these powerful systems.

The microcomputer segment of the hardware industry is vastly different from the mainframe, supercomputer, and minicomputer sectors. Barriers to entry into the microcomputer market are not so high as the other markets; therefore, a considerable number of both microcomputer and micro peripheral manufacturers have ventured into the waters. In many cases, microcomputer manufacturers simply purchase standard parts in large quantities from other companies and assemble the parts into a computer with their name on it. Some of the more popular microcomputer manufacturers include IBM, Apple, Compaq, Tandy, CompuAdd, Northgate, and Dell. A number of companies have become successful by selling their computers through the mail.

Large computer vendors do more than just sell their systems. A computer is useless to an organization that lacks the knowledge needed to operate it. Most vendors provide support services along with the initial purchase. These services normally include education and training for all levels of users from top executives to data-entry personnel. Training can involve classes and seminars of self-study in which users pace their own learning while studying manuals and practicing hands-on exercises. Other services such as maintenance and repair may be included in the purchase or lease price of a computer system. Recent technological advances have contributed to a yearly decline in hardware costs. In contrast, service costs have increased significantly each year, making good vendor support after the initial purchase even more important to users.

Since a large percentage of the money spent on hardware goes toward the purchase of peripherals such as printers, monitors, and disk drives, many of the major companies

FIGURE 2–17

Laser Printer
The HP LaserJet IIISi printer from Hewlett-Packard Company.

mentioned earlier also produce peripheral equipment to support their computers. For example, IBM and Hewlett-Packard manufacture printers, monitors, and disk drives (see Figure 2–17). Leading exclusive manufacturers of peripherals include NEC (monitors), Epson (printers), and Kodak (disk drives).

Because of rapidly changing technology in the computer industry, many new product announcements are made over the course of a year. New technology leads to new companies. Often a new company will introduce a product that incorporates the latest technology, creating a highly successful business year for them. That successful year may be followed by a lean one after a competitor introduces an even more sophisticated product a short time later. Many times in the past, situations such as this have led to the failure of peripheral companies, so the market is in a constant state of flux.

The Software Industry

Early computer systems came complete with software that was specially designed to operate on a specific system. Most of the software consisted of programs to control the operation of the computer and its peripherals which were designed by the manufacturer. Users were responsible for designing programs to meet their own specific needs, and companies hired programming staffs to write the programs in-house. Companies found this practice very expensive and looked for other ways to solve their programming needs. During this period, a court decision in 1969 forced IBM, the industry leader, to "unbundle" its software, or offer hardware and software for sale separately. This action, more than any other, led to the development of independent software companies and the emergence of a new industry.

Early software companies often consisted of one person working at home, developing a clever idea. Today there are thousands of software companies in existence, creating programs capable of running on all sizes and brands of computers. Many companies specialize in producing a particular type of program to satisfy a particular industry or need; other companies create "generic" software for a variety of applications. A few software companies work under contract, custom-designing programs to meet the needs of specific customers. Some hardware companies still offer their own company-designed software to hardware buyers. Of all the options presently available to users, off-the-shelf software is generally the most cost-effective; programming your own is expensive because it is labor-intensive and requires a high degree of skill.

■ THE MICROCOMPUTER REVOLUTION

Few technological events have been as fascinating as the evolution and growth of the microcomputer industry. In only one decade, microcomputers grew from relatively primitive build-it-yourself kits to sophisticated machines more powerful than the early mainframe computers. Interest in microcomputers quickly spread from computer hobbyists to small business owners, managers, engineers, teachers, teenagers, and homemakers. This strong interest then led computer manufacturers to design and produce microcomputers to meet consumer demand.

Microcomputers have become a lasting part of society because they have so many uses. The growing number of microcomputer users have special information needs. Their hardware and software requirements often differ from users of larger computers. Also, microcomputer users sometimes require special support that may be obtained through services such as users groups and electronic bulletin boards. The following sections will discuss the evolution of microcomputers.

The New Technology

Actually, the first microprocessor was not designed to be used in microcomputers. Ted Hoff, an engineer at Intel Corporation, designed the first microprocessor chip for a Japanese company that wanted a programmable integrated circuit chip for its line of calculators. At the time, calculators used circuit chips that could perform only one function. Hoff's chip, the Intel 4004, could be programmed to perform numerous calculator functions.

The Intel 4004 microprocessor had a very limited set of instructions; it could only process four bits of data at a time. By 1974, however, microprocessors could process 8 bits (one byte) of data at a time. These microprocessors included the MOS Technology 6502, the Zilog Z-80, the Intel 8080, and the Motorola 6809. These 8-bit processors were used in the first microcomputers, among them the MITS Altair 8800 and the Apple II. In the early 1980s, 16-bit microprocessors were developed. The most popular of these microprocessors were the Intel 8088 and 8086. In the mid-1980s, 32-bit microprocessors were developed to meet the ever increasing demand for speed and accuracy in microcomputers. The Motorola 68000 family of processors and the Intel 80386 and 80486 are the most popular of the 32-bit microprocessors. So far, the most powerful microprocessor is the 64-bit microprocessor developed by Control Data Corporation.

Microprocessors are being used to control the functions of many devices other than microcomputers. They are commonly found in microwave ovens, calculators, typewriters, vending machines, traffic lights, and gasoline pumps. Microprocessors have also been incorporated into the design of automobiles. They control the ignition

Will Your Next Personal Computer Be Able to Read Your Handwriting?

One of the most recent innovations in computer technologies are personal computers that can read hand writing directly from a screen. The computers include a special pen and screen which allow the computer to identify exactly where the pen is on the screen and to read each pen stroke made. Current versions of these personal computers, however, can only read block-printed writing, not script.

One of the first companies to put these personal computers to use will be the Southern Pacific Transportation Company. The company will be issuing these computers to freight train conductors to record information that has formerly been recorded on standard paper forms. Southern Pacific hopes this new technology will allow the information to be captured more accurately and that billing errors previously caused by poor paperwork will be reduced significantly. Once the information is captured on the new personal computers it will be transmitted to office computers over telephone lines. This innovation will also allow more timely recording of required information.

The potential uses of such technology seem almost limitless. Other applications include salespeople entering orders while still on the road, nurses updating patient charts, traffic cops writing tickets—virtually any task that requires filling out a form. These computers are lightweight (normally less than eight pounds), operate on battery power, and can be carried almost anywhere. Many companies have already begun to work on software capable of reading script handwriting. Once this technology is developed, the success of these ingenious personal computers seems almost guaranteed.

system, the flow and mix of gasoline, and the timing of the spark in the engine. They also monitor and give to the driver information about speed, fuel supply, and other basic operations.

Microcomputer Pioneers

Ed Roberts, the founder of a company called MITS, foresaw the start of the microcomputer revolution. He saw a computer that could be assembled from a kit. In 1974, MITS introduced one of the first microcomputers available to the general public, the Altair 8800. The computer came unassembled for $397 or fully assembled for $498. It used the Intel 8080 8-bit microprocessor and had only 1,024 bytes (1 K) of memory. The Altair 8800 was featured in the January 1975 issue of *Popular Electronics* and created so much interest that the company received over 5,000 orders. The overwhelming response indicated that the market for microcomputers was well worth pursuing.

In 1976, not long after the introduction of the Altair 8800, Stephen Wozniak, an employee of Hewlett-Packard, finished building a small, easy-to-use computer. His computer, the Apple I, used the MOS 6502 microprocessor which, at $20, was inexpensive enough to be used for home computers. Steven Jobs, a friend of Wozniak's and a former Hewlett-Packard employee, persuaded Wozniak to leave Hewlett-Packard and start a business with him. The two men raised $1,300 and began building Apple computers. Their first commercial microcomputer, the Apple II, was a remarkable success (see Figure 2–18). Since then, the company has produced a number

FIGURE 2–18

Steven Jobs and Stephen Wozniak, the original Apple I, and the Apple II

of microcomputers, including the Apple II Plus, IIe, IIc, IIGS, the Apple III, and the Macintosh and Macintosh II families.

Also in 1976, Commodore Business Machines, headed by Jack Tramiel, acquired MOS Technology, the semiconductor manufacturer that had developed the 6502 microprocessor. With additional financing supplied by Commodore, the 6502 microprocessor was built into the Commodore PET microcomputer. In 1977, the PET was introduced at an electronics show (see Figure 2–19). Tramiel also sold the 6502 microprocessor to Apple and Atari. Later, Commodore developed the VIC 20, Commodore 64, Commodore 128, and Amiga microcomputers.

A year later, in 1977, the chairman of Tandy Corporation, John Roach, was busy persuading Tandy president, Charles Tandy, to manufacture a microcomputer and market it through the Radio Shack stores that Tandy had bought in 1963. Roach had the foresight and marketing skill to create a situation where, for the first time, a person could walk into a retail store and purchase a low-priced personal computer. The TRS-80 and Tandy families of microcomputers made Radio Shack and Tandy Corporation a driving force in the microcomputer industry (see Figure 2–20).

IBM entered the microcomputer race in 1981. The IBM Personal Computer, or PC, quickly became the standard in small business computers (see Figure 2–21). It used the Intel 8086 microprocessor which could process 16 bits of data at a time. The success of the IBM PC prompted other microcomputer manufacturers to develop 16-bit microcomputers. Since then, IBM has introduced a number of microcomputers, including the IBM PCjr, IBM PC-XT, IBM PC-AT, and the IBM PS/2 family.

FIGURE 2–19

The Commodore PET Microcomputer

FIGURE 2–20

John Roach and the TRS-80 Model 4 Microcomputer

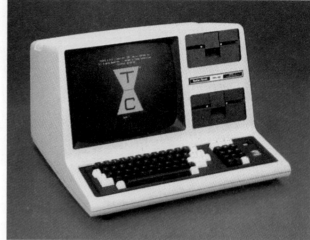

FIGURE 2–21

The IBM PC, 1981

CONCEPT SUMMARY 2–2	
The Microcomputer Revolution	
Year	**Event**
1971	Ted Hoff develops the first programmable integrated circuit chip (or microprocessor).
1974	Ed Roberts and MITS introduce the Altair 8800 microcomputer.
1976	Stephen Wozniak and Steven Jobs introduce the Apple II.
1977	Commodore Business Machines introduces the PET and Tandy/Radio Shack introduce the first TRS-80.
1981	IBM introduces the IBM PC.

CHAPTER 2: THE EVOLUTION OF COMPUTERS

■ SUMMARY POINTS

■ Humans have been searching for ways to calculate answers to problems and keep track of the results for thousands of years. Early attempts to succeed at this goal include the abacus, Napier's Bones, Pascal's and von Leibniz's machines, and Jacquard's punched cards.

■ Charles Babbage, the father of computers, designed the analytical engine, a machine that was similar in design to a computer, but it was doomed to failure because it was too advanced to be produced by the technology of its time.

■ Punched cards played an important role in the advance toward automatic machines when Dr. Herman Hollerith designed a tabulating machine that could read census data from the 1890 census punched onto cards.

■ Hollerith's tabulating machine became the basis for a company that Thomas Watson joined and later led. Today that company is known as IBM. During the 1920s accounting machines evolved that could perform many record-keeping and accounting functions.

■ Howard H. Aiken invented the first large-scale electromechanical automatic calculator, the Mark I.

■ John W. Mauchly and J. Presper Eckert, Jr. are usually considered to be the builders of the first electronic digital computer. However, a recent lawsuit brought forward evidence that John V. Atanasoff began to build an electronic digital computer before Mauchly and Eckert but was unable to complete it because of World War II.

■ John W. Mauchly and J. Presper Eckert, Jr. built the ENIAC, which was huge and required tremendous amounts of electricity, but it was much faster than Aiken's Mark I.

■ To solve the problem of manually feeding operating instructions into ENIAC and setting switches, John von Neumann proposed the idea of storing both instructions and data in the computer's memory. This is the stored-program concept. The first computer of this type in the United States was called EDVAC.

■ First-generation computers relied on vacuum tubes for power and used magnetic drums for memory. Instructions were coded in machine language until symbolic languages (mnemonic symbols representing instruction) were invented.

■ Second-generation computers were characterized by magnetic core memory and transistors for power. Memory was supplemented by storage on magnetic tapes and disks. More sophisticated, English-like languages such as COBOL were commonly used.

■ The integrated circuit developed by Jack S. Kilby of Texas Instruments and Robert Noyce at Fairchild Semiconductor led to the third computer generation. These machines were even smaller, faster, and more powerful than computers in earlier generations. They were also less costly, more reliable, and used less electricity.

■ A major third-generation innovation resulted when IBM developed the System/360 computers, the first series designed to run the same programs and use the same input, output, and storage equipment. Other developments in this period included minicomputers and the emergence of the software industry.

■ Fourth-generation computers rely on large-scale integration and very-large-scale integration to cram more circuits onto a chip. Ted Hoff, an engineer at Intel Corporation, introduced the microprocessor, or "computer on a chip."

■ Trends in miniaturization led to the development of the largest and most powerful of computers, the supercomputers. These machines perform complex calculations required in aircraft design, weather forecasting, nuclear weapons research, and energy conservation.

■ Fifth-generation computers will most likely perform artificial intelligence operations.

■ The hardware industry encompasses manufacturers of computer equipment, including makers of different sizes of computer systems and makers of peripheral devices such as monitors, disk drives, communications equipment, and printers.

■ Large computer vendors generally offer support services to users. While hardware costs are declining, costs associated with training, maintenance, and repair are increasing, making good vendor support an important consideration for potential buyers.

■ A large percentage of the money spent on hardware goes toward the purchase of peripherals such as printers, monitors, and disk drives. Rapidly changing technology leads to the rise and fall of many makers of peripheral equipment.

■ Early computer systems came complete with software that was specially designed to operate on that specific system. A court decision in 1969 forced IBM, the industry leader, to "unbundle" its software, or offer hardware and software for sale separately. This action, more than any other, led to the development of independent software companies.

■ Today software companies offer users many options to meet their computing needs, from custom-designed programs to off-the-shelf software. Off-the-shelf software is generally the most cost-effective way of meeting needs because programming is labor-intensive and requires a high degree of skill.

■ The first microprocessor, the Intel 4004, could only process 4 bits of data at a time. It was programmable and was designed for use in calculators.

■ The first 8-bit microprocessors included the MOS 6502, Zilog Z-80, Intel 8080, and Motorola 6809.

■ Microcomputer pioneers included Ed Roberts, the founder of MITS, which developed the Altair 8800. The Altair 8800, introduced in 1974, was one of the first microcomputers available to the general public.

■ Stephen Wozniak and Steven Jobs began marketing the Apple II microcomputer in 1976.

■ In 1977, Commodore introduced the PET microcomputer and Radio Shack and Tandy introduced the first of the TRS-80 microcomputers.

■ In 1981, IBM entered the microcomputer race by introducing the IBM PC.

■ TERMS FOR REVIEW

abacus, p. 29

accounting machines, p. 32

analytical engine, p. 31

artificial intelligence, p. 41

Bletchley Park computer, p. 32

EDVAC, p. 34

ENIAC, p. 32

first-generation computers, p. 35

fourth-generation computers, p. 39

integrated circuits (IC), p. 38

large-scale integration (LSI), p. 39

machine language, p. 36

magnetic cores, p. 36

magnetic drums, p. 36

Mark I, p. 32

Napier's Bones, p. 29

Pascaline, p. 30

punched cards, p. 30

remote terminals, p. 39

second-generation computers, p. 36

Stepped Reckoner, p. 30

stored program concept, p. 34

symbolic languages, p. 36

third-generation computers, p. 38

transistors, p. 36

UNIVAC I, p. 34

vacuum tubes, p. 35

very-large-scale integration (VLSI), p. 39

◘ REVIEW QUESTIONS

1. What role did the Stepped Reckoner play in the development of computers? Who developed the Stepped Reckoner?

2. What concepts important to computer theory were emphasized by Jacquard's loom? Who was the first person to use these concepts in a computing machine?

3. What was Dr. Herman Hollerith's contribution to the development of modern computers? What modern day company was founded by Hollerith?

4. How did World War II contribute to the development of modern computers?

5. What important feature of modern computers was introduced by John von Neumann in the EDVAC?

6. Identify five characteristics of first-generation computers. How do these features compare with similar characteristics in fourth-generation computers?

7. What contribution to modern computers was made simultaneously by Jack Kilby and Robert Noyce? What did this development mark?

8. What role did Ted Hoff play in the development of the microcomputer?

9. How does the microcomputer segment of the hardware industry differ from the mainframe, supercomputer, and minicomputer segments of the industry?

10. What impact did the IBM PC have on the microcomputer industry when it was introduced in 1981?

11. Name ten ways in which microcomputers are currently being used. Base your answer on personal experiences as far as possible.

APPLICATION

Kodak

George Eastman began his business career at age fourteen as an office boy in an insurance company and followed that with a job as a clerk in a local bank. In 1879, he invented and patented a machine for coating dry plates. Used in photography, the dry plates were coated with a gelatin emulsion that could dry without harming the silver salts used to record images. He resigned his bank clerk position in 1881 and formed a partnership called the Eastman Dry Plate Company, the firm that eventually became Eastman Kodak Company.

Shortly after forming his company, Eastman introduced a technology that would change photography completely. He made flexible film in rolls, with the roll holder for winding the films adaptable to nearly every plate camera on the market.

With the gelatin emulsions on a paper base, negatives could be much smaller; thus, cameras could be much smaller. In 1888, Eastman introduced the Kodak box camera that held this new smaller film. This camera, loaded with enough film for 100 exposures and priced at $25, could be easily carried and handheld during operation. After exposure, the camera and film were returned to Rochester, New York, where the company was located. There the film was developed, prints were made, and new film was inserted—all for $10. By 1990, Eastman was manufacturing a camera that sold for just $1.

KODAK'S BUSINESS PRINCIPLES
Eastman had four principles for his business that he saw as closely related:

- to achieve mass production at low cost
- to use internal distribution
- to apply extensive advertising
- to keep a focus on the customer

Mass production could not be justified without wide distribution, which, in turn, needed the support of strong advertising. From the beginning, he imbued the company with the conviction that fulfilling customer needs and desires is the only road to success.

To his basic principles of business, he added these policies:

- to foster growth and development through continuing research
- to treat employees fairly, in a way that fostered self-respect
- to reinvest profits to build and extend the business

The history of Eastman Kodak Company is one of progress in development of these basic principles and policies. Today, the business of the Eastman Kodak Company has expanded into four sectors—imaging, chemicals, health, and information.

KODAK'S BUSINESS SECTORS
Although the average person thinks of Kodak as only a photographic company, its business today is actually divided into four sectors—imaging, chemicals, health, and information. At the center is imaging. From there, the other three sectors form natural growth lines.

Kodak is pioneering new forms of creating, storing, manipulating, and reproducing images in ways undreamed of in Eastman's time.

From the very start, the manufacture of film as well as its processing required chemicals. Kodak's chemicals sector traces its roots to 1920, when the company began to manufacture methanol (wood alcohol) for use in the manufacture of films. Today, Kodak chemicals are used in products that people recognize and use daily, such as toys, apparel, home furnishings, beverage bottles, plastic food wrap, cosmetics, and more.

Kodak's entry into the health market started with x-ray films. Through its extensive knowledge of controlled chemical reactions in the photographic process, the company was able to expand this market by developing dry chemistry slides for clinical testing. This same knowledge also allowed the company to begin supplying chemical intermediates (substances obtained as the necessary intermediate stages between the original materials and the final product) to the pharmaceuticals industry, a practice that has continued for more than 70 years.

In the information market, Kodak began by manufacturing graphics films and microfilms. Depth in imaging science has further led the company to more electronically linked and computer-related developments in copiers and optical storage. For this high-growth sector at Kodak, the increasing use of electronics in newly developed products has greatly expanded the demand for internal software support.

EVOLUTION OF COMPUTING
AND IMAGING AT KODAK

Kodak's use of computers to support all phases of the business has kept step with the evolution of the industry. The company has always been on the leading edge in the use of new equipment and software to support its internal needs. What began with simple payroll and accounting systems on a central computer has grown today to include a vast worldwide network of personal computers, minicomputers, and mainframes that are used in sales support, order entry, manufacturing, testing and monitoring, distribution, decision support, electronic mail, artificial intelligence, process control, robotics, and more.

In the information sector today, Kodak is pioneering the development of new forms of imaging technology—creating, storing, manipulating, and reproducing images in ways that were undreamed of in Eastman's time. While not actually developing computers, the company is developing the products to capture images, store them efficiently, and reproduce them in hard copy. It is also developing the software to both create and manipulate these images.

Electronic image capture through scanners and sensors is key to Kodak's intent to be the world's leader in imaging. The Image Acquisition Products Division manufactures and markets an electronic imaging sensor with the world's highest resolution—4 million pixels (picture elements). It also produces the Imagelink scanner 900, capable of scanning 120 two-sided documents a minute, and a smaller PC-based scanner that reads letter-sized documents in 2.3 seconds.

Photographic-quality output is produced from digitized images.

The Integrated and System Products Division produces software and systems engineering solutions for customers worldwide. The software systems are designed to enable customers to add Kodak imaging products to a variety of computing environments. The division is regarded as a premier designer and supplier of UNIX-based systems, now standard for many computing environments.

High-resolution electronic digital images require enormous amounts of storage. The Mass Memory Division is meeting that need through the development of an optical disk system that is the world's highest-capacity, highest-performance electronic storage system. It uses a 14-inch optical disk that can be written to once and can store 8.2 billion bytes of information—the equivalent of information on a stack of paper as tall as the World Trade Center in New York City. For smaller information storage needs, the division has built an automated disk library, something like a high-tech jukebox, that offers up to 75 gigabytes of storage on 5.25-inch optical disks in the space of only three square feet.

Using light-emitting diode (LED) technology, the Copy Products Division has produced the industry's fastest networked color printer compatible with the Postscript® page description language. The Printer Products Division is exploiting thermal printing to produce photographic-quality output from digitized images. It is also using ink-jet technology to produce light-weight, high-speed portable printers for use with personal computers.

Meeting the challenge of using a variety of components synergistically to meet customer needs is one of the major goals of the information sector. One example of a system that combines the efforts of all these divisions is the Kodak Image Management System (KIMS). KIMS was designed to help government agencies and service businesses such as banking and insurance forge solutions to information overload. The system, which integrates scanners, workstations, optical disks, microfilm, and printers, is capable of storing nearly 6 million pages of information, any page of which can be accessed electronically in only 12 seconds. At one agency, paperwork that could have risen six times higher than the Empire State Building made customers wait days while clerks searched for data. Those same clerks, using the KIMS system, now respond to queries in seconds. Filing space, frustration, and response time have been reduced; productivity has increased by more than 250 percent.

The entrepreneurial spirit that began with George Eastman's quest to simplify the complex art of photography remains very much alive at Kodak, more than 100 years later. As the twenty-first century approaches, Kodak continues to explore and define the convergence of conventional imaging science with electronics.

The Kodak Image Management System integrates scanners, workstations, optical disks, microfilm, and printers.

DISCUSSION POINTS

1. How did Kodak originally use computers?
2. How are Kodak's products contributing to the continued evolution of the use of computers?

CHAPTER 3

Introduction to Information Systems

ARTICLE

The Next Frontier
is the Text Frontier

John W. Verity, *Business Week*

Like most law offices, Xerox Corp.'s legal department in the mid-1980s found itself awash in documents. Its word processing equipment was only making matters worse, churning out briefs, memos, patent filings, and letters in record numbers. Copies of all those documents—now totaling 300,000 and growing by 120,000 a year—were dutifully filed away on computer disks, but that really didn't help. How, for instance, could a lawyer locate relevant information buried in documents created years before? Who could possibly grasp the contents of so much verbiage well enough to cross-index it all successfully?

Take the problem of Xerox's 150-employee legal department and multiply it by several million, and you have an inkling of what big business is up against. Textual material—letters, field reports, wire-service stories, memos, electronic-mail messages, faxes—pours into corporations each day from dozens of sources. But swirling in that flood are nuggets of information that may provide a company with a competitive edge, if only they can be found quickly and correlated.

Panning for those data nuggets amid a rush of unorganized electronic text is the next big challenge for computer software developers. More than a dozen companies, including IBM, Digital Equipment Corp., and several startups, are plugging away at it.

Computers have no trouble processing data that fit naturally into lists of structured records—inventory updates, for instance. Each piece of data can be stored with an index, making it easy to find and to relate it to other data. That's how a data-base management program can quickly add up the inventory of pink widgets held in 50 different stores.

BRUTE FORCE

Text is another matter. It's generally just a long, unindexed string of words whose sentences and paragraphs convey ideas in ways that remain mysterious even to experts. Even now, computers can do little more than scan individual words, albeit at blinding speed. But such brute-force searches often turn up irrelevant documents and miss important ones. Finding precisely what you're looking for in a mass of unorganized text—nothing more, nothing less—is "a problem of nearly intractable complexity," notes Christopher Locke, director of industrial relations at Carnegie Mellon University's Robotics Institute.

Still, text retrieval is a $98 million business that, according to market researcher International Data Corp., will grow to $261 million by 1993. And it's the focus of intense research, because solving the text problem will be a big step toward computers that understand human speech and, in time, information systems that are vastly more accessible. "Text is the next great frontier of information processing," says Cliff Conneighton, who tracks the office automation market at Gartner Group in Stamford, Conn.

Much of the technology has its origins in research originally funded by the Central Intelligence Agency and the military. They needed a way to pore over the millions of words collected from spies, intercepted messages, foreign broadcasts, and publications. Verity Inc., in Mountain View, Calif., for example, developed its Topic software from such work. GESCAN International Inc., a spin-off of General Electric Co., built its text-retrieval computer for the military. It can scan 1 billion characters per second.

Early text-retrieval systems ran on mainframes and were used mostly for searching large, commercial data bases. But now they're running on minicomputers and desktops. Verity's workstation-based Topic, for instance, helps scientists scan enormous National Science Foundation files on research projects and grants. GE uses a GESCAN machine to plow through notes on phone calls to a customer hot line, helping identify patterns in reported problems.

The leader in large-scale text retrieval is Information Dimensions Inc., a unit of Battelle Memorial Institute in Columbus, Ohio. More than 1,300 copies of its Basis software are in use, including the one Xerox adapted for its lawyers. In seconds, the software can pluck out every passage in which "Trump" and "cash," for example, show up. Verity's product lets you "weight" such keywords by relative importance. Moreover, keywords can be grouped together into "topics." That makes it easier to zero in on relevant documents.

'JUNK-MAIL FILTER'
Interest in text systems is growing almost as fast as the torrent of electronic words. In late May, DEC endorsed a variety of text-searching products for use with its All-in-1 office automation system. Among them

was GESCAN's computer, which "you could use as an electronic junk-mail filter," says Howard Woolf, manager of network-applications support and electronic-publishing systems. "It's turning paperwork into profit."

In the future, managing text promises to change how computers are used. Its big benefit: Customers can collect reams of information without having to decide ahead of time how to organize or search it. In traditional computing, data has to fit into a data base's predefined slots. Hoping to feed customers' growing "textbases" is Dow Jones & Co., whose recently announced Dow-

Vision news wire delivers a daily stream of some 10 million bytes, or characters, of business information. Dow leaves it to customers to do their own scanning and sorting of the bulk data. Sifting all that information will be the job of the "business intelligence" departments that Herbert E. Meyer, a CIA-trained consultant, helps set up for large corporations. Sorry, he says, he can't name them.

Still, text processing has a ways to go. The computer "can't yet tell me what I ought to know," says Carnegie Mellon's Locke. But when it does, you can be sure there'll be lots of people listening.

◼ INTRODUCTION

In the eighteenth century the United States changed from an agricultural country to an industrial society. Most of the country's workers no longer worked on farms, but were employed in jobs related to manufacturing. Since then, the United States has evolved from an industrial society into an information-oriented society. The amount of accessible information is increasing at an astounding rate. Today, U.S. workers process over 35 billion pieces of paper each year. In order to meet this demand for information, more people are now employed in information-related jobs than in manufacturing jobs.

This chapter discusses how technology developed to meet information needs as the United States evolved from an industrial to an information-oriented society. The chapter includes discussions of qualities and value of information. The term *system*, so frequently associated with computers, is defined, and the relationship among systems, subsystems, and information systems is explored. The chapter also examines the ways businesses use information systems.

◼ QUALITIES OF INFORMATION

As explained in Chapter 1, information is data that has been processed. Information increases understanding and helps people make intelligent decisions. Yet not all information is equally valuable. The value of information varies depending upon when and how the data was gathered and processed.

A business manager does not need outdated information, or information that is not complete. Furthermore, managers only want accurate, relevant information. The most valued information is accurate, verifiable, timely, relevant, complete, and clear.

Information should be *accurate* (error-free). It is difficult to provide error-free information; inaccuracies can occur when data is put into the system, or it can be inappropriately processed. Erroneous data entered into the computer system brings about a situation known as **"GIGO"** or **"garbage in—garbage out."** The degree of accuracy acceptable to most decision makers depends on the circumstances. When decisions must be made quickly, there are trade-offs between speed and accuracy. Information produced quickly may not be error free.

Accurate information is *verifiable*. In other words, it can be confirmed. Verification can be accomplished in different ways. One approach compares the new information with other information that is accurate. Another approach involves reentering new data and comparing the processed information with the original. A third approach, an **audit trail,** traces the information back to its original source. An audit trail describes the path that leads to the data on which information is based. A decision maker evaluates the audit trail description to verify the accuracy of information. Any well-designed information system should include a plan for an audit trail. Information that cannot be verified cannot be depended upon for decision making.

The *timeliness* of information is important because information frequently loses its value as it ages. Information necessary for routine business operations must be current. For example, a warehouse manager needs up-to-the-minute reports on inventory levels to fill orders promptly. A report generated last year would be useless in determining inventory levels for the current week. The type of information needed for long-term planning, however, may require more than current information. A future sales campaign may be based on sales figures that span a five-year period, revealing past sales trends. Therefore *timely* does not always mean *current;* timely information is appropriate information that is available when needed.

Even the most timely information is useless if it does not actually contribute to making a good decision. Extraneous information can complicate decision making, whereas relevant information makes it easier. *Relevant* information is information that a manager or a staff specialist "needs to know" in order to make a particular decision. A company comptroller performing an audit does not need the plant maintenance schedule for the past year, he needs financial records. Relevant information is new knowledge that actually assists the appropriate person in decision making.

Before making decisions, managers must determine if the information is *complete* or if more is needed. Accurate, verifiable, timely, relevant information is meaningless if it is incomplete. The completeness of information refers not to the quantity of information, but rather its content. Large volumes of information may be present, but one crucial detail may have been overlooked. Circumstances influence whether or not the missing information hampers decision making. At one time incomplete information may have little effect, whereas at another the missing information could have serious consequences. For example, a fire department will respond immediately to a report of a fire in a chemical plant. Once at the scene, however, firefighters may need more complete information to fight the fire effectively. The chemicals inside the building affect decisions about techniques used to combat the blaze. Without this information, firefighters could use the wrong containment techniques and actually spread the fire instead of putting it out.

Finally, information should be *clear*. It should contain no ambiguous terms and should be stated in a way that leaves no doubts concerning the meaning of facts. A report that contains vague generalities and ambiguous terms quickly loses its value to an organization.

All these qualities are equally important if the receiver of the information is to have complete confidence in using the information for decision making. Unfortunately, limitations in time and money may necessitate compromises in any of these areas.

Qualities of Information

Quality	Explanation
Timely	Information frequently loses value as it ages. Different management levels have different information needs.
Accurate	Information should be without errors. The degree of accuracy depends on different circumstances.
Verifiable	The accuracy of information can be confirmed by comparing, rekeying, or implementing an audit trail.
Relevant	Information should contribute to making decisions more easily or more successfully. Extraneous information can complicate decision making.
Complete	Information may be meaningless if it is not complete. Circumstances help determine if more information is needed.
Clear	Information should leave no doubts and contain no ambiguous terms.

■ FUNDAMENTAL PRINCIPLES OF INFORMATION SYSTEMS

What Is a System?

A **system** is a group of related elements that work together toward a common goal. The term *system* is often associated with computers, but it actually refers to a wider concept, used in many areas such as science and the social sciences. For example, physiologists see the human body as a system made up of smaller subsystems such as the respiratory system and the circulatory system. In our study, an information system is made up of input, processes, and output. **Input** enters the system from the surrounding environment and is transformed by some **process** into output. Information can flow within the system or between it and its larger environment. Most **output** leaves the system and flows into the external environment. Some may remain in the internal environment.

A system requires **feedback,** which can come from either internal or external sources. Feedback keeps the system functioning smoothly. In system theory, a system's primary goal is survival. Feedback helps the system survive by pinpointing the system's strengths and weaknesses (Figure 3–1).

A newspaper is an example of a system with input, processes, output, and feedback. Input consists of the news items that are collected by reporters. The writing, editing, typesetting, and printing of the stories are the processes that turns the news items into output (the printed paper). Feedback to this system may come from internal or external sources. The opinions of the publisher are a source of internal feedback. Letters to the editor from readers and people dropping their subscriptions are sources of external feedback.

A System's Interaction with Other Systems

Every system can be viewed in terms of inputs, processes, outputs, and feedback

FIGURE 3–1

The Environment of a System

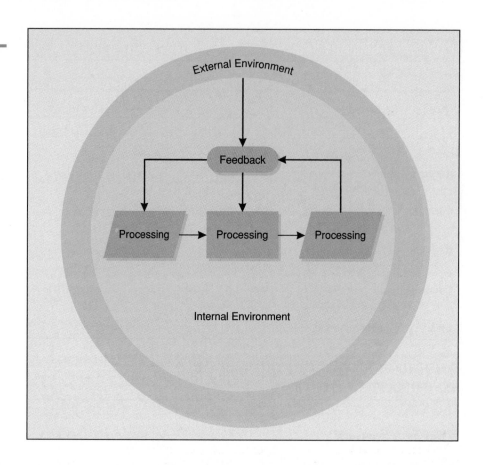

mechanisms, but the boundaries between systems are not always clear. Which elements of a system are actually subsystems? The boundaries and elements of a system depend upon the level from which one views the system. In medicine, for instance, a general practitioner views the human body as the system, whereas an ophthalmologist views just the eye as the system. In a business, payroll, accounts receivable, and accounts payable can all be subsystems of the accounting system. An important concept in system theory is that subsystems (such as payroll in accounting) interact with the system. Accounting is, of course, a subsystem of the business and interacts with other departments such as marketing.

The Organization as a System

System theory is also applicable to organizations. Organizations have groups of related elements (departments and employees) working toward common goals (survival, growth, or profit). Figure 3–2 shows a state university as a subsystem of a larger system, the community. The university uses inputs from the surrounding environment and transforms them into useful outputs.

As shown in Figure 3–2, the university is affected by external factors beyond its control. Examples of external factors are the economy; federal, state, and local legislation; and competition from other universities. Internal factors affecting the university include the quality of its faculty and students, relationships among administrators, departmental relations, and internal communication channels. An analysis of its information needs must consider both internal and external factors.

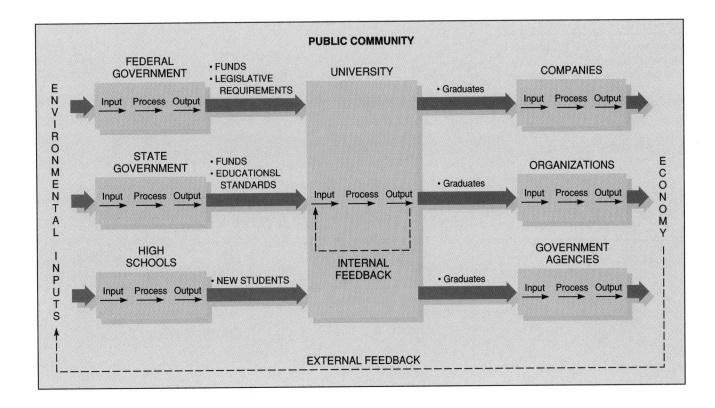

FIGURE 3–2

The University as an Interacting System

Each department in a university is a subsystem within the university. The goal of each department is to educate students according to predetermined standards. But each department must interact with other departments. The history department must obtain enrollment and eligibility information from the registrar. The registrar finds out from the bursar's office which students have not paid their tuition.

External information, such as the number of high school graduates, SAT scores, and new tax laws affecting education, comes from state agencies among other sources. Information about present and future economic conditions that will affect university enrollments is supplied by external sources such as federal agencies. Some of the many interactions are shown in Figure 3–3.

◘ COMPONENTS OF AN INFORMATION SYSTEM

Information is data that has been processed and made useful for decision making. Decision makers use information to increase knowledge and reduce uncertainty. Organizations cannot function without information. An information system, therefore, is designed to transform data into information and make it available to decision makers in a timely fashion. An information system consists of many components. The four major components—hardware, software, data, and people—are discussed in the following sections.

Hardware as Part of an Information System

In a computer-based information system, hardware consists of equipment, or the parts

FIGURE 3–3

The Internal and External Interactions of a University

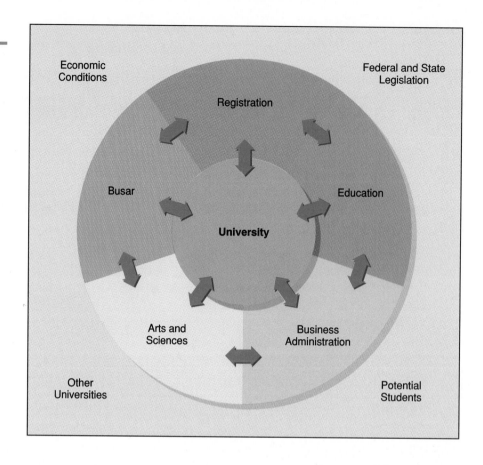

of the computer that can be seen. Hardware is used to input the data into the computer system (see Figure 3–4). Once inside the computer the data is processed by the hardware into information. Output equipment is then used either to place the information on storage devices or to present the information in human-readable form such as on a display screen.

Software as Part of an Information System

Software programs are specific sequences of instructions needed to run computers. Without specific instructions provided by software, a computer-based system could not function. Software not only processes the information needed by users, but also provides the instructions needed just to get the computer running.

Data as Part of an Information System

Before it can flow through an information system, data must be collected and changed into a form on which the computer can operate. Although collection methods vary widely, the most common data-input method is using a keyboard to "type" the data. Data can also be input directly from sources by scanning devices such as the ones used at the check-out counters of grocery stores. Remember that data refers to raw facts collected from various sources, facts not yet organized or defined in a meaningful way. Information is processed data that helps people make intelligent decisions.

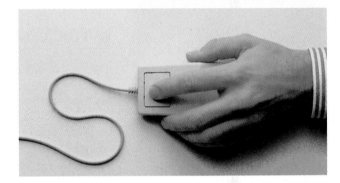

Processing data through an information system involves manipulating data by hardware and software.

People as Part of an Information System

People are an essential part of an information system. They put together and coordinate all activities within the system (Figure 3–5). People in an information system can be categorized by their roles, such as providers, users, and clients.

Providers are the people who design and operate the computer information system. They include system analysts, programmers, and operators. Information system careers are discussed later in this chapter. Users interact directly with the information system. They provide input or use the output in their jobs. Users often are clerks or data-entry personnel, although more and more managers are becoming "hands-on" users. Clients, on the other hand, may not interact directly with the system, although they do benefit from it in other ways. A customer purchasing a product through a computer-based information system benefits when the product is received even though the customer does not enjoy direct use of the computer.

FIGURE 3–4

Input Equipment
Clockwise: keyboard, voice input, mouse, graphic tablet.

FIGURE 3–5

*People are an important component of
an information system*

■ THE VALUE OF INFORMATION SYSTEMS

The number of businesses and organizations with computer-based information systems is growing. Companies find that combining hardware, software, data, and people to create information systems is so successful that the term **synergism** is frequently used to describe the relationship. A synergistic relationship is one in which the combined effort of all the parts is greater than the sum of the efforts of each part operating independently.

Science has many synergistic relationships. In chemistry, an area in which synergism abounds, tensile strength is one example. Chrome-nickel steel has a tensile strength of approximately 350,000 pounds per square inch. That figure exceeds, by 100,000 pounds per square inch, the sum of the tensile strength of each of the several elements that, when combined, form chrome-nickel steel. In other words, the whole is greater than the sum of its parts.

We can also observe synergistic relationships in a political campaign. Suppose a candidate's staff must decide the most effective way to use personal appearances, television ads, and direct-mail flyers in a campaign. The staff knows that when used one at a time, a direct-mail flyer will generate 5,000 votes, personal appearances will generate 7,000 votes, and television ads will generate 10,000 votes. If each of the tactics is used in succession over the course of three separate months, the candidate can depend on receiving 22,000 votes. However, voter surveys show that if all three tactics are used in combination the month before an election, the joint effect will generate 30,000 votes. With this information, a knowledgeable staff would combine the techniques.

Regardless of the situation, political campaign or information system, combining resources for maximum effectiveness demonstrates good management practice. A person working alone to input data in an information system is slower than a computer and more prone to errors. A computer can input data faster and more accurately than humans, but it can only input data that people have found a way to put in computer-readable form. Thus, humans and computers working together can input huge amounts of data with a high degree of accuracy.

After the input phase, recall that data is processed to be turned into useful information. The question that businesses face is, since a computer-based information system is a major expense, what is the value of that processed information to the organization?

Decisions are made with the hope that they will produce the best outcome either by maximizing or minimizing a result. A major consideration in determining the value of information is whether it reduces the uncertainty that surrounds the outcome of a decision. A decision is generally chosen from among a number of options, or choices, each with a different degree of uncertainty. The degree to which information reduces uncertainty determines its value to the organization or firm.

Businesses quantify the value of information by determining the cost of obtaining the information and comparing that with the cost of making a decision without the information. If the cost of obtaining information exceeds the ill effects of making a decision without that information, then the information loses its value to the firm.

■ HOW BUSINESSES USE INFORMATION SYSTEMS

Businesses use computer-based information systems in a variety of ways. When computers were first introduced to businesses, the machines were used to solve specific processing problems. Little emphasis was placed on centralized planning or on using computers in the most effective way to benefit the entire organization. The primary applications for computers were clerical and record-keeping tasks. Today, computer-based information systems have expanded and developed into information systems that include all types of applications from record keeping to operational functions to strategic planning. The following sections show how businesses are using computers to improve their effectiveness.

Accounting/Payroll

Payroll, essentially a record-keeping function, is a common application of information systems in the accounting department of most businesses (see Figure 3–6). Accounting machines were among the first forms of automated machines. Accountants, therefore, made some of the first applications of electronic computers. Since a major purpose of accounting is to maintain and represent financial data accurately, the speed, accuracy, and memory advantages offered by computers make them ideal for such applications.

A payroll system designed to compute wages for hourly employees has informational requirements above mere hours and rate of pay. A typical payroll system also computes taxes and appropriate deductions for each employee. Vacation time and sick leave must be reflected in the paychecks. Checks and W-2 forms must be printed. A payroll system must also accommodate changes in employee information, such as change of address or number of deductions. Although these information requirements are complex, most systems break them into phases so that they may be performed without error.

Finance/Budgeting

Budgeting, a subsystem of finance, is an indispensable function in all businesses. An

FIGURE 3–6

Rockwell International's Graphics Systems Division in Reading, PA, which manufactures newspaper printing presses, monitors factory time, attendance, and labor productivity with a Honeywell factory data collection system. Terminals on the factory floor and in the managers' offices supply the factory's 1200 employees with timely information on job status, job cost, and payroll.

information system designed for budgeting can process data and generate reports that are used to manage financial resources. Reports in cost accounting are used to determine how and where money is spent. It is essential for managers to have this information whether they are planning their payroll or the purchase of new materials or equipment.

A budgeting system receives input from several sources, including marketing, production, accounts payable, and accounts receivable. After processing all the data, the system produces a projected budget. Management can use the projected budget to keep track of actual spending and identify discrepancies in spending before expenditures get out of control. Because information systems are capable of processing huge amounts of data, some firms use their budget systems to process hypothetical data for planning purposes.

Marketing/Sales Order Processing

In the area of marketing, sales order processing is a frequent application of an information system. Order processing must provide for a fast and accurate fulfillment of customer orders. A computerized inventory system is often used in conjunction with order processing. By combining the two in the same information system, orders can be filled more quickly, accurately, and efficiently.

Most businesses receive orders placed alternately in person, by phone, by mail, or by online computer systems. Items are also returned for credit. The firm's information system must be designed to handle all of these situations.

An inventory control system can help process orders. Inventory control systems facilitate sales by preventing delays in filling orders that are caused by running out of stock. For example, a computerized inventory system may indicate reorder points when inventory levels are low. Inventory control systems also help keep costs down by making sure that warehouses do not become overstocked with items that tie up operating capital.

Human Resources Management/Personnel

Human resources management departments are involved in many functional areas of businesses. Employee assistance programs, such as relocation and benefits, fall under human resources management, as do training and development, policies and procedures, and personnel record keeping.

Personnel record keeping is a functional area ideally suited to computerization because the volume of processed information is large and records must be updated frequently. Most organizations keep employee records in a centralized data base to which additions, deletions, and other changes can be made. Each record may include information such as the employee's name, address, phone number, social security number, date of hiring, job assignment, salary, and performance ratings. Human resource management seeks to bring about efficient planning and control for career path planning and skills development. By computerizing the personnel record-keeping functions, organizations can reach this goal.

Production Management/ Materials Requirement Planning (MRP)

Manufacturers transform raw materials into finished products. This transformation usually involves many complex activities: products are designed and engineered; raw materials are purchased; components are assembled; and facilities and equipment must be scheduled. **Materials requirement planning (MRP)** assists in the planning, purchasing, and control of raw materials used in the manufacture of goods (see Figure 3–7).

A well-designed MRP system has many interacting subsystems. Inventory control regulates the quantity of raw materials available. The scheduling of facilities helps eliminate wasted machine time and scheduling conflicts. Engineering systems assist in designing and testing new products. Sophisticated engineering systems speed up the design process and hold down costs by reducing the need for building and testing prototypes (see Figure 3–8).

FIGURE 3–7

MRP is being used increasingly by manufacturers.

FIGURE 3–8

Using computers to assist in product design and engineering can speed up the design process and reduce manufacturing costs.

Engineering/Computer-Aided Engineering

Engineering departments are responsible for product design. In the early 1970s, **computer-aided design (CAD)** systems were first introduced to help engineers draw and analyze physical structures. CAD systems were and still are used to convert designs into production drawings, and are therefore considered ''tail end'' systems. While CAD systems have greatly reduced product development time and costs, computer-aided engineering (CAE) systems go one step beyond CAD.

Computer-aided engineering (CAE) systems, which are used in the design of products, are tools for the ''front end'' of product design. Engineers use CAE systems for everything from the initial design concept to production drawings. A CAE system works a little like a word processing system. Word processors allow users to make changes to text at any point during the creation of a document. Users can correct mistakes as soon as they are identified. Similarly, CAE systems allow engineers to interact with the computer during simulation runs as errors are identified. Most CAD systems, on the other hand, run through an entire simulation before mistakes are identified, and a simulation for a complex computer chip design, for example, can take several days. Because CAE allows engineers to make design changes as they are identified, product prototypes frequently work on the first try. Using a CAE system, Hewlett-Packard designed a computer chip in seven months that normally would have taken two years to design. By cutting design time, CAE systems can significantly affect company profits.

Businesses are continually looking for ways to use computers to improve efficiency and increase profits. In many instances those companies that have developed creative ways of using computers have gained a competitive edge over their competition. For example, Ford Motor Company introduced an information storage system to improve customer relations and create dealer loyalty. Ford recognized that dealers who needed parts for repairs often had difficulty locating them. While dealers were trying to locate the necessary parts, customers waited impatiently for repairs. Together with AT&T Information Systems, Ford developed a greatly improved parts inventory system for dealers. A digital network, Net/1000, helps dealers search the inventories of other dealers for needed parts. Now customers are enjoying faster service; Ford is enjoying improved customer relations; and dealers are experiencing improved customer loyalty. In order to compete, other companies must also develop sophisticated information systems like the one used at Ford.

◘ CAREERS IN COMPUTERS

Today a great many organizations, including businesses, hospitals, schools, government agencies, banks, and libraries, are using computers to help organize and store information. This has created the demand for a large class of professionals who can design and operate effective computer systems. This section describes various career opportunities in the computer field.

Data-Processing Operations Personnel

Data-processing operations personnel are responsible for entering data and instructions into the computer, operating the computer and attached devices, retrieving output, and ensuring the smooth operation of the computing center and its associated libraries. An efficient operations staff is crucial to the effective use of an organization's resources.

HIGHLIGHT

Futuristic Security

For many years companies and government agencies have limited access to their buildings—or areas within their buildings—by means of security systems. These systems have normally included either a key or a card bearing a magnetic stripe that had to be carried by the employees and inserted into a lock or into a card reader in order to gain entry into the work area. These types of systems, however, are fast becoming outdated. The future of security systems lies in biometric technologies. Biometric security systems use such techniques as fingerprint recognition, retinal blood vessel pattern recognition, hand shape recognition, handwriting recognition, and vocal intonation recognition to uniquely identify an individual.

In the past, security systems relied on the assumption that the people who wanted to gain entry would always have their keys or magnetic stripe cards with them and, in fact, be the workers that the devices were issued to. Such, of course, was not always the case. Biometric systems, however, rely on identifiers that are truly unique to an individual, cannot be stolen or misplaced, and cannot be duplicated or changed in any way. The majority of biometric security systems used today are fingerprint scanners. Connecticut Bank & Trust, for example, uses a fingerprint scanner to identify the approximately 340 employees that enter its building daily. The system used by the bank is controlled by an IBM PS/2 Model 30 microcomputer. Employee access

to the building can be managed by simply adding, deleting, or changing the unique information about an employee stored on the computer.

Biometric security systems have existed for a number of years, but their reliability was low and their price was extremely high compared to other more reliable, less costly alternatives. However, recent technological advances have helped render these types of security systems more reliable and less costly. It is likely that the use of these types of security systems will burgeon dramatically in the near future.

The **librarian** is responsible for classifying, cataloging, and maintaining the files and programs stored on tapes, disks, and diskettes, and all other storage media in a computer library. The librarian's tasks include transferring backup files to alternate storage sites, purging old files, and supervising the periodic cleaning of magnetic tapes and disks. As for job qualifications, the librarian should have a high-school diploma, clerical record-keeping skills, and a knowledge of basic data-processing concepts.

A **computer operator's** duties include setting up equipment; mounting and removing tapes, disks, and diskettes; and monitoring the operation of the computer. A computer operator should be able to identify operational problems and take appropriate corrective actions. Most computers run under sophisticated operating systems that direct the operator through messages generated during processing. However, the operator is responsible for reviewing errors that occur during operation, determining their causes, and maintaining operating records.

An operator should be able to read and understand technical literature. Although few operators have a four-year college degree, some have degrees from technical schools and junior colleges. Many operators receive apprentice and on-the-job training.

A **data-entry operator's** job involves transcribing data into a form suitable for computer processing. A **keypunch operator** uses a keypunch machine to transfer data from source documents to a form that can be processed by a computer. Operators of key-entry devices normally transfer data to magnetic tape and magnetic disk for subsequent processing.

A **remote terminal operator** is involved with the preparation of input data. The operator is located at a site that is probably some distance from the computer itself. The data is entered into the computer directly from the remote location at which it is generated.

Data-entry jobs usually require manual dexterity, typing or keying skills, and alertness. They do not require more than a high school education. Usually data-entry personnel receive several weeks of on-the-job training so they can become familiar with the documents they will be reading. This training minimizes errors.

Occupations in computer operations are affected by changes in data-processing technology. For example, the demand for keypunch operators has declined as new methods of data preparation have developed. Yet the expanding use of computers, especially in small businesses, will require additional computer operating personnel.

System Development Personnel

PROGRAMMERS. Generally, three types of programming are done in an organization:

1. *Application programming,* that is, developing programs for specific functions such as accounting.
2. *Maintenance programming,* which is keeping already developed programs current and error free.
3. *System programming,* which is developing and maintaining the programs that operate the computer.

Persons working in any of these areas should possess the following basic skills:

- Good command of the programming language(s) in which programs are written.
- A knowledge of general programming methodology and the relationships between programs and hardware.
- Analytical reasoning ability and attention to detail.
- Creativity and discipline for developing new problem-solving methods.
- Patience and persistence.

Application programmers convert a design for a system into instructions for the computer. They are responsible for testing, debugging, documenting, and implementing programs. Applications programmers in business generally have at least a two-year degree. They should know the objectives of an organization and have a basic understanding of accounting and management science in addition to the skills outlined earlier.

Scientific application programmers work on scientific or engineering problems, which usually require complex mathematical solutions. Thus, scientific application programming usually requires a degree in computer science, information science, mathematics, engineering, or a physical science. Some jobs require graduate degrees. Few scientific organizations are interested in applicants with no college training.

Program maintenance is an important but often neglected activity. Many large programs are never completely **debugged;** furthermore, there is a continuing need to change and improve major programs. In some organizations, maintenance programming is done by application programmers. To be effective, a **maintenance**

programmer needs extensive programming experience and a high level of analytical ability. Occasionally, personnel in computer operations are promoted to maintenance programming positions, but they often are required to take additional data-processing courses.

System programmers are responsible for creating and maintaining system software. System programmers do not write programs that solve day-to-day organizational problems. Instead, they develop utility programs; maintain operating systems, database packages, compilers, and assemblers; and are involved in decisions concerning additions and deletions of hardware and software. Because of their knowledge of operating systems, system programmers typically offer technical help to application programmers. A system programmer should have at least one year of assembly language programming experience or a college degree in computer science. He or she should have (a) a background in the theory of computer language ·structure and syntax, and (b) extensive and detailed knowledge of the hardware being used and the software that controls it. Some employers may look for specialized skills in system programmers. For example, the advanced technology of today's communication networks offers excellent opportunities for programmers skilled in designing, coding, testing, debugging, documenting, and implementing data communication software. Application and system programmers will continue to be in high demand.

SYSTEM ANALYSTS. The **system analyst** plays a significant role in the analysis, design, and implementation of a formal system. The analyst has the following responsibilities:

■ Helping the user determine information needs.
■ Gathering facts about existing systems and analyzing them to determine the effectiveness of current processing methods and procedures.
■ Designing new systems, recommending changes to existing systems, and being involved in implementing these changes.

The analyst's role is critical to the success of any information system. He or she acts as an interface between users of the system and technical personnel such as programmers, machine operators, and data-base specialists. This role becomes more important as the cost of designing, implementing, and maintaining information systems rises.

An effective system analyst should have:

■ A general knowledge of the firm, including its goals, objectives, products, and services.
■ Familiarity with the organizational structure of the company and management's rationale for selecting that structure.
■ Comprehensive knowledge of data-processing methods and current hardware; familiarity with available programming languages.
■ The ability to plan and organize work and to cooperate and interact effectively with both technical and nontechnical personnel.
■ A high degree of creativity.

Minimum requirements for a job as a system analyst generally include work experience in system design and programming and specialized industry experience. System analysts seeking jobs in a business environment should be college graduates with backgrounds in business management, accounting, economics, computer science, information systems, or data processing. For work in a scientifically oriented organization, a college background in physical sciences, mathematics, or engineering is

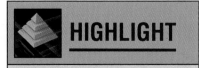

HIGHLIGHT

A New Twist in Advertising

Promotion Technology, Inc. has introduced a system that—as grocery item checkout scanners did a number of years ago—will revolutionize the look of grocery store checkout counters. The system, named Vision, is designed to show customers ten-second, full-motion video advertisements while the customer is waiting at the checkout counter. The system uses a Macintosh II microcomputer, a color monitor, and a laser disc player to beam these advertisements at the customers.

In addition to displaying advertisements, Vision is also capable of recording and tracking frequent-shopper information. This system is an electronic version of the system that used to give customers stamps to be pasted into books. Once enough books had been accumulated, they were redeemable for merchandise. The Vision system will record information on a card carried by the customer that is similar to a credit card but contains a microchip. The Vision Value Club card gives customers electronic credit and prints paper coupons and other incentives at the checkout counter. The credit accumulated on the Vision Value Club card can then be redeemed for merchandise from a Vision Value Club catalog. It all preserves the fun of stamps, without needing to lick the glue.

preferred. Many universities offer majors in management information systems; their curricula are designed to train people to be system analysts.

The need for system analysts is growing. There is a continuing high demand for system professionals by computer manufacturers, and the increasing use of mini-computers and microcomputers will create even greater need for analysts to design systems for small computers.

Data-Base Specialists

Data-base specialists are responsible for designing and controlling the use of data resources. A **data-base analyst**—the key person in the analysis, design, and implementation of data structures—must plan and coordinate data use within a system. A data-base analyst has the following responsibilities:

- Helping the system analyst or user analyze the interrelationships of data.
- Defining the physical data structures and logical views of data.
- Designing new data-base systems, recommending changes to existing ones, and being involved in the implementation of these changes.
- Eliminating data redundancy.

A data-base analyst needs technical knowledge of programming and system methodologies. A background in system software is valuable for persons planning physical data-base structures. The job requires a college education and courses in computer science, business data processing, and data-base management system design. Many colleges offer courses in data-base management to train people to be data analysts.

The person who controls all the data resources of an organization is called the **data-base administrator (DBA).** The primary responsibilities of this position include:

- Developing a dictionary of standard data definitions so that all records are consistent.
- Designing data bases.
- Maintaining the accuracy, completeness, and timeliness of data bases.
- Designing procedures to ensure data security and data-base backup and recovery.
- Facilitating communications between analysts and users.
- Advising analysts, programmers, and system users about the best ways to use data bases.

A data-base administrator must have a high level of technical expertise, as well as the ability to communicate effectively with diverse groups of people. He or she also needs supervisory and leadership skills. The demand for data-base specialists is high. With the increasing trend toward data-base management, the need for people with the technical knowledge to design data-base application systems is increasing.

Information System Managers

Historically, data processing managers have been programmers or system analysts who worked their way up to management positions with little formal management training. But the increasing emphasis on information systems and information management has brought a change; professional managers with demonstrable leadership qualities and communication skills are being hired to manage information system departments.

The **management information system (MIS) manager** is responsible for planning and tying together all the information resources of a firm. The manager is responsible for organizing the physical and human resources of a department. He or she must devise effective control mechanisms to monitor progress toward company goals. The following knowledge and skills are useful assets for an MIS manager:

■ A thorough understanding of an organization, its goals, and its business activities.
■ Leadership qualities to motivate and control highly skilled people.
■ Knowledge of data-processing methods and familiarity with available hardware and software.

A person seeking a career in information system management should have a college degree. A degree in business administration with a concentration in the area of management information systems is desirable for managing business data-processing centers. Some employers prefer an individual with an MBA degree. To handle high-level management responsibilities, a candidate should have at least two years of extensive management experience, advanced knowledge of the industry in which the individual hopes to work, and competence in all technical, professional, and business skills.

❑ PROFESSIONAL ASSOCIATIONS

Societies have been formed that increase communication among professional people in computer fields. The purposes of these organizations vary, but most attempt to share current knowledge through the publication of professional journals and encourage the ongoing professional education of members.

AFIPS

The American Federation of Information Processing Societies (AFIPS), organized in 1961, is a national federation of professional societies established to represent member societies on an international basis and to advance and disseminate knowledge of these societies. There are two categories of AFIPS participation: (a) member societies that have a principal interest in computers and information processing; and (b) affiliated societies that, although not primarily concerned with computers and information processing, have a major interest in this area. Some of the prominent constituent societies of AFIPS are the Association for Computing Machinery (ACM), the Data Processing Management Association (DPMA), the Institute of Electrical and Electronic Engineers (IEEE), and the American Society for Information Science (ASIS). Affiliated societies of AFIPS include the American Institute of Certified Public Accountants (AICPA) and the American Statistical Association (ASA).

ACM

The Association for Computing Machinery (ACM) is the largest scientific, educational, and technical society of the computing community. Founded in 1947, this association is dedicated to the development of information processing as a discipline and to the responsible use of computers in increasingly complex and diverse applications. The objectives of the association are:

■ To advance the science and art of information processing, including the study, design, development, construction, and application of modern machinery, computing techniques, and programming software.

■ To promote the free exchange of ideas in the field of information processing in a professional manner, among both specialists and the public.

■ To develop and maintain the integrity and competence of individuals engaged in the field of information processing.

DPMA

Founded in Chicago as the National Machine Accountants Association, the Data Processing Management Association (DPMA) was chartered in December 1961. At that time the first electronic computer had yet to come into commercial use. The name "machine accountants" was chosen to identify persons associated with the operation and supervision of punched-card equipment. The society took its present name in 1962.

DPMA is one of the largest worldwide organizations serving the information-processing and management communities. It comprises all levels of management personnel. Through its educational and publishing activities, DPMA seeks to encourage high standards in the field of data processing and to promote a professional attitude among its members.

One of DPMA's specific purposes is to promote and develop educational and scientific inquiry in the field of data processing and data-processing management. It sponsors college student organizations interested in data processing and encourages members to serve as counselors for the Boy Scout computer merit badge. The organization also presents DPMA's Distinguished Information Sciences Award for outstanding contributions to computer use in information management.

ASM

The Association of Systems Management (ASM), founded in 1947, is headquartered in Cleveland, Ohio. The ASM is an international organization engaged in keeping its members abreast of the rapid growth and change occurring in the field of systems management and information processing. It provides for the professional growth and development of its members and of the systems profession through:

■ Extended programs in local and regional areas in the fields of education and research.

■ Annual conferences and committee functions in research, education, and public relations.

■ Promotion of high standards of work performance by members of the ASM and members of the systems profession.

■ Publication of the *Journal of Systems Management,* technical reports, and other works on subjects of current interest to systems practitioners.

ICCP

The Institute of Certification of Computer Professionals is a nonprofit organization established in 1973 for the purpose of testing and certifying the knowledge and skills of computing personnel. A primary objective of the ICCP is to pool the resources of constituent societies so that the full attention of the information-processing industry can be focused on the vital tasks of development and recognition of qualified personnel.

The establishment of the ICCP was an outgrowth of studies made by committees of the DPMA and the ACM, which developed the concept of a "computer foundation" to foster testing and certification programs of DPMA. The ICCP has four certificates: Associate Systems Professional (ASP), Certified Systems Professional (CSP), Certificate in Computer Programming (CCP), and Certificate in Data Processing (CDP). Candidates for certificates must pass examinations on material related to their area. For example, a candidate for the CDP certificate must pass exams covering data processing equipment, computer programming and software, principles of management, quantitative methods, and system analysis and design. In addition, certification requirements require varying degrees of work experience.

Because the computer field changes so rapidly, certificate holders must be recertified every three years. Candidates for recertification can either take a new exam or they can earn recertification credit by participating in educational activities such as attending seminars or writing for publication.

SIM

The Society for Information Management (SIM) was founded in 1968 to serve persons concerned with all aspects of management information systems in the electronic data-processing industry, including business system designers, managers, and educators. The organizational aims include providing an exchange or marketplace for technical information about management information systems and enhancing communications between MIS directors and executives responsible for the management of business enterprises. SIM also offers educational and research programs, sponsors competitions, bestows awards, and maintains placement programs.

CONCEPT SUMMARY 3–2	
Professional Associations	
Association	**Purpose**
AFIPS	To represent member societies on an international basis and to advance and disseminate knowledge of the member societies.
ACM	To develop information processing as a discipline and promote responsible use of computers in diverse applications.
DPMA	To encourage high standards in the field of data processing and to promote a professional attitude among members.
ASM	To keep members abreast of rapid change and growth in the field of systems management and information processing.
ICCP	To test and certify knowledge and skills of computing personnel.
SIM	To provide an exchange or marketplace for technical information about MIS and to enhance communications between MIS directors and executives.

◼ SUMMARY POINTS

◼ As information needs increase, information systems are in great demand for processing information and presenting it in meaningful ways to decision makers.

◼ In order to be meaningful and appropriate for decision making, information must be timely, relevant, accurate, verifiable, complete, and clear. Information that meets these criteria is suitable for decision making.

◼ A system is a group of related elements that work together toward a common goal. A system includes inputs, processes, outputs, and feedback. Many systems are subsystems of larger systems.

◼ The boundaries between systems are seldom easy to define. It is also difficult to identify the elements of a system that might stand alone as systems in themselves. The determination of boundaries and elements depends on the level or scope with which we view the system.

◼ System theory can be applied to an organization: it has a group of related elements (departments and employees) working together toward a common goal (survival, growth, or profit).

◼ The four main components of an information system include hardware, software, data, and people.

◼ Hardware consists of equipment, or the parts of the computer that can be seen. An information system has several kinds of hardware. Input equipment is used to place data in the computer. Processing equipment performs operations on data placed in the computer. Output equipment transfers data or information from one location to another. Storage devices hold data before and after processing.

◼ Software consists of the specific sequences of instructions required to run a computer.

◼ People are a necessary part of an information system, for they bring together the other parts and coordinate all activities within the system. People in an information system are categorized by the roles they perform: providers, users, and clients.

◼ Synergistic relationships are those in which the combined effort of all the parts is greater than the sum of each part operating independently.

◼ One consideration in determining the value of information to a firm is whether it reduces the uncertainty that surrounds the outcome of a decision. The degree to which information reduces uncertainty determines its value to the organization.

◼ Businesses quantify the value of information by determining the cost of obtaining the information and then comparing that with the cost of making a decision without the information.

◼ Businesses use computer-based information systems in different ways to meet the needs of management, employees, and customers. Information systems are commonly used in accounting, finance, marketing, human resources, product management, and engineering.

◼ Businesses that develop creative ways of using computers to improve efficiency and increase profits gain an edge over their competition.

◼ Computer-related personnel such as programmers, analysts, data-base specialists and information systems managers are increasingly in demand.

◼ Programmers perform three types of programming: application programming, maintenance programming, and system programming.

◼ As more and more people have chosen careers in computer-related fields, societies have been formed that increase communication among professionals. Most of these societies attempt to share current knowledge through the publication of professional journals and to encourage the ongoing professional education of members. Some of these societies are AFIPS, ACM, DPMA, ASM, ICCP, and SIM.

■ TERMS FOR REVIEW

application programmer, p. 70

audit trail, p. 58

computer-aided design (CAD), p. 68

computer-aided engineering (CAE), p. 68

computer operator, p. 69

data-base analyst, p. 72

data-base administrator (DBA), p. 72

data-entry operator, p. 69

debug, p. 70

feedback, p. 59

GIGO (garbage in–garbage out), p. 58

input, p. 59

keypunch operator, p. 69

librarian, p. 69

maintenance programmer, p. 70

management information system (MIS) manager, p. 73

materials requirement planning (MRP), p. 67

output, p. 59

process, p. 59

remote terminal operator, p. 70

synergism, p. 64

system, p. 59

system analyst, p. 71

system programmer, p. 71

■ REVIEW QUESTIONS

1. What does GIGO stand for? Why is GIGO an important concept in information processing?

2. What is an audit trail? Why would an audit trail be used? How does it work?

3. What are the six qualities of information? Give a brief description of each.

4. In general terms, what is a system? What fundamental elements comprise an information system?

5. Name five common ways information systems are used in businesses. Name five additional ways that are not discussed in the text.

6. Take one of the five uses of information systems you named in the second part of Question 5 and give a brief description of how such an application works.

7. Give a brief description of how a materials requirement planning (MRP) system works?

8. What tasks are performed by a data-processing librarian? What qualifications are required in order to be a librarian?

9. What types of programmers are considered system development personnel? Give a brief description of each of these programming positions.

10. Briefly describe what role a system analyst plays in the development of information systems.

Chase Manhattan

The Chase Manhattan Corporation started out in 1799 as a New York City water company, the brainchild of Aaron Burr. Through Burr's lobbying in the New York State Legislature, the company was permitted to use capital not required in the water business in other money transactions or operations. Thus on Sept. 1, 1799, the Bank of the Manhattan Company broke the monopoly of Alexander Hamilton's federal institution, The Bank of the United States.

In 1955 the Chase Manhattan Bank was formed by a merger between Chase National, the nation's third largest bank, and the Bank of The Manhattan Company, the fifteenth largest.

From its earliest days, the Bank of The Manhattan Company supported the nation's economic development. The bank made its first ship construction loan in 1805. It frequently financed East India trade in the early 1800s. It provided major funding for the construction of the Erie Canal.

In the years following World War II, Chase solidified its position as the bank to corporate America, and the bank's retail branch capabilities continued to grow. In the 1950s Chase developed one of the first corporate computer facilities. Then, in 1961, Chase installed a fully automated check processing and demand deposit accounting computer system, the first of its kind in New York City.

Today Chase is a global wholesale and consumer financial institution doing business in more than 100 countries. Quality—in people, products and technology—makes Chase a recognized leader and innovator worldwide, providing corporations and individuals with superior products and service.

INFORMATION TO THE DESKTOP
A major goal of computer technology in business today is information delivery—getting the right information to the right people in ways and in a timeframe that meet their decision-making needs. This means finding ways to bring focused information to the desktop computers of business professionals and making sure the access to the information is easy to use and easy to share.

CFIX. Business people who have information before their competitors are positioned to be the first to identify profit-able opportunities. Chase Manhattan Bank's deal makers often have such an advantage, in large part because of the Corporate Finance Information Exchange (CFIX), a communications network that supplies timely market data to the desktops of some 1,200 banking professionals in North America and Europe.

CFIX, which went online in September of 1988, provides access to many internal and external information services and products, such as real-time news wires, data bases, and global electronic mail. These features give Chase deal makers key business information and the opportunity to close lucrative business deals quickly.

Chase's "client/server computing" finds the balance between the need for integration and the traditional independence of business units.

CFIX presents information in a straightforward, predictable, responsive, easy-to-use format. The system can be accessed not only at work, but also at home or on the road using microcomputers such as laptop terminals. Chase employees can therefore tap into information around the globe and around the clock. CFIX products are also standardized, thus enabling users to send, receive, and process information with an identical "look and feel" all across the nation. Finally, CFIX integrates every information technology a business requires into a seamless network, thereby obviating the need to change terminals to access different applications.

In short, CFIX gets critical business information to the front lines quickly, giving Chase a competitive edge.

Chase-Mail. A generic form of information delivery is electronic mail or "e-mail." Chase's electronic mail network, called Chase-Mail, enables more than 10,000 Chase employees to send messages and documents reliably to colleagues around the world. Highly specialized, complex software integrates otherwise incompatible e-mail systems put in place from multiple vendors by Chase's decentralized businesses. The goal is to create a single network that will have 20,000 Chase users by 1992.

Chase-Mail serves not only as a messaging system, but also as the infrastructure for the delivery of all kinds of information to the desktop. (CFIX, for example—described above—taps into Chase-Mail to deliver its news items and business information.) Chase-Mail transcends time zones and geographies, and eliminates communications blockages. In May, 1990, Chase-Mail was also linked to a public electronic mail network operated by MCI, allowing Chase to do business electronically with customers who subscribe to MCI's system.

CHASE SYSTEMS ARCHITECTURE

At Chase, the technological byword today is integration. For a large global organization, systems integration is a necessity, requiring a technological infrastructure that provides for the rapid exchange of information across all products and markets. At Chase, this integration is taking place against a long-term commitment to decentralization.

Chase employs over 4,000 information systems people in a wide variety of data-processing centers around the world, with hundreds of products and systems of all sizes and makes. Since the mid-1970s, responsibility for these people and computers has been distributed among the various business units. This brought systems and business people closer together, making it possible for technology to become an integral part of many of the bank's lines of business and for individual business units to make the technology trade-offs they deemed worthwhile. The challenge today is finding the balance between the need for integration and the traditional independence of the business units.

To help meet this challenge, Chase has developed a Computing Environment Strategy (CES) to act as a framework for developing competitive systems into the 1990s. Specifically, the goal of Chase's CES is to define the infrastructure on which applications would run. At the heart of CES lie basic business objectives, including the following:

■ timely, accurate, and secure delivery of global financial products
■ improved ability to share, as well as provide, information and processing across business lines

■ increased cost efficiencies by leveraging modern technologies
■ rapid development of computer-based products

To move toward Chase's CES, much effort has been directed towards the definition of an infrastructure called "client/server computing." Unlike the host/terminal, hierarchical model of the 70s and 80s, client/server computing emphasizes distributed intelligence in a peer environment. Some of its key characteristics are listed:

1. Workstations, or "clients," are independent of processors.
2. Workstations see a network of available applications and computing resources.

3. Workstations can access any server (host, minicomputer, PC server).

4. Workstations are separate and distinct from applications.

5. Servers communicate with each other as peers, in a non-hierarchical manner.

6. Access to applications requires no knowledge of communications pathways or routing.

7. Access methods are uniform across systems.

8. A standard set of security management approaches will be used.

Chase's CES and its architectural principles are intended to provide an optimum network and applications development infrastructure. The goal is to allow Chase to develop competitive products for today's banking environment. As we head into the 90s, this promises to be a challenging and exciting goal for the bank to fulfill.

DISCUSSION POINTS

1. How does the Chase philosophy exemplify the qualities of useful information?

2. Define the word *synergism* in terms of the Chase information system.

CHAPTER 4

Hardware

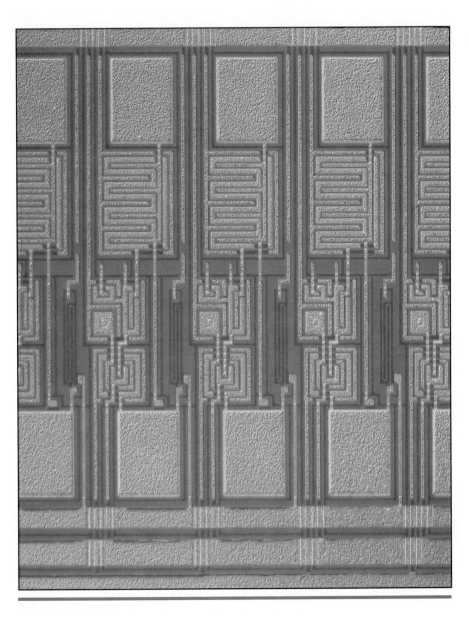

'Biochips': Life Mimics Electronics

Neil Gross, *Business Week*

In elementary school in a Tokyo suburb, Isao Karube dreamed of becoming a ship's captain. After high school, he enrolled in the Tokyo University of Fisheries. But his career was very short. The reason: seasickness. "My first day on the open sea was also my last," he recalls wistfully.

Today, 48-year-old Karube is one of Japan's most prolific scientists. At Tokyo University's Research Center for Advanced Science & Technology, he heads one of the world's largest laboratories pursuing bioelectronics, a new science that combines semiconductor fabrication techniques and biochemistry to produce novel electronic devices and sensors from living organisms. The ultimate goal: biochips, in which organic molecules will be made to mimic the electronic circuitry in computers.

"The work is very far-reaching," says Jonathan Cooper, a biochemist at Britain's University of Newcastle-upon-Tyne, who recently worked in Karube's lab. To make a sensor that warns of certain toxic chemicals, for example, one team cloned the gene for the enzyme that makes a firefly glow, implanting it in a microorganism. Photodetectors monitor the light-emitting bacteria, which weaken in the presence of toxins.

Most of Japan's cutting-edge R&D today is done in companies, but Karube has built a flourishing university-based empire. His team of 44 staff and graduate students is tackling a staggering array of projects. One group has linked neural-network computers and an array of 10 membrane-based sensors that detect odors. The result: an experimental machine that can be programmed to test perfumes—or sniff out hidden explosives or cocaine. Another team is crafting ultrathin sensors that doctors will someday be able to insert directly into a patient's brain to test for chemical compounds. Others are working on artificial photosynthesis.

Karube acknowledges that Americans did the trailblazing. Thirty years ago, Leland C. Clark of the Children's Hospital Research Foundation in Cincinnati developed the world's first sensors used to measure oxygen and glucose in the blood. But they required removing blood by syringe, and the test took half an hour. Karube's researchers made the sensors the size of sewing needles, so the test could be done quickly in the bloodstream. The first commercial application is a glucose analyser for diabetics, developed with Fuji Electric Co.

Karube maintains close ties with industry. Seventeen of his researchers are on loan from corporate labs. For example, a long collaboration with auto-parts giant Nippondenso Co. yielded a wrist-watch-like sweat sensor that monitors a driver's heart rate and general alertness. Another project, with a major food distributor, resulted in sensors to test the freshness of fish.

Karube's influence doesn't stop at the lab door. He advises the Japanese government on half a dozen research projects in biotechnology. They include a $10 million project in artificial membranes, another in wastewater disposal, and one that will screen algae from all over the world in search of microorganisms that absorb ozone-depleting gases.

Although the technology of biosensors and biochips is still in its infancy, Karube believes it will have a major impact in the 21st century. Someday, he predicts, the synthesis of molecular biology and microelectronics will enable direct communication between computers and the human brain. That goal will undoubtedly keep him running breathless for a long time. "I'd still like to be a sailor," says the professor, "but there's plenty to be done on dry land."

◘ INTRODUCTION

It is possible to obtain a general understanding of electronic data processing without undertaking a detailed study of computer technology, just as it is possible to generally comprehend how a car operates without undertaking a detailed study of the internal combustion engine. However, with cars as well as computers, a general understanding of the machines' capabilities and limitations can be useful.

This chapter focuses on the parts of a computer system. The central processing unit, or CPU, and its key components are identified and their functions explained. The chapter also examines various forms of memory and briefly discusses random-access memory (RAM), read-only memory (ROM), and programmable read-only memory (PROM). Data representation in relation to computer processing is discussed. Binary, octal, and hexadecimal number systems are covered, along with computer codes. The chapter concludes with a brief discussion of code checking.

◘ CENTRAL PROCESSING UNIT

The **central processing unit (CPU)** is the heart of the computer system. It is composed of three parts that function together as a unit. These components are the control unit, the arithmetic/logic unit, and memory. Although memory is considered to be part of the CPU, it is normally located on separate circuit boards which are then connected to the CPU. Each part of the CPU performs its own unique functions (see Figure 4–1).

While the CPU incorporates all three components, the control unit and the arithmetic/logic unit are often referred to collectively as the **processor.** A processor may incorporate one or more circuit elements, or ''chips.'' In a large computer, the processor may be built on several circuit boards in boxlike structures or frames, hence the term *mainframe.* Processors in microcomputers have been reduced in size to fit onto a single plug-in chip and are referred to as microprocessors.

When data and programs enter the CPU, they are held in memory. Since memory is volatile, or nonpermanent, data or programs will be erased when the electric power to the computer is turned off or disrupted in any other way. When any changes or results are to be preserved, they must be saved on an external form of storage, for example, on disks or magnetic tapes.

To begin work, programs and data to be manipulated are written into memory. What happens to the contents of memory depends on the processor. The processor, as stated earlier, consists of two processing units: the control unit and the arithmetic/logic unit. The **control unit** maintains order and controls activity in the CPU. It does not process or store data; it directs the sequence of operations. The control unit interprets the instructions of a program in memory and produces signals that ''command'' circuits to execute the instructions. Other functions of the control unit include communicating with an input device in order to begin the transfer of instructions and data into memory and, similarly, communicating with an output device to initiate the transfer of results to storage.

The manipulation of the data occurs in the **arithmetic/logic unit (ALU)** of the CPU. The ALU performs arithmetic computations and logical operations. Arithmetic computations include addition, subtraction, multiplication, and division. Logical comparisons include six combinations of equality: equal to, not equal to, greater than, less than, equal to or greater than, and equal to or less than. Since the bulk of internal

FIGURE 4–1

Computer System Components

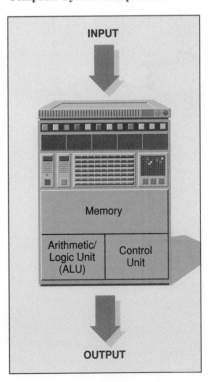

processing involves calculations or comparisons, computer capabilities often depend upon the design and capabilities of the ALU.

Memory (also known as **primary memory, internal memory,** or **main memory**) holds instructions, data, and intermediate and final results of processing. At the start of processing, data is transferred from some form of input media by an input device to memory, where it is kept until needed for processing. Data being processed and intermediate results of ALU calculations are also stored here. After all computations and manipulations are completed, the final results remain in memory until the control unit causes them to be transferred to an output device. See Concept Summary 4–1 for a review of the central processing unit.

FIGURE 4–2

Memory Segmentation

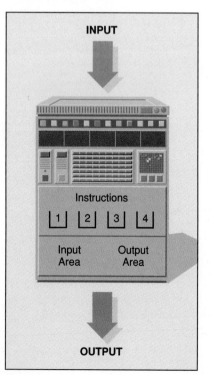

▣ INSTRUCTIONS

A computer functions by processing a series of instructions. Each computer instruction has two basic parts: the operation code and the operand. The **operation code (op code)** indicates to the control unit what function is to be performed (such as ADD, MOVE, DATA, or COMPARE). The **operand** indicates the location within memory of the data on which to operate. (Op codes and operands will be discussed in more detail in Chapter 12.)

The computer performs instructions sequentially, in the order they are given, unless instructed to do otherwise. This **next-sequential-instruction** feature requires that instructions be placed in consecutive locations in memory. Otherwise, the computer would be unable to differentiate between instructions and data. Since input must be brought into the computer for processing, a separate area must be designated for the input. The output generated by processing also requires an area isolated from the instructions (see Figure 4–2).

Input to a computer can take many forms. In one form, data and instructions can be entered into the computer by pressing keys on a terminal keyboard. Another method relies on data that is stored on magnetic disks or tapes. No matter what method is used to enter data into a computer, once the process begins, the control unit directs the input device to transfer instructions and data to memory. Then the control unit takes one instruction from memory, examines it, and sends electronic signals to the ALU and memory, which causes the instruction to be carried out. The signals sent to memory may tell it to transfer data to the ALU, where it is manipulated. The result may then be transferred back to memory.

After an instruction has been executed, the control unit takes the next instruction from the memory unit. Data may be transferred from memory to the ALU and back several times before all instructions are executed. When all manipulations are complete, the control unit directs the memory unit to transfer the processed data (information) to the output device.

The most widely used output devices are printers, which provide results on paper; visual-display units, which project results on a television-like screen; and tape and disk drives, which produce machine-readable magnetic information. (These devices will be discussed in Chapters 5 and 6).

If more than one input record is to be processed, the steps that have been described will be repeated for each record. These steps can be summarized as shown in Figure 4–3. Notice that, like humans, computers can execute only one instruction at a time.

FIGURE 4–3

CPU Operations

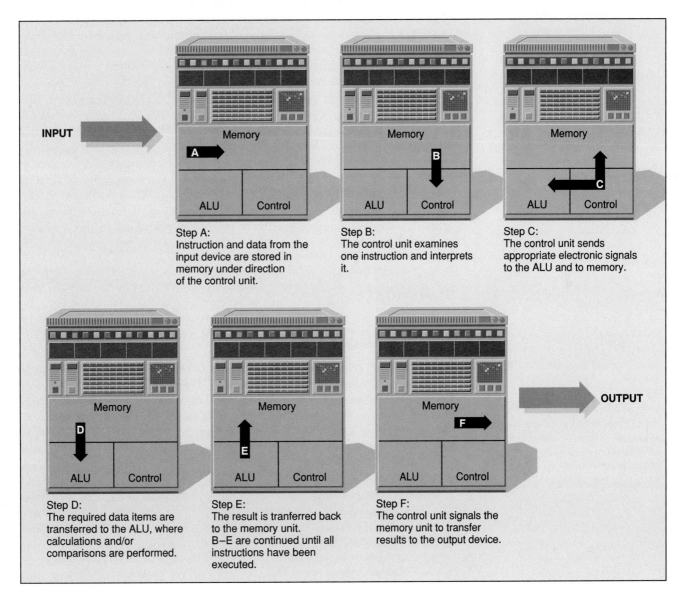

INPUT

Memory

A

ALU | Control

Step A:
Instruction and data from the input device are stored in memory under direction of the control unit.

Memory

B

ALU | Control

Step B:
The control unit examines one instruction and interprets it.

Memory

C

ALU | Control

Step C:
The control unit sends appropriate electronic signals to the ALU and to memory.

Memory

D

ALU | Control

Step D:
The required data items are transferred to the ALU, where calculations and/or comparisons are performed.

Memory

E

ALU | Control

Step E:
The result is tranferred back to the memory unit. B–E are continued until all instructions have been executed.

Memory

F

ALU | Control

OUTPUT

Step F:
The control unit signals the memory unit to transfer results to the output device.

A Glimpse into the Future of Supercomputers

According to Superperformance Computing Service (SCS), a market research firm located in Mountain View, California, supercomputers in the year 2000 will have incredible processing power. SCS has based its projections on research done by the Semiconductor Research Corporation. The Semiconductor Research Corporation's members include IBM, AT&T, Control Data Corporation, Digital Equipment Corporation, Hewlett-Packard Company, Texas Instruments, Inc., Intel Corporation, National Semiconductor Corporation, and Motorola, Inc.

SCS predicts that by the year 2000 supercomputers will have as many as 256 processors and contain from 1 trillion to 100 trillion bytes of memory. The processors contained in these computers will be no larger than 16 cubic centimeters, but will be capable of executing 10 trillion floating-point mathematical operations per second. The prices of these supercomputers are estimated to be around $100 million, which is considered cheap compared to the incredible processing power they will offer. However, in order for this type of supermachine to be built, a number of advances in computer chip manufacturing must be made in the 1990s.

Remember, the power of computers comes from the fact that they are accurate when processing and can work at incredibly high speeds.

◼ STORED-PROGRAM CONCEPT

In Chapter 1 a program was defined as a series of instructions that direct the computer to perform a given task. In early computers, instructions had to be either wired on control panels and plugged into the computer at the beginning of a job or read into the computer from punched cards in distinct steps as the job progressed. This approach slowed down processing because the computer had to wait for instructions by a human operator. To speed up processing, the memory of the computer began to be used to store the instructions as well as the data. This development, the **stored-program concept,** was significant; since instructions were stored in computer memory in electronic form, no human intervention was required during processing. The computer could proceed at its own speed—close to the speed of light!

Modern computers can store programs. Once instructions required for an application have been determined, they are placed into computer memory so the appropriate operations will be performed. The memory unit operates much as a tape recorder. Once instructions are stored, they remain in memory until new ones are stored over them. This same process holds true for data as well. Data in the computer is held until new data is placed over top of it. Therefore, the same instructions or data can be used over and over again until they are changed. The process of accessing the same instructions or data over and over is called **reading.** Storing new instructions or data in computer memory is called **writing.** The basic characteristic, therefore, is known as **nondestructive read/destructive write.** When instructions or data are read, they do not replace or destroy previous instructions or data. When new instructions or data are written into the computer memory, whatever was formerly in that area of memory is destroyed. A series of instructions placed into memory is called a **stored program.**

◼ MEMORY

Memory Locations

In order to direct processing operations, the control unit of the CPU must be able to locate each instruction and data item in memory. Therefore, each location in memory is assigned an **address.** One way to understand this concept is to picture computer memory as a large collection of mailboxes. Each mailbox is a specific location with its own number or address (see Figure 4–4). Each can hold one item of information. Since each location in memory has a unique address, items can be located by use of stored-program instructions that provide their addresses. Sometimes data at a location must be changed, added to, or deleted during execution of the program. The programmer assigns a **variable,** or symbolic name, to the piece of data that is stored at that memory location.

To understand variables, consider this example. Suppose the computer is directed to subtract TAX from GROSS PAY to determine an employee's NET PAY. Suppose further that TAX is stored at location 104 and has a value of 55.60 and that GROSS PAY is stored at location 111 and has a value of 263.00. To determine an employee's

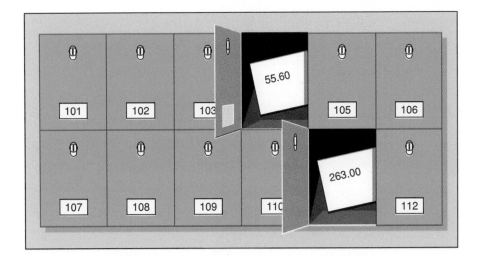

FIGURE 4–4

Each mailbox represents a storage location with a unique address.

NET PAY, the programmer instructs the computer to subtract TAX from GROSS PAY. The computer interprets this to mean that it should subtract the contents of location 104 from the contents of location 111.

Programmers must keep track of what is stored at each location, and variable names help in this task. It is easier for the programmer to use names such as TAX and GROSS PAY and let the computer translate them into addresses assigned to memory locations. The term *variable* means that while the variable name (memory address) does not change, data stored at the location may. The values of TAX and GROSS PAY are likely to change with each employee. The addresses of TAX and GROSS PAY will not.

Primary Memory

Primary memory is the section of the CPU that holds instructions, data, and intermediate results during processing. It may, in some cases, be supplemented by **storage** (also called auxiliary, external, or secondary storage) which is separate from the CPU. Information is transferred between memory and storage through electrical lines. The most common storage media are discussed more fully in Chapter 6.

Second- and third-generation computers contained memory units composed of magnetic cores. Each core could store one bit (short for *bi*nary digi*t*). When electricity flowed through the wires making up the cores, a magnetic field was created. The direction of the magnetic field determined which binary state a core represented. A magnetic field in one direction indicated an "on" (1) condition; a magnetic field in the other direction indicated an "off" (0) condition (see Figure 4–5).

Technological developments have led to the use of semiconductors in memory units. **Semiconductor memory** is composed of circuitry on **silicon chips.** Each chip, only slightly bigger than a single core, can hold as much data as thousands of cores, and operate at significantly faster speeds. Memory for most computers in use today consists of semiconductors (see Figure 4–6).

Semiconductors are designed to store data in locations called **bit cells,** which are capable of being either "on" or "off." An "on " state is represented by a 1, an "off" state by a 0. The bit cells are arranged in matrices; often these matrices are eight rows by eight columns. Unlike core memory, semiconductor memory does not

FIGURE 4–5

Magnetizing a Core

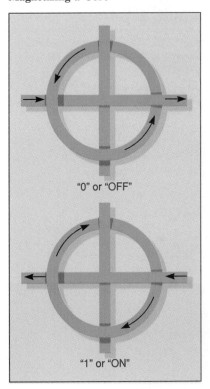

"0" or "OFF"

"1" or "ON"

FIGURE 4-6

IBM 3090 1-Megabit Memory Chip
This 1-megabit memory chip can hold as much data as thousands of cores.

store data magnetically. With semiconductor memory, electrical current is sent along the wires leading to the bit cells. At the points where the electrically charged wires intersect, the bit cells are in ''on'' states. The remaining cells are in ''off'' states (see Figure 4–7).

There are many different kinds of semiconductor memory, but most require a constant power source. Since they rely on currents to represent data, all data in memory

FIGURE 4-7

The shaded areas represent electrically charged bit cells. At the point where electrically charged wires intersect, the bit cells are ''on.''

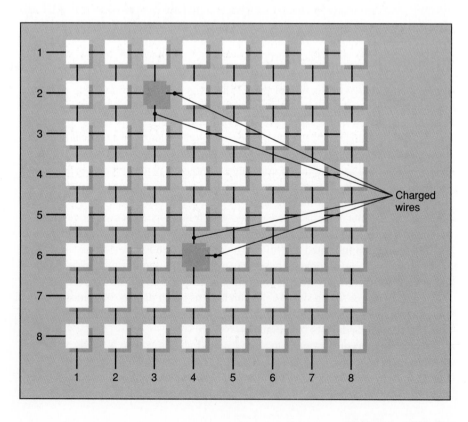

are lost if the power source fails and no emergency (backup) system exists. Core memory retains its contents even if the power source fails because it relies on magnetic charges rather than on currents. Despite this disadvantage of semiconductor memory, its speed makes it a more desirable form of memory than core.

A form of memory called **bubble memory** has been introduced as a replacement medium for both memory and storage. This memory consists of magnetized spots, or **magnetic domains,** resting on a thin film of semiconductor material. The magnetic domains (called bubbles) have a polarity opposite that of the semiconductor material on which they rest. Data is stored by shifting the bubbles into place on the surface of the material (see Figure 4–8). When data is read, the presence of a bubble indicates a 0 bit. Bubbles are similar to magnetic cores in that they retain their magnetism indefinitely. They are much smaller than magnetic cores and store more data in a smaller area. A bubble memory module only slightly larger than a quarter can store 20,000 characters of data. While some manufacturers are using bubble memory in computers, high costs and production problems have led to the limited use of it.

Random-Access Memory

Random-access memory (RAM) is the most widely used type of computer memory. The memory used to store programs and data during processing is RAM. RAM is the working area of the computer. As we have learned, this type of memory is not permanent. It relies on electrical current to store data and instructions. If the power to the computer is turned off or fails, the contents of RAM are lost. As the name suggests, the data and instructions stored in RAM can be accessed randomly, or directly. This is to say that instructions or data can be referenced by only their address. There is no need to search memory for the desired instruction or piece of data. The control unit is able to go directly to the desired instruction or piece of data based on its address.

The size of a computer's memory can be increased by installing additional RAM chips. In some cases, users can increase the size of their computer's memory simply by plugging more RAM chips into the memory circuit board(s) of the computer. Other RAM chips must be installed by the computer manufacturer or by trained service personnel. The method of installation depends on the design of the computer's circuit boards. RAM chips are commonly used to install additional memory in microcomputers.

Read-Only Memory (ROM)

Computers are capable of performing complex functions such as taking square roots and evaluating exponents. Such functions can be built into the hardware or software of a computer. When the functions are built into the hardware, they provide the advantage of speed and reliability since the operations are part of the actual computer circuitry. Building functions into software allows more flexibility, but carrying out functions built into software is slower and more prone to error.

When functions are built into the hardware of a computer, they are placed in **read-only memory (ROM).** Read-only memory instructions are **hard-wired** and cannot be changed or deleted by other stored-program instructions. Since ROM is permanent, it cannot be occupied by common stored-program instructions or data and can only be changed by altering the physical construction of the circuits. Sometimes ROM chips are called *firmware*. Building instructions into ROM makes the distinction between hardware and software less clear-cut (see Figure 4–9).

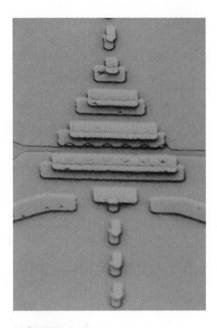

FIGURE 4–8

Bubble Memory

FIGURE 4–9

ROM Chip

Microprograms are a direct result of hard wiring. Microprograms are sequences of instructions built into read-only memory to carry out functions (such as calculating square roots) that otherwise would have to be directed by stored-program instructions at a much slower speed. Although some machines can be programmed by users at the microprogram level, microprograms are usually supplied by computer manufacturers and cannot be altered by users. Vendors can, however, tailor microprograms to meet the specific needs of users. If all instructions that a computer can execute are located in ROM, a new set of instructions can be obtained by changing the ROM. When selecting a computer, users can get the standard features of the machines plus their choice of the optional features available through microprogramming.

Read-only memory is different from nondestructive read. With nondestructive read, items stored in memory can be read repeatedly without loss of information. New items can then be stored over old ones if the stored program instructs the computer to do so. Read-only memory, on the other hand, is hard-wired into the computer and can only be changed by rewiring.

A version of ROM that can be programmed by the end user is **programmable read-only memory (PROM)**. PROM can be programmed by the manufacturer, or it can be shipped "blank" to another company that will program it for use by the end user. Once programmed, its contents are unalterable. With PROM the end user has the advantages of ROM along with the flexibility to meet unique needs. A problem with it, though, is that mistakes programmed into the unit cannot be corrected. To overcome this drawback, **erasable programmable read-only memory (EPROM)** has been developed (see Figure 4–10). EPROM can be erased but only when it is submitted to a special process, such as being bathed in ultraviolet light. Concept Summary 4–2 presents a review of RAM and ROM.

FIGURE 4–10

EPROM Chip

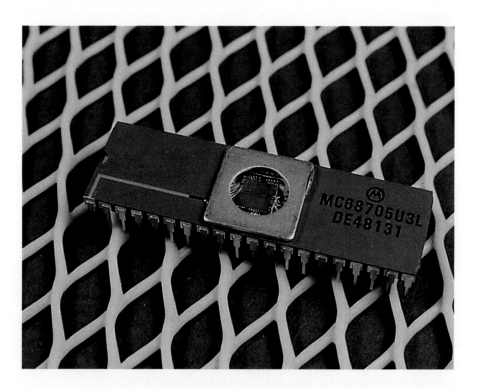

RAM and ROM

RAM	ROM
Stands for random-access memory	Stands for read-only memory
Form of memory for holding temporary data and instructions	Form of memory for holding permanent data and instructions
Volatile: Programs and data are erased when the power is disrupted	Permanent: Programs and data remain intact even when power is off
	Other forms of ROM: PROM—Programmable ROM EPROM—Erasable PROM

Registers

Registers are temporary holding areas in the CPU for instructions and data, but they are not considered part of memory. Registers can receive information, hold it, and transfer it very quickly as directed by the control unit of the CPU.

The CPU has a number of different types of registers, but essentially they all operate in the same way. A register functions much as a standard pocket calculator does. The person using the calculator acts as the control unit by transferring numbers from a sheet of paper to the calculator. This paper is analogous to the memory unit of the CPU. When the calculation is complete, the calculator (register) displays the result. The person (control unit) then transfers the result displayed on the calculator back to the sheet of paper (memory). This process is very similar to the way most modern computers work. Intermediate calculations are performed in registers, and the final results are transferred back to memory.

Cache Memory

Cache memory, also called a **high-speed buffer,** is a portion of memory used to speed the processing operations of the computer. Cache memory serves as a working buffer or temporary area to store both instructions and data. The program looks ahead and tries to anticipate what instructions and data must be accessed often and places these in cache memory. By storing the data or instructions in a temporary area of memory, the computer does not need to access storage. Accessing storage slows down the processing considerably. Although more expensive than storage, cache memory increases processing speeds, which sometimes warrants its use.

■ THE MICROPROCESSOR

As discussed earlier, the microprocessor of a microcomputer differs slightly from the CPU of a minicomputer, mainframe computer, or supercomputer. The microprocessor

FIGURE 4–11

A 32-bit Microprocessor

is a silicon chip only fractions of an inch wide (see Figure 4–11). Microprocessors are typically categorized by their speed and the amount of memory they can directly, or randomly, access. The speed at which the microprocessor can execute instructions affects the overall speed of the microcomputer. Microprocessor speed is dependent on two factors: word size and clock speed.

The **word size** is the number of bits that can be processed by the microprocessor at one time. An eight-bit microprocessor, for example, can manipulate eight bits, or one byte, of data at a time. The majority of microcomputers being used today contain microprocessors capable of processing either sixteen or thirty-two bits of data at a time.

The **clock speed** of a microprocessor represents the number of electronic pulses the chip can produce each second. Clock speed is built into a microprocessor and is measured in **megahertz (MHz).** *Mega* means million and *hertz* means number of cycles, or pulses, per second. One megahertz is equal to one million cycles per second. The electronic pulses affect the speed at which the computer executes instructions. Therefore, increasing the word size and clock speed of a microprocessor can increase the microcomputer's overall speed. Microcomputers sold today have clock speeds ranging from 12.5 MHz to 33 MHz.

◻ DATA REPRESENTATION

Humans communicate information by using symbols that have specific meanings. Symbols such as letters or numbers are combined in meaningful ways to represent information. For example, the twenty-six letters of the English alphabet can be combined to form words, sentences, paragraphs, and so on. By combining individual words in various ways, we construct various messages. This enables us to communicate with one another.

HIGHLIGHT

Ceramic Computer Chips

Can computer chips be made out of materials other than silicon? Ramtron International Corporation of Colorado Springs, Colorado, is betting the answer to that question is yes. Ramtron is currently working to develop integrated circuits made out of a combination of ceramic material and silicon. Ramtron is etching integrated circuits into a thin ceramic film layered on top of silicon semiconductors. The advantage to this type of memory is two-fold: first, the new computer chips are much faster than traditional silicon circuits; secondly, the data stored in their memory will not be lost when the power is turned off.

Richard L. Horton, President of Ramtron International, believes that ceramic memory will replace nearly all types of computer memory, including hard disk drives. Ceramic-based memory is faster than silicon-based memory because the bit cells where data is stored can be packed much closer together than is possible in silicon. When these bit cells are closer together, electronic signals do not have to travel as far—which means that operations performed with this new type of memory are much faster. In addition, once ceramic bit cells are charged they stay that way for years. This allows for the use of ceramic memory as a form of storage as well.

Although the people at Ramtron hold that ceramic circuits will be the wave of the future in computer memory and storage, others in the computer chip industry are somewhat skeptical. Just exactly what the future holds for ceramic circuits may be uncertain. However, it is almost a sure thing that researchers will go on trying to find alternatives to silicon-based circuits in a continuing effort to improve computer chip performance and data storage reliability.

The human mind is much more complex than the computer. A computer is only a machine; it is not capable of understanding the inherent meanings of symbols used by humans to communicate. To use a computer, therefore, humans must convert their symbols to a form the computer is capable of ''understanding.'' This is accomplished through binary representation and the ''on'' and ''off'' states of electricity discussed earlier.

Binary Representation

Data is represented in the computer by the electrical state of the machine's circuitry: magnetic states for core memory, current for semiconductor memory, and the position of magnetic bubbles for bubble memory. In all cases, only two states are possible, ''on'' and ''off.'' This two-state system is known as the **binary system,** and its use to represent data is known as **binary representation.**

The **binary (base 2) number system** operates in a manner similar to the way the familiar **decimal number system** works. For example, the decimal number 4,672 can be analyzed as follows:

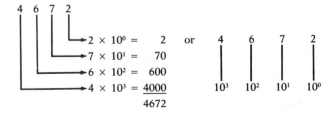

FIGURE 4–12

Decimal Place Value

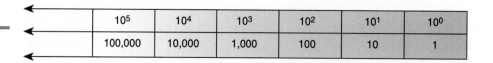

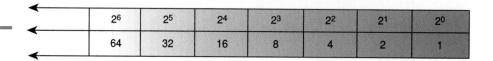

10^5	10^4	10^3	10^2	10^1	10^0
100,000	10,000	1,000	100	10	1

FIGURE 4–13

Binary Place Value

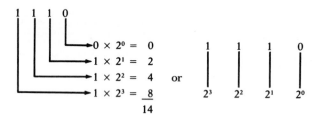

2^6	2^5	2^4	2^3	2^2	2^1	2^0
64	32	16	8	4	2	1

Each position represents a specific power of 10. The progression of powers is from right to left; that is, digits further to the left in a decimal number represent larger powers of 10 than digits to the right of them (see Figure 4–12).

The same principle holds for binary representation. The difference is that in binary representation each position in the number represents a power of 2 (see Figure 4–13). For example, consider the decimal number 14. In binary, the value equivalent to 14 is written as follows:

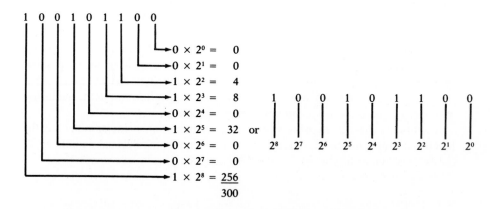

```
1  1  1  0
         →0 × 2⁰ =  0        1   1   1   0
      →1 × 2¹ =  2           |   |   |   |
   →1 × 2² =  4     or       |   |   |   |
→1 × 2³ =  8                2³  2²  2¹  2⁰
        14
```

As a further example, the value represented by the decimal number 300 is represented in binary form below:

```
1  0  0  1  0  1  1  0  0
                        →0 × 2⁰ =  0
                     →0 × 2¹ =  0
                  →1 × 2² =  4     1   0   0   1   0   1   1   0   0
               →1 × 2³ =  8        |   |   |   |   |   |   |   |   |
            →0 × 2⁴ =  0           |   |   |   |   |   |   |   |   |
         →1 × 2⁵ = 32     or       |   |   |   |   |   |   |   |   |
      →0 × 2⁶ =  0                 2⁸  2⁷  2⁶  2⁵  2⁴  2³  2²  2¹  2⁰
   →0 × 2⁷ =  0
→1 × 2⁸ = 256
        300
```

As indicated by the examples above, the binary number system uses 1s and 0s in various combinations to represent various values. Recall that each digit position in a binary number is called a bit. A 1 in a bit position indicates the presence of a specific power of 2; a 0 indicates the absence of a specific power. As in the decimal number system, the progression of powers is from right to left.

Octal Number System

Although all digital computers must store data as 0s and 1s, the sizes of the memory locations vary. Memory locations are referred to as **words,** and one word is equal to one "mailbox" (see discussion on memory locations and addresses earlier in this chapter). Word sizes are measured in bits and are typically 8, 16, 24, 32, 48, and 64 bits in length.

The **octal (base 8) number system,** which uses digits 0 to 7, can be employed as a shorthand method of representing the data contained within one word, or addressable memory location. In the case of 24 - and 48-bit word size computers, the octal number system provides a shorthand method of representing what is contained in memory. This is true because three binary digits, or bits, can be represented by one octal digit and both 24 and 48 are divisible by three.

As noted above, three binary digits can be represented by one octal digit. This is done by considering the first three binary place values from right to left that sum to seven, the highest digit value in the octal number system.

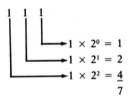

If we wanted to represent a binary value that was contained in a 24-bit word as an octal value, it could be converted as follows:

The octal value can be converted to its decimal equivalent. The octal number 1,702 is equivalent to the decimal number 962. Consider the conversion below, keeping in mind that each digit of the octal number represents a power of 8.

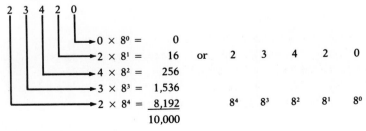

For another example, the value represented by the decimal number 10,000 is displayed in octal form below.

FIGURE 4-14

Core Dump

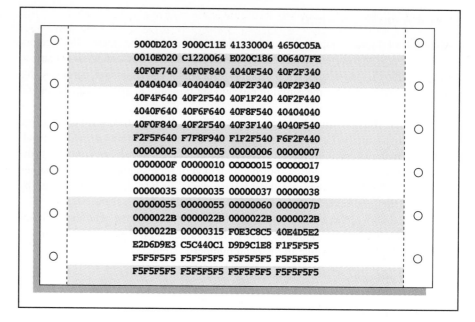

Hexadecimal Number System

When a program fails to execute correctly, it is sometimes necessary to examine the contents of certain memory locations to discover what is wrong. This can be done by obtaining a printout, or **dump,** of the contents of the memory locations (see Figure 4-14). If everything were printed in binary representation, the programmer would see page after page of 1s and 0s. Error detection would be difficult.

To alleviate this problem, the contents of memory locations in computers can be represented by the octal number system or the **hexadecimal (base 16) number system.** In the hexadecimal number system, sixteen symbols are used to represent the digits 0 through 15 (see Figure 4-15). Note that the letters A through F designate the numbers 10 through 15. The fact that each position in a hexadecimal number

FIGURE 4-15

Binary, Hexadecimal, and Decimal Equivalent Values

BINARY SYSTEM (PLACE VALUES)				HEXADECIMAL EQUIVALENT	DECIMAL EQUIVALENT
8	4	2	1		
0	0	0	0	0	0
0	0	0	1	1	1
0	0	1	0	2	2
0	0	1	1	3	3
0	1	0	0	4	4
0	1	0	1	5	5
0	1	1	0	6	6
0	1	1	1	7	7
1	0	0	0	8	8
1	0	0	1	9	9
1	0	1	0	A	10
1	0	1	1	B	11
1	1	0	0	C	12
1	1	0	1	D	13
1	1	1	0	E	14
1	1	1	1	F	15

represents a power of 16 allows for easy conversion from binary to hexadecimal since 16 is equal to 2^4. A single hexadecimal digit can be used to represent four binary digits.

As noted above, four binary digits can be represented by one hexadecimal digit. This is done by considering the first four binary place values (from right to left) that sum to 15, the highest single digit value in the hexadecimal number system.

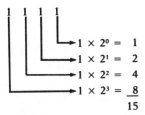

$$1 \times 2^0 = 1$$
$$1 \times 2^1 = 2$$
$$1 \times 2^2 = 4$$
$$1 \times 2^3 = \underline{8}$$
$$15$$

A binary value contained in a 32-bit word as a hexadecimal value could be converted as follows:

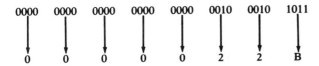

0000	0000	0000	0000	0000	0010	0010	1011
0	0	0	0	0	2	2	B

The hexadecimal value can be converted to its decimal equivalent. Keep in mind that each digit of the hexadecimal number represents a power of 16.

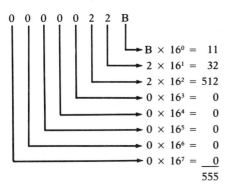

0 0 0 0 0 2 2 B

$$B \times 16^0 = 11$$
$$2 \times 16^1 = 32$$
$$2 \times 16^2 = 512$$
$$0 \times 16^3 = 0$$
$$0 \times 16^4 = 0$$
$$0 \times 16^5 = 0$$
$$0 \times 16^6 = 0$$
$$0 \times 16^7 = \underline{0}$$
$$555$$

Easy-to-Do Conversion

The division multiplication method is a simpler way to convert any decimal number to its equivalent in any other base system. Following this method, first, divide the number by the value of the base you have chosen until nothing is left to divide. The remainders of each division, written in each place starting with the ones place, form the new equivalent number. Here's how it works in base 2:

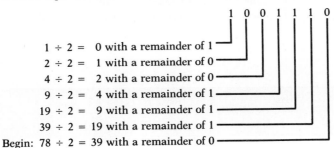

1 0 0 1 1 1 0

$$1 \div 2 = 0 \text{ with a remainder of } 1$$
$$2 \div 2 = 1 \text{ with a remainder of } 0$$
$$4 \div 2 = 2 \text{ with a remainder of } 0$$
$$9 \div 2 = 4 \text{ with a remainder of } 1$$
$$19 \div 2 = 9 \text{ with a remainder of } 1$$
$$39 \div 2 = 19 \text{ with a remainder of } 1$$
$$\text{Begin: } 78 \div 2 = 39 \text{ with a remainder of } 0$$

Now convert the decimal number 325 to a base 2 number. Did you get 101000101? Very good! So try something more difficult: Change 325 to a base 8 number. Was your answer 505? Good! That means 5 in the 64s place, 0 in the 8s place, and 5 in the 1s place. Try some more problems you make up.

Computer Codes

Many computers use coding schemes other than simple binary notation to represent numbers. One of the most basic coding schemes is called **four-bit binary coded decimal (BCD).** Rather than represent a decimal number as a string of 0s and 1s (which gets increasingly complicated for large numbers), BCD represents each decimal digit in a number by using four bits. For instance, the decimal number 23 is represented by two groups of four bits, one group for the "2," the other for the "3." Representations of the number 23 in four bit BCD and in binary are compared below:

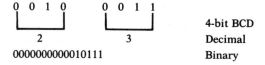

0 0 1 0	0 0 1 1	4-bit BCD
2	3	Decimal
0000000000010111		Binary

The representation of a three-digit decimal number in four-bit BCD consists of three sets of four bits, or twelve binary digits. For example, the decimal number 637 is coded as follows:

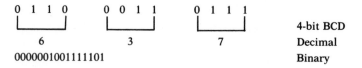

0 1 1 0	0 0 1 1	0 1 1 1	4-bit BCD
6	3	7	Decimal
0000001001111101			Binary

Use of a four-bit BCD saves space when large decimal numbers must be represented. Furthermore, it is easier to convert a four-bit BCD to its decimal equivalent than to convert a binary representation to decimal.

The four-bit code allows sixteen (2^4) possible unique bit combinations. We have already seen that ten of them are used to represent the decimal digits 0 through 9. Since that leaves only six remaining combinations, this code in practice is used only to represent numbers.

To represent letters and special characters as well as numbers, more than four bit positions are needed. Another coding scheme, called **six-bit BCD,** allows for sixty-four (2^6) unique combinations. Thus, six-bit BCD can be used to represent the decimal digits 0 through 9, the letters A through Z, and twenty-eight characters, such as the period and the comma.

The four rightmost bit positions in six-bit BCD are called **numeric bits.** The two leftmost bit positions are called **zone bits** (see Figure 4–16). The zone bits are used in various combinations with the numeric bits to represent numbers, letters, and special characters.

FIGURE 4–16

Bit Position in 6-Bit BCD Representation

ZONE BITS		NUMERIC BITS			
B	A	8	4	2	1

CHAPTER 4: HARDWARE

Another approach to data representation is an eight-bit code known as **Extended Binary Coded Decimal Interchange Code (EBCDIC).** An eight-bit code allows 256 (2^8) possible bit combinations. Whereas six-bit BCD can be used to represent only upper case letters, eight-bit EBCDIC can be used to represent uppercase and lowercase letters and additional special characters, such as the cent sign and the quotation mark. The EBCDIC bit combinations for uppercase letters and numbers are given in Figure 4–17.

In EBCDIC, the four leftmost bit positions are zone bits, and the four rightmost bit positions are numeric bits. As with six-bit BCD, the zone bits are used in various combinations with the numeric bits to represent numbers, letters, and special characters.

The **American Standard Code for Information Interchange (ASCII)** is a seven-bit code developed cooperatively by several computer manufacturers who wanted to develop a standard code for all computers. Because certain machines are designed to accept eight-bit rather than seven-bit code patterns, an eight-bit version of ASCII, called **ASCII-8,** was created. ASCII-8 and EBCDIC are similar, the key difference between them being in the bit patterns used to represent certain characters.

As described earlier, a fixed number of adjacent bits operated on as a unit is called a byte. Usually, one alphabetic character or two numeric characters are represented in one byte. Since eight bits are usually sufficient to represent a character, eight-bit groupings are basic units of memory. In computers that accept eight-bit characters, then, a byte is a group of eight adjacent bits. When large amounts of memory are described, the symbol **K** for kilobyte) is often used. Generally, one K equals 1,024 (2^{10}) units. Thus, a computer that has 256K bytes of memory can store $256 \times 1,024$, or 262,144 characters.

Code Checking

Computers do not always function perfectly; errors can and do occur. For example, a bit may be lost while data is being transferred from the ALU to the memory unit

Character	EBDIC Bit Configuration		Character	EBDIC Bit Configuration	
A	1100	0001	S	1110	0010
B	1100	0010	T	1110	0011
C	1100	0011	U	1110	0100
D	1100	0100	V	1110	0101
E	1100	0101	W	1110	0110
F	1100	0110	X	1110	0111
G	1100	0111	Y	1110	1000
H	1100	1000	Z	1110	1001
I	1100	1001	0	1111	0000
J	1101	0001	1	1111	0001
K	1101	0010	2	1111	0010
L	1101	0011	3	1111	0011
M	1101	0100	4	1111	0100
N	1101	0101	5	1111	0101
O	1101	0110	6	1111	0110
P	1101	0111	7	1111	0111
Q	1101	1000	8	1111	1000
R	1101	1001	9	1111	1001

FIGURE 4–17

EBCDIC Representation: 0–9, A–Z

FIGURE 4–18

Bit Positions of 6-Bit BCD with
Check Bit

CHECK BIT	ZONE BITS		NUMERIC BITS			
C	B	A	8	4	2	1

FIGURE 4–19

Detection of Error with Parity Check
(Odd Parity)

	C	B	A	8	4	2	1
Invalid – –➔	1	0	0	0	1	1	0
Valid ◀– –	1	0	0	0	0	1	0

or over telephone lines from one location to another. This loss can be caused by varied factors such as dust, moisture, magnetic fields, or equipment failure. Thus, it is necessary to have a method to detect the occurrence of an error and to isolate the location of the error.

Most computers accomplish this by having an additional bit, called a **parity bit,** or **check bit,** at each memory location. Computers that use parity bits are specifically designed always to have either an even or an odd number of 1 (or ''on'') bits in each memory location. If an odd number of 1 bits is used to represent each character, the characters are said to be written in **odd parity.** If an even number of 1 bits is used to represent each character, the characters are written in **even parity.** Internal circuitry in the computer constantly monitors its operation by checking to ensure that the required number of bits is present in each location.

For example, if the six-bit BCD code is used, a seventh bit is added as a check bit (see Figure 4–18). Suppose the number 6 is to be represented in six-bit BCD using odd parity (see Figure 4–19). In this case, the check bit must be set to 1, or ''on,'' to make the number of 1 bits odd. If a parity error is detected, the system may retry the read or write operation occurring when the error was detected. If retries are unsuccessful, the system informs the computer operator that an error has occurred.

Notice that the checking circuitry of the computer can only detect the miscoding of characters. It cannot detect the use of incorrect data. In the previous example, for instance, the computer circuitry could determine whether a bit had been dropped, making the representation of the number 6 invalid. However, if the number 5 had been mistakenly entered into the computer instead of 6 (perhaps because of incorrect keying), no code checking error would be detected.

■ SUMMARY POINTS

■ The central processing unit, the heart of the computer, is composed of three parts: the control unit, the arithmetic/logic unit (ALU), and memory. The control unit maintains order and controls what is happening in the CPU; the ALU performs arithmetic and logical operations; and the memory unit holds all data and instructions necessary for processing.

■ Instructions are placed in consecutive locations in memory so that they can be accessed one after the other. This is called the next-sequential-instruction feature.

■ The stored-program concept involves storing both data and instructions in the computer's memory, eliminating the need for human intervention during processing.

■ The nondestructive read/destructive write characteristic of memory allows a program to be re-executed, since the program remains intact in memory until another is stored over it.

■ Each location in memory has a unique address, which allows stored-program instructions and data items to be located by the control unit of the CPU as it directs processing operations. Variables (names for memory addresses) are used by programmers to facilitate data location.

■ One method of storing data in memory uses electrical currents to set magnetic cores to "on" and "off" states. Another form of memory is semiconductor memory, which uses circuitry on silicon chips. Semiconductor units are smaller and faster than cores, but they usually demand a constant power source. Bubble memory consists of magnetized spots that rest on a thin film of semiconductor material. These bubbles retain their magnetism indefinitely and have the ability to store much more data in a smaller space than core memory.

■ The type of memory used to store data and instructions is called random-access memory (RAM). RAM is a nonpermanent form of memory.

■ Read-only memory (ROM), part of the hardware of a computer, stores items in a form that can be deleted or changed only by rewiring. Microprograms are sequences of instructions built into read-only memory to carry out functions that otherwise would be directed by stored-program instructions at a much slower speed.

■ Programmable read-only memory (PROM) can be programmed either by the manufacturer or by other companies to meet unique user needs. Thus, it provides greater flexibility and versatility than ROM.

■ Registers are devices that facilitate the execution of instructions. They act as temporary holding areas and are capable of receiving information, holding it, and transferring it very quickly as directed by the control unit of the CPU.

■ Cache memory is a portion of memory designed to speed the CPU's processing of instructions or data by anticipating what instructions or data a program will need and placing these in this high-speed buffer area.

■ The speed at which a microcomputer can execute instructions is dependent upon the word size and clock speed of the microprocessor.

■ Microcomputers sold today normally have microprocessors with word sizes of either 16 or 32 bits and contain clocks that can operate at speeds ranging from 12.5 MHz to 33 MHz.

■ Data representation in the computer is based on a two-state, or binary, system. A 1 in a given position indicates the presence of a power of 2; a 0 indicates its absence. The four-bit binary coded decimal (BCD) system uses groups of four binary digits to represent the decimal digits 0 through 9.

■ The six-bit BCD system allows for sixty-four unique bit combinations; alphabetic, numeric, and twenty-eight special characters can be represented. Both EBCDIC and ASCII-8 are eight-bit coding systems and are capable of representing up to 256 different characters.

■ Octal (base 8) and hexadecimal (base 16) notation can be used to represent binary data in a more concise form. For this reason, the contents of computer memory are sometimes viewed or printed in one of these notations. Programmers use these number systems to help in locating errors.

■ Parity bits, or check bits, are additional bits in a coding scheme used to detect errors in the transmission of data. They can detect only the miscoding of characters and cannot detect the use of incorrect data.

SUMMARY POINTS

■ TERMS FOR REVIEW

■ REVIEW QUESTIONS

1. What is a CPU? What components make up the CPU?

2. What two processing units make up the processor? Give a brief description of the functions performed by each of these units.

3. Why is the stored-program concept so important to modern computing? Describe what is meant by the term *nondestructive read/destructive write*.

4. How does random-access memory (RAM) differ from read-only memory (ROM)? What is PROM? What is EPROM?

5. How does the clock speed of a microprocessor affect the overall speed of a microcomputer? How is microprocessor clock speed measured?

6. What are the advantages of using the binary, octal, and hexadecimal number systems when working with computers?

7. What is the decimal (base 10) equivalent of binary 11010010? Show how you arrive at your answer.

8. What is the decimal (base 10) equivalent of the hexidecimal number E0. Show how you derive your answer.

9. What are computer codes? How are these codes used by computer manufacturers? What are some of the more common computer codes?

10. Why is code checking used on computers? What is a parity or check bit?

IBM

GENERAL CORPORATE INFORMATION

In the 1880s, Herman Hollerith developed a mechanical method of processing census data for the United States Bureau of Census. His method included two devices: one that coded population data as punched holes in cards and another that sensed the data. The success of his method led Hollerith to form his own company in 1896 to manufacture and sell these devices. In 1911, the company became part of the Computing-Tabulating-Recording (CTR) Company, which manufactured recording equipment. In 1924, CTR became the International Business Machines (IBM) Corporation.

Today, IBM is a leader of the worldwide data-processing community and is the leading vendor of mainframe computers. IBM's Entry Systems Division is the second largest producer of small computers. IBM's products include data-processing machines and systems, information processors, electric typewriters, copiers, dictation equipment, educational and testing materials, and related supplies and services. Most products can be either leased or purchased through IBM's worldwide marketing organizations.

IBM'S FAMILY SERIES

IBM's major business is information handling. IBM computers range from small, powerful microcomputers to ultra-high-performance computers for high-speed, large-scale scientific and commercial applications. The wide range of computer applications in scientific, industrial, and commercial areas today requires machines of different sizes and capabilities. For example, a computer used to forecast the weather has capabilities different from those of a computer used mainly for payroll processing. Consequently, computers with similar characteristics are usually grouped together into a family, series, or system. The family members differ from each other in range of available memory, number of input-output channels, execution speed, and types of devices with which interface can be established.

In the spring of 1987, IBM introduced the Personal System/2, a new family of microcomputers to replace the existing IBM PC. New proprietary technology was implemented to differentiate this product from existing personal computers and make it difficult for other companies to imitate (clone) the PS/2. In addition, IBM launched a massive advertising campaign to assure consumer awareness

of the advantages of these new personal computers.

The smaller models (Model 25 and Model 30) both incorporate a faster version of the older processor chip found in the IBM PC, an Intel 8086. Moreover, the graphics and sound capabilities of these PS/2 models are significantly more sophisticated than comparable PCs. These computers are totally compatible with existing IBM PC software, including the operating system (DOS). Therefore, the transition for an existing user has been made painless; most of the vast number of existing PC programs will run without modification on these machines. These models have been advertised as the choice for education.

The middle of the line models in this family (Model 50 and Model 60) use a more advanced processor chip, the Intel 80286. In addition to providing faster operating speeds, the computer has the ability to address a significantly larger block of internal memory, up to 15 million bytes, and provides attractive graphics capabilities. Associated with many of the advanced applications for this computer is a different operating system, IBM Operating System/2 (OS/2).

As the world's data-processing needs have expanded, hardware provided by IBM has developed to give the necessary support.

At the top of the PS/2 line, IBM offers the Model 95 XP SX. It is differentiated from the rest of the family by its implementation of a much more sophisticated processor chip, the Intel 80486. The computer is designed to use the most advanced components to achieve optimum performance in power, speed, storage, memory, and graphics resolution. With the high end of the family exhibiting such processing power, the distinction formerly afforded microcomputers is blurring. Desktop publishing, numeric-intensive applications such as financial modeling and CAD/CAM, and other uses of graphics along with large-scale data manipulations will benefit from these advances.

IBM's new POWERserver 930 system.

The newest series, the RISC System/6000, is the industry's most powerful workstation family. The computers are designed to provide the accuracy, power, and speed needed by technical users, but can also advance office productivity for commercial users. They can fulfill a wide range of needs at attractive costs.

IBM is the originator of the RISC design. The letters RISC stand for "Reduced Instruction Set Computer," but a more meaningful wording of the acronym is "reduced instruction set cycles." A RISC computer does have a smaller instruction set—the fundamental logic and arithmetic procedures that a computer performs—than many of today's powerful microprocessors; however, it also reduces the number of clock cycles required for executing critical instructions. The instructions execute not only faster but also concurrently with others in the same cycle among three different processor chips.

The computers use AIX Version 3, IBM's implementation of the UNIX operating system. They can access a vast amount of memory rapidly, and permit high-speed transference of data among peripherals. They have a PC simulator that runs existing DOS software. RISC computers provide three-dimensional and motion graphics capabilities used in science, engineering, desktop publishing, and other professional uses. They facilitate high-level technical functions such as quantitative analysis, yet have an easy-to-understand user interface.

Some models are meant to be used as workstations called POWERstations for individual users, and other models are POWERservers designed to be network servers for multiple users. (The acronym POWER stands for Performance Optimization With Enhanced RISC.) There are desktop, deskside, and rack-mounted models.

The IBM Application System/400 series is a family of high-function, easy-to-use processors designed to provide solutions in multi-user medium-sized business environments. There are currently eight processor models in the family, ranging from the compact C10 to the rack-mounted B70. This family of computers has been designed to replace the existing System/36 and System/38 computers. Many industry observers believe that the AS/400 will become the standard for the 1990s for the medium-sized business as well as an attractive, cost-effective system for small businesses and departments in large businesses.

The AS/400 system can be sold as a Total System Package (TSP). This concept includes a prepackaged, preconfigured system shipped to a location "ready to go," including preloaded software. Online educational and support software is also available with the system. In addition, the computer has been designed so that transferring (migrating) data and programs from existing computers is extremely simple.

The AS/400 series incorporates the latest hardware and software technology. Its architecture accommodates the needs of advanced applications such as voice, image, and artificial intelligence. The Operating System/400 integrates a powerful relational data-base system with a simple menu-driven interface for users to provide ease of connectivity and flexibility with other computer systems.

For the large system user, IBM has taken a slightly different product approach. The System/370 family of computers was introduced in the 1970s for large-scale, high-speed scientific and commercial applications. As new technology was implemented, more advanced computer models were added to the series. This allowed the user to expect total compatibility for software developed for an older machine in the 370 line. In 1985, IBM introduced the Enterprise Systems/3090 processor family based upon the System/370 architecture. Thus there was created a specialized family of powerful computers within the System/370 family of large-scale general-purpose systems. The new design has been named the ESA/370, for Enterprise Systems Architecture/370, to further identify its position within the existing family. The processing power of the ES/3090 is based upon high-speed buffers, large data paths, multiprocessing, and advanced chip packaging. This new processor family has been identified by IBM as "the base for growth into the 90s."

APPLICATION
IBM

Table 4–1 summarizes the major IBM series and their various models. As data-processing requirements have expanded, hardware capabilities such as those provided by IBM have been developed to give the necessary support.

DISCUSSION POINTS

1. What characteristics do computers within a family have in common?
2. Why is it important for new computer systems to maintain compatibility with existing computers?

TABLE 4–1

Major IBM Computers					
Series	Date Introduced	Comments	Series	Date Introduced	Comments
700	1953	Vacuum tubes	System/34	1977	Small system for business
Type 650	1954	Magnetic-drum machine	Series/1	1976	Versatile small computer for experienced users
1400	1960	Oriented to business	System/38	1973	Powerful, general-purpose, supporting extensive data bases
7000	1960	Transistors, business-oriented and scientific-oriented			
1620	1960	Scientific-oriented, decimal minicomputer	5100	1975	Portable computer
			5110	1978	Small business computer
1130	1962	Integrated circuits, small, special-purpose	5120	1980	Small business system
1800	1963	Integrated circuits, small, special-purpose	Datamaster	1981	Small system with data, word processing
360	1965	Systems designed for all purposes—business and scientific	Personal Computer	1981	Microcomputer for home and office
System/3	1969	Midi-small computer	S/36	1983	Small business system
System/7	1970	Replacement for 1800	9370	1986	Mid-range departmental system
370	1973	IBM's most popular system— extends capabilities of System/360	PS/2	1987	New generation of personal computers
3031	1977				
3033	1980		AS/400	1988	Replaced S/36 and S/38; relational data base system; middle-range family of computers based upon a relational data-base system
3090	1985	IBM's most powerful processors—became known as Enterprise Systems/3090 within the new sub-family ESA/370, for Enterprise Systems Architecture/370	RISC/6000	1990	High speed and power workstations and network servers for technical uses as well as for office productivity
System/32	1975	Small system for business			

Input and Output

Trump-eting Use
of Wireless Terminals

Ellis Booker, *COMPUTERWORLD*

ATLANTIC CITY—Win or lose at the blackjack tables, diners at the Trump Taj Mahal Casino Resort can bet on a speedy meal.

Waiters and waitresses at two of the 12 restaurants in the glittering gambling casino use handheld radio-frequency data terminals to send food orders from customers' tables to the kitchen.

The handheld units are part of a $1 million contract with NCR Corp. for point-of-sale systems at the casino resort, which opened amid characteristic Donald Trump excess and media hoopla.

A total of 48 NCR Hand-Held Order Entry Systems have been deployed. They are linked to a personal computer-based system, the NCR 2760 Food Service System, which prints or displays incoming orders for cooks and generates detailed management reports. In turn, this system communicates, over conventional wiring, with an NCR point-of-sale computer at the cash register station, which prints out the guest check.

"The rationale is to get orders passed along quickly and accurately," said Taj Mahal Vice-President of Administration Tom Adams. Adams, who spent a year looking into the viability of the data terminal approach, said he expects "a very successful rollout" and hopes to move the movable data terminals into other parts of the 17.3-acre complex, such as the four bars and lounges and the pool bar area.

While some workers may resist giving up their time-honored pencil and paper, the use of handheld terminals for restaurants and other retail establishments is expected to accelerate, according to observers. . . .

The handheld units, made for NCR by Seiko Co., weigh just a few ounces and open wallet-like to reveal function keys and a two-line LCD screen.

In addition to sending an order from the table, the data terminal interacts with the base station to prompt the waiter or waitress through an order. For example, after a customer asks for a New York steak, the terminal asks the waiter to

choose a second function key corresponding to a degree of doneness indicated on the second line of the LCD.

Of the two restaurants, the 348-seat New Delhi Deli, with its neon lights and high-tech feel, would seem at first the better-suited for the data terminals. By comparison, the 417-seat Bombay Cafe coffee shop is fashioned after the Brighton Pavilion in England, complete with marble floors, carved glass and crystal chandeliers.

According to Adams, however, the terminals are "a fairly cut-and-dried application of technology to solve a problem . . . in our case, how to get food to a customer."

The Trump casino, now the tallest building in New Jersey and christened the "Eighth Wonder of the World" by Trump publicists, was inspired by India's famed Taj Mahal and includes carved stone elephant statues at its main gate and a roof adorned by no fewer than 70 colorful minarets and onion-shaped domes.

A computer system is much more than a central processing unit with different kinds of storage. Auxiliary devices enter data into and receive output from the CPU. **Input** is data submitted to the computer for processing. **Output** is the information produced by the computer as a result of computer processing. The input and output operations are often referred to as **I/O.** I/O operations are important activities in any computer-based system because they are the communication links between people and the machine. If these interfaces are weak, the overall performance of the computer system suffers. This chapter describes a number of the methods used for computer input. The field of source-data automation is also examined. A discussion of printers and other forms of output concludes the chapter.

■ INPUT DEVICES

The past thirty-five years have seen many advances in techniques used to enter data into computer systems. Compared to the early days of computing, when punched cards were used to enter programs and data, today's data-entry techniques have become quite sophisticated. One of the most significant advances in automated data entry has been the use of scanners. These input devices will be discussed in a section all their own.

Even though many significant advances in the area of automated data entry have occurred, the majority of data entered into computer systems is still done manually by human data-entry personnel. This is usually accomplished through the use of a computer keyboard. The data typed in is then stored on one of the computer system's storage devices. (Storage devices will be discussed in detail in Chapter 6.) This process of manually entering data into a computer system is referred to as key-to-magnetic media, or keyboarding.

Other input devices work especially well in a microcomputer environment. These devices must be easy to use because a large number of microcomputer users are not experienced computer users. Business users in particular may be discouraged from using microcomputers if the input devices are not easy to use.

Keyboards

Key-to-magnetic media data entry comprises the most widely used method of input today. Data is entered by using a keyboard similar to a typewriter (see Figure 5–1). Most keyboards have the standard typewriter arrangement for keying letters, numbers, and some special characters. Many keyboards have additional keys for issuing commands to the computer. The data keyboarded onto **magnetic tapes** or **magnetic disks** is stored in the form of magnetized spots on the surface of a tape or disk.

Before the data is accepted and stored on the computer system, however, it usually is checked for accuracy by the computer system, using stored-program instructions. If an error is detected, the system interrupts the data entry person and waits until a correction has been entered.

Mice

In addition to the keyboard, the **mouse** has become a very important input device. A **mouse** is a hand-movable input device that controls the position of the cursor on

FIGURE 5-1

Manual Data Entry Using a Keyboard

the computer's screen. (The cursor is a symbol on a computer display that shows where the next typed character will appear.) On the bottom of a mouse is either a small ball similar to a ball bearing or a light sensor that detects that the mouse is being moved across a flat surface. On the top of the mouse are from one to three pushbuttons that are used for activating commands. When the mouse is moved across a flat surface, the cursor on the computer's display moves accordingly. Using a mouse eliminates a considerable amount of typing (see Figure 5–2).

FIGURE 5-2

A Mouse
Some microcomputers allow the user to bypass the keyboard by using a mouse. The mouse is similar to a track ball: in the mouse, the roller is on the under surface of the device, and in the track ball the roller is on the upper surface. The user rolls the mouse around on the desk, making a cursor on the screen move accordingly. A click of the button on the mouse commands the computer.

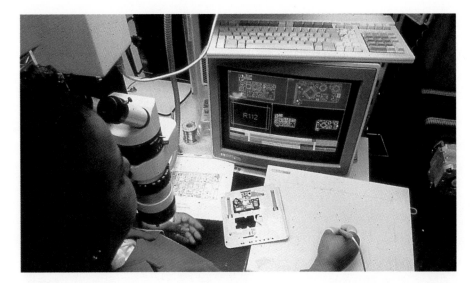

FIGURE 5–3

Graphics Tablet
A graphics tablet allows the user to enter data by writing on a flat pad that transfers impulses of the movements of the writing to the proper positions on the screen.

Graphics Tablets

Graphics tablets are flat, boardlike surfaces directly connected to a computer display (see Figure 5–3). The user draws on the tablet using a pencil-like device, and the image is transmitted to the display. Graphics tablets enable the user to employ colors, textures, and patterns when creating images.

Light Pens

A **light pen** is a pen-shaped object with a light-sensitive cell at its end. Users can select from a list of choices displayed on the computer's screen by touching a light pen to the proper item. Light pens may also be used in highly technical fields for altering graphs and other drawings.

Scanners

Somewhat new input devices are scanners. **Scanners** are devices that read printed material so that it can be put in a computer readable form without having to retype, redraw, reprint, or rephotograph the material. Scanners have become very popular as desktop publishing software has become more and more popular (see Figure 5–4 and Chapter 12). Scanners, in many different forms, also play an important role in source-data automation.

Microphones

It is also possible for people to perform data entry by speaking into a microphone connected to a computer system. This capability is known as **voice recognition.** At present, computers can identify and process a vocabulary of several dozen words or numbers. Eventually, computers are expected to be able to recognize an extensive vocabulary and be able to respond by creating transcripts of spoken text.

FIGURE 5–4

A Full-Page Scanner

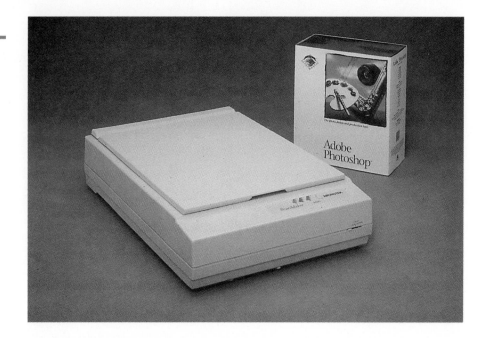

■ SOURCE-DATA AUTOMATION

Data entry has traditionally been the weakest link in the chain of data-processing operations. Although it can be processed electronically at extremely high speeds, significantly more time is required to prepare the data, enter it, and then check its accuracy before it can actually be processed. Another method of data entry, **source-data automation,** collects data about an event, in computer-readable form, when and where the event takes place. This eliminates the possibility of keying incorrect information into the computer. Source-data automation improves the speed, accuracy, and efficiency of data-processing operations.

Source-data automation is implemented in several ways. Each requires special machines for reading data and converting it into machine language. The most common forms of source-data automation are discussed in the following paragraphs.

Magnetic-ink was introduced in the late 1950s to speed check processing in the banking industry. Because magnetic-ink characters can be read by both humans and machines, no special data-conversion step is needed. Magnetic-ink characters are formed with magnetized particles of iron oxide. Each character is composed of certain sections of a seventy-section matrix (see Figure 5–5). The characters can be read and interpreted by a **magnetic-ink character reader.** This process is called **magnetic-ink character recognition (MICR).**

With MICR each character area is examined to determine the shape of the character represented. The presence of a magnetic field in a section of the area represents a 1 bit; the absence of a magnetic field represents a 0 bit. Each magnetic-ink character is composed of a unique combination of 0 bits and 1 bits. When all sections in a character area are combined and translated into binary notation in this manner, the character represented can be determined. MICR devices automatically check each character read to ensure accuracy.

Processing bank checks is a major application of magnetic-ink character recognition. The magnetic ink characters are printed along the bottom of the check (see

FIGURE 5–5

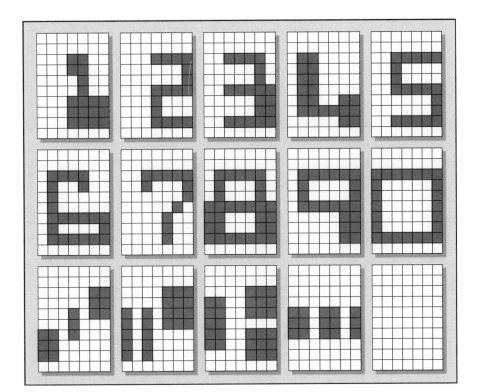

Figure 5–6). The **transit field** is preprinted on the check. It includes the bank number, which is an aid in routing the check through the Federal Reserve System. The customer's account number appears in an **"on-us" field.** A clerk manually inserts the amount of the check in the **amount field** after the check has been used and received at a bank.

All magnetic-ink characters on checks are formed with the standard fourteen-character set shown in Figure 5–7. Other character sets may be used in other applications. As the checks are fed into the MICR device, it reads them and sorts them by bank number at a Federal Reserve Bank and by account number at the issuing bank. In this manner, checks are routed back to each issuing bank and then back to its customers. A MICR device can read and sort hundreds of checks per minute.

In another form of source-data automation, optical recognition devices read marks or symbols coded on paper documents and convert them into electrical pulses. The pulses can then be transmitted directly to the CPU or stored on magnetic tape for input at a later time. The simplest approach to optical recognition is known as **optical-mark recognition (OMR),** or **mark-sensing.** This approach is often used for machine scoring of multiple-choice examinations (see Figure 5–8). A heavy lead pencil is used to mark the location of each desired answer. The marks on an OMR document are sensed by an **optical-mark page reader** as the document passes under a light source. The presence of marks in specific locations is indicated by light reflected at those locations. As the document is read, the optical-mark data is automatically translated into machine language. When the optical-mark page reader is directly connected to the computer, thousands of forms of the same type can be read and processed in an extremely short period of time compared to entering the data by hand.

Optical-mark recognition is also used in order writing, inventory control, surveys

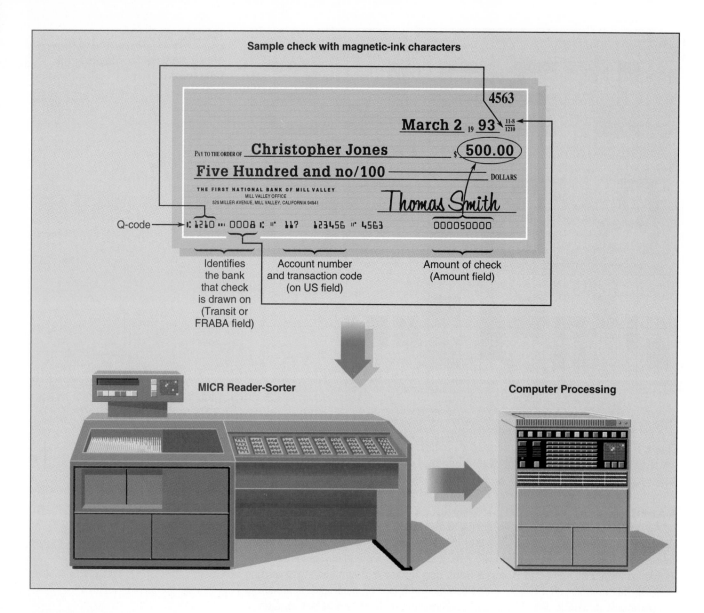

Sample check with magnetic-ink characters

4563

March 2 19 93 11-8/1210

PAY TO THE ORDER OF **Christopher Jones** $ **500.00**

Five Hundred and no/100 _____ DOLLARS

THE FIRST NATIONAL BANK OF MILL VALLEY
MILL VALLEY OFFICE
525 MILLER AVENUE, MILL VALLEY, CALIFORNIA 94941

Thomas Smith

Q-code ⟶ ⑆1210⑆ 0008⑆ ⑈ 117 123456⑈ 4563   000050000

Identifies the bank that check is drawn on (Transit or FRABA field)

Account number and transaction code (on US field)

Amount of check (Amount field)

MICR Reader-Sorter

Computer Processing

FIGURE 5–6

Magnetic-Ink Character Recognition

and questionnaires, and payroll applications. Since optical-mark data is initially recorded by people, forms that are easy for them to understand and complete must be devised. Instructions, with examples, are generally provided to aid those who must use the forms. Good design helps prevent errors and lessens the amount of time required to complete forms.

FIGURE 5–7

Magnetic-Ink Character Set

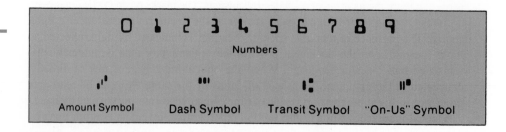

0 1 2 3 4 5 6 7 8 9

Numbers

Amount Symbol   Dash Symbol   Transit Symbol   "On-Us" Symbol

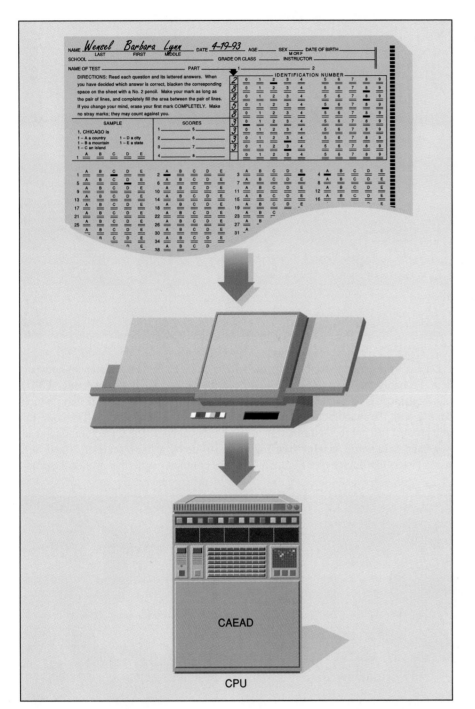

FIGURE 5–8

Optical-Mark Recognition for a Multiple-Choice Test

Another type of optical reader, the **bar-code reader,** can read special line or bar codes. Bar codes are patterns of optical marks that represent information about the object on which the code appears. They are suitable for many applications, including **point-of-sale (POS) systems,** credit card verification, and freight identification to facilitate warehouse operations (see Figure 5–9).

FIGURE 5–9

The Universal Product Code being read by a bar code reader.

Data is represented in bar code by the widths of the bars and the distances between them. Probably the most familiar bar code is the **Universal Product Code (UPC)** found on most grocery items. This code consists of pairs of vertical bars, which identify both the manufacturer and the item, but not the item's price. The code for each product is a unique combination of these vertical bars. The UPC symbol is read by a hand-held **wand reader** (see Figure 5–10) or by a fixed scanner linked to a cash register–like device (see Figure 5–11). The computer system identifies the prod-

FIGURE 5–10

UPC Wand Reader

FIGURE 5–11

Point-of-Sale Terminal with Fixed Scanner

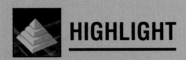
Can Computers Read Chinese?

The Chinese language is posing a unique problem for computer specialists. Chinese is based on the use of graphic symbols (ideograms) to represent ideas. This is in contrast to languages such as English, which are phonetic languages that use words to represent ideas. Unfortunately, there is currently no phonetic translation of Chinese, and Chinese keyboards are very difficult to use. Since the Chinese ideograms cannot currently be entered into a computer, the huge computer market that China represents has largely been ignored by Western computer and software companies.

Recently, however, a company based in New York's Chinatown developed a computer program that can read all of the 7,000 characters in the Chinese language. These characters are written by hand on an electronic writing tablet. The company, BusinessPlus Corporation, has developed the program using techniques used to interpret satellite photographs in China. David Dai is the senior project leader at BusinessPlus and the author of the program that interprets the Chinese language characters. The company hopes that this innovative approach will help to unlock the vast potential market for microcomputers that exists in China.

uct, its brand name, and other pertinent information and uses this data to find the item's price. It then prints out both name and price. The computer keeps track of each item sold and thus helps the store manager to maintain current inventory status.

Optical-character readers can read special types of characters known as **optical characters.** Some **optical-character recognition (OCR)** devices can read the characters of several type fonts, including both uppercase and lowercase letters. The most common font used in OCR is shown in Figure 5–12.

A major difference between optical-character recognition and optical-mark recognition is that optical-character data is represented by the shapes of characters rather than by the positions of marks. However, both OCR and OMR devices rely on reflected light to translate written data into machine-readable form.

Acceptable OCR input can be produced by computer printers, adding machines, cash registers, accounting machines, and typewriters. Data can be fed into the reader via a **continuous form** such as cash register tape or on **cut forms** such as phone or utility bills. When individual cut forms are used, the reader can usually sort the forms as well.

FIGURE 5–12

OCR Characters

ABCDEFGHIJKLMN
OPQRSTUVWXYZ,.
$/*-1234567890

The most advanced optical-character readers can even read handwritten characters. Handwritten characters must be neat and clear, however, or they may not be read correctly. The system is not foolproof because handwriting can vary so much from person to person. The optical-character readers reject any characters that cannot be interpreted. Devices that must read handwriting are often very slow.

Machine-produced optical-character recognition has been used in credit card billing, utility billing, and inventory-control applications. Handwritten optical-character recognition has been used widely in mail sorting. The reliability of optical-character recognition systems is generally very good.

Remote terminals collect data at its source and transmit the data to a central computer for processing. Generally, data is transmitted over telecommunications equipment. The many types of remote terminals available can increase the versatility and expand the applications of the computer.

Remote terminals that perform the functions of a cash register and also capture sales data are referred to as **point-of-sale (POS) terminals.** Such terminals have a keyboard for data entry, a panel to display the price, a cash drawer, and a printer that provides a cash receipt. A POS terminal typical of those found in many retail stores is pictured in Figure 5–13.

Some POS terminals have wand readers that can read either the Universal Product Code (UPC) or the OCR characters stamped on or attached to an item. The sale is registered automatically as the checkout person passes the wand reader over the code; there is no need to enter the price via a keyboard unless the wand malfunctions. Thus, POS terminals enable sales data to be collected at its source. If the terminals are directly connected to a large central computer, useful inventory and sales information can be provided to the retailer almost instantaneously.

Touch-tone devices are remote terminals used together with ordinary telephone lines to transfer data from remote locations to a central computer. The data is entered via a special keyboard on the terminal. Generally, slight modifications need to be made to the telephone connection to allow data to be transferred over the line (see Figure 5–14).

FIGURE 5–13

Point-of-Sale Terminal
This NCR 7000/Department Store System is one of a new generation of advanced point-of-sale systems. It consists of a programmable terminal 7050 and 7830 hand-held scanner.

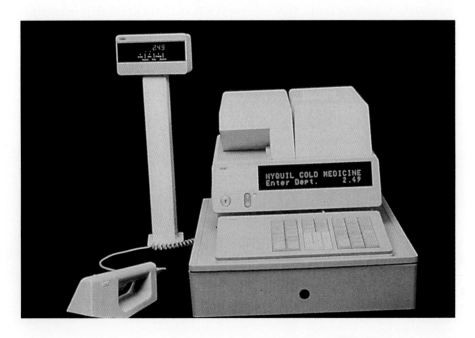

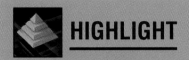

The Reading Machine

Raymond Kurzweil has had a significant impact in a number of computer related fields. However, the area in which he has had perhaps the greatest impact is in the development and use of scanners. After he graduated from college, Kurzweil set out to develop a technology that could reliably read any type of printed document. His hope was to be able to read any type font, regardless of its style. In 1974, Kurzweil started Kurzweil Computer Products to develop this technology.

Today, the Kurzweil scanning and character-recognition products are among the most sophisticated and highest quality available. One quite remarkable scanning device that has achieved great popularity among those involved with learning disabilities is the Kurzweil reading machine. The reading machine scans printed text and reads its contents aloud.

The current version of the reading machine, The Personal Reader, is used in a number of settings to aid

students who are for various reasons capable, but cannot read. The Personal Reader can be used much like a copying machine is used. The document, article, or book is placed on top of the machine and the machine then proceeds to read the text aloud to the student in one of nine voices. The personal reader combines both input and output devices to produce a tremendous learning tool to those who have the terrible learning disability of illiteracy.

FIGURE 5–14

Touch-Tone Device

There are several types of touch-tone devices. One that reads a magnetic strip on the back of plastic cards is often used to verify credit card transactions. Another stores large amounts of data on a magnetic belt similar to a magnetic tape before transmitting it. This type of terminal is best suited for large-volume processing. Concept Summary 5–1 reviews the various types of input devices.

CONCEPT SUMMARY 5–1

Input Devices

Device	Use
Keyboards	Used to manually enter data into a computer system.
Mice	Typically used on small computer systems to reduce the amount of typing required by the user.
Graphics Tablets	Allow users to draw pictures that are then turned into computer readable drawings.
Light Pens	Used to reduce typing and to draw images on a computer display device.
Scanners	Used to read printed material.
Microphones	Allow a user to speak and have the words recognized and saved by the computer system.

◼ OUTPUT DEVICES

Output is data that has been processed into information by the computer. Output must be in a form that is convenient for the users. Output can be produced by printers, plotters, and visual display terminals. Printers and plotters produce hard copies of output, while visual display terminals (VDT) produce soft copy.

Printers

Printers print processed data in a form humans can read. To produce hard copy, the printer first receives electronic signals from the central processing unit. In an **impact printer,** these signals activate print elements that are pressed against paper. Newer, **nonimpact printers** use heat, laser technology, or photographic techniques to print output.

IMPACT PRINTERS. Impact printers come in a variety of shapes and sizes. Some print one character at a time, while others print a line at a time. Dot- or wire-matrix printers and daisy-wheel printers are the principal types of impact printers.

Dot-matrix (also called **wire-matrix**) **printers** are based on a design principle similar to that of a football or basketball scoreboard. The matrix is a rectangle composed of pins. Certain combinations of pins are activated to represent characters. For example, the number 4 and the letter L are formed by a combination of pins being pressed against paper (see Figure 5–15). The dot combinations used to represent

FIGURE 5–15

Character Patterns for Dot-Matrix Printers

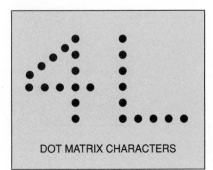

DOT MATRIX CHARACTERS

CHAPTER 5: INPUT AND OUTPUT

FIGURE 5–16

Dot-Matrix Character Set

various numbers, letters, and special characters are shown in Figure 5–16.

The quality of characters produced by a dot-matrix printer is determined by the resolution of the matrix used to produce the character. The more dots that can be printed in the matrix, the higher the quality of print. Near-letter-quality (NLQ) characters produced by dot-matrix printers contain more dots placed closer together. Most dot-matrix printers sold today have either 9- or 24-pin printheads. They print at speeds ranging from 80 characters per second in NLQ mode to 400 characters per second in draft mode.

Daisy-wheel printers use a daisy wheel, which is a flat disk with petal-like projections (see Figure 5–17). Daisy wheels come in several type fonts that can be interchanged quickly to suit application needs. The daisy-wheel printer offers high-quality type and is often used in word-processing systems to give output a typewriter quality appearance. Daisy-wheel printers can produce up to 3,000 characters per minute.

Types of line-at-a-time printers include print-wheel, chain, and drum printers. A **print-wheel printer** typically contains 120 print wheels, one for each of 120 print positions on a line (see Figure 5–18). Each print wheel contains forty-eight alphabetic, numeric, and special characters. The wheel rotates until the desired characters move into the corresponding print position on the current print line. When all wheels are in their correct positions, a hammer drives the paper against the wheels and an entire line of output is printed. Print-wheel printers can produce about 150 lines per minute, which makes them rather slow compared to other line-at-a-time printers.

A **chain printer** has a character set assembled in a chain that revolves horizontally past all print positions (see Figure 5–19). The printer has one print hammer for each column on the paper. Characters are printed when hammers press the paper against an inked ribbon, which in turn presses against appropriate characters on the print chain. The fonts can be changed easily on chain printers, allowing a variety of fonts, such as italic or boldface, to be used. Some chain printers can produce up to 2,000 lines per minute.

A **drum printer** uses a metal cylinder with rows of characters engraved across its surface (see Figure 5–20). Each column on the drum contains a complete character set and corresponds to one print position on the line. As the drum rotates, all characters are rotated past the print position. A hammer presses the paper against the ink ribbon and drum when the appropriate character is in place. One line is printed for each revolution of the drum, since all characters eventually reach the print position during one revolution. Some drum printers can produce 2,000 lines per minute.

FIGURE 5–17

Daisy Print Wheel

FIGURE 5-18

Print Wheel

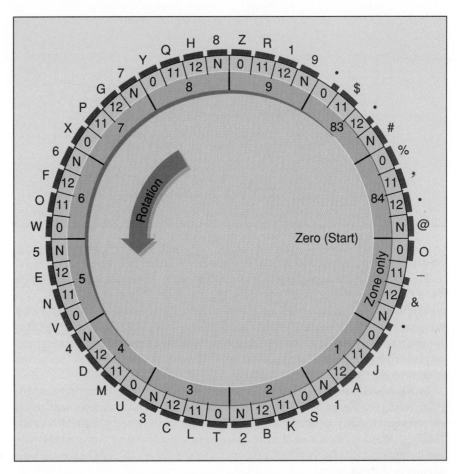

FIGURE 5-19

Chain Printer Print Element

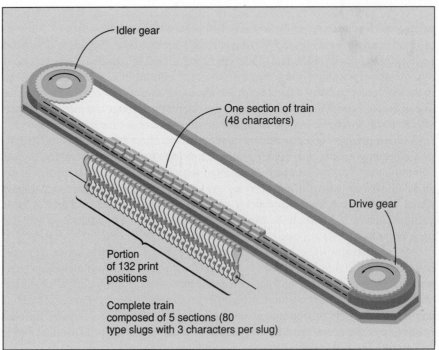

Idler gear

One section of train
(48 characters)

Drive gear

Portion
of 132 print
positions

Complete train
composed of 5 sections (80
type slugs with 3 characters per slug)

FIGURE 5–20

Print Drum

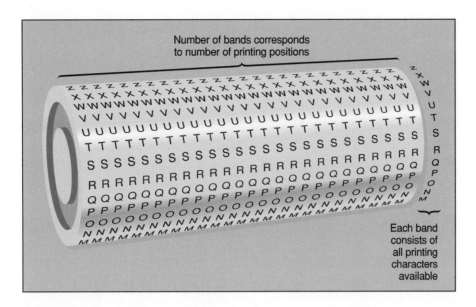

Number of bands corresponds to number of printing positions

Each band consists of all printing characters available

NONIMPACT PRINTERS. Nonimpact printers do not print characters by means of a mechanical printing element that strikes the paper. Instead, a variety of other methods are used. Electrostatic, electrothermal, ink-jet, laser, and xerographic printers are some of these types.

An **electrostatic printer** forms an image of a character on special paper using a dot matrix of charged wires or pins. The paper is moved through a solution containing ink particles that have a charge opposite that of the pattern. The ink particles adhere to each charged pattern of the paper, forming a visible image of each character.

Electrothermal printers generate characters by using heat and heat-sensitive paper. Rods are heated in a matrix. As the ends of the selected rods touch the heat-sensitive paper, an image is created. Both electrothermal and electrostatic printers operate quietly. They are often used in applications where noise may be a problem. Some of these printers are capable of producing 5,000 lines per minute. The paper required for use in electrothermal printers, however, is expensive and in many cases cost prohibitive.

In an **ink-jet printer,** a nozzle is used to shoot a stream of charged ink toward the paper. Before reaching it, the ink passes through an electrical field that arranges the charged particles into characters. These printers can produce up to 12,000 characters per minute.

Laser printers combine laser beams and electrophotographic technology to create output images (see Figure 5–21). A beam of light is focused through a rotating disk containing a full font of characters. The character image is projected onto a piece of film or photographic paper, and the print or negative is developed and fixed in a manner similar to that used for ordinary photographs. The output consists of high-quality, letter-perfect images. The process is often used to print books. Laser printers, which can operate at speeds of up to 21,000 lines per minute, are often replacing the slower printers that have been used with word-processing systems in the past.

Xerographic printers use printing methods much like those used in common xerographic copying machines. For example, Xerox, the pioneer of this type of printing, has one model that prints on single 8½-by-11-inch sheets of plain paper rather than on the continuous-form paper normally used. Xerographic printers operate at speeds of up to 4,000 lines per minute.

FIGURE 5–21

Laser Printer—Hewlett-Packard
LaserJet III

Nonimpact printers are generally faster than impact printers because they involve less physical movement. They offer a wider choice of typefaces and better speed-to-price ratios than impact printers, and their technology implies a higher degree of reliability because they use fewer movable parts in printing. The disadvantages of nonimpact printers include the special paper requirements and the poor type-image quality of some printers. Also, nonimpact printers cannot make carbon copies. Yet nonimpact printers can produce several copies of a page in less time than it takes an impact printer to produce one page with several carbon copies.

New print systems now on the market combine many features of the printing process into one machine. For example, collating, routing, hole punching, blanking out of proprietary information, and perforating may be performed. Some printers produce both text and form designs on plain paper, reducing or eliminating the need for preprinted forms. Furthermore, some laser and ink jet printers can also print in color. For a summary of the types and speeds of impact and nonimpact printers, see Concept Summary 5–2.

Plotters

Sometimes the best way for a computer to present information to a user is not in the form of text, but in graphic form. A **plotter** is an output device that prepares graphic, hard copy of information. It can produce lines, curves, and complex shapes. Plotters are often used to produce line and bar charts, graphs, organizational charts, engineering drawings, maps, trend lines, and supply and demand curves, among other things.

A typical plotter has a pen, a movable carriage, a drum, and a chart-paper holder (see Figure 5–22). Shapes are produced as the pen moves back and forth across the paper along the x-axis while the drum moves the paper up and down along the x-axis. Both the paper movement and the pen movement are bi-directional. The pen is raised from and lowered to the paper surface automatically. Many plotters use more than one pen at a time. The colors of graphics can be changed by changing the colors of the pens.

Impact and Nonimpact Printers

Impact Printers	Speed
Printer-Keyboard	Very slow
Dot Matrix	Up to 24,000 characters per minute
Daisy Wheel	Up to 3,000 characters per minute
Chain Printer	Up to 2,000 lines per minute
Drum Printer	Up to 2,000 lines per minute

Nonimpact Printers	Speed
Electrostatic	Up to 5,000 lines per minute
Electrothermal	Up to 5,000 lines per minute
Laser	Up to 21,000 lines per minute
Xerographic	Up to 4,000 lines per minute
Ink-jet	Up to 12,000 characters per minute

Visual Display Devices

Visual display devices display data on cathode-ray tubes (CRTs) similar to television screens (see Figure 5–23). A typical screen can hold twenty-four lines, each containing eighty characters. These terminals supply soft copy output, which means the screen image is not a permanent record of what is shown. CRTs are well suited for applications involving inquiry and response, where no permanent (printed) records are

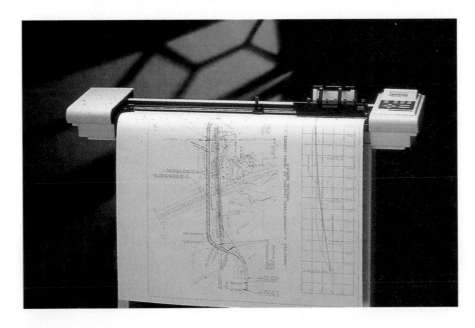

FIGURE 5–22

Plotter

FIGURE 5–23

required, and can be used for capturing data transmitted to the screen for verification as it is keyed.

Visual display devices have some advantages over printers. First, they can display output much faster than printers—some CRT terminals can display up to 10,000 characters in a second. Also, they are much quieter in operation than impact printers. It is usually possible to connect a printer or a copier to a CRT terminal, making it possible to obtain hard copy output of the screen contents.

Another type of CRT, known as a **graphic display device,** is used to display drawings as well as characters on a screen. Graphic display devices are generally used to show graphs and charts, but they can also display complex curves and shapes. Graphic display devices are being used in highly technical fields such as the aerospace industry to aid in the design of new wing structures. They are also being used heavily in computer-assisted design/computer-assisted manufacturing (CAD/CAM) areas, where objects can be designed and tested and the manufacturing process specified on the computer system in an interactive fashion.

Display devices are commonly referred to as monitors. Like the display devices described above, the information displayed on a monitor can be in either character or graphic form. Monitors are generally divided into three categories: (a) monochrome, (b) composite color, and (c) RGB (red-green-blue). **Monochrome monitors** display a single color, such as white, green, or amber, against a black background. They display text clearly and are inexpensive, ranging from $100 to $300. Most monochrome monitors are composite monitors, so-called for their single video signal. They usually require no additional video circuitry in the computer.

Composite color monitors display a composite of colors received in a single video signal and are slightly more expensive than monochrome monitors. They deliver less clarity in displaying text than monochrome monitors, however. Images on a composite color monitor are also less crisp than images on RGB monitors.

RGB monitors receive three separate color signals, one for each of three colors— red, green, and blue. Commonly used for high-quality graphics displays, they display sharper images than the composite color monitors, but produce fuzzier text than monochrome monitors (see Figure 5–24). They are more expensive than composite

FIGURE 5–24

RGB Color Monitor

color monitors, generally costing from $500 to $900. A color graphics display adapter (circuit board) is necessary for using RGB monitors with most computers.

Another type of display device is the flat panel display. **Flat panel displays** are used on portable microcomputers. They are less bulky and require less power than the cathode ray tubes (CRTs) used in most display devices. They show the image less clearly; looking at a flat panel display from an angle or in direct lighting makes the image faint or even invisible. Two common types of flat panel displays are liquid crystal display (LCD) and electroluminescent.

Voice Synthesizers

Audio output is becoming a more and more popular form of computer output. A **voice synthesizer** is used by the computer to output information to users in sequences of sound that resemble the human voice. The computer generates sounds electronically from texts entered by human operators or stored within the system. Two common forms of audio output in use today are the voice that gives you a telephone number when you call information and the voice that tells you the price of grocery items at automated grocery store checkout counters.

■ SUMMARY POINTS

■ The most common form of data entry is through keyboards. However, input devices such as scanners are becoming quite popular.

■ Some of the most common input devices in use today (other than keyboards) include mice, graphics tablets, light pens, and scanners.

■ Source-data automation is the collection of data at the point where a transaction occurs. Common approaches to source-data automation employ optical-recognition devices and other types of remote terminals.

■ Magnetic-ink characters can be read by humans and by machines, since they are magnetically inscribed. Magnetic-ink character recognition (MICR) devices can convert the magnetic characters into machine code for computer processing. MICR devices are used extensively by the banking industry for processing checks.

■ Optical-mark recognition devices can sense marks made with a heavy lead pencil and convert them into machine code. Other optical-character recognition devices are capable of reading bar codes, documents printed in various type fonts, and even handwritten characters. The main advantage of optical-character recognition is that it eliminates the intermediate process of transcribing data from source documents to an input medium.

■ Remote terminals can collect data at its source and transmit it over communication lines for processing by a central computer. Each device satisfies distinct needs for input and output. Which device is most appropriate for a certain application depends on the particular input/output requirements.

■ Printers provide output in a permanent (hard copy) form, which people can read. Impact printers can be classified as either character-at-a-time (such as dot-matrix printers and daisy-wheel printers) or line-at-a-time (such as print-wheel printers, drum printers, and chain printers).

■ Nonimpact printers use more recent technological developments such as photographic, thermal, or laser techniques to print output. They are typically faster than impact printers, offer a wider choice of type faces, better speed-to-price ratios, and are very reliable.

■ Plotters produce hard copy in graphic form. They are used to present information in the form of charts and graphs.

■ Visual display devices display data on cathode-ray tubes (CRTs). Typically a CRT screen can hold twenty-four lines, each containing eighty columns of soft copy output. A graphic display device can display drawings as well as characters.

■ TERMS FOR REVIEW

amount field, p. 113

bar-code reader, p. 115

chain printer, p. 121

composite color monitors, p. 126

continuous form, p. 117

cut forms, p. 117

daisy-wheel printer, p. 121

dot-matrix (wire-matr ix) printer, p. 120

drum printer, p. 121

electrostatic printer, p. 123

electrothermal printer, p. 123

flat panel displays, p. 127

graphic display device, p. 126

graphics tablet, p. 111

impact printer, p. 120

ink-jet printer, p. 123

laser printer, p. 123

light pen, p. 111

magnetic disks, p. 109

magnetic tapes, p. 109

magnetic-ink character reader, p. 112

magnetic-ink character recognition (MICR), p. 112

monochrome monitors, p. 126

mouse, p. 109

nonimpact printer, p. 120

"on us" field, p. 113

optical character recognition (OCR), p. 117

optical characters, p. 117

optical-mark page reader, p. 113

optical-mark recognition (OMR) (mark sensing), p. 113

plotter, p. 124

■ REVIEW QUESTIONS

1. What input device is used to enter the majority of data into information systems? How might this change in the future?

2. Briefly describe how a mouse can be used as an input device. In your opinion, does a mouse make working on a computer easier or harder? Why?

3. How are scanners used for input? Name five situations in which you personally have seen scanners used.

4. In what way are microphones used as input devices? What is the term used to describe this capability? Describe two or three circumstances in which you feel the use of microphones might greatly enhance the use of a computer.

5. Why is source-data automation an important technology? Identify five methods of data entry currently in use that could be improved by some form of source-data automation.

6. What is the Universal Product Code (UPC)? How does the use of the UPC benefit retailers?

7. Identify one common use of touch-tone devices. Why is using a touch-tone device in this particular situation beneficial?

8. Name the most common types of nonimpact printers? What are some of the advantages of nonimpact printers versus impact printers?

9. What are three categories of monitors?

10. What is the most common use of flat panel displays? Why are these types of displays preferred for this use?

Federal Express

Federal Express is the world's largest express transportation company. It provides time-definite services for important documents, packages, and freight, delivering over 1.5 million items in 127 countries each working day.

Federal Express flies to over 300 airports via a transport fleet of over 200 different kinds of jets. It also owns over 200 turboprop feeder aircraft, which serve small communities. More than 30,000 computer and radio equipped vehicles are in service around the globe. Federal Express also maintains a network of over 1600 staffed facilities and more than 29,000 drop-off locations. It employs more than 90,000 people and has been honored on numerous occasions as an outstanding employer.

To provide real-time package tracking for each shipment, the corporation utilizes one of the world's largest computer and telecommunications networks. The employees operate tens of thousands of small hand-held computers called Supertrackers to record the transit of shipments through the FedEx system. That information is promptly transmitted to the company's mainframe computers. This enables Federal Express customers to access information concerning a shipment's status around the clock and around the world.

BACKGROUND
The Federal Express Corporation is based in Memphis, Tennessee. It was founded in April 1973 by Frederick Smith and began showing a profit in 1976. It soon became established as the high-priority carrier in the market place.

Federal Express invented the ''hub and spokes'' system of distribution, which has been copied not only by other air cargo companies, but by the passenger airlines as well. The company's growth gained impetus following air cargo deregulation in 1977. Deregulation allowed Federal Express to begin use of large aircraft, such as the Boeing 727s and later the McDonnell Douglas DC-10s. Recently it has added McDonnell Douglas MD-11s to its fleet for use in international operations, and has placed orders for Airbus A300-600 F aircraft to be used primarily in U.S. domestic operations. After deregulation, the smaller Falcon aircraft, which had been the backbone of the company, were used to expand into medium-sized and smaller markets. The domestic expansion has continued, and today

Federal Express provides direct service to virtually all of the U.S. population.

During the late 1970s and into the first half of the 1980s, the company entered its maturing phase. Federal Express was well established, and the competition was trying to catch up. Growth rate was compounded at about 40 percent per year. Revenues currently are in excess of $7 billion.

Federal Express acquired Tiger International Inc., in February 1989, and became the world's largest full-service all-cargo airline with the integration of Flying Tigers' network into its system on August 7, 1989. Included in the acquisition were Flying Tigers' routes to 21 countries; a fleet of aircraft that included Boeing 747s, DC-8s, and 727s; facilities throughout the world; and Tiger's expertise in international air freight. Since then, the company has continued expansion into the international marketplace.

Worldwide, over 60,000 pocket-sized, hand-held Supertrackers are scanning packages for FedEx each time a shipment changes hands.

POLICIES AND INNOVATIONS
Federal Express was the first express transportation company to lower its service commitment from noon to 10:30 a.m., and the first to offer money-back guarantees on its service commitments. As the company expanded, it increased weight limits for express shipments from 70 pounds to 120 pounds to 150 pounds per package, and finally to virtually any size shipment. FedEx continually reinvests profits into state-of-the-art equipment and aircraft to support expansion. It also emphasizes employee training and benefits, which results in satisfied employees who in

turn provide the "value-added" type of service necessary to stay ahead of the competition.

While the concept of picking up and delivering documents and packages is simple, the systems to make it operate quickly and efficiently are innovative, complicated, and expensive. Federal Express has been the industry leader in the use of high technology to improve its services, and despite its rapid growth, has kept pace with innovations in its never-ending efforts to retain its leadership role. The innovations include the following:

■ Development of a computerized tracking system designed to tell the company and the customer the location of any package or document at any given time from pickup to delivery.

■ Development of a customer service system with 29 call centers throughout the world that handle upwards of 297,000 requests for service and inquiries daily.

■ Development of a computerized, digitally assisted dispatch system (DADS) which communicates to couriers through computer screens in their vans. DADS provides quick courier response to dispatches and allows couriers to manage their time and routes with extreme efficiency and accuracy.

■ Expansion of the central sorting system in Memphis, which is continually undergoing refinements in technologies and techniques in order to meet the ever-increasing volumes of items being shipped. In order to meet the next-morning delivery commitment, the nightly sort system

must operate in a tight time frame. Whether the number of packages is 35,000 as it was in 1978 or over 1.5 million systemwide as it is today, all of the packages must be sorted in the same amount of time—about two hours. A second hub has been established in Indianapolis, Indiana, and there are now regional sorting facilities in Newark, New Jersey; Oakland, California; Los Angeles, California; Anchorage, Alaska; and Brussels, Belgium.

■ Introduction of the Overnight Letter in 1981, offering a lower-priced way of sending documents overnight. The original weight limit for the Overnight Letter was 20 pages, or 6 ounces, but that weight limit was increased to 30 pages, or 8 ounces. The product has grown to an average of more than 300,000 shipments per day.

■ Introduction of the Federal Express POWERSHIP systems, which are on-premise computers that process approximately one-third of FedEx shipments. The systems provide automated billing, allow customers direct access to their package information, and give international shippers detailed directions for their particular needs.

■ Establishment of the Business Logistics Services division, a separate, independent division of Federal Express that provides a full range of logistics services for customers. Inventory management and distribution solutions, including warehousing services, customer service, information systems, transportation, credit and collections, or technical support, can be totally customized to a company's "just-in-time" needs.

APPLICATION
Federal Express

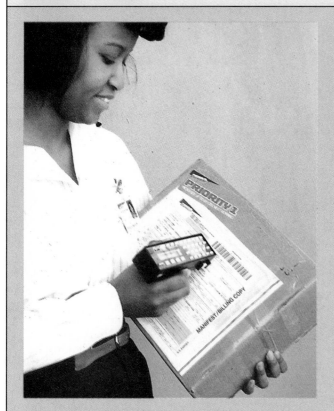

THE COSMOS II POSITIVE TRACKING SYSTEM

In order to track the large number of packages shipped every day, Federal Express needed a system that is accurate, simple to use, and extremely efficient. Thus the company developed the COSMOS II tracking system, which met the criteria so well that it won the Computerworld Smithsonian Award in the Transportation Category.

The developers of the system designed and produced a pocket-sized, hand-held scanner called the Supertracker that could stand rigorous treatment in all weather conditions. In addition, each van contains a Digital Access Dispatch System computer and a Courier printer designed in-house to issue a ''very smart'' label for each package. Using these basic tools and linking them to sophisticated communications and data-processing equipment and techniques has enabled Federal Express to track every single item entrusted to its care, anywhere in the world.

Each package receives a ''smart'' label marked with a bar code and printed with the Courier printer. The Super-

tracker scanner reads the bar code. Then another COS-MOS II component, software called Astra (which resides in the Supertracker scanner), interprets the bar code and helps route and sort packages so not one of them goes astray. The Supertrackers relay data back to mini-computers in the dispatch stations through couplers on the Digital Access Dispatch systems in each van. Worldwide, over 60,000 Supertrackers are scanning packages each time a shipment changes hands.

At the end of each business day, the Supertrackers are stored in mechanical cradles located in the dispatch stations. There, they download information to the company's mainframe computers, updating the company's data bases overnight.

Thus each package is scanned at pick-up. Its location is updated at the SuperHub in Memphis and at the distribution locations. When the package arrives at a processing center, it is put onto a moving belt. Each package is coded and loaded onto the proper delivery slide as it comes off the belt, so that there is no accumulation of package inventory which could create confusion and errors. When each item is delivered, the courier notes the time, day, and name of the person who signs for the item. That information is also entered into the company's computer system.

A significant volume of packages still passes through the hub at Memphis but now a comprehensive network of regional hubs and sorting centers helps create efficiency and speed in package delivery. A distributed system of computing offloads some transaction processing from the company's mainframe computers to the minicomputers at the dispatch centers. This lets each dispatch station have the data it needs to manage its own deliveries, as opposed to locating all data in central mainframes. The stations then access only the data they need from the mainframes.

This system enables Federal Express to think of distribution as marketing, and thus serve its customers better. Because of its ability to continually adapt to changing market circumstances, Federal Express has established its leadership as the world's largest full-service all-cargo airline.

DISCUSSION POINTS

1. Describe some input and output features of the FedEx system.
2. Explain how the Federal Express COSMOS II system demonstrates the principles of source data automation.

Storage Devices

Library Releases Data via Laser Disc

Gary H. Anthes, *Computerworld*

WASHINGTON, D.C.—The Library of Congress has tapped seven universities and a municipality to join in an experiment that may point the way to the libraries of the 21st century—digital depositories of text, photos, movies and recordings tied together by hypertext software and navigated with clicks of a mouse.

Beginning this fall, libraries at the eight institutions will get a series of test packages from the Library of Congress' American Memory project. They will include software and, in some cases, hardware with optical laser discs and videodiscs containing images of U.S. photographs, manuscripts, sheet music, motion pictures and recordings, most depicting life around the turn of the century.

The Library of Congress has distributed printed catalog cards since 1901 and machine-readable catalogs since the 1960s. Now, in what the library modestly calls the "next phase," it is gearing up for a fundamental extension of its mission, from the distribution of catalog information to the electronic dissemination of key portions of its vast collections.

The American Memory project is at the leading edge of this revolution in the Library of Congress' mission. Between 1990 and 1995, the project will use its $1 million annual budget to prepare between 15 and 20 collections for the electronic library at the rate of two or three per year.

The first package, a cluster of logically related Library of Congress collections, covers roughly the period from the U.S. Civil War to the start of World War I. Major components include the following:

■ 25,000 photographs of historic scenes from 1890 to 1920.
■ A collection of 400 pamphlets written by black authors between 1820 and 1920.
■ Films of U.S. cities and people from 1898 to 1910.
■ Sound recordings of spoken-word recordings of political figures, stage performers and orators of the period.

The photographs and films are stored in analog format on videodiscs. All other items are stored digitally on compact disc/read-only memory discs, indexed by subject and key words much as books are catalogued in conventional libraries.

The Library of Congress ties it all together with Apple Computer, Inc.'s Hypercard running on a Macintosh computer and using Hypersearch from Discovery Systems, Inc. for information retrieval. Carl Fleischhauer, project coordinator, said the project is not committed to use of those products. The Library of Congress will later experiment with IBM Personal Computer implementations, he said.

Users of the system prototype can trace a theme across the components of the collection. For example, a researcher reading about turn-of-the-century architecture might find a reference to the neoclassical style and click the mouse on the word neoclassical to retrieve a definition of the style from another source. The student might then click on a reference to Thomas Jefferson found in that definition to retrieve a picture of Jefferson's Virginia home, Monticello.

In one of the first menus seen after logging on, the user may decide to go to the reading room for independent, self-directed research or to the Exhibit Hall, where tutorial information may have been predefined for a student or trainee.

Fleischhauer said the challenge of American Memory is not a technological one. "We're using existing technology. We're following the computer marketplace, not leading it," he said.

The hard work is getting information from thousands of faded, crumbling pages onto machine-readable media, Fleischhauer said. "We have a lot of wonderful things pertaining to history. How do you get it off of paper and into these kinds of gadgets so lots of people can get it?"

Libraries getting the first installment of American Memory are at Brigham Young University, Northwestern University, Oklahoma State University of Agriculture and Applied Science, West Virginia University, Willamette University, the U.S. Naval Academy, the University of Nevada and the Washoe County Library in Reno, Nev.

■ INTRODUCTION

Organizations store large amounts of data for a variety of purposes. Many businesses commonly store data regarding their employees, customers, suppliers, inventory levels, sales figures, and expenses, in addition to the specific types of data required to perform their particular business functions. Organizations that use electronic methods of processing data must store it in computer-accessible form. The arrangement of computer-based files and, ultimately, the type of media used for data storage depend on the needs and constraints of the organization. Each type of storage media has certain characteristics that must be considered.

This chapter examines the two most popular types of data storage media, magnetic tape and magnetic disk, and begins the discussion of two of the most common types of file arrangement using these media, sequential and direct-access. (These topics are elaborated upon in the next chapter.)

■ CLASSIFICATION OF STORAGE MEDIA

As was discussed in Chapter 4, memory is part of the CPU and is used to store instructions and data needed for processing. Semiconductor memory, the circuitry on silicon chips capable of extremely fast processing, is the most widely used form of memory.

In most cases, the amount of data required by a program exceeds the capacity of memory. To compensate for limited memory, data can be stored on storage devices. Storage is not part of the CPU. The most common types of storage are magnetic tapes and magnetic disks. Mass storage devices are also useful in some situations. Storage media costs much less than memory. Therefore, they make the storage of large amounts of data economically feasible for most organizations.

Storage media are connected to the CPU. Once data has been stored on a storage device, it can be retrieved for processing as needed. However, the retrieval of items from storage is significantly slower than retrieval of items from memory. After processing has been completed, the data or results can be written back onto the storage media (see Figure 6–1).

■ SEQUENTIAL-ACCESS MEDIA

Magnetic Tape

A **magnetic tape** is a continuous plastic strip wound onto a reel, quite similar to the tape used in reel-to-reel audio recorders. The magnetic tape's plastic base is treated with an iron oxide coating that can be magnetized. Typically, the tape is one-half inch in width. It is wound in lengths from 400 to 3,200 feet. Some magnetic tapes are also packaged in plastic cartridges and cassettes for use with personal computers.

Data is stored on magnetic tape by magnetizing small spots of the iron oxide coating on the tape. Although these spots can be read (detected) by the computer, they are invisible to the human eye. Large volumes of information can be stored on a single tape; densities of 1,600 characters per inch are common, and some tapes can store up to 6,250 characters per inch. A typical tape reel 2,400 feet long can store as much data as 24,000 pages of doubled-spaced text, while costing only $20 to $30.

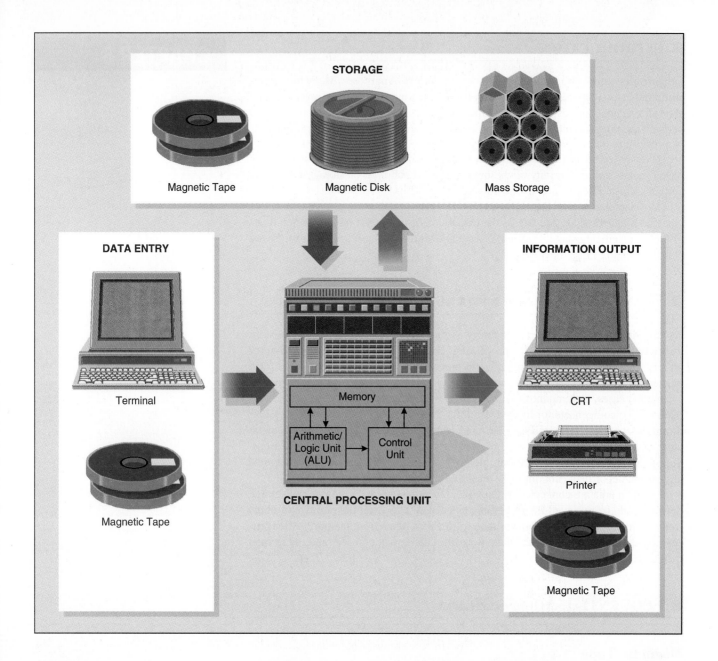

FIGURE 6–1

Computer System Utilizing Storage Media

The most common method of representing data on magnetic tape uses a nine-track coding scheme, although other coding schemes are also used. When the nine-track method is used, the tape is divided into nine horizontal rows called **tracks** (see Figure 6–2). Data is represented vertically in columns, one character per column. This method of coding is identical to the Extended Binary Coded Decimal Interchange Code (EBCDIC) used to represent data in some computers' memory. In this way, eight bits and eight of the nine tracks are used to represent each character. The ninth bit and ninth track function as a parity bit.

A magnetic tape is mounted on a **tape drive** when a program needs the data it contains (see Figure 6–3). The tape drive has a **read/write head** (which is actually an electromagnet) that creates or detects the magnetized bits as the tape moves past

136   **CHAPTER 6: STORAGE DEVICES**

FIGURE 6–2

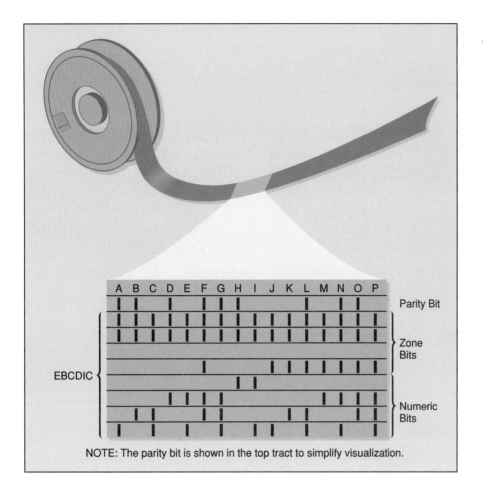

Nine-Track Tape with Even Parity

NOTE: The parity bit is shown in the top tract to simplify visualization.

FIGURE 6–3

Magnetic Tape Drive

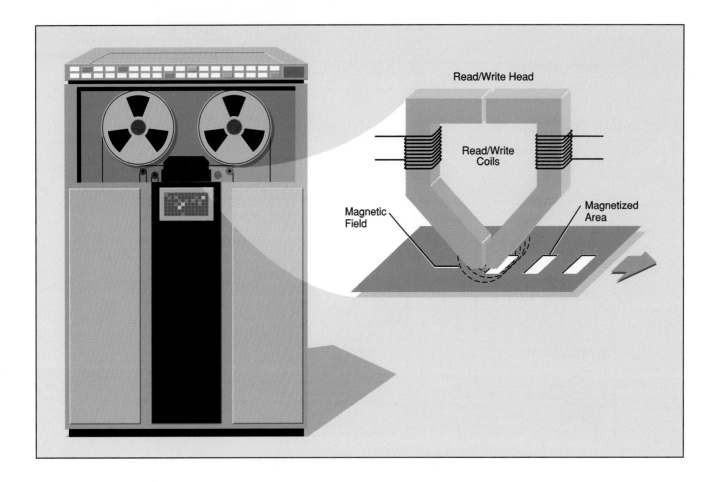

Read/Write Head

Read/Write
Coils

Magnetic
Field

Magnetized
Area

FIGURE 6–4

Recording on Magnetic Tape

it (see Figure 6–4). When the read/write head is reading data, it detects the magnetized spots and converts them into electrical pulses to send to the CPU. When writing data, the head magnetizes the appropriate spots on the tape, while erasing any data stored there previously.

Individual records on magnetic tape are separated by **interrecord gaps (IRGs),** as shown in Figure 6–5. These gaps do not contain data but they perform a specific function. When a tape is being read, its entire contents are rarely read all at once. Rather, it is stopped when the end of a record is reached. The tape must then be accelerated to the proper speed before the next record can be read accurately. If this were not the case, the result would be similar to what happens when a phonograph record is played at the wrong speed. The IRG gives the tape time to regain the proper speed before the next record is read. The length of the IRG depends on the speed of the tape drive. If the tape drive is very fast, longer gaps are needed. A slower tape drive requires shorter gaps.

If the records stored on a tape are very short and the IRGs are long, it would be possible for the tape to be more than 50 percent blank, causing the tape drive to stop and accelerate constantly. To avoid this situation, records may be grouped, or blocked, together. These **blocked records,** or **blocks,** are separated by **interblock gaps (IBGs)** as shown in Figure 6–6. Instead of reading a short record and stopping, then reading another short record and stopping, the read/write head reads a block of records at

FIGURE 6–5

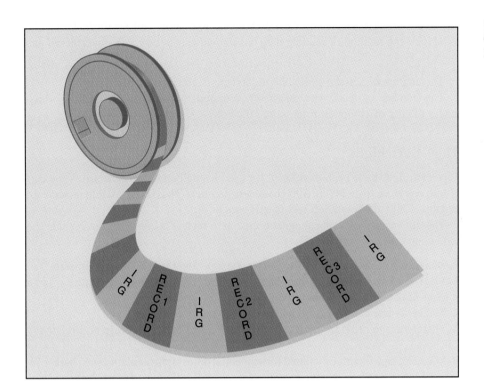

Magnetic Tape with Interrecord Gaps

FIGURE 6–6

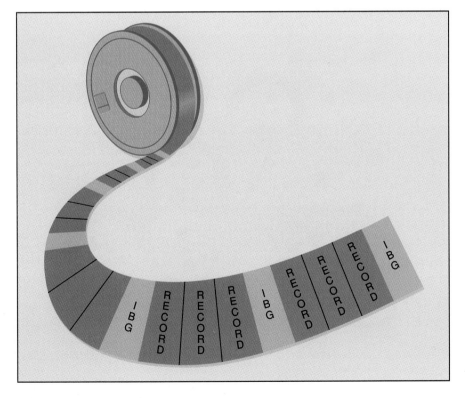

Magnetic Tape with Interblock Gaps

SEQUENTIAL-ACCESS MEDIA

one time and stops, then reads another block and stops, and so forth. Using the interblock gap method of reading data has two advantages over the interrecord gap method:

1. The amount of storage available on the tape is used more efficiently.
2. The number of read/write operations required is significantly reduced, which makes the use of computer time more efficient.

Tape Cartridges

Tape cartridges have been developed for use on small computer systems. Tape cartridges can store from 200 to 800 characters per inch. They are available in standard lengths of 300, 450, and 555 feet (see Figure 6–7).

The advantages of using magnetic tape as a means of data storage include the following:

■ Data can be transferred between magnetic tape and the CPU at high speeds.
■ Magnetic tapes have high recording densities; therefore they can store a large amount of data in a small amount of space.
■ Magnetic tape can be erased and used over and over again.
■ Magnetic tape provides high-capacity storage and backup storage at a relatively low cost.
■ Magnetic tape is perfectly suited for sequential processing (explained in Chapter 7). It is the most common storage medium for systems utilizing sequential processing.

Use of magnetic tape has the following disadvantages:

■ Magnetic tape is a sequential medium, which means the entire tape must be read from beginning to end when changes are made in the data. The amount of time required to retrieve data precludes its use when instantaneous retrieval is required.

FIGURE 6–7

Tape Cartridges Used for Data Storage

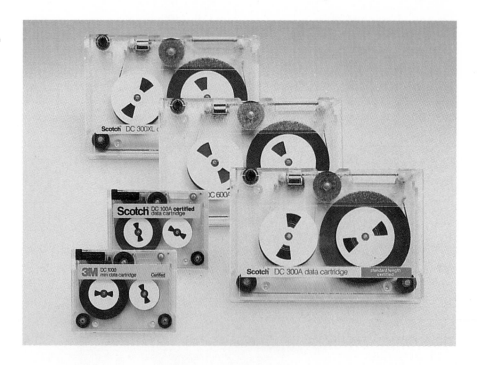

■ All tape and reel containers must be properly labeled to identify the contents.

■ The data on the tape must be printed in order for humans to read the data.

■ Environmental factors can distort data stored on magnetic tape. Dust, moisture, extreme heat or cold, and static electricity can alter the data. **Backup copies,** that is, second copies of original tapes, must be made to prevent data loss.

CONCEPT SUMMARY 6–1

Characteristics of Magnetic Tape

Features	Advantages	Disadvantages
A continuous strip of plastic tape wound onto a reel	Transfers data between tape and the CPU rapidly	Data must be read sequentially
Tape is treated with a magnetizable iron oxide coating		Tapes require proper labels for content identification
Data are represented as magnetized spots on the surface of the tape	Stores large amounts of data in a small space	Environmental factors can distort data stored on tape
Data is accessed sequentially	Erasable and reusable	Humans cannot read the data stored on tape
	Low-cost backup media	
	Well suited for sequential processing	

■ DIRECT-ACCESS MEDIA

Magnetic Disk

A **magnetic disk** is a cylindrical metal platter coated on both sides with a magnetizable material such as iron oxide. In many respects, a magnetic disk resembles a phonograph record. However, it does not have grooves etched onto its surface like a phonograph record; the surface of a magnetic disk is smooth.

A magnetic disk stores and retrieves data in much the same fashion as a phonograph record is played. The disk is rotated while a read/write head is positioned above its magnetic surface. Instead of spiraling into the center of the disk as the needle does on a phonograph record, the read/write head stores and retrieves data in concentric circles. Each circle is referred to as a **track.** One track never touches another (see Figure 6–8). Some magnetic disks contain thousands of tracks per side.

In most disk storage devices, several disks are assembled to form a **disk pack** (see Figure 6–9). The disks are mounted on a central shaft. The individual disks are spaced on the shaft to allow room for a read/write mechanism to move between them

FIGURE 6-8

Top View of Disk Surface Showing
200 Concentric Tracks

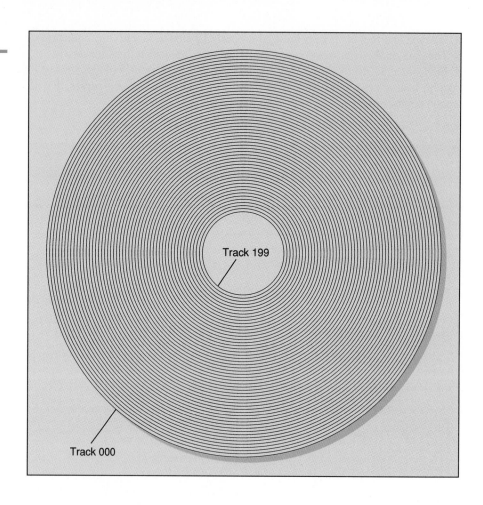

Track 199

Track 000

FIGURE 6-9

Disk Packs

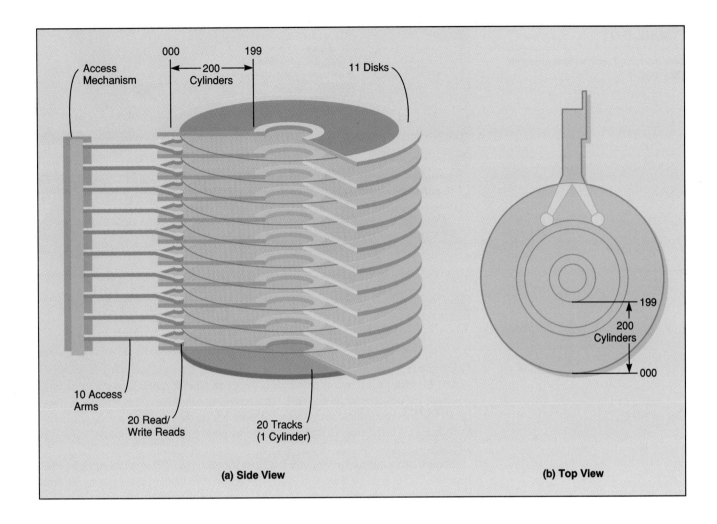

000   **199**

← **200** →
Cylinders

Access
Mechanism

11 Disks

10 Access
Arms

20 Read/
Write Reads

20 Tracks
(1 Cylinder)

(a) Side View

199

200
Cylinders

000

(b) Top View

(see Figure 6–10). The disk pack in Figure 6–10 has eleven disks and provides twenty usable recording surfaces. The top and bottom surfaces are not used for storing data because they are likely to become scratched or nicked. A disk pack may contain anywhere from five to one hundred disks.

A disk pack is positioned in a disk drive when the data on the pack is to be processed. The **disk drive** rotates all disks in unison at speeds up to 3,600 revolutions per minute. In some models, the disk packs are removable; in others, the disks are permanently mounted on the disk drive. Removable disk packs allow disks to be removed when the data they contain is not needed (see Figure 6–11). Users of removable disk packs typically have many more disk packs than disk drives.

The data on a disk is read or written by the read/write heads located between the disks. Most disk units have one read/write head for each disk recording surface. All the heads are permanently connected to an **access mechanism.** When reading or writing occurs, the heads are positioned over the appropriate track by the in-and-out movements of the access mechanism.

When data stored on the surface of one disk in the disk pack is required, all heads move to the corresponding tracks on the surfaces of the other disks because they are

FIGURE 6–10

Side View (a) and Top View (b) of a Disk Pack

FIGURE 6–11

Disk Storage Units with Removable
Disk Packs

connected to the same access mechanism. Since all the read/write heads move together, they are positioned over the same tracks on all disk surfaces at the same time. All the number-1 tracks on the disk surfaces form a **cylinder;** the number-2 tracks on all surfaces form another cylinder enclosed within the first; and so on (see Figure 6–10 again). The number of cylinders per disk pack equals the number of tracks per surface.

Some disk units have one read/write head for each track. The access time is much faster with this type of disk unit since the access mechanism does not move from track to track. Units such as this are rarely used because they are very expensive. The placement of data on the disk pack, therefore, can be an important factor if the amount of access time is critical. When access time is an important factor, it is best to store data that is accessed more frequently on the same or adjacent tracks of the disk surfaces. This will reduce the motion of the read/write heads and thus reduce the access time.

Each track on a disk can store the same amount of data even though the tracks get smaller toward the center of the disk. Consider a disk pack with 4,000 usable tracks (20 surfaces × 200 tracks per surface) on which 7,294 characters can be stored on each track. The disk pack could conceivably store 29,176,000 characters of data (4,000 tracks × 7,294 characters per track).

The computer locates data stored on a magnetic disk by its disk surface number, track number, and record number. The numbers make up the data's **disk address.** The disk address of a record is stored immediately before the record (see Figure 6–12). Disk records are separated by gaps similar to the interrecord gaps on magnetic tape. Also similarly, the presence of gaps in each track reduces the amount of data that can be stored on a disk. Therefore, the usable storage capacity in the disk pack described in the previous paragraph would be slightly less than the potential 29,176,000 characters.

Since disks provide direct access, they are typically used to store data that is accessed frequently (direct-access systems are discussed in Chapter 7). Depending on the disk drive, it is possible for up to 850,000 characters to be read per second.

FIGURE 6–12

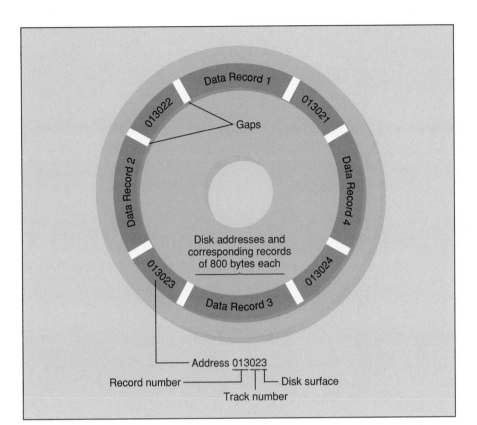

Floppy Disk

The **floppy disk, flexible disk,** or **diskette,** was introduced in 1973 to replace punched cards as a medium for data entry, but it can also store programs and data files. Today, diskettes are produced in two sizes, 5¼ inches and 3½ inches (see Figure 6–13). The term microfloppy disks is often used to refer to the 3½″ diskettes. Floppy disks are made of plastic and coated with a magnetizable oxide substance. In most respects, they are miniature magnetic disks. Since the diskettes are relatively inexpensive (most sell for less than $1.00), they are popular for use with microcomputer systems and point-of-sale terminals. They are reusable, easy to store, and weigh less than two ounces. Floppy disks can even be mailed. In addition, they can add security to a computer system because they can be removed and stored in a safe place.

Data is stored on a floppy disk as magnetized spots in tracks, as on conventional magnetic disks, and elements are addressed by track number and sector number (see Figure 6–14). The read/write head accesses the disk through the oblong or rectangular opening in the jacket, called the **read/write notch** (see Figure 6–15). The head moves back and forth to read the data or write data to the disk. Unlike the one used in hard disk systems, this read/write head actually rides on the surface of the disk rather than being positioned slightly above it. The disk rotates at a speed of 360 revolutions per minute (as compared to as many as 3,600 revolutions per minute for hard disk drives).

Magnetic disks have several advantages over magnetic tapes:

■ Disk files on magnetic disks can be organized sequentially and processed in the

FIGURE 6–13

Floppy Disks

FIGURE 6–14

Sectors and Tracks on a Floppy Disk

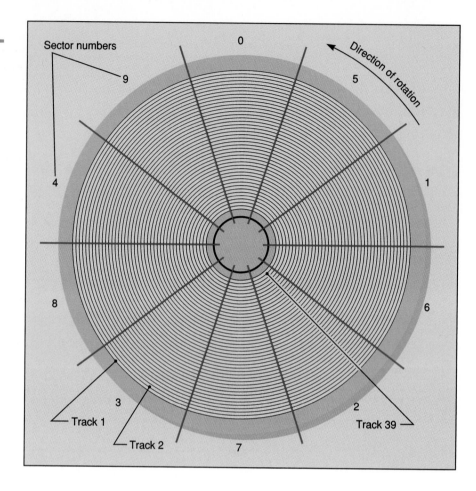

FIGURE 6–15

Parts of a Floppy Disk

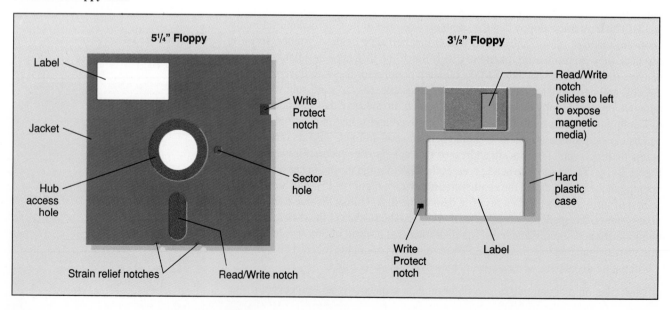

same way as magnetic tape, or they can be organized for direct-access processing.

■ The fast access time offered by magnetic disk storage allows data files to be accessed or changed immediately.

■ Quick response can be made to inquiries (normally, response is made in seconds).

■ With the appropriate software, a single transaction can simultaneously update or change several files stored on disks.

The major disadvantages of magnetic disk storage include the following:

■ Magnetic hard disks are a relatively expensive storage medium; their cost may be ten times that of magnetic tape in terms of cost per character stored. However, reductions in disk cost and the introduction of floppy disks are making these storage devices more affordable.

■ When data stored on a disk is changed, the original data is erased and the new data is stored in its place. Therefore, magnetic disks do not provide backup files. Data can be lost if there are inadequate provisions for error checking and backup files.

■ Disk storage requires more complicated programming to gain access to records and to update files. The technicians who maintain the complicated hardware must be highly skilled.

■ The ease of gaining access to data stored on disk files can create security problems.

CONCEPT SUMMARY 6–2

Characteristics of Magnetic Disks

Features	Advantages	Disadvantages
A metal platter coated on both sides with a magnetizable material	Files can be organized for sequential or direct-access storage	More expensive than magnetic tape
Data is represented as magnetized spots on the surface of the disk	Data can be accessed immediately	Require backup files so data is not lost when changes are made
Disks come in varying sizes	Files can be altered simultaneously	Require complex programming to gain access to files
		Easy access to data may pose security problems

◘ MASS STORAGE

As stated earlier, accessing data and instructions from memory is very fast because it requires no physical movement of hardware devices. The speed of electricity is, in effect, the only limiting factor. However, the capacity of memory is limited and

FIGURE 6–16

A Mass Storage Device Using Cartridge Tape

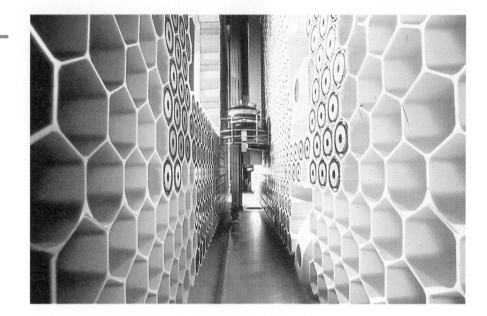

also very expensive. Disk storage is less expensive and provides direct-access capabilities, but even disk storage tends to be expensive when very large amounts of data must be stored for direct-access processing.

To meet the need for a low-cost method of storing vast amounts of data, mass storage devices have been developed. They allow rapid access to data. Large files, backup files, and infrequently used files can be placed in mass storage at a relatively low cost.

One type of mass storage uses a cartridge tape as the storage medium (see Figure 6–16). The cartridges are similar to cassette tapes and permit sequential access of data. The high-density tape used requires 90 percent less storage space than common magnetic tapes. A mass storage system such as this can hold the equivalent of up to 1,000 tape reels. Tape mounting is controlled by the system, rather than by a human operator, and tends to be much faster than the traditional operator-controlled mounting of magnetic tapes.

Mass storage is not limited to high-density magnetic tape. A mass storage system for minicomputers using small floppy disks as the storage medium has been introduced. However, unlike the cartridge system described above, most mass storage systems such as this require extensive physical movement because the needed files must first be found and then mounted (or loaded) mechanically before data can be read or written. Although direct access is possible, the retrieval time is relatively slow (although still measured in seconds) compared to systems utilizing magnetic tapes and disks.

■ MODERN METHODS OF DATA STORAGE

Charge-Coupled Devices

As technology continues to advance, smaller, faster, and less-expensive storage devices will become commonplace. Advances are rapidly being made in semiconductor

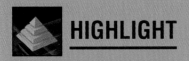
Fighting Crime with Modern Technology

Optical disk mass storage systems are making a significant contribution to the fight against crime. Agencies such as local police and fire departments are using optical (laser) disk systems to store large amounts of information that is up-to-date and can be retrieved for review almost instantaneously.

The Multiuser Archival and Retrieval System (MARS) from Micro Dynamics Ltd. is being used by the El Paso, Texas, Police Department to store thousands of photographs, ar-

rest records, and witness statements. The new system replaces a microfiche system that contained information that was five months old. The MARS system uses Sony Corporation WORM drives connected to an Apple Macintosh local area network (LAN) to store the equivalent of the contents of approximately 400 two-drawer file cabinets. The information stored on the system is up-to-date and can be accessed almost instantaneously. El Paso Police Department officials estimate that the $100,000

system will pay for itself in approximately twelve months. Their estimate is based upon the amount saved in labor costs and in increased employee productivity.

With mass storage systems such as MARS, agencies such as the El Paso Police Department can be extremely effective in performing their job. In El Paso, they are really taking a byte out of crime.

and laser technology. An innovation in semiconductor technology is the development of **charge-coupled devices (CCDs)** for use in data storage. CCDs are made of silicon similar to semiconductor memory. They are nearly 100 times faster than magnetic bubble memory but are somewhat slower than semiconductor RAM. As in semiconductor memories, data in CCDs can be lost if a power failure occurs. CCDs are used primarily with large computer systems such as minicomputers and mainframes.

RAM Disks

Accessing data on disks is relatively slow compared to the speed at which a microprocessor can manipulate data. **Random-access memory (RAM) disks** are currently the only type of storage device that can approximate the speed of a microprocessor. A peripheral device using RAM chips is available (see Figure 6–17). A RAM card that contains RAM chips plugs into the computer in the same slot as the disk drive card. The computer treats the RAM card just as it does a disk drive. Even though RAM disks are not separate physical disks, they function like regular diskettes. A RAM disk instructs the computer to set aside storage space in RAM to function like a disk. Some RAM disks used with microcomputers can store up to 128 Mb of data and have a retrieval rate fifty times faster than a floppy disk.

The advantage of using RAM disks is speed. Data stored in RAM can be transferred from one part of RAM to another faster than it can be transferred from a disk to RAM. The disadvantage of RAM disks is that they require a continuous power supply. As with any memory, when the power supply is discontinued, data is erased from memory. However, some manufacturers provide battery backup units for use with RAM disks in case of power failure.

MODERN METHODS OF DATA STORAGE

149

FIGURE 6–17

RAM Disk Chip

Laser Technology

Laser technology provides an opportunity to store mass quantities of data at greatly reduced costs. A **laser storage system** can store nearly 128 billion characters of data at about one-tenth the cost of standard magnetic media. In a laser storage system, data is recorded when a laser beam forms patterns on the surface of a polyester sheet coated with a thin layer of rhodium metal. To read data from this sheet, the laser reflects light off the surface, reconstructing the data into a digital bit stream. Data stored by laser resists alterations and any attempt to change it can easily be detected. Therefore, it provides a very secure storage system. In addition, unlike magnetic media, laser storage does not deteriorate over time and it is immune to electromagnetic radiation. Another advantage is that there is no danger of losing data as a result of power failures.

A more recent development is a laser system used as a mass storage device for minicomputers. This system uses a helium-neon laser, delivering about ten milliwatts of optical power to a disk coated with a film of a nonmetallic substance called tellurium. Data is recorded when the laser creates a hole approximately one micrometer in diameter in the film. The disk used in this system is thirty centimeters in diameter and can store ten billion bits on its 40,000 tracks. The data cannot be erased once it is written, so this system is best suited for archival storage purposes.

Another development in laser technology is the optical, or laser, disk (see Figure 6–18). **Optical disks** are much faster than hard disks but are still fairly slow compared to semiconductor RAM. One big advantage, though, is their large capacity. A single optical disk can hold more than 600 megabytes (Mb) of data. That is over 225,000 pages of manuscript, or the entire contents of the *Encyclopedia Britannica* with space left over. Bits of data are stored on an optical disk as the presence or absence of a tiny pit burned into the disk by a pinpoint laser beam. A single line one inch long contains about 5,000 pits, or bits of data.

FIGURE 6–18

Optical Disk

Compact Disks

Compact disks (CDs), similar to the type used for high quality audio recordings, are now being used as a storage medium for microcomputers. These disks use the laser technology discussed in the previous section. The 5¼ inch disks can store up to 1,000 times more data than a 1 Mb floppy disk. Although the retrieval time of compact disks is slower than magnetic media, CDs are effective in searching data bases to locate data.

Because they can store large amounts of data, compact disks are being used in a number of different areas including customer service, libraries, public service, and **multimedia** applications. In the area of customer service, compact disks are used by travel agencies to store mass amounts of data about hotels and resorts on CDs rather than in travel books. The Library of Congress is also using compact disks to distribute some of its vast amounts of information to the microcomputer-using public. Fire and police departments are also using compact disks to store large amounts of data that can be updated and accessed quickly.

Compact disks, and in some cases videodisks and compact disks together, are being used to create what is being referred to as multimedia applications. These applications combine data with pictures. The Grolier Electronic Encyclopedia, for example, includes information and more than 1500 color photographs that can be displayed on a computer monitor.

Presently, CDs come in several forms, including a read-only version (CD-ROM), a write-once read-many version (WORM), and also an erasable, or nonpermanent, version. The information on CD-ROM is placed on the CD when it is manufactured. A company buying a CD-ROM uses it to access information, but cannot place information on the disk. In the case of CD-WORM, a company can place information on the CD, but it is a permanent copy.

What's All the Hype?

Computers themselves are very powerful tools. But combine computers with interactive videos, slides, stereo music, and a vast amount of data storage and you have—hypermedia. Hypermedia uses optical disks to store not only large amounts of text, but the other data, such as videos, as well. Most hypermedia systems require two video monitors, a computer keyboard, and a mouse. The user employs the keyboard and mouse to access the stored data in any order desired. So far, universities are the main users of hypermedia.

For example, Apple Computer's HyperCard, used on a Macintosh, has a system called Slice of Life. It is used at the University of Utah to teach brain anatomy. The student can read text about the brain while at the same time viewing any of the 22,000 images on file. In addition, medical students can review the actual case studies of patients. Another medical system, used at Cornell University Medical College, allows the student to view an organ such as a liver on one screen and then view a diseased organ for comparison on the second screen. If surgery is required, the student can watch a video of surgeons performing the necessary operation.

Hypermedia is used in many areas other than medicine. In history classes the system not only provides text about the era, it also plays music and talk shows, displays still photography, and presents TV news programs, all from the era the student is studying.

Many businesses have not yet explored the possibilities of hypermedia but it can be used there as well. Imagine a travel video that allows the user to see and hear the waves on the beach and actually see the different hotel options.

The hardware for a hypermedia system, sometimes called compact disc interactive (CD-I) or interactive multimedia, costs about $3,000. Some manufacturers such as Sony and Philips hope to develop a system that will connect to a regular TV, so that only one monitor would be needed. This could lower the cost to less than $1,000. Hypermedia may soon be as common as TV.

The erasable version of compact disks comes in a cartridge which is inserted into an erasable-optical (E-O) drive. These drives are relatively new and are not yet being sold in mass quantities. For this reason the drives are still somewhat expensive, ranging in price from $4000 to $7000. In addition, the drives operate at speeds that are slower than conventional hard disk drives; therefore, the E-O drives are currently not replacing hard disk drives with similar storage capacities.

Superconductors

Superconductors are metals that are capable of transmitting high levels of current. Until recently superconductors have been impractical for most applications because they have a very limiting quality; they can be used in only extremely cold environments. In 1911, when superconductors were first discovered, they had to be cooled to almost absolute zero, which is −459°F. Since 1986, however, scientists have made great progress in developing superconductors. A superconductor compound that contains bismuth can function at −243°F. Scientists feel they will continue to discover superconductors that can function at even warmer temperatures.

Why all the excitement about superconductors? Scientists and businesses feel superconductors will have a major impact on technology. For example, once superconductors are perfected some scientists feel supercomputers will no longer be so large they fill a room; instead, they may be reduced to about the size of a minicomputer! (see Figure 6–19).

Technology advances so rapidly that accurate predictions of what future storage media will be like is nearly impossible. Even though the state of the art changes from day to day, the objectives of making storage less expensive, faster, and more compact will continue to be pursued.

❑ SUMMARY POINTS

■ Storage, which is not part of the CPU, can hold large amounts of data and instructions at a lower cost than memory. The most-common storage media are magnetic tapes and magnetic disks.

■ Magnetic tape consists of a plastic base coated with iron oxide. Data is stored as small magnetized areas on the surface of the tape.

■ Records are separated on magnetic tape by interrecord gaps (IRGs). After the tape is stopped while reading records, these gaps allow the tape to regain the proper speed before the next record is read.

■ Data is often recorded on magnetic tape in groups of records called blocks. Blocks are separated from each other by interblock gaps (IBGs). Blocking reduces overall input/output time and makes more efficient use of available storage.

■ Tape cartridges are used to store large amounts of data and are commonly used to backup microcomputer hard disks.

■ Magnetic disks provide direct access to data. Any record can be located by referring to its address—disk surface number, track number, and record number.

■ A disk pack is positioned on a disk drive, which rotates all disks in the pack in unison. Some disk packs are removable; others are permanently mounted on disk drives.

■ Floppy, or flexible, disks provide low-cost, direct-access storage. Floppy disks are easy to store and are frequently used with minicomputers and microcomputers.

■ Mass storage devices are appropriate when large amounts of data must be stored at low costs. Commonly used mass storage media are cartridge tapes and floppy disks. Floppy disk mass storage devices provide direct access, but the retrieval time is much slower than with standard disk storage.

■ Compact disks are an excellent form of storage for data base retrieval, but the medium is used by few companies because the initial investment in a CD system is expensive and it is difficult to develop an appropriate data base.

■ A RAM disk is an area of RAM that temporarily functions like a storage diskette.

■ Optical disks allow faster access to data than hard disks, but they provide fairly slow data retrieval compared to RAM. The advantage of optical disks as a storage medium is their storage capacity.

FIGURE 6–19

Superconductivity
Some scientists feel supercomputers may be reduced to the size of microcomputers once superconductors are perfected.

❑ TERMS FOR REVIEW

◻ REVIEW QUESTIONS

1. Why is storage required on computer systems? What are two of the most common types of storage?

2. What purpose do interrecord gaps (IRGs) serve on magnetic tapes? What determines the length of an IRG?

3. How are interblock gaps (IBGs) different from IRGs? Which method of blocking is preferred and why?

4. What are some of the advantages of using magnetic tape as a storage media? What are some of its disadvantages?

5. What is a disk drive? What is an access mechanism?

6. What is one way of reducing the amount of time required for data to be accessed on a hard disk drive?

7. List the advantages magnetic disks have over magnetic tapes. List the disadvantages of magnetic disks.

8. What is the primary purpose of mass-storage devices? Name three applications in which you feel mass storage would be required.

9. Identify some modern trends in data storage. Are there any applications you know of that use these methods of data storage?

10. What is multimedia? What storage device has made multimedia possible? Name some areas in which you think multimedia may be used in the future.

General Dynamics

General Dynamics is one of the free world's largest defense firms. It is engaged in the design, development, and manufacture of highly sophisticated defense systems and in the production and delivery of general aviation aircraft, construction materials, and natural resources. The company uses its broad technological capabilities in the assembly of military aircraft, space vehicles, electronic products, land vehicles, and nuclear-powered submarines.

HISTORY OF GENERAL DYNAMICS

Nine divisions and six major operating subsidiaries make up General Dynamics. Some of them were independent companies in existence for many years before joining General Dynamics.

An example is the founding division of General Dynamics, Electric Boat, headquartered in Groton, Connecticut. Electric Boat, which today makes nuclear-powered attack and ballistic missile–firing submarines, traces its history to the formation in 1880 of a predecessor company, Electro Dynamic. (Electro Dynamic exists today as Electric Boat's facilities in Avenel, New Jersey.) Electro Dynamic's birth coincided with the introduction of electricity into everyday life; the light bulb was patented in the same year. Electro Dynamic made electric motors, batteries, and other electrical equipment.

Electric Boat received its name in 1899 when the Electric Launch Company merged with the Holland Company. Electric Launch built electrically powered pleasure boats, while the Holland Company built the U.S. Navy's first operational submarine. In the years since, Electric Boat has concentrated on submarine design and construction, although its Elco division turned out more than half of the PT boats built during World War II. Electric Boat built 85 submarines during World War I and 78 during World War II. The division brought submarines into a new age by making the first nuclear-powered submarine, the USS Nautilus, which was launched in 1954.

After World War II, Electric Boat expanded into other lines of business, prompting the company to change its name to General Dynamics in 1952 and designate Electric Boat as a division of the company.

Just two years later, General Dynamics merged with Convair, an aviation giant formed in 1923. During World War II, Convair, known before the war as Consolidated Aircraft Co. and during the war as Consolidated Vultee, produced the Allies' most widely used heavy bomber, the B-24 Liberator, and a family of amphibious aircraft that included the PBY Catalina.

After joining General Dynamics, Convair continued to produce military aircraft such as the B-36 Peacemaker and B-58 Hustler bombers and the F-102 and F-106 delta-wing interceptors. Today, Convair manufactures Cruise missiles and airline fuselages.

Four more divisions have evolved out of Convair: Pomona (1961), which produces antiaircraft and antiship weapons such as the Sparrow and Standard missiles and the Phalanx gun system; Electronics (1961), which makes military avionics and communications systems; Space Systems (1985), which makes the Atlas I and II launch vehicles for military and commercial customers; and Fort Worth (1961), which turns out the F-16 Falcon fighter for the United States and many of its allies.

GENERAL DYNAMICS

Inside the 12-sided honeycomb that stores up to 6000 tape cartridges in its cells, the robot moves, searching for, mounting and demounting cartridges surely, effortlessly—this is ACS at General Dynamics.

The F-16 is one of General Dynamics' major product lines. Worldwide deliveries of the Fighting Falcon are expected to exceed 4,000 aircraft.

The next major firms to join General Dynamics after its merger with Convair were Material Service Corporation and Marblehead Lime in 1960. Material Service produces construction materials in the Midwest. Marblehead mines lime and produces brick. Freeman United Coal Mining Co. became part of GD in 1972.

General Dynamics expanded into the tank business in 1982 by buying the U.S. Army's only tank builder, Chrysler Defense, Inc. Renamed Land Systems Division, it has made over 50,000 tanks since 1941. Its current product, the M1A1 Abrams, the world's most advanced ground weapon system, is descended from a long line of tanks that include the M4 Sherman. The Sherman was the Western Allies' most widely used tank during World War II.

General aviation became General Dynamics' next activity when it bought Cessna Aircraft Company in 1985. Cessna has made over 177,000 aircraft since its formation in 1927, including the U.S. Air Force's first jet trainer, the T-37. Today Cessna makes light utility aircraft and business jets. It has produced the world's largest fleet of business jets.

In 1985, the company also established Valley Systems Division in Rancho Cucamonga, California. Valley Systems, formed out of Pomona Division, makes Stinger portable antiaircraft weapons and the Rolling Airframe Missile, which defends against antiship missiles.

Other units of General Dynamics include Data Systems Division, which provides in-house computer services; General Dynamics Services Co., which supplies product support services, operations and maintenance, and construction management; and American Overseas Marine Corporation, which mans and services Maritime Prepositioning Ships that are stocked and ready to serve as supply points for U.S. forces overseas during crises.

With more than 12,000 of its 105,000 employees working as scientists and engineers, General Dynamics has a strong technological research and development capability. It is one of three firms that worked on the preliminary design of the National Aero-Space Plane, which will take off like a conventional aircraft and achieve orbit at greater than five times the speed of sound. GD was picked to build the Air Force's Medium Launch Vehicle, an expendable rocket to boost payloads into orbit, and has started its own commercial launch vehicle program by funding the construction of eighteen Atlas I's to boost commercial spacecraft. The company is also involved in the design of the Navy's newest attack submarine type, the Seawolf.

GENERAL COMPUTER USE

The Data Systems Division (DSD) provides corporate-wide guidance for, direction to, and management of the company's information resources and the information services required by the company's operating divisions.

Chartered in 1973 as Data Systems Services, the unit was intended by General Dynamics to ensure that data-processing functions that were being performed by individual operating units be organized and consolidated to achieve more efficient and effective use of resources.

Over the next three years, seventeen separate data-processing functions were organized into three regional Data Centers which were geographically located in close proximity to General Dynamics' major operating divisions.

In 1981, Data Systems Services was elevated to divisional status in recognition of the importance of its services to the overall business of General Dynamics.

With division headquarters located in St. Louis, Missouri, DSD currently provides information services to General Dynamics from four regional Data Centers. Data Center management works closely with General Dynamics' product divisions, which are viewed as "customers," through the product divisions' Information Resource Management (IRM) functions. Each product division's IRM function acts as a focal point to coordinate computing requirements for the various departments within the product division. In this respect, user demand and DSD supply can be negotiated to continue efficient and effective use of resources and provide for optimum benefit to the corporation.

Information services provided by DSD include a full range of computer processing and systems development activities. Processing represents equipment and services relating to the processing of data. Development represents services relating to the design, development, and implementation of computer-based systems. These services are provided for all facets of company operations and include business systems, computer-aided design and manufacturing (CAD/CAM) systems, scientific and engineering systems, and deliverable software, which is software actually embedded in various product division products.

Business processing services are mainly run on IBM mainframe computers located within a central computing complex at each Data Center. CAD/CAM processing utilizes a variety of processors, including large-scale mainframe computers as well as engineering workstations. Scientific and engineering systems processing is performed on a wide range of mainframes and minicomputers, with a Cray XMP supercomputer as the top of the line.

Development services are provided for all of the areas outlined above; however, concentration is heaviest in the business systems and deliverable software areas.

DATA STORAGE AT GENERAL DYNAMICS

Like many other large corporations, General Dynamics relies on direct-access devices (DADs) for data storage. The company uses nonremovable magnetic disks. General Dynamics also uses cartridge tapes for sequential storage of some of their data. Most of these tapes are retrieved and mounted manually; however, the Western Center of the Data Systems Division has introduced a method of automating tape storage in its computer operations center.

The Western Center began its pilot project in April 1988, installing an Automatic Cartridge Store (ACS) system to reduce costs in tape operations and save time in retrieving data stored on cartridges. According to the center, the system eliminates errors previously experienced with the manual mounting of tapes. The first tapes stored in the module were those that received the highest use for read/write operations.

The ACS system is based on a library storage module, a 12-sided structure that can store up to 6,000 tape cartridges in its cells. Inside the module is a robotic assembly that retrieves, mounts, and demounts cartridges. The robot finds the cartridge, then validates that the cartridge is the correct one by reading its bar code label. Then the robot takes the cartridge from its cell, moves it to a transporting device, and mounts it in a tape drive for reading. When the tape is no longer needed, the robot removes it from the drive and replaces it in its cell. The robot operates around the clock, mounting hundreds of tapes per day. The entire operation occurs rapidly, taking 12 to 15 seconds for the mount/demount cycle.

A tiny television camera is mounted on one of the robots. It feeds images of the continuous motion in the mount/demount cycle to a television screen in the center. Visitors to the center can see what is going on inside the module by watching the screen.

Currently, the Western Center has two library storage modules and is installing a third. The new system enables the center to significantly improve the services provided to the division customers, thus helping to fulfill General Dynamics' vision of achieving total customer satisfaction.

DISCUSSION POINTS

1. Relate the advantages of using tape storage listed in the chapter to the Western Center's use of the Automatic Cartridge Store system.

2. Explain how the use of a robotic system improves the use of tapes as a storage medium.

File Organization and
Data Base Design

ARTICLE

But Can You Read It Like a Book?

Michael Alexander, *Computerworld*

Even though electronic databases contain massive amounts of information, they are more like warehouses than libraries. While all of the information is contained under one "roof," it may not be readily apparent where and in what form the information is stored. Walk into a library, on the other hand, and you have a pretty good idea what aisle contains the information you are looking for, and you can expect it to be contained in a book.

That is the basic premise of an "electronic library," which aims to combine the massive amounts of information in an electronic database with the logic and facile use of a library.

About 150 chemistry students and faculty members at Cornell University in Ithaca, N.Y., are experimenting with such an electronic library, an on-line system that enables users to retrieve information contained in thousands of articles published by the *Journal of the American Chemical Society.* Unlike on-line databases, the electronic library is not limited to textual information: Users are also able to retrieve graphics, illustrations and other images.

It is the first test of its kind, according to officials at Cornell's Albert R. Mann Library, where the Chemistry On-Line Retrieval Experiment (CORE) is being conducted, and Bellcore, where the system's ex-

perimental Superbook software interface and database engine was developed.

"Chemists tend not to use or find on-line services that useful because the graphical components are key to understanding," said Howard Curtis, head of the information technology section at the Mann Library. "Take away the schematics, photos, illustrations, and there's not much left."

One objective of CORE will be to determine whether on-line text and image retrieval and reading the material on screen is more practical than actually scouring the shelves for chemistry articles.

"It is not just a question of how willing researchers are to search and browse electronically but also whether they will want to read on their screens," Curtis said.

In the current test phase, . . . students and faculty can retrieve text and images from 1,000 articles. By the end of next spring, the database is scheduled to contain 70,000 articles, or about seven years' worth of articles from 20 scientific journals.

The database consists of four parts: text stored as ASCII files, an index, graphics that have been extracted from the articles and 300 dot/in. reproductions of complete pages. Text, the index and graphics are stored on magnetic media; the page reproductions are stored on optical discs. Although little of the informa-

tion contained in the publications is in color, the 70,000 articles and related graphics will take up about 160G bytes of storage space.

"We need to figure out exactly what is required in the database structure, especially the storage of graphics," Curtis explained. "To what degree do we have to replicate the printed page and to what degree is the electronic journal a new entity?" Students and faculty are using Sun Microsystems, Inc. and Digital Equipment Corp. workstations during the test. Eventually, other workstations and operating systems will be used.

Cornell plans to test three electronic library user interfaces: Superbook and Pixlook, developed at Bellcore, and Diadem, developed by OCLC. It's too early to determine what interface users will prefer, mainly because the initial testing has been limited to Bellcore's Superbook, Curtis said.

"We launched the Superbook project to try to make the screen presentation of text better than paper rather than worse," said Tom Landauer, manager of Bellcore's cognitive research division in Morristown, N.J. "We believe that Superbook is the first and only on-line hypertext application that makes it easier to use than harder."

■ INTRODUCTION

All organizations maintain a wide variety of files containing data about employees, customers, inventory levels, productions, sales, and other information pertinent to the firm. An organization's method of processing this data is determined largely by its information needs. Does new data need to be processed immediately, or can data be held and grouped and processed at a later time? The structure of the organization's files is also based on its information needs; file structures can minimize overall processing time and increase processing efficiency.

This chapter examines three types of file arrangement, or data design: sequential, direct-access, and indexed-sequential. It discusses the characteristics of each method and offers representative applications of these methods to illustrate how they are used. The chapter also explains the concept of a data base and describes what is meant by physical and logical data design.

■ FILE PROCESSING

File processing is the activity of updating permanent files to thoroughly reflect any changes in data. Files can be organized in several ways, with or without a computerized system. Without computers, files must be recorded on paper and updated manually. Some companies do not need their file system computerized in order to be efficient; perhaps the small amount of paperwork they have would not justify the cost of computer hardware and software. In other companies, however, a computerized system could increase efficiency and profits. For example, consider the case of American Sporting Goods, a small supplier of sports equipment. The company carries an inventory of 110 items, supplies equipment to thirty customers and maintains a staff of twenty employees. All of American Sporting Goods' records are kept on paper and transactions are recorded manually.

Every time a customer places an order, a clerk must prepare a sales order. The customer's file is checked to obtain all necessary data about the customer, such as billing address, shipping address, and credit status. The clerk fills in the type and quantity of item ordered, and the sales order is sent to the warehouse where the inventory is stored. At the warehouse, an employee determines if the requested items are available. To do this, the employee must actually count the number of items in stock. If the items are available, they can be packaged and prepared for shipping. If the order cannot be filled, the employee must prepare a back order. The sales order is sent on to the accounting department, where the customer's bill is prepared. In the accounting department, a clerk checks the company catalog to determine the current cost of each item on the order. The total bill is calculated, including tax and shipping charges. The total amount is recorded on the customer's record, and the order is then shipped.

Even this simplified transaction includes many time-consuming activities. In addition to handling customer orders, the company must prepare monthly payrolls, sales reports, purchase orders to replenish inventory supplies, and many other types of records. The American Sporting Goods Company could save time and money by computerizing its activities.

Several computerized files could be designed to facilitate American Sporting Goods' operations. An employee file could be set up containing records of each employee. An employee record might contain the employee's home address, social security number, company identification number, hourly wage, withholding tax bracket, and gross income. In order for this data to be used in a variety of ways by several departments, it must be stored in a file accessible by all departments that require the data. Figure 7–1 shows a portion of an employee file and reintroduces several terms useful in a discussion of data design. Recall from Chapter 1 that a field is one data item, a record is a group of data items related to a single unit, and a file is a group of related records.

The company could also use an inventory file with one record for each item carried in inventory. Each record could contain a description of the item, its cost, the quantity in stock, and information about the manufacturer of the item. Finally, a customer file containing fields such as billing and shipping addresses, current balance due, and credit status would be useful.

Each of these files would be accessed, or read, in different ways. For example, the entire employee file would be read every time the payroll was prepared. The inventory file, however, would only need to be accessed one record at a time; that is, only one record would be read each time an order was placed for a certain item. The customer file would be accessed in two ways. When a customer placed an order, only the record containing the data about the customer would be read. The entire file would be read each time the American Sporting Goods Company prepared customer bills or needed a report on overdue accounts.

FIGURE 7–1

Employee File for the American Sporting Goods Company

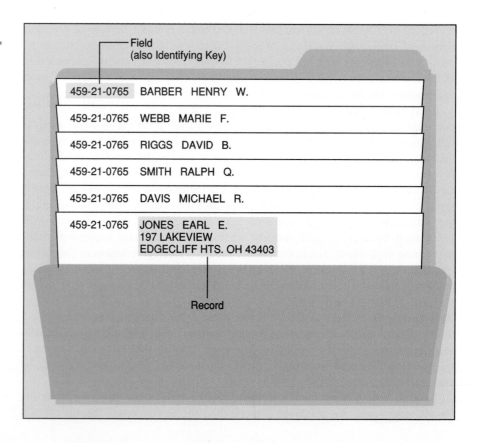

Field (also Identifying Key)

459-21-0765   BARBER   HENRY   W.

459-21-0765   WEBB   MARIE   F.

459-21-0765   RIGGS   DAVID   B.

459-21-0765   SMITH   RALPH   Q.

459-21-0765   DAVIS   MICHAEL   R.

459-21-0765   JONES   EARL   E.
197 LAKEVIEW
EDGECLIFF HTS. OH 43403

Record

■ METHODS OF FILE ACCESS

Two important considerations in determining the best file design for an organization are how quickly data must be processed and the manner in which data will be retrieved. An organization must consider these factors when determining whether to use batch file access or online file access.

Batch File Access

With **batch file access,** all transactions to be processed are gathered for a certain period of time and then processed all at once. The length of time during which transactions are gathered before processing may be one work shift (eight hours), one calendar day (twenty-four hours), or any other logical time period dictated by the information needs of the user(s).

Batch file access is most useful when current information is needed only at set times, rather than at all times. For example, student grades can be processed at the end of a term or employee payrolls at the end of a pay period.

Online File Access

Online file access provides the ability to retrieve current information at any time. Each time a transaction occurs, the affected records are simultaneously updated. Online file access is often used for inventory control, airline reservations, and banking transactions.

■ FILE DESIGNS

A computer file can be arranged in a number of ways. Generally, file arrangement depends upon the method used to access the file. If the information in the file is retrieved by batch file access, then the best file design may be sequential. If the file will be accessed online, a direct-access file design or indexed-sequential file design must be used.

Sequential File Design

If a particular record must be found in a file and the number of records in the file is very small, then it may not be difficult to search the file from beginning to end to find the desired record. For files containing large numbers of records, however, this method is inefficient. A special ordering technique is needed so that records can be retrieved more easily. For this reason, records may be arranged according to a **key value.** The key is one data field chosen to identify the record. Since a key is used to locate a particular record, it must be unique; that is, no two records in a file can have the same key value. In Figure 7–1, the social security number field is used as the key. Social security numbers are excellent keys for employee records because no two people in the United States have the same number. An employee record is located by searching for the appropriate value in the social security field. The key value in an inventory file could be the item number. When records are ordered according to their key values, a **sequential file** is formed.

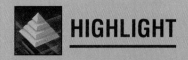
Data Bases Aid Environmental Scientists

Much of the scientific research conducted today is possible because of sophisticated computer technology. Two important functions provided by this technology are the ability to store large amounts of data and the means to retrieve and manipulate this data in a time-critical manner. One such research project has led to the development of the "Reality Globe"—a 7-foot diameter replica of the planet Earth. The goal of the project was to produce a computer-generated view of the Earth that could be manipulated and used to conduct research.

The view of the Earth is created by projecting satellite images of the planet onto the Reality Globe. The globe is made of fiberglass and the satellite images are stored in a data base designed to be used on a Stardent Computer, Inc. Model 1000 supercomputer. The project is the

dream of two men: Thomas Van Sant, a sculptor, and Van Warren, a scientist. Their goal in producing the Reality Globe was to enhance the research conducted by scientists and environmentalists on how we can best use and preserve the Earth's natural resources. Their research effort resulted in the first ever unclouded, unobstructed view of the Earth.

The system used to project the Earth's image is based on software written by Warren which takes individual satellite images of the Earth and stores them in digital format in a data base. Van Sant reviews the satellite images to determine, from a visual standpoint, which of them should be included in the database. Once the digital version of the images are stored in the data base, they must be retrieved and then manipulated by the software to form the im-

age of the Earth that is being requested by the researcher. This retrieval and display of the satellite images requires very rapid manipulation of a considerable amount of data.

The images of the Earth created by the system can be displayed on the computer's graphical display devices as well as projected onto the Reality Globe. Displaying the Earth's image on the Stardent Computer's display devices requires a matrix that is 4,000 by 8,000 pixels (picture elements). Approximately 150 million bytes of computer memory are required to manipulate the satellite data and produce the Earth's image. This incredible computing power is only available through recent technological advances.

Updating a sequential file involves two sets of files: the master file and transaction file. The **master file** is the file containing all existing records. The **transaction file** is the file containing the changes to be made to the master. During the updating process a third file, the new master file, is created.

Before updating begins, the old master file must be in sequential order according to the key field. The transaction file should then be sorted on the same key as the master file. The computer compares the key of the first master file record with the key from the first record in the transaction file. If the keys do not match, the computer writes the record to the new master file as is, and then it reads the next record on the master file. When a match between the master and transaction records occurs, the computer updates the master record. Sometimes if a transaction record has no matching master record, the computer may generate an error message.

Some transactions may add a new record, while others may delete an existing record. Since records are stored one after another on a sequential file, these types of transactions cannot be handled using the old master file alone. To allow for the insertion or deletion of records, a new master file is created whenever changes are made to the old master file. Each master record not deleted from the file must be written into a new master, whether or not it is changed during the update. The process of creating an entirely new master file each time transactions are processed is called **sequential processing.**

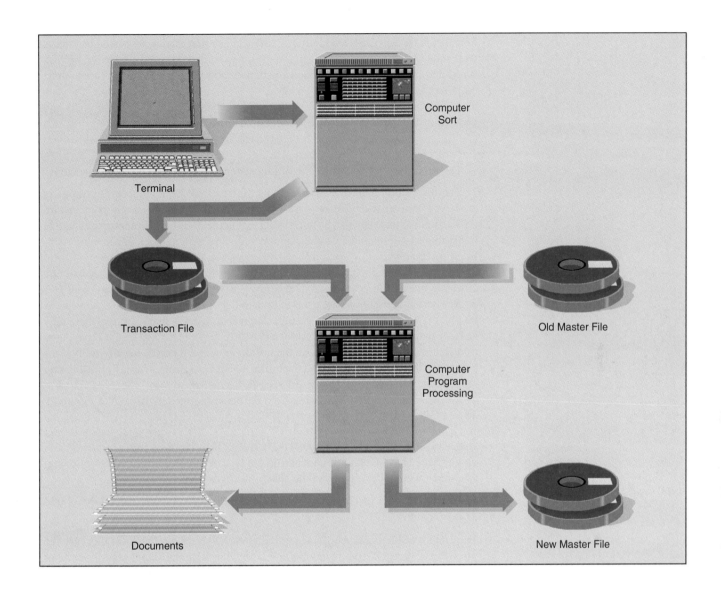

Terminal

Computer Sort

Transaction File

Old Master File

Computer Program Processing

Documents

New Master File

With sequential processing there is no direct way to locate the matching master record for a transaction. Each time a certain master record is to be updated, the entire master file must be read and a new master file created. Since this makes updating one record in a file very time-consuming, transactions are collected over a period of time and processed in one run (see Figure 7–2). Therefore, batch file access must be used with sequential file design.

The amount of time required to update a record with sequential processing includes the time needed to process the transaction, read and rewrite the master file until the proper record is reached, update the master record, and finish rewriting the master file. To reduce the time needed, the transactions are sorted in the same order as the master file. For security, the old master file and the transaction records are kept for a period of time; then if the new master is accidentally destroyed, it can be reconstructed from the old master and the transaction files. In many instances, two generations of old masters are kept, giving rise to ''father'' and ''grandfather'' backup copies.

FIGURE 7–2

Sequential Processing

EXAMPLE OF SEQUENTIAL PROCESSING. The preparation of customer bills is well suited to sequential processing. Customers' bills are usually prepared only at scheduled intervals. Standard procedures apply and large numbers of records must be processed.

Processing customer records results in the preparation of bills for customers and updates of the amount they owe. Magnetic tape is an appropriate medium for this application because the customer records can be arranged in order by customer number and processed in sequence accordingly.

The procedure for preparing the billing statements involves the following steps:

1. The transaction records indicating which items have been shipped to customers are keyed and verified. The key-to-tape operation also provides a report of invalid transactions so that they can be corrected (see Figure 7–3a). This report may include transactions with invalid customer numbers, invalid item numbers, or invalid quantities, for example.

2. The transaction records are sorted according to customer number because the customer master file is arranged in order by customer number (see Figure 7–3b).

3. The sorted transactions are used to update the customer master file. The process involves reading the transaction records and master records into memory (there may be more than one transaction record for a master record). The master record is updated to reflect the final amount owed by the customer, and a report is usually printed for management. For example, during the billing update, the computer may print a listing of customers who have exceeded their credit limits (see Figure 7–3c).

4. The customers' bills are prepared from the data generated in Step 3 (see Figure 7–3d).

MAKING INQUIRIES TO SEQUENTIAL FILES. How inquiries into a sequential file on magnetic tape are handled depends on the type of inquiry. Consider the following two inquiries into the employee file shown in Figure 7–1.

1. List the records of employees with social security numbers 234–02–1532 and 372–84–7436.

The employee file is sequenced according to social security number. In this case the file will be searched from beginning to end by checking the social security number key. As soon as the required social security numbers are located and the required records listed, the search is stopped. Of course, if the numbers are the last two records on the file, then the entire file must be searched.

2. List all employees from the area with zip code 43403.

For this inquiry the entire file will again be searched. In this case, the zip code field of each record must be checked to see if it matches 43403. This illustrates one problem with referring to a non-key field on sequential files. If an inquiry is based on a field other than the key, a great deal of time may be wasted in the search process. To alleviate this problem a second employee file, ordered by zip code, could be created; however, this approach requires multiple files with duplicate data.

ASSESSMENT OF SEQUENTIAL FILE DESIGN. In determining if sequential file design is appropriate for a particular application, two factors must be considered—activity and volatility. **Activity** refers to the number of records that must be updated during a batch processing run. For example, if 400 of a total of 500 records must be updated during a run, the activity rate would be 80 percent. This would be considered

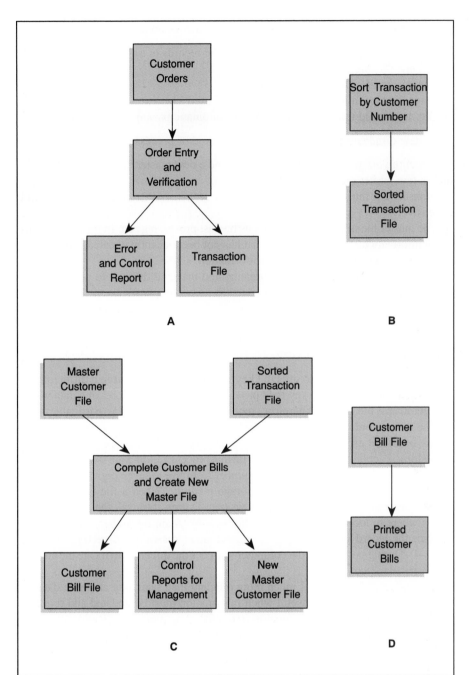

FIGURE 7–3

Billing Operations Using Sequential
Processing

a high rate of activity. **Volatility** refers to how often a particular record may be updated during some period of time. If a record gets updated once every two weeks, the volatility might be considered low. Sequential processing and file design are suitable for applications with high activity and low volatility. Examples of such applications (requiring large numbers of records to be updated at specific times) include payroll processing, updating the addresses of magazine subscribers, and preparing student grades.

Advantages of sequential file design include the following:

■ It can be cost effective when at least half the records in a master file are updated during one processing run.
■ The design of sequential files is simple.
■ Magnetic tape, a low-cost medium, can be used to maximum advantage.
■ Old master and transaction files provide automatic backup for the system.

Certain disadvantages characterize this method of processing, however:

■ The entire master file must be processed and a new master file created even when only a few master records have to be updated.
■ Transactions must be sorted in a particular sequence; this takes time and can be expensive.
■ The master file is only as up to date as the last processing run. In many instances, using information from a master file that has not been recently updated results in the use of old, and sometimes incorrect, information.
■ The sequential nature of the file organization makes it difficult to provide information for unanticipated inquiries such as the status of a particular record, because all information is retrieved by reading the file from beginning to end.

Direct-Access File Design

Direct-access file design also uses the key field of the records but in a different way from sequential design. The key field provides the only way of accessing data within a direct-access file design. Therefore, records are not stored in any particular order.

The data record being sought is retrieved according to its key value, so records before or after it are not read. Usually, a mathematical process called **randomizing** or **hashing** is applied to the record key, with that process yielding the storage addresses of the records. The address is usually a number from five to seven digits that is related to the physical characteristics of the storage medium. When a file is created, this address determines where the record is written. During retrieval, the address determines where to locate the record. Another way to obtain the address of a record is to place the record keys and their corresponding addresses in a **directory** (see Figure 7–4). During processing, the computer searches the directory to locate the address of a particular record.

Direct-access file design is much more efficient than searching an entire data file for a particular record. It is useful when information must be updated and retrieved quickly and when current information is crucial. A common application of direct-access file organization is for airline seat reservations. Current information about available flights and seats must be available at all times so that flights are not overbooked.

In contrast to a batch-processing system, a direct-access system does not require transaction records to be grouped or sorted before they are processed. Data is submitted to the computer in the order it occurs, usually using an online access method. **Direct-access storage devices (DASDs),** such as magnetic-disk drive units, make this type of processing possible. A particular record on a master file can be accessed directly, using its assigned keys, and updated without all preceding records on the file being read. Only the key to the record needs to be known. Thus, up-to-the-minute reports can be provided. For example, assume Ralph Smith's address in the employee master file in Figure 7–1 had to be changed. With direct-access processing, the computer

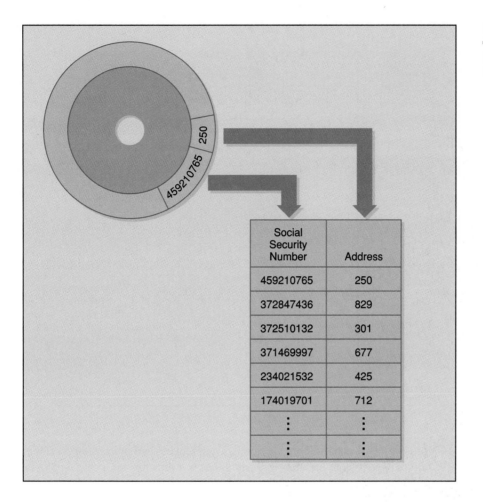

FIGURE 7–4

Sample Directory for Social Security Number

Social Security Number	Address
459210765	250
372847436	829
372510132	301
371469997	677
234021532	425
174019701	712
⋮	⋮
⋮	⋮

can locate the record to be updated without processing all records that precede it. Figure 7–5 shows how direct-access processing would be used in a business.

MAKING INQUIRIES TO DIRECT-ACCESS FILES. Consider again the two inquiries discussed in connection with sequential files. This time the inquiries will be made to direct-access files.

1. List the records of employees with social security numbers 234–02–1532 and 372–84–7436.

With the social security number as the key to the employee file, these two employee records can be located directly. The computer retrieves each record from the address assigned for each social security number. It does not have to read all the records in the file.

2. List all employees from the area with zip code 43403.

The approach used for this inquiry will depend on the organization of the file. If the file is large and much processing is done based on a geographic breakdown of employees, a directory using zip codes and their record addresses can be created (as

FIGURE 7–5

Direct-Access Processing

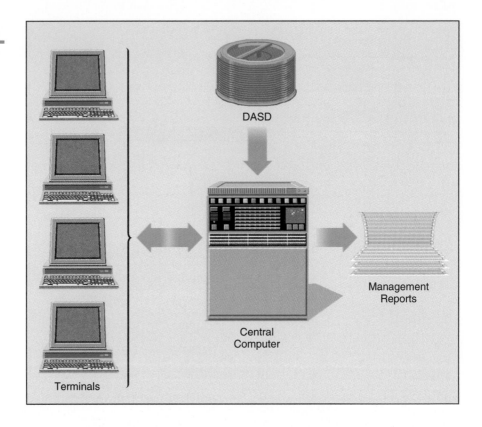

DASD

Central
Computer

Management
Reports

Terminals

in Figure 7–6). However, if there are not many employees and processing is seldom based on the geographic breakdown of employees, a directory to locate employee records by zip code may have little value. In this case, the situation is the same as with sequential files—the entire file must be read to obtain the desired information.

ASSESSMENT OF DIRECT-ACCESS FILE DESIGN. Direct-access processing and file design is suitable for applications with low activity and high volatility. Examples of such applications (systems requiring only a few records to be updated frequently) include banking operations and hotel and airline reservation systems.

Advantages of direct-access processing and file design are the following:

■ Transaction data can be used directly to update master records via online terminals without first being sorted. Transactions are processed as they occur.

■ The master file is not read completely each time updating occurs; only the master records to be updated are accessed. This saves time and money.

■ Gaining access to any record on a direct-access file takes only a fraction of a second.

■ Direct-access files provide flexibility in handling inquiries.

■ Several files can be updated at the same time by use of direct-access processing. For example, when a credit sale is made, the inventory file can be updated, the customer file can be changed to reflect the current accounts receivable figure, and the sales file can be updated to show which employee made the sale. Several runs would be required to accomplish all these operations if sequential processing were used.

FIGURE 7–6

Directory for Zip Codes

ZIP CODE	ADDRESS
43403	12043
43403	12140
44151	12046
44153	12143
44200	12146
44201	12045

Disadvantages of direct-access design include the following:

■ During processing, the original record is replaced by the updated record. In effect, it is destroyed. (In batch processing, a completely new master file is created, but the old master file remains intact.) Consequently, to provide backup, an organization may have to make a magnetic-tape copy of the master file weekly and also keep the current week's transactions so that master records can be reconstructed if necessary.

■ Since many users may have access to records stored on direct-access devices in online systems, the chances of accidental destruction of data are greater than with sequential processing. Special programs are required to edit input data and to perform other checks to ensure that data is not lost.

■ Direct-access could present security problems for organizations. Users may be able to access confidential information. Therefore additional security procedures must be implemented.

■ Implementation of direct-access systems is often difficult because of the complexity and the high level of programming (software) support that such systems need. In addition, the cost of developing and maintaining a direct-access system is greater than the expense of a sequential processing system.

Indexed-Sequential File Design

Sequential processing is suitable for applications in which the proportion of records processed in an updating run is high. However, sequential files provide slow response times and cannot adequately handle file inquiries. On the other hand, direct-access processing is inappropriate for applications like payroll, where most records are processed during a single run. When a single file must be used for both batch processing and online processing, neither direct-access nor sequential file organization is appropriate. The same customer file that is used in a weekly batch run for preparing bills by the accounting department may be used daily by order-entry personnel to record orders and check credit status. To some extent, the limitations of both types of file design can be minimized by using another approach to file organization, indexed-sequential design.

In this structure, the records are stored sequentially on a direct-access storage device according to a primary key. A **primary key** is a field that will be unique for each record on the file. In addition, secondary keys can also be established. **Secondary keys** are fields that are used to gain access to records on the file but may not be unique. For instance, if zip code is chosen as a secondary key, there may be several records with the same value. Records on an indexed-sequential file can be accessed randomly by using either the primary or one of the secondary keys, or the file can be read sequentially, in order according to primary key.

The method used to gain access to a record on an indexed-sequential file is a little different from the method used for a direct-access file. Every record on an indexed-sequential file may not have its own unique address. Rather, several records may be grouped together and one address given for the entire group. An index table is created for all fields that are primary or secondary keys. The index table lists the value of the key (such as social security number) and the corresponding address on the direct-access storage device at which the group containing that record can be found. (The index table can either be stored at the beginning of the file or a separate file of indexes may be created.) A key given by the user is matched against the index table to get an approximate address for the required record. The computer then goes to that

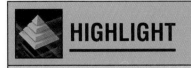

HIGHLIGHT

Dictionary Data Base

Today, even the task of creating a dictionary is dependent upon computer systems that can store large amounts of data. In this case, the data stored is information that pertains to the meanings of words. The Merriam-Webster company, publishers of Webster's Dictionary, is using a Hewlett-Packard minicomputer to store word meanings and passages of text. Since the turn of the century, the company has been saving these meanings and passages so that future versions of the dictionary can be published with definitions that are up to date. These meanings and text passages are saved by the company and then reviewed prior to publication to ensure that the published word meanings are consistent with current uses of the words.

In the past, word meanings and passages were saved on photocopies, carbon copies, and on 3 × 5 cards that had been typed from articles in magazines and periodicals. Today, the company employs six people to enter citations and text passages into a computer system that allows for their storage, retrieval, and cross-reference in a time-efficient and consistent format. Currently there are over 500,000 text passages and 30 million words stored in the Merriam-Webster system. By year's end the company expects to have the text passages transferred to a mass-storage medium such as CD-ROM.

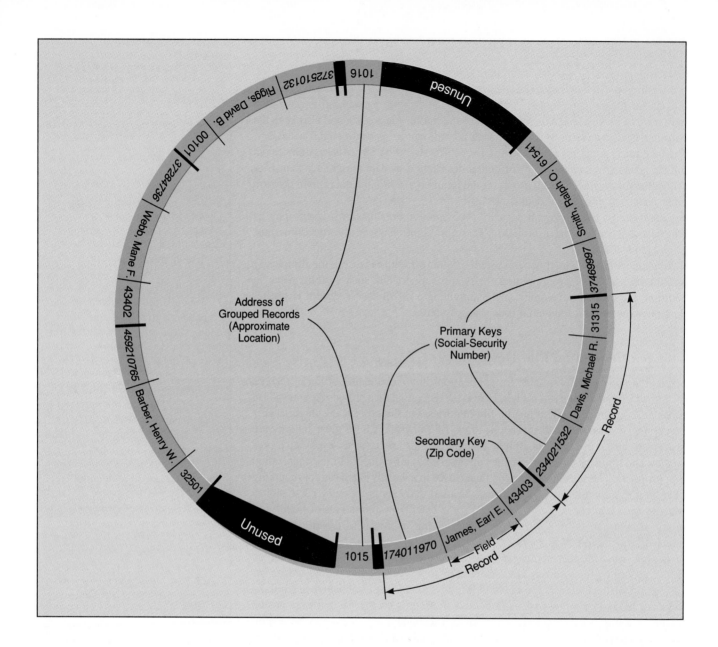

FIGURE 7–7

The Physical Layout of Records on a Disk for Indexed-Sequential Design

location on the direct-access storage device and checks records sequentially until the desired record is found. In the case of secondary keys, all records with that key may be retrieved.

Figure 7–7 shows the employee file from Figure 7–1 set up as an indexed-sequential file. The primary key is the social security number, while zip code is a secondary key. Notice how the records are in sequence according to the social security number on the file. To locate an employee with a zip code of 43403, the computer goes to the index table for zip code (see Figure 7–8). Next to the value 43403 is the address on the direct-access storage device at which the group containing the record can be found, 1015. The computer goes to that address and reads each record in the group until the one with zip code 43403 is found. In this case, it is the first record in the group.

FIGURE 7–8

Index Tables of Primary and
Secondary Keys

PRIMARY KEY (Social Security Number)		SECONDARY KEY (Zip Code)	
Number	Address	Number	Address
174-01-1970	1015	00101	1016
234-02-1532	1015	31315	1015
371-46-9997	1015	32501	1016
372-51-0132	1016	43402	1016
372-84-7436	1016	43403	1015
459-21-0765	1016	61541	1015

Thus, an indexed-sequential file provides direct-access capability. Since all the records are ordered according to a primary key, it also allows efficient sequential processing.

MAKING INQUIRIES TO INDEXED-SEQUENTIAL FILES. The customer file referred to earlier in this chapter is an example of a file suitable for indexed-sequential processing. The file could be read sequentially for the billing operation. In addition, it could be accessed one record at a time for order-entry transactions. The following steps outline the procedures involved in preparing a customer order:

1. A customer sends an order to American Sporting Goods for equipment. The clerk receives the order and enters the customer number on a visual display terminal. This number acts as a key to the file.

2. The index to the customer number on the customer file is searched until it is located. The record's approximate address is used to begin the search on the disk file. Once at that location, records are searched sequentially until a match is found between the number entered and the appropriate record. Once the appropriate record is found, the information appears on the terminal screen. The clerk verifies shipping and billing addresses.

3. The order is entered at the keyboard, and a sales order is generated by a printer connected to the system.

4. The customer's record is updated to reflect the current order.

ASSESSMENT OF INDEXED-SEQUENTIAL FILE DESIGN. Indexed-sequential files have a built-in flexibility that is not available with either sequential or direct-access designs. They work well in an environment where transactions are batch processed and inquiries require the fast response of direct-access processing.

Advantages of indexed-sequential design include the following:

■ Indexed-sequential files are well suited for both inquiries and large processing runs.
■ Access time to specific records is faster than it would be if the file were sequentially organized.

Disadvantages of indexed-sequential design include the following:

■ More direct-access storage space is required for an indexed-sequential file than for a sequential file holding the same data because of the storage space required for indexes. Therefore this type of system is more costly.
■ Processing time for specific record selection is longer than it would be in a direct-access system.

Comparison of File Designs

	Sequential	Direct-Access	Indexed-Sequential
Types of Access	batch	online	batch or online
Data Organization	sequentially by key value	no particular order	sequentially and by index
Flexibility in Handling Inquiries	low	high	very high
Availability of Up-to-Date Data	no	yes	yes
Speed of Retrieval	slow	very fast	fast
Activity	high	low	high
Volatility	low	high	high
Examples	payroll processing and billing operations	airline reservations and banking transactions	customer ordering and billing

◼ DATA BASES

Organizations such as hospitals, banks, retailers, and manufacturers have special information needs. Usually, data is collected and stored by many departments in these organizations, which often results in duplication of data. A hospital, for example, may keep files on patients treated in the emergency room. If a patient is then admitted, separate records may be compiled and kept for admissions, surgical procedures, X-rays, insurance, and billing purposes. The patient's name, address, personal physician, and medical history might be repeated in most or all of the records.

A data-base approach to file design treats all data from every department as one entity. A **data base** is a single collection of related data that can be used in many applications. Data is usually stored only once in a data base, which minimizes data duplication.

In a data base, data is stored in such a way that the same data can be accessed by many users for various reasons. Data is grouped to fit the needs of all departments in the organization rather than the needs of one particular department. Eliminating duplication of data also increases efficiency. When a piece of data is updated, the change needs to be made only once because the data files are shared by all users. Once the update is made, current information is readily available to all departments.

Consider the case of a student at a large university. The student's name, home address, and social security number are often stored in a student file by a number of offices, such as the registrar, financial aid office, housing office, and the health center. If the student's home (permanent) address is changed, all these offices will need this information. Without a data base the student would need to notify each office individually about the change of address. If the university has a data base, the information needs to be changed only once because all the offices would share the student data file.

FIGURE 7–9

Example of a Data Base

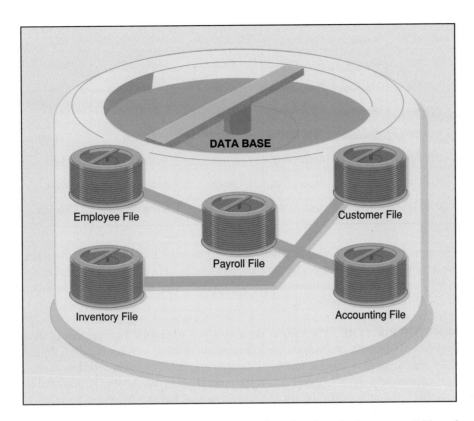

The task of determining the design of data in a data base is the responsibility of the system analyst and the data-base analyst. The system analyst helps the users define their data-base needs. The data-base analyst is responsible for the analysis, design, and implementation of the data base. Together, they try to model the actual relationships that exist among pieces of data. The physical design of the data base is performed by the data-base administration (DBA) team. The DBA team must consider the problems of data redundancy, access time, and storage constraints in order to develop a logical design that works for the physical records and files actually stored in the data base.

The key to a successful data base is to incorporate more than one physical file into a logical file. The **physical file** is the way data is stored by the computer. The **logical file** is the combination of data needed to meet a user's needs. What one user views as a logical unit of data may include data from several physical files. For example, if a user needs an employee's identification number, address, and salary, all that information can be obtained from two files, the employee file and the payroll file (see Figure 7–9).

Data-base systems depend on direct-access storage devices (DASDs) to allow easy retrieval of data elements. The capabilities of DASDs are needed to handle the many logical relationships that exist among data elements. Combinations of data elements can be retrieved from a number of DASDs.

Structuring Data

Data stored in a computer file can be arranged in many ways according to how the fields and records are related to one another. These relationships, called **data structures,** represent the ways in which data elements can be joined together logically.

FIGURE 7–10

File with Simple Structure

ADDRESS	NAME	TITLE	EDUCATION	DEPARTMENT	SEX
018021	Borgeit	Asst. Prof.	Ph.D.	Marketing	Male
018024	Henkes	Professor	D.Sc.	Management	Male
018046	Pickens	Instructor	M.S.	Accounting	Male
018020	Deluse	Asst. Prof.	Ph.D	Marketing	Female
018416	Kozak	Assoc. Prof.	Ph.D.	Accounting	Male
018412	Gadus	Assoc. Prof.	Ph.D.	Accounting	Male
018318	Cross	Asst. Prof.	M.B.A.	Management	Female

The user determines the way in which pieces of data are related to each other. The most common data structures are: simple, hierarchical, network, and relational structures. These structures determine the possible ways in which data contained in a data base can be logically organized.

SIMPLE STRUCTURE. The **simple structure** is a sequential arrangement of data records. All records are viewed as independent entities, as illustrated in Figure 7–10. Each record in this file has five characteristic fields called **attributes**—name, title, education, department, and sex. If the records are ordered—that is, arranged in a specific sequence—then the list is referred to as a **linear structure.** Simple file structure is appropriate for generating large reports but cumbersome for handling inquiries. To overcome this limitation, an **inverted structure** can be used. The inverted structure contains indexes for selected attributes in a file, similar to those used in indexed-sequential files; the addresses of records having those attributes are also listed so that these records can be referenced by address. Figure 7–11 demonstrates an inverted file. Thus, the computer can handle complex inquiries because it searches the indexes rather than the actual files.

An advantage of the inverted structure is that it enables a variety of inquiries to be handled quickly and efficiently. A major disadvantage is that the attributes to be used in searches must be indexed. In some cases, the indexes for a particular file may be larger than the file itself.

FIGURE 7–11

File with Inverted Structure

NAME Value	Address	TITLE Value	Address	EDUCATION Value	Address	DEPARTMENT Value	Address	SEX Value	Address
Borgeit	018021	Instructor	018046	M.S.	018046	Marketing	018021	Male	018021
Henkes	018024	Asst. Prof.	018021	M.B.A.	018318		018020		018024
Pickens	018046		018020	Ph.D.	018021	Management	018024		018046
Deluse	018020		018318		018020		018318		018016
Kozak	018016	Assoc. Prof.	018016		018016	Accounting	018046		018412
Gadus	018412		018412		018412		018016	Female	018020
Cross	018318	Professor	018024	D.Sc.	018024		018412		018318

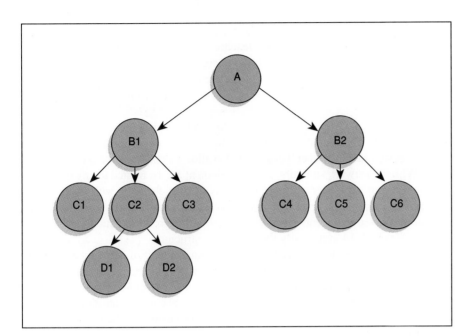

FIGURE 7–12

Hierarchical Data Structure

HIERARCHICAL STRUCTURE. When a primary data element has many secondary data elements linked to it at various levels, it is called a **hierarchical** (or **tree**) **structure.** The primary data element is the parent element. Each parent may have many children (secondary elements) related to it, but each child may have only one parent. Figure 7–12 shows a hierarchical structure. A is the parent of B1 and B2; B1 is the parent of C1, C2, and C3; and so forth. The organization of corporations is typically a hierarchical structure.

A school system may use the hierarchical data structure for its student records. Figure 7–13 shows the relationship between data elements of a student's course

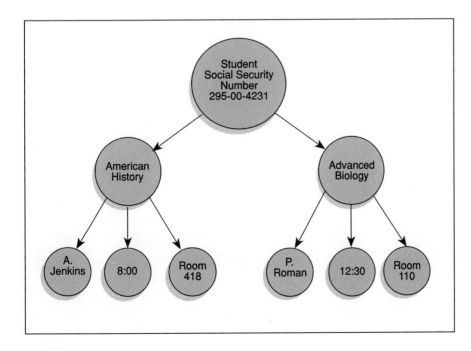

schedule. A student's social security number is linked to the courses in which he is enrolled. Each course is linked to one teacher's meeting time and a room number. Therefore, if the principal needs to know where a particular student is at 1:00, for example, she could enter the student's social security number into the computer and the student's course schedule would be displayed on the terminal screen.

NETWORK STRUCTURE. Similar to the hierarchical data structure, a **network structure** allows a parent data element to have many children. It differs from a hierarchical structure, however, because it also allows a child to have more than one parent. With the network structure, any data element can be related to any other data element. There is no longer a simple hierarchy of data elements with relationships flowing only from a high level to a lower level. Data elements at a lower level can be related to several elements at a higher level, although these structures are quite complex. Figure 7–14 graphically illustrates this structure.

Figure 7–15 shows the relationship between data elements of a student course file. Each course is related to a student, a teacher, a meeting time, and a room number. Courses may have two parents, a student's social security number and a teacher's name. With this relatively simple example, the principal could locate either a student or a teacher by entering the student's social security number or the teacher's name.

RELATIONAL STRUCTURE. The newest type of data base is the **relational structure.** Relational data bases were developed to provide a more user-friendly approach to accessing data. Although relational data bases are easy for the user to access, they are the most sophisticated of the types of data bases discussed in this chapter. A relational data structure places the data elements in a table (called a relation) with columns and rows. The rows represent records, and the columns represent fields or individual data elements. With this structure, a data element can be related to other elements in the column in which it is located or to elements in the row in which it is located. With a relational data structure, the user can access either the data elements

FIGURE 7–14

Network Data Structure

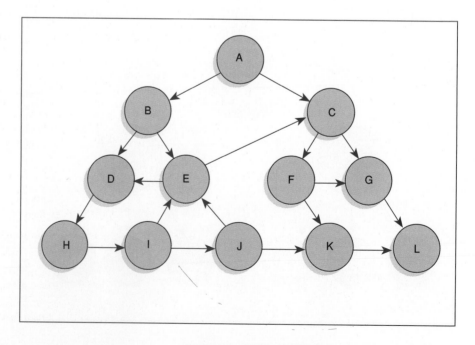

FIGURE 7–15

Student Course Schedule Shown in a
Network Data Structure

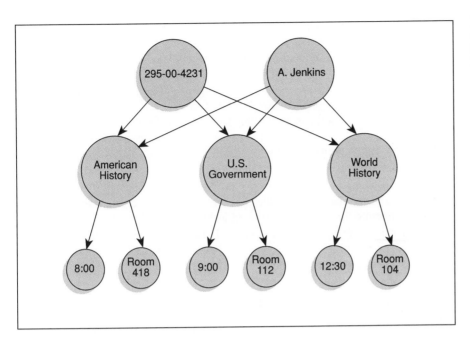

that comprise a record (one row) or the data elements contained in one field (one column). It is also possible to join two or more relations to develop a third relation, or to select records within a record according to user-specified criteria.

Table 7–1 shows a relational data structure of authors, books, publishers, and copyright dates. Each record contains one author, one title, a book publisher, and a copyright date. For example, Ernest Hemingway, *The Sun Also Rises,* Charles Scribner's Sons, and 1926 make up one record. Every record has those four fields.

TABLE 7–1					
Relational Data Structure					
		Columns **(Fields)**			
		Author **(1)**	**Book** **(2)**	**Publisher** **(3)**	**Copyright** **(4)**
Rows **(Records)**	(1)	Ernest Hemingway	The Sun Also Rises	Charles Scribner's Sons	1926
	(2)	F. Scott Fitzgerald	The Last Tycoon	Charles Scribner's Sons	1941
	(3)	Richard Adams	Watership Down	Avon	1972
	(4)	J. R. R. Tolkien	The Simarillion	George Allen 7 Unwin	1977
	(5)	James Joyce	Ulysses	Random House	1934
	(6)	William Faulkner	The Sound and the Fury	Random House	1946
	(7)	J. D. Salinger	The Catcher in the Rye	Bantam Books	1945

Each data element has a unique location in the table identified by the column number and row number. The row and column numbers are called subscripts. For example, the subscript (1,5) identifies the data element James Joyce, located in column 1, row 5.

This sample data structure in Table 7–1 might be used at a bookstore. A clerk could then obtain all the records with J. R. R. Tolkien data, for example, or a list of all book titles carried at the store (all the data elements in the Book field).

DATA-BASE STRUCTURE SUMMARY. From a logical perspective, a relational data-base structure is easier to understand than a hierarchical or network structure. This is because in hierarchical and network structures, the user establishes the logical relationships of the data fields at the time the data base is created. In a relational data-base structure, however, logical relationships among data fields do not have to be established when the data base is created. Therefore, when compared to either hierarchical or network data bases, users find relational data bases more flexible and useful for processing inquiries and producing ad hoc reports.

Data-Base Management Systems

An organization can use a **data-base management system (DBMS)** to help set up a data base. A DBMS is a set of programs that serves as the interface between the data base and the programmer, operating system, and users. With a DBMS, the programmer does not have to pay attention to the physical nature of the file; the programmer's main concern is the specific data the program needs.

A DBMS can perform the following functions:

■ Organizing the data into logical structures that model the actual relationships among the data elements.
■ Storing the data required to meet the needs of multiple users.
■ Providing for concurrent retrieval and updating of data.
■ Arranging data to eliminate data duplication.
■ Providing privacy controls to prevent unauthorized access to data.

Assessment of the Data-Base Approach

Using a data base has a number of advantages:

■ Data redundancy is minimized.
■ Data can be stored in a manner that is useful for a wide variety of applications.
■ Updating involves only one copy of the data.
■ The system can handle requests that previously may have spanned several departments.

Limitations of the data-base approach include the following:

■ An error in one input data record may be carried throughout the data base.
■ Design and implementation of a data-base system requires highly skilled, well-trained people.
■ Major attention must be given to the security of the system since all the data resources of the organization are collected in a place that is readily accessible to data-base users.
■ Traditional processing jobs may run more slowly.

◘ SUMMARY POINTS

■ Batch file access methods require transactions to be gathered for processing at one time.

■ Online file access methods provide the ability to retrieve data and update it at any time.

■ In sequential file design, all data is stored in sequential order on a master file; it must be ordered by some key field. Transactions to be processed against the master file are stored in a transaction file. Transactions are usually collected and processed against the master in one batch. During processing, transactions are matched against the master file, and updates to the master file are made by writing a new master during processing. The entire master file must be read when sequential processing is used.

■ Batch access methods are generally used with sequential file design.

■ In direct-access processing, records are accessed according to their key. The computer determines the location of the record on the disk by a transformation process on the key or by using a directory. Once the physical address is known, the record can be retrieved.

■ Direct-access file designs are accessed using online methods.

■ Indexed-sequential processing is used when the same file may be required for sequential processing and for single-record updates. A primary key is used to identify each unique record, and records are stored in sequence according to the primary key. Secondary keys are set up for those fields used to gain access to the file. The computer uses the key value to determine the approximate physical location of the record (or records), and then reads the records sequentially until the desired one is found.

■ A data base is a grouping of data elements structured to fit the information needs of all departments of an organization. The data base reduces data duplication and increases efficiency and flexibility.

■ Data within a data base can be structured in many ways. Four ways are the simple structure, the hierarchical structure, the network structure, and the relational structure.

■ In a simple structure, records are arranged sequentially. Inverted structures are used to index files with simple structures according to attributes which are characteristic fields.

■ In a hierarchical structure, a given parent element may have many children, but a given child can have only one parent. In network structures, on the other hand, a parent can have many children, and each child can also have more than one parent.

■ The newest type of data-base structure, the relational structure, has data elements placed in tables called relations. The rows represent records and the columns contain fields.

■ A data-base management system is a set of programs that provides a method of arranging data to limit duplication, the ability to make changes to the data easily, and the ability to handle direct inquiries.

◘ TERMS FOR REVIEW

activity, p. 166

attributes, p. 176

batch file access, p. 163

data base, p. 174

data base management system (DBMS), p. 180

data structure, p. 175

◻ REVIEW QUESTIONS

1. Describe what is meant by the term *file processing?* Does file processing require the use of a computer?

2. Describe what is meant by accessing a file using the batch access method. Describe the online access method. Which is preferable?

3. Briefly explain the process required to update a master customer file when the customer records are stored in sequential order.

4. Define the terms *activity* and *volatility* when they are used in relation to sequential processing. Why are these two items important when considering file designs for computer applications?

5. What are the advantages of sequential file design? What are its disadvantages?

6. How does direct-access file design differ from sequential-access file design?

7. Would it be possible to design an application using direct-access file design and magnetic tape as a storage media? Why or why not?

8. What types of applications are best suited for a direct-access file design?

9. What are some of the drawbacks to a direct-access file design?

10. Why was the indexed-sequential method of file design created? What are the advantages to this type of file design as compared to sequential and direct-access file designs? What are its disadvantages?

11. What is the primary reason for using a data base rather than data files when designing computer applications? Please explain your answer.

12. What is a DBMS? Name three DBMS packages that you have heard of.

Art Connection Network

Art Connection Network, Inc., (ACN) is an electronic clearinghouse for retailing art reproductions. Art reproductions are divided into four categories of quality: mass copies, posters, commercial art, and collectibles. The mass produced lithographic copies are printed in great numbers and prepackaged for sale from $2 to $10 each through major discount chains. The most popular subjects are sports, entertainers, models, and cartoon/movie characters. Poster art is targeted toward a market that warrants a higher quality paper stock and state-of-the-art four color off-set printing. The posters are good quality reproductions of contemporary art, museum masterpieces, and graphic art commonly used for interior decorating purposes. The prices range from $15 to $75. These are marketed through retail stores such as art galleries, frame shops, poster shops, and department stores.

Commercial art has an even higher quality of reproduction with greater artistic integrity. Editions in this category range in price from $75 to $300. The fourth group, collectibles, consists of fine art reproductions in limited editions that have been signed by the artist and range in price from $200 to $50,000 or more.

Normally, poster art is purchased at art galleries or framing stores, although it may also be acquired at museum shops or even by mail order catalog. There are currently over 20,000 posters available, making it impossible for a shop to carry even a representative inventory from the standpoint of cost, space, and "trend perishability." Thus, a customer either finds a poster that is acceptable from the limited supply on hand or must look through the endless—and many times out-dated—catalogs. After studying the marketing and distribution of poster art, one of the founders of ACN, Jim Barrett, initiated research in May of 1989 to design an alternate method of getting poster art into the hands of the customers.

The research led to the formation of ACN. ACN combines computers, laser disc imagery, and communications technology to bring images of the reproductions to the customer. As a marketing strategy, ACN's concept is simple. Each participating frame shop, gallery, interior decorator, or poster shop has ACN equipment for displaying the images of art works. The customer looks at the choices and selects the art he or she wants. Then the shop prepares the order and transmits it to the ACN central computer, where it is recorded and sent directly to the publisher, bypassing a "middleman" distributor. The concept increases the profits of art publishers and retailers, and provides the customer with a wide range of current art.

A prototype laser disc containing the images was completed and exhibited at the largest trade show in the United States in New York City in April of 1991. ACN was pleased with the enthusiastic response, and began plans for enlisting publishers and retailers and also for completing the programming of the art data base. The company had 100 publishers representing over 5,000 images on the system by summer of 1991. Programming for the retail systems and the central computer system was completed by fall of 1991.

At first, ACN concentrated on poster art. Once it had established a strong base of publisher and retail membership, however, it began adding commercial art and collectible reproductions.

ACN can search through over 5,000 posters, commercial art prints, and collectible reproductions, searching according to almost any field you can imagine.

ACN DATA BASES AT THE RETAIL LEVEL

The ACN network design consists of computer systems at retail stations, a central computer system, and computers or FAX machines at publisher locations. The computer system at the retail location consists of a laser disc containing the images of the art posters; a data base manage-

APPLICATION
Art Connection Network

ment system for locating, displaying, and ordering the appropriate work of art; a television for displaying the images; and a printer for printing records of sale for the customer.

The retail stores can access several data bases containing information about the artists, images, and publishers. The artist data base contains data such as the artist code, the artist's last name, the artist's first name, the city of residence, the style of art, and so on. The image data base contains image number, availability, image title, list price, general subject category, specific subject category, and many other items. The publisher data base includes data such as the publisher code, the publisher's name, shipping options, packing options, payment terms, and shipping costs. Although the ACN concept is simple, the data bases required a great deal of planning. They are designed to avoid duplication of data where possible, provide convenient access, and allow multi-level searches.

The image and artist data bases bring current offerings of many publishers directly to the customer. With the help of the sales representative, the customer can request particular works of art by image number or the image title. If the customer wants to view a wider range of works, the sales representative enters a search field. A search field can direct the system to find art of a particular style, subject, predominant color, or size. The search can be conducted using the artist data base also, by using the artist's last name, first name, awards, country of residence, and so forth. Once the search is activated, a list of "matches" appears on the computer screen. The customer then selects an image to view from this reference list. Any number of searches can be conducted.

When the customer makes a selection, the sales representative enters information for generating the order and the transaction record. For example, the representative enters data such as the gallery operator, date, invoice number, customer name, customer address, image title, publisher, quantity, and price. At this time, information from the publisher data base is needed to complete the order. This information includes packing and shipping options, payment terms, and shipping costs. Each order generates a transaction record that contains data such as transaction number, date, time, ACN member number, customer invoice number, shipping name, shipping address, image title, and so on.

The retail orders are transmitted to the central computer in one of two modes: batch or immediate. Most customer

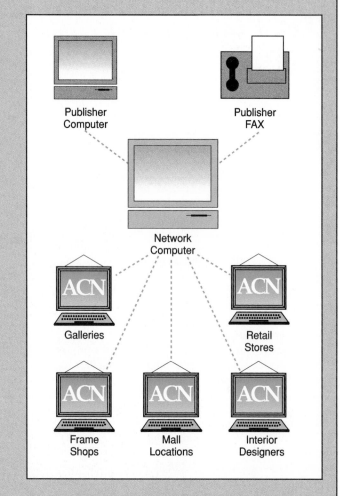

orders are collected for batch transmission to the ACN central computer system during a closing operation at the end of the business day. If a customer is bidding on a numbered and signed art print, the bid is relayed by immediate mode. If the bid is accepted, the customer receives a certificate of acquisition.

ACN CENTRAL COMPUTER OPERATIONS
The retail system actually acts as a point-of-sale (POS) terminal to print an invoice and transmit the sale information to the ACN central clearinghouse computer through telephone lines. The retail store can also access the central computer in order to check the status of an order or bid.

Before the retail orders are transmitted to the central computer, they are sorted and compiled into master retail purchase orders. When the orders are received by the central computer, they are recorded and compiled into master publisher purchase orders, which are directed to the appropriate publisher for fulfillment and shipping. Compiling all of the retail orders in this manner enables the stores to take advantage of special rates for large quantities.

The central computer also handles the electronic mail and billing functions between retail outlets and publishers. Communication from the central computer to the publisher usually occurs in batch mode, but can occur in immediate mode for bidding purposes. The user at the central level can request reports according to his or her specifications of any transactions, customer invoices, or retail/publisher purchase orders during the past eighteen months. The user can also update the data bases according to images offered, prices, or artists.

THE PUBLISHERS

Each member publisher must have a FAX machine or a computer to receive orders and bids from the central computer. The publisher should be able to receive orders by batch and also to conduct activities in immediate mode. When the orders are received, the publisher can fill the orders and send the prints either to the retail member or to the customer's shipping address. Since the transactions are sorted according to the various shipping options, the ACN system allows the publisher to send all those images going to the same location by the same shipping method in the same shipping package. The publishers can also send messages to the central computer about changes to the data base via an electronic mail function.

The data base system at ACN is complex and required a great deal of planning to handle the various types of information about the images and the publisher's policies, but it is current and fast. To many small shops and small poster art publishers, the system that may have existed only in dreams is now a reality in ACN.

DISCUSSION POINTS

1. Describe the ACN data base in terms of batch processing and online processing.

2. How can the user at the retail level manipulate the data base? How is the retail user limited in manipulating the data base?

Microcomputers

ARTICLE

Rivals IBM, Apple Team Up for Open Platform

**By Kristi Coale and
Ed Scannell,** *INFO World*

IBM and Apple—spectators over the last few years as Microsoft has come to dominate the market—are positioning themselves to once again be the standard bearers for the computer industry.

IBM is proposing to be Apple's full partner in developing an open platform and operating system based on the Power PC, the chip used in IBM's RS/6000, and the Pink operating system, which other vendors will support. Basically, it is an attempt at self-determination.

"IBM must come up with a workable plan to stave off the clones, otherwise its future will be determined by all comers," said Dick Shaffer, editor of *Technologic Letter,* in New York.

Apple, which is looking to Big Blue to help it be a serious player in the corporate market, has experienced a change of heart as well—the old religion is dead.

"Apple needs access to IBM's customer base and a credible server strategy to make [the Mac] succeed," said Shaffer.

While IBM offers its size and clout, Apple has plenty to offer IBM in operating system technology and reputation as a producer of technology that is exciting and easy to use, said Esther Dyson, editor of *Release 1.0,* in New York.

Individual needs aside, the deal has left no room for Microsoft's participation, industry observers noted.

"This is a slap in the face for Bill Gates. In the long term, they are trying to establish a new platform and it is not clear how [Gates] fits in," said one developer.

Still, Microsoft and other competitors will not feel any heat for a while, because any progeny of the IBM-Apple union won't see daylight until 1993, at the earliest. Meanwhile, Microsoft will continue to sell Windows into the desktop market, which is dominated by Intel-based systems.

"I can't believe that IBM and Apple are going to take over the market and tromp Microsoft and Intel into the mud [right away], because Microsoft is clearly established with Windows," said Will Fastie, editor of the *Fastie Report,* in Baltimore. In the long run, the alliance could hurt Microsoft's efforts in the workstation market. The company is a critical part of the Advanced Computing Environment (ACE) initiative. How the two efforts match up is hard to tell, as Microsoft's New Technology (NT) kernal and Pink exist only in a laboratory, Shaffer said. Shaffer and others give the edge to Apple and IBM because they—along with Motorola—are

three companies collaborating, whereas ACE must overcome the difficulties inherent in getting 21 vendors to agree on anything.

More immediately, Microsoft may face stiff competition in the multimedia arena as a result of this alliance, said Michael Gould, an analyst with Open Systems, in Boston.

Apple, armed with QuickTime and a load of multimedia credibility, is a formidable foe technologically to Microsoft's Multimedia PC, said Tony Bove, editor of the *Bove and Rhodes Inside Report,* in Gualata, California.

In fact, with IBM's installed base and Apple's willingness to make QuickTime a standard, Microsoft could be in for a tough fight.

One certain effect of the alliance is the confusion that will abound in the marketplace and serve to depress sales, said Bob Holmes, manager of systems evaluation for Southern California Gas Co., in Los Angeles. Holmes also questioned IBM's commitment to its current agendas, given this new deal.

■ INTRODUCTION

Few technological changes can equal the impact microcomputers have had on our lives. Since their introduction in the mid-1970s, microcomputers have evolved from primitive toys for hobbyists to sophisticated machines that far surpass the early mainframe computers in both speed and capabilities. Microcomputers have become so common that they now appear in every aspect of our lives, from work to play.

The proliferation of microcomputers has forced nearly all of us to personally come in contact with computer technology in one form or another. An ever increasing number of us have microcomputers, or personal computers as they are often called, in our homes. In addition, the majority of those in the workplace have had to learn the basics about computers in order to remain competitive and to be able to function in today's workplace. Education too has been greatly affected by the proliferation of microcomputers. The introduction of microcomputers at all levels of education will soon result in entire generations that are computer literate.

Along with the proliferation of microcomputers has come a new set of terms and capabilities to be explored. This chapter will examine some of these terms as well as describe some of the microcomputer's capabilities. The chapter will conclude with a discussion of steps to be followed and considerations to be kept in mind when purchasing a microcomputer.

■ MICROCOMPUTERS: AN OVERVIEW

Microcomputers, also called personal computers or home computers, are the smallest computers. They differ from minicomputers, mainframes, and supercomputers in capability, price, and size. The list of things they can do is rapidly expanding, however, and a clear distinction no longer exists between their capabilities and those of the next class of computers, minicomputers. Some microcomputers, often referred to as supermicrocomputers, are so powerful that they are being used instead of mini-computers by some organizations. (These machines are discussed later in the chapter.)

Microcomputers can usually sit on a desk top (see Figure 8–1). They are less

FIGURE 8–1

Microcomputer
Microcomputers, the least expensive category of computers, are general-purpose machines used in many applications in homes, schools, and offices.

expensive than minicomputers and mainframes, due largely to their less complex and less expensive operating systems. Microcomputer prices range from about $100 to $15,000.

The prefix *micro* should be thought of as applying more to size and cost than to capability. Microcomputers are very powerful for their size. Today's microcomputers exceed the power of the early room-sized mainframe computers. Although they cannot perform as many complex functions as the large computers available today, technology continues to give them more speed and more memory at an ever-decreasing cost.

Microprocessor

The invention of the microprocessor ushered in the fourth generation of computers in 1971. The microprocessor is a single electronic circuit chip containing arithmetic and logic circuitry as well as control capability for memory and input/output operations (see Figure 8–2). It controls the sequence of operations and the arithmetic and logic operations. It also controls the storage of data, instructions, and intermediate and final results of processing, much as the CPU of a mainframe computer does.

During the late 1970s and the 1980s, microprocessors increased in power while they decreased in size. This combination of power and miniaturization paved the way for microcomputers as they exist today.

As mentioned previously in Chapter 2, the first microprocessor was not even designed for microcomputers. Ted Hoff, an engineer at Intel, designed the first microprocessor chip for a Japanese company that wanted an integrated, programmable circuit chip for its line of calculators. At the time, calculators used several circuit chips, each chip performing only one function. Hoff's chip, the Intel 4004, could be programmed to perform numerous calculator functions.

The Instruction Set

The instructions used for performing arithmetic and logic operations and storage and retrieval functions are designed into a microprocessor's circuitry. The set of instructions that a microprocessor can perform is called its **instruction set.** The number of

FIGURE 8–2

The Intel 80486 Microprocessor
This microprocessor has as much processing power as some minicomputers.

instructions in an instruction set is often quite limited, typically ranging from one- to three-hundred. By using the instruction set (through programming languages— see Chapter 12), programmers produce software that harnesses the microcomputer's power to achieve the desired results.

Instruction sets approaching 300 instructions on 32-bit microprocessors occupy a lot of space on the chip, leaving less room for other components and slowing processing speeds. A recent development, the Reduced Instruction Set Computer (RISC), uses a very simple and small instruction set. This technology simplifies the design of the microprocessor. (Until very recently, however, RISC technology was not cost-effective.) Because RISC technology encourages the more efficient use of space on microprocessors, more and more companies are beginning to use this technology in the design of new microprocessors.

The Machines Themselves

Most microcomputers today are desktop models (see Figure 8–3). They are small enough to place on a desk, but too large to carry around easily. A fairly versatile system includes the computer, a keyboard for input, a disk drive or two as storage devices, and a monitor and a printer for output. Other peripheral devices can be added to most systems.

Inside the computer itself is a main system board, often called the motherboard, that holds the microprocessor, other circuits, and memory chips (see Figure 8–4). The system board may contain slots for plugging in cards that expand the capabilities of the computer. For example, you can insert cards for adding memory, disk drives, storage devices, or using printers, modems, voice recognition units, music synthesizers, and bar code readers (see Figure 8–5). Of course, there is a limit to the number of cards that can be added.

Microcomputers can also have ports that can be used for plugging in peripherals (see Figure 8–6). A port may be designed for serial communication, in which the bits are transferred one at a time much as people pass through a turnstile, or parallel

FIGURE 8–3

Desktop computers fit on the surface of work spaces but are too large to be carried around comfortably.

FIGURE 8-4

The Main System Board
This main system board, sometimes called the motherboard, holds the microprocessor, some memory chips, slots for additional cards, and other electronic components necessary for running a microcomputer.

communication, in which the bits are transferred eight at a time much as cars drive down an eight-lane expressway. Cables for telephone connections and some printers require serial ports, while parallel ports are used for communicating with most printers.

Although most computers are desktop models, there are two other major groups of microcomputers: portables and supermicrocomputers.

PORTABLES. In general, portable computers are microcomputers that can easily be carried from one place to another. One way to categorize portables is according to

FIGURE 8-5

Add-on Card

FIGURE 8-6

Ports

their overall weight. The smallest microcomputers available are referred to as **notebook portables.** These portable microcomputers typically weigh less than eight pounds and have one 3½-inch floppy diskette drive. In some cases, notebook portables can even be purchased with small capacity (20 Mb to 40 Mb) hard disk drives. These microcomputers do not need an external power source to run and operate for two to five hours before their batteries require recharging or replacing.

The next category of portable microcomputers is the **laptop portable.** Laptops are powered by rechargeable batteries and weigh between eight and twelve pounds. Laptop portable computers commonly include both a hard disk drive and a 3½-inch floppy diskette drive. The hard disk drives used in laptops range in capacity from 20 Mb to 175 Mb. In many cases, the new laptop microcomputers are as powerful as many of the desktop microcomputers currently being used.

A **portable** is slightly larger than a laptop and normally weighs between twelve and seventeen pounds. Like laptop and notebook portables, these microcomputers do not require an external power source but run on rechargeable batteries. This category also comes with both a hard disk and floppy diskette drive.

The largest of the portable microcomputers is referred to as a **transportable.** This category of portable microcomputers includes computers that weigh more than seventeen pounds. As was true with portables, nearly all transportables contain hard disk drives that range in capacity from 40 Mb to 185 Mb. Today, transportables are equal in power to the majority of desktop microcomputers being used. Transportables are normally distinguished from notebook portables, laptop portables, and portables because they do require an external power source to operate. Figure 8–7 shows portable computers in each of the four categories that have been discussed.

FIGURE 8–7

The Four Types of Portable Computers
(a) *Notebook Portable*
(b) *Laptop Portable*
(c) *Portable*
(d) *Transportable*

(a)

(b)

(c)

(d)

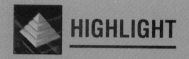
Fishing by Computer

Today, even the commercial fishing industry is starting to run on computer technology. The Mississippi Department of Economic and Community Development is currently testing a system in the Gulf of Mexico that helps commercial fisherman identify locations in the gulf where fish are most likely to be found.

The experimental personal computer system has been installed in four commercial fishing boats to test the feasibility of accurately locating fish by computer. The software used on the PC was developed at The National Marine Fisheries Service. A portion of the software was origi-

nally developed by NASA and is designed to calculate water-temperature contours from data supplied by satellites orbiting the Earth. Data provided by satellite can be updated as often as 52-minute intervals if the fisherman wish. The National Marine Fisheries Service used the NASA software and added logic to display water depth and under-water obstacles and also added data on species of fish living in the Gulf to create a fish-finding software package.

In one case, only twenty minutes of training on the system was required. The overall results of the testing have been excellent. In fact,

the results have been so good that the system has drawn criticism from environmental groups.

The value of such a system used by commercial fishermen worldwide has been recognized by a company that has licensed the software. Gulf Weather Corporation, a Mississippi company, intends to eventually market the software worldwide. Gulf Weather will sell subscriptions to the satellite data and will also be constantly updating the software to include species of fish contained in all the oceans of the world. It's getting so a fish hardly has a fighting chance these days.

FIGURE 8–8

Supermicrocomputer
The Compaq System Pro

Nearly all portable microcomputers have flat display screens that are slim and can be folded or positioned so the computer is easy to carry. Portables can range in price from $500 to $8,000 depending on the features included on the computer. Each portable has different features, so users must evaluate their particular needs before selecting a portable. Some useful features include built-in **modems** and software for transmitting and receiving data by telephone. Some portables have ports for connecting floppy disk drives, cassette recorders, or bar code readers. Some portables have built-in software such as a word processor, spreadsheet, or database manager (see the section on software later in this chapter). Built-in programming languages such as BASIC may also be included.

Portables are especially useful for reporters, businesspeople, and students. For example, a salesperson might use a portable to compose reports that are sent to the main office via telephone lines. Journalists use portables in similar ways. A reporter can cover an event 2,000 miles from the newspaper's headquarters, write the story using a word processor and a portable computer, and use a modem to send the article over telephone lines to the editor's desk. Students carry notebook computers to classes in order to take decipherable lecture notes and prepare assignments.

SUPERMICROCOMPUTERS. Some microcomputers are so powerful that they can compete with low-end minicomputers. These **supermicrocomputers** are usually built around powerful 32-bit microprocessors, can store large amounts of data, and can support multiple users (see Figure 8–8). Because microprocessors are inexpensive compared to the CPUs of minicomputers, supermicrocomputers offer a significant price advantage over minicomputers. The low cost of microprocessors also makes it possible to build supermicrocomputers with multiple processors, each dedicated to a particular task.

Supermicrocomputers must be able to store large amounts of data. Hard disks can store much more data than the floppy disks often used with microcomputers. The prices of hard disk drives have fallen in recent years, making them ideal storage devices for supermicrocomputers.

One problem hindering full-scale implementation of supermicrocomputers is the limited amount of available software. But as they gain in popularity, there will be more interest in developing software for these machines just as a great deal of software was developed for traditional microcomputers.

Another problem is the loyalty of minicomputer users to their machines. Many users are skeptical of the power a supermicrocomputer has and would not readily choose a supermicrocomputer over a minicomputer system. Time will remedy this problem as the power of the small supermachines increases and as more uses are found for them. In fact, the minicomputer market is already weakening as more customers upgrade their systems by linking microcomputers to existing minicomputers or mainframes. Several developments, including lower prices, networking capabilities, better software packages, and increased storage capacity, help explain the current market's preference for microcomputers.

CONCEPT SUMMARY 8-1		
Microcomputer Sizes		
Desktop Models	**Portables**	**Supermicrocomputers**
Small enough to put on a desk.	Small enough to be easily carried from one place to another.	Are, in some cases, as powerful as minicomputers.
Too large and bulky to carry comfortably.	Generally put in four categories according to weight: notebook, laptop, portable, and transportable.	Store large amounts of data.
	All categories except the transportable can run for some period of time without an external power supply.	Support multiple users.

■ MICROCOMPUTER OPERATING SYSTEMS

A computer operating system is a collection of programs used by the computer to manage its operations and provide an interface between the user or application program and the computer hardware. Operating systems will be discussed in detail in Chapter 10. Without an operating system, a computer cannot even recognize that a key on the keyboard has been pressed, much less what it means. A number of operating systems and user interface programs have been designed for use with microcomputers (see Table 8–1). Microsoft Windows and the Apple Macintosh Finder are programs that serve as an interface between the user and the microcomputer's operating system.

TABLE 8–1

Operating Systems for Microcomputers

	MS DOS	Apple DOS	MS Windows	Finder
Manufacturer	Microsoft	Apple Computer	Microsoft	Apple Computer
Microprocessor	Intel 8088, 8086, 80286, 80386, and 80486	MOS 6502	Intel 80286, 80386, and 80486	Motorola 68000, 68020, 68030, and 68040
Microcomputers	IBM PC, IBM PCjr, IBM PC/AT, IBM PS/2 family, and IBM PC compatible computers	Apple II family of microcomputers	IBM PC/AT, IBM PS/2 family, and IBM PC/AT compatible computers	Macintosh family of microcomputers
Important Facts	The system was first licensed for use on the original IBM PC. The system quickly became the most popular operating system for 16-bit microcomputers. Over 100 types of MS-DOS microcomputers currently use it. A very large selection of application software for businesses and education is available. The system limits programs to the use of 640 K of memory.	The system was designed to be used by nonprofessional computer users. The system is easy to learn and easy to use. The system allows limited utilities and file usage. The system is closely related to Apple's version of BASIC. Apple ProDOS overcomes Apple DOS's problems; ProDOS can be used with hard disks. A very large selection of educational application software and a large selection of business application software is available.	The system is a graphical user interface that is intended to be easier to learn and use. The system allows programs to use more than 640 K of memory. The system supports multiple programs running at the same time. A limited selection of business application software is currently available. The number of application software packages should increase as the program gains in popularity.	The system was designed to be used with a mouse. The system was designed to be an easy to use and learn operating system. The system supports the use of shared devices such as hard disks and laser printers. A large selection of business and educational application software is available. This system is currently the most popular operating system for use with desktop publishing applications.

Operating systems can be loaded into memory from either floppy diskettes or hard disks. This process is what is known as **booting.** The word *boot* derives from the expression "to lift yourself up by your own bootstraps," which is essentially what a computer does when it is first turned on. In order to read from and write to a disk, the disk operating system (or DOS) must be in memory. However, the disk operating system itself is stored on disk. Therefore, it seems impossible for the computer to load its operating system into memory when it must have the operating system in memory in order to read from a disk. In actuality, the computer already has a small portion of its operating system built into its ROM. This part of the operating system starts the process of reading the remainder of the operating system from the disk. Some systems require you to turn on the computer before inserting the operating system diskette; others require you to insert the diskette into the drive first. Hard disk systems normally do not require a diskette because the operating system is stored on and booted from the hard disk. Care should be taken that the proper procedure is followed for booting the microcomputer you are using.

The first operating system developed for use with microcomputers was Digital Research's CP/M (Control Program for Microprocessors). CP/M was stored on a floppy disk so that it could be loaded into any microcomputer, provided the computer used the Intel 8080 or 8085 or the Zilog Z-80 eight-bit microprocessor.

In 1981 IBM introduced the IBM PC and along with it IBM PC-DOS. IBM PC-DOS was developed for IBM by Microsoft. As a result of its agreement with IBM, Microsoft was able to market its own version of the operating system, called MS-DOS. Although the two operating systems are nearly identical from a user's perspective, IBM does hold the copyright to PC-DOS and could, in the future, change it in a way that may make it incompatible with MS-DOS. Today, more than 100 different microcomputers—IBM compatibles—use the MS-DOS operating system. IBM PC-DOS and MS-DOS are designed to run on Intel 8088, 8086, and 80286 sixteen-bit microprocessors and 80386 and 80486 thirty-two-bit microprocessors.

Other microcomputer operating systems include Apple DOS and Apple ProDOS, which are used on the Apple II family of microcomputers; Unix (or Xenix), which is used on microcomputers as well as minicomputers; and TRS-DOS (Tandy/Radio Shack Disk Operating System), which is used on the TRS-80 family of microcomputers. Newer, **transparent user interfaces** have been introduced to lessen the amount of operating system knowledge required by the user of the microcomputer. The Macintosh Finder and Microsoft Windows allow the user to point to *icons* and use pull-down menus on the screen with the help of a mouse (see Figure 8–9). An **icon** is a pictoral representation or graphic image that appears on the computer screen. Icons represent commands or menu choices. On the Apple Macintosh, for example, an icon of a trash can is used to signify that a file is being deleted or thrown away.

These transparent user interfaces are often called graphic user interfaces. The type of user interface provided by IBM PC-DOS and MS-DOS is referred to as a command-

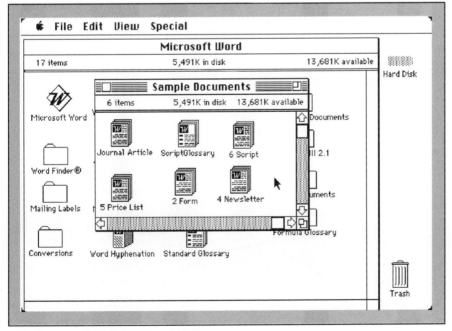

FIGURE 8–9

The icons (graphic images) on the screen are used with a mouse to enter commands on the Macintosh. Icons and pull-down menus make the Macintosh one of the most user-friendly microcomputers on the market.

line user interface. The differences between the two are discussed in the following section.

Graphic User Interfaces vs. Command-Line User Interfaces

Graphic user interface programs such as the Apple Macintosh Finder or Microsoft Windows use a computerized desktop as their interface between the user and the operating system. Microcomputers that use IBM PC-DOS or MS-DOS use what is referred to as a command-line user interface. The operating system issues the user a **prompt** which signifies to the user that a command can be entered. Normally, the command is typed on one line and the issuing of the command is signified by pressing the Enter key. There are several basic differences between a graphic user interface and a command-line user interface.

A graphic user interface uses pictures, or icons, to represent such items as disks, files, and programs. A graphic user interface also has pull-down or pop-up menus that allow the user to select from a predefined list of command choices. The combination of icons and menus gives users a complete picture of the items that can be used and the functions that can be performed. A graphic user interface normally makes use of a mouse (see Chapter 5). The mouse allows the user to point at and choose the items or commands that he or she would like to use. A user interface that combines icons, menus, and a mouse is easy to learn and natural to use. In addition, a graphic user interface ensures its users of a consistent means of interacting with all computers using the interface and the applications designed to run on them.

A **command-line user interface** requires a user to type in a specific command that then must be interpreted and acted on by the operating system. The user of the command-line interface must remember the commands required to perform certain tasks and type them in precise form to have the computer act on them.

The Macintosh User Interface was the first graphic interface designed for use on a microcomputer. The Macintosh User Interface was introduced along with the first Macintosh microcomputer in 1984. Microsoft Windows is a graphic user interface that runs in conjunction with MS-DOS. Windows has become popular on MS-DOS microcomputers because it is easier to use than the command-line interface normally found on these types of computers. The following two sections discuss some of the conventions that are common to Macintosh and IBM PC-DOS/MS-DOS microcomputers.

CONCEPT SUMMARY 8–2

Graphic User Interfaces vs. Command-Line User Interfaces

Graphic User Interface	Command-line User Interface
Uses icons, menus, and a mouse.	Uses a prompt to tell the user a new command can be entered.
Designed to be easy to learn and use.	Designed to give the user direct access to the operating system through typing in specific commands.
All available commands are accessible from the menu bar.	The user must memorize commands and enter them exactly as required by the operating system.

Apple Macintosh Conventions

The Apple Macintosh Operating System consists of three primary parts: the operating system itself (a portion of which permanently resides in the Macintosh's memory), the System file, and the Finder. Apple Macintosh operating system 7 is the most recent version of the operating system used on the Macintosh microcomputers. As was discussed earlier, the operating system manages all the activities taking place on the computer. The majority of the Macintosh's operating system is stored in ROM. A smaller portion of the Macintosh Operating System is stored in the System file on disk. This portion of the operating system is loaded into RAM from the System file at startup (boot) time. The **Finder** serves as the interface between the Macintosh user and the Macintosh Operating System.

THE SYSTEM FILE. Since the System file contains a vitally important part of the Macintosh Operating System, the computer must have access to the System file at startup. Without the portion of the operating system stored in the System file, the Macintosh cannot operate.

In addition to part of the operating system, the System file also contains desk accessory and font programs which are referred to as resources. These resources provide such tools as an alarm clock and a calculator. The font resources allow you to control the size and style of the characters that are displayed on the Macintosh screen.

THE FINDER. The Finder performs two very important functions on the Macintosh. It displays the computerized desktop to the user and acts on commands issued to the operating system through the desktop. The Finder also manages the data stored on either floppy or hard disks. To perform these functions, the Finder must work very closely with the Macintosh Operating System. For this reason, the System file and the Finder must be compatible. In other words, the System file and Finder must be able to understand each other perfectly in order to carry out the user's commands. If the System file and Finder are not compatible, the operating system will not understand what is being requested of it, and it will be unable to carry out commands it is given.

THE DESKTOP. The Macintosh User Interface refers to the user's on-screen working environment as the **desktop.** The desktop includes icons and pull-down menus and requires the use of a mouse. As you move the mouse, a pointer, which represents the location of the mouse on the screen, also moves (see Figure 8–10). There are four different pointers that are used by the Macintosh. These are the arrow, crosshair, I beam and wristwatch (see Figure 8–11).

The icons that appear on the Macintosh desktop represent either an application, a document, a folder, or a disk. An **application** is a program. Programs like MacWrite, MacPaint, MacDraw, Microsoft Word, Aldus Pagemaker and Microsoft Works are all applications. A **document** is a file where data is stored on a Macintosh. A document may contain the data entered into a spreadsheet or it may contain the text of a business letter. For example, one chapter of a dissertation created using Microsoft Word would be considered a document. A **folder** is a place where applications, documents, and other folders can be stored. Like paper file folders used to organize paper documents, folders on a Macintosh are used to organize the data and information stored on disks. If, for example, you were writing your dissertation in graduate school, you could organize all of the documents related to the manuscript by placing them in one folder.

FIGURE 8–10

The Arrow Pointer

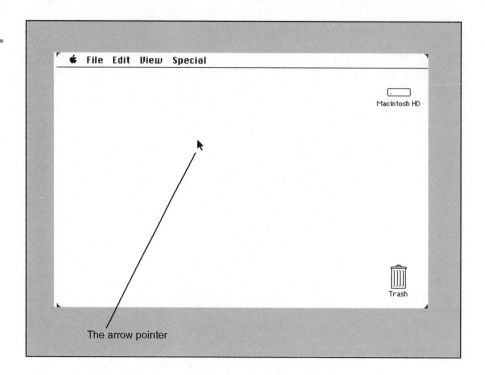

The arrow pointer

FIGURE 8–11

The Macintosh Pointers

> ➤ **Arrow pointer**; used for choosing, pointing, and dragging.
>
> ╋ **Crosshair**; used in the Control Panel, for example, for choosing and pointing.
> Also used to create shapes, such as circles and squares
>
> Ⅰ **I-beam**; used when editing text to identify the mouse's location on the screen.
>
> ⌚ **Wristwatch**; displayed when a particular operation will take some time to complete.

Within the pull-down menus on the Macintosh desktop are the various commands that can be selected by a user. The menu names are part of the menu bar which is located on the top line of the Macintosh screen. To choose a command from one of the menus, simply position the pointer on either the Apple icon or one of the menu names on the menu bar (see Figure 8–12). Once the pointer is positioned in the proper location on the menu bar, press and hold down the mouse button. The menu that corresponds to the Apple icon or menu name will be pulled down. As you continue to hold the mouse button down, drag the pointer to the command you want to choose (see Figure 8–13). When the command you want to choose is highlighted, release the mouse button.

IBM PC-DOS and MS-DOS Conventions

In the sections that follow, the conventions used by IBM PC-DOS and MS-DOS to manage data and programs stored on a computer will be described. MS-DOS version 5.0 is the most recent release of the operating system typically used on IBM and IBM compatible microcomputers. The IBM PC-DOS and MS-DOS conventions that relate specifically to naming files, managing directories, and specifying the location of files will be discussed. A thorough understanding of these conventions is essential

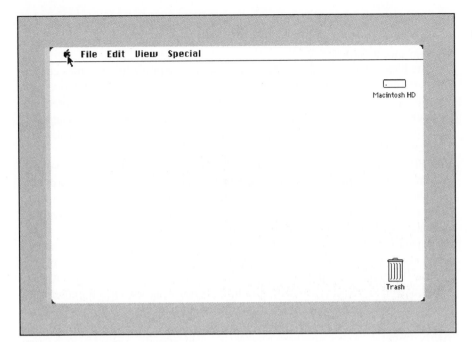

FIGURE 8–12

The Arrow Pointer Positioned on the
Apple Menu Icon

if a user of the IBM PC-DOS and MS-DOS operating systems is to understand the
commands that can be issued.

FILES. Within the MS-DOS operating system, there are two basic types of files—
executable files and data files. Executable files include both program files and MS-
DOS batch files. Program files are directly understandable by the microprocessor and
are the result of translating (or compiling) a source code program (see Chapter 4).

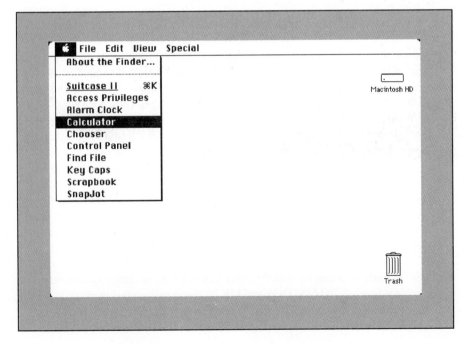

FIGURE 8–13

The Apple Menu Pulled Down and
the Calculator Desk Accessory
Selected

Batch files, in contrast, are interpreted by the operating system as they are run. Both of these types of files ask the operating system to execute commands required to perform specific tasks.

Data files contain data that can be manipulated by a program. Data files can take on many different forms. For example, one data file may contain employee data records (see Chapter 1). Another may contain a letter written using a word processor.

Each file that is stored on a diskette or hard disk must have a unique name. The name of a file consists of two parts, the file name and the file name extension. The file name and file name extension are separated by a period (.). The name SAMPLE.FIL, for example, has a file name of SAMPLE and a file name extension of FIL. A name does not require a file name extension, but it is often helpful in providing an indication of what is contained within a particular file. For example, files with a file name extension of EXE or COM represent executable program files, and files with a BAT extension represent batch files.

A name can consist of from one to eleven characters. A maximum of eight characters can be used for the file name, and a maximum of three characters can be used for the file name extension. The set of valid file name characters includes A–Z, a–z, 0–9, $, %, ', −, @, {, }, ~, ', !, #, (,), and &. When using MS-DOS file commands, a valid file name must be included within the command.

DIRECTORIES. As a way to keep files better organized and separated on both floppy diskettes and hard disks, IBM PC-DOS and MS-DOS allow for the creation of directories. Directories can be likened to file folders. All the information, for example, that pertains to employee Smith can be kept in a file folder labeled Smith; information that pertains to employee Jones can be kept in a file folder labeled Jones. If we were keeping the information on a floppy diskette instead of in file folders, we could have one directory labeled Smith and another labeled Jones. All the information (files) required for employee Smith would be stored in the directory Smith, and all information required for employee Jones would be stored in the Jones directory.

There are two types of directories that can be created. The first is a **root directory.** The root directory is created by default (or automatically) when a floppy diskette or hard disk is formatted, and there can be only one root directory per disk. In addition, a root directory is fixed in size and is stored in a fixed location on the disk. The size of the root directory will vary depending on the type of disk being used. A double-sized, double-density (360 K capacity) floppy diskette, for example, can contain up to 112 files and/or directories.

The other type of directory is known as a **subdirectory.** A subdirectory is created as an extension to the root directory. See Figure 8–14 for a graphic representation of a root directory and its subdirectories. A subdirectory can grow to be any size and is stored anywhere on the disk. The directory that a computer user is currently in is referred to as the **working directory.**

Again, directories simply give the user the ability to better organize and separate files that are being stored on floppy diskettes and hard disks. Commands that create and remove directories, show the user a list of the files in a directory, and move from one directory to another are discussed in Appendix A.

PATHS. A **path** is a way in which a user can tell the operating system where a specific file is located. IBM PC DOS and MS-DOS use path names in much the same way that file names are used. File names combined with path names form what is sometimes referred to as a fully qualified file name. The backslash character (\) is

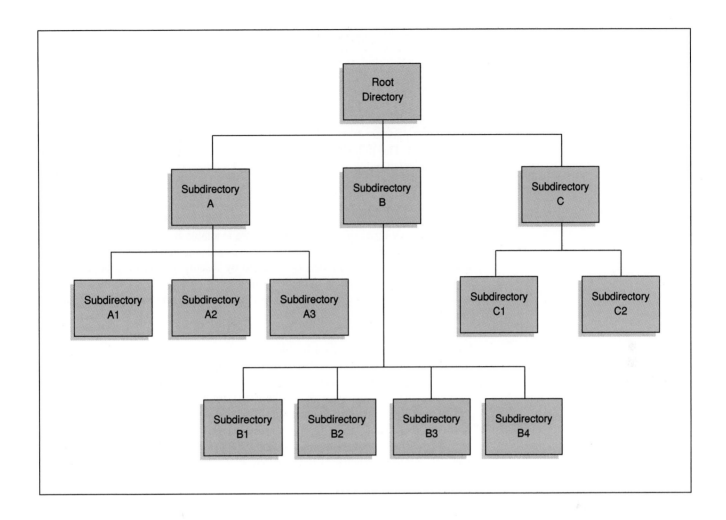

FIGURE 8–14

A Root Directory and Subdirectories

used to separate path names from file names. For example, if there was a file named SAMPLE.DAT in the directory XYZ on Drive A, the fully qualified file name for SAMPLE.DAT would be:

A:\XYZ\SAMPLE.DAT

By using a fully qualified file name, the user has explicitly told the operating system where a particular file is located. As mentioned previously, the directory that you are currently in is the working directory. If a command requiring a file name is used and the file name that is provided does not contain a path name, the working directory is assumed to be the path name and the operating system acts accordingly. In the example given above, if the user was in the XYZ directory on Drive A, the working directory within the operating system would be set to the following:

A:\XYZ

Therefore, for any command requiring a path name, the operating system would add A:\XYZ\ to the beginning of the file name supplied by the user. Path names are used in many of the examples provided in the following sections.

❑ USING MICROCOMPUTERS

Microcomputers are general-purpose machines; that is, they are designed to perform a variety of tasks. The people who buy and use microcomputers are a diverse group—businesspeople, teachers, students, doctors, lawyers, and farmers—and their computing needs are just as diverse. They may need different types of peripheral equipment. They may need various types of services, such as information services and users groups. The following section describes some of the many options available for microcomputers.

Software Packages

There are many types of application software available for microcomputers. A discussion at this time of word processors, electronic spreadsheets, data-management software, and graphics software is followed by discussions on integrated software and utility software. Chapter 13 contains more detailed discussions on these types of application software packages as well as discussions on other application software used by businesses.

THE BIG FOUR. Software for business use often fills the needs of four basic tasks: doing word processing jobs, analyzing financial data, filing data, and producing pictures that summarize data.

Word processing software allows the user to manipulate text in four basic ways: writing, editing, formatting, and printing. What is written appears on a screen during the first three stages (the soft copy) and on paper during the printing process (the hard copy). During the writing and editing stages, text can be entered, moved, deleted, or searched. When text is formatted, it is designed for appearance on paper. Formatting may entail spacing between lines, setting margins, adding page numbers, underlining or boldfacing text, merging two or more documents, or centering headings. Printing may involve producing a rough draft or a final copy of the text on paper.

Electronic spreadsheets are used in preparing financial data for summaries (see Figure 8–15). Many are prepared like tables with data arranged in columns and rows. Each column and row has a heading. The user looks across the desired row and down the desired column in order to find the needed data. Some parts of the spreadsheet contain formulas using data from other parts of the spreadsheet. As the data is changed, the results of the calculations in the formulas change.

Data can be filed using data-management software. One type is the file handler, which copies traditional filing methods. Material is filed by category and data can appear in several files. The other type is the data-base manager, which allows entry of thousands of records that can be accessed in many types of ways.

Graphics software packages are designed for displaying data in chart form. Depending upon the hardware, the charts are displayed on the monitor screen or are printed using printers or plotters. Common charts drawn by graphics software are bar charts, line graphs, and pie charts.

INTEGRATED SOFTWARE. Integration suggests the blending of two or more parts into a whole. When the term *integration* is used in conjunction with software, it means that two or more types of software are blended into one application package. Integrated software generally conforms to three standards:

FIGURE 8–15

Electronic Spreadsheet

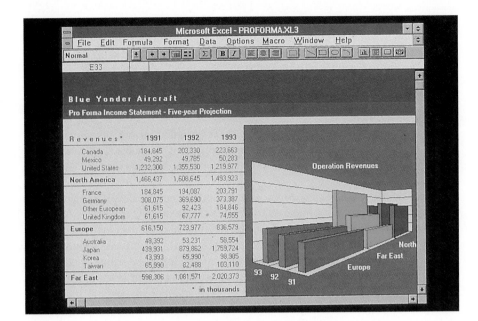

1. The software consists of what are usually separate application packages.
2. The software provides easy movement of data among the applications.
3. A common group of commands is used for all the applications in the package.

Integration may occur when several applications are combined into one, such as a data manager, spreadsheet, and graphics package, which can share data and pass data to each other. Integration can also occur when one type of software is enhanced. An example would be the addition of a spelling program, thesaurus, or grammar program to a word processor.

UTILITIES AND OTHER FUNCTIONS. Software can be used for many other functions that a typical office employee or businessperson might encounter every day. Some software provides a calendar for entering appointments and business functions. Others set alarm clocks, dial telephone numbers, or act like calculators and notepads. Some programs provide the mechanism for writing outlines in preparation for a paper or presentation. Other programs check spelling and grammar, offer alternate word choices, and allow you to program functions into one or two keys in order to save you time while typing.

Compatibility

When a microcomputer does not perform a desired task, the owner may solve the problem by adding peripheral equipment to the system, such as disk drives, color monitors, printers, and modems. Internal circuitry can even be added to expand the memory, increase the speed, or change the text windows of most computers. It is not always necessary to choose peripherals from the manufacturer of the microcomputer. Another manufacturer's equipment may have the same or better capabilities at a less expensive price. The peripherals do have to be **compatible,** however. The word *compatible* describes the ability to use one manufacturer's equipment or software with another manufacturer's equipment. The term *compatible* is also used to refer to entire computers that are compatible with other manufacturers' computers. A number of companies have become successful by manufacturing and or selling microcomputers that are compatible with the IBM PC line of microcomputers. Compaq, for example, has become a very successful and profitable company by manufacturing and marketing microcomputers that will run software that is identical to the software that runs on the IBM PC.

Software also must be compatible. Programs designed for one operating system cannot be used on computers with different operating systems. Compatibility in software includes the ability to read from and write to the same diskette and to use common data files.

Compatibility can be extended by adding another microprocessor to a computer. The second microprocessor makes the computer compatible with another operating system. It is a microprocessor that can be plugged into the original computer to replace or work with the original microprocessor. It allows software written for its operating system to be run on a machine that could not run the software otherwise. The second microprocessor usually comes on a plug-in board or card, along with other chips necessary for it to run. The original microprocessor and the second microprocessor share the computer's disk drives, keyboard, and other peripherals.

In addition to a second microprocessor, a coprocessor can also be added to a microcomputer to assist the microprocessor with such things as arithmetic functions. A math coprocessor can be added to IBM and IBM compatible microcomputers to speed up complicated calculations.

Users Groups

Where can a microcomputer owner go for help in getting the machine to operate? When a $150 software package will not run on the machine, who can identify the problem? Which word-processing package priced under $200 works best on a certain microcomputer? Questions such as these often baffle the proud new owner of a microcomputer. One source of answers is a **users group.** A users group is a relatively informal group of owners of a particular microcomputer or software package who exchange information about hardware, software, service, and support. Users groups may also form around applications and related topics, such as real estate, medicine, telecommunications, education, and desktop publishing.

The value of users groups comes from the accumulation of knowledge and experience ready to be shared by members. The best evaluation of hardware and software comes from one who has actually purchased and used it. As software becomes more sophisticated and more hardware becomes available for enhancing microcomputers, users groups will become even more valuable.

Users groups may be beneficial to small companies because their internal computing experience is limited. Top management may join users groups to learn about new technology and how it can be used in maintaining a competitive position in a particular business field. Individual businesspeople may be interested in improving personal productivity.

Since users groups do not normally have telephones or office space, finding a local group is not always easy. However, dealers who sell microcomputers usually know how to contact users groups, and groups often post notices and flyers in computer stores. Information on national groups is sometimes included in the microcomputer package when it is sold. Contacting the manufacturer directly may also yield the name of the person to contact about a local group.

◾ PURCHASING MICROCOMPUTERS

For a number of reasons, buying a microcomputer and software can be a difficult and time-consuming task. As with stereo components and other appliances, there are many models of microcomputers. Choosing one out of 150 models can seem impossible. Add to that choice the hundreds of peripheral devices, add-ons, and worthwhile software packages from which to select and the task is indeed complex and confusing.

The purchase of a computer is a major investment for most people, so care must be taken not to make expensive mistakes. Spend time learning about the different systems on the market and analyzing what you want to do with a computer before making a decision. Otherwise, your computer purchase may end up in the closet gathering dust.

The Big Picture

Experts often recommend that you choose the software and then match the hardware needs to the software. Although this is a good policy, there may be important hardware factors involved in a final decision. Use the following list as a general guide before considering specific requirements.

1. You should have a good idea of what you want to do with your computer and software. Do you want to write papers, analyze financial data, file data, create graphs and charts, publish a newsletter, or use the same data interchangeably among several programs?

2. Know about how much data you will be using at once—ten pages or fifty pages of text, a day's figures or a month's figures of financial data. Both software needs and data needs determine how much memory and speed you need in hardware as well as required storage capacities.

3. Know the functions and names of basic hardware devices.

4. Know some basic functions of various software packages. (See Chapters 10, 11, and 12, for details about software, programming, and languages.)

5. Test computers and programs at the store. Test programs with data similar to what you will be entering. You may narrow your choice of software to two or three packages, then list a few machines that will run your software.

6. Find out whether the machines on your final list can be used for other purposes in the future.

7. Decide whether the hardware and software must be compatible with those used at work.

8. Be sure that all equipment and software is compatible within the system. Printers, for example, require certain types of connections. Be sure you have the proper connections.

9. Check with friends, computer magazines, and users groups for further information about the software and hardware you are considering.

10. Try different products at different stores.

11. Get firm prices. Find out how much is included in the basic package. The price may include the CPU only, or the CPU, monitor, and disk drive. You may need additional cash outlays for cards that drive a printer or produce graphics.

12. Find out about warranties, service, and exchange policies.

13. Set price limits, but don't be too price conscious. By identifying your intended uses, you already will have defined some price limits.

Mail-Order Mania

When personal computers first became available the majority of people purchasing them were hobbyists and technically oriented individuals. If something broke on their computers or if they wanted to update or upgrade some part of their system, they did it themselves. Some of these early computers could even be ordered by mail in the form of a kit.

After personal computers become popular for everyday use by those that were not hobbyists or "techies," the vast majority of the machines bought were sold by local computer dealers who provided training and service after the sale.

However, recently, PC mail-order houses have experienced a tremendous increase in the number of computer systems they sell. In 1989 5 percent of the personal computer systems sold were sold by mail.

The primary motivation for someone to purchase a PC from a mail-order house is price. In some cases a savings of up to 50 percent can be realized by buying a computer by mail. The majority of personal computers sold through the mail are IBM-compatible, or clone, computers. However, a number of issues need to be considered if you think you would like to buy a PC by mail.

If you are a first-time computer buyer and are not experienced in the use of a personal computer, buying through the mail is probably not your best bet. In fact, in some large metropolitan areas, discount stores may be able to match—or come close to matching—the prices offered by mail-order houses. The important thing to remember is that, if you should have any problems, you can take the computer back to a local

dealer easier and in many cases faster than you can try to resolve the problem with a mail-order house. Support after the sale is a key consideration. This is one area where the mail-order houses have improved; however, be cautious and check out the company's policies on returns and replacement parts very carefully. Ideally, replacements for defective parts should be sent using an overnight service and should carry a 30-day money-back guarantee. An additional item to consider, wherever you buy, is the purchase of an extended warranty. It is believed that approximately 60 percent of all repairs occur after the warranty has expired and that the average cost to repair a PC is $250. Therefore, an extended warranty for about $200 may not be a bad investment.

WHERE TO BUY. Once you have analyzed your needs and determined the appropriate software, you can purchase your computer from several sources: microcomputer vendors, retailers, and mail-order houses.

Computer vendors such as IBM, DEC, Unisys, and NCR offer their line of microcomputers through a direct sales force. Buying through a computer manufacturer can have several benefits. Often, the salespeople are highly trained in the use of microcomputers in business and can assist you in determining which microcomputer system will meet your needs. Microcomputer vendors can also provide maintenance contracts for on-site repair and can offer replacement equipment if some part of your system should be down for a period of time.

Microcomputer manufacturers also market their products through department stores and computer specialty stores. The sales personnel at some outlets may lack the knowledge you need in making your choices. Be sure you feel comfortable with the salespeople. Computer specialty stores are often staffed with knowledgeable people and in most cases have an in-house service department.

Buying from a mail-order house can be to your advantage if you know exactly what you want to purchase. In many cases, mail-order houses offer products for less than computer specialty stores. Before you buy from a mail-order house, determine what you can expect in the way of services, and make sure you are dealing with a reputable dealer.

OTHER CONSIDERATIONS. You may wonder whether you should buy your system now or wait for newer technology. This question should always be considered before making a decision. Of course, advances will be made and prices will continue to fall. On the other hand, waiting could prevent you from realizing the benefits that technology has already provided.

If you do not have enough money for purchasing the system you want, you may be tempted to buy a cheaper system. Money spent on a cheaper system may be wasted if you do not like the software or hardware and do not use it. Under these circumstances, it may be better to wait a few months while you earn extra money or make alternative arrangements for purchasing the system you do want.

When you are considering various software and hardware for purchase, one of the most important factors should be the documentation. Documentation includes both the manuals that accompany hardware and software and on-screen help. The importance of documentation can be overlooked by hardware and software vendors; however, you will undoubtedly refer to documentation for resolving questions you will have. Good documentation is complete, accurate, and easy to use.

TRAINING. If you will require some training after purchasing your hardware and software, there are a number of options. Seminars offered by microcomputer software vendors and independent training firms are available for some of the more popular software packages. These seminars will guide you in using all the features of the packages. Local computer stores often offer similar classes and seminars (see Figure 8–16).

Colleges and high schools also offer classes in computer use and programming through the normal curriculum or adult education programs. User groups can help resolve questions you have about equipment or programs. A final form of training is through individual home study. Many hardware and software vendors provide tutorials on the use of their products. Tutorials may also be available from independent sources and can be purchased in many bookstores.

FIGURE 8–16

Computer Store Training
Local computer stores frequently offer training seminars to new computer owners. Here a customer receives hands-on experience with a Macintosh in a computer store.

Evaluating Software

You must know what you plan on doing with your software before you can evaluate the features of software packages. Consider the following specific factors in your final decision.

LEARNING. Gain knowledge about software by reading computer magazines, asking a knowledgeable friend, or joining a users group.

TESTING. Test several programs of the type you are considering. Use data similar to what you plan to use after the purchase. Have a checklist of requirements.

HARDWARE REQUIREMENTS. Check the hardware requirements for using the software. Be sure there are no problems with compatibility.

FLEXIBILITY. Be sure the software can grow as your needs expand. A good program will let you run the program using only the basic commands needed to accomplish the application, and then allow you to incorporate more sophisticated commands as you learn and need them.

ORGANIZATION. Look for a clear and logical screen appearance. A screen that is cluttered and poorly organized will take more time to learn and will not be efficient to use. Some programs are so clear that they let you learn almost by instinct. Look at how the program handles movement between the program modes.

ERROR HANDLING. Determine how the program deals with errors. Error handling capability is an area that, if overlooked in the selection of a program, can spring up as one of the most annoying and disastrous aspects of the program. You should consciously try to make the program you are testing fail, in order to see how it handles the error conditions. A good program will let you recover from common errors. For example, if you are in the middle of a save operation and you get an error message that the disk is full, the program should allow you to replace the disk and then redo the save operation without losing any data.

DATA REQUIREMENTS. Be sure the program will handle the amount of data you will be entering. For example, check the number of records a data manager can support, the number of pages of text a word processor can work with, or the number of columns and rows that a spreadsheet can support.

COMMAND STYLES. Check the type of command style used in the program. Command style refers to the approach used to command the program. Several approaches are the full menu with explanation, the menu alone, a single command with explanation, memorization of all commands with no menus available, or menus with alternative key command options. Although menus are helpful to beginners, experienced users may find that menus slow down the input and processing stages.

HELP SCREENS. Make sure the help screens are really helpful. Help screens that you can call from any point in the program and that return you to where you left off are the most efficient and helpful.

COPY PROTECTION. The question of copy protection can be important. Being able to copy a program allows a great deal of flexibility. If the software cannot be copied, you may not be able to use it with a hard disk, local area network, or electronic disk simulator because you cannot move the copy from a floppy disk. You should also be able to make backup copies of the program. Software developers now offer special versions of their software for use with hard disks.

VENDOR POLICIES. Find out the policy of the vendor if the software is updated or if there are programming errors in the software.

MACROS. Not essential, but very helpful, is the program's ability to use macro commands. A macro command allows you to string together several commands and define them as a single key. When that key is struck, the sequence of commands is executed automatically. For example, in a word processing program it may be necessary to search for a word or phrase, replace the word or phrase with another, and save the change. Performing operations such as this with a single keystroke increases the efficiency and ease of use of a program. Macros may be offered in a separate software package that is compatible with the one you will be using.

DEFAULTS. Examine the program for default values. A default is a value that the computer assumes when you do not tell it what value to use. For example, many word processors are set up to produce a standard business letter on 8½ by 11 inch paper without your having to specify this size. Default values make the program more flexible. They should be easy to change, allowing you to set them so the most often used formats will automatically be used when the program is run. They should also be easy to override temporarily while you are using the program.

Choosing the Hardware

The most important consideration in buying hardware is whether it can handle the software you have chosen. Other factors include ease of use, expected output, storage, and devices that can be added to expand the capabilities of your system.

THE MICROPROCESSOR. Early microcomputers had 8-bit microprocessors. These computers are still popular today and will remain so because software for them is proven, and many users do not need the speed and memory offered by 16-bit and 32-bit microprocessors.

The 16-bit and 32-bit microprocessors have greater memory capacities and allow the computer to process instructions at a much faster rate. If you intend to use your computer for jobs like financial analysis or want to run two or three programs at once, a larger microprocessor is necessary.

MONITORS. Some computers have a built-in video display. Most, however, require the purchase of a separate video display or monitor. There are several things to consider when purchasing a monitor. First, you must decide whether you want a color monitor or a monochrome monitor.

Second, decide on screen dimensions. Microcomputer monitors come in various sizes. If you are going to use your system for word processing or desktop publishing, a monitor that displays an entire page of text may be more desirable than one that only displays a portion of a printed page.

FIGURE 8–17

Monitor, CPU, and Keyboard
Choosing the appropriate hardware is an important step in the computer buying process.

Third, consider the resolution of the characters displayed on the monitor. Resolution refers to the clarity of those characters. Characters are created using small dots called pixels (picture elements). The smaller the dots and the more closely packed they are, the clearer the images on the screen.

Fourth, make sure there is a way to control the brightness, contrast, and focus of the display. Controlling these factors permits you to adjust the display to suit the lighting conditions of the room in which you are working. Glare can be a stubborn nuisance, too. Most monitors now incorporate some kind of antiglare coating, either inside or outside the glass. Snap-on glare covers are available for most monitors as well. Tilt and swivel display stands, an extra for most monitors, can provide a better viewing angle for the elimination of glare and muscle tension in the neck.

Fifth, check whether the image leaves a ghostlike trail or flickers and blurs when text is scrolled or when you enter data.

KEYBOARDS. Keyboards for microcomputers can come in one of two forms. They can be attached to the computer enclosure or detached from it. Detached keyboards may be either connected to the computer by a cord or operated by batteries (see Figure 8–17).

The angle of the keyboard is important. Keyboards that are part of the machine's enclosure cannot be adjusted, and typing for long periods on these can be tiresome. Detachable keyboards adjust to various angles.

Keyboard touch is another consideration. Most microcomputers have standard touch-sensitive keys that make a noise similar to typewriter keys. A few offer pressure-sensitive keyboards (membrane keyboards). These may be more suitable for use around small children or heavy industry because they protect the keyboard from dirt and spills. Pressure-sensitive keyboards are difficult for touch-typing and would not be a wise choice for word processing.

Some keyboards offer special features such as repeating keys, function keys, and numeric keypads. Numeric keypads are helpful when a considerable amount of numeric data is to be entered.

STORAGE. Storage for microcomputers typically includes floppy disks, hard disks, and tape cartridges. When selecting which type of storage to buy, consider price, amount of storage, access time, and security.

Floppy disks are fairly inexpensive and provide direct access to data, thereby making data retrieval faster than tape storage. Floppy disks commonly come in two sizes: 5¼-inch and 3½-inch. To date, the 5¼-inch size has been the most common. The 3½-inch disks are usually packaged in hard plastic for better protection when handling outside the disk drive.

Hard disks are the most expensive form of storage but allow very rapid access to data. They may be shared by more than one microcomputer, and offer more system flexibility. Some software cannot be placed on hard disks without also inserting the program disk in a regular disk drive.

Tape cartridges are typically used on microcomputers for online backup. A separate peripheral hardware device is required for this application.

PRINTERS. Printers can be one of the most expensive peripherals you purchase. There are a number of features that should be considered when shopping for a printer:

■ The speed of printing.
■ The amount of noise the printer makes. If the printer of your choice makes considerable noise, purchase a sound shield to cover the printer during operation.

212

- The availability of supplies such as ribbons, cartridges, or special paper required by the printer.
- The number of characters per inch (the pitch).
- The size of the platen (the carriage roller). (A larger size may be needed in printing spreadsheets, for example.)
- The type of paper feed—tractor feed, which uses tiny pins in pulling the paper through the printer, and friction feed, which is the type of paper feed used by typewriters.
- The quality of print. Letter-quality printers produce solid characters suitable for formal communication, while dot-matrix printers produce characters made of tiny dots. Some dot matrix printers produce near-letter-quality characters and can be used for most purposes.
- The flexibility of different fonts and sizes of print. Letter-quality impact printers produce one size of print. The font can be changed by exchanging the removable print element. Dot-matrix printers allow flexibility in printing many fonts, or styles of type, and many sizes of type. These printers may be more suitable for newsletters. For a more expensive printer with high-quality output and a high degree of flexibility in fonts and sizes, consider the laser printer.
- The number of copies to be made. Laser printers do not print through multiple copies, so an impact printer is needed if carbon copies are to be made.

ADD-ONS. Add-ons are printed circuit boards or expansion boards that can increase the capabilities of your computer. They can be used for several purposes:

- Adding a modem to the computer.
- Adding graphics capabilities to the computer.
- Adding a coprocessor to the computer so that software for a different operating system can be run.
- Adding memory.
- Providing interfaces for input and output devices such as printers, mice, graphics tablets, and tape backup units.

The software you choose may require the use of one or more add-on circuit boards. Check the requirements carefully before purchasing equipment. Some computers are sold with interfaces for video displays and graphics, for example, while others need additional boards.

When buying an expansion board, test it at the dealer's, making sure all the functions work. If you are not knowledgeable about computers, it is best to have the board installed in your machine by the dealer. Power to the computer should be off and cords removed from wall outlets before installation takes place. In addition, you should discharge static from your body before touching the components. The best way is to touch the metal chassis of any grounded appliance, such as an office copier.

Again, be sure the expansion board is compatible with all the other elements of your computer system.

OTHER HARDWARE DEVICES. Depending on your intended uses and specific needs, your microcomputer system may require other specialized hardware devices. For example, a particular graphics package may require the use of a graphics tablet or light pen for data input. Special hardware devices include the following: joystick, Koala pad or other graphics tablet, game paddle, modem for using a telephone with your computer, track ball, light pen, mouse, digitizer, touch screen, voice recognition or voice synthesizer system, and music synthesizer. Descriptions of these items are found in this text and in popular computer literature such as magazines and books.

Buyer's Checklist

When selecting a microcomputer, a checklist is often helpful. The following checklist can help you identify the items you need.

1. List the expected uses of your computer.
2. List the software requirements for handling your intended uses.
3. List the application programs that can meet your designated needs.
4. Given the software requirements listed above, check the specific hardware requirement below.

THE MICROPROCESSOR
_____ 8-bit
_____ 16-bit
_____ 32-bit
_____ K internal memory needed

THE MONITOR
_____ Screen dimensions
_____ Monochrome display
      _____ White
      _____ Green
      _____ Amber
_____ Color display
      _____ Good Resolution
      _____ Very Good Resolution
_____ Glare shield

THE KEYBOARD
_____ Detachable
_____ Upper- and lower-case letters
_____ Repeating keys
_____ Numeric keypad
_____ Function keys

THE PRINTER
_____ Dot-matrix
_____ Letter-quality
_____ Friction feed
_____ Tractor feed
_____ Individual sheet feed
_____ Carriage width
      _____ 80-column
      _____ 132-column
_____ Speed
_____ Pitch
_____ Noise shield

ADD-ON (EXPANSION) CIRCUIT BOARD
_____ Graphic display
_____ Printer interface
_____ Interface for other devices such as joystick, graphics tablet, and so on
_____ Additional memory
_____ Coprocessor

OTHER HARDWARE DEVICES
_____ Joystick
_____ Graphics tablet

_____ Track ball
_____ Paddle
_____ Modem
_____ Light pen
_____ Mouse
_____ Touch screen
_____ Voice recognition
_____ Voice synthesizer
_____ Music synthesizer
_____ Digitizer
_____ Plotter
_____ Scanner

❏ SUMMARY POINTS

■ Microcomputers are the smallest and least expensive computers; they differ from minicomputers, mainframes, and supercomputers in capability, price, and size. The distinctions between microcomputers and larger systems are fading as microcomputers become more powerful.

■ The increased power and miniaturization of microprocessors paved the way for the development of microcomputers.

■ Instructions for basic computer functions such as arithmetic and logic operations and storage and retrieval functions constitute the instruction set of the computer.

■ Portable computers can be classified by size as laptop, notebook, or portable. They are light enough to be carried and do not need an external power source. Transportables are larger than portables but are still light enough to be carried. They require an external power source.

■ Supermicrocomputers are less expensive than minicomputers and provide users with high performance at a relatively low cost.

■ An operating system is a collection of programs used by the computer to manage its operation and provide an interface between the user and the operating system.

■ A graphic user interface uses icons, pull-down or pop-up menus, and a mouse to make the user interface natural to use and easy to learn.

■ A command-line user interface requires the user to type in specific commands. The user must remember the command required to perform a certain task and type it in exactly in order to have the operating system act on it.

■ The Macintosh Operating System is made up of the operating system, the System file and the Finder. The System file contains the portion of the operating system that is loaded into memory from disk; the Finder is an application that acts as an interface between the user and the operating system.

■ The Finder displays the Macintosh desktop to the user and acts on commands issued through the desktop.

■ The Macintosh User Interface calls the area where you work on-screen the desktop.

■ The icons displayed on the Macintosh desktop represent either an application, a document, a folder, or a disk. An application is a program; a document is a file where data is stored; and a folder is used to organize applications, documents, and other folders.

■ There are two types of files in the IBM PC-DOS and MS-DOS operating system— executable files and data files.

■ Names of files in the IBM PC-DOS and MS-DOS operating systems consist of the file name and the file name extension.

■ Directories are a way of keeping files better organized and separated on both floppy diskettes and hard disks.

■ There are two types of directories: a root directory and a subdirectory. The directory that you are currently in is called the working directory.

■ Paths are used to tell the operating system exactly where a file is located on the computer system. The backslash character (\) is used to separate path names from file names.

■ Popular software includes programs for word processing, electronic spreadsheets, data management, and graphics. Combinations of programs—such as a data manager, spreadsheet, and graphics package, or a word processor and spelling program—are called integrated software.

■ Users groups offer owners advice and information from other microcomputer users about machines, programs, and topics of special interest such as electronic publishing or telecommunications.

■ It is recommended that when purchasing a microcomputer you first select the software you will require and then match the hardware to the needs of the software.

■ Microcomputer training is available in a number of forms, including seminars provided by manufacturers and microcomputer dealers, college and high school classes, users groups, and self study.

■ The parts of the microcomputer to be considered before purchasing include the microprocessor, monitors, keyboards, storage, printers, and other add-on devices such as modems, a mouse, a light pen, and a graphics tablet.

■ TERMS FOR REVIEW

application, p. 199

booting, p. 196

command-line user interface, p. 198

compatible, p. 205

"desktop", p. 199

document, p. 199

finder, p. 199

folder, p. 199

graphic user interface, p. 198

icon, p. 197

instruction set, p. 190

laptop portable, p. 193

modem, p. 194

notebook portable, p. 193

path, p. 202

portable, p. 193

prompt, p. 198

root directory, p. 202

subdirectory, p. 202

supermicrocomputer, p. 194

transportable, p. 193

transparent user interface, p. 197

users group, p. 206

working directory, p. 202

■ REVIEW QUESTIONS

1. What differentiates microcomputers from larger computers?

2. What is an instruction set? Why is it important to the operation of a microcomputer?

3. Explain what is meant by *booting* the microcomputer.

4. What is a graphic user interface? What is a command-line user interface?

5. Why are icons, menus, and a mouse important to a graphic user interface?

6. Which of the two types of interfaces discussed do you think is best from a user's perspective? Why?

7. Explain what a "desktop" is.

8. How does a folder on the Macintosh compare to a directory in the IBM PC-DOS or MS-DOS operating system?

9. Why are paths an important part of the IBM PC-DOS and MS-DOS operating systems?

10. What is a users group?

11. What should be considered first when purchasing a microcomputer—software or hardware? Why?

12. List four factors that you feel would be important in selecting a word processor. Describe why you feel these factors are important.

13. What types of storage are most common on microcomputers? How are tape cartridges typically used on microcomputers?

APPLICATION

Compaq Computer Corporation

Compaq Computer Corporation is a world leader in the manufacture of personal computer systems and desktop, portable, and laptop personal computers and a leading supplier of desktop personal computers based on the advanced Intel® 80386 microprocessor. Compaq employs over 10,000 people worldwide, with U.S. and international manufacturing facilities and office facilities worldwide totaling more than 4 million square feet.

BEGINNINGS

Compaq was founded in February 1982 by Rod Canion, Jim Harris, and Bill Murto, three senior managers who left Texas Instruments and invested $1,000 each to form their own company. Sketched on a paper placemat in a Houston pie shop, the new company's first product was a portable personal computer, able to run all of the software being developed for the original IBM PC, introduced in 1981.

The founders presented their idea to Ben Rosen, president of Sevin-Rosen Partners, the high-tech venture capital firm that would later fund Compaq and other fast-growth companies, including Lotus Development Corp. The venture capitalists were impressed with the idea of a portable product innovating within the emerging IBM PC standard and agreed to fund the new company.

In the years following its founding in February 1982, the Houston, Texas-based company has set sales and financial records, rapidly expanded its work force and facilities, and built a corporate organization poised to achieve even greater long-term growth. In 1983, its first full year of operation, Compaq achieved revenues of $111.2 million, a record in U.S. business history for the most successful first year of sales. The company's 1984 sales of $329 million also set a record for the greatest second-year sales in the history of the U.S. computer industry.

In 1985, when many other computer companies reported lower revenues, Compaq Computer Corporation reported record sales of $503.9 million, making it the first company to achieve "Fortune 500" status in less than four years. In 1987, Compaq surpassed $1 billion in annual sales, just five years after shipping the first COMPAQ® Portable computer. The company reached this milestone faster than any other company in business history. Since then, it has shown other dramatic increases in sales.

INDUSTRY STANDARDS

COMPAQ personal computers are compatible with personal computer industry standards, meaning they support the largest base of business software programs, peripherals, and hardware add-ons. The company is resolute in its dedication to maintaining full compatibility with established industry standards, and believes that innovation within these standards is a key to success. It has established standards for performance, quality of design, reliability, and superior features that meet real user needs.

Compaq's first two products, the COMPAQ Portable and COMPAQ PLUS® personal computers, were introduced in 1983 and quickly set the standard for full-function portable personal computers. Within a year, they were the world's best-selling portable personal computers.

A company that began with a sketch on a placemat in a pie shop grossed over $111 million its first full year.

In June 1984, the company introduced the COMPAQ DESKPRO® family of 8086-based desktop personal computers and within four months it became one of the top-selling lines of desktop business personal computers.

The company continued developing the COMPAQ DESKPRO series in 1985 with the 286 personal computer that was compatible with the IBM PC AT®. In 1986, Compaq established a new high-performance personal computing standard by introducing the COMPAQ DESK-

PRO 386®, the first industry standard personal computer based on the 32-bit architecture of the 80386 microprocessor. In doing so, the company achieved a major technology breakthrough and ushered in the third generation of personal computer technology. Compaq again revolutionized the personal computer industry in 1987 with its introductions of the COMPAQ DESKPRO 386/20™ and the COMPAQ PORTABLE 386™, pound-for-pound the most powerful computers ever built.

In 1988, Compaq introduced the COMPAQ DESKPRO 386/25 and the COMPAQ DESKPRO 386s, the first personal computer to use the new Intel 80386SX microprocessor, which delivered breakthrough performance to a broad range of business users. The COMPAQ DESKPRO 286e, an enhanced, small-footprint 286-based personal computer, was introduced in 1989 and became the company's best selling product in the U.S. and Canada in the first full month of availability. On May 22, 1989, Compaq introduced the COMPAQ DESKPRO 386/33, designed for demanding applications such as computer-aided design, financial modeling, and software development, and also for use as a file server or multi-user host system.

In the meantime, Compaq continued its development of portable computers. In February of 1986, the company introduced the COMPAQ Portable II®, which at the time set the standard as the world's smallest and lightest high-performance, portable personal computer. A new portable, the COMPAQ PORTABLE III®, was unveiled in 1987. It provided the power and functionality of a high-performance desktop computer in a small and rugged self-contained unit weighing only 18 pounds.

Compaq's first laptop personal computer, the 14-pound COMPAQ SLT/286, was introduced in 1988. Among this computer's many features were advanced VGA display; a unique, power-saving battery pack; and a removable keyboard. It quickly became the most popular portable computer Compaq has ever introduced.

Compaq introduced the COMPAQ LTE/286 and COMPAQ LTE in 1989. These computers were the first notebook-sized computers to offer full PC functionality in a package measuring just 8½ by 11 inches and weighing only 6 pounds. They fit in a briefcase with room to spare, offering mobile professionals "go-anywhere" portability with more than 3½ hours of battery life. A newer COMPAQ LTE is model 386S/20.

On November 6, 1989, Compaq unveiled a host of advanced computer products that expanded the frontier of

COMPAQ PORTABLE 386™

COMPAQ SLT 386S/20

industry-standard PC computing power and flexibility. Two of the products were the COMPAQ SYSTEMPRO Personal Computer System and the COMPAQ DESKPRO 486/25. The COMPAQ SYSTEMPRO is the first of an emerging class of extremely powerful personal computers capable of application solutions heretofore the exclusive territory of minicomputers. More recent products include the DESKPRO 386/25e for business users and the DESKPRO 486/50L for engineers, software developers, and scientists. These new Compaq products offer unprecedented levels of power and performance based on user-defined rather than vendor-specific industry standards.

APPLICATION
Compaq Computer Corporation

COMPAQ DESKPRO 486/336

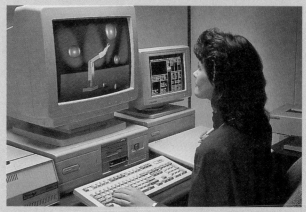

COMPAQ SYSTEMPRO

DISTRIBUTION

The company sells its personal computer products exclusively through more than 3,000 Authorized COMPAQ Computer Dealers in 63 countries. Gaining valuable shelf space while developing and maintaining strong relationships with authorized COMPAQ computer dealers has been a major factor in the company's success.

Compaq has established a network of manufacturing facilities to better meet the particular needs of international users and provide enhanced support for the company's Houston-based assembly operations. These include a portable and desktop production facility in Erskine, Scotland, and a printed-circuit board assembly plant in Singapore, Compaq's first satellite manufacturing facility outside the U.S. Compaq also purchased the former Wang Laboratories manufacturing facility in Stirling, Scotland, to be used as a base for the company's expanding service and repair operations. In addition, the company markets its full line of personal computer products through wholly-owned overseas subsidiaries in Australia, Austria, Belgium, Canada, Denmark, Finland, France, Germany, Italy, the Netherlands, Norway, Singapore, Spain, Sweden, Switzerland, and the United Kingdom.

DISCUSSION POINTS

1. What corporate design strategy has been critical to the success of Compaq?
2. Discuss the product mix of Compaq computers.

Telecommunications and Networks

ARTICLE

Marist Creating a High-Tech Campus

Carol Hildebrand, *Computerworld*

POUGHKEEPSIE, N.Y.—By the time Marist College is through, about the only things you will not be able to do there electronically will be either illegal, immoral or fattening.

As part of a $13 million partnership the tiny liberal arts school has formed with IBM, every room on campus will eventually be wired to take advantage of state-of-the-art voice and data systems.

Marist, which has a student population of about 3,200, has had a good relationship with IBM for years, according to Dennis Murray, president of the college. Marist is in the heart of IBM country, and about 10% of its graduates find jobs there when they graduate, he said.

The program originally emerged from a study aimed at gauging the impact of large mainframe capabilities on a small environment, for which Marist received an IBM 3090 Model 200E.

After starting to network the campus together to take advantage of all this horsepower, "we started to realize that what we were doing for data also made sense for voice," Murray said. So the study was expanded to include voice capabilities as well.

IBM is providing Marist with a Rolm Systems 9751 CBX switch, as well as Rolm phone mail and IBM Token-Ring local-area networks. The college is paying for cabling and a fiber-optic backbone to connect campus buildings to each other as well as to the mainframe.

When the study is complete, Murray said, he expects every room on campus to be wired for voice and data transmission. "If a student has a personal computer, they can just walk into their room and plug into the network," he said, adding that they hope to get the wiring done by the fall.

Each student will also have a voice mailbox. "You can get to any phone on campus and punch in your code and get voice messages," Murray said. He added that he hopes it will smooth out a lot of organizational hassles. For instance, a faculty member can advise seminar attendees of a switch in location by leaving a phone-mail message.

Making Connections

According to Carl Gerberich, vice president of information services at the college, each floor of a residence hall, for example, will have its own Token-Ring connected to a building-wide ring, which in turn will hook into the campuswide fiber backbone.

Although Marist will not provide each student with a PC, each dormitory will boast several common terminal rooms, with even greater access available at the academic buildings. For example, the new Dyson Center for Management Studies, which was constructed to take advantage of the data and telephone network, has two laboratories with a total of approximately 45 IBM Personal System/2 55SXs.

Murray sees almost limitless opportunities for the new system. The card catalog at the library is already on-line. "It can tell you if a book is checked out and when it is due back, so you don't have to look through the stacks for books," he said. "Next year, you'll be able to reserve the book right over the lines." Murray said he wants the final phase of the study to examine methods to exploit optical storage technologies in the library.

Murray said general reaction has been positive: "Initially, there's a bit of grousing, but once they start to see how information technology can be useful to them, the students become very excited about it."

◼ INTRODUCTION

Earlier chapters have presented information on both large and small computer systems. Discussions have focused on the physical components of computer systems and on file organization and data design. This chapter focuses on data communications and what is required to transmit data from one component to another within a computer system as well as from one computer system to another.

Managing today's diverse and multinational businesses is a complex task. Managers often require up-to-date data pertaining to company operations in order to effectively control their business. In many cases, decisions must be made on short notice and on the basis of data gathered and analyzed from geographically dispersed locations. Therefore, an efficient and timely way to capture and process data is required. Telecommunications systems designed to meet these needs help to accomplish the task of providing timely and accurate data to today's managers.

This chapter discusses telecommunications and the equipment that makes up a telecommunication system. Included in this discussion is information on how data is transmitted from one device to another and from one location to another. The chapter also presents information on how computer systems can be configured to take advantage of data transmission and telecommunication technology. Networking and applications such as electronic banking, telecommuting, and information services are built upon and continue to be dependent upon data transmission and telecommunication technologies. All these topics provide insight as to how telecommunications technologies can be used to benefit today's businesses.

◼ TELECOMMUNICATIONS

Data communication is the electronic transmission of data from one location to another, over communication channels such as telephone or telegraph lines or microwaves. Data communication occurs between components of a computer system and between two or more computer systems. As people and equipment become geographically dispersed, the computer and input and output devices, or **terminals,** are hooked into a communication network. The communication network provides the means for the input and output devices to communicate with both themselves and the computer(s) tied into the network. The combined use of communication facilities, such as telephone systems, and data-processing equipment is called **telecommunication.**

Data transmission using communication channels can take place between terminals that are in the same room or separated by an ocean. The difference between these two situations is the type of communication channel through which the data flows.

◼ COMMUNICATION CHANNELS

A **communication channel** is the link that permits transmission of electrical signals (data) between **distributed data processing (DDP)** locations. The purpose of a communication channel is to carry data from one location to another. Communication channels can be classified in a number of different ways. The following discussion classifies channels by type, grade, and mode.

Types of Channels

Several types of media are used as communication channels for data transfer, the most common of which are telephone lines, coaxial cables, fiber-optic cables, and microwaves.

Telephone lines are one of the most widely used communication channels for the transmission of both voices and data. Ordinary telephone lines are composed of strands of copper wire that are twisted into pairs. Copper is an excellent conductor of electrical signals, and data travels along the wire from one location to another.

Coaxial cable is composed of groups of both copper and aluminum wires. The wires are insulated to reduce the distortion that interferes with signal transmission (see Figure 9–1). Coaxial cables permit high-speed transmission of data and can be used to replace ordinary telephone lines.

Fiber optics is also being used as a medium that permits digital transmission. In fiber-optic cables, light impulses (laser beams) are sent along clear, flexible tubing approximately half the diameter of a human hair (see Figure 9–2). A fiber-optic cable is about one-tenth the diameter of a wire cable. Because fiber-optic cables permit data to be transmitted without conversion to analog form, there are few errors in data transmission. The small tubing makes the cables easy to install. One drawback of fiber-optic cables, however, is that the light impulses lose signal strength over distance. However, fiber optic cables are not susceptible to electrical interference; hence, they are ideal for data transmission because of the reduced chance of error.

Microwave communication channels transmit data in analog form. Microwaves are sent through the atmosphere at high speeds in a way that is similar to radio or television transmission. Microwaves are transmitted from one ground station to another or from earth to satellite or vice versa. Unlike other communication channels, however, microwaves cannot bend. Since they must be transmitted in a straight line between two points, microwave transmission is frequently used in conjunction with satellites. Communication satellites rotate about the earth at approximately the same speed that the earth rotates about the sun. Microwaves are sent in a straight line from an earth station to the satellite and then redirected from the receiving satellite to another satellite or earth station (see Figure 9–3).

FIGURE 9–1

Coaxial Cable

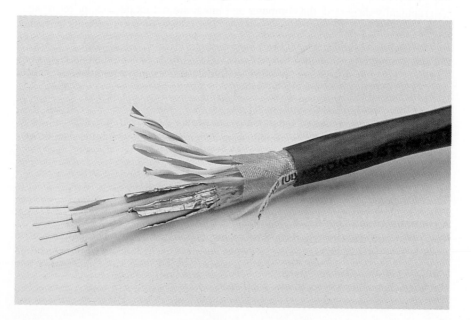

 FIGURE 9–2

Fiber-Optic Cable

FIGURE 9–3

Satellite Communication System Using Microwaves

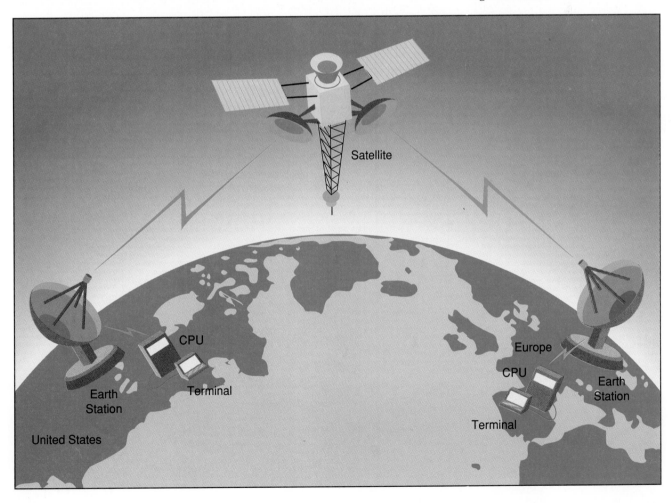

Microwave transmission is relatively error-free and offers a great deal of flexibility because there is no need for a physical link between transmission points. On the negative side, microwave transmission is expensive because of the high cost of constructing ground stations and launching satellites.

Grades of Channels

Communication channels can also be classified by grade. The **grade** or **bandwidth** of a channel determines the range of frequency at which it can transmit data. The rate at which data can be transmitted across the channel is directly proportional to the width of the frequency band. **Narrow bandwidth channels,** such as telegraph lines, can transmit data at rates between 45 and 90 bits per second.

Voice-grade channels have wider frequency ranges. They can transmit at rates between 300 and 9,600 bits per second. Voice-grade channels such as telephone lines are used by AT&T for the Wide Area Telephone Service (WATS) line.

For applications that require high-speed transmission of large volumes of data, **broad-band channels** are most suitable. Coaxial cables, microwaves, and fiber-optic cables fall into this category. Broad-band transmission services can be leased from both Western Union and AT&T. Broad-band channels can transmit data at a rate of up to 120,000 bits per second.

Modes of Channels

Communication channels operate in one of three basic transmission modes: simplex, half-duplex, or full-duplex. The mode of transmission is dependent upon the application and the terminal equipment used. A simplex transmission is unidirectional, or

CONCEPT SUMMARY 9–1		
Communication Channels		
Type of Channel	**Characteristics of Channel**	**Grade of Channel**
Telephone line	Twisted copper strands Excellent conductor of electricity Most widely used media Analog transmission	Voice-grade
Coaxial cable	Copper and aluminum wires insulated to reduce distortion High-speed analog transmission	Broad-band
Fiber-optic cable	Flexible, narrow tubing Light impulses are sent along clear flexible tubing Digital transmission	Broad-band
Microwave	Similar to radio or television transmission Transmission must be in a straight line Used with satellites Analog transmission	Broad-band

one-way. A simplex modem can either send or receive data; it cannot do both. Half-duplex transmission permits data to flow in two directions but only one way at a time. Modems capable of half-duplex transmission are commonly used in telephone services and networks. Full-duplex transmission permits data to flow in both directions simultaneously. A modem capable of full-duplex transmission is the most versatile type available. Figure 9–4 illustrates the channel transmission modes.

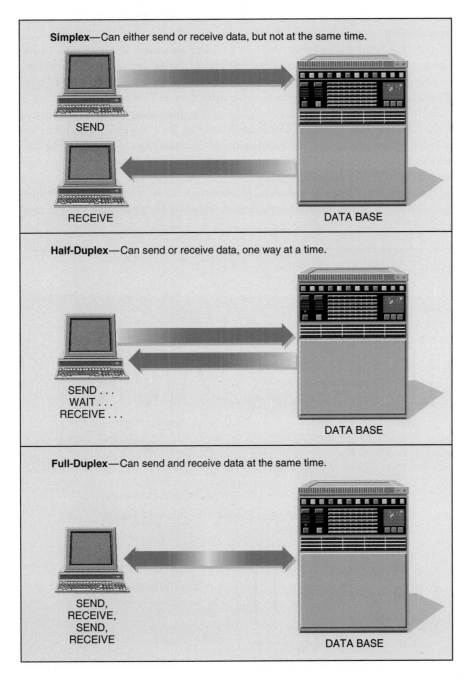

Simplex—Can either send or receive data, but not at the same time.

SEND

RECEIVE

DATA BASE

Half-Duplex—Can send or receive data, one way at a time.

SEND . . .
WAIT . . .
RECEIVE . . .

DATA BASE

Full-Duplex—Can send and receive data at the same time.

SEND,
RECEIVE,
SEND,
RECEIVE

DATA BASE

FIGURE 9–4

Channel Transmission Modes

■ DATA TRANSMISSION

Data can be transmitted through communication channels in one of two forms: analog or digital. Transmission of data in continuous wave form is referred to as **analog transmission.** An analog transmission can be likened to the waves created in a pan of still water when a stick is inserted. By sending "waves" down a wire electronically, messages are sent and received. In the past, analog transmission was the major means of relaying data over long distances. This was due largely to the type of telephone and telegraph lines provided by American Telephone and Telegraph (AT&T). **Digital transmission,** on the other hand, involves the transmission of data as distinct on and off pulses. Digital transmission tends to be faster and more accurate than analog transmission. Figure 9–5 illustrates the concepts of digital and analog transmission.

Analog transmission requires that the sender convert the data from the digital form in which it is stored to wave form before transmitting it. This conversion process is called **modulation.** The opposite conversion—from wave to digital form—is required at the receiving end before the data is understood by the computer. This conversion is called **demodulation.** Both modulation and demodulation are accomplished by devices called **modems** or **data sets.** The term *modem* is derived from the terms *mod*ulation and *dem*odulation.

There are three types of modems: (a) acoustic coupler, (b) direct connect, and (c) internal. An **acoustic-coupler modem** is linked to a terminal and has a special

FIGURE 9–5

Analog and Digital Transmission

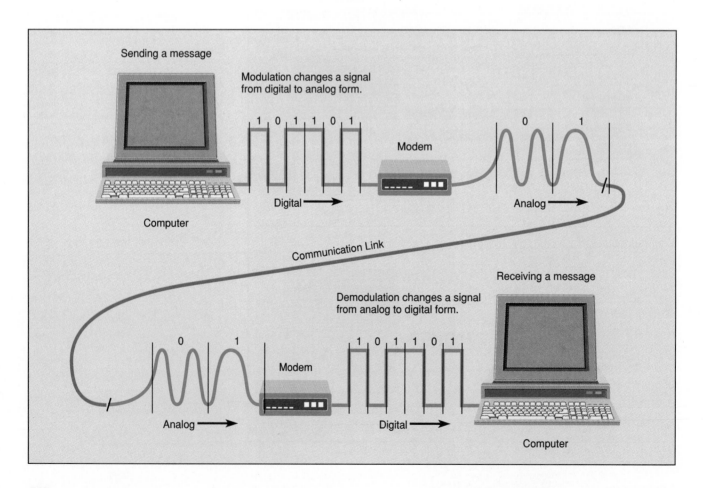

(a)

(b)

(c)

cradle that holds a standard telephone handset (see Figure 9–6a). The modem processes audible analog tones that pass through the receiver, thus the term *acoustic* coupler. A **direct-connect modem** connects a computer directly to a telephone line (see Figure 9–6b). An **internal modem** consists of a circuit board that is plugged into the internal circuitry of the computer. This type of modem also connects a computer directly to a telephone line (see Figure 9–6c).

Since the computer stores data in an on/off (digital) form, when digital transmission is used there is no need to convert data from wave to digital form. This reduces the time required to send messages and eliminates the data errors that frequently occur in the conversion process. Users can transmit large amounts of data faster and more reliably with digital transmission.

FIGURE 9–6

The Three Types of Modems:
(a) Acoustic-Coupler Modem
(b) Direct-Connect Modem
(c) Internal Modem

◼ INPUT/OUTPUT OPERATIONS

As stated in earlier chapters, a computer system consists of peripheral devices, or input/output devices—printers, terminals, storage devices, etc.—connected to a CPU (central processing unit). In order for the system to operate properly, the CPU must be able to communicate with the peripheral devices. In turn, the peripheral devices must be able to communicate with the CPU. This two-way communications between the CPU and its peripherals must take place in order for the system to function properly. These communications operations are discussed in the remainder of this section.

One of the key functions of the input/output (IO) devices of a computer system is the conversion of data into a machine-readable form. For instance, data entered through a computer terminal must be converted from a form understood by humans into a machine-readable form such as ASCII or BCD (see the section on computer codes in Chapter 4). Code conversion must be performed when data is input from devices such as remote terminals and magnetic-ink character recognition devices and also at output when information is sent to a printer or display terminal. Code conversion is performed by the **input/output (I/O) control unit.** This unit is different from the control unit of the CPU. It is located between one or more I/O devices and the CPU and is used only to facilitate I/O operations.

In addition to code conversion, I/O control units perform **data buffering.** A **buffer** is a separate storage unit (normally contained in the I/O control unit) for a particular input or output device. It is used as a temporary holding area for data being transferred to or from the CPU.

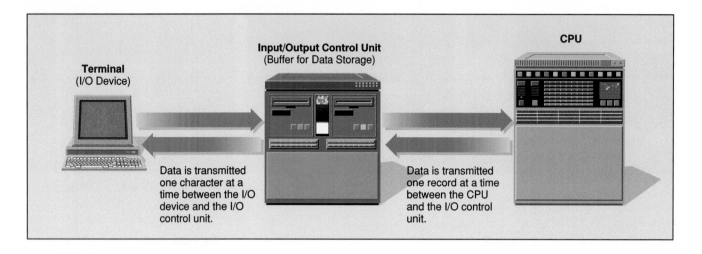

FIGURE 9–7

Data Buffering

When data is read by an input device, it is converted to a machine-readable form and stored in a buffer. Once a specific amount of data has been collected in the buffer, it is transferred to the CPU. The buffer allows a large quantity of data to be transferred much faster than if the data items were transferred individually. For example, a buffer is used to temporarily hold data being entered from a remote terminal; this allows a large block of data to be keyed on the terminal, held, and transferred all at once to the CPU. While the data is being keyed, the CPU processes other data (see Figure 9–7). The buffer serves a similar purpose when information is transferred from the CPU to a printer or terminal as output.

Although the CPU is very fast and accurate, it can execute only one instruction at a time. If it executes an instruction that requires input or output, it must wait while data is retrieved from or sent to an input/output device. Compared with the CPU's internal processing speeds, I/O device speeds are extremely slow. Even high-speed I/O devices often work only one-tenth as fast as the CPU. When the CPU slows down to wait for input/output operations to take place, it is **input/output bound.**

The flow of data shown in Table 9–1 indicates that in this system the CPU does the process step when it has the necessary data but sits idle while input and output occur. To increase use of the CPU, **channels** have been developed to take over the task of transferring data to and from the CPU (see Table 9–2). Each channel is a small, limited-capacity computer that serves as a data roadway. The channel may be within the CPU or a separate piece of equipment connected to it. During processing,

TABLE 9–1			
Input/Output Bound			
	Time 1	**Time 2**	**Time 3**
Input	Item 1		
Process		Item 1	
Output			Item 1

The CPU is input/output-bound—it can operate on only one item at a time.

TABLE 9–2			
Processing with Channels			
	Time 1	**Time 2**	**Time 3**
Input	Item 1	Item 2	Item 3
Process		Item 1	Item 2
Output			Item 1

With the aid of channels, the CPU can be active a greater percentage of the time.

when the CPU encounters an instruction requiring input or output, the CPU indicates to the channel what is needed. The channel then goes to the required input device for data or sends information to the appropriate output device. The CPU, meanwhile, is free to execute other instructions; it is relieved of its responsibility to transfer data and can process the data more efficiently.

Communication hardware devices are often used to manage the transmission of data over a computer system's communication channels. These hardware devices are discussed in the following section, Communication Hardware.

▣ COMMUNICATION HARDWARE

Often, data communication requires the use of special hardware to speed the transfer of data. There are several types of communication hardware devices, including multiplexers, concentrators, and selectors. These devices manage the data communication that takes place on a computer system's communication channels.

Multiplexers, Concentrators, and Selectors

Multiplexers, concentrators, and **selectors,** also known as **datacom handlers,** increase the number of input/output devices that can use a communication channel. They allow multiple I/O devices to share one channel. It is advantageous to increase the number of I/O devices because these devices operate at much lower speeds (100 to 150 bits per second) than communication channels (300 to 9,600 bits per second for voice-grade channels). Thus, a channel is not used to full capacity by a single I/O device.

Multiplexing can promote more economical use of a communication channel; it acts as a communication interface, combining the input streams from several devices into a single stream that can be sent over a single channel to the computer system. This allows a single communication channel (typically voice-grade) to substitute for many slower subvoice channels that might otherwise have been operating at less than full capacity. Once the computer system has completed processing, the data is sent to the multiplexer, which then routes the data to the appropriate device.

A concentrator differs from a multiplexer in that it allows data to be transmitted from only one terminal at a time over a communication channel. The concentrator **polls** the terminals one at a time to see if they have any messages to send. When a communication channel is free, the first terminal ready to send or receive data will

FIGURE 9–8

Communication Systems with and without Multiplexers and Concentrators

get control of the channel and continue to control it for the length of the transaction. The use of a concentrator relies on the assumption that not all terminals will be ready to send or receive data at a given time. Figure 9–8 shows examples of communication systems with and without multiplexers and concentrators.

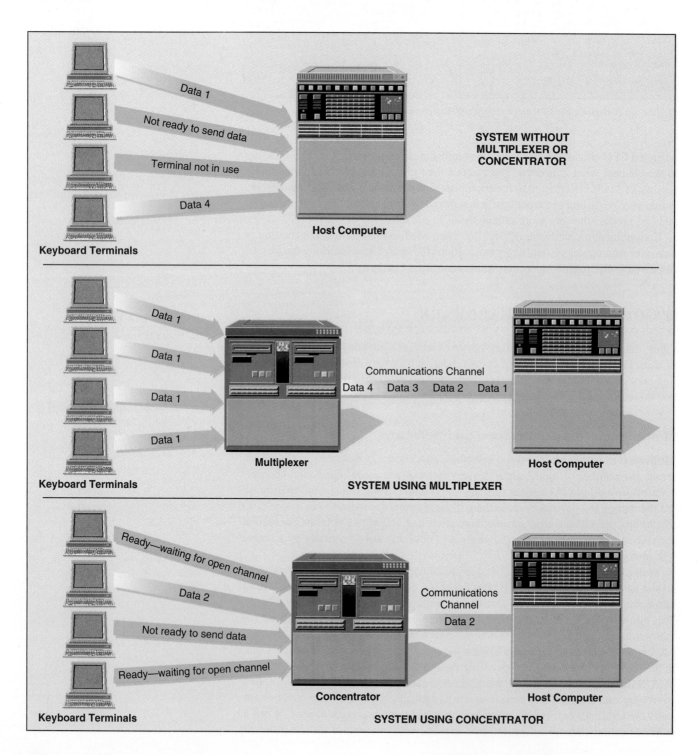

SYSTEM WITHOUT MULTIPLEXER OR CONCENTRATOR

Data 1

Not ready to send data

Terminal not in use

Data 4

Keyboard Terminals

Host Computer

Data 1

Data 1

Data 1

Data 1

Communications Channel
Data 4   Data 3   Data 2   Data 1

Keyboard Terminals

Multiplexer

Host Computer

SYSTEM USING MULTIPLEXER

Ready—waiting for open channel

Data 2

Not ready to send data

Ready—waiting for open channel

Communications Channel
Data 2

Keyboard Terminals

Concentrator

Host Computer

SYSTEM USING CONCENTRATOR

A selector is similar to a concentrator in that it allows data to be transmitted from only one input/output device at a time. Selectors are normally used with high-speed devices such as a magnetic-tape or magnetic-disk unit.

Programmable Communications Processors

A **programmable communications processor** is a device that relieves the CPU of many of the tasks typically required in a computer system. When the volume of data transmission surpasses a certain level, a programmable communications processor can handle these tasks more economically than the CPU. Examples of such tasks include handling messages and priorities, terminating transmission after messages have been received, requesting retransmission of incomplete messages, and verifying successfully transmitted messages.

The two most frequent uses of communications processors are message switching and front-end processing. The principal task of the processor used for **message switching** is to receive messages and route them to appropriate destinations. A **front-end processor** performs message switching as well as more sophisticated operations, such as validating transmitted data and processing data before it is transmitted to the central computer.

◼ NETWORKS

The development of the communication channels discussed earlier made possible the development and widespread use of computer networks. A computer **network** is the linking together of CPUs and terminals via a communication system. A network allows users at different locations to share files, devices, and programs. Many terminals may share the resources of one CPU, or multiple CPUs may be linked together. Terminals and CPUs may be geographically dispersed or situated within the physical constraints of a single office or building.

Single CPU Networks

A typical computer system consists of a single mainframe linked to a variety of peripherals. When peripherals are connected directly to the CPU, the system is called a **local system.** Advancements in computer technology have made it possible to place terminals (or other devices) in locations removed from the CPU and connect them to the central computer by a communication channel. The resulting system is called a **remote system.**

Many businesses could benefit from a computer facility but find the costs prohibitive. For organizations that only infrequently need the power of a large computer system, **time-sharing systems** have been developed. Under time sharing, many different businesses with diverse requirements can access the same central computer and receive what seems to be simultaneous responses. Each user seems to have total control of the computer, but in reality the computer divides its time among the users. Each user is charged only for the computer resources actually used. This time-sharing system may be accessed by remote users via I/O devices and communication channels or by local users whose I/O devices are connected directly to the system.

A system that supports time sharing must allocate computing time to users. The purpose of the time-sharing system would be defeated if one user had to wait a long time while another monopolized the CPU's processing facilities. A technique called

time slicing can solve this problem. Each user is allocated a small portion of processing time. If the user's program is completely executed during this time, or if the program reaches a point at which input or output activity must occur before the allotted time is used up, the CPU begins (or resumes) execution of another user's program. If execution of the program is not completed during that allocated time, control of the CPU is transferred to another user's program and the first program is placed at the end of a waiting list. Once the program returns to the top of the list, execution is resumed at the point where it was stopped when control of the CPU was transferred to another user's program. This switching of programs occurs at such a rapid rate that users are generally unaware of it.

There are two methods of establishing time-sharing capability. One is to set up a time-sharing system **in-house** to obtain quick answers to such problems as production and cost analysis, forecasting, and accounts receivable. The other is to purchase time-sharing capability from a service company that owns and maintains one or more computer systems. Because of the intense competition in this area, many service companies have expanded to provide not only time-sharing capability but also specialized programs and technical assistance.

The major advantages of time-sharing systems include the following:

■ They provide an economical means for small users to access the resources of a large computer system.
■ They allow each user to seem to possess a private computer.
■ They offer the advantage of quick response capabilities.
■ Through resource poolings, they provide access to greater numbers of application programs at a lower unit cost than privately owned and maintained computers.
■ They relieve worry about equipment obsolescence.

Time sharing also has some inherent problems:

■ Users connected to the system by telephone lines must worry about breakdowns in the lines or increases in amount of communication; these lines are not the best medium for transmission of data. Thus, applications involving extensive I/O operations may not be suited to time sharing.
■ Because data can be accessed quickly and easily in a time-sharing system, concern for security must be increased. All programs and data must be safeguarded from unauthorized persons or use.
■ When quick response is not a necessity, time-sharing capability may be a needless expense.
■ System reliability may be lower than in non-time-sharing systems. The additional equipment and communication channels are possible areas for both mechanical and system-related problems.

Multiple CPU Networks

As with a single CPU and its terminals, a network's CPUs can be hooked together to form either local or remote systems. All networks are comprised of two basic structures: nodes and links. A **node** refers to the end points of a network. Nodes consist of CPUs, printers, terminals, and other physical devices. **Links** are the communication channels that connect the nodes.

Nodes and links can be arranged in a number of different ways to form a network configuration or topology. Some of the more common are star, ring, hierarchical, bus, and fully distributed. Figure 9–9 illustrates these configurations.

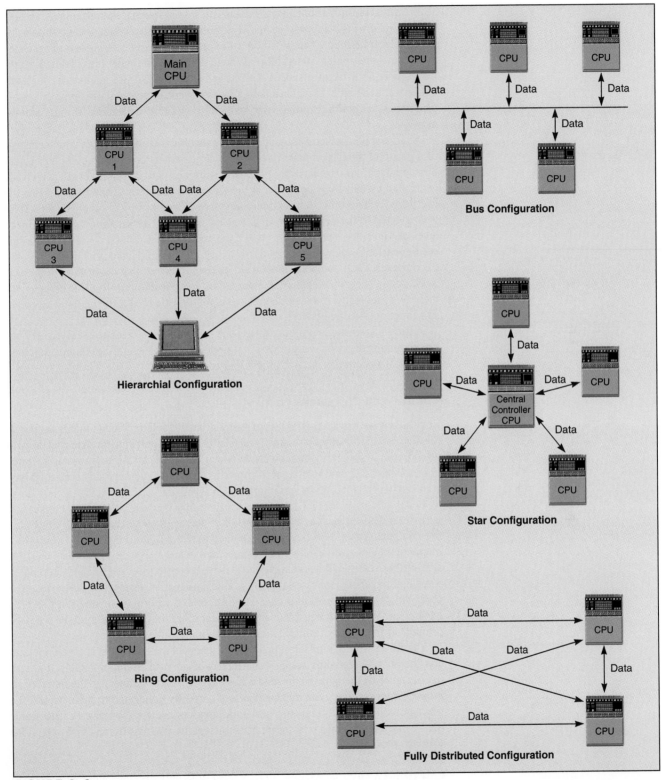

FIGURE 9–9

Network Configurations

In a **star configuration,** all transactions must go through a central computer before being routed to the appropriate network computer. This creates a central decision point, which facilitates workload distribution and resource sharing but exposes the system to single-point vulnerability. When the central computer breaks down, all the nodes in the network are disabled. An alternative approach uses a number of computers connected to a single transmission line in a **ring configuration.** This type of system can bypass a malfunctioning unit without disrupting operations throughout the network.

A more sophisticated approach is the **hierarchical configuration,** which consists of a group of small computers tied into a large central computing complex. Under this approach, an organization's needs are divided into multiple levels, which are controlled by the single computer at the top of the hierarchy. The lowest level is the user level, where only routine transaction-processing power is supplied. This level is connected to the next higher level and its associated information system. At each level, the machine size increases while the need for distribution decreases. In a **bus configuration,** each computer plugs into a single bus cable that runs from computer to computer. Each computer must have its own interface that connects it to the network. As messages travel along the bus cable, stations monitor the cable and retrieve their own messages. If one node in a bus configuration breaks down, the system can still function effectively.

A **fully distributed configuration** is one in which every set of nodes in the network can communicate with every other set of nodes through a single communication link. Each local system has its own processing capabilities.

Local-Area Networks (LANs)

Local-area networks (LANs) were originally designed to connect microcomputers together so that they could share peripheral devices and information and also to provide the ability to communicate between members of the network. Local-area networks are designed to operate within a well-defined and generally self-contained area, such as a small office building.

Local-area networks have become very popular because of the fact that sharing peripheral devices such as printers and mass storage devices can reduce costs on a per computer basis. For example, in some LAN configurations, up to twenty-four microcomputers can share a laser printer and a large capacity hard-disk unit. By sharing these types of devices, the cost per computer is reduced significantly compared to a situation where twenty-four printers and storage devices must be purchased. The ability to share information is also very important; information stored at a central location provides greater data integrity (accuracy and timeliness) and can be accessed or updated in a timely fashion from any location on the network.

The ability to communicate among the members of the network is also an important consideration. **Electronic mail** is one means of network communication. It allows one member of the network to send a message to other members of the network. If the members receiving the message are not currently connected to the network, the message will be saved until the next time they connect to the network. Electronic mail can eliminate many of the unnecessary calls and return calls of a telephone message process.

LAN HARDWARE. The members of a local-area network are identified by one of two terms—file server or workstation. A **file server** is the part of the LAN that allows for the sharing of peripheral devices and information. Devices such as printers and

Logistical LAN

As you can imagine, moving a mountain of military supplies and equipment can be an overwhelming and complicated task. In Operation Desert Shield the Military Traffic Management Command used a microcomputer-based local-area network to accomplish the incredible task of moving tons of equipment and provisions to Saudi Arabia. Issues such as what to send, how to send it, where to send it, and when it should arrive were all worked out through the use of a LAN and software such as Ashton-Tate's Multimate and Dbase III+ and Lotus 1-2-3. Since 1983, the Military Traffic Management Command has been installing local-area networks. Currently, 3,500 workstations and 64 file servers running the Novell network operating system software are in use. These independent LANs are connected together and to mainframe systems through a wide-area network that spans the globe.

A very important part of the mobilization of troops and equipment to Saudi Arabia was the establishment of a shipping terminal at Elounte Island near Jacksonville, Florida. Prior to the build-up in the Middle East, there was no terminal at Elounte Island. The military realized that it would need such a staging point to accomplish the task of shipping supplies and equipment to the Middle East. In three days the new terminal had been established and its network of PCs was up and running, accomplishing the needed logistical tasks. As a result, thirty-five ships were loaded with supplies for the Middle East at the Elounte Island Terminal.

One of the things that the network provides is an up-to-date status of shipments. All sorts of people need to know where the items being shipped are at any moment, and the network can provide this information to them in a timely fashion. As a result of its success, military commanders have become dependent upon the logistical network. In addition to the application software that accomplishes the task of scheduling and tracking the shipments, the users of the network are also taking advantage of its electronic mail capabilities. Generals who were moving from location to location during the mobilization process used the electronic mail to keep in touch with what was happening. The electronic mail system allowed the top brass to monitor and control the operation even when they were on the move.

hard-disk units are connected to the network's file server. In addition, the software that controls the operation of the network is installed on the hard-disk unit attached to the file server. The name file server is given to this member of the LAN because it serves other members' requests to access data in files that are stored on the network. The other microcomputers connected to the network are referred to as workstations. **Workstations** are the members of the LAN where work on applications such as payroll or order processing takes place.

One of the primary hardware components of a local-area network is the Network Interface Card (NIC). A **NIC** allows the members of a local-area network to communicate with each other. Network interface cards are integrated circuit boards that plug into the internal circuitry of the microcomputer.

The NIC has two primary functions in the network. It first provides for the physical connection of the members of the network. The cable that connects each microcomputer is plugged into the network interface card. The second function of the NIC is to control the communication that takes place between the members of the LAN. The NIC contains logic (software) that allows the members of the LAN to send and receive data. This transmission of data between members of the network is accomplished through the use of a communication protocol. A **protocol** describes the rules of communication when transmitting and receiving data on the network. Protocols that are used by network interface cards normally conform to standards published by organizations such as the International Organization for Standards (ISO), American National Standards Institute (ANSI), or others (see the section on Telecommunications Standards). The three standards normally used in local-area networks are Ethernet, ARCNET, and Token Ring. These standards employ either the star, ring, or bus network topologies discussed in the previous section.

The file server and workstations are connected together with either coaxial, twisted-pair (similar to telephone cable), or fiber-optic cable. The members of a local-area network must normally be positioned within 800 to 1,000 feet of each other. The distance between the members of the network are limited by the time and distance required for data to travel from one member to the next. This is a limiting factor because the strength of the transmission signal decreases as it travels. Therefore, in order for a signal to be received properly,it must arrive at its destination at a strength that will allow it to be understood.

LAN SOFTWARE. The software used to control network operations is referred to as the network operating system (NOS). The **network operating system** is the software that controls member access to the network's shared resources. If, for example, two or more members on the network request access to the printer at the same time, the network operating system will control the order in which the requests are processed. In addition to the control of access to shared resources, the network operating system normally includes programs that oversee network security and the processing of electronic mail.

The network operating system that has gained the widest acceptance for use on LANs is Novell's NetWare. This network operating system is capable of being used on a number of different LAN configurations as well as on a significant number of network hardware manufacturers' equipment. Other local-area network operating systems in use today include 3Com's 3+, Microsoft LAN Manager, Banyan Systems' VINES (*VI*rtual *NE*twork Operating *S*ystem) and Apple Computer's AppleTalk.

CONCEPT SUMMARY 9–2

Network Configurations

Structure	Feature
Star	All transactions go through a central computer; single-point vulnerability
Ring	All computers connected to a single transmission line, and malfunctioning units are bypassed
Hierarchical	Organizational needs are divided into multiple levels; a single computer controls the hierarchy
Bus	Each computer must have an interface to connect to the bus cable that links the machines
Fully Distributed	Every set of nodes can communicate directly with every other set of nodes; local systems have their own processing capabilities

■ TELECOMMUNICATION STANDARDS

Telecommunication standards are a set of rules that are agreed upon by government agencies that make and enforce standards and by leading companies within the telecommunication industry. The standards are proposed and adopted so that telecommunication architectures, physical design specifications, and communication protocols can be dealt with in a consistent fashion. The fact that leading companies within the telecommunication industry participate in the process of developing standards demonstrates the companies' willingness to produce products that adhere to the standards. Organizations that are involved in the establishment of telecommunication standards include the International Organization for Standardization (ISO), American National Standards Institute (ANSI), Consultative Committee on International Telephone and Telegraph (CCITT), Institute of Electrical and Electronics Engineers (IEEE), Electronic Industries Association (EIA), National Bureau of Standards (NBS), Exchange Carrier Standards Association, and the Corporation for Open Systems (COS).

The Consultative Committee on International Telephone and Telegraph (CCITT) has proposed standards that relate to how electrical connections used in telecommunication systems should be accomplished. The X.nn series of standards describes how digital equipment should be connected to public data networks using digital data transmission. The X.25 standard in particular describes how the interface between microcomputers with modems and public data networks should be accomplished. The CCITT has also proposed a standard that deals with the transmission of voice, data, and images over worldwide networks in a digital format. The Integrated Services Digital Network (ISDN) standard would lead to a single, consistent, worldwide telecommunication network from a user's viewpoint. The X.25 and ISDN are just two of a number of telecommunication standards that are being developed by international standards making organizations.

In the area of LANs, two committees and a number of companies have been involved with developing and publishing applicable standards. Committee 802 of IEEE has published standards for the Ethernet and Token-ring local-area networks, while ANSI is expected to publish an ARCNET standard sometime in the near future.

■ TELECOMMUNICATION AND NETWORK APPLICATIONS

The technologies used to facilitate telecommunications and networking are being used in a number of practical ways. In the following sections some of the more popular applications of these technologies are described.

Electronic Banking

Banks process huge amounts of paper in the form of checks, loan records, deposits, savings clubs, investment information, and so forth. The account balance of every customer must be kept up to date and funds and data must be exchanged among banks. Computers are used to facilitate these activities in every banking institution across the country.

HIGHLIGHT

Scheduling Communication Satellites

Intelsat (short for the International Telecommunications Satellite Organization) is in the process of transferring its communication satellite scheduling operations from IBM 4381 mainframes to a microcomputer based local-area network. The Intelsat company currently schedules the communication channels for fifteen communication satellites orbiting the earth. Intelsat provides 180 countries access to its communications satellites, which carry approximately 120,000 communication channels handling international telephone, television, facsimile (FAX), and data communication.

The local-area network being put in place by Intelsat will be running the OS/2 operating system and the Microsoft LAN Manager network operating system. The company is switching from its outdated mainframe equipment to a LAN in order to provide more flexibility in its scheduling operations. The flexibility comes from the fact that more than one user of the LAN can be accessing the same data to accomplish different tasks related to the scheduling of the satellites' communication channels. This scheduling will be accomplished using two applications, the Operational Planning System (OPS) and Operations Frequency Planning System (OFPS). Both applications will be written in the C programming language and will utilize the OS/2 Presentation Manager as a user interface. In the past,

scheduling a satellite could take up to three weeks to perform using the old system. The new system will be able to accomplish the same task in as little as eight hours.

The company feels that the LAN solution to their scheduling problems has provided them with a cost-effective option as compared to alternative mainframe solutions. Intelsat also believes that the new OPS and OFPS systems running on IBM PS/2 workstations, a Compaq Systempro file server, and an IBM Token-Ring network will go a long way toward making their satellite scheduling tasks effective, efficient, and much simpler.

Telecommunication technology is now being used by banks in the form of **electronic funds transfer (EFT).** In an EFT system, the accounts of a party or parties involved in a transaction are adjusted by electronic communication between computers and/or computer terminals. No cash or checks actually change hands. Many banks now offer automated services such as direct deposit of checks into customers' accounts by their employers and automatic payment of bills.

One popular form of EFT is the **automatic teller machine (ATM).** ATMs are unattended remote devices that communicate with a bank's computer. Many banks have installed the machines in the outside walls of bank buildings. The machines are also located at supermarkets, airports, college campuses, and shopping malls. Bank customers can use them twenty-four hours a day to check their account balances, transfer funds, make deposits or withdrawals, and draw out cash from a credit card account. Customers identify themselves by inserting plastic cards (either their credit cards or bank cards) and entering identification codes. The cards contain account numbers and credit limits encoded on strips of magnetic tape. Once identification is approved, the customers select transactions by pushing a series of buttons.

Another application of EFT involves home banking. Using a telephone or a microcomputer and a modem, a customer can perform banking transactions by entering account numbers and transaction codes through the keypad of the telephone or the keyboard of the microcomputer. A voice synthesizer, which is programmed to give transaction instructions and information, may respond to the customer. The same tasks can be performed if a customer has a keypad device attached to a television set and two-way cable television lines.

Some institutions accept the use of the ''smart'' card. A customer obtains from the bank a plastic card about the size of a normal credit card. Embedded in the thin plastic is a microcomputer—a chip that has programmable functions and a memory. Rather than operating on the basis of a credit limit, the card functions on a debit basis. To use the card, the customer transfers money from a savings account to the card account. When a purchase is made, the card is inserted into the reader at the store. The amount of a purchase is deducted from the customer's account and added to the store's account. Fraud is less likely than with an ordinary charge card since this card is personalized by a sequence of four digits, which make up the personal identity number (PIN). After three incorrect PINs are entered, part of the codes on the card self-destruct, rendering the card useless. An unauthorized user can almost never guess the correct PIN in three tries.

Banks also perform transactions with each other by computers. The Federal Reserve System, for example, operates the Fed Wire transfer network for use by member banks. Another EFT network, BankWire, serves several hundred banks in the United States. EFT facilitates international banking through a system called SWIFT (Society for Worldwide Interbank Financial Telecommunications).

Telecommuting

Perhaps one of the most interesting aspects of telecommunications to contemporary office workers is **telecommuting**—commuting to the office by computer rather than in person. The system offers advantages in cities where office rent is high and mass transit systems or parking facilities are inadequate, and in businesses that do not require frequent face-to-face meetings among office workers. Telecommuting also provides greater flexibility for disabled employees and working parents.

Salespeople and journalists, who are often away from their offices, have successfully used a kind of telecommuting by taking portable computers and tiny printers with them on assignments. The portable computer is used to type memos, letters, stories, or reports. Using a modem, the person sends information over telephone lines to the office. Once the information has been received at the office, phone messages, edited copy, or other information can be sent back to the original writer.

Telecommuting does have disadvantages, however. Some employees may not have the discipline to work away from the office. They may fear that ''out of sight is out of mind,'' particularly when promotions and raises are considered. In addition, managers may be uneasy about the amount of control they have over employees who work away from the office.

Information Services

One of the benefits of buying a microcomputer is having the opportunity to access computer networks. Accessing a network through your microcomputer's modem can provide you with an opportunity to obtain resources and information and communicate with other computer users.

Information services, also known as commercial data bases, allow the personal computer user to gain access to vast storehouses of information. Most services require payment of an initial fee. You are then issued a special user identification number and/or a password. This ensures that only paid subscribers have access to the service. All services also charge an hourly connect rate, which will vary with the time of the day you are connected and the type of information you wish to access. The information services will provide their rates to subscribers and all interested persons. The hours of availability of the services also vary; not all services can be accessed twenty-four hours a day. Another cost that may be associated with the services is telephone line charges by your local telephone company. There may be local phone numbers for you to use, but these are available only in areas where there are a lot of potential users. If local numbers exist, the services will provide them.

COMPUSERVE. CompuServe is the largest information service available to individual and family users. Hourly connect rates vary depending on the day and time of day you use the service and the type of modem you have. Some of CompuServe's special services (such as stock price and dividend information) may have additional charges. The company also publishes *CompuServe* magazine, which provides helpful information on using the firm's services.

CompuServe uses a menu-choice and word-search approach. Menu-choice allows the user to access the desired information by selecting a topic and entering the numbers (see Figure 9–10). Word-search allows the user to enter a word or topic into designated areas of CompuServe while the computer looks for the related information. CompuServe also offers many computer games and allows users to shop at home by browsing through an electronic catalog.

You can send messages to other subscribers by using CompuServe's EMAIL. In addition to the Associated Press wire service, you can also access newspapers such as the *St. Louis Post-Dispatch,* the *Middlesex Daily,* and the *Washington Post.* CompuServe also links together special-interest groups. Each group shares a common interest such as music or owning an IBM-PC. Subscribers can communicate directly with CompuServe, giving their comments and suggestions, which may be used to add new services. CompuServe is always changing and adding to its resources.

FIGURE 9–10

CompuServe Menu

Users of CompuServe make menu selections from among a wide range of topics.

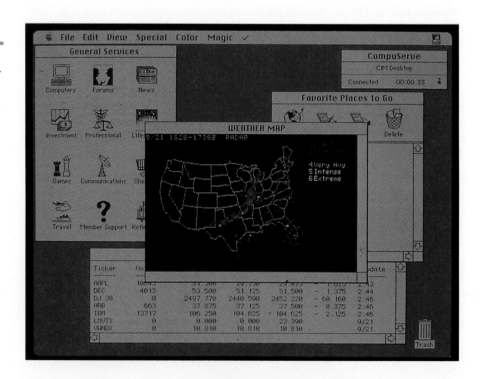

CHAPTER 9: TELECOMMUNICATIONS AND NETWORKS

THE SOURCE. Like CompuServe, The Source is geared toward individual and family users. There is a one-time subscription fee plus a monthly minimum charge. Hourly connect rates vary. Again, some services may charge additional fees. The Source also uses a menu-choice approach.

When connected to The Source, you can consult the *Official Airline Guide Electronic Edition,* to find the best route and fare for your next flight. If your destination is New York, Washington, or other major U.S. cities, you can even select restaurants before you go, by using the restaurant guide. The Source also offers you the convenience of shopping at home or playing computer games.

Through the EMPLOY option, you can look for job openings or potential employees in about forty different fields, ranging from accounting to utilities. The Source also allows you to send messages to other subscribers through the Mailgram service. If you want to talk with others who are connected to The Source at the same time, you can use the CHAT option. Do you need help with finances? The Source offers programs that figure depreciation schedules, balance your checkbook, and amortize a loan. As a Source subscriber, you can access the United Press International (UPI) wire service.

The Source calls its special-interest groups Private Sector. There are special-interest groups, groups for school administrators, public utilities, and radio stations. A group sponsor pays a service charge for twenty-five membership account numbers and the ability to put data bases on The Source. Like CompuServe, The Source is always updating its services and keeps its users informed through its newsletter, *SourceWorld.*

DOW JONES NEWS/RETRIEVAL. The Dow Jones News/Retrieval Service is designed with business information in mind and its primary users are business professionals and individuals interested in business. There are various user levels available with varying subscription fees. Connect rates per hour also vary. Dow Jones News/Retrieval uses a menu-choice approach to its services.

The Dow Jones News/Retrieval system provides information on every company listed on the New York and American stock exchanges, as well as some selected companies whose stock is traded over the counter. You can get historical stock market quotes and current information that is only fifteen minutes behind the action on the exchange floors. The service also gives corporate earnings estimates and price/volume data.

With a Dow Jones News/Retrieval subscription, you can get UPI summaries of local and national news, news stories from various financial newspapers and magazines, and access to the *Academic American Encyclopedia.* The service also has movie reviews and weather information, and allows you to shop at home.

Three software packages are available with which you can record and manipulate information from the News/Retrieval data bases. The Market Analyzer performs seventeen analytical functions and charts the results. The Market Microscope ranks companies and industries by sixty-eight financial indicators. The Market Manager monitors and updates investment portfolios.

DIALOG INFORMATION SERVICES. DIALOG Information Services offers two different data base collections for the serious researcher. The Information Retrieval Service data base collection has no subscription or minimum fee; however, there is a charge for a user's manual. Online hourly fees vary, depending on the data base you wish to access. The Knowledge-Index data base has variable hourly rates and limited hours of access. DIALOG uses a word-search approach for both of these services.

DIALOG Information Retrieval Service has comprehensive coverage of virtually every area of study—history, science, arts and humanities, law, medicine, and current affairs. More than 60,000 journals have been referenced as well as books, dissertations, patents, and pamphlets. You enter the word or words about which you want to gather information and DIALOG gives you a list of all references.

The Knowledge Index consists of about fifteen of the Information Retrieval data bases containing data from 10,000 journals. Some of the topics include computers, government publications, magazines, and psychology. Subscribers use a simplified word search to get the abstracts and references to the articles.

PRODIGY. A relatively new competitor in the information service market is Prodigy. Prodigy is a joint venture between Sears and IBM. It is geared toward individuals and families. Prodigy is a menu-driven, user-friendly service that allows subscribers to shop at home, perform banking tasks, make airline reservations, and access a wide variety of news and entertainment sources of information. Prodigy costs subscribers $9.95 a month and allows for unlimited use of the services for that price. The user must, of course, pay telephone usage charges to connect to the Prodigy service.

In addition to the services offered to subscribers, Prodigy also serves as an advertising medium for approximately 200 companies. These companies pay for advertising on the Prodigy system according to how many times an advertisement is accessed by subscribers and also by the number of products sold to subscribers.

Although the information-service market is quite competitive, Prodigy believes it can be successful by appealing to the large number of home computer users at an inexpensive price. Prodigy currently has a network of 22 minicomputer centers located around the country that serves approximately 200,000 subscribers.

SPECIALTY SERVICES. In addition to the networks mentioned above, there are also many specialty services. BRS/After Dark, which operates evenings and weekends, is a bibliographic retrieval service. LEXIS is a service for the legal profession that includes cases, regulations, laws, and decisions in the United States, Britain, and France. AMA/NET has four different data bases that provide medical personnel with information on drugs, diagnosing, medical legislation, and public health issues. HORSE has information on the breeding and race records of more than one million racehorses in North America. The number of information services or commercial data bases is increasing daily and the variety of information available is always expanding.

Bulletin Board

Electronic bulletin boards provide a place for users to post notices of all kinds. Although information services such as CompuServe and The Source provide bulletin board space for their subscribers, all you need to access most boards is the phone number and the proper communications link on your computer. Bulletin boards are normally free to the users (unless long-distance phone calls are placed). There are thousands of bulletin boards throughout the country, and the number is constantly rising.

Bulletin board users log onto a ''host'' computer. Once they are connected, users can send or receive data, messages, and information, copy programs from the board, and leave programs to be copied. The ''host'' computer is frequently another microcomputer whose owner decided to start the bulletin board. The flexibility of the board depends upon the host.

Bulletin boards are usually good sources for hardware and software reviews, new product information, and free programs. They also offer users the opportunity to meet other computer enthusiasts. Local computer dealers and user groups can provide information on bulletin boards in the areas near you.

◻ SUMMARY POINTS

◼ Data communication is the electronic transmission of data from one location to another, usually over communication channels such as telephone, telegraph, or microwaves. The combined use of data-processing equipment and communication facilities such as telephone systems is called telecommunication.

◼ A communication channel is the link permitting transmission of electrical signals from one location to another. Types of communication channels include telegraph lines, telephone lines, coaxial cables, and microwaves. Communication channels can also be classified by grade, or bandwidth, and mode of transmission (simplex, half-duplex, and full-duplex).

◼ Modulation is the process of converting data from the pulse form used by the computer to a wave form used for message transmission over communication lines. Demodulation is the process of converting the received message from wave form back to pulse form. These functions are performed by devices called modems, or data sets.

◼ Digital transmission involves transmitting data as distinct on and off pulses rather than as waves. This mode of transmission eliminates the specialized steps of conversion from pulse to wave form and subsequent reconversion from wave to pulse form at the destination.

◼ I/O control units and channels are used in an I/O subsystem to increase the efficiency of the CPU. A control unit converts input data into machine-readable form, and vice versa. It is also used in data buffering.

◼ Channels control I/O operations and free the CPU to do other processing; this allows input, output, and processing to overlap.

◼ Multiplexers, concentrators, selectors, and programmable communications processors are hardware devices that reduce the costs associated with data transmission in a communication system.

◼ The development of communication channels led to the development and widespread use of computer networks.

◼ A commuter network links together CPUs and terminals via a communication system.

◼ Communication networks may have single or multiple CPUs and may be either local or remote. A time-sharing system allows several users to access the same computer at the same time. An in-house time-sharing system can be installed, or time-sharing capability can be purchased from a service company.

◼ Multiple CPU networks are characterized by several computers linked together to form either local or remote systems. Five common multiple CPU configurations are star, ring, hierarchical, bus, and fully distributed.

◼ The star configuration directs all transactions through a central computer. A ring configuration uses a number of computers connected to a single transmission line. A malfunctioning unit can be bypassed without disrupting operations throughout the network. A hierarchical configuration consists of a group of small computers tied into a large central computing complex.

■ In a bus configuration, each computer plugs into a single bus cable that runs from workstation to workstation. A fully distributed network is one in which every set of nodes can communicate directly with every other set of nodes through a single communications link.

■ Local-area networks involve interconnecting computers in a single building or a complex of buildings. Electronic mail is a means of network communication in which one member of the network sends a message to another member.

■ Local-area networks (LANs) are designed to connect microcomputers together so they may share peripheral devices and information and communicate with other members of the network.

■ Members of a LAN are referred to as file servers or workstations. A file server controls the sharing of the peripherals and information, while the workstations make requests for the shared resources of the network.

■ A Network Interface Card (NIC) is the hardware device that allows members of a LAN to communicate with each other. The NIC contains a communication protocol that is common to all NICs on the network.

■ The network operating system (NOS) is the collection of software that controls the operation of a LAN.

■ Information services, or commercial databases, allow personal computers equipped with a modem to access vast banks of information that are stored on a central computer system.

■ Information services such as CompuServe, The Source, and Dow Jones News/ Retrieval offer a variety of types of information.

■ Bulletin boards are also accessed by microcomputers through modems and provide a place for users to post notices and communicate with each other.

❏ TERMS FOR REVIEW

■ REVIEW QUESTIONS

1. What is telecommunication?

2. How does a data buffer help speed up data communication?

3. Distinguish among simplex, half-duplex, and full-duplex transmission modes.

4. How does the manner in which a concentrator communicate with an I/O device differ from the way in which a multiplexer performs the same function?

5. What is a programmable communications processor?

6. Explain the difference between digital and analog transmission.

7. What are modems and what purpose do they serve in data communication systems?

8. Which configuration for multiple CPU networks has the disadvantage of single-point vulnerability? Why?

9. What are some advantages of a time-sharing system?

10. What is a local-area network?

11. What is a file server? What is a workstation?

12. What is a NIC? Why is it important to a LAN?

13. What is an information service? How do information services charge for the services they provide?

14. How do bulletin boards differ from information services?

APPLICATION

The Dow Chemical Company

The Dow Chemical Company markets over 2,000 products and services, including chemicals, plastics, hydrocarbons, energy, agricultural products, pharmaceuticals, and consumer products such as plastic wrap, Styrofoam plastic foam, adhesive films, cleaners, and hair care products. The company has 181 manufacturing sites in 32 countries and employs 62,000 people around the world. It is active in conservation practices such as using recycled plastics and finding ways to use less energy in manufacturing.

The company is known for its T.I.M.E. data base that contains listings for nearly 4,000 materials. Each material is reviewed and evaluated from toxicology, industrial hygiene, medical, and environmental perspectives. Employees around the world draw upon the data base continually.

COMPANY BACKGROUND

Herbert Henry Dow was an early leader in the U.S. chemical industry. In 1892, he founded the Midland Chemical Company, in Midland, Michigan. Then, in 1897, he founded the Dow Chemical Company, a bleach plant to use the wastes from Midland. In 1900, the two companies combined under the Dow Chemical name.

Through research, which Dow emphasized, the company was able to manufacture a variety of products including carbon tetrachloride and an inexpensive phenol (carbolic acid). Dow developed uses for bromine extracted from sea water. He extracted chlorides, magnesium, and calcium from brine deposits near Midland. In 1916, the company produced the first synthetic indigo in the United States, and later was the first important producer of iodine. Dow's headquarters remain to this day in Midland.

COMPUTER USE AT DOW

Recognizing the link between technology and success, the Dow Chemical Company uses computers to closely integrate information systems with business strategy. Office, financial, and accounting functions are computerized, and the company makes use of various networks. Electronic Data Interchange (EDI) functions at Dow allow customers to order products electronically with ease. According to *Computerworld Premier 100,* Dow ranks high in the use of information systems.

The *Computerworld* ranking is based on six criteria:

1. Information systems (IS) budget as a percentage of annual revenue (compared with industry averages from a survey of Fortune 1,000 companies).
2. Currentness of equipment (measured by the market value of systems as a percentage of total revenue).
3. Five-year company profitability, recognizing the relationship of IS and business performance.
4. Management of staff costs, with more points going to the companies with lower staff costs.
5. Commitment to training staff in computer procedures (measured by the amount of IS budget allowed for the training).
6. Ability to provide user access to technology, (measured as a ratio of PCs and terminals to total employees).

All of the criteria are given weight factors in evaluation.

Dow ranked favorably in each area. Its IS budget runs over $300 million. Its IS strategy combines data center consolidation and global systems integration toward the goal of improving customer service.

A Dow salesperson anywhere in the world can find out almost instantly what is available from any Dow facility through their worldwide network.

Almost all of Dow's employees worldwide have an electronic mail (E-mail) address, and almost half of these are active users. The E-mail network is considered to be the prototype for the new customer-oriented systems that Dow is initiating. Dow is beginning a five-year program to enable its salespeople to access relevant business information in any Dow data base throughout the world. The program would create a centralized order service for the company's units worldwide. It should simplify order entry, order management, and inventory control from IBM mainframes that are accessible from desktop computers. A salesperson anywhere in the world can find out what is available from any Dow facility through a worldwide network based on IBM's Systems Network Architecture and Token-Ring and Digital Equipment Corporation's Decnet.

This system helps Dow's customers obtain reliable information for making decisions and purchasing materials by "just-in-time" guidelines. Customers can deal with one Dow person who has access to all the information needed for placing an order, rather than dealing with a salesperson, an inventory person, and someone in marketing who knows the prices of each item. The salesperson can quote current inventory, prices, and the best available shipping methods by accessing the data base with either Apple Macintosh or IBM personal computers.

Dow's managers use the IS system on a regular basis. Through the worldwide system, they gain knowledge of Dow's operations in Canada, Europe, Latin America, and Asia. The system helps managers track orders, plan manufacturing schedules and goals, and maintain relations with suppliers.

The company has consolidated three U.S. data centers into one and integrated two data centers in Brazil. This consolidation will give Dow greater control over global operations and costs. In developing its customer service systems and IS systems, the company plans to take advantage of the many innovative hardware and software products on the market rather than developing the program completely in-house.

DISCUSSION POINTS

1. Name several criteria that would help a company evaluate its use of information systems.
2. How does Dow's IS system help both Dow and its customers?

System Software

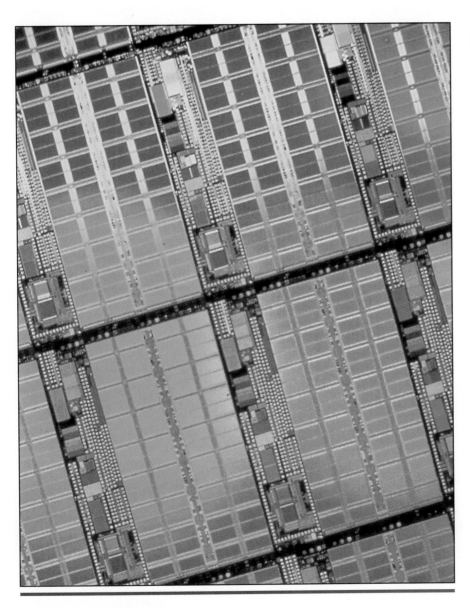

ARTICLE

Fishing Around with Virtual Computing

Maryfran Johnson, *Computerworld*

Imagine that the machine on your desktop was capable of changing identities on command—one minute an IBM Personal Computer, the next minute an Apple Macintosh.

Impossible, right? Those processor chips with their myriad functions were etched into silicon back at the factory. That's why they call it hardware.

Well, swing off the logic gate into the abstract world of virtual computers, where the boundaries of software encroach on hardware's territory, and the rules of the game can be changed.

"The idea behind a virtual computer is basically taking the notion of software to its logical extreme," said Brian Silverman, director of research at Logo Computer Systems, Inc. in Montreal. Silverman is the author of Phantom Fish Tank, a $30 recreational software package that allows users to design a two-dimensional virtual computer on their PC screen and then watch it in action.

The screen of Phantom Fish Tank is divided into 1,600 tiny cells or squares—cellular automata—that represent the logic gates on a silicon chip. Each cell is in either an "input" or "output" state and by following a few simple rules can change its state (and color) with each tick of the computer clock.

The whimsical name of the program, which runs on IBM Personal Computers, PC-compatibles and Apple Computer, Inc. IIs, refers to the strange undulating patterns made by the cellular automata as they move around the screen.

A FUZZY LINE

That imaginary PC-to-Macintosh quick-change act described above is one way Silverman explains what virtual computing may one day accomplish.

"That hardware/software boundary could be pushed back a little," he said. "The stuff people think of as hardware could itself be implemented in software."

Another way to think about the possibilities of virtual computing is

to picture the grid of a silicon chip as a city map, with roads and intersections etched in concrete. "Now imagine that instead of something solid, you could make it in more reshapeable materials," he explained. "When you graphically changed the map, you would change the function or direction of the road."

The Phantom Fish Tank is more a "proof of concept" than a serious demonstration of virtual computing, Silverman emphasized, and practical uses for virtual computers are at least a decade away.

Still, the game seems to appeal to a diverse collection of users. The software designer remembers one particular day when two teachers told him how useful they found Phantom Fish Tank in their philosophy discussions with their classes. "What grade do you teach?" he asked them.

"Graduate school," the first teacher said.

"Third grade," the other replied.

■ INTRODUCTION

The computer is a powerful machine that can be used to solve a variety of problems. Previous chapters have covered the major hardware components of a computer system and have shown how these components are used to store and process data and generate information. However, the computer cannot solve problems without using programs. Programming is a critical step in data processing. If the computer is not correctly programmed, it cannot deliver the needed information. This chapter explains the differences between system programs and application programs and discusses the various functions performed by operating system software. The chapter also describes some of the more advanced software developments that have been made in recent years. The concepts of multiprogramming and multiprocessing are introduced, and the use of virtual storage to overcome memory limitations is discussed.

■ CATEGORIES OF PROGRAMS

Despite the apparent complexity and power of the computer, it is merely a tool manipulated by humans. It requires step-by-step instructions to reach a solution to a problem. As stated earlier, this series of instructions is known as a program, and the individual who creates the program is the programmer. There are two basic categories of programs: (1) **system programs,** which coordinate the operation of computer circuitry and assist in the development of application programs; and (2) **application programs,** which solve particular user problems.

System Programs

System programs directly affect the operation of the computer. They are designed to facilitate the efficient use of the computer's resources and aid in the development and execution of application programs. For example, one system program allocates storage for data being entered into the system; another system program instructs output to be sent to the appropriate device such as a line printer. We have already seen that computers differ in memory capacity, in the methods used to store and code data, and in the number of instructions they can perform. Consequently, system programs are written specifically for a particular type of computer and cannot be used (without modification) on different machines.

A system programmer maintains the system programs in good running order and tailors them, when necessary, to meet organizational requirements. Because system programmers serve as a bridge between the computer and application programmers, they must have the technical background needed to understand the complex internal operations of the computer. Because each organization uses a different set of application programs, system programs must be modified to execute the needed application programs in the most efficient manner and obtain the resulting information in an appropriate form.

System programs are normally provided by the computer manufacturer or a specialized programming firm. Thus, they are initially written in a general fashion to meet as many user requirements as possible. However, they can be modified, or tailored, to meet a particular organization's specific needs.

Application Programs

Application programs perform specific data-processing or computational tasks to solve an organization's information needs. They can be developed within the organization or purchased from software firms. Typical examples of application programs are those used in inventory control and accounting; in banks, application programs update checking and savings account balances.

The job of the application programmer is to use the capabilities of the computer to solve specific problems. A programmer need not have an in-depth knowledge of the computer to write application programs. Instead, the programmer concentrates on the particular problem to be solved. If the problem is clearly defined and understood, the task of writing a program to solve it is greatly simplified. Application software will be discussed in greater detail in Chapter 13.

▢ OPERATING SYSTEMS

In early computer systems, human operators monitored computer operations, determined the order (or priority) in which submitted programs were run, and readied input and output devices. While early electronic development increased the processing speeds of CPUs, the speed of human operators remained constant. Time delays and errors caused by human operator intervention became a serious problem.

Development of Operating Systems

In the 1960s, operating systems were developed to help overcome this problem. An **operating system** consists of an integrated collection of system programs that control the functions of the CPU, input and output, and storage facilities of the system. This portion of the operating system is often referred to as the supervisor, monitor, executive, or resource manager. By performing these tasks, the operating system provides an interface between the user or the application program and the computer hardware. Concept Summary 10–1 shows the relationship among the user, operating system, and computer hardware.

Functions of Operating Systems

The functions of an operating system are geared toward attaining maximum efficiency in processing operations. As already mentioned, eliminating human intervention is one method. Allowing several programs to share computer resources is another; the operating system allocates these resources to the programs requesting them and resolves conflicts that occur when, for example, two or three programs request the use of the same tape drive or memory locations. In addition, the operating system performs an accounting function; it keeps track of the computer system's resources that are used and who is using them. This is done so that user fees can be calculated and so the efficiency of the computer system can be determined.

Another important function performed by the operating system is scheduling jobs on a priority basis. Although it may seem logical to run programs in the order in which they are submitted, this is not always the most practical approach. For instance, assume that five programs are submitted for processing within a short period of time. Suppose one program requires one minute of CPU time and the other four require one hour each. It may be reasonable to process the short program first. Or suppose one program will produce a vital report and the output of the others is less important.

Relationships Among User, Operating System, and Computer Hardware

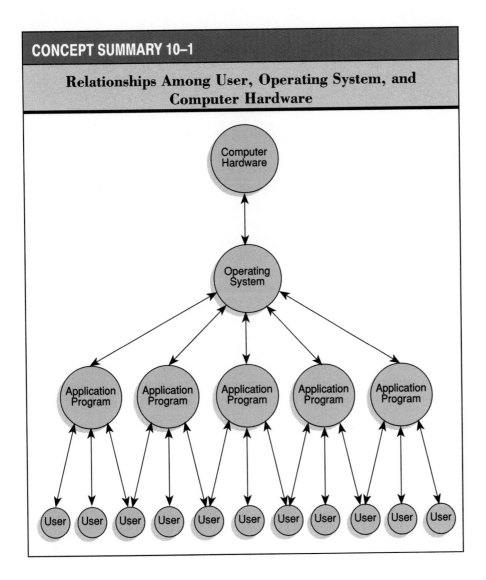

The more important program should probably be processed first. A system of priorities can be established based on considerations such as the required processing time and the need for the expected output.

Types of Processing Handled by Operating Systems

There are two basic types of operating systems: batch and online. In a batch operating system user programs ("jobs") are grouped into a batch to be processed one after the other in a continuous stream. For example, in the morning an operator may load all jobs to be processed during the day onto a tape. The batch operating system will direct processing without interruption until all jobs on the tape are completed, thus freeing the operator to perform other tasks.

An online operating system can respond to spontaneous requests for system resources, such as management inquiries entered from online terminals.

Operating systems currently in use can handle both batch and online applications simultaneously. These operating systems direct the processing of a job but also respond to **interrupts** from I/O devices such as online terminals (or workstations), printers, and storage devices which communicate with the CPU through the operating system. When an I/O device sends a message to the CPU, normal processing is suspended (the CPU is interrupted) so that the CPU may direct the operation of the I/O device. It is the function of the operating system, therefore, to manage the resources of the CPU in its handling of batch and online processing and its control of peripheral devices.

Components of Operating Systems

As previously mentioned an operating system is an integrated collection of system programs. Each program performs specific duties. Because all operating system programs work as a "team," CPU idle time is avoided and utilization of computer facilities is increased. Operating system programs are kept online on a storage device known as the **system residence device.** The storage media most commonly used are magnetic tape drives (TOS—tape operating system) and magnetic disk drives (DOS—disk operating system). Magnetic-drum technology has the fastest processing time, but many existing operating systems use magnetic-disk technology.

Two types of programs make up the operating system: **control programs** and **processing programs.** Control programs oversee system operations and perform tasks such as input/output, scheduling, handling interrupts, and communicating with the computer operator or programmer. They make certain that computer resources are used efficiently. Processing programs are used by programmers to aid in the development of application and system programs.

CONTROL PROGRAMS. The **supervisor program** (also called the **monitor** or **executive**), the major component of the operating system, coordinates the activities of all other parts of the operating system. When the computer is first put into use the supervisor is the first program to be transferred into memory from the system residence device. Only the most frequently used components of the supervisor are initially loaded into memory. These components are referred to as **resident routines,** because they remain in memory as long as the computer is running. Certain other supervisor routines known as **transient routines** remain on the storage device with the remainder of the operating system. Resident routines call for these transient routines as needed and load them into memory. The supervisor schedules I/O operations and allocates communication channels to various I/O devices. It also sends messages to the computer operator indicating the status of particular jobs, error conditions, and so forth. Figure 10–1 illustrates how supervisor routines control access to the programs on the system residence device.

The operating system requires job-control information in order to instruct it as to how a particular job is to be carried out. (A *job* is a task to be processed by the CPU.) A **job-control language (JCL)** serves as the communication link between the programmer and the operating system. Job-control languages are typically used in conjunction with the batch oriented portion of operating systems.

The term JCL was introduced by IBM; however, nearly all systems have a job-control language to instruct the computer system on how particular jobs should be carried out. A JCL can be a very complex language with a large number of commands. Although other manufacturers have different names for their job-control languages, the term JCL has become so widely accepted that programmers generally use it to refer to any type of job-control language, regardless of the system.

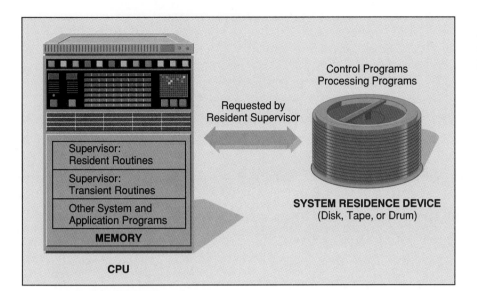

FIGURE 10–1

Operating System in Memory and
System Residence Device

In a batch operating system, job-control statements must be placed at the beginning of the job. These statements identify such things as the beginning of the job, the user, and the specific program to be executed, describe the work to be done, and indicate the I/O devices required. The **job-control program** translates the job-control statements written by a programmer into machine-language instructions that can be executed by the computer.

In most computer systems, the data to be processed is kept on storage media such as magnetic tape or disk. On these systems, job-control statements and programs often are entered from a source other than that on which the data files are stored. For example, the JCL and program may be entered as a series of statements from magnetic tape, as shown in Figure 10–2a. Among other things, these JCL statements must specify which data files and I/O devices are required by the program.

On other systems, programs and data are read into memory from the same device used to submit the JCL (see Figure 10–2b). No additional I/O devices are required, but this is not an efficient method for processing large programs or data files. It is most often used when programs are being tested, before they are stored on a secondary-storage medium. Figure 10–3 shows a sample JCL used to translate a COBOL program into machine-readable form (that is, the 1s and 0s that the computer is capable of executing), which reads program data, processes the data, and then sends the results to a line printer.

The first statement uniquely identifies the job and indicates what system message will be displayed concerning the translation. The second statement identifies the particular step of the overall job and invokes the COBOL language translator program. Although this JCL contains only one step, multiple steps can be contained in a single job, as demonstrated in Figure 10–2. The third statement identifies the beginning of the COBOL source program, and the fourth statement identifies the beginning of the program data. The source program would be placed between statements three and four and the data between statements four and five. Statement five defines the master file to be used, which in this case is a disk file. The final statement simply identifies the line printer as the output device.

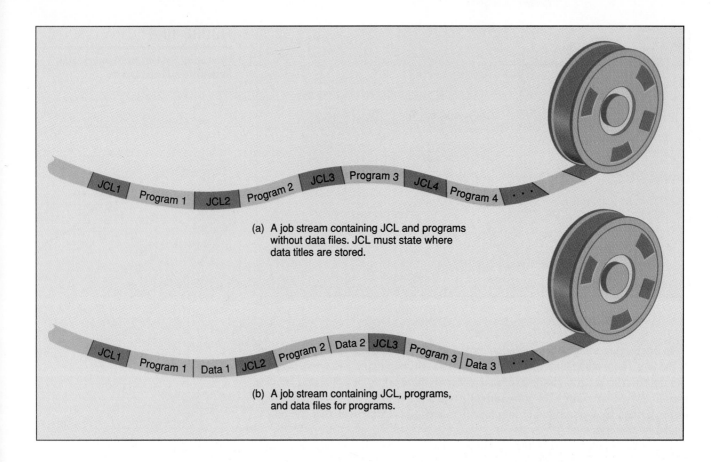

(a) A job stream containing JCL and programs without data files. JCL must state where data titles are stored.

(b) A job stream containing JCL, programs, and data files for programs.

FIGURE 10–2

Continuous Job Streams for a Batch Processing System

A job is often thought of as a single program entered by a user into the computer. In fact, most data-processing jobs require the execution of many related programs. Thus, several job-control statements would be needed to indicate which operations should be performed and the devices needed to perform them.

The control programs of the operating system must be able to control and coordinate the CPU while receiving input from communication channels, executing instructions of programs in memory and regulating output. I/O devices must be assigned to specific programs and data must be moved between them and specific memory locations. The **input/output management system** oversees and coordinates these processes.

FIGURE 10–3

Sample JCL

```
//PAY JOB ACCT, '***PAYROLL***', MSGLEVEL=(1,1)
//STEP1 EXEC COBVCG
//COB. SYSIN DD *

//GO. SYSIN DD *

//GO.FILE1 DD DSN=MASTER.FILE , DISP = SHR
//GO.OUTPUT DD SYSOUT=A
```

Why Are Open Systems Important?

What, you ask, *is* an open system? Not yet in existence, but envisioned, it is a computer operating system that would run on different types and even different brands of computer hardware. For example, a true open operating system could be used on a microcomputer, on a minicomputer, or even on a mainframe. In addition, it could be used on computer systems manufactured by any number of hardware manufacturers. The advantages to using open operating systems are legion. This is why the concept excites computer users and manufacturers.

An open system provides application software developers a consistent environment for which to create new applications. Developers know no matter what type or brand of computer the application will be running on, their package will work. This provides two key advantages. The first is that the time it takes to develop application software for various systems will be significantly cut. (Today, it is not uncommon to have to reprogram an application in order to move it from one operating

system to another.) The second advantage is that, under open systems, users would be provided with a user interface and applications that have a consistent look and feel, no matter what computers they are using. Such a familiar feel would reduce—if not eliminate—the lag in productivity and user enjoyment when an individual or company switches from one brand of hardware to another.

Open operating systems have been discussed for years. It now appears that some of the goals of open systems are being realized. IBM continues to develop and improve its Systems Application Architecture (SAA), which it designed to allow IBM mainframes, minis and micros to be connected together in networks. The goal of SAA is to provide IBM computer users with a consistent user interface and consistent applications no matter what IBM computer they are using on the network.

In addition, IBM and a number of other computer manufacturers and software developers have formed the Open Software Foundation (OSF).

This organization's intent is to set standards for the development of both operating systems and application software. Their hope is that adherence to these standards by hardware manufacturers and software developers will eventually lead to open operating systems.

The increased use and acceptance of the UNIX operating system has also helped to emphasize the benefits of an open operating system. UNIX is currently available for use on microcomputers and minicomputers built by a wide variety of computer manufacturers. UNIX is not currently available for all categories of computers and it is also not quite implemented uniformly on all the computer systems where it is used. However, the fact that applications developed for the UNIX operating system can easily be moved from one type or one brand of computer to another is proof that the basic open systems concepts are sound. Thus the movement toward open operating systems, with all the benefits they bring, inches forward.

PROCESSING PROGRAMS. The operating system contains several processing programs that facilitate efficient processing operations by simplifying program preparation and execution for users. The major processing programs contained in the operating system are the language translators, linkage editor, library programs, and utility programs. Language translators, linkage editors, and library programs will be discussed in greater detail in Chapter 12.

Operating systems also include a set of **utility programs** that perform specialized functions. One such program transfers data from file to file, or from one I/O device to another. For example, a utility program can be used to transfer data from tape to tape, tape to disk, disk to tape, or tape/disk to printer. Other utility programs known as **sort/merge programs** are used to sort records into a particular sequence to facilitate the updating of files. Once sorted, several files can be merged to form a single, updated file. Job-control statements are used to specify the sort/merge program to be accessed; these programs or routines are then called into memory when needed. See Concept Summary 10–2 for a summary of the types and purposes of operating system programs.

CONCEPT SUMMARY 10–2	
Types of Operating System Programs	
Control Programs	**Purpose**
Supervisor program	Coordinates activities of all other parts of the operating system
Job-control program	Translates job-control statements into machine language
I/O management system	Coordinates the CPU while receiving input, executing instructions, and regulating output
Processing Programs	**Purpose**
Utility programs	Perform specialized functions such as transferring data from one file to another
Sort/merge programs	Perform tasks such as sorting files into a particular order and merging several files into a single file.

ADDITIONAL SOFTWARE. As mentioned at the beginning of the chapter, system programs are available from a variety of sources. Each data-processing department must decide which system programs should be included in its operating system. The original operating system is usually obtained from the manufacturer of the CPU. However, in some cases alternative operating systems can be purchased from software vendors.

Once the essential operating system has been purchased, optional programs may be obtained. These programs can either improve an existing operating system or provide additional capabilities to the existing operating system. For example, the operating system for a bank's computer might be supplemented with a program to interface with MICR equipment (discussed in Chapter 4). Applications requiring the use of light pens with display terminals also demand special system programs.

■ MULTIPROGRAMMING

When the CPU is very active, the system as a whole is more efficient. However, the CPU frequently must remain idle because I/O devices are not fast enough. The CPU can operate on only one instruction at a time; furthermore, it cannot operate on data that is not in memory. If an input device is slow in providing data or instructions, the CPU must wait until I/O operations have been completed before executing a program.

In the earliest computer systems with simple operating systems, most programs were executed using **serial processing:** one at a time, one after the other. Serial processing was highly inefficient because the high-speed CPU was idle for long periods of time as slow input devices loaded data or output devices printed or stored the results.

Multiprogramming, or **multitasking,** increases CPU active time by effectively allocating computer resources and offsetting low I/O speeds. Under multiprogramming, several programs reside in memory at the same time. Although the CPU still can execute only one instruction at a time, it can execute instructions from one program, then another, then another, and back to the first again. Instructions from one program are executed until an interrupt for either input or output is generated. While the I/O operation is handled by a communication channel, the CPU can shift its attention to another program in memory until that program requires input or output. This rotation occurs so quickly that the execution of the programs appears to be simultaneous. More precisely, the CPU executes the different programs **concurrently** which, in this context, is used to mean "within the same time interval." Figure 10–4 illustrates this process.

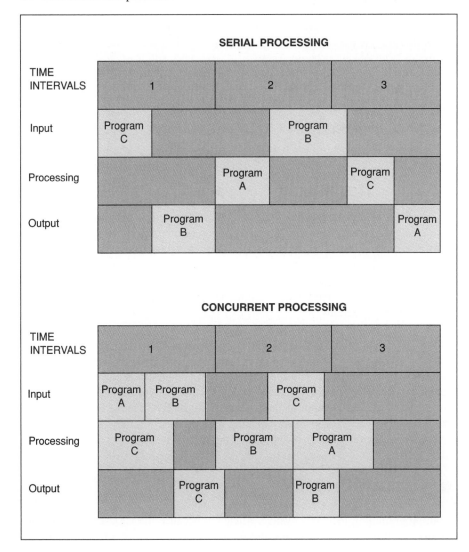

FIGURE 10–4

Comparison of Serial Processing and Concurrent Processing

Although multiprogramming increases the system's flexibility and efficiency, it also creates some problems. First, the programs in memory must be kept separate. This is accomplished through the use of **regions** or **partitions.** Keeping programs in the correct region or partition is known as **memory management** or **memory protection.** A similar situation exists with I/O devices—two programs cannot access the same tape or disk drive at the same time. These problems are handled by operating system control programs.

A second problem that arises with multiprogramming is the need to schedule programs to determine which will receive service first. This requires that each program be assigned a priority. For large systems, scheduling is not a simple task. Two programs of the same priority may request CPU resources at the same time. The method of deciding which program gets control first may be arbitrary; for example, the program that has been in memory longer may receive control first. Fortunately, the operating system is capable of handling such problems as they occur and in most instances makes the process of multiprogramming invisible to the user.

■ VIRTUAL MEMORY

Multiprogramming increases system efficiency because the CPU can execute programs concurrently instead of waiting for I/O operations to occur. A limitation of multiprogramming, however, is that each partition must be large enough to hold an entire program; the program remains in memory until its execution is completed. Therefore, all the instructions of a program are kept in memory throughout its execution. As processing requirements increase, the physical limitations of memory become a critical constraint and the productive use of memory becomes increasingly important.

For many years, the space limitations of memory were a barrier to applications. Programmers spent much time trying to find ways to trim the size of programs so that they could fit into the available memory space. In some cases, attempts were made to segment programs (break them into separate modules) so that they could be executed in separate job steps; but doing this manually is both tedious and time consuming. While hardware costs have decreased and memory capacities have increased, this memory problem still exists in high-volume processing·systems that require large programs.

To alleviate the problem, an extension of multiprogramming called **virtual memory** (sometimes called **virtual storage**) has been developed. Virtual memory is based on the principle that only the immediately needed portion of a program must be in memory at any given time; the rest of the program and data can be kept in storage. Since only part of a program is in memory at one time, more programs can reside in memory simultaneously, allowing more programs to be executed within a given time interval. Using virtual memory gives the system the ability to treat storage as if it were merely an extension of memory. This technique gives the illusion that memory is unlimited, or "virtual."

To implement virtual memory, a direct-access storage device such as a magnetic-disk drive is used to augment memory. The term **real memory** is usually given to memory within the CPU, while virtual memory refers to the direct-access storage (see Figure 10–5). Both real and virtual memory locations are given addresses by the operating system. If data or instructions needed are not in the real memory area, the portion of the program containing them is transferred from virtual memory into real memory, while another portion currently in real memory may be written back to virtual memory. This process is known as **swapping.** If the portion of the program in real memory has not been modified during execution, the portion from virtual memory may be simply laid over it, because copies of all parts of the program are kept in virtual memory.

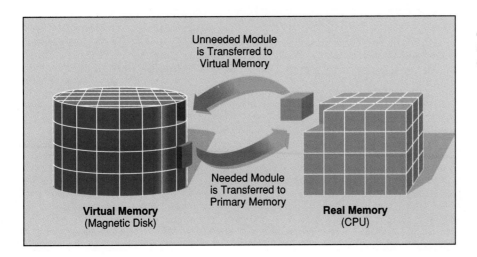

Virtual Memory
(Magnetic Disk)

Unneeded Module
is Transferred to
Virtual Memory

Needed Module
is Transferred to
Primary Memory

Real Memory
(CPU)

FIGURE 10–5

Schematic Drawing of Virtual Memory and Swapping

There are two main methods of implementing virtual-memory systems, both of which use a combination of hardware and software to accomplish the task. The first method is called **segmentation.** Each program is broken into variable-sized blocks called **segments,** which are logical parts of the program. For example, one segment may contain data used by the program; another segment may contain a **subroutine** of the program; and so on. The operating system software allocates memory according to the size of these logical segments.

A second method of implementing virtual storage is called **paging.** Here, memory is divided into physical areas of fixed size called **page frames.** All page frames for all programs are the same size, and this size depends on the characteristics of the particular computer. In contrast to segmentation, paging does not consider the logical portions of the programs. Instead, the programs are broken into equal-sized blocks called **pages.** One page can fit in one page frame of memory (see Figure 10–6).

In both paging and segmentation, the operating system handles the swapping of pages or segments whenever a portion of the program that is not in real memory is needed during processing.

Virtual memory offers tremendous flexibility to programmers and system analysts designing new applications; they can devote their time to solving the problem at hand rather than fitting programs into memory. Moreover, as already explained, the use of memory is optimized, because only needed portions of programs are in memory at any given time.

One of the major limitations of virtual storage is the requirement for extensive online storage. Also, the virtual-storage operating system is highly sophisticated and requires significant amounts of memory itself. If virtual storage is not used wisely,

FIGURE 10–6

Paging

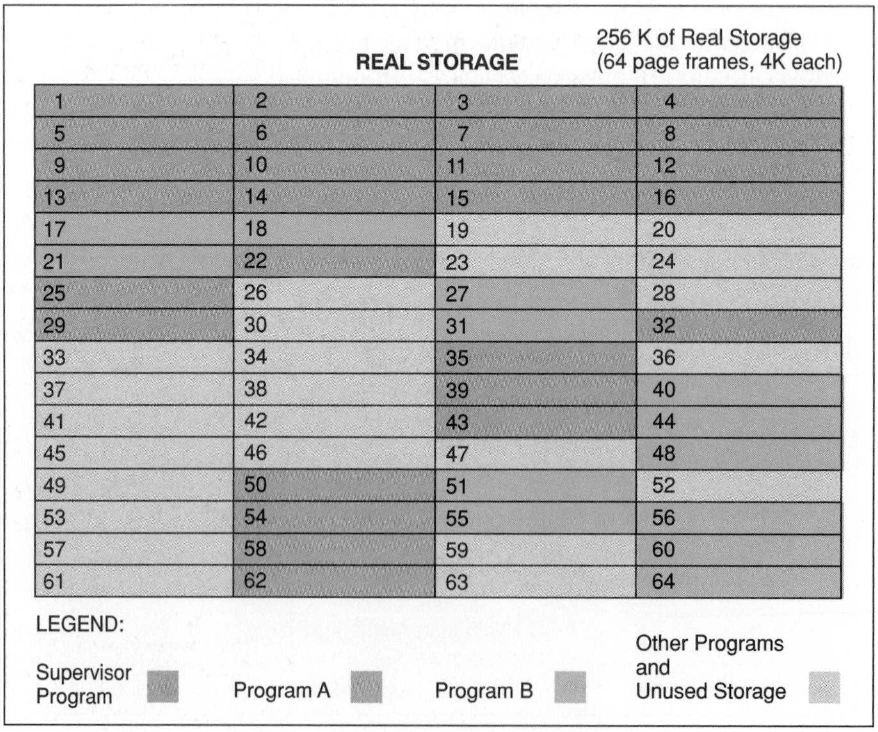

REAL STORAGE			256 K of Real Storage (64 page frames, 4K each)
1	2	3	4
5	6	7	8
9	10	11	12
13	14	15	16
17	18	19	20
21	22	23	24
25	26	27	28
29	30	31	32
33	34	35	36
37	38	39	40
41	42	43	44
45	46	47	48
49	50	51	52
53	54	55	56
57	58	59	60
61	62	63	64

LEGEND:

Supervisor Program ▦   Program A ▦   Program B ▦   Other Programs and Unused Storage ▦

much time can be spent locating and changing program pages or segments; in some programs, little actual processing occurs compared with the amount of swapping. (This is known as **thrashing.**)

◼ MULTIPROCESSING

Multiprocessing involves the use of two or more CPUs linked together for coordinated operation. Stored-program instructions are executed simultaneously, but by different CPUs. The CPUs may execute different instructions from the same program, or they may execute totally different programs. (In contrast, under multiprogramming, the computer appears to be processing different jobs simultaneously but is actually processing them concurrently, or within a given time interval.)

Multiprocessing systems are designed to achieve a particular objective. One common objective is to relieve a large CPU of tasks such as scheduling, editing data, and maintaining files so that it can continue high-priority or complex processing without interruption. To achieve this goal, a small CPU is linked to the large CPU. All work coming into the system from remote terminals or other peripheral devices is first channeled through the small CPU, which coordinates the activities of the large one. Generally, the small CPU handles all I/O interrupts and so on, while the large CPU handles the "number crunching" (large mathematical calculations). A schematic diagram of this type of multiprocessing system is shown in Figure 10–7. The small CPU in Figure 10–7 is commonly referred to as a **front-end processor.** It is an interface between the large CPU and peripheral devices such as online terminals.

A small CPU may also be used as an interface between a large CPU and a large data base stored on direct-access storage devices. In this case, the small CPU, often termed a **back-end processor,** is solely responsible for maintaining the data base. Accessing data and updating specific data fields are typical functions that a small CPU performs in this type of multiprocessing system.

Many large multiprocessing systems have two or more large CPUs. These large CPUs are no different from those used in single-CPU (stand-alone) configurations. Each may have its own separate memory, or a single memory may be shared by all of them. The activities of each CPU can be controlled in whole or in part by a common supervisor program. This type of system is used by organizations with extremely large and complex data-processing needs. Each large CPU may be dedicated to a specific task such as I/O processing or arithmetic processing. One CPU can be set up to handle online processing while another handles only batch processing. Alternately, two CPUs may be used together on the same task to provide rapid responses in the most demanding applications. Many multiprocessing systems are designed so that one or more of the CPUs can provide backup if another malfunctions. A configuration that uses multiple large CPUs is depicted in Figure 10–8. This system also uses a small CPU to control communications with peripheral devices and perform "housekeeping chores" (input editing, validation, and the like).

Coordinating the efforts of several CPUs requires highly sophisticated software and careful planning. The scheduling of workloads for the CPUs involves making the most efficient use of computer resources. Implementing such a system is a time-consuming endeavor that may require the services of outside consultants as well as those provided by the equipment manufacturers. The payoff from this effort is a system with capabilities extending far beyond those of a single-CPU system. See Concept Summary 10–3 for a review of multiprogramming, virtual storage, and multiprocessing.

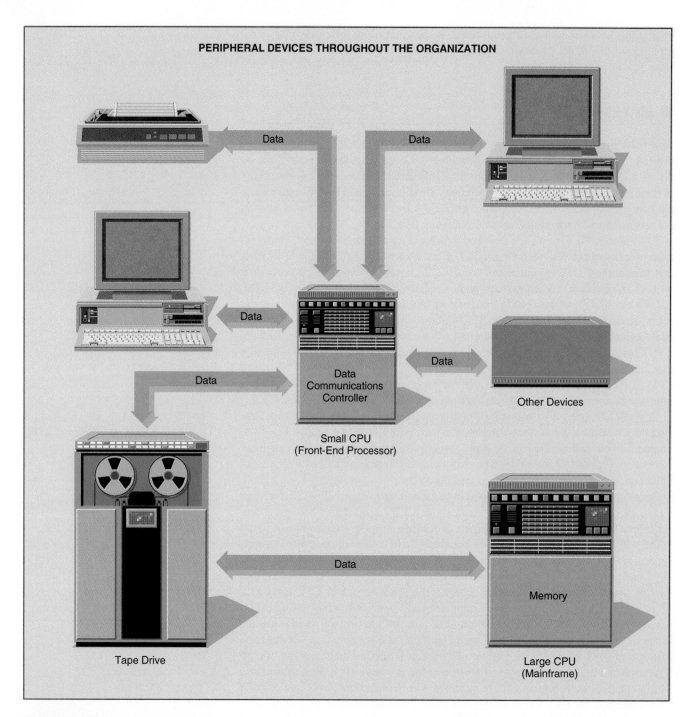

PERIPHERAL DEVICES THROUGHOUT THE ORGANIZATION

Data

Data

Data

Data

Other Devices

Data
Communications
Controller

Small CPU
(Front-End Processor)

Data

Tape Drive

Memory

Large CPU
(Mainframe)

FIGURE 10–7

**Multiprocessing System with Small
Front-End Processor and Large
Mainframe**

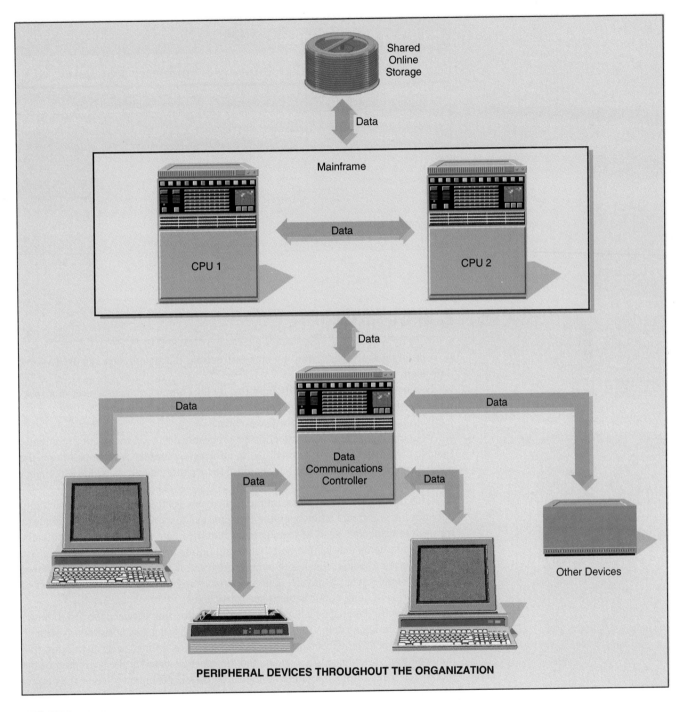

Shared Online Storage

Data

Mainframe

Data

CPU 1

CPU 2

Data

Data Communications Controller

Data

Data

Data

Data

Other Devices

PERIPHERAL DEVICES THROUGHOUT THE ORGANIZATION

FIGURE 10–8

Multiprocessing System Using Multiple Large CPUs

CONCEPT SUMMARY 10–3

Developments that Improved Computer Efficiency

Multiprogramming	Virtual Storage	Multiprocessing
Involves storing several programs in memory at one time.	Involves use of pages or segments of a program	Involves use of two or more CPUs linked together
Processes programs concurrently (that is, within a given time interval) by shifting back and forth among programs	Only needed portions of program reside in memory, giving illusion that memory is unlimited	Stored-program instructions are executed simultaneously

◘ SUMMARY POINTS

■ A program is a series of step-by-step instructions that a computer can use to solve a problem.

■ System programs are generally provided by the computer manufacturer or a specialized programming firm. Application programs can be developed within the organization or purchased from a software firm.

■ An operating system is a collection of programs designed to permit a computer system to manage its own operations. It allocates computer resources among the users, keeps track of all information required for accounting purposes, and establishes job priorities.

■ Batch operating systems allow uninterrupted processing of a batch of jobs without operator intervention. Online operating systems can respond to spontaneous requests for system resources, such as management inquiries entered from online terminals. Operating systems that handle both batch and online applications are standard.

■ An operating system consists of control programs and processing programs stored on the system residence device. The supervisor program, the major component of the operating system, controls the other subsystems.

■ A job-control language (JCL) is the communication link between the programmer and the operating system. Job-control statements instruct the operating system in how the job is to be executed. When using batch processing, each instruction that the operating system needs to execute the job must be stated at the beginning of the job. When using online operating systems, the user is prompted to enter the correct operating instruction when it is needed.

■ The input/output management system is part of the operating system control programs. It receives input from communication channels, regulates output, assigns I/O devices to specific programs, and coordinates all I/O activities.

■ Utility programs perform specialized functions like sorting and merging and transferring data from one I/O device to another.

■ Operating systems can be configured in a modular fashion by the addition of components to the original operating system.

■ The CPU may be idle for a significant amount of time because of the speed disparity between the CPU and the I/O devices. Multiprogramming is used to increase the efficiency of CPU utilization through the use of concurrent processing.

■ With multiprogramming several programs reside in memory at the same time. Instructions from one program are executed until an interrupt for either input or output is generated. Then the CPU shifts its attention to another program in memory until that program requires input or output.

■ When multiprogramming is used, the programs in memory are kept separate by use of partitions or regions. Memory protection and a method of assigning priorities to programs are required.

■ Multiprogramming is limited by memory space; a complete program may not fit into a partition. These problems are alleviated by the use of virtual memory.

■ Virtual memory involves loading only the part of a program needed in memory, while keeping the remainder of the program in storage. This technique gives the illusion that memory is unlimited.

■ Segmentation is a method of implementing virtual memory whereby each program is broken into segments of variable size. Each segment is a logical subunit of the complete program. Paging, another method of implementing virtual memory, uses equal-sized blocks called pages without considering logical parts of the program.

■ Multiprocessing involves the use of two or more CPUs linked together for co-ordinated operation. Separate programs or separate parts of the same program can be processed simultaneously by different CPUs.

■ Small computers can be linked to mainframes as either front-end processors or back-end processors. The former act as interfaces between the CPU and the I/O devices; the latter act as interfaces between large CPUs and data bases stored on direct-access storage devices.

■ Large CPUs can be linked together to handle extremely large and complex data-processing needs. Each CPU may be assigned to a specific task, or it may be used with other CPUs on the same task to provide rapid response.

■ TERMS FOR REVIEW

application program, p. 253

back-end processor, p. 265

concurrently, p. 261

control program, p. 256

front-end processor, p. 265

input/output management system,
    p. 258

interrupt, p. 256

job-control language (JCL), p. 256

job-control program, p. 257

memory management (memory
    protection), p. 262

multiprogramming (multitasking),
    p. 261

operating system, p. 254

pages, p. 264

page frame, p. 264

paging, p. 264

processing program, p. 256

real memory, p. 263

region (partition), p. 262

resident routine, p. 256

segment, p. 264

segmentation, p. 264

serial processing, p. 261

sort/merge program, p. 259

subroutine, p. 264

supervisor program (monitor or
    executive), p. 256

swapping, p. 263

system program, p. 253

◼ REVIEW QUESTIONS

1. How do system programs and application programs differ?

2. Why were operating systems developed? What is the name given to the portion of the operating system that controls the CPU, input and output, and storage?

3. What is the primary objective of an operating system? How does it accomplish this objective?

4. Briefly explain the differences between batch and online operating systems.

5. What two types of programs comprise an operating system? Give a brief description of each type.

6. What is a job-control language (JCL)?

7. What types of programs are considered operating system processing programs? Describe some of the tasks performed by operating system utility programs.

8. Compare multiprogramming to multiprocessing. Include within your comparison a brief definition of each.

9. Why are regions or partitions an important aspect of multiprogramming?

10. Describe the basic concept behind virtual memory. Why is it necessary?

Microsoft Corporation

The microcomputer industry began in the mid-1970s and since then has experienced rapid growth. Most visible have been the successes of various hardware suppliers—Apple Computer, Tandy Corporation, and IBM, to name but a few. It was the marked achievements of these suppliers that stimulated the development of a number of related businesses—most notably companies that designed and manufactured software to run on the new machines. One of these software companies was Microsoft Corporation.

EARLY DEVELOPMENTS
Founded in 1974, Microsoft Corporation has quickly become the largest developer of software for microcomputers in the United States, establishing itself as a pioneer. Since 1977, sales have increased dramatically and staffing has jumped from 5 persons to some 5,200 employees. Corporate headquarters in Redmond, Washington, occupy a 53-acre site that resembles a college campus.

Beginning with Microsoft's initial product, the first BASIC language for microcomputers (still an industry standard), the company established a reputation for developing innovative, state-of-the-art products. One of the most notable features of Microsoft's design standards is that each new generation of software is compatible with the software of the previous generation.

Microsoft began as a partnership between William H. Gates and Paul G. Allen. It was reorganized as a privately held corporation in 1981 with Gates as executive vice president and chairman of the board and Allen as executive vice president. Jon Shirley joined the company as president in August 1983. Today, Microsoft is the leading independent software supplier of easy-to-learn and well-supported productivity tools, languages, and operating systems. Microsoft established foreign subsidiaries around the world that have contributed to making it the undisputed leader in international software, with more than 40 percent of total revenues generated outside the United States. It realized over $1 billion in revenues in 1990.

PRODUCT LINE
Most IBM Personal Computer users will recognize Microsoft as the developer of the popular computer game, Flight Simulator. Flight Simulator has become one of the best selling programs for the IBM PC. In the game, the players "pilot" an aircraft similar to a Cessna Skylane through takeoff and landing at more than 20 airports. They may alter the environment to simulate various weather conditions, as well as daytime or nighttime flight.

Microsoft does much more than develop entertainment software, however. The company has the most comprehensive range of microcomputer software products of any company in the world, maintaining a full line of language compilers, interpreters, operating systems, and business tools.

After its success in developing the first BASIC for microcomputers, Microsoft adapted Bell Labs' UNIX operating system for micros, calling it XENIX—all these triumphs even before Windows emerged.

In 1980, Microsoft licensed the UNIX operating system from Bell Labs and began to develop its own enhanced version for microcomputers, which is called XENIX. UNIX is a powerful, multi-user operating system designed for microcomputers, and Microsoft successfully adapted it, with a number of improvements, to run on the 16-bit microprocessor. With the release of the XENIX operating system, Microsoft began providing maintenance, support, and even application assistance to original equipment manufacturers and end users. As a result, Microsoft rapidly became the main supplier of a popular, standardized, high-level 16-bit operating system that was powerful and also accessible to almost every microprocessor on the market. The XENIX operating system was developed to run on multi-user computers with 16-bit microprocessors and on DEC's PDP-11 series. To date, forty companies in eight different countries have licensed XENIX.

APPLICATION
Microsoft Corporation

In 1988, Microsoft introduced an Intel 80386 based version of XENIX. An agreement between AT&T and Microsoft will permit the development of a new version of UNIX for the 80386 that will combine the best features of XENIX and AT&T System V technology. This marks the first time that AT&T has licensed its trademark UNIX.

Also in 1980, Microsoft developed and introduced the Microsoft SoftCard, a plug-in board that allowed Apple II owners access to both Microsoft BASIC and the CP/M operating system for the Zilog Z-80 microprocessor, and thereby tens of thousands of software packages. The first year on the market, Microsoft sold 25,000 units; since then SoftCard has been installed in more than 100,000 Apple systems.

Approached by IBM and working closely with them, Microsoft developed a new 16-bit operating system. When IBM introduced its personal computer in August 1981, Microsoft MS-DOS was the only operating system for which IBM provided additional software. Within a year, IBM had announced full support of twelve Microsoft products, and by June 1982, thirty other companies had released software designed to run on Microsoft MS-DOS. Since then, over 40 million copies of MS-DOS/PC-DOS have been sold. The most recent MS-DOS is version 5.0, which is easy to use, frees more memory, and enables the user to switch applications quickly.

In 1983, Microsoft introduced a low-cost, hand-held input device called the Microsoft Mouse. Mouse is small and lightweight and is used to quickly insert, delete, and reposition the cursor or blocks of text within a document without having to use the keyboard. Microsoft Mouse has been developed for use with the IBM Personal Computer and other systems that run on the MS-DOS operating system. A new mouse product, Microsoft BallPoint Mouse, is designed for use with laptop computers.

With the release of the Microsoft Mouse, Microsoft also introduced a highly sophisticated word-processing software package, Microsoft Word. Features like style sheets, footnotes, glossaries, columnar formatting, and multiple windows have helped make Word an industry leader. Typical of Microsoft's careful planning, Word was designed to take advantage of anticipated developments in computer printers by allowing users to specify not only paper and type sizes but also special character sizes, ink colors, and many different type fonts. Word has become a best seller among users of the Apple's Macintosh computer and Laserwriter printer.

Microsoft continued its expansion into application software with Excel, a complete spreadsheet with integrated business graphics and data base for both the Macintosh and IBM PC computers. The company also introduced Microsoft Works, which integrates word processing, database management, spreadsheets, and communications.

In May of 1990, Microsoft released version 3.0 of Windows. Windows, while still requiring the use of the MS-DOS or PC-DOS operating system, completely changes the user's interface with the computer. Instead of typing key commands to accomplish a task, the user works in a visual, or graphical, environment. Options are shown on the screen as icons or are listed in menus that are pulled down from a bar across the top of the screen. The user can use a mouse to manipulate the objects on the screen. In addition, Windows enables the user to use multiple applications simultaneously and cut, copy, and paste between applications.

Other software companies have adapted over 700 programs to be compatible with the Windows environment, and Microsoft itself has released versions of Word, Excel, and other programs to be used with Windows. The company is also introducing networking software usable with Windows, and PenWindows, a set of operating system extensions designed to recognize handprinted text and accept commands from gestures made with a pen or stylus.

As if these programs were not enough, Microsoft has continued in the development of computer languages. The company offers Business BASIC, Pascal, COBOL, C, and FORTRAN, as well as the new QuickBASIC. It also has released versions of BASIC (Visual Basic) and FORTRAN (Fortran Professional Development System version 5.1) that enable users to develop their own Windows applications.

Microsoft, while continuing to develop other consumer applications and tools, is committed to the philosophy of constantly improving software and developing upwardly compatible versions of all established products for the newer generations of personal computers. Its vision depends on keeping user needs at the forefront.

DISCUSSION POINTS

1. What key issues does Microsoft consider critical to software developers in the future, and why are these issues important?

2. Why is the development of standards for user interface an important consideration for a software developer?

CHAPTER 11

Software Development

An Endless Campaign to Simplify Software

Jonathan B. Levine

From his Zurich office, Niklaus Wirth can look across to the cupola of the main lecture hall at the Swiss Federal Institute of Technology, known as ETH, which is short for its name in German. For Wirth, the view is a constant reminder of a favorite maxim of Albert Einstein, who taught physics in the hall 80 years ago: "Make solutions as simple as possible, but no simpler."

If computer software is often complicated, it's not Wirth's fault. Now head of the influential computer science department at ETH, dubbed "Europe's MIT," Wirth, 56, has spent his career trying to make it simpler. Wirthian languages such as Pascal force programmers to write leaner, more bug-free programs than they do using Fortran, Cobol, and older languages. Since software glitches can cause everything from telephone network crashes to train wrecks, that's important.

Wirth never intended Pascal for the commercial market, thinking of it instead as a tool for teaching programming. But after 20 years, it is still one of the most widely used languages. That's because Pascal is particularly well suited to writing programs for microprocessors—the heart of personal computers. Because of that, thousands of young programmers have learned their trade using the language. "Niklaus changed the way people think about programming," says Philippe Kahn, a former ETH student and president of California's Borland International Inc., which has sold more than 1.5 million copies of a version of Pascal.

Wirth learned economy of design while repairing model airplanes as a boy in rural Switzerland. "If you have to pay out of your own pocket money, you learn not to make the fixes overly complicated," he says. His introduction to programming came in the early 1960s while he was earning a PhD at the University of California at Berkeley. In 1967, after a stint as one of Stanford's first computer science professors, he returned to ETH, where he devised Pascal. He named the language after the 17th century French mathematician who invented one of the first calculating machines. Wirth has since churned out many innovations.

His perennial peeve is that companies waste exorbitant sums on inefficient, bug-ridden programs. That wouldn't happen if they used more disciplined programming methods instead of older free-wheeling languages, Wirth contends. But companies stick with outdated techniques because of the huge investment they have in software and the training it takes for employees to use it.

For his latest project, Wirth and a colleague devised a warehouse of reusable software modules, from which they built a lean new operating system, or basic computer program. Known as Oberon, it gives programmers mix-and-match building blocks from which they can create complex programs faster—and with fewer bugs.

Wirth is now finishing translation software that will let Oberon run on workstations from Digital Equipment, Sun Microsystems, Apple Computer, and IBM. He wants Oberon to catch on with business so that it will have wide influence. But he has never worried much about making money. As an employee of a Swiss institution, his innovations belong to the public domain, and he doesn't profit from them. "I don't need a villa or a Porsche," he says. For Wirth, simplicity is an end in itself.

■ INTRODUCTION

Augusta Ada Byron, Countess of Lovelace, made the following statement concerning the analytical engine which she helped Charles Babbage to develop, ''The Analytical Engine has no pretensions whatever to originate anything. It can do whatever we know how to order it to perform. It can follow analysis; but it has no power of anticipating any analytical relations or truths. Its province is to assist us in making available what we are already acquainted with.''

This statement briefly explains the basic problem in programming: the programmer must know how to instruct the computer, in an ordered way, in the exact steps it must take to solve a programming problem. People often solve problems intuitively, without identifying each step they perform. Computers lack this human capability. Therefore, using a computer to help solve a problem requires planning. In the early days of the computer, the most significant changes came in the area of improvements to the hardware. Changes in the methodology of software development did not keep pace with these hardware advances. Only in recent years have the methods used to develop software become the object of intensive research. It has been determined that to efficiently develop a well-designed solution to a programming problem, four steps, collectively referred to as the **software development process,** should be followed:

1. Define and document the problem.
2. Design and document a solution.
3. Write and document the program.
4. Debug and test the program and revise the documentation if necessary.

Each of these steps will be discussed in detail in this chapter. Concept Summary 11–1 graphically portrays the steps of the software development process.

■ DEFINING AND DOCUMENTING THE PROBLEM

It is next to impossible to get somewhere if you do not know the way. Likewise, in programming, a clear and concise statement of the problem must be given before anything else is done. Despite this fact, many programming disasters have occurred because this step was glossed over. Often this situation occurs because the person who writes the program is not the same person who will be using it. Communication between these two people (or groups) can be inadequate, leading to misunderstandings concerning the desired results of the program and ultimately to programs that do not meet the user's needs. Therefore, before the project proceeds, the problem must be clearly defined and documented in writing and agreed upon by all parties involved. Because such analysis skills often differ from the skills required of a programmer, many corporations use system analysts to define and design a solution to the programming problem. The tasks of actually writing, debugging, and testing the program are then performed by members of the corporation's programming staff.

The documentation of the problem definition should include a description of:

■ *The desired output.* All output and the manner in which it is to be formatted should be described here. Formatting refers to the way in which the output is to be displayed or printed to make it easy for the user to read and use. For example, placing output in table form with appropriate headings is one way of formatting it.

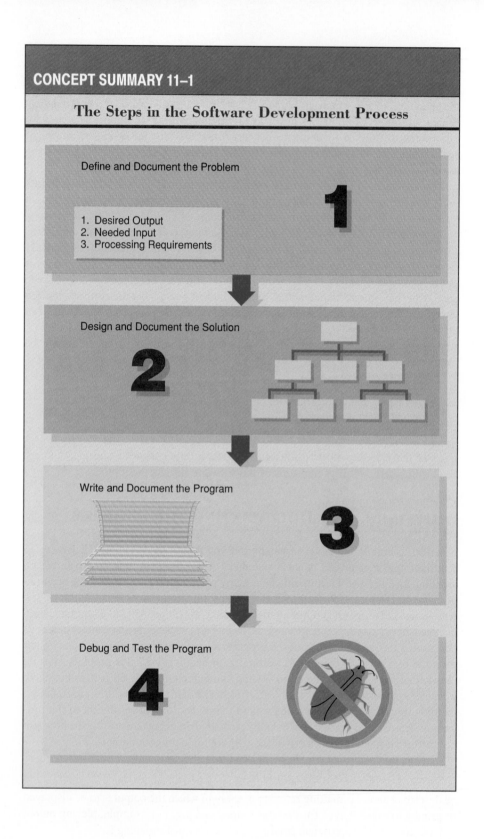

CONCEPT SUMMARY 11–1

The Steps in the Software Development Process

Define and Document the Problem

1. Desired Output
2. Needed Input
3. Processing Requirements

1

Design and Document the Solution

2

Write and Document the Program

3

Debug and Test the Program

4

■ *The input.* What data is needed to obtain the desired output? From where will this data be obtained? How will this data be formatted? The programmer or system analyst should make it as easy as possible for the user to enter the data that a program needs.

■ *The processing requirements.* Given the stated output specifications and the required input, the processing requirements can be determined.

The documentation for these three items, the input, output, and processing steps, is referred to as the **program specifications.**

As an example of this process, let's define and document a specific programming problem. The accounting department's payroll section is not functioning properly. Checks are issued late, and many are incorrect. Most of the reports to management, local and state governments, and union officials are woefully inadequate. The payroll section's personnel often work overtime to process the previous week's payroll checks.

The problem is fairly obvious—company expansion and new reporting requirements have strained the accounting department beyond its capacity. A new computerized payroll system has been suggested. Management has agreed with this assessment and has contacted the computer services department for help in solving the problem. The accounting department and computer services department, working together, have defined the problem as shown below.

Problem Definition: Write a program to process the company's payroll. This program will generate not only individual paychecks but appropriate summary reports.

Desired Output: First of all, the payroll program must issue the paychecks. It must also send a statement of weekly and monthly payroll expenses to management and an updated list of changes in employee salaries and positions to the personnel department. The local, state, and federal governments require a monthly report of income taxes withheld, and the union receives payment of employee dues deducted by the payroll section. Not only the checks but all of these reports must be printed by the program. The content and format (layout) of the reports should be determined at this time.

Needed Input: The next step in defining the problem is to determine the input needed to generate the output listed above. This input includes each employee's time card, which contains the employee number and the hours worked each day of the week. Another input, dealing with new employees and changes in pay scales, is sent by the personnel department. Supervisors provide a special form regarding employee promotions. The tax section sends updates of tax tables used to calculate local, state, and federal withholdings. The union provides information about the withholding of union dues. The format and content of the forms used for input must also be determined as part of the process of identifying the needed input.

Processing Requirements: Given the needed output and input, the processing required of the new computerized payroll system is illustrated in Figure 11–1. First, each employee's gross pay must be calculated from the employee's time card and pay scale. Second, each deduction regarding taxes and union dues must be determined from the tax rates provided by the tax department and the information regarding union dues provided by the union, and these deductions must be subtracted from the gross pay to arrive at the net, or take-home, pay. Third, each employee's paycheck must be printed. Totals must be kept of all employees' gross pay and net pay values as well as of taxes and union dues withheld. These totals are used to generate reports to management, government, and union officials. In addition, changes in any employee's work status must be reported to the personnel department.

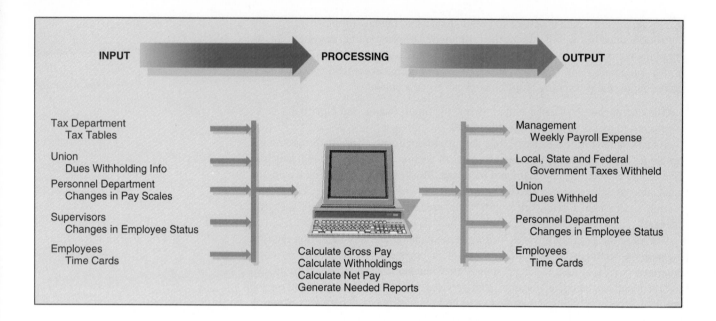

INPUT → PROCESSING → OUTPUT

Tax Department
   Tax Tables

Union
   Dues Withholding Info

Personnel Department
   Changes in Pay Scales

Supervisors
   Changes in Employee Status

Employees
   Time Cards

Calculate Gross Pay
Calculate Withholdings
Calculate Net Pay
Generate Needed Reports

Management
   Weekly Payroll Expense

Local, State and Federal
   Government Taxes Withheld

Union
   Dues Withheld

Personnel Department
   Changes in Employee Status

Employees
   Time Cards

FIGURE 11–1

Problem Definition Step for Payroll Example

The programmer or system analyst must not only thoroughly understand the problem, but also must write the statement of the problem in a clear, concise style. By documenting the problem, it becomes apparent whether or not it is clearly understood. This written documentation should be shown to the potential user(s) of the program to determine if the analyst's understanding of the problem is the same as that of the user(s). Making certain of this early in the programming process will save time and increase the probability that everyone involved will be satisfied with the end product.

◘ DESIGNING AND DOCUMENTING A SOLUTION

Once the necessary program input, output, and processing requirements have been determined, it is time to design a solution. It is not necessary to know what programming language will be used in order to develop the logic of a tentative solution. (In fact, knowing the processing requirements first helps the programmer to select the language best suited to those requirements.)

The Four Basic Logic Patterns

After the processing requirements are known, the actual logic of the solution can be determined. In order to do this, it is necessary to know the basic logic patterns that the computer is able to execute. The power of the computer comes in large part through the programmer's ability to specify the sequence in which statements in a program are to be executed. However, the computer can execute only four basic logic patterns: the simple sequence, the selection pattern, the loop, and the branch. Programming languages may have more complicated statements, but they all are based on various combinations of these four patterns.

SIMPLE SEQUENCE. In a **simple sequence** the computer executes one statement after another in the order in which they are listed in the program. It is the easiest

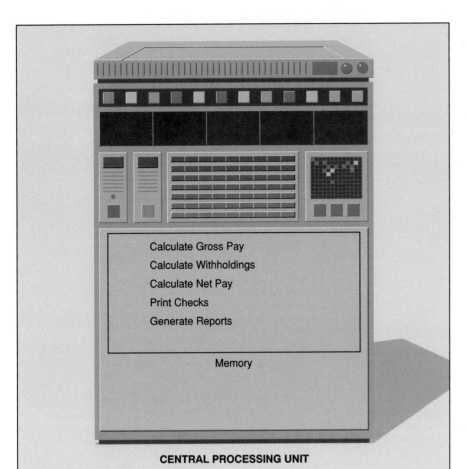

FIGURE 11–2

Simple Sequence Logic Pattern

Calculate Gross Pay

Calculate Withholdings

Calculate Net Pay

Print Checks

Generate Reports

Memory

CENTRAL PROCESSING UNIT

pattern to understand. Figure 11–2 demonstrates the simple sequence pattern as it relates to the payroll example.

SELECTION. The **selection** pattern requires that the computer make a choice. The choice it makes, however, is based not on personal preference but on pure logic. Each selection is made on the basis of the results of a comparison. The computer can determine if a given value is greater than, equal to, or less than another value; these are the only comparisons the computer is capable of making. Complex comparisons are made by combining two or more simple comparisons. This process of requiring the computer to make a selection or choice is often referred to as conditional programming logic. Figure 11–3 illustrates the selection pattern by demonstrating how the logic of the payroll example would consider overtime pay.

LOOP. The **loop** or iterative pattern enables the programmer to instruct the computer to alter the normal next-sequential-instruction process and loop back to a previous statement in the program, so that a given sequence of statements can be performed as many times as needed. This is especially useful if the same sequence of statements is to be executed, say, for each employee in a payroll program; the programmer need not duplicate the sequence of statements for each set of employee data processed. The looping pattern is illustrated in Figure 11–4.

FIGURE 11-3

Selection Logic Pattern

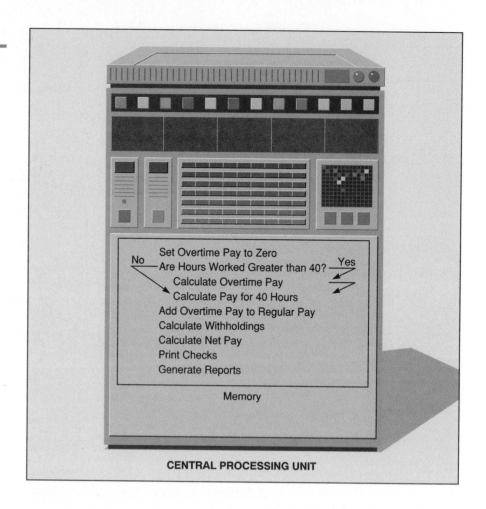

Set Overtime Pay to Zero

No — Are Hours Worked Greater than 40? — Yes

Calculate Overtime Pay

Calculate Pay for 40 Hours

Add Overtime Pay to Regular Pay

Calculate Withholdings

Calculate Net Pay

Print Checks

Generate Reports

Memory

CENTRAL PROCESSING UNIT

BRANCH. The last and most controversial pattern is the **branch** (also called the GOTO), which is often used in combination with selection or looping (see Figure 11–5). This pattern allows the programmer to skip statements in a program, leaving them unexecuted.

Branching is controversial for several reasons. If a program uses branches too often, the logic of the program becomes very difficult to follow. Such programs are difficult and time consuming for programmers to maintain and modify. Therefore, the use of the branch statement is strongly discouraged in most situations. When using most of the newer programming languages such as Pascal, Ada, and C, referred to as structured programming languages, there is very little need to use branch statements. Loops and selection patterns are used instead. These languages and their advantages will be discussed in Chapter 12.

Structured Programming Techniques

Data processing has come a long way since the days of the UNIVAC I, when the leading scientists of the period projected that the world would need only seven such machines for the rest of time. Today the world has millions of computers with

FIGURE 11–4

Loop Logic Pattern

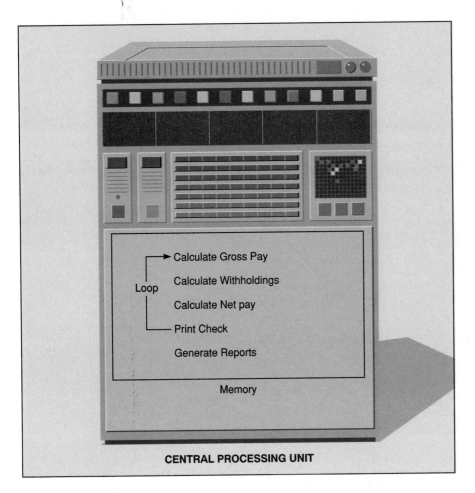

CENTRAL PROCESSING UNIT

processing capabilities billions of times greater than ten UNIVAC Is, and the demand for computing power continues to increase. In the first generation of computers, hardware was expensive, accounting for 80 percent of the total cost, whereas software accounted for approximately 20 percent. Today those figures are reversed, and it appears this trend will continue for some time. Figure 11–6 graphically depicts this situation.

As the sophistication of hardware increased rapidly, software technology did not keep pace. In the early days of software development, programming was very much an art. There were no standards or concrete rules. Many programmers approached their work haphazardly. Their main objective was to develop a program that executed properly, but they were not concerned about how this was accomplished. This situation created the following problems:

■ Programmer productivity was low. Developing a usable program of any significant size was a long, tedious process.

■ The programs often were not reliable. **Reliability** is the ability of a program to always obtain correct results. These early programs often produced incorrect results.

■ The programs could not always correctly handle invalid input. A well-written program should be able to handle any type of input. For example, if the user types

FIGURE 11-5

Branch Logic Pattern

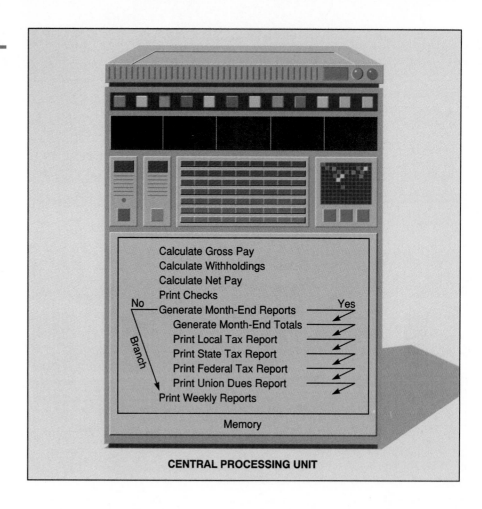

Calculate Gross Pay
Calculate Withholdings
Calculate Net Pay
Print Checks
No Generate Month-End Reports Yes
Branch
Generate Month-End Totals
Print Local Tax Report
Print State Tax Report
Print Federal Tax Report
Print Union Dues Report
Print Weekly Reports

Memory

CENTRAL PROCESSING UNIT

FIGURE 11-6

Trends in the Relationship between Hardware and Software Costs

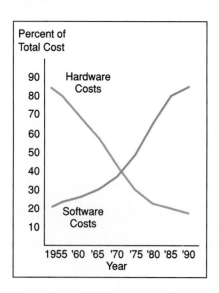

in a letter of the alphabet when a number should have been entered, the program should be able to handle the situation appropriately by, for example, printing an error message.

■ The programs were not easy to maintain (that is, keep in working order). The original programmers did not concern themselves with making the logic of the program easy for others to understand. Therefore, if a different programmer had to modify an existing program at a later date (a situation that happens continually in industry), it was a difficult task.

As programmers became aware of these difficulties, their attention was turned to developing methods of improving programming techniques. One of the earliest developments was the discovery by two mathematicians, Guiseppe Jacopini and Corrado Bohm, that any programming problem could be solved using a combination of three basic logic patterns: the simple sequence, the selection pattern, and the loop. Therefore, the fourth pattern, the branch, was unnecessary. Until this point, branches were used often, leading to programs with convoluted, difficult-to-follow logic.

Another milestone in the development of structured programming was reached in 1968 when E. W. Dijkstra published a letter in the Communications of the ACM (Association for Computer Machinists) titled ''Go To Statements Considered Harmful.'' Dijkstra stated in this now-famous letter that using the GOTO statement (which uses the branch logic pattern) made the logic of a program virtually impossible to

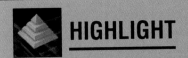
The Art of Programming

Will programmers of the future be required to have a degree in art as well as computer science? Hardware and software technologies have so greatly improved the possibilities of computer screen display, a degree in art would be a definite plus for software designers and programmers of the future. Computer systems allowing for nearly 17 million colors to be displayed to the user, databases that store the elements of a multimedia presentation (text, graphics, sound, and full-motion video), graphic user interfaces (GUIs)—all these innovations put pressure on designers and programmers to produce displays that are visually appealing and easily recognizable.

In some cases, designers and programmers have called in outside design consultants to help them create esthetic, functional computer screen displays. In other cases, programmers have resorted to taking art classes to improve their ability to judge what constituted good visual design. As computer technology improves, users also become more sophisticated. As a result, they expect more attractive and creative screen designs.

Graphic user interfaces are anticipated to be the choice of the majority of computer users in the future. Such user interfaces typically are easier to learn and easier to use. However, if they are not properly

designed, if they do not clearly represent the computer's functions pictorially (through icons), GUIs can be confusing and actually hinder learning and computing.

Therefore, future software designers and programmers will have the responsibility to develop good graphics. In essence, the computer's display screen will become the programmer's canvas. Designers and programmers will be required to compose a picture that is visually appealing, exact in what it intends to convey, and readily understandable by users. Believe it or not, before long a degree in art may not be an unreasonable requirement in this field.

follow because execution skipped haphazardly from one part of the program to another. At this stage computer scientists began to realize that it was important to develop programming languages that allowed programs to be written without the use of the GOTO statement.

At about this time, computer scientists also determined that program structure could be obtained by breaking a program into more manageable subprograms or **modules,** each designed to perform a specific task. These subprograms can be compared to the chapters in a textbook; each chapter deals with a specific topic and has specific goals. The chapters are combined to present a unified whole. Dividing a program into modules makes the program's logic easier to follow just as dividing a book into chapters (and subsections within those chapters) makes the facts and concepts presented easier to comprehend. The ability to easily divide a large program into fairly independent modules is an important characteristic of structured programming languages. Languages with this characteristic will be discussed in Chapter 12. Programs developed in this manner tend to have fewer errors than unstructured programs because the logic is readily apparent.

These events led to the development of a set of techniques, referred to as **structured programming.** Structured programming encourages programmers to think about the problem first and thoroughly design a solution before actually beginning to write the program in a programming language. Using structured programming encourages the development of well-written modular programs that have easy-to-follow logic and tend to be more error-free than other programs. There are many characteristics that distinguish structured programming. These characteristics can be divided into two broad categories: those that affect the manner in which the program solution is designed (structured design techniques) and those that affect the style in which the actual program is written (structured coding). Structured coding will be discussed in the section on writing programs (step 3 of the software development process). Structured design techniques will be presented next.

Top-Down Design

Using a computer to solve a problem is considerably different than most people think. The programmer needs to know only a little about the computer and how it works, but he or she must know a programming language. The most difficult aspect of programming is learning to organize solutions in a clear, concise way. One method of organizing a solution is to define the major steps or functions first, then expand the functions into more detailed steps later. This method, which proceeds from the general to the specific, is called **top-down design.** Top-down design employs the **modular approach,** which consists of breaking a problem into smaller and smaller subproblems. Sometimes this is referred to as the ''divide-and-conquer'' method, because it is easier to deal with a large job by completing it a small step at a time. When the actual program is written, these small steps can be written as separate modules, each of which performs a specific task. These modules are then joined together to form the entire program.

STRUCTURE CHARTS. **Structure charts** are used to document the results of the top-down design process by graphically illustrating the various modules and their relationship to one another. The most general level of organization is the main control module; this overall definition of the solution is the most critical to the success of the program. Modules at the next level contain broad descriptions of the steps in the solution process. These steps are further detailed in lower-level modules. The lowest-level modules contain the specific individual tasks the program must perform.

Figure 11–7 contains a structure chart that was developed to solve the payroll processing problem. Note that this structure chart has a total of four levels. The topmost level, Level 0, contains a statement of the general problem. Level 1 contains three basic processing steps the program must perform: read the needed data, process that data, and print the results. Level 2 contains further refinements of the steps in Level 1. In Level 3, only three steps from Level 2 are further refined.

Using top-down design has several advantages. It helps to prevent the programmer from becoming overwhelmed by the size of the job at hand. Also, the programmer is more likely to discover early in the programming process whether a specific solution will work. When the program is actually coded (written in a programming language), each box in the structure chart can be written as a separate module performing a specific task.

HIPO PACKAGES. The term **HIPO (Hierarchy plus Input-Process-Output)** is applied to a kind of visual aid commonly used to supplement structure charts. Whereas structure charts emphasize only structure and function, HIPO packages highlight the inputs, processing, and outputs of program modules.

A typical HIPO package consists of three types of diagrams that describe a program or system of programs from the general level to the detail level. At the most general level is the **visual table of contents,** which is almost identical to the structure chart but includes some additional information. Each block in the visual table of contents is given an identification number that is used as a reference in other HIPO diagrams. Figure 11–8 shows a visual table of contents for the payroll processing application.

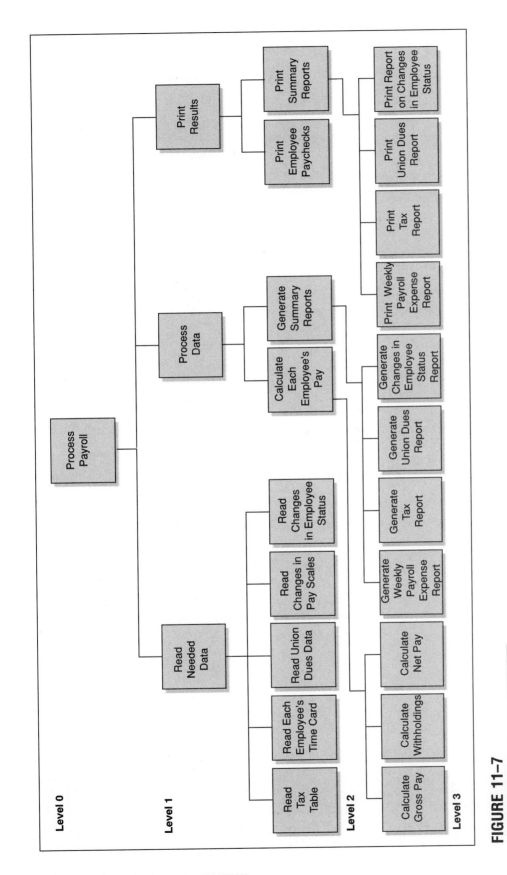

FIGURE 11–7

Structure Chart for Payroll Processing Problem

FIGURE 11-8

Visual Table of Contents for Payroll Processing Example

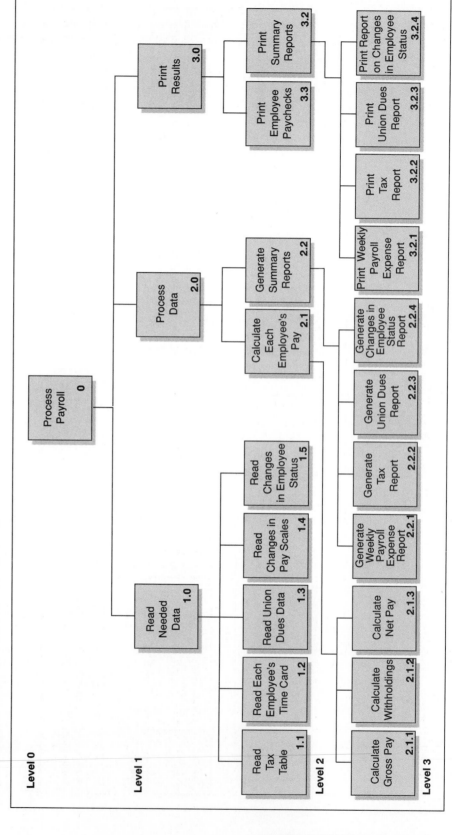

Level 0

Level 1

Level 2

Level 3

Each module in the visual table of contents is described in greater detail in an **overview diagram,** which includes the module's inputs, processing, and outputs. The reference number assigned to the overview diagram shows where the module fits into the overall structure of the system as depicted in the visual table of contents. If the module passes control to a lower-level module in the hierarchy for some specific processing operation, that operation is also given a reference number. An overview diagram for the payroll processing module (2.1), ''Calculate Each Employee's Pay,'' is shown in Figure 11–9.

Finally, the specific functions performed and data items used in each module are described in a **detail diagram.** The amount of detail used in these diagrams depends on the complexity of the problem involved. Enough detail should be included to enable a programmer to understand the functions and write the code to perform them.

HIPO diagrams are an excellent means of documenting systems and programs. The varying levels of detail incorporated in the diagrams allow them to be used by managers, analysts, and programmers to meet needs ranging from program maintenance to the overhaul of entire systems.

Pseudocode

Once a structure chart has been developed for a program, the actual logic of the solution can be documented; one method often used is pseudocode. **Pseudocode** is a narrative, or English-like description, representing the logic of a program or program module. The programmer arranges these descriptions in the order in which corresponding program statements will appear. Using pseudocode allows the programmer to focus on the steps required to perform a particular process, rather than on the syntax (or grammatical rules) of a particular programming language. Each pseudocode statement can be transcribed into one or more program statements.

Pseudocode is easy to learn and use. Although it has no rigid rules, several key words often appear. They include PRINT, IF/THEN/ELSE, END, and READ. Some statements are indented to set off repeated steps or conditions to be met. The statements

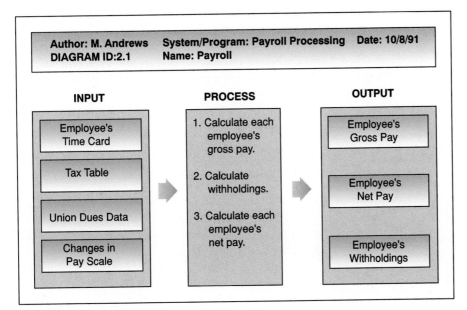

FIGURE 11–9

HIPO Overview Diagram for ''Calculate Each Employee's Pay'' Module

FIGURE 11-10

Pseudocode Illustrating Three Logic Patterns

1. Simple Sequence Pattern

Read Name
Read hours worked
Read hourly rate
Multiply hours worked by hourly rate to obtain gross pay

2. Selection Pattern

If hours worked is greater than 40
    Then subtract 40 hours worked to obtain overtime hours

3. Loop Pattern

Begin loop; perform until no more records
    Read name
    Read hours worked
    Read hourly rate
    Mutiply hours worked by hourly rate to obtain gross pay
End loop

cannot be translated for execution by the computer, therefore *pseudo-* is an appropriate prefix for this type of programming code. Figure 11–10 shows how the three basic logic patterns used in structured programming could be written in pseudocode. The pseudocode for the payroll program is shown in Figure 11–11.

Flowcharts

One way of graphically representing the logic of a solution to a programming problem is by using a **flowchart.** A flowchart shows the actual flow of the logic of a program, whereas a structure chart simply contains statements of the levels of refinement used to reach a solution. Each symbol in a flowchart has a specific meaning, as shown in Figure 11–12. Flowchart symbols are arranged from top to bottom and left to right. Flowlines connect the symbols and visually represent the implied flow of the program's logic. Arrowheads indicate the direction of flow. A disadvantage of flowcharts is that they can take up many pages and grow more confusing as programs become more complex. Flowcharting is becoming outdated as more and more programming environments use pseudocode to represent a program's logic. Figure 11–13 shows examples of how the four basic logic structures could be flowcharted.

FIGURE 11-11

Pseudocode for Payroll Processing Example

Begin
Begin loop; perform until no more employee records
    Read employee's name, hours worked, and hourly rate
    Calculate gross pay
    Calculate withholdings
    Calculate net pay
    Print check
    End loop
Generate summary reports
End

FIGURE 11–12

Flowchart Symbols

 Terminal, Interrupt — A start, stop, or interruption point in a program.

 Input / Output — General input / output operations.

 Process — Any processing funcitons.

 Decision — A comparison operation that determines which of two paths is followed.

 Connector — Connection between parts of a flowchart.

 Comment, Annotation — Additional descriptive comments.

 Predefined Process — Operations or program steps specified in a subroutine or another set of flowcharts.

 Arrowheads — The direction of processing or data flow.

DESIGNING AND DOCUMENTING A SOLUTION

FIGURE 11–13

Flowchart Examples for Each of the Four Basic Logic Patterns

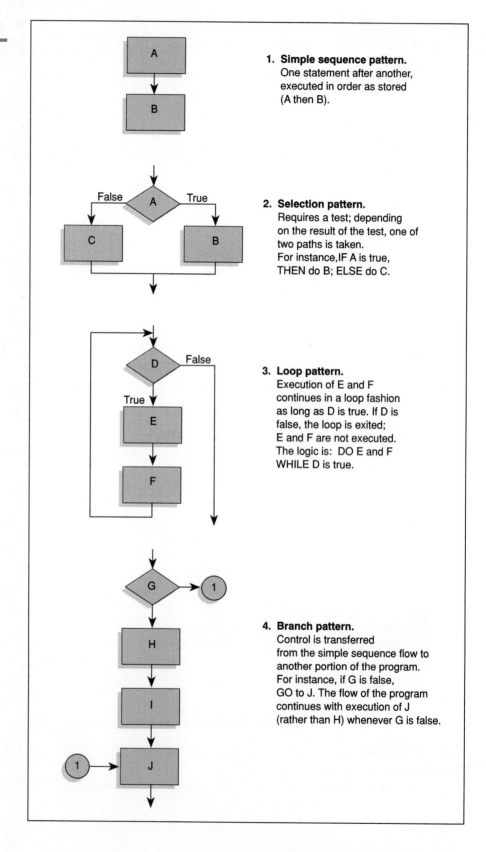

1. **Simple sequence pattern.**
   One statement after another, executed in order as stored (A then B).

2. **Selection pattern.**
   Requires a test; depending on the result of the test, one of two paths is taken.
   For instance, IF A is true, THEN do B; ELSE do C.

3. **Loop pattern.**
   Execution of E and F continues in a loop fashion as long as D is true. If D is false, the loop is exited; E and F are not executed.
   The logic is: DO E and F WHILE D is true.

4. **Branch pattern.**
   Control is transferred from the simple sequence flow to another portion of the program. For instance, if G is false, GO to J. The flow of the program continues with execution of J (rather than H) whenever G is false.

Action Diagrams

Action diagrams are an alternative form of documenting a designed solution to a problem. Action diagrams lend themselves to a top-down design because they can be used to document each level of the design. They can be used at a high level where structure charts or HIPO diagrams might be used as well as at a detailed level where pseudocode might typically be used. By using action diagrams, there can be a natural progression from a high level to a low level of detail because of the consistent method of documenting each level of the solution. This eliminates the need to mix alternate methods of documenting such as mixing structure or HIPO charts with pseudocode or flowcharts.

Action diagrams also use notation that supports structured programming techniques including modularization, functional decomposition, structured control constructs, and hierarchical organization. Action diagrams use brackets ([) as their basic building blocks. Each bracket begins with a label which describes the task done in that block, and each one except simple sequence also ends with a label to mark the end of the task. Figure 11–14 illustrates how the four basic logic patterns would be documented using action diagrams, while Figure 11–15 shows an action diagram for

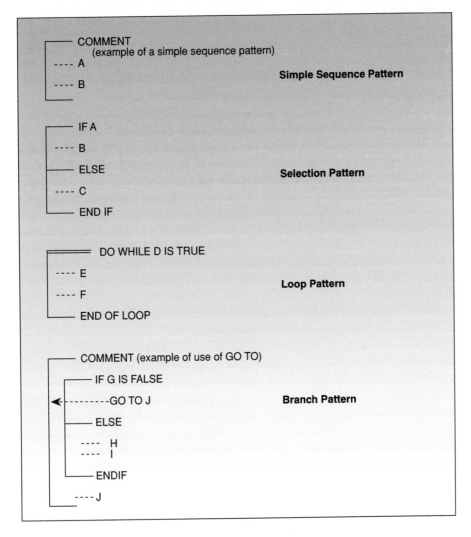

FIGURE 11–14

Action Diagram for the Four Basic Logic Patterns

FIGURE 11-15

Action Diagram for the Payroll Processing Example

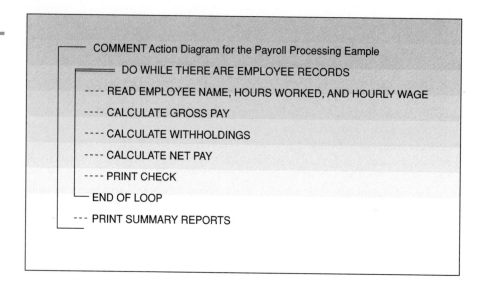

the payroll processing example. Note that a bracket with a double bar at the top is used to denote a loop pattern and an arrow extending out through a bracket is used to indicate a GOTO.

Using Structured Design Techniques in Industry

The program to generate a company's payroll would be long and complex, having many modules. In large corporations, programs such as this are developed by programmers working in teams. These programmers would use the structured design methods such as top-down design that we discussed earlier. They also would generally employ other methods to develop the software in an organized manner. Two commonly used methods, the chief programmer team and the structured walkthrough, are discussed below.

CHIEF PROGRAMMER TEAM. An important first step in coordinating a programming effort involves the formation of a **chief programmer team (CPT),** which is a group of programmers under the supervision of a chief programmer. The number of team members varies with the complexity of the project. The purpose of this approach is to use each team member's time and abilities as efficiently as possible.

The chief programmer primarily is responsible for the overall coordination, development, and success of the programming project. He or she meets with the user(s) to determine the exact software specifications. Usually a backup programmer is assigned as an assistant to the chief programmer to help design, test, and evaluate the software. Separate modules of the software are written and tested by programmers on the team. These modules are then integrated into a complete system.

The CPT also includes a librarian to help maintain complete, up-to-date documentation on the project and to relieve the team programmers of many clerical tasks. A librarian enhances communication among team members because he or she makes all program description, coding, and test results readily available to everyone involved in the effort. Figure 11-16 shows the organization of the chief programmer team.

The CPT approach facilitates top-down design and ongoing documentation of programs because each team member's tasks are clearly defined and coordinated as a team effort. This approach also helps with the testing of programs.

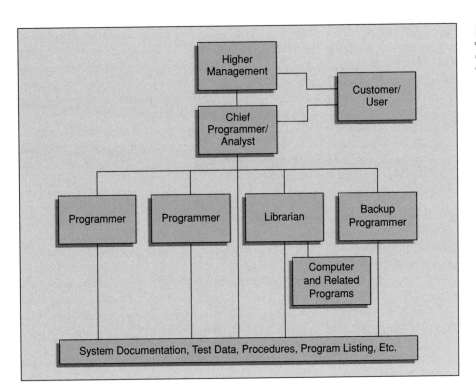

FIGURE 11–16

Organization of Chief Programmer
Team

STRUCTURED REVIEW AND EVALUATION. An important goal of a programming effort is to produce an error-free program in the shortest possible time. Meeting this goal requires the early detection of errors in order to prevent costly modifications later. One approach used to try to detect program errors at an early stage is an **informal design review.** The system design documentation is studied by selected management, analysts, and programmers, usually before the actual coding of program modules. After a brief review period, each person responds with suggestions for additions, deletions, and modifications to the system design.

A **formal design review** is sometimes used after the detailed parts of the system have been sufficiently documented. The documentation at this point may consist of structure charts, HIPO charts, flowcharts, pseudocode, or any combination of these methods. Sometimes called a **structured walkthrough,** the formal design review involves distributing the documentation to a review team of two to four members, which studies the documentation and then meets with the program designers to discuss the overall completeness, accuracy, and quality of the design. The reviewers and program designers often trace through the programs checking for errors. In large ongoing projects, formal design reviews are often held at various points in the software development process. Because other programmers have a fresh outlook on the program, they can often identify problem areas that the original programmer is not able to recognize.

◘ WRITING AND DOCUMENTING THE PROGRAM

After the programming problem has been defined and a solution designed, the program is written in a specific programming language; this process is referred to as **coding.**

Sometimes the proposed solution will limit the choice of languages that can be used in coding the program. Other constraints outside the scope of the problem and its solution may also affect the choice of a programming language. A programmer may have no choice in the selection of a language for a particular application; for instance, a business may require the use of COBOL because of its readability and because it is used in the company's existing software.

Once the programming language is chosen, the programmer should proceed to code the program according to the **syntax** (the grammatical rules) of the particular language and the rules of structured programming.

Structured Coding

When structured programming techniques are used to create a program, certain rules are followed during coding. Four major rules govern the use of branching statements, the size of program modules, the definition of a proper program, and thorough documentation.

As previously discussed, one characteristic of structured programming is the lack of branching (GOTO) statements. The programmer writes the program within the confines of three logic patterns: the simple sequence, selection, and the loop. This discipline limits the use of the branch to jump from one program statement to another in a random fashion.

When branching statements are avoided, the programmer can code each module as an independent segment. Each module should be relatively small (generally no more than 50 or 60 lines) to facilitate the translation of modules into program statements. When module size is limited in this manner, the coding for each module fits on a single page of computer printout paper, which simplifies program testing and debugging.

Yet another rule of structured coding dictates that modules should have only one entrance point and one exit point. A program segment that has only one entrance point and one exit point is called a **proper program** (see Figure 11–17). Following

FIGURE 11–17

Illustration of a Proper Program

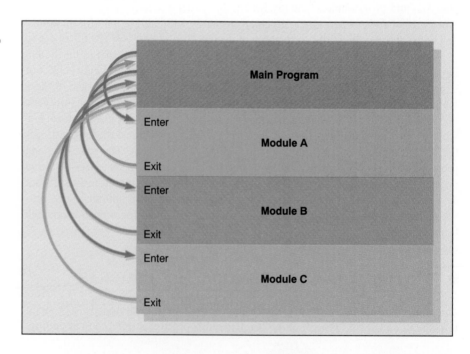

this rule makes the basic logic flow easy to follow and simplifies the modification of a program at a later date.

A final rule to follow in writing structured programs is to include documentation, or comment statements, liberally throughout the program. The comments should explain the data items being used in the main module and document each of the lower-level modules. Documentation aids in testing and debugging programs, which should occur at intervals throughout the coding phase. Documentation is also helpful when the program needs to be modified at a later date. See Concept Summary 11–2 for a review of structured programming techniques.

CONCEPT SUMMARY 11–2

Structured Programming Techniques

Structured Design Techniques	
Top-Down Design	Reaches a problem solution by dividing a problem into more and more specific modules
Chief Programmer Team	Uses a team approach to develop software, wherein a group of programmers work under the supervision of a chief programmer
Structured Review and Evaluation	A formal review of the design of a program to locate errors and problem areas as efficiently as possible
Structured Coding	
Avoidance of branching (GOTO) statements	Branching statements are discouraged so that program logic is easy to follow
Short program modules	The ideal length of a module is generally considered to be 50 to 60 lines
Proper program modules are used	Each program module has a single entrance point and a single exit point
Programs are well documented	The program is thoroughly documented to aid in testing, debugging, and later modification

Types of Statements

Certain types of programming statements are common to most high-level programming languages; they are comments, declarations, input/output statements, computations, comparisons, and loops.

COMMENTS. The type of statement known as the remark or comment has no effect on program execution; the computer simply ignores these statements. Comments are inserted at key points in the program as documentation—notes to anyone reading the program to explain the purpose of program statements. For example, if a series of statements sorts a list of names into alphabetical order, the programmer may want to include a remark to the effect: "This segment sorts names in ascending alphabetical order."

DECLARATIONS. The programmer uses declarations to define items used in the program. Examples include definitions of files, records, modules, functions, and variables.

INPUT/OUTPUT STATEMENTS. Input statements bring data into memory for use by the program. Output statements transfer data from memory to output media such as hard-copy printouts or displays on terminal screens. These statements differ considerably in form (though not so much in function) from one programming language to another.

COMPUTATIONS. Computational instructions perform arithmetic operations such as addition, subtraction, multiplication, division, and exponentiation.

COMPARISONS. This type of statement allows two items to be compared to determine if one is less than, equal to, or greater than the other. The action taken next depends on the result of this comparison.

LOOPS. The final type of statement is the loop, which allows a specified section of a program to be repeated as long as stated conditions remain constant.

◘ DEBUGGING AND TESTING THE PROGRAM

Using structured programming techniques encourages the development of programs with easy-to-follow logic, thus making them much less error-prone than unstructured programs. Nonetheless, programs of any significant length virtually always contain some errors, and correcting them can account for a large portion of the time spent in developing and maintaining software. Therefore, numerous techniques have been developed to make debugging easier and more reliable.

The language translator can detect grammatical or syntax errors such as misspellings and incorrect punctuation. Such errors often occur because the programmer does not fully know the programming language being used. Errors in programs are called **bugs,** and the process of locating, isolating, and eliminating bugs is called **debugging.** The amount of time that must be spent in debugging depends on the quality of the program. However, a newly completed program rarely executes successfully the first time it is run. In fact, one-third to one-half of a programmer's time is spent in debugging.

After all of the syntax errors are located and corrected, the program can be **tested.** This involves executing the program with input data that is either a representative sample of actual data or a facsimile of it. Often, sample data that can be manipulated easily by the programmer is used so that the computer-determined output can be compared with the programmer-determined correct results.

A complex program is frequently tested in separate modules so that errors can be isolated to specific sections, helping to narrow the search for the cause of an error. The programmer must correct all mistakes; running and rerunning a specific module

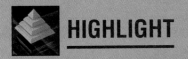
Software Development: 2000

As we approach the 21st century, our reliance on computer technology will undoubtedly increase. The question on many peoples' minds is, "Can software development keep pace with new hardware technologies?" The time it takes new application software to catch up with new hardware can seem an eternity. Some say that software development is the major obstacle to getting better products to market faster.

Many believe that this scenario *must* change if we are to remain competitive in a world-wide economy. However, the experts don't always agree as to how this change can be brought about. Right now, there are companies producing quality software effectively and efficiently. Watching these companies at work, four critical factors emerge. These software developers all:

- Manage time effectively
- Sufficiently prepare for the programming process
- Maintain effective communication
- Don't over manage

Managing time effectively is essential. Often, as a result of competitive and market forces, a piece of software must be developed by a specified date. Within this (often severe) time constraint, sufficient time must be allocated for producing a realistic design of the software and for programming and testing that design. Once these time allocations have been agreed upon, the project team must be managed effectively with respect to meeting fixed project milestones. In accomplishing these goals on time, quality need not be sacrificed.

Sufficiently preparing for the programming process allows the team to meet deadlines with quality programs. All programming tools required for the project should be developed or secured before coding starts. This way, no time delays will hold up a portion of the programming while a tool or library is being acquired.

Effective communications among the software development team is essential to meeting their goals, as it is in nearly all relationships.

Over management of a programming project must be avoided. Over management can lead to delays and a loss of commitment on the part of team members, which can lead to errors, more delays, and ultimately more over management. The worst fallout from over management often is the stifling of creativity in hopes of achieving a deadline. Though it should be kept in a disciplined framework, creativity should be allowed to flourish.

As we approach the year 2000, creative, well-managed software development is our best hope of remaining competitive in this critical world market.

---

may be necessary before the cause of an error can be found. The programmer then rewrites the part in error and resubmits it for another test. Care must be taken that correction of one error does not lead to several others.

Each section of the program must be tested (even sections that will be used infrequently). The programmer often finds **desk checking** helpful. With this method, the programmer pretends to be the computer and, reading each instruction and simulating how the computer would process a data item, attempts to catch any flaws in the program logic.

After a programmer has worked for a long time to correct the logic of a program, he or she may tend to overlook errors. For this reason, programmers sometimes trade their partially debugged programs among themselves. The programmer tracing through a "fresh" program may uncover mistakes in logic that were hidden to the original programmer.

In some cases, program errors prove especially difficult to locate. Two commonly used diagnostic procedures usually available to the programmer in such cases are dump programs and trace programs.

A dump lists the contents of registers and memory locations. The dump is often useful in locating an error because the values that were in the registers and memory at the time the error occurred can be checked for correctness. If an incorrect value is found, it can be used to help locate the error.

A trace, produced by a trace program, is apt to be easier to use than a dump. The trace lists the steps followed during program execution in the order in which they occurred. The programmer can specify that all or portions of a program be traced. The trace is often used in combination with the desk-checking procedure described above to see if the correct flow of execution has occurred. The values of selected variables (memory locations) can also be displayed in the trace; this can be helpful in determining whether the necessary calculations have been performed correctly.

Although program testing, if conducted properly, will uncover most of the errors in a program, it is no guarantee that a program is completely correct. There may be errors that were overlooked in the testing process because of the extremely large number of execution paths a program can take. Therefore, the area of program **verification** is receiving increasing attention in the software development field. Verification involves the process of mathematically proving the correctness of a program through the use of predicate calculus. Although this area of study is still not refined to the level of commercial use, it is likely that it will be widely used in the near future.

It is important to remember that each time a program is modified, the documentation must also be modified to reflect any changes that were made to the program. This updating of documentation when changes are made is critical in industry because programs are continually being altered and expanded. If the documentation no longer matches the program, program maintenance can become very difficult.

◨ SUMMARY POINTS

■ A sequence of steps, collectively referred to as the software development process, is used to efficiently develop a programming problem solution. The steps are: (1) Define and document the problem. (2) Design and document a solution. (3) Write and document the program. (4) Debug and test the program and revise the documentation as necessary.

■ When a programming problem is defined, it is necessary to state the desired output, the needed input, and the processing requirements. These three items collectively are referred to as the program specifications.

■ After the problem is defined, a solution can be designed. When designing a solution, the programmer must realize that the computer is capable of executing only four basic logic patterns: a simple sequence (in which statements are executed in the order in which they occur), a selection pattern (in which a comparison is made), a loop (which allows for the repetition of a sequence of statements), and a branch (which allows for program execution to skip over statements). The branch pattern is controversial because its overuse can lead to programs with difficult-to-follow logic.

■ Numerous problems were encountered in the early days of software development. Some of these problems were that programmer productivity was low, programs often were not reliable and did not correctly handle invalid input, and programs were not easy to maintain. Consequently, structured programming techniques were developed. Structured programming can be divided into two categories: structured design techniques and structured coding.

■ When using structured design, top-down design is used to break a problem into smaller and smaller subproblems. Structure charts are used to graphically illustrate the result of the top-down design process. Each box in the structure chart can be written as a separate module when the program is coded.

■ HIPO packages are visual aids that supplement structure charts. Typically, an HIPO package consists of three types of diagrams: a visual table of contents, an overview diagram, and a detail diagram.

■ Pseudocode consists of an English-like description of the logic of a program.

■ Flowcharts graphically represent the logic of a programming problem solution. Each symbol has a specific meaning; flowlines and arrows indicate the direction of flow.

■ In business and industry, a number of programmers are typically assigned to work together on large programming projects. Several structured design techniques are often used in developing these large projects. Two of these are chief programmer teams and structured review and evaluation.

■ The chief programmer team (CPT) is a small group of programmers under the supervision of a chief programmer. Usually the chief programmer is assisted by a highly qualified backup programmer. A librarian is responsible for maintaining up-to-date documentation on the project. Other programmers are included on the team according to the needs of the particular project.

■ Software designs must be reviewed before they are implemented. In an informal design review, the design documentation is reviewed before coding takes place. Later, a formal design review may be held to discuss the overall completeness, accuracy, and quality of the design.

■ The process of writing the program in a programming language is referred to as coding. In structured coding, a number of rules are followed, including avoiding branch (GOTO) statements, dividing the program into independent modules of manageable length, each working together to form the entire program, writing each module so that it is a proper program (that is, containing only one entrance point and one exit point), and fully documenting the program.

■ Some of the general types of statements in a program are: comments, declarations, input/output statements, computations, comparison, and loops.

■ Although using structured programming techniques encourages the development of programs that are less error-prone than unstructured programs, programs of any length nearly always contain some bugs, or errors. Debugging is the process of locating and correcting these errors.

■ Testing programs involves running them with a variety of data to determine if they always obtain correct results. It is difficult to locate all program errors through testing. Therefore, program verification, which involves mathematically proving the correctness of a program, is an area of increasing interest in the software development field. Although program verification is not yet practical on a large scale, it is likely to prove useful in the near future.

◘ TERMS FOR REVIEW

branch, p. 280
bug, p. 296
chief programmer team (CPT),
   p. 292

coding, p. 293
debugging, p. 296
desired output, p. 275
desk checking, p. 297

■ REVIEW QUESTIONS

1. What are the four steps of the software development process?

2. What items make up a program specification? Give a brief description of what information is included in each item.

3. What concept (discussed in Chapter 1) does the program specification coincide with?

4. What are the four basic logic patterns a computer can perform? Using flow-charting symbols, give an example of each of these patterns.

5. Why has structured programming become an important issue? What are the benefits of using structured programming techniques?

6. What are the advantages of using top-down design to solve a problem? Name two tools used to document a top-down design.

7. How is pseudocode used when documenting the solution to a particular problem? Write the pseudocode required to document the conversion of a Celsius temperature to a Fahrenheit temperature.

8. What are the advantages of using action diagrams to document a solution to a particular problem?

9. Describe the chief programmer team concept and explain why it is a successful way to coordinate a large-scale programming task.

10. Provide brief descriptions for each of the types of statements that can be used in high-level programming languages.

APPLICATION

Allied Van Lines

The business of Allied Van Lines, Inc. is interstate, local, and long-distance moving. It hauls household goods, U.S. government and military shipments, and special products shipments. With over 800 agency and branch locations, Allied is one of the largest companies in the relocation business. In 1988, the company was purchased by NFC, the largest freight consortium in Great Britain. Allied's headquarters are in Broadview, Illinois.

In a highly competitive business, Allied has initiated a new information systems strategy called Allied Transportation System (ATS). ATS integrates many of Allied's business functions into a single, efficient, and effective computerized system.

BACKGROUND OF ATS

Allied recognizes three critical elements in its business. First, the company operates as a partnership in terms of its agents and its drivers. Second, quality of service is essential in differentiating Allied from other companies and building a satisfied customer base. Third, Allied's personnel—its agents, drivers, and employees—are critical resources to its success. In 1980, however, the regulated environment in which the transportation industry operated was relaxed, and the industry became highly competitive. Allied had to rethink these key elements in terms of increasing automation to lower overhead and increase service levels, particularly in the area of detailed tracking and reporting on the status of shipments.

Through studies of its past operation, Allied found that there were several operational problems that presented obstacles toward reaching its goals. One problem involved the excessive manual paperwork and duplication of data. Data related to a shipment was collected throughout its lifetime on a series of manually prepared forms, often by different agents at different locations. Some of the separate forms included the bill of lading and freight bill, the statement of additional services, certificate of weight and measure, booker control form, the shipment document transmittal form, the notice to the agent, household goods descriptive inventory, and condition report. Often, the rates, terms, and conditions of a contract had to be looked up in hard copy form, and the computations were performed manually.

Another problem was that accounting for payments and revenues was complex and unwieldy. It was often hard to find out just what the revenues were for agents, drivers, and the company. This led to the problems of diminished accuracy and timeliness of reporting. Thus, the reports could not always support critical decision making, as they should have. A final problem was that Allied had no clearly defined tracking and communications capabilities.

ATS provides Allied employees and managers with online, complete, accurate, and timely information about sales, shipments, equipment, customers, rating, billing, and revenue distribution.

DEVELOPMENT

For studying its current system and implementing ATS, Allied relied on a methodology called STRADIS—*STR*uctured *A*nalysis, *D*esign, and *I*mplementation of Information *S*ystems. STRADIS, marketed by McDonnell Douglas Corporation, is an organized set of step-by-step procedures and guidelines for developing and maintaining information systems. It integrates the best practices known today in the information systems industry, while remaining flexible to changes based on experience and new developments. According to McDonnell Douglas, STRADIS decreases the risk of wasting money on system development and saves time on projects because all of the personnel involved are using a standard approach. The methodology is used not only for developing a new system, but also for evaluating and maintaining the system during its entire life cycle.

INSTALLING ATS

ATS addresses all of the problems Allied was facing. Although there is still manual entry of data at initial registration of a shipment, agents and drivers subsequently have real-time access to relevant files, a capability that reduces

errors and speeds overall processing. Access can be gained either by telephone or through the use of portable, hand-held computers. Billing and accounting is improved because Allied maintains a central repository of data available to the appropriate parties. The information can be updated quickly and online, thus reducing errors and additional work. ATS also helps the company's management to control all aspects of the business because the reporting features of ATS provide current information, including market share data. Finally, ATS automation greatly improves the tracking of shipments by linking data files and providing access to data on a real-time basis.

Thus, ATS provides the necessary tools for Allied employees to do their jobs. It provides online, complete, accurate, and timely information about sales, shipments, equipment, customers, rating, billing, and revenue distribution. It reduces errors by accepting and validating data at the point of origin, improving data integrity and reducing data redundancy. It reduces paperwork for everyone.

ATS is a user friendly system. It is menu-driven, includes a HELP feature, prompts the user at crucial points, has descriptive error messages, and utilizes pop-up windows. ATS provides online tutorial capabilities for agents and other users to reduce training time and cost. It has both summary and detail-level data at the user's request. It is also user friendly for future enhancements and changes because it is a flexible, modular, and integrated system.

ATS provides summary reports on a timely and accurate basis to assist users in making decisions. It allows exception reporting when appropriate and reflects company performance and industry trends.

ATS uses state-of-the-art equipment and software, including relational data base components. The majority of ATS' automated processes are designed to run under the IBM 3090 200E host computer. Some front-end user processing can occur on the intelligent workstations (PCs). ATS runs under IBM's MVS/ESA operating system and uses DB2 as the relational data base management system. AT&T's ISN network is used for connecting ATS' internal customers to Allied's host computer. The agent community is linked using a remote network through leased or dial-up lines or both.

ATS IN ACTION
Consider one example of how ATS is used to track a routine household move. The initial customer contact begins when an agent receives a call or a shipment request. Information such as the customer name, address, and preliminary move requirements would be entered into ATS. The

agent uses ATS to determine the location of a booking agent if the shipment's origin is outside his or her own area. Before a salesperson calls at the customer's household, the origin agent would use ATS to generate reports that the salesperson would use when describing Allied's services. These reports include a partially completed sales information sheet, a tariff sheet, and price discounting terms. The salesperson returns the completed information to the origin agent, who then updates the shipping request information in the ATS system.

The request is tracked until it becomes a registration or a "lost sale." When a shipment is registered, the ATS system determines its assigned trip. Any changes in service or price are entered into the system as soon as they occur and ATS automatically notifies the affected parties.

The system helps track the status of the shipment at the location of loading, throughout the actual trip, and at the destination. Agents and drivers both update the information as needed. Billing functions and distribution of revenue are then facilitated by ATS. When possible, electronic data interchange is used to bill the customer.

DISCUSSION POINTS
1. What strategy did Allied use for studying its current system and implementing ATS?
2. After studying the features of ATS, suggest some ways ATS would help Allied to reduce costs and make decisions.

Programming Languages

Cobol: The Successful Failure

John M. Bradley, *Computerworld*

It's not often that a computer programming language is pronounced dead before it is even born. That, however is precisely what one person implied about Cobol while it was being designed in the 1950s.

The gentleman in question disagreed with a number of design decisions and believed that Cobol was doomed as a computer programming language. To make his point, he presented the committee with a tombstone engraved "Cobol—R.I.P."

Retrospectively, it seems that this gesture was somewhat premature, since Cobol is currently the most widely used commercial computer programming language in the world. Nevertheless, it also appears to have been an omen, since Cobol has been declared dead more often than any other programming language in the history of computer science.

The first postbirth announcement of Cobol's death came in the late 1960s, when IBM started predicting that it would be replaced by PL/1 within a few years. As it turned out, of course, the vast majority of the computing world stayed with Cobol, and within 10 years, PL/1 was largely dead as a commercial programming language (at least outside of IBM).

Later, the academic community took its turn, pushing its ill-fated favorite, Pascal. Then, in the early 1980s, panic over the Japanese fifth-generation computer project spurred the development of another class of contenders, the so-called fourth-generation languages (4GLs).

A LONG WAY TO GO

The computing world is still awash with hype about 4GLs and their cousins, the computer-aided software engineering (CASE) tools. It is clear that these products hold much promise in the long term. However, it is also clear that there is still a long way to go before any of these products can be standardized.

One of the most formidable recent challengers to Cobol is the C language, which is currently advancing under the banners of Unix and open systems.

Despite its strong lobby, the idea of C as the dominant commercial programming language is clearly pure fantasy. Most computer scientists acknowledge that there are some obvious flaws in Cobol and that working on some 100,000-line Cobol programs can be very distasteful. However, any seasoned C programmer knows that the only thing worse is working on most 100,000-line C programs. Moreover, although C is a very good scientific and systems programming language, it is very weak in the areas of numerical accuracy, range and I/O, which are somewhat important in commercial programming.

All this talk about "open systems" is humorous because Cobol has been an open systems programming language from the very beginning. Moreover, this is one of the main reasons why it has been so successful. Veterans of commerical programming remember how much effort and expense went into converting systems from assembly language to Cobol and how they swore at the time that they would never do anything like that again. They also remember why they chose Cobol—so they wouldn't have to do it again.

As the price/performance ratio swings away from mainframes and toward open systems, it is likely that companies will start to move their Cobol systems into the open systems arena in droves. This will not weaken Cobol but will strenghten its position.

There are several reasons why I say this. One is that institutions will not rewrite their software unless there is a commercial benefit to doing so, such as greater portability, reduced maintenance or improved future development options. Wise customers who have resisted the extensions and proprietary Job Control Languages offered by the larger computer vendors in an effort to lock sites into their product lines still have all of these benefits in Cobol.

Furthermore, Cobol's portability will become increasingly important as the trend toward open systems brings about increased competition and lower profit margins. In the long run, the weaker suppliers will almost certainly go bankrupt, leaving some customers high and dry. Under such conditions, portability will become vital.

It is probable that improvements in technology will ultimately render Cobol obsolete. At this time, nobody knows exactly what event will cause this or what the replacement will be. It may turn out to be 4GL, a CASE tool, a new form of programming or something else.

One thing is certain though: Cobol will be declared dead several more times before it really dies. Even when it is finally killed off, a lot of people probably still won't believe it.

◼ INTRODUCTION

Languages are systems of communication. Programming languages are communication systems that people can use to communicate with computers. The earliest computers were programmed by arranging various wires and switches within the computer components. Up to 6,000 switches could be set on the ENIAC to execute one program. However, when a new program was to be run, all the switches had to be reset. This was clearly inefficient. The EDSAC, the first stored-program computer, allowed instructions to be entered into memory without rewiring or resetting switches. Codes that corresponded to the required on/off electrical states were needed to enter these instructions. These codes were called **machine language.** Later, **assembly language** (which uses simple codes to represent machine-language instructions) was developed to offset the tedium of writing machine-language programs. A disadvantage of both machine and assembly languages is that they are dependent on the type of computer system being used; the programmer must be familiar with the hardware for which the program is being written.

The development of FORTRAN in the mid-1950s signaled the beginning of a trend toward high-level languages that were oriented more toward the programmer than the computer. Since that time, a wide variety of high-level languages have been developed. At the present time there are more than two hundred distinct computer programming languages.

This chapter discusses some of the programming languages most commonly used today. As with languages such as English and German, each of these programming languages has a history of development and specific characteristics. The unique features, characteristics, advantages, and disadvantages of each language are explained in this chapter and sample applications are shown.

◼ STANDARDIZATION OF LANGUAGES

One of the advantages of using high-level languages is the potential for these programs to be **portable;** that is, to be able to be executed on a wide variety of computer systems with minimal changes. The necessary restriction, though, is that the language must be standardized; that is, rules must be developed so that all of the language translator programs for a particular language will be able to translate the same program. Therefore, it is necessary that standards be established for programming languages. A number of agencies authorize these standards. The most influential is the

American National Standards Institute (ANSI), which has developed or adopted widely used standards for many languages including FORTRAN, Pascal, BASIC, COBOL, Ada, and C (all of which will be discussed in this chapter). One difficulty is that many computer manufacturers and language translator developers do not entirely adhere to these standards. They often add extra features (referred to as "enhancements") to their language translator programs to make them more useful. This means that if a program uses any of these enhancements it may not run on other computer systems without modification.

◻ CATEGORIZING LANGUAGES

Computer scientists have long tried to categorize programming languages. Categorization helps the programmer in determining which language might be most useful in a particular situation. Some different ways in which it is possible to categorize languages are listed below:

◼ *Low-level or high-level.* This refers to the degree to which the language is oriented toward the hardware as compared to the programmer. Low-level languages are oriented toward the computer, whereas high-level languages are oriented more toward the programmer. Therefore, low-level languages are easier for the computer to execute, but high-level languages are easier for people to use and understand.

◼ *Structured or unstructured.* The characteristics of structured programming languages were discussed in Chapter 11. Briefly, these languages allow programmers to easily divide programs into modules, each performing a specific task. Also, structured programming languages provide a wide variety of control structures such as loops (to perform repetitive tasks) and selection statements (to make comparisons). These features result in programs with easy-to-follow logic that are easy to modify and maintain. Many languages that were developed before the widespread acceptance of structured programming have since been modified to include structured techniques (COBOL is an example).

◼ *Procedure-oriented or problem-oriented.* Procedure-oriented languages place programming emphasis on describing the computational and logical procedures required to solve a problem. Commonly used procedure-oriented languages include COBOL, FORTRAN, and Pascal. A problem-oriented language is one in which the problem and solution are described without the necessary procedures being specified, therefore requiring little programming skill.

◼ *General purpose or special purpose.* General-purpose languages are those languages that can be used to solve a wide variety of programming problems. BASIC and Pascal are examples of general-purpose languages. Some examples of categories of special-purpose languages might be educational languages, business languages, and scientific languages. For example, FORTRAN, a language used mostly for mathematical and scientific applications, is a scientific language.

Although it would be nice to be able to neatly categorize each language, many languages fall somewhere in between one extreme or the other in any specific category. For example, C, a programming language discussed in more detail later, is often considered to be neither a low-level nor a high-level language, but somewhere in between. Nonetheless, these categories can prove useful in making generalized statements about languages and their typical uses. Therefore, where appropriate we will attempt to categorize the languages discussed in this chapter.

■ TRANSLATING LANGUAGES

Translating a computer programming language is conceptually very similar to translating one spoken language into another. In order for an English-speaking person to understand Russian, for example, someone must translate the Russian language into English. This process of translating one language to another is also required by computers. Since machine language is the only language a computer can understand, all other languages must be translated into machine language.

Assembly and high-level languages are much more widely used by programmers than machine language. Since these languages cannot be executed directly by computers, they are converted into machine executable form by language-translator programs. The language-translator program translates the source program (that is, the sequence of instructions written by the programmer) into machine language. The translator program for assembly language programs is called an **assembler program.** A high-level language translator can be either a **compiler program** or an **interpreter program.** Assemblers, compilers, and interpreters are designed for specific machines and languages. For example, a compiler that translates a source program written in FORTRAN into a machine-language program can translate only FORTRAN programs.

This translated program (called the **object program**) is then ''linked'' with other object programs which reside in a **system library** to form what is referred to as the load module. It is the load module that is then executed by the CPU. The process of linking the application object program with the object programs in the system library is handled by the **linkage editor.** The object programs in the system library are combined to form the library and managed by the object module **librarian program.**

An interpreter, unlike assemblers and compilers, evaluates and translates a program one statement at a time. The interpreter reads each program statement checking for syntax errors and, if errors are found, generates an appropriate error message. If there are no errors, the interpreter translates the statement into machine language and executes it before proceeding to the next statement. This is in contrast to an assembler or a compiler, which first checks the entire program for syntax errors and then translates the entire program into an object program that is executed. An interpreter program is typically smaller than an assembler or compiler program. An interpreter, however, can be inefficient. Program statements that are used more than once during a program's execution must be evaluated, translated, and executed each time the statement is used.

■ LOW-LEVEL LANGUAGES

Machine Language

Remember from Chapter 3 that all data in digital computers is stored as either on or off electrical states which we represent through the use of 1s and 0s. Machine language must take the form of 1s and 0s to be understood by the computer. But coding a program in this binary form is very tedious; therefore machine language is often coded in either octal (base 8) or hexadecimal (base 16) codes.

The programmer using machine language must specify everything to the computer. Every step the computer must take to execute a program must be coded; therefore,

48	00	23C0	
4C	00	23C2	
40	00	2310	
D2	01	2310	2310
48	00	2310	
4E	00	2028	
F3	17	3002	
9G	F0	3003	2028

FIGURE 12–1

Machine-Language Instructions Expressed in the Hexadecimal (Base 16) Number System

the programmer must know exactly how the computer works. The actual numerical addresses of the memory locations containing instructions and data must be specified.

In order to accomplish the necessary specificity, each machine-language instruction has two parts. The **op code** (short for operation code) tells the computer what function to perform, such as adding two values. The **operand** tells the computer what data to use when performing that function. The operand takes the form of the specific memory address where the data is located. Figure 12–1 shows some examples of machine-language instructions.

The greatest advantages of machine language are that the computer can execute it efficiently and that generally it uses less memory space than high-level languages. It also allows the programmer to fully utilize the computer's potential because the programmer is interacting directly with the computer hardware.

On the other hand, this type of programming is extremely tedious, time consuming, and error prone. The instructions are difficult to remember and to use. In addition, programs written in machine language will execute only on the specific type of system for which they were written. Therefore, machine language is used only in rare instances today.

Assembly Language

Assembly languages were developed to alleviate many of the disadvantages of machine-language programming. When programming in an assembly language, the programmer uses **mnemonics** (symbolic names) to specify machine operations; thus, coding in 0s and 1s is no longer required. Mnemonics are alphabetic abbreviations for the machine-language op codes. Table 12–1 shows some common arithmetic

TABLE 12–1

Examples of Assembly-Language Mnemonic Code

Operation	Typical Assembly-Language Op Code	Typical Binary (Machine Language) Op Code
Add memory to register	A	01011010
Add (decimal) memory to register	AP	11111010
Multiply register by memory	M	01011100
Multiply (decimal) register by memory	MP	11111100
Subtract memory from register	S	01011011
Subtract (decimal) memory from register	SP	11111011
Move (numeric) from register to memory	MVN	11010001
Compare memory to register	C	01011001
Compare (decimal) memory to register	CP	11111001
Zero register and add (decimal) memory to register	ZAP	11111000

operations coded in assembly language and in machine language. Assembly-language instructions differ depending on the type and model of computer being programmed. Thus, assembly-language programs, like machine-language programs, can be written only for the type of computer that will execute them.

There are three basic parts to an assembly-language instruction: an op code and an operand, as in machine language, and a label. Table 12–2 shows a section of an assembly-language program with the parts of the instructions labeled. The **label** is a programmer-supplied name that represents the location in which a particular instruction will be stored. When the programmer wishes to refer to that instruction, he or she can simply specify the label, without regard to the actual address of the memory location.

The op code, as in machine language, tells the computer what operation to perform, but it is in mnemonic form. The operand, also in mnemonic form, represents the address of the item that is to be manipulated. Each instruction may contain one or two operands. The remainder of the line can be used for remarks that explain to humans the operation being performed (the remarks are optional and are simply ignored by the computer).

There are several advantages to using assembly language. The main advantage is that it can be used to develop programs that use memory space and processing time efficiently. As with machine language, the programmer is able to fully utilize the computer's processing capabilities. Second, the assembler program (the program that translates the assembly program into machine language) performs certain error-checking functions and generates error messages, if appropriate, that are useful to the programmer when debugging the program.

The main disadvantage of assembly language is that it is more cumbersome to use than high-level languages. Generally, one assembly-language instruction is translated into one machine-language instruction; this one-for-one relationship leads to

TABLE 12–2			
The Parts of an Assembly-Language Instruction			
Label	**Op Code**	**Operands A and B**	**Remarks**
OVERTIME	AP	OVERTIME, FORTY	BEGIN OVERTIME COMPUTATION
	MP	OVERTIME, WKRATE	
	AP	GROSS, WKRATE	
	SP	WKHRS, FORTY	COMPUTE OVERTIME PAY
	MP	WKHRS, ONEHLF	
	MP	GROSS, WKHRS	
	MVN	GROSS +5(1), GROSS +6	
	ZAP	GROSS(7), GROSS (6)	
	AP	GROSS, OVERTIME	
TAXRATE	CP	GROSS, = P′25000′	BEGIN TAX COMPUTATION

That Really Bugs Me!

As in other professions, programmers have their own language. One of their often used phrases is to "debug" a program or find "the bugs" in a program, that is, to find the errors in a program. Few people realize that the phrase originated because a real live bug once caused problems in a computer system.

In the summer of 1945, something went wrong with the Mark II, a large electromechanical machine used by the Department of Defense. Though the machine was not working properly, the operating personnel could find no obvious problems. A continued search revealed a large moth beaten to death by one of the electromechanical relays. The moth was pulled out with tweezers and taped to a log book. "From then on," said Rear Admiral Grace Hopper, one of the people working with the machine, "when the officer came in to ask if we were accomplishing anything, we told him we were 'debugging' the computer."

And where is that infamous bug today? The insect is exhibited in the Naval Museum at the Naval Surface Weapons Center, in Dahlgren, Virginia.

long program preparation time. However, this feature makes it easier for the computer to translate the program into machine language than to translate a high-level language into machine language. Another disadvantage of assembly language is the high level of skill required to use it effectively. As with machine language, the programmer must know the computer to be used and must be able to work with binary or hexadecimal numbers. Finally, assembly language, like machine language, is machine-dependent; a program written for one computer generally cannot be executed on another.

Assembly language is often used for writing operating system programs. Because operating systems are designed for particular computers, they are machine-dependent. The potential efficiency of assembly language also makes it well suited for operating-system programming.

■ HIGH-LEVEL LANGUAGES

In this section we will discuss a cross-section of high-level languages. High-level languages are much easier to understand than low-level languages because they use meaningful words such as READ and PRINT in their instructions. One high-level statement may generate several machine-language statements. Therefore, high-level language programs are more difficult to translate into machine language than are assembly-language programs. Traditionally, high-level languages have not made as efficient use of computer resources as machine and assembly languages. However, with the ever-increasing sophistication of translator programs, this is no longer necessarily true.

FORTRAN

FORTRAN (FORmula TRANslator) is the oldest high-level programming language. It originated in the mid-1950s, when most programs were written in either assembly language or machine language. Efforts were made to develop a programming language that resembled English but could be translated into machine language by the computer. This effort, backed by IBM, produced FORTRAN—the first commercially available high-level language.

Early FORTRAN compilers contained many errors and were not always efficient in their use of computer resources. Moreover, several manufacturers offered variations of FORTRAN that could be used only on their particular computers. Although many improvements were made, early implementations of FORTRAN continued to suffer from this lack of standardization. In response to this problem, the American National Standards Institute laid the groundwork for a standardized FORTRAN. In 1966, two standard versions of FORTRAN were recognized, ANSI FORTRAN and Basic FORTRAN. A more recent version, FORTRAN 77, provides more enhancements to the language. A new FORTRAN standard (FORTRAN 8X) is also under consideration by the American National Standards Institute. In spite of the attempts to standardize FORTRAN, however, most computer manufacturers have continued to offer their own extensions of the language. Therefore, compatibility of FORTRAN programs remains a problem today.

In 1957, when the language was first released, computers were used primarily by engineers, scientists, and mathematicians. Consequently, FORTRAN was developed to suit their needs and its purpose has remained unchanged. FORTRAN is a procedure-oriented language with extraordinary mathematical capabilities. It is especially applicable when numerous complex arithmetic calculations are necessary. In general, FORTRAN is not a good business language. Its capabilities are not well suited to programs involving file maintenance, data editing, or document production. However, use of FORTRAN is increasing for certain types of business applications, such as feasibility studies, forecasting, and production scheduling. Another disadvantage of FORTRAN is that it does not resemble English as closely as many high-level languages; therefore, the programs must be well documented to be understandable. Figure 12–2 contains a simple FORTRAN program that calculates a payroll.

BASIC

BASIC, an acronym for Beginner's All-purpose Symbolic Instruction Code, was developed in the mid-1960s at Dartmouth College by Professors John Kemeny and Thomas Kurtz. It was originally developed for use on time-sharing systems to help students learn to program. Inspired by FORTRAN, BASIC is a simplified version of that first high-level language.

The growth in the use of time-sharing systems has been accompanied by an increase in the use of BASIC. Although BASIC was originally intended to be used by colleges and universities for instructional purposes, many companies have adopted it for their data-processing needs. In addition, the increased popularity of microcomputers in homes is furthering the use of BASIC, since it is the language most often sold with these computers.

Among BASIC's most attractive features are its simplicity and flexibility. Because it is easy to learn, it can be used by people with little or no programming experience; a novice programmer can write fairly complex programs in BASIC in a matter of a few hours. It is a general-purpose language that can be used to write programs to solve a wide variety of problems. A BASIC program is shown in Figure 12–3.

The simplicity of BASIC has led many manufacturers to offer different versions of the language. Although there is an established standard (American National Standards Institute BASIC), few manufacturers adhere to this standard and virtually all of them have added their own quirks to the language. Therefore, BASIC programs written for one system often need substantial modification before being used on another.

The main criticism of BASIC focuses on the fact that traditionally it has not been a structured programming language. This means that many popular versions of BASIC do not encourage dividing the program into modules nor do they contain adequate control statements. In many implementations of BASIC it is often necessary to use unconditional branches (GOTO statements) that can cause program logic to be convoluted and difficult to follow.

Some newer versions of BASIC do encourage the development of structured programs. One of these is True BASIC, which was developed by the original developers of BASIC, Kemeny and Kurtz, and was put on the market in 1984. True BASIC retains many of the strengths of the first version produced twenty years ago; it is an economical language, using English-like commands. Yet it provides extensions and options that allow programmers to develop properly structured programs and sophisticated graphics and perform text processing. In addition, ANSI has adopted new standards for a structured BASIC. It will be interesting to see how widely implemented these new standards will be.

FIGURE 12–2

Payroll Program in FORTRAN
Figure continues next page

```fortran
C     *********************************************
C     **         Payroll Program           **
C     *********************************************
      Character*20 fname
      Character*16 employee_name
      INTEGER*2 hours_worked, overtime_hours
      Real net_pay

C     ** Opening an input file **
C     * Prompt the user for the file name *
      write(*, '(A\)') 'ENTER EMPLOYEE MASTER FILE NAME --> '

C     * Read the file name *
      read (*, '(A)') fname

C     * Opening the file *
      open (5, file = fname)

C     ***********************
C     **** MAIN PROGRAM ****
C     ***********************

C     * Print heading *
      write(1,5) 'EMPLOYEE NAME' , 'NET PAY'
5     format(//,1x,A13,8x, A7)

10    read(5,12,END = 99,ERR = 90) employee_name,hours_worked
     1 wage_per_hour
12    format(a16,i2,f5.2)

      if (hours_worked .gt. 40) goto 20

      gross_pay = hours_worked * wage_per_hour
      goto 25

C     * Overtime pay *
20    regular_pay = wage_per_hour * 40
      overtime_hours = hours_worked - 40
      overtime_rate = wage_per_hour * 1.5
      overtime_pay = overtime_rate * overtime_hours
      gross_pay = regular_pay + overtime_pay

C     * Tax calculation *
25    if (gross_pay .gt. 250.00) then
        tax = gross_pay * 0.20
      else
        tax = gross_pay * 0.14
      endif

      write(1,30) employee_name, net_pay
30    Format(/,1x,a16,5x,f7.2

      goto 10

90    write(*,*) 'Error Reading File'
      close(5)
99    stop
      end
```

FIGURE 12–2

Payroll Program in FORTRAN
continued

```
                 EMPLOYEE NAME        NET PAY

                 LYNN MANGINO         224.00
                 THOMAS RITTER        212.42
                 MARIE OLSON          209.00
                 LORI DUNLEVY         172.00
                 WILLIAM LUOMA        308.00
```

FIGURE 12–3

Payroll Program in BASIC

```
10 REM *********************************************
20 REM **        PAYROLL PROGRAM          **
30 REM *********************************************
40 REM
50 PRINT "EMPLOYEE NAME",," NET PAY"
60 PRINT
70 READ NME$,HOURS,WAGE
80 WHILE NME$ <> "END OF DATA"
90   IF HOURS <= 40 THEN GROSS = HOURS * WAGE ELSE GOSUB 1000
100  IF GROSS > 250 THEN LET TAX = .2 ELSE LET TAX = .14
110  LET TAX2 = TAX * GROSS
120  LET PAY = GROSS - TAX2
130  PRINT NME$,,
135  PRINT USING "$$###.##";PAY
140  READ NME$,HOURS,WAGE
150 WEND
999 END
1000 REM
1010 REM *******************************************
1020 REM **            OVERTIME PAY         **
1030 REM *******************************************
1040 REM
1050 LET REGULAR = 40 * WAGE
1060 LET OVERTIME = (HOURS - 40) * (1.5 * WAGE)
1070 LET GROSS = REGULAR + OVERTIME
1080 RETURN
1090 REM
2000 DATA "LYNN MANGINO",35,8.00
2010 DATA "THOMAS RITTER",48,4.75
2020 DATA "MARIE OLSON",45,5.50
2030 DATA "LORI DUNLEVY",40,5.00
2040 DATA "WILLIAM LUOMA",50,7.00
2050 DATA "END OF DATA",0,0
```

```
          EMPLOYEE NAME        NET PAY

          LYNN MANGINO         224
          THOMAS RITTER        212.42
          MARIE OLSON          209
          LORI DUNLEVY         172
          WILLIAM LUOMA        308
```

Pascal

Pascal was the first major programming language to implement the ideas and methodology of structured programming. Niklaus Wirth, a Swiss computer scientist, developed Pascal between 1968 and 1970; in 1971 the first compiler became available. Wirth named the language after the French mathematician and philosopher Blaise Pascal, who invented the first mechanical adding machine. In 1982, ANSI adopted a standard for Pascal.

Like BASIC, Pascal was first developed to teach programming concepts to students, but it rapidly expanded beyond its initial purpose and has found increasing acceptance in business and scientific applications.

Pascal increasingly is becoming the first programming language taught to students at the college level; at present, it is the introductory programming course for computer science students at the majority of universities. It is relatively easy to learn, like BASIC; in addition, it is a powerful language capable of performing a wide variety of tasks including sophisticated mathematical operations. The main reason for the widespread use of Pascal as a teaching tool is that it is a structured language. Each

FIGURE 12–4

Payroll Program in Pascal
Figure continues next page

```
(*      Payroll Program        *)

program payroll (emplfile, output);

type
  array20 = array[1..20] of char;

var
  emplfile : text;
  name : array20;
  wage, hours, grosspay, tax, netpay : real;

procedure readname (var name : array20);

var
  i : integer;
  count : integer;

begin  (* readname *)

  i := 1;
  while not eoln (emplfile) and (i <= 20) do
  begin (* while *)
    read (emplfile, name[i]);
    i := i + 1
  end; (* while *)

  for count := i to 20 do
    name[count] := ' '

end;   (* readname *)

begin  (* payroll program *)

  Assign (emplfile, 'PAYROLL.DAT');
  reset (emplfile);
```

Pascal program is made up of modules called procedures that can be nested within one another. Pascal contains a wide variety of useful control structures such as the IF/THEN/ELSE decision statement and the WHILE/DO loop. Pascal also forces the programmer to declare a variable before it can be used within the program. This declaration requires the programmer to identify the variable's type—whole number, real number, string of characters, or whatever. As a result, variables cannot be used to store an improper type of data. These features encourage students to develop good programming habits. Figure 12–4 contains a short program written in Pascal.

At first Pascal's availability was limited, but more computer manufacturers are now offering Pascal compilers for their machines. Some compilers developed for microcomputers, such as the popular TURBO Pascal implementation, are surprisingly inexpensive and versatile. Many of these compilers have good graphics capabilities. Programmers can create intricate, detailed graphic objects using properly equipped display terminals. This feature is attractive to scientists and increasingly to business personnel as well. A disadvantage of Pascal is that many people believe it has poor input/output capabilities. Therefore, it is not particularly well suited to applications involving manipulation of large data files.

FIGURE 12–4

Payroll Program in Pascal
continued

```
writeln;
  writeln ('EMPLOYEE NAME':13, 'NET PAY':27);
  writeln;

  while not eof (emplfile) do
  begin   (* while *)
    readname (name);
    readln (emplfile, hours, wage);

    (* Calculate gross pay *)
    if hours <= 40
      then grosspay := hours * wage
      else grosspay := hours * wage + (hours - 40) * wage * 0.5;

    (* Calculate net pay *)
    if grosspay > 250
      then tax := 0.2 * grosspay
      else tax := 0.14 * grosspay;
    netpay := grosspay - tax;
    writeln (name:20, '$':14, netpay:3:2)

  end (* while *)
end.   (* payroll program *)
```

EMPLOYEE NAME	NET PAY
LYNN MANGINO	224.00
THOMAS RITTER	212.42
MARIE OLSON	209.00
LORI DUNLEVY	172.00
WILLIAM LUOMA	308.00

COBOL

COBOL (COmmon Business-Oriented Language) is the most frequently used business programming language. Before 1960 no language was well suited to solving business problems. Recognizing this inadequacy, the Department of Defense met with representatives of computers users, manufacturers, and government installations to examine the feasibility of developing a common business programming language. That was the beginning of the CODASYL (Conference Of DAta SYstems Languages) Committee. By 1960 the Committee had established the specifications for COBOL and the first commercial versions of the language were offered later that year. The government furthered its cause in the mid-1960s by refusing to buy or lease any computer that could not process a program written in COBOL.

One of the objectives of the CODASYL group was to design a machine-independent language—that is, a language that could be used on any computer with any COBOL compiler, regardless of who manufactured it. Thus, when several manufacturers began offering their own modifications and extensions of COBOL, the need for standardization became apparent. In 1968 ANSI published guidelines for a standardized COBOL that became known as ANSI COBOL. In 1974 ANSI expanded the language definition in a revised version of the standard. These standards have been widely accepted in industry. After many years of difficult analysis and compromise, a new set of ANSI standards for COBOL was published in 1985. These new standards made many changes to the language including the addition of structured programming facilities.

A key objective of the designers of COBOL was to make the language similar to English. Their intent was that a program written in COBOL should be understandable even to casual readers, and hence self-documenting. You can judge how successful they were by looking at Figure 12–5, which shows a payroll application program written in COBOL.

COBOL programs have a formal, uniform structure. Many types of statements must appear in the same form and the same position in every COBOL program. The basic unit of a COBOL program is the sentence. Sentences are combined to form paragraphs; paragraphs are joined into sections; and sections are contained within divisions. COBOL programs must have four divisions: IDENTIFICATION, ENVIRONMENT, DATA, and PROCEDURE. The divisions appear in the program in this order and are identified by headings, as shown in Figure 12–5.

COBOL offers many advantages for business users. Because of its English-like nature, programs require very little additional documentation; well-written COBOL programs tend to be self-explanatory. This feature makes programs easier to maintain and modify. This is very important because large business programs are always being altered, expanded, and so forth. Since the logic of the program is easy to follow, testing and debugging procedures are simplified. In addition, programmers other than the original ones can read the program and quickly discern what the program does and how it does it. COBOL also has strong file-handling capabilities; it supports sequential, indexed, and direct-access files (see Chapter 6). This feature is very important to large corporations that must deal with enormous quantities of data stored in files.

Because COBOL is standardized, a firm can switch computer systems with little or no rewriting of existing programs. Its standardization also has implications for programmers: once programmers learn COBOL through college training or previous experience, they can transfer their learning with little adjustment to various computer systems and organizations.

```
            IDENTIFICATION DIVISION.
            PROGRAM-ID. PAYROLL.
            INPUT-OUTPUT SECTION.
            FILE-CONTROL.
               SELECT CARD-FILE ASSIGN TO UR-S-SYSIN.
               SELECT PRINT-FILE ASSIGN TO UR-S-OUTPUT.


            DATA DIVISION.
            FILE SECTION.
            FD  CARD-FILE
                LABEL RECORDS ARE OMITTED
                RECORD CONTAINS 80 CHARACTERS
                DATA RECORD IS PAY-RECORD.
            01  PAY-RECORD.
                03  EMPLOYEE-NAME     PIC A(16).
                03  HOURS-WORKED      PIC 99.
                03  WAGE-PER-HOUR     PIC 99V99.
                03  FILLER            PIC X(58).


            FD  PRINT-FILE
                LABEL RECORDS ARE OMITTED
                RECORD CONTAINS 132 CHARACTERS
                DATA RECORD IS PRINT-RECORD.
            01  PRINT-RECORD          PIC X(132).


            WORKING-STORAGE SECTION.
            77  GROSS-PAY             PIC 9(3)V99.
            77  REGULAR-PAY           PIC 9(3)V99.
            77  OVERTIME-PAY          PIC 9(3)V99.
            77  NET-PAY               PIC 9(3)V99.
            77  TAX                   PIC 9(3)V99.
            77  OVERTIME-HOURS        PIC 99.
            77  OVERTIME-RATE         PIC 9(3)V999.
            77  EOF-FLAG              PIC X(3)      VALUE 'NO'.
            01  HEADING-LINE.
                03  FILLER            PIC X         VALUE SPACES.
                03  FILLER            PIC X(21)       VALUE 'EMPLOYEE NAME'.
                03  FILLER            PIC X(7)        VALUE 'NET PAY'.


            01  OUTPUT-RECORD.
                03  FILLER            PIC X         VALUE SPACES.
                03  NAME              PIC A(16).
                03  FILLER            PIC X(5)        VALUE SPACES.
                03  AMOUNT            PIC $$$$.99.
                03  FILLER            PIC X(103)      VALUE SPACES.

            PROCEDURE DIVISION.
            MAIN-LOGIC.
               OPEN INPUT CARD-FILE
                  OUTPUT PRINT-FILE.
               PERFORM HEADING-ROUTINE.
               READ CARD-FILE
                  AT END MOVE 'YES' TO EOF-FLAG.
               PERFORM WORK-LOOP UNTIL EOF-FLAG = 'YES'.
               CLOSE CARD-FILE
                  PRINT-FILE.
               STOP RUN.
```

FIGURE 12–5

Payroll Program in COBOL
Figure continues next page

FIGURE 12–5

Payroll Program in COBOL
continued

```
        HEADING-ROUTINE.
           WRITE PRINT-RECORD FROM HEADING-LINE
              BEFORE ADVANCING 2 LINES.
        WORK-LOOP.
           IF HOURS-WORKED IS GREATER THAN 40
              THEN
                 PERFORM OVERTIME-ROUTINE
              ELSE
                 MULTIPLY HOURS-WORKED BY WAGE-PER-HOUR
                    GIVING GROSS-PAY.
           PERFORM TAX-COMPUTATION.
           PERFORM OUTPUT-ROUTINE.
           READ CARD-FILE AT END MOVE 'YES' TO EOF-FLAG.

        OVERTIME-ROUTINE.
           MULTIPLY WAGE-PER-HOUR BY 40 GIVING REGULAR-PAY.
           SUBTRACT 40 FROM HOURS-WORKED GIVING OVERTIME-HOURS.
           MULTIPLY REGULAR-PAY BY 1.5 GIVING OVERTIME-RATE.
           MULTIPLY OVERTIME-HOURS BY OVERTIME-RATE
              GIVING OVERTIME-PAY.
           ADD REGULAR-PAY, OVERTIME-PAY GIVING GROSS-PAY.

        TAX-COMPUTATION.
           IF GROSS-PAY IS GREATER THAN 250
              THEN
                 MULTIPLY GROSS-PAY BY 0.20 GIVING TAX
              ELSE
                 MULTIPLY GROSS-PAY BY 0.14 GIVING TAX.
           SUBTRACT TAX FROM GROSS-PAY GIVING NET-PAY.

        OUTPUT-ROUTINE.
           MOVE EMPLOYEE-NAME TO NAME.
           MOVE NET-PAY TO AMOUNT.
           WRITE PRINT-RECORD FROM OUTPUT-RECORD
              BEFORE ADVANCING 1 LINES.
```

```
        EMPLOYEE NAME           NET PAY

        LYNN MANGINO            $224.00
        THOMAS RITTER           $212.42
        MARIE OLSON             $209.00
        LORI DUNLEVY            $172.00
        WILLIAM LUOMA           $308.00
```

However, the effort to make COBOL as English-like and self-explanatory as possible has created two disadvantages. First, COBOL programs tend to be wordy and rather long. Using COBOL usually requires more statements to solve a problem than using a more compact language such as Pascal. Second, a large, sophisticated translator program is needed to turn a COBOL source program into machine language. Such a program occupies a large portion of memory.

Regardless of COBOL's disadvantages, it is likely to remain a popular language for many years. Converting the hundreds of thousands of COBOL programs to other languages and retraining thousands of programmers and users would be neither inexpensive nor easy.

Ada

Ada is a state-of-the-art programming language developed by the Department of Defense. Ada is named after Augusta Ada Byron, Countess of Lovelace and daughter of the poet Lord Byron. Augusta Ada Byron worked with Charles Babbage, programming his difference engine (see Chapter 2), and for this reason is often referred to as the first programmer. Ada is derived from Pascal and like Pascal is a structured language with many useful control statements.

The need for a language such as Ada was determined by a Department of Defense study conducted in 1974, which found that more than $7 billion was spent on software in 1973. Through further study it was found that no current high-level language could meet the needs of the Department of Defense and a new language would have to be developed. In 1980 the Department of Defense approved the initial Ada standard, and in 1983 ANSI approved it. Because of the considerable influence the Department of Defense has had and continues to have in this area, some people believe that Ada will someday replace COBOL as the most widely used programming language in business.

Ada is not a beginner's language; a skilled programmer may take six months to become proficient in the language. However, it has the sophistication and reliability (that is, the ability to always obtain correct results) that is necessary for programming in areas of defense, weather forecasting, oil exploration, and so forth.

Ada has the advantage of supporting the use of multiprogramming, which, as discussed in Chapter 10, is the capability of a single CPU to execute more than one program (or subpart of a program) at the same time. Multiprogramming allows computer resources to be used very efficiently.

C

Developed in 1972, **C** has become popular for both system and application programming. It has some capabilities similar to those of assembly languages, such as the capability to manipulate individual bits and bytes in memory locations. Yet it also offers many high-level language features, such as a wide variety of useful control structures. Therefore, it sometimes is referred to as a *middle-level language.*

C is popular for several reasons. First, it is independent of machine architecture, so that C programs are portable. That is, the same program can be run on different computers. Second, C can be implemented on a wide variety of systems, from eight-bit microcomputers to supercomputers such as the Cray-1. Third, it includes many structured programming features found in languages like Pascal. Figure 12–6 contains a payroll program written in C.

C was designed by Dennis Ritchie at Bell Laboratories. One of the first uses was in the rewriting of Bell Laboratories' UNIX operating system. UNIX and its utilities include more than 300,000 lines of C source code, a very ambitious programming project. Today, many of the largest microcomputer manufacturers and software developers use C for system programs, utility programs, and graphics applications.

```
/*      Payroll Program      */

#include <stdio.h>
#include <string.h>

/* Function prototypes */

int main(void);
static float calc_gross_pay(float hours, float wage);
static float calc_net_pay(float gross_pay);

int main(void)
{
  FILE *emplfile;
  char input_buf[133];
  char output_buf[81];
  char emp_name[21];
  float hours, wage, gross_pay, net_pay;

  /* Open payroll data file */
  if ((emplfile = fopen("PAYROLL.DAT", "r")) != NULL)
  {
    /* Print headers */
    sprintf(output_buf, "%-20.20s %s\n\n", "EMPLOYEE NAME",
      "NET PAY");
    printf(output_buf);

    while (fgets(input_buf, 132, emplfile) != NULL)
    {
      /* Separate input line from file into name, hours and wage */
      sscanf(input_buf, "\"%[^\"]\",%f,%f", emp_name, &hours, &wage);

      /* Calculate gross pay */
      gross_pay = calc_gross_pay(hours, wage);

      /* Calculate net pay */
      net_pay = calc_net_pay(gross_pay);

      /* Print results */
      sprintf(output_buf, "%-20.20s $%6.2f\n", emp_name, net_pay);
      printf(output_buf);
    }
```

FIGURE 12-6

Payroll Program in C
Figure continues next page

Companies such as Digital Research, Microsoft, Ashton-Tate, and Novell have used C in the programming of some of their products.

C is a general-purpose language that features economy of expression, modern data structures, and a rich set of operators. Although it is considered a system programming language, it is also useful for numerical, text-processing, and data-base programs. It is a "small" language, using many built-in functions. Therefore, the compilers are simple and compact. Unlike Pascal, which assumes that the programmer is often wrong and thus limits the chances for the programmer to write incorrect statements, C assumes that the programmer is always right and allows the programmer a freer programming style. Therefore, truly spectacular errors are easier to make in C. C is a compiled language and also contains rather cryptic error messages that can confuse a novice programmer. For these reasons, C is clearly intended for the professional programmer.

```
                        /* Close data file */
                        fclose(emplfile);
                    }
                    else
                        printf("\nError Opening File\n");

                    return 0;
                }

                float calc_gross_pay(float hours, float wage)
                {
                    float gross;

                    if (hours <= 40.0F)
                        gross = hours * wage;
                    else
                        gross = hours * wage + (hours - 40.0F) * wage * 0.5F;

                    return gross;
                }

                float calc_net_pay(float gross_pay)
                {
                    float tax, net;

                    if (gross_pay > 250.0F)
                        tax = 0.2F * gross_pay;
                    else
                        tax = 0.14F * gross_pay;
                    net = gross_pay - tax;

                    return net;
                }
```

```
                    EMPLOYEE NAME        NET PAY
                    LYNN MANGINO         224.00
                    THOMAS RITTER        212.42
                    MARIE OLSON          209.00
                    LORI DUNLEVY         172.00
                    WILLIAM LUOMA        308.00
```

Logo

Logo is a procedure-oriented, interactive programming language developed initially by Seymour Papert and the MIT Logo group in the late 1960s. Like BASIC and Pascal, it was originally designed as a teaching tool. Logo's main attraction is that it allows children and adults of all ages to begin to program and communicate with the computer in a very short period of time. Logo allows the user to draw images, animate them, and color them using very simple instructions.

Logo accomplishes this interactive programming of graphics through a triangular object called a turtle, which leaves a graphic trail in its path. The user can easily command the turtle to draw straight lines, squares, or other objects as his or her skill level increases. Figure 12–7 contains a Logo program that illustrates statements that can be used to draw a triangular figure.

FIGURE 12–6

Payroll Program in C
continued

FIGURE 12-7

Logo Program to Draw a Triangular
Figure

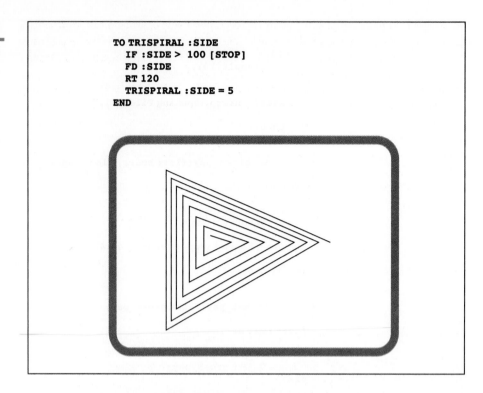

```
TO TRISPIRAL :SIDE
  IF :SIDE > 100 [STOP]
  FD :SIDE
  RT 120
  TRISPIRAL :SIDE = 5
END
```

Logo was developed as an education-oriented language; its strengths lie in its ability to help the inexperienced user learn logic and programming. Because it is a structured language, it encourages the beginning programmer to develop good programming habits. Logo helps the user to determine and develop the procedures required to solve a given problem using the computer. It also helps the user learn to communicate with the computer and to develop an understanding of what programming is all about, including how to debug programs.

The word- and list-processing capabilities of Logo add more power to an already powerful programming language that is used in teaching geometry, language, physics, art, music, and architecture, to name only a few subject areas.

■ VERY-HIGH-LEVEL LANGUAGES

Very-high-level, or fourth-generation, languages are programming languages that still require a specific or exact syntax but are much easier to learn and use. For example, someone who is not a professional computer programmer can use a very-high-level language to develop application software. Very-high-level languages allow the user to specify "what" needs to be accomplished without having to specify "how" it should be accomplished. The fourth-generation language itself is designed such that the user can designate what problem is to be solved. Once the problem has been defined, the fourth-generation language determines what program instructions will be required to solve the problem.

Very-high-level languages typically contain three tools that can be used in the development of an application program. These include query languages, report generators, and application generators. In addition, some very-high-level languages also include a data-base manager. The fourth-generation language FOCUS would be an example. The query language portion of the language requires the user to construct English-like statements to extract and manipulate data in the data base. Although easily understood, these English-like statements must still maintain an exact syntax.

The report generator portion of a very-high-level language allows a user to designate the format of reports that are created from data contained in the language's data base. Application generators give the user a simplified method of developing an application program. This program can then be used to enter and manipulate data within the data base. The application generator can be used to create "user friendly" applications by allowing the user a way of designing input screens. The application generator may also be used to designate verification rules to be performed on the data being entered. Calculations that are required may also be specified when using an application generator. Although they are easy to use, very-high-level languages are still limited in their capabilities. They are often not capable of developing complex programs such as those that may be created using COBOL, FORTRAN, or C.

CONCEPT SUMMARY 12–1		
Special-Purpose Languages		
Category	**Characteristics**	**Examples**
Education	Should teach good programming concepts and be fairly easy to learn; should be able to be used to write a variety of programs to give the beginner a range of experiences	Pascal Logo, BASIC
Scientific	Able to perform complex mathematical operations with a high degree of accuracy	FORTRAN FORTH
Business	Able to handle large data files efficiently and to perform the types of data processing necessary in business	COBOL

◼ NATURAL LANGUAGES

Computer scientists have always realized that computers can't achieve their full potential if only a few people know how to use them. Programmers have helped to make software "user friendly" by using menus and other devices to make the machines interact in humanlike ways. One way in which people's interaction with these machines could be greatly improved would be to allow data bases to be queried in plain English.

Natural languages are programming languages that attempt to allow the user to state queries in English sentences. The question is then translated into a form that the computer can understand. A sentence such as "HOW MANY WOMEN HOLD A POSITION AT LEVEL 10 OR ABOVE?" may be entered by a member of the

Object-Oriented Programming

Object-oriented programming (OOP) is a new—and extremely useful—way of looking at how to write a computer program. In the past, programs were written with a particular function in mind. Say a doctor's office needed a program for printing patient billing statements. Not surprisingly the program would be written to perform that function. Programming in this fashion put the program's functionality ahead of the data that needed to be accessed and manipulated by the program. This was—and remains—the functional view to programming.

Object-oriented programming, on the other hand, can be called the data view to programming. As you might have guessed, object-oriented programming places the data in a program ahead of its overall function. An object-oriented program is a collection of elements (objects) that, when combined, accomplish the required task. Each object is defined in terms of the data it can access and what it does to that data. By combining objects that access and manipulate the data you need, you can write

a program that does everything you want it to.

Let's consider how a patient billing statement program might be written using object-oriented programming. Two objects in the billing program might be "patient" and "account." The "patient" object accesses and can manipulate the patient's name, address, telephone number, and medical condition. The "account" object accesses the patient's account balance, insurance coverage, and finance charges. If the "patient" object needed to know the patient's account balance it would simply ask the "account" object for that sum. This approach to programming offers several advantages.

If such a data view is maintained throughout a program, it follows that a particular piece of data is manipulated in only one location in the program. This helps since any maintenance required to fix the way that piece of data is accessed or manipulated need be done only once in one place within the program. In addition to easily maintained code, object-oriented programming lends itself to

code reusability. An object used in one program can be used in any number of other programs provided the data it accesses and the way it manipulates the data is consistent with the requirements of those new programs. This feature of object-oriented programming could ultimately lead to significant reductions in the time required to write programs.

Although object-oriented programming has not yet won widespread acceptance, it is sure to play an important role in the development of future computer applications. Software vendors have begun to produce and market object-oriented language translators. ANSI, the American National Standards Institute, has started to develop standards for object-oriented languages. Some companies are beginning to report the benefits they have realized from projects developed using object-oriented programming languages. The wave of the future in computer programming might well be an object-oriented wave.

personnel department to gain information for reporting purposes. In some cases, if the natural language processor does not fully understand the inquiry, it may request further information from the user in order to process the given inquiry.

Natural languages have been designed primarily for the novice computer user for use as online, data-base query languages. Natural-language processors normally are designed to be used with a vocabulary of words and definitions that allows the processor to translate the English sentences to machine-executable form. Currently, natural-language sentences are typed at the keyboard; however, in the future the combination of voice recognition technology and natural languages could result in a very powerful tool for computer users. The ability to interface natural-language systems with graphics software also provides a valuable tool for managers in decision making. Although limited to mainframe computers in the past, natural-language systems are being developed for minicomputer and microcomputer systems as well.

◼ PROGRAMMING LANGUAGES—A COMPARISON

Implementing an information system involves making an important decision concerning the type of programming language to use. Some questions must be asked:

◼ What languages does the selected (or available) computer system support?
◼ Does the company require that the system be written in a particular language? For example, in some businesses, all application programs must be written in COBOL.
◼ Will the application require mostly complex computations, file processing, or report generation?
◼ Are equipment changes planned for the future? If so, is it important that the chosen language be implemented on a wide variety of computer systems?
◼ How frequently will programs need modification?
◼ What languages do the programmers who will program and maintain the system know?

The size of the computer system is an obvious constraint on language choice. The size of the memory of microcomputers limits the use of languages such as ADA. But languages such as Pascal, C, and BASIC are widely available on microcomputers.

For large systems, the type of processing is the key consideration in choosing a language. Business applications typically involve large amounts of data on which relatively few calculations are performed. Substantial file processing (requiring many I/O operations) is required; thus, many business applications are **input/output bound.** In such cases, COBOL is the language generally chosen, although Ada is growing in popularity.

Scientific programming applications usually require many complex calculations on relatively small amounts of data. Therefore, they tend to be **process-bound.** The computational capabilities of FORTRAN make it ideal for such applications although Pascal also is often used because it is structured better than FORTRAN.

Because of the diversity of programming languages, many firms choose to use several. For example, a firm can write scientific programs in FORTRAN and file-updating programs in COBOL. It is also possible to write part of a program in one language and another part in a different language; this involves compiling the various portions of the program in separate steps and linking together the resultant object programs. For example, a program written in COBOL may call up an assembly-language program to perform extensive sorting of alphanumeric data, because assembly language can perform sorting tasks more efficiently than COBOL and thus save processing time.

Nevertheless, there has been a definite trend away from programming in assembly language. Because of the one-to-one relationship between assembly-language instructions and machine-language instructions, programming in assembly language is very time consuming. Assembly-language programs may be efficient, but writing them is laborious. In contrast, high-level languages shift the programming emphasis away from detailed computer functions toward procedures for solving problems. If it is necessary to use low-level language commands such as those involving bit and byte manipulation, a so-called ''middle-level'' language such as C should be considered. These languages incorporate the advantages of both high-level and low-level languages.

◘ SUMMARY POINTS

■ Machine language and assembly language, which are low-level languages, require extensive knowledge of the computer system being used.

■ Machine language, consisting of 1s and 0s, is the only language that the computer is capable of executing directly. It is different for each type of computer.

■ Assembly-language statements use symbolic names (called mnemonics) to represent machine operations, making assembly-language programming less tedious and time-consuming than machine-language programming. Before assembly-language programs are executed, they must be translated into machine language. Because there is generally a one-to-one correspondence between assembly- and machine-language statements, this translation is easier to make than when a high-level language is used.

■ Programming languages can be divided into various categories, such as high level or low level, structured or unstructured, procedure-oriented or problem-oriented, and general or special purpose. Dividing programming languages into categories helps programmers in making generalizations about languages and in chosing the right language to meet a specific need.

■ Assembly-language programs are translated into machine language by an assembler. There are two types of translator programs for high-level language programs—compilers and interpreters. Compilers translate the entire source program into machine code, thereby creating an object program, which is then executed. Interpreters translate the source program one statement at a time. In general, interpreters are smaller than compilers and therefore take up less space in memory. However, interpreters can be less efficient than compilers because statements that are used more than once in a program must be retranslated each time.

■ High-level language statements contain English-like words such as READ and PRINT; these statements must be translated into machine language before execution. High-level languages are oriented toward the user, whereas low-level languages are oriented toward the computer hardware. A single high-level language statement may translate into many machine-language statements.

■ FORTRAN is the oldest high-level language and is commonly used for scientific applications because of its ability to perform mathematical calculations with a great deal of accuracy.

■ BASIC is an easy-to-learn language that is widely implemented on microcomputers and is often taught to beginning programmers.

■ Pascal is a structured language that was developed as an instructional language. It is relatively easy to learn and is useful in both business and scientific applications.

■ COBOL is the most popular business programming language. It was designed to be English-like and self-documenting. The main disadvantage of COBOL is that a large and sophisticated compiler is required to translate programs. A main advantage of COBOL is its ability to handle large data files efficiently.

■ Ada is a structured high-level language that was developed for use by the Department of Defense. It allows for the use of multiprogramming and is a sophisticated language that obtains the level of accuracy necessary for programming in areas such as defense, weather forecasting, and oil exploration.

■ C is a structured high-level language that also includes low-level·language instructions; therefore it is sometimes referred to as a middle-level language. It is a general-purpose language that features economy of expression, modern data structures, and a wide variety of operators. C is used for both system and application programming.

■ Logo is an interactive, education-oriented language that uses an object called a turtle to help beginners become familiar with the computer and computer graphics.

■ Very-high-level languages require adherence to a programming syntax but are much easier to use than high-level languages.

■ Natural languages are designed to allow the novice computer user to access the computer's capabilities more easily. For example, easy to write and understand English sentences allow the user to access information in a data base.

■ Factors to consider when selecting an appropriate programming language include: What languages can the computer support? Does the company require that application programs be written in a particular language? Are computations simple? Does the application require much handling of large data files? Are equipment changes planned in the future? How often will programs be modified? What languages do the programmers who will work on the project know?

❑ TERMS FOR REVIEW

◼ REVIEW QUESTIONS

1. What are some of the ways in which programming languages can be categorized? Why is it necessary to categorize programming languages?

2. What does an assembler program do? How does it differ from an interpreter program?

3. What is a linkage editor? Why is a linkage editor needed?

4. What is a mnemonic? How does it help programmers?

5. Outline the advantages and disadvantages of using low-level programming languages.

6. Briefly describe why high-level programming languages were developed.

7. Why was the BASIC programming language developed originally? What are some of the advantages of BASIC? What are BASIC's disadvantages?

8. Describe some of the key advantages of programming in C.

9. List and discuss the factors that should be considered when selecting a programming language for a particular application program.

10. How does a very-high-level language differ from a high-level language? How does a very-high-level language differ from a natural language?

APPLICATION

First Information Processing Co., Inc.

First Information Processing Co., Inc. (FIPCO) in Lima, Ohio, is a consulting firm specializing in information management services. The company assists businesses and financial institutions in data processing procedures from initial planning, design, setup, testing, and final implementation. It can support a client through many product choices including personal computers, mainframe systems, networks, custom software, and popular microcomputer software packages.

FIPCO'S BUSINESS

FIPCO began as a subsidiary of First Federal Savings and Loan Association of Lima. When First Federal wanted to sell the subsidiary, Thomas M. Eversole, once vice president of data processing at First Federal, decided to buy it. Eversole, as president of FIPCO, remains at the consulting offices in Lima, but FIPCO also has a sales operation in Toledo.

The company is an "IBM business partner," specializing in the investigation, recommendation, installation, and support of IBM mid-range systems including the S/36, AS/ENTRY, and AS/400 computers. It also provides services on IBM personal computers, mainframes, and the new RISC System/6000 computers and installs Novell, IBM Token Ring, IBM LAN, and PBX/ROLM networks. FIPCO delivers a wide range of software and operating system support, custom software, industry specific software, education, and maintenance.

In addition, FIPCO helps clients choose and install from a variety of PC software packages including Lotus 1-2-3, dBase, WordPerfect, WordStar, and FoxPro. Recently, FIPCO acquired the local ComputerLand store, which gives its clients an even broader base of products and services from which to choose.

FIPCO arranges disaster planning and testing for clients. It also prepares microfilm from source documents.

FIPCO'S CONSULTING PROCEDURES

FIPCO takes a structured approach to all projects. The first step is project planning. In this stage, the company and client determine the long term goals, set management priorities, and prepare the stage for the installation process.

The second step, systems design, involves an output-process-input approach. The desired results—that is, the output—determines the processing needed in a system. The process then determines what input is needed to achieve these results. Regardless of whether the client is installing a commercial package or developing a home-grown system, FIPCO performs the systems design step in order to insure that project goals are met.

Installation—the longest running phase of setting up any project—is the third step. During this stage, the design is drawn up in detail and the software is constructed or custom-tailored. Hardware and software are installed, and personnel are trained to use the system.

The fourth step is support. FIPCO provides periodic evaluations and continued education to insure the success of each installed project.

The First Collections System has been so successful that FIPCO is marketing it nationwide to financial institutions.

A FIPCO SOFTWARE PROJECT

In 1986, interest rates dropped and the inflation rate leveled. First Federal Savings was able to increase its mortgage production. The company had developed its mortgage banking division to handle a large servicing operation and had the data processing resources—the origin of FIPCO—to handle the computing operations of the new business. First Federal was not prepared for the inevitable increase in delinquent accounts, however. Instead, the collections department had stagnated until it was overwhelmed by the paperwork of the manual card file system and the lack of personnel. It needed a computerized operation that provided networking capability and accessed customer information from the host servicing system.

First Federal had an IBM 4300 series mainframe with Canton Automated Systems software. It was able to produce delinquent notices and reports, apply late charges, and generate billing records, but needed a tool to help with collections. The first improvement was to purchase Canton's on-line service card, which enabled the company to track collections automatically on the mainframe.

The new system fit nicely into First Federal's existing computer resources and contained a direct link to the loan servicing system. On the other hand, information in the loan servicing system was duplicated in the collections system. The collections system was inflexible and required a great deal of programmer maintenance time. It used a third-generation data base language and took up enormous amounts of disk storage space and access time.

As the First Federal staff used the collections system, it began forming ideas about what an automated collections system should do. The data processing department did a major redesign of the system, trying to stay within the limitations of the existing software. Using the COBOL language, the department defined new on-screen forms, designed new collection letters, and developed a better interface between the collections system and the loan servicing software.

The redesigned system was used for another few months in 1988, during which Eversole formed FIPCO as a subsidiary of First Federal. By this time, Eversole and his colleagues had acquired the expertise in personal computers needed to develop the kind of collections system he had envisioned. It was only as they studied their needs that they decided that a PC-based system was obvious.

The majority of collection efforts take place between 3 p.m. and 7 p.m., when people are home from work. Yet the mainframe at First Federal shut down at 5:15 p.m. A freestanding PC system would be available when needed. The PC concept would let the collectors feel as if they were working with a ledger card file at their desks. They could interact with the system to enter comments and produce letters. They would have access to accounts and be able to link with other PC programs such as Lotus 1-2-3. The system would also have automatic archiving abilities.

The information in the system would be updated on a nightly basis from the host computer.

The FIPCO people decided to write the new system in dBase IV, a product of Borland Corp. The language is a fourth-generation language—that is, a language that is closer to human use of English than typical high-level languages. It was chosen because it is user-friendly and the FIPCO programmers had experience with it. At first, the new system was slow, the networking proved problematic, and records duplicated themselves. Transferring the information from the old system to the new posed a problem, too. Soon, however, the problems were corrected. As a result, the delinquency rate improved to 3.37 percent from 5.99 percent five years earlier.

FIPCO notes two highlights of the new system. One is the extract subsystem, which allows a manager in the collections department to generate and modify reports on his schedule rather than wait for the data processing department to do programming. The second is the user-defined letter function, which enables collectors to prepare special letter formats without outside programming help.

The system has been so successful that the now-independent FIPCO is marketing it nationwide to other financial institutions either as a system the client can install or as a turnkey system—that is, a complete hardware and software system that basically starts up when the client "turns the key." (See Chapter 13 for more on turnkey systems.) For marketing, FIPCO developed the system in another fourth-generation language, FoxPro, from Fox Software in Perrysburg, Ohio. Most clients require some custom coding. FIPCO also provides updates to the system two or three times a year as needed. The system, called the First Collections System, runs in stand-alone or LAN environments.

DISCUSSION POINTS

1. How was COBOL used in the major redesign of the first improvement in the First Federal collections system?
2. How does the fourth-generation-language-based collections system demonstrate user-friendliness?

CHAPTER 13

Application Software

ARTICLE

Si, This Word Processor Is Bilingual

James Daly, *Computerworld*

SANTA CRUZ, Calif.—A small start-up software house has created a bilingual English/Spanish word processing program that is intended to offer dramatic benefits for firms in places where a large Hispanic population resides.

Westcliff Software, Inc.'s Dos Amigos program, or "two friends" in Spanish, allows users to work in English, Spanish or both at the same time, thus allowing computer access to a heretofore untapped labor pool, company officials said. The program creates, edits and checks the spelling in a document in both languages and comes with a bilingual dictionary of more than 291,000 words.

Dos Amigos, which has been enthusiastically received by the Hispanic Chambers of Commerce, was designed by a pair of former Borland International, Inc. developers who said a burgeoning market was largely overlooked.

"Hispanics are one of the fastest growing population segments in America, yet somehow the computer industry has failed to recognize this," President Mark Andrews said. He and Executive Vice President Jim Moody estimated that there are more than 900,000 Hispanics working in the San Francisco Bay Area alone.

CHOICE OF DEFAULT

The user chooses English or Spanish as the default that appears on the screen when the program is started, but second-language interpretations of all aspects of the product are available: menus, Help screens, manuals and software tools.

While Dos Amigos is not a translator, single-word translation duties can be performed, Andrews said. For example, if a user wanted to interpret "powerful" into Spanish, he would press a key and the words "poderoso" and "fuerte" would be pre-

sented. The user would then insert the chosen word. Westcliff officials admitted that cultural and linguistic nuances make it nearly impossible to develop a 100% accurate automatic translation program but said they are moving in that direction.

The application allows the user to do mail merges, print and share files with other personal computers.

The suggested retail price of Dos Amigos is $149, but Westcliff officials said they are offering the program at an introductory price of $124.50.

◼ INTRODUCTION

In Chapter 11 we examined the software development process. This process can be used by a company to develop an application software package for in-house use or by a company to develop application software packages to sell. In recent years, the use of commercially written application software packages has increased dramatically. There are commercial packages available for everything from running a doctor's office to performing sophisticated statistical analysis on research data. We will discuss some of the advantages and disadvantages of using commercially developed application software. Included in the chapter are discussions of different kinds of application packages—productivity tools, functional tools, and end-user development tools. The chapter concludes with some guidelines for choosing an application software package.

◼ ADVANTAGES AND DISADVANTAGES OF COMMERCIAL APPLICATION SOFTWARE

Many factors have contributed to the increased availability of commercially developed software packages. You may recall from Chapter 2 that a court decision forcing IBM to "unbundle" its software had a major impact on the growth of the software industry. During that period companies also began to realize that developing programs in-house required a staff of highly talented and skilled programmers. Many found the cost of in-house software development prohibitive, so they began using commercially developed packages. Other factors contributing to the increased use of commercial packages include, first, the speed at which commercial packages can be implemented. Usually less time is needed to implement a commercial application package than to develop software in-house. Second, the quality and sophistication of commercial packages means that often a commercial package will contain more features than could realistically be included in a package developed in-house. Third, the reliability of the packages can be assumed. Because the package is already on the market, presumably it will work properly (or at least well enough to be usable). The reputation of the commercial developer is on the line; therefore, the developer is eager to market a package that will work properly. Because of the strong competition in the field, commercial software developers also have an incentive to provide good quality support for the user. Software support involves a variety of services including on-site training of users and "hot line" telephone support, which allows the users to talk to a staff of trained support representatives. These support representatives are typically employees of the company that has developed the application software package, who have been trained to answer user questions and solve user problems.

While there are benefits to using commercially developed software, there are also disadvantages. A commercially developed package may not meet the user's exact needs and therefore may require extensive modification. In industry, a general rule of thumb is that about 85 percent of an application package can be used exactly as it is written. The other 15 percent of the package must be modified according to user needs. The commercially developed packages can be modified, or customized, by the developer for a user, or, in some cases, commercial software developers sell the source code to users so it can be modified to meet their needs. In addition, the customer usually depends on the vendor from whom the package was purchased to provide support. In the early days of commercial application packages, there were considerable problems in this area. Software developers did not have the personnel or the facilities to provide the needed support. Vendors would make impossible promises concerning the capabilities of their software, leaving many users highly dissatisfied. However, word quickly spread concerning unreliable software developers and vendors. Today most developers and vendors are extremely concerned about their reputations and produce and market high-quality products. Therefore, for many companies, buying and using commercial application software has become a way of life. For most companies, developing and maintaining application software has become costly; this cost can be reduced by purchasing commercial application software.

◼ GENERAL CATEGORIES OF APPLICATION SOFTWARE PACKAGES

The computer industry has grown at a rate unmatched by any other industry. Because of this rapid growth, some areas of the industry are not clearly defined or are the subject of disagreement among industry professionals. Commercial application software development is one area in which some confusion exists. There is a lack of consensus among professionals about how to label or categorize software packages. In this chapter we will divide application software into three broad categories: productivity tools, functional tools, and end-user development tools. Although these categories overlap to some extent, they do provide a useful method of making generalized statements about the different types of application software currently available.

◼ PRODUCTIVITY TOOLS

Productivity tools are software packages that can increase user productivity. Common examples of productivity tools are word processors, graphics packages, spreadsheets, and file managers. These tools can be used for a wide variety of tasks. Productivity tools are simply aids in achieving a goal; the exact goal may vary depending on the particular situation.

Word Processors

Software packages that allow the user to manipulate documents consisting of text, such as letters, reports, and manuscripts, are referred to as **word processors.** Anyone who has ever used a word processor knows how helpful they are when creating and editing these types of documents. No longer are typing mistakes and organizational problems a major difficulty. Portions of the text can be easily deleted, inserted, or moved. Other features often included in word processors are the ability to justify the left and right margins and center headings. Footnotes can be inserted at the bottom of pages and pages can be numbered automatically. Most word processors allow the user to specify options such as italics, underlining, or boldface type.

Often word processors will include extensions such as **spelling checkers,** which compare each word in a specified document with the contents of an online dictionary. If a particular word does not appear in the dictionary, it is flagged so that the user can check it for correct spelling. Most spelling checkers allow the user to add words to the dictionary so that it can be customized to meet the user's needs and vocabulary.

Another popular extension to word processors is a mail-merge capability, which allows users to merge a mailing list with a form letter. This extension can allow users to create a form letter that can then be customized for each recipient from information contained in the mailing list. In some cases, the mailing list can be maintained in a file manager or data base (file managers and data bases will be discussed later in this chapter).

Graphics Packages

Graphics packages allow the user to create bar graphs, line graphs, pie charts, and so forth. Figure 13–1 shows examples of the different types of graphics that might be created with this type of application software. Normally, the user need only specify the type of graph desired and the size of each field within the graph. Different parts of the graph can be appropriately labeled. When using color display devices, the user can specify the colors for various parts of the graph, creating an attractive, professional-looking product in minimal time. Graphics packages are very useful for managers who must prepare reports summarizing complex information.

There are many specialized graphics packages available. Some allow geologists to create color-coded graphics of the earth's surface; these graphics are based on aerial photographs. Presentation graphics packages are especially designed for managers and educators to use when preparing presentations of slidelike shows for groups. The packages allow figures and graphs to be pulled easily from other sources. Composite screens can be created and a wide range of display and dissolve techniques are generally available. Special cameras can create slides from images on terminal screens. In addition, special projectors designed to be attached to computer terminals can be used to project the images onto a screen.

Spreadsheets

A spreadsheet, or electronic ledger sheet, is primarily used in business by accountants for performing financial calculations and recording transactions. An **electronic spreadsheet** is simply a computerized version of a traditional spreadsheet. Electronic

FIGURE 13–1

Examples of graphics developed with Aldus Persuasion. ®

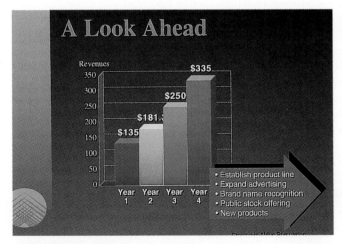

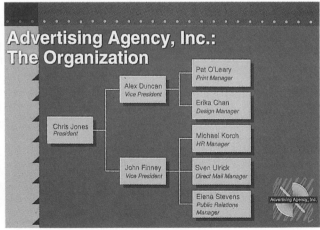

spreadsheets, however, are being used for more than just doing financial calculations and recording transactions. An electronic spreadsheet consists of a table of rows and columns used to store and manipulate any kind of numerical data. The point in a spreadsheet where a particular row and column meet is called a **cell.** Each cell is a unique location within the spreadsheet. Cells can contain labels, values, and formulas.

The use of formulas is what makes spreadsheets powerful. A formula can be applied to the contents of specified cells to obtain a result. For example, a user could calculate the amount of monthly payments on a loan, depending on the interest rate being charged. It would also be a simple matter to determine how much monthly payments would be if the length of payment time varied, say for thirty-six, forty-eight or sixty months. The ability to alter variables within the spreadsheet and easily see what happens to all those values dependent upon the variables is what makes such "what-if" analysis a useful tool.

File Managers

File managers are designed to duplicate the traditional manual methods of filing. Before the use of computers for filing, sections or departments in a business generally kept records that pertained only to their particular area of interest. The payroll department, for example, might keep an employee's name, number, address, salary, and number of deductions to facilitate the writing of paychecks. The personnel department might keep each employee's name, employee number, salary, job title, address, employment history, and spouse's name. Each department would keep its own information independently for its own use.

Computers and computerized recordkeeping made it possible for the procedures and methods of recording, filing, and updating data to be converted from paper file folders and file cabinets to computer software and storage devices. These computerized files can be updated easily and also can be accessed by more than one person at a time.

Other Productivity Tools

Microcomputer software vendors have developed a number of software packages to aid a computer user's productivity. Desktop organizers such as Sidekick combine a number of functions into one software package. These functions are made available to the user with a single keystroke. Functions such as a notepad, calculator, calendar, and telephone dialer for modems can help to improve a computer user's productivity. Text outliners like ThinkTank are designed to allow users to quickly produce outlines. Integrated software packages such as Framework increase a user's productivity by combining a word processor, spreadsheet, file manager, and graphics package into one with a common user interface. Keyboard macro packages such as Superkey can also be used to increase productivity. Keyboard macro packages allow the user to define a series of keystrokes that can be played back as if they were being typed by the user. These macros can be played back by pressing one or two keys to activate them.

■ FUNCTIONAL TOOLS

Functional tools are software packages that perform a specific function. For example, an inventory program used by a grocery store has only one purpose: to keep track of the inventory. An enormous variety of functional tools are currently available, and the number increases daily.

Businesses are the most common users of these commercial application packages. Uses for the packages include accounting, manufacturing, sales, and marketing. We will discuss some popular types of packages here.

Desktop Publishing Packages

Desktop publishing software packages allow users to create near-typeset quality documents by using a laser printer in conjunction with their computer system. Desktop publishing can be used for documents such as company newsletters that may not require the quality of a typeset document. This can result in a significant savings to organizations that would normally send documents out to be typeset. Desktop publishing software allows both text and graphics to be placed on the same page without any cutting and pasting. A typical microcomputer-based desktop publishing system with a laser printer and hard disk drive would cost between $5,000 and $12,000. This can be a very insignificant cost to a business that would spend considerably more to have documents professionally typeset and printed. Desktop publishing software packages such as Aldus Corporation's PageMaker allow a user to view exactly what the printed page will look like on the computer monitor. This is known as a "what-you-see-is-what-you-get" (WYSIWYG) page description desktop publishing software package. With recent decreases in the cost of microcomputer hardware and laser printers, desktop publishing has become a viable alternative for small companies that might require a limited amount of near-typeset quality printing. Microcomputer systems purchased for desktop publishing can also be used by small companies to run other software packages to assist in the management of the business.

Accounting Packages

Most accounting packages are designed as a series of integrated modules. For example, a particular package might have payroll, billing, accounts receivable, and accounts payable modules. When a company purchases a particular package, only those modules needed are obtained. Others can be added on later, if desired. Therefore, the package is tailored to individual needs. Because these modules are then integrated into an entire package,they can interact with one another, passing data between them. These packages can be customized to generate well-designed reports that meet the needs of a specific company. Balance sheets and income statements can be produced, as well as other reports. Figure 13–2 shows a screen for an accounts payable package. Such packages can generate a wide variety of output (see Figure 13–3).

Manufacturing Packages

Manufacturing application packages, like other functional packages, tend to be composed of a number of integrated modules. The modules used depend on the needs of the particular company. In manufacturing, application packages are used to determine material requirements so that inventory needs can be projected to maintain a steady inventory of items on hand. This is important because keeping excess inventory on hand is expensive and ties up capital that could be used elsewhere. If a company maintains multiple warehouses, application packages can track down needed material, making overall operations run more smoothly and making efficient use of stock on hand.

```
AP08
                    GLOBAL SOFTWARE, INC. - ACCONTS PAYABLE
                           VENDOR MASTER INQUIRY

         COMPANY NUMBER   : 10
         VENDOR NUMBER    : A123      X-REF : 8003347192
         VENDOR NAME-1    : GLOBAL SOFTWARE
         VENDOR NAME-2
         VENDOR ADDRESS   : P.O. BOX 19646
         VENDOR CITY      : RALEGH      STATE: NC ZIP CODE: 27619
         TELEPHONE                     COUNTRY:
         ATTENTION      :
         SPEC. INSTRUCTIONS:
         TAX IDENTIFICATION:          SIC CODE :
         DEFAULT G/L DIST. : 102000001020
         RATING        :      ONE TIME :
         OFFICER       :       TERMS   :
         DISCOUNT DAYS   :       TYPE   :
         NET DAYS      :      1099 FORM:
         EMPLOYEE      :       599 FORM :
         SEP CHECK     :       ALT PAYEE:

         CONTINUE: N    END:
```

FIGURE 13–2

This screen demonstrates Global Software, Inc.'s Accounts Payable Ledger Inquiry.

Manufacturing resource planning (MRP) packages have been developed to meet these needs. MRP combines a variety of functions in the areas of business planning and production planning and scheduling. Such a system can maximize resources by helping to route materials efficiently; in addition, overhead is kept at a minimum because only needed inventory is kept on hand. Another important aspect of manufacturing is the scheduling of equipment and people. Often, equipment must be carefully scheduled so that it can be used in the most efficient way possible. A large amount of manufacturing time is used in setting up equipment. For example, if a lathe must be set up in a special way to turn the arms for a certain type of chair, all of the arms that will be needed over an established period of time should be cut at once.

MRP software has become popular and indeed essential because, if implemented correctly, it can save a company large amounts of money; the average return on the investment varies from 50 to 200 percent. In addition, the average MRP user reduces inventory by 17 percent, increases manufacturing productivity by 10 percent, and realizes cost reductions of approximately 7 percent.

In addition to MRP packages, computer-aided design (CAD), computer-aided engineering (CAE), and computer-aided manufacturing (CAM) packages have be-

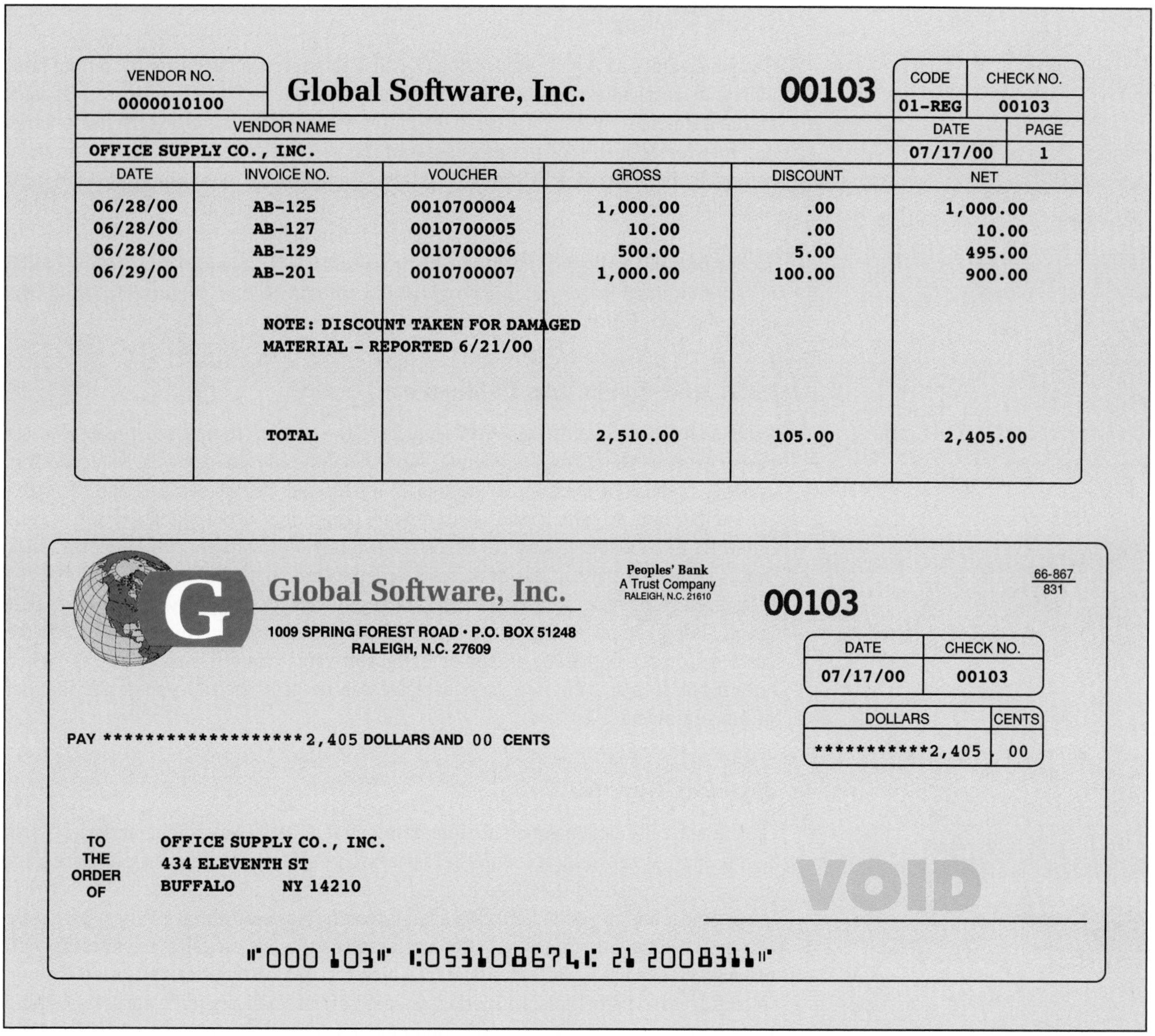

VENDOR NO.	Global Software, Inc.			00103		CODE	CHECK NO.
0000010100						01-REG	00103
VENDOR NAME						DATE	PAGE
OFFICE SUPPLY CO., INC.						07/17/00	1

DATE	INVOICE NO.	VOUCHER	GROSS	DISCOUNT	NET
06/28/00	AB-125	0010700004	1,000.00	.00	1,000.00
06/28/00	AB-127	0010700005	10.00	.00	10.00
06/28/00	AB-129	0010700006	500.00	5.00	495.00
06/29/00	AB-201	0010700007	1,000.00	100.00	900.00
	NOTE: DISCOUNT TAKEN FOR DAMAGED MATERIAL – REPORTED 6/21/00				
	TOTAL		2,510.00	105.00	2,405.00

Global Software, Inc.

Peoples' Bank
A Trust Company
RALEIGH, N.C. 21610

66-867
831

1009 SPRING FOREST ROAD · P.O. BOX 51248
RALEIGH, N.C. 27609

00103

DATE	CHECK NO.
07/17/00	00103

DOLLARS	CENTS
**********2,405	00

PAY ******************2,405 DOLLARS AND 00 CENTS

TO
THE
ORDER
OF

OFFICE SUPPLY CO., INC.
434 ELEVENTH ST
BUFFALO   NY 14210

VOID

⑈000 103⑈ ⑆053108674⑆ 21 2008311⑈

come an essential part of the overall manufacturing process. Computer-aided design allows a user to create a design for a single part or an assembly of parts by using two- or three-dimensional computer graphics. The CAD package allows an engineer or draftsman to rotate, enlarge, or quickly modify a portion of the design. These capabilities allow the user to be significantly more productive than if the design had to be created and modified using pencil and paper. Computer-aided engineering packages allow the design created by the CAD package to be tested and analyzed prior to the actual manufacture of the part or assembly. A CAE package, for example, can be used to conduct stress tests on parts that may ultimately fit into a car's suspension. Once the part or assembly has been designed and tested, a computer-aided manufacturing package can be used to actually create the end product.

FIGURE 13-3

Global Software, Inc.'s Accounts Payable System can perform a variety of tasks such as generating correctly formatted checks.

CASE Packages

Computer-aided systems engineering (CASE) software packages are becoming popular with companies that develop application software. CASE software packages automate the step-by-step process of developing software by capturing the information required for each step of the process from the user. Once the information has been entered by the user, the CASE package then completes the requirements for the steps in an automated fashion. For example, some CASE packages are capable of allowing the user to design an input/output screen and then generate the program required to accept the input or display the output on the screen. CASE packages are very appealing because, in many cases, they can reduce the amount of time required to produce a particular application software package.

Sales and Marketing Packages

Sales analysis software is used to analyze data on sales transactions over a given period of time. The software generates reports stating sales made by each salesperson, quantity of sales of a particular item or in a particular region, profits, and so forth.

Another area in which sales departments commonly use application software is ordering. Excellent software packages are available to maintain order records. New orders are entered, the status of existing orders can be updated, and filled orders can be deleted. This type of package can be integrated with inventory and billing operations. For example, when an order is filled, the data concerning how much the customer owes can then be passed on to the software that performs the billing. When an order is shipped, the inventory package can be instructed to update the number of units in inventory.

Turnkey Systems

Functional tools can be aimed at either horizontal markets or vertical markets. A tool for the horizontal market would be an accounting package that was designed for general use and could therefore be used by any type of user that needed to perform general accounting tasks. Such a package would not be customized for a particular business. On the other hand, a set of application software packages to run a doctor's office is an example of a functional tool aimed at the vertical market. Such a group of packages has a very specific market, doctors' offices, and a specific purpose, helping to perform those tasks that can be computerized. Therefore, the package is designed to meet user's needs in ways that a more general package cannot.

Developing functional tools for the vertical market is a rapidly expanding field. Some software companies not only set up a complete system of integrated packages designed to meet the user's needs but also supply the necessary software. These packages, in which everything is provided for the user, including hardware, software, training, and support, are referred to as **turnkey systems.** These types of systems are very popular with small businesses that do not have the in-house expertise to locate and implement the appropriate hardware and software.

For example, a company that implements turnkey systems for dentists' offices might first determine the exact needs of a particular office and then set up a minicomputer or microcomputer system that will be capable of efficiently running the needed application packages such as scheduling, billing, storing patient records, and generating needed reports. This provides a single integrated system that is designed to meet a variety of needs in a specific situation.

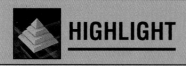

HIGHLIGHT

On the Leading Edge: Cartography

Cartography, or map making, is beginning to realize significant benefits from advances in computer hardware and software technology. Hammond, Inc., makers of maps and atlases, has developed map-making application software that allows artists to create a map of anywhere in the world, at any scale, in a visually appealing format.

Since the art of map making requires taking a picture of something round (the earth) and turning it into a flat piece of art work (a map or atlas), the logic required in a cartography application can be quite complex. The Hammond software is designed to take into consideration the distortion that occurs when creating maps and atlases from aerial pictures of the earth's surface.

The software allows the cartographer to review the effects of scaling and distortion prior to the final printing of a map. If the effects are determined to be undesirable, a new scale can be requested and the effects reviewed.

The software used by Hammond also allows cartographers to control the typesetting of the labels that appear on the map. This leads to a map that is visually more appealing and technically more accurate.

The placement of labels on maps, however, can be a difficult and time-consuming task. Most cartographers still place labels on their maps manually. Oftentimes, labels take more room on the map than the location they are identifying. In densely populated areas, it can be difficult to find space for labels that does not require overlaying an important portion of the map. A professor of geography at the State University of New York at Albany, Jim Mower, is working on software that will automatically place labels on maps. Although he is still developing his program, he has found that the set of rules required to determine where a label can be placed is very complex. On a conventional computer system, the program took as long as thirty minutes to place a single label. With the help of a parallel processing computer, the time has been reduced to three minutes.

The ability to automatically create maps has some very interesting possible future applications. For example, car rental agencies could provide access to a computer that would provide customized maps to its clients. Someone renting a car in an unfamiliar city, for example, might request a map complete with directions from the airport to their hotel or business meeting. Automobile manufacturers could also use this technology to build map displays into future cars. The impact computer technology can have on an application such as map making can be quite significant. These applications are often overlooked by the rest of us, who do not think of the work involved in producing the map in the glove compartment.

Ortho-Track is one company that has designed a specific system for use in orthodontists' offices. Not only does Ortho-Track provide the hardware and software for the business, it also provides on-site training when the system is first implemented and a telephone hotline to handle later questions or problems. The software used by this system, like that for other systems, is modularized. Therefore, the office personnel can choose only those modules that are suited to their needs. The user can also customize the way in which output is displayed on the screen. The Ortho-Track system is typical of many of the systems aimed at the vertical market. The number of companies providing this type of specialized service is growing daily.

■ END-USER DEVELOPMENT TOOLS

End-user development tools (also referred to as **fourth-generation software development tools**) are software packages that allow a user to develop a software application to meet the specific needs of a particular situation. There are several reasons why end-users may choose to develop their own package rather than to buy a commercial package. Sometimes the user's needs are highly specialized; therefore the market for such a package is small and an appropriate one may not be available. In addition, by developing its own package, a company can tailor the software to the exact needs of the particular situation. There is a wide variety of end-user development tools on the market, including simulation software, statistical packages, decision support systems, and data-base management systems.

Creating a software package using these tools requires less skill than that required to program a system. Often development tools allow users to solve problems that ordinarily would require the attention of data processing departments. This frees users from dependency upon data processing departments and is an important advantage in many companies where the data processing department may have a backlog of projects.

Fourth-generation programming languages, or query languages as they are often called, are used with these end-user development tools. The end-user can quickly learn to use these languages because they are similar to English. These languages allow managers to manipulate corporate data in a fast, friendly, flexible way. The user must learn the necessary commands and syntax, but because the statements are similar to English, they require little time or skill to learn.

Simulation Software

People establish theories based on what they observe and measure in reality. Models are then built to test the theory to see if it is correct. If the model works properly, it can be used for **simulation,** which is the use of a model to project what could possibly happen in a particular situation. A simple example of this process would be the development of a formula for converting Fahrenheit temperatures to Celsius. The reality is that any given temperature can be stated in terms of both the Fahrenheit and the Celsius scales. Therefore, a theory could be proposed that because these two scales are based on an absolute value (temperature), it should be possible to come up with a formula to convert a temperature stated in one scale to the other. Once a theory has been created, a model can be developed. One way of developing a model is to take a range of Fahrenheit and Celsius temperatures and determine the relationship. From this a model could be stated:

$$\text{Celsius} = \frac{5}{9} \times (\text{Fahrenheit} - 32)$$

If this model consistently yields correct results when used in simulation, it can be assumed to be reasonably accurate; if not, the model will have to be altered accordingly. After it has been shown that using the model in simulation consistently yields accurate results, it is no longer necessary to check the results against reality. Therefore, results are considered accurate simply by using the model. Concept Summary 13–1 explains the relationship between reality and simulation.

Simulation is particularly useful in making business decisions. For example, if a manager needs to know how cost-effective building a new plant would be, a simulation package can help in making such a decision. Usually such software makes use of a wide variety of information stored in the company's data base to arrive at a conclusion.

An example of a general-purpose simulation software package is GPSS (General Purpose Simulation System), developed by IBM. This package allows the user to establish variables and then alter the relationships between the variables. The software package will determine how these alterations will affect output.

DECISION SUPPORT SYSTEMS. **Decision support systems (DSS)** help managers to make and implement decisions. These software packages are capable of obtaining data from a wide variety of sources such as different departments within a company; they allow the user to analyze this data on an interactive basis. These systems also generally include a number of productivity tools that were previously discussed, such as graphics packages and spreadsheets. What makes the decision support system unique is the way in which these tools are integrated into a highly sophisticated package. Such systems are widely used by financial institutions, oil companies, automobile manufacturers, and other similar industries. The theory behind decision support systems will be discussed in detail in Chapter 15; our emphasis here is on the software used to implement these systems. Decision support systems use fourth-generation languages to query data bases to obtain necessary information; in addition they can be used to simulate specified conditions to determine the output of a particular situation. An example of such a system is the SAS System, developed by SAS Institute Inc. It is an integrated decision support system that includes 125 applications including spreadsheets, statistical analysis, and decision support. Sophisticated graphics and report-generating features allow the output to be attractively displayed or printed. Figure 13–4 demonstrates the SAS System, which can also be used as a statistical package. (Statistical packages will be discussed later in this chapter.)

There are a number of application software packages available that allow the manager to interactively probe a computerized model for results concerning various decision alternatives. These packages include MARKETPLAN and BRANDAID, which help in preparing marketing plans; CALLPLAN and DETAILER, which aid in the allocation of a sales force; and MEDIAC, which helps to prepare advertising media schedules.

Another package is the Interactive Financial Planning System (IFPS). IFPS is an interactive planning package that centers around a model based on a manager's

FIGURE 13–4

The results generated by the SAS decision support system can be displayed in a variety of ways, including easy-to-understand graphs.

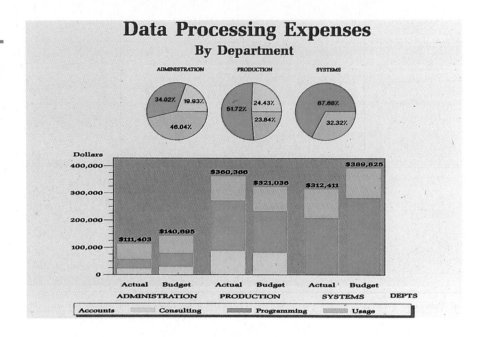

perception of the real-world system. Marketed by EXECUCOM Systems Corporation, IFPS can be considered a generalized planning or modeling system. As a generalized system, IFPS can be used for such applications as balance sheet and income statement preparation, operating budgets, forecasting, strategic planning, risk analysis, and capital budgeting. Because IFPS does not incorporate a specific model, it offers management a great deal of flexibility. See Figure 13–5 as an illustration of the decision support aspect of IFPS.

FIGURE 13–5

The What-If? feature of IFPS enables the user to calculate the effect of changes on selected values to the remaining values with a single menu selection.

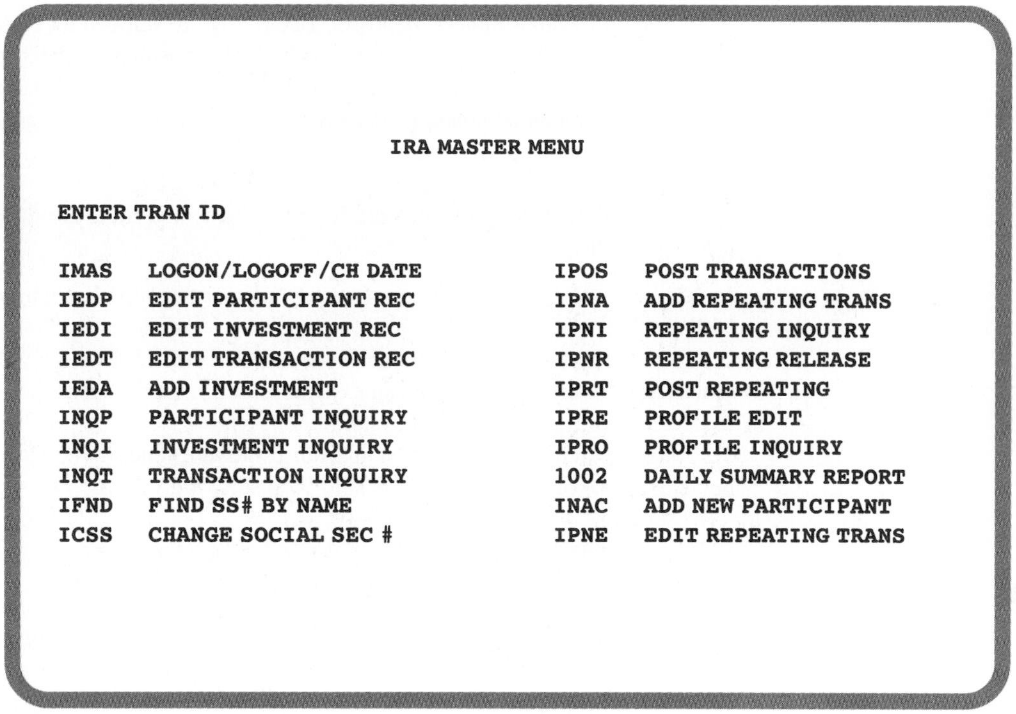

```
                        IRA MASTER MENU

        ENTER TRAN ID

            IMAS   LOGON/LOGOFF/CH DATE      IPOS   POST TRANSACTIONS
            IEDP   EDIT PARTICIPANT REC       IPNA   ADD REPEATING TRANS
            IEDI   EDIT INVESTMENT REC        IPNI   REPEATING INQUIRY
            IEDT   EDIT TRANSACTION REC       IPNR   REPEATING RELEASE
            IEDA   ADD INVESTMENT             IPRT   POST REPEATING
            INQP   PARTICIPANT INQUIRY        IPRE   PROFILE EDIT
            INQI   INVESTMENT INQUIRY         IPRO   PROFILE INQUIRY
            INQT   TRANSACTION INQUIRY        1002   DAILY SUMMARY REPORT
            IFND   FIND SS# BY NAME           INAC   ADD NEW PARTICIPANT
            ICSS   CHANGE SOCIAL SEC #        IPNE   EDIT REPEATING TRANS
```

◼ EXPERT SYSTEMS

Expert systems are built using what is known of the human thought processes to mimic the decision-making processes of human experts in narrowly defined fields. Software designers try to program the computer to follow the same path of thinking as top experts in the specified field. Expert systems are different from decision support systems in that they cover only very small fields of knowledge; decision support systems attempt to allow managers to make decisions based on a wide range of data and factors (see Figure 13–6).

The heart of the system is a knowledge base that contains facts and rules used by experts. The user asks questions of the system through the use of fourth-generation programming languages. When responding to these questions, the expert system draws on its knowledge base.

Although the quality of these systems is growing rapidly, as yet they are unable to make the type of sophisticated inferences that a human expert can make. Nonetheless, expert systems offer a number of advantages over human experts. For example, knowledge is not lost as it may be when a human expert dies or moves to another job.

One expert system is MYCIN, which is used to diagnose infectious diseases and recommend appropriate drugs. Another interesting expert system is XCON, developed by J. McDermott at Carnegie-Mellon University, which is used to determine

FIGURE 13–6

IRA Master from Fogle Computing Corp. is an expert system used for investment purposes.

the best configuration of Digital Equipment Corporation (DEC) minicomputer system components for a particular user. PROSPECTOR is an expert system that helps geologists in locating mineral deposits. Taxadvisor, developed by R. Michaelsen at the University of Illinois, helps users with estate planning. It determines ways in which the client can minimize income and death taxes and also makes investment and insurance recommendations. ILPRS, an expert system that assists businesses in long-range planning, and IPPMS, an expert system that assists businesses in managing projects, are expert systems developed by DEC. More expert systems in every conceivable field are being designed all the time. Typically, there are three approaches to the use of expert systems:

1. You can write your own expert system using programming languages such as LISP or PROLOG.

2. You can use an expert system shell such as VP-EXPERT, M.1, LEVEL5 OBJECT, Goldworks, or Exsys to develop an expert system. Expert system shells can be used to develop a customized expert system.

3. You can purchase an expert system from a software vendor. The Taxadvisor would be an example of an expert system sold by a software vendor.

Statistical Packages

An interesting application of prewritten software packages is in the area of statistics. Before the advent of these packages, scientists and statisticians spent many hours analyzing data, using calculators and complex mathematical formulas. Today, elaborate statistical procedures can be performed accurately and quickly with the aid of **statistical packages.** The user must write a simple program that then generates the needed statistics, but because the program is written in a fourth-generation language, these packages are easy for people with no programming experience to use. Three commonly used statistical packages are SAS (Statistical Analysis System), SPSS (Statistical Package for the Social Sciences), and Minitab. These packages can provide a wide variety of arithmetic and trigonometric functions. In addition, statistical functions calculating means, ranges, variances, and standard deviations, as well as more complicated statistics, are easily performed.

To use a statistical package, the user must write a program in a fourth-generation programming language designed specifically for that package. Figure 13–7 shows a sample SAS program and its output. In addition to performing a wide variety of statistical operations, SAS also allows the user to determine how the output will be printed. Statistical packages are often included as part of a decision support system, thereby allowing managers to analyze data as desired.

Data-Base Management Systems

Data-base management systems (DBMS) consist of a series of programs that are used to design and maintain data bases. A data-base management system is more complex than a file manager because programs can be developed to access the data base in a variety of ways.

For example, if the accounting department accessed employee records contained in a data base, the records could be displayed in a way that was most convenient for their needs. Also, only the information needed by the accounting department would be displayed. On the other hand, a different program could be written to access the same employee records for the personnel department. This program would display only the information needed by personnel.

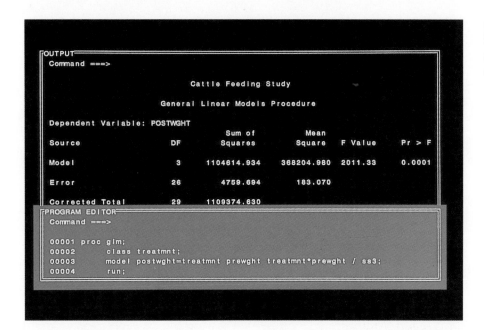

FIGURE 13–7

SAS/STAT® software performs simple and complex statistical analysis.

Data-base management systems are divided into three categories depending on the way in which data contained in them is stored. The categories, which were explained in Chapter 7, are hierarchical, network, and relational. The oldest data-base structure is the hierarchical structure. An example of a hierarchical data base is IMS, which was developed by IBM and has been widely used for some time. A commonly used network data base is MDBS.

When using hierarchical or network systems, programs called **schemas** are written that determine the manner in which the records stored in the data base will be related to one another. These schemas are written in a **data definition language (DDL).** Once the **DDL** is written, a program written in a **data manipulation language (DML)** accesses the data base defined by the DDL. In these programs, data manipulation language statements are embedded in another language, such as COBOL. Therefore, writing a program to access a hierarchical or network data base requires a significant amount of programming skill.

On the other hand, when using a relational data base, the user simply accesses the data base directly through the use of a fourth-generation language. The American National Standards Institute (ANSI) has approved SQL (Structured Query Language) as the standard fourth-generation language to query relational data bases. Three relational data bases currently available are DB2, developed by IBM; ORACLE, developed by Oracle Corporation; and INGRES, developed by Relational Technology. All of these data bases can be queried by using the fourth-generation language SQL. Data bases provide an enormous amount of flexibility in allowing users to access data in a wide variety of ways.

◻ CHOOSING AN APPLICATION SOFTWARE PACKAGE

The user who needs to decide whether to buy a commercial application package or to develop the needed software system in-house is facing a difficult decision. Some of the questions that should be asked are:

G-Fit to the Rescue

One of the most difficult and time-consuming tasks associated with NASA's space shuttle missions is determining how to fit all the mission's cargo into the shuttle's cargo bay. The task is doubly complex in that the cargo must be placed on board the shuttle while it is in a vertical position. In addition, pins that hold each piece of cargo in place must fit into their designated holes within a tolerance of one-hundredth of an inch.

Over the past fifteen years, two Rockwell International employees have been largely responsible for the loading of the shuttle's cargo bay. Recently, however, one of those employees retired, and the second is now nearing retirement age. As a result, Rockwell had to determine some way of capturing the vast amount of knowledge and experience these two workers had accumulated in their fifteen years of loading the shuttle's cargo bay. The answer: G-Fit, an expert system designed to incorporate all the experience of the two experts before it was lost.

G-Fit (Ground System to Flight Payload Integration Tool) runs on an Apple Macintosh II microcomputer and allows engineers working on the shuttle program to interactively design how a mission's cargo can be placed in the cargo bay. Cargo including satellites, telescopes, and scientific experiments can be loaded and reloaded as necessary within G-Fit until the right configuration is found.

The knowledge built into G-Fit includes the cargo bay's dimensions, information about devices mounted to the sides of the cargo bay, and the rules and requirements for using the cargo bay's available space. Once G-Fit creates a possible configuration for a mission's cargo, it prints out a diagram and also a report that is reviewed for feasibility. This process continues until an acceptable cargo configuration is agreed upon. When agreement is reached, the cargo is then loaded into a test cargo bay identical in shape and size to that of the shuttle.

Without expert systems such as G-Fit, the many years of knowledge and experience gained by human experts would be lost. It is for this reason that research in the area of expert systems has been so intense. As with many other emerging technologies, expert systems will undoubtedly play an ever increasing role in our daily lives.

■ Does the data processing department have the needed system analysts and/or programmers with the needed skills to develop the package in-house?

■ Is there commercial application software that can meet the stated needs (or at least be easily modified to meet these needs)?

■ Will the appropriate commercial software run on the available computer system?

■ Is there adequate documentation?

■ Will the vendor or manufacturer provide the needed support?

■ Is there time available to write the software in-house, or is obtaining a package that can be quickly implemented a critical factor?

If after carefully considering the above factors it has been decided to purchase a commercial application package, it then must be determined which package will best meet the user's needs. If possible, the user should arrange to try the package on a trial basis to determine how well it will work day in, day out. Another source of information on the quality of application software is user surveys. Several publications conduct such surveys on a regular basis. For example, *DATAMATION* conducts a yearly survey of data processing managers called the Applications Software Survey, asking them to evaluate packages they are using. The results of this survey can be a very helpful guide in choosing software. According to *DATAMATION,* there are four areas of primary concern in evaluating these packages: performance, operations,

I/O functionality, and vendor support. Performance is concerned with such factors as the efficiency of hardware utilization and the ease of use. I/O functionality covers data entry provisions and how quickly and easily output format changes can be made. The applications software packages covered in the survey fall into business categories such as general accounting, payroll and personnel, and business management and forecasting.

When choosing application software packages, customers often turn to resources within their specific field. Another method of evaluating application packages is simply word-of-mouth. Company management within a specific industry often have frequent contact with management in similar companies and can ask these people what types of packages they are using and how they would evaluate the performance of the software.

Probably the best method of choosing a package is to use a number of them on a trial basis to determine how each will actually perform on the job. Because the application package will probably be used for some time to come, the time spent in making an informed choice is well spent.

CONCEPT SUMMARY 13–2

Categories of Application Software Packages

Category	Explanation	Examples
Productivity tools	Used to increase user productivity	Word processor Graphics package Spreadsheet File Manager
Functional tools	Perform a specific purpose	Payroll Billing Accounts receivable Inventory control Manufacturing resource planning
End-user development tools	Allow the end-user to develop software tailored to a specific situation, often through the use of a fourth-generation programming language	Decision support system (DSS) Data-base management system (DBMS)

■ SUMMARY POINTS

■ The use of commercially written application software packages has increased dramatically in recent years. Such packages have a number of advantages over software written in-house, including generally lower cost, faster implementation, better quality, and reliability. There are some disadvantages, however, including the fact that a commercial package may not meet the user's needs as precisely as one developed in-house. Also, the user is dependent upon the vendor or the developer for support.

■ Application software can be divided into three broad categories: productivity tools, functional tools, and end-user development tools.

■ Productivity tools are packages that can be used in a wide variety of ways to increase the productivity of the user. Examples are word processors, graphics packages, spreadsheets, and file managers.

■ Functional tools perform a specific function or purpose. Functional packages are generally built from modules so that they can be customized to meet the user's needs. Accounting packages produce payrolls, balance sheets, and income statements. Desktop publishing packages are used to produce near-typeset quality printed documents. Manufacturing resource planning (MRP) packages are commonly used in manufacturing to handle inventory and schedule employees and equipment efficiently. In sales and marketing, software packages keep track of order status and generate sales reports.

■ Turnkey systems are popular with small businesses. Companies specializing in these systems supply the user with a complete package, including hardware, software, training of staff, and ongoing support. Because the software is usually modularized, it can be customized easily to meet the user's needs.

■ End-user development tools allow the end-user to use fourth-generation programming languages to develop an application package to exact specifications. Fourth-generation programming languages are more English-like than high-level languages such as COBOL and require only a short time to learn.

■ Simulation software uses a model to project what will happen in a particular situation. Decision support systems help managers to make and implement decisions. They obtain data from a wide variety of sources, most commonly data bases. In addition, they incorporate a wide variety of packages such as graphics and spreadsheets. IFPS is a decision support system that allows the user to manipulate variables to determine how various results will be affected.

■ Expert systems attempt to mimic the decision-making processes of experts in narrowly-defined fields. These systems use a knowledge base to answer questions posed by the user.

■ Statistical packages quickly and accurately perform statistical analysis of data. SAS, SPSS, and Minitab are three examples of statistical packages.

■ Data-base management systems consist of a series of programs that are used to design and maintain data bases. When using hierarchical or network data bases, a data definition language (DDL) must be used to write a program that determines how the data base is organized. Then programs are written in data manipulation languages (DML) that allow the user to access the data base. The end-user can then access the data base through the use of a fourth-generation language. Relational data bases do not require the use of data definition languages or data manipulation languages. These data bases can be accessed directly by using fourth-generation languages.

■ When choosing an application package, many factors must be taken into account. Some of them are: (1) Can the package be written by the company's data processing department? Are the needed analysts and programmers available? (2) Is there a commercial package available that can meet the stated need and will this package run on the available computer system? (3) Is there adequate documentation for the commercial software and will the vendor or manufacturer supply the needed support? (4) Is there time to develop the package in-house?

■ If a company decides to buy a commercial package, a particular package must be chosen. User surveys conducted by magazines and journals are one helpful method

350

of determining if current users are satisfied with their software. Another method is to ask other companies in the same field how happy they are with the software they are using. The best test of how well it will perform in a particular setting is using the software on a trial basis.

■ TERMS FOR REVIEW

cell, p. 336

data base management system (DBMS), p. 346

data definition language (DDL), p. 347

data manipulation language (DML), p. 347

decision support system (DSS), p. 343

electronic spreadsheet, p. 335

end-user development tools (fourth-generation software development tools), p. 341

expert system, p. 345

file manager, p. 336

functional tools, p. 336

graphics packages, p. 335

productivity tools, p. 334

schema, p. 347

simulation, p. 342

spelling checker, p. 334

statistical package, p. 346

turnkey systems, p. 340

word procesors, p. 334

■ REVIEW QUESTIONS

1. What are some of the factors that contribute to a company's selection of commercially developed software over software developed in house?

2. What types of application software packages are included in the productivity tools category?

3. Briefly describe five common features found in word processors. List two common extensions to word processors.

4. What are some common uses of electronic spreadsheets? (Consider uses mentioned in the text as well as others you may know about or have had experience with.)

5. What is a cell? What types of things can be put in a cell?

6. Give a brief description of some of the software packages found in the functional tools category.

7. What is WYSIWYG? Why is it important?

8. What does CASE stand for? Why do you feel software developers are looking very seriously at CASE packages?

9. Describe what is meant by the term *turnkey system*. Why do you think businesses such as doctors' offices prefer turnkey systems?

10. What is an expert system? What is the basis for an expert system? Where is this basis found?

Ford Motor Company

On June 16, 1903, Ford Motor Company entered the business world with little fanfare when Henry Ford and eleven associates filed incorporation papers in Lansing, Michigan. With an abundance of faith, but only $28,000 in cash, the pioneering industrialists gave birth to what was to become one of the world's largest corporations. At the time of its incorporation, Ford was but a tiny operation in a converted Detroit wagon factory staffed with ten people.

Today, the company is one of the world's largest industrial enterprises with active manufacturing, assembly, and sales operations in 25 countries on six continents. Ford employs 366,600 men and women and its products are sold in nearly 200 nations and territories by some 10,500 dealers. The company's annual sales exceed the gross national products of many industrialized nations. In 1989, Ford Motor Company had profits of $3.2 billion. It is ranked number three on the Fortune 500 list of the largest U.S. industrial corporations, based on sales, and is the second largest manufacturing company in the United States.

GENERAL COMPUTER USE

Today, computer use at Ford falls into four broad categories. Centralized mainframe computers are used to support the major information-processing requirements of the company. Specialized computers and workstations are used in the computer-aided design, engineering, and manufacturing (CAD/CAM/CAE) areas. Plant floor automation strategies help improve manufacturing efficiency and use a wide range of computer equipment. Finally, a comprehensive office automation program provides employees with a variety of productivity tools such as word processors and spreadsheets.

Corporate and divisional systems require capabilities of large mainframe computers for transaction-intensive applications. The mainframe computers are organized in clusters of processors serving a community of interests. Major centers housing these computers are linked by high-speed communication channels to allow the sharing of information and backup facilities. This environment plays a major role in information processing by offering the most efficient and manageable mode of operation for the large application systems.

Corporate strategies to reduce costs while improving quality, timeliness, and customer satisfaction have increased demands for CAD/CAM/CAE support. Other pressures for CAD/CAM/CAE support come from the growth in the number of customers, requirements for data exchange with suppliers, and greater emphasis on worldwide product programs. A major effort is being deployed to make optimum use of engineer skills by providing engineers with state-of-the-art computer-assisted engineering tools.

DOES II allows Ford's dealers and others to prepare parts orders on their own computers as time is available and then send information to the mainframe when convenient—all through "transaction streaming."

Computer-related technologies used in factory floor automation offer considerable potential for improving manufacturing efficiency. These plant-floor systems fall into two categories. The first consists of business systems which typically involve the use of computer terminals on the shop floor for online entry or display of centralized data. The second category is used in the actual manufacturing process and includes robots or flexible machining systems, the grouping of similar parts into families for manufacture, and better overall design of shop floor processes.

On a world-wide basis, each major Ford company component has a program to establish an internal solution for office automation and end-user computing that is compatible with the rest of the corporation. The objective is to facilitate communications and integration across the entire organization and to realize economic advantages on a company-wide scale. Ford employees use a variety of commercial computers and software tools for office automation, but one commonly used computer is the IBM PS/2 system. Among the software tools that support the system are the spreadsheet Excel from Microsoft Corp., the word-processing package WordPerfect from WordPerfect Corp., and the data-base program DataEase from International, Inc. When this variety of hardware and software tools is fully deployed, end-users have available an array of common, integrated, easy-to-use tools to improve their personal productivity. They can communicate effectively with each other, share computer resources, and access information on both corporate and commercial data bases.

DOES II: A DIVISION-WIDE SYSTEM

The Direct Order Entry System (DOES II) at the Ford Parts and Services Division is an example of a divisional mainframe computer application. The system couples local and mainframe interaction by allowing customers (that is, dealers and others) to prepare parts orders on their own computers as time is available and then send information to the mainframe computer when convenient. To support this offline concept, a new and innovative computer technique called "transaction streaming" was developed. The technique is unique in the service parts industry and has helped to increase service and business flexibility for the customer and to decrease costs for both the customer and Ford. In addition, having the central computer control the major processing functions enables program revisions and enhancements to be implemented with minimal impact to customer computer operations. By providing the capability for direct order entry and immediate access to parts information at the central computer, DOES II lets customers retrieve order information and answer questions at their convenience. DOES II is a "best-in-class" customer parts-ordering and information system.

AuTOPS: A GROUP PRODUCTIVITY TOOL

Automated Team-Oriented Problem Solving (AuTOPS) is a systems-based productivity tool used by Light Truck Product Development activities at Ford. Employees in engineering, manufacturing, purchasing, and other activities work in teams to solve problems and produce "best-in-class" products. Because hundreds of people from different activities can become involved, coordination and com-

munication of up-to-date information is essential for success in the team-oriented approach.

AuTOPS provides the necessary communication by using a combination of data-base and electronic-mail technologies. It enables team members to document problems online and route them to the appropriate individuals for comment and resolution. AuTOPS also provides additional features that enhance the team process, including the following:

- A common format for specifying, updating, re-routing, and responding to problems
- Up-to-date online information
- Ad-hoc reporting
- Summary information reporting

By providing these capabilities, the AuTOPS system reduces the need to conduct meetings and distribute paper documents. Online interaction also avoids the delays associated with using the telephone and mail, and allows individuals to more effectively manage their time.

DISCUSSION POINTS

1. In what ways does Ford use computer-related technology to improve efficiency on the factory floor?
2. How do the DOES II system and AuTOPS increase employee productivity and customer satisfaction at Ford?

System Analysis and Design

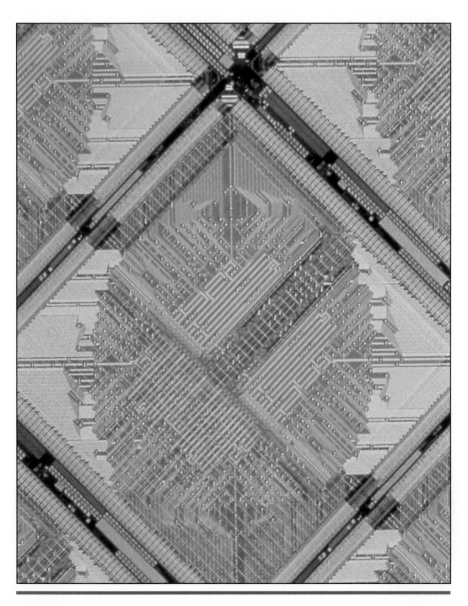

Simon Says Soup Is Good Food

Johanna Ambrosio, *Computerworld*

CAMDEN, N.J.—How does Campbell Soup Co. ensure that its soup is "mm-mm good"? An expert system, chosen and implemented by an end-user department, helps the company determine when something goes wrong with the processing of the soup and what to do about it.

The expert system, dubbed Simon, was installed two years ago and became fully operational a year later. "We tested it for a year to make sure it's right," said Michael S. Mignogna, corporate process authority at Campbell. "We wanted to make sure that when it decided something, it was the same as if one of our people had made the decision." Thus far, the system has saved Campbell's about $5 million. Simon was written using Aion Corp.'s Aion Development System shell.

Mignogna's department, thermal process development, sets the standards for how soup should be cooked to ensure sterility and to avoid conditions such as botulism. It also makes the calls about what to do if something goes wrong.

For instance, a batch of cream of mushroom needs to be cooked for 50 minutes at 250 degrees, and halfway through the cooking, the plant loses steam pressure or the conveyor belt slows down. Mignogna's group has to decide whether to OK that batch

for sale or destroy it. The goal is to destroy as few items as possible while guaranteeing quality. "It's that one can of soup that we worry about," he said.

Before Simon was installed, Mignogna's department used a General Electric Co. time-sharing arrangement. Then in 1985, Mignogna and his engineers converted the time-sharing application to run on an IBM Personal Computer. "I wouldn't say it was the most efficient system," Mignogna said, "but it worked." And it saved the approximately $4,500 a month that the time-sharing system cost.

All told, Simon has saved Campbell between $2 million and $3 million a year. Most of this is accounted for by products that would have been destroyed under the old system but that were really safe. "That sounds like a lot of money," Mignogna said, "until you realize that Campbell makes five billion to 10 billion cans of soup a year."

With the old PC system, whenever there was a problem the plant would notify Mignogna's people and send data about all the conditions. Thermal process would look at the data and use the PC program to do mathematical simulations to decide whether the product was safe. This process took up to eight weeks, and the product in question needed to be

held in a warehouse until a decision was made.

With Simon, however, that decision-making process is cut to about three minutes, and most of the decisions are made by Simon with little human intervention. When something goes wrong at the plant, a quality control person enters data into Simon on a personal computer. Four plants have PCs that run Simon locally. Mignogna's group also has a PC with Simon on it.

If the expert system determines that the problem will not impact quality, it authorizes the product to be released. "It's the same as if I signed it off," Mignogna said. If the problem is determined to be more serious, the product is put into isolation in a warehouse, and Mignogna's group reviews the paperwork and does a risk analysis.

Simon makes the decisions about 90% of the time, Mignogna said. In the other 10%, all the data may not be immediately available. Nor does Simon contain rules for all the possible combinations—such as container defects, for instance. "These are the sorts of things that are not toxic and won't kill anyone," Mignogna said.

Because the expert system can separate the business rules from the mathematical calculations, Mignogna said, either can be changed without affecting the other. This can come in handy when Campbell adds new products or changes the recipes for old ones. When the company introduced its low-salt soups, for example, Simon needed to be changed to accommodate. "Salt is a preservative, so when you take it out, there's some impact," Mignogna said.

Besides the cost savings, benefits include improved efficiency of the decision-making process and improved morale at the plants, Mignogna said. Plant employees feel more in control of things because they no longer have to wait for his group to make a decision.

In the future, the Simon systems in the plants and Mignogna's group will be linked so Mignogna can pull information out of the plant PCs.

Currently, the only way Mignogna can update his files is to dial into the plant PCs. "We're waiting for our MIS department to make all the connections," he said.

◻ INTRODUCTION

In computer-based information systems, the hardware and software technologies discussed in earlier chapters are applied as tools for the collection, storage, and retrieval of information that is either helpful to management or required for routine business practices. Information that is helpful to management might include sales analyses, while information that is required for normal business practices might include payroll processing or income tax reporting. It is necessary to understand the hardware and software technologies in order to develop an effective management information system.

This chapter focuses on how hardware and software technologies are used in the development of computer-based information systems and explains the various phases involved in designing and implementing such systems. Topics covered include system analysis, design, programming, implementation, and audit and review.

◻ SYSTEM ANALYSIS

The first step of **system analysis** is to formulate a statement of overall business objectives—the goals of the system. Identifying these objectives is essential to the identification of information the system will require. The next step is for the analyst to acquire a general understanding of the scope of the analysis.

By viewing the system from the top down, the analyst determines on what level the analysis should be conducted. Figure 14–1, for example, illustrates the potential levels at which analysis could be conducted for a company's marketing information system. Other information systems such as an accounting information system or a personnel information system may also exist within a company's organizational information system. The level at which the analysis should be conducted should be agreed upon with management and reviewed in the form of a proposal to conduct a system analysis. The proposal should provide management with the following:

■ A clear and concise statement of the problem or reason for the system analysis.
■ A statement clearly defining the level of the system analysis and its objectives.
■ An identification of the information that must be collected and the potential sources of this information.
■ A preliminary schedule for conducting the analysis.

CHAPTER 14

FIGURE 14–1

Top-Down View of an Organization's Information System

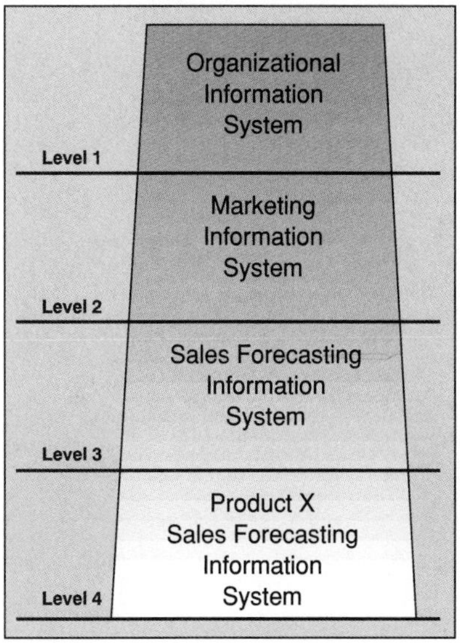

Level 1 — Organizational Information System

Level 2 — Marketing Information System

Level 3 — Sales Forecasting Information System

Level 4 — Product X Sales Forecasting Information System

The proposal ensures that management knows what resources will be required during the system analysis. It also helps the system user to make sure the analyst has identified the problem correctly and understands what the analysis should accomplish. Because system analysis is costly and time consuming, the scope of the analysis should be clarified in this way before the analyst continues.

Once the proposal has been accepted, the analysis can proceed. Data relevant to decision makers' information needs is gathered and analyzed. When the analysis is completed, the analyst communicates the findings to management in the **system analysis report.** On the basis of this report, management decides whether or not to continue with the next step in system development—system design.

Reasons for Conducting System Analysis

System analysis is performed for various reasons, which determine its scope or magnitude. An analysis may be required because of a need to solve a problem, as a response to new information requirements, as a method of incorporating new technology into a system, or as a means of making broad system improvements. The gathering and analyzing of data occur at different levels of intensity, depending upon the scope of the analysis. The reasons for conducting system analysis are discussed in the following sections.

SOLVING A PROBLEM. Sometimes information systems that do not function properly require adjustment. Perhaps a particular manager is not getting a report at the time it is needed, or an insufficient number of copies of a certain report are being printed, or the information a report provides is incorrect, or the information system is not effective in helping the company's management run the business.

In attempting to solve problems like these, the analyst may find that the effort expands into broad system improvements. One problem may lead to another, which may then lead to another, and so forth. Because this snowball effect frequently occurs, it is important for the analyst to determine the scope of the system analysis at the outset of the project, as described earlier. Analysts must use discretion and discipline in solving the problem at hand.

RESPONDING TO NEW REQUIREMENTS. Information systems should be designed to be flexible so changes can be made easily. Unfortunately, it is often difficult to anticipate future information needs; new requirements more often than not cause changes that require a new system analysis. For example, oil companies have experienced a series of changes in government regulations in recent years. Passage of the windfall profits tax followed by the earlier-than-expected deregulation of domestic oil prices created instant headaches for the companies and instant projects for system analysts. Information systems, especially for the accounting departments, had to be updated very rapidly in order to comply with new laws.

There are other areas in which government regulations have affected business information systems. Personnel is one of those areas; regulations governing hiring and firing practices are constantly changing. Another area affected by government regulations is privacy. New laws designed to protect the rights of citizens mandate that more and more information must be kept confidential.

New requirements also originate from nongovernment sources. A company may add a new product line, necessitating a whole new series of reports. A new labor agreement may require additional benefits and deductions or a different way of calculating base pay.

IMPLEMENTING NEW TECHNOLOGY. The introduction of new data-processing technology can cause major changes in information systems. Many companies started with punched-card, batch-processing environments. When magnetic tape became available, larger files could be processed and more information could be stored. The introduction of magnetic-disk technology opened up direct-access processing, causing major changes to information systems in the late 1960s. New input devices such as visual display terminals began to replace paper forms and punched cards for data entry.

In banking alone, the introduction of MICR (magnetic-ink character recognition) technology eliminated thousands of bookkeeping jobs because it allowed electronic posting of entries to accounts instead of manual posting. In grocery stores and other retail stores, bar-code readers and optical-character readers are being combined with point-of-sale devices to dramatically change internal accounting and checkout procedures. There are dozens of other ways in which new technology has led to changes in information systems. We could list many other examples, but the important thing to remember is that changes in technology often lead to changes in information systems.

MAKING BROAD SYSTEM IMPROVEMENTS. There may be times when an organization wants to update its entire information system. An increase in size or sales volume may make such a change necessary. Competition from a rival may provide an incentive to improve efficiency.

One example of a broad system improvement is the introduction and use of online ticketing by major airlines. As soon as the first company converted to this new method, other airlines had to follow suit to remain competitive. The new method forced changes in the airlines' entire accounting and reservations systems.

During the boom years of the 1950s and 1960s numerous companies discovered that their information systems were out of date because of mergers and acquisitions. Many companies found that it was advantageous to update their entire information system rather than to just keep patching it.

A broad system improvement normally requires an extensive system analysis because it has a very broad scope.

Data Gathering

After the proposal to conduct system analysis has been accepted, the analyst sets out to gather data. The type and amount of data gathered depends upon the scope and goal of the system analysis. Data can be supplied by internal and external sources.

INTERNAL SOURCES. Some common sources of internal information are interviews, observations, system flowcharts, questionnaires, and formal reports. A brief description of each source follows.

Interviews. Personal interviews can be a very important source of data. Preliminary interviews provide data about current operations and procedures as well as the users' perception of what the system should do. The analyst must be diplomatic yet probing. Often during an interview the analyst discovers informal information in the form of reports, personal notes, and phone numbers that indicates how the current information system really works. Without interviews, these "extras" might never appear.

Observation. When an analyst is gathering data on an existing information system, observation can be used both to confirm data already obtained and to gather data on aspects of the system for which none exists. By observing an existing information system's data flow, a system analyst can gather data about the system on a first-hand basis.

System Flowcharts. After gathering the documents that provide the system input, the analyst turns to the system flowchart to identify the processing steps used in the system. Devices and files used in the system, the resulting output, and the departments that use the output are identified. (A more detailed discussion of system flowcharts will appear later in this chapter.)

Questionnaires. Questionnaires are used to collect details about system operations (see Figure 14–2). By keying questions to specific steps in a system flowchart, the

FIGURE 14–2

Sample Questionnaire

TITLE   Report Analysis–Batch Payroll Report
NUMBER   378-Batch-Pay
PURPOSE To determine demand for and timing of Batch Payroll Report

1. Do you currently receive, or would you like to receive the Paryoll Report?
   - ❑ Yes   If yes, please answer the remaining questions.
   - ❑ No   If no, please fo to the end of th4e questionnaire.

2. How often would you like to receive the Paryoll Report?
   - ❑ Weekly   ❑ Quarterly   ❑ Annually
   - ❑ Monthly   ❑ Semiannually

3. What would you be using the report for?
   - ❑ Department budgeting of payroll expenses.
   - ❑ General information only.
   - ❑ Other_____.

4. How do you rank this report in relation to other reports you receive?
   - ❑ Above average   ❑ Average   ❑ Below average

5. Do you require more payroll information than is contained on the report?
   - ❑ Yes   ❑ No
   If yes, please list the additional information you require:
   _____
   _____
   _____

6. Please indicate any other information that would be useful in revising or updating the Payroll Report.
   _____
   _____
   _____

Thank you for your cooperation.

Signed_____ Title_____

Department _____ Date_____

analyst can obtain detailed data on the volume of input and output. Information such as the frequency of processing, the time required for various processing steps, and the personnel used can also be identified.

Questionnaires are useful only if they are properly constructed. Further, the analyst must be careful to take note of who filled out a particular questionnaire; a manager might respond differently from an employee. The analyst must be sure to follow up if a questionnaire is not returned.

Formal Reports. Formal reports, the major output of many systems, should be studied carefully by the analyst (see Figure 14–3). The processing steps taken to convert data to information usually become apparent when these reports are examined. The number of copies of each report made and the people who receive them help to identify the flow of information within an organization. Where and how a report is stored may indicate the degree of sensitivity and the importance of the information it contains. The advent of inexpensive paper copiers makes the task of determining all users of a particular report extremely difficult. The ease with which copies are made can be a disadvantage.

EXTERNAL SOURCES. System analysts should examine external sources of information during the data-gathering stage. Standard external sources are books, periodicals, brochures, and product specifications from manufacturers. Customers and suppliers are sometimes good sources. For example, asking customers what information they would like to see on an invoice might aid in the analysis of an accounts receivable system. Analysts should also attempt to contact other companies that have developed or implemented similar information systems.

CONCEPT SUMMARY 14–1	
Types of Data Gathering	
Internal Sources	**External Sources**
Interviews	Books
Observation	Periodicals
System flowcharts	Brochures
Questionnaires	Manufacturers' product specifications
Formal reports	Customers and suppliers

Data Analysis

After data has been collected, it must be organized so that it can be seen in proper perspective. While the focus during data collection is on *what* is being done, the focus during data analysis is on *why* certain operations and procedures are being used. The analyst looks for ways to improve these operations.

INFORMATION NEEDS. An analysis should be conducted to determine both management's information needs and the data that will be required to meet those needs.

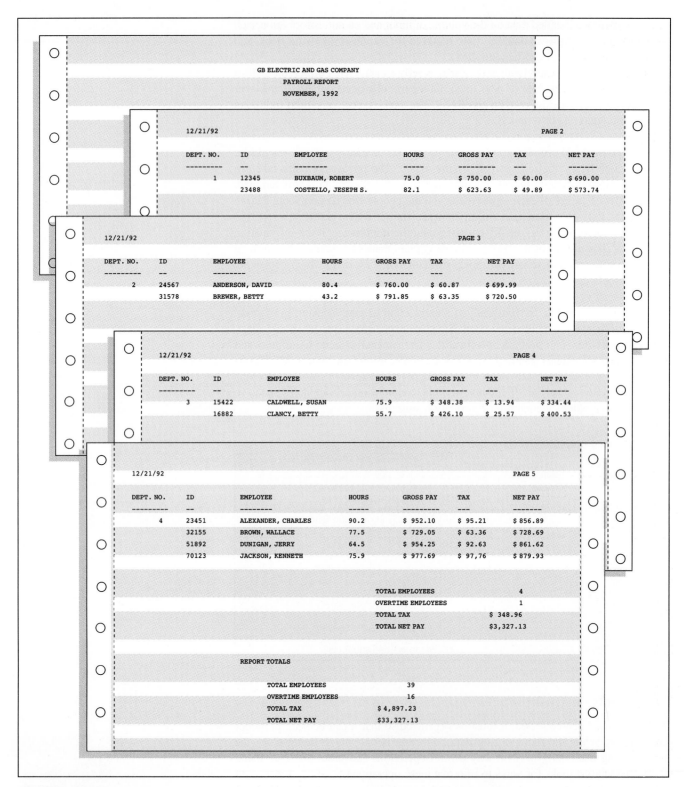

FIGURE 14–3

Example of a Formal Report

This will have a significant impact later when input/output requirements are being determined.

Determining information needs requires that the analyst use a top-down approach. In a file-processing environment, it is relatively easy to create and manipulate files. But many companies are rapidly moving into data-base environments. Creating and maintaining an effective data base requires that data items be maintained independently. This means that the data must be analyzed and organized from a corporate-wide perspective. A file can no longer be created for use by a single department; data must be accessible to many other departments as well. The goal is to properly relate each data item to all other data items, ignoring departmental boundaries.

Some techniques used to analyze data and determine information needs are grid charts, system flowcharts, and decision logic tables. While these techniques are some of the most frequently used, there are many others. Analysts should use the tools and techniques that are best suited for analyzing gathered data. In the following paragraphs grid charts, system flowcharts, and decision logic tables are explained.

Grid Charts. The **tabular** or **grid chart** is used to summarize the relationships among the components of a system. Relationships among components such as inputs, outputs, and files are often depicted on grid charts. Figure 14–4 is a grid chart indicating which department used what documents of an order-processing, billing, and inventory-control system. For example, the billing department uses shipping and invoice documents, while accounts receivable uses invoices, credit authorization, and monthly reports.

System Flowcharts. In Chapter 11, program flowcharts were concerned with operations on data. In contrast, **system flowcharts** emphasize the flow of data through the entire data-processing system, without describing details of internal computer operations. A system flowchart represents the interrelationships among various elements of the information system.

The general input/output symbol used in program flowcharting is not specific enough for system flowcharting. A variety of specialized input/output symbols are

FIGURE 14–4

Grid Chart

Department / Document	Order Writing	Shipping	Billing	Inventory	Marketing	Accounts Receivable
Sales Order	✔				✔	
Shipping Order	✔	✔	✔	✔		
Invoice			✔		✔	✔
Credit Authorization					✔	✔
Monthly Report					✔	✔

FIGURE 14–5

Specialized Input/Output Symbols for System Flowcharting

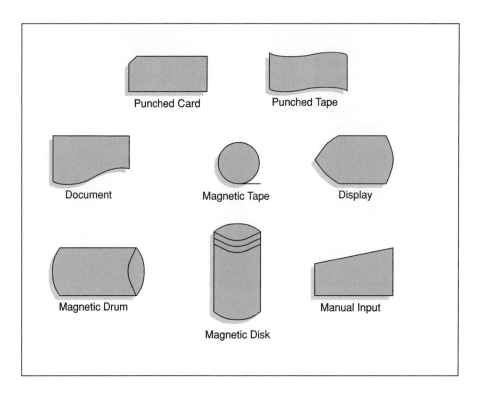

needed to identify the wide variety of media used in input/output activities. The symbols are miniature outlines of the actual media (see Figure 14–5).

Similarly, specialized process symbols are used instead of the general process symbol (▭) to represent specific processing operations. For example, a trapezoid is used to indicate a manual operation such as key-to-tape data entry (see Figure 14–6).

FIGURE 14–6

Specialized Process Symbols for System Flowcharting

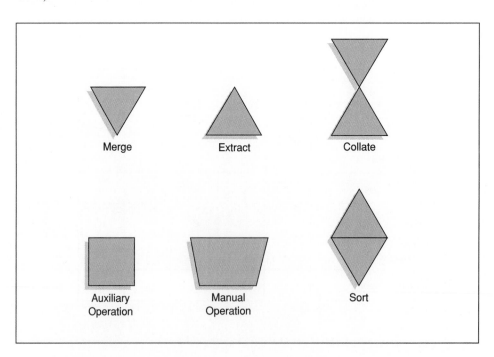

The difference in emphasis in the two forms of flowcharting is due to the differences in the purposes they serve. A program flowchart aids the programmer by providing details necessary to the coding of the program. In contrast, system flowcharts are designed to represent the general information flow; often one process symbol is used to represent many operations.

Figure 14–7 is a sample system flowchart that shows the updating of an inventory master file. The **online storage** symbol (⬚) indicates that the file is kept on an online storage medium such as disk or tape. The file is used to keep track of the raw materials and finished products of the organization. Whether or not this information is current depends on how often the master file is updated. If it is updated as soon as a product is shipped or a raw material supply depleted, then the information it provides is up-to-date. Usually, however, the updating is done on a periodic basis. All changes that occur during a specific time period are batched and then processed together to update the inventory master file. Reports from the shipping, receiving,

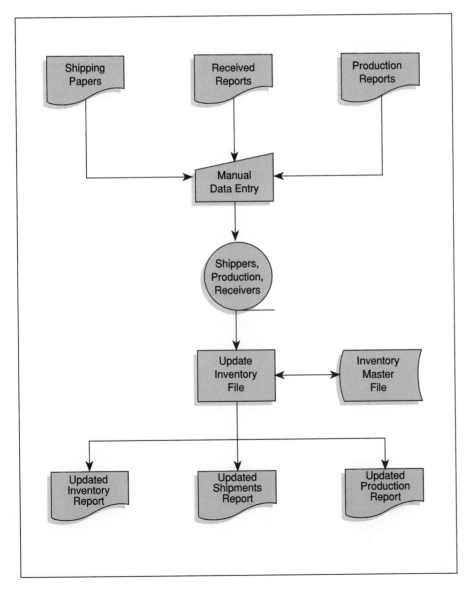

FIGURE 14–7

Sample System Flowchart

and production departments are collected. The data from this set of documents is entered into the computer via a CRT. The data entered on the CRT and the inventory master file then serves as input for the updating process.

The flowchart in Figure 14–7 outlines the steps in this process. In addition to updating the inventory master file, the system generates three reports, which give management information about inventory, order shipments, and production. Notice that in the system flowchart one process symbol encompasses the entire updating process. A program flowchart must be created to detail the specific operations to be performed within this process.

Decision Logic Tables. A **decision logic table (DLT)** is a tabular representation of the actions to be taken under various sets of conditions. The decision table expresses the logic for arriving at a particular decision under a given set of circumstances. The structure within the table is based on the proposition ''if this condition is met, then do this.''

The basic elements of a decision logic table are shown in Figure 14–8. The upper half lists conditions to be met and the lower half shows actions to be taken. That is, the **condition stub** describes the various conditions; the **action stub** describes the possible actions. **Condition entries** are made in the top right section. **Action entries** are made in the bottom right section.

A decision table is not needed when conditions can be communicated and understood easily. However, where multiple conditions exist, a decision table serves as a valuable tool in analyzing the decision logic involved. Figure 14–9 shows a decision table for selecting applicants for an assembly-line job.

The rules for selecting applicants are based on the age, education, and experience of the candidates. The applicants must be at least eighteen years old to be considered for the position. They must have at least a high school education or a year's experience to be interviewed for further evaluation. If they meet both requirements, they are hired directly. The Ys in the table mean yes, the Ns mean no, and the Xs indicate what actions are to be taken. The decision table is read as follows:

■ Rule 1: If the applicant's age is less than eighteen years, then reject him or her.
■ Rule 2: If the applicant is at least eighteen years old but has no high school education and less than one year's experience, then reject him or her.
■ Rule 3: If the applicant is at least eighteen years old, has no high school education, but has experience of more than one year, then call him or her for an interview. Once

FIGURE 14–8

Decision Logic Table

	Rule Numbers							
HEADING	1	2	3	4	5	6	7	8
CONDITION STUB				Condition Entries				
ACTION STUB				Action Entries				

FIGURE 14–9

Decision Logic Table for Selecting Applicants

SELECTING APPLICANTS		Rules				
		1	2	3	4	5
CONDITIONS	Age < 18 Years?	Y	N	N	N	N
	High School Education?		N	N	Y	Y
	Experience > 1 Year?		N	Y	N	Y
ACTIONS	Reject	X	X			
	Interview			X	X	
	Hire					X

a candidate has been selected for an interview, another decision table may be needed to evaluate the interviewee.

■ Rule 4: If the applicant is at least eighteen years old, has a high school education, but has less than one year's experience, then call him or her for an interview. Again, another decision table might be used to evaluate the interviewee.

■ Rule 5: If the applicant is at least eighteen years old, has a high school education, and has more than one year's experience, then hire him or her.

A more detailed decision logic table is shown in Figure 14–10. The first step in constructing such a table is to determine which conditions must be considered. In this case, the conditions are: (1) Is the customer's credit rating AAA? (2) Is the quantity ordered above or equal to the minimum quantity for a discount? (3) Is there enough stock on hand to fill the order? The conditions are listed in the condition stub section of the decision table.

FIGURE 14–10

Decision Logic Table for Order Processing

ORDER PROCESSING	Rules							
	1	2	3	4	5	6	7	8
Credit Rating of AAA	Y	Y	Y	Y	N	N	N	N
Quantity Ordered >= Minimum Discount Quantity	Y	N	N	Y	Y	N	Y	N
Quantity Ordered <= Stock on Hand	N	Y	N	Y	N	Y	Y	N
Bill at Discount Price	X			X				
Bill at Regular Price		X	X		X	X	X	X
Ship Total Quantity Ordered		X		X		X	X	
Ship Partial and Back-Order Remaining Amount	X		X		X			X

The next step is to determine what actions can take place. These are: Either (1) bill at a discount price or (2) bill at a regular price; and either (3) ship the total quantity ordered or (4) ship a partial order and back-order the rest. These possibilities go in the action stub section.

Once the conditions and possible courses of action have been identified, the conditions can be related to corresponding action entries to indicate the appropriate decision. Thus, Rule 4 could be interpreted as follows: "If the customer has a credit rating of AAA and the quantity ordered is equal to or above the minimum discount quantity and there is enough stock on hand, then the customer is to be billed at the discount price and the total order is to be shipped."

Decision tables summarize the logic required to make a decision in a form that is easy to understand. They are used to record facts collected during the investigation of the old system and can also be used to summarize aspects of the new system. In the latter case, they guide programmers in writing programs for the new system.

System Analysis Report

After collecting and analyzing the data, the system analyst must communicate the findings to management. The system analysis report should include the following items:

■ A restatement of the scope and objectives of the system analysis.

■ An explanation of the present system, the procedures used, and any problems identified.

■ A statement of all constraints on the present system and any assumptions made by the analyst during this phase.

■ A preliminary report of alternatives that currently seem feasible.

■ An estimate of the resources and capital required to either modify the present system or design a new one. This estimate should include costs of a feasibility study.

The system analyst proceeds to the detailed system design only if management approves this report.

■ SYSTEM DESIGN

If, after reviewing the system analysis report, management decides to continue the project, the system design stage begins. Designing an information system demands a great deal of creativity and planning. It is also very costly and time consuming. In system analysis, the analyst has focused on what the current system does and on what it should be doing according to the requirements discovered in the analysis. In the design phase, the analysis changes focus and concentrates on how a system can be developed to meet information requirements.

Several steps are useful during the design phase of system development:

■ Reviewing goals and objectives.
■ Developing a system model.
■ Evaluating organizational constraints.
■ Developing alternative designs.
■ Performing feasibility analysis.
■ Performing cost/benefit analysis.
■ Preparing a system design report and recommendation.

HIGHLIGHT

The Design Team

Designing application software is a long and complex process. Designers decide what the program should do and how it should be done. The programmers then transform the design into computer code. Software development groups are adding two new members to the development team—a trainer and a documentation specialist.

The trainer is the person responsible for training new users on the system. For example, when the system is sold, the trainer may hold on-site seminars to show users how to operate the application. The documentation specialist is the person who writes the text for the user manuals. Even if the new user has been trained, all the procedures in the system cannot be covered in a seminar. The user will consult the user manuals as needed. The trainer and the

documentation specialist are important to design teams because they view the emerging system through the eyes of a user. They can point out parts of a system that are unclear or inconsistencies that might confuse the user.

For example, a trainer and documentation specialist would not assume that the user is familiar with common computer terms. They would determine the level of expertise of the user and define any terms that might be unfamiliar. Another example is the need to eliminate inconsistencies that may exist within the application. If the designer requires the use of the same screen a number of times, but refers to the screen by two different names, the user might get confused. Again, a documentation specialist or trainer would catch and help resolve the

problem.

In the product services department of the Online Computer Library Center (OCLC) in Dublin, Ohio, manager Janet Mushruch says trainers and documentation specialists are included on their design teams because they head off problems early in the development phase. Robert Stahl, a consultant with Interface Design Group in Oakland, California, agrees with Mushruch saying that management must support the concept of trainers and documentation specialists on the design team in order for the process to work.

All good systems begin with good design. For many companies, that means having a design team that includes a trainer and a documentation specialist.

Reviewing Goals and Objectives

The objectives of the new or revised system were identified during system analysis and stated in the system analysis report. Before the analyst can proceed with system design, these objectives must be reviewed, for any system design offered must conform to them.

In order to maintain a broad approach and flexibility in the system design phase, the analyst may restate users' information requirements to reflect the needs of the majority of users. For example, the finance department may want a report of customers who have been delinquent in payments. Since this department may be only one subsystem in a larger accounts-receivable system, the analyst may restate this requirement more generally. It might more appropriately be stated as follows: (1) maintain an accurate and timely record of the amounts owed by customers, (2) provide control procedures that ensure detection of abnormal accounts and report them on an exception basis, and (3) provide, on a timely basis, information regarding accounts receivable to different levels of management to help achieve overall company goals.

A well-designed system can meet the current goals and objectives of the organization and adapt to changes within the organization. In discussions with managers, the analyst may be able to determine organizational trends that help to pinpoint which subsystems require more flexibility. For instance, if the analyst is developing a system for an electric company, strong consideration should be given to providing flexibility in the reporting subsystem in order to respond to changing regulatory reporting requirements.

Developing a System Model

The analyst next attempts to represent symbolically the system's major components to verify understanding of the various components and their interactions. The analyst may use flowcharts to help in the development of a system model or may simply be creative in the use of diagrammatic representations.

In reviewing the model, the analyst refers to system theory to discover any possible omissions of important subsystems. Are the major interactions among subsystems shown? Are the inputs, processes, and outputs appropriately identified? Does the model provide for appropriate feedback to each of the subsystems? Are too many functions included within one subsystem?

Once a satisfactory system model has been developed, the analyst has an appropriate tool for evaluating alternative designs (discussed later in this section). Each alternative can be evaluated on the basis of how well it matches the requirements of the model. Figure 14–11 is an example of a conceptual model of an accounts-receivable system.

Evaluating Organizational Constraints

No organization has unlimited resources; most have limitations on financial budgets, personnel, and computer facilities and time constraints for system development. The system analyst must recognize the constraints on system design imposed by this limited availability of resources.

Few organizations request the optimal design for their information requirements. Businesses are profit-seeking organizations. Only in an extremely rare case does an

FIGURE 14–11

Model of an Accounts-Receivable System

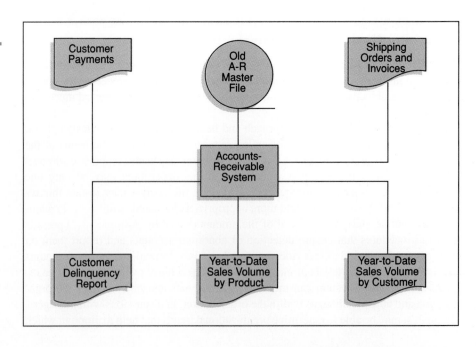

organization request an all-out system development with no cost constraints. (Competition or technological developments, for example, may make such an uncharacteristic decision mandatory.)

The structure of the organization also affects subsequent designs developed by the analyst. A highly centralized management may reject a proposal for distributed processing. Similarly, an organization with geographically dispersed, highly autonomous decision centers may find designs that require routing reports throughout the central office unsatisfactory.

Human factors are also an organizational constraint that must be evaluated during the system design phase. Special consideration must be given to the users of the system. A proposed system design should be **user friendly.** In other words, the system must be designed not only to meet the needs of the user, but also to meet those needs through an easy-to-use, understandable design.

A **menu-driven** system design, for example, guides the user through the computerized system helping him or her attain the needed information. A menu-driven system displays menus (lists of available choices or actions) to the user (see Figure 14–12). With the menu-driven system, the user can be guided through the process of using the system.

Technological advances such as a mouse, touch-sensitive screens, or a voice recognition system may also help make a system design more compatible for its human users. The human factors of system design are extremely important.

Before proceeding with system design, the analyst must be fully aware of the various organizational constraints and critically evaluate their impact on the system design.

Developing Alternative Designs

Systems can be either simple or complex. Simple systems require simple controls to keep processes working properly. Complex systems, on the other hand, require complex controls. A business is a complex system; it requires vast numbers of interactions

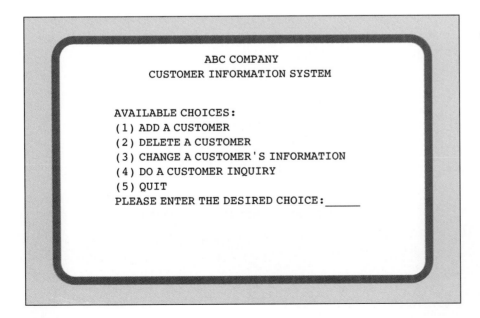

FIGURE 14–12

Sample Menu

among its many interrelated subsystems. It naturally follows that information systems developed for business use must be complex, since they model the actual business.

There is more than one way to design a complex information system, and system analysts are generally required to develop more than one design alternative. This requirement is useful because it forces the analyst to be creative. By designing several possible systems, the analyst may discover valuable parts in each that can be integrated into an entirely new system. The alternative systems may also be designed in ascending order of complexity and cost; since management often desires alternatives from which to choose, designing alternative systems in this fashion is quite appropriate.

The analyst must work with a number of elements in designing alternative systems. Computerized information systems have many components. Inputs, outputs, hardware, software, files, data bases, clerical procedures, and users interact in hundreds of different ways. Processing requirements may also differ in each alternative. For example, one may require batch processing and sequential organization of files; another may provide random-access processing using direct-access storage and online terminals. The data collection, processing, storage, retrieval, and update procedures vary, depending on the alternative selected.

Each alternative developed by the analyst must be technically feasible. In some instances, analysts try to design at least one noncomputerized alternative. Although this may be difficult, it often reveals unique methods of information processing that the analyst has not considered when developing the computerized systems.

In designing each alternative, the analyst should include tentative input forms, the structures and formats of output reports, the program specifications needed to guide programmers in code preparation, the files or data base required, the clerical procedures to be used, and the process-control measures that should be instituted.

With the increasing use of online systems, the input forms are often input screens. These screens must be designed in as much detail as their hard-copy counterparts. The analyst, in consultation with those who will be inputting the data, must design each screen to maximize efficiency in data input. The screen format must be easy for users to view and understand (see Figure 14–13).

FIGURE 14–13

Screen Format

```
                        CUSTOMER INQUIRY


CUSTOMER NAME: XXXXXXXXXXXXXXXXXXXXXXXXXXXXXXXXX
CUSTOMER NUMBER: ########
STREET: XXXXXXXXXXXXXXXXXXXXXXXXXXXXX
CITY: XXXXXXXXXXXXXXXXXX  STATE: XX  ZIP: #####
PHONE: (###) ###-####
LAST INVOICE: ######
DATE ORDER WAS SHIPPED: ##/##/##
WOULD YOU LIKE TO DO ANOTHER INQUIRY? (Y/N):
```

Output reports must be designed so that users can quickly and easily view the information they require. The analyst often prepares mock-up reports that approximate how the actual computer-generated report will look (see Figure 14–14). Most contain sample data. It is easier for users to relate their needs to such sample reports than to discuss them in abstract form with the analyst in an interview. Mock-up reports also allow the analyst to verify once again what is required of the system.

Once the input forms or screens and output reports have been designed, a detailed set of programming specifications for each alternative must be prepared. The analyst must determine what kind of processing is to occur in each of the system designs. The analyst often works in conjunction with the programming staff to determine these requirements and to develop cost estimates for program coding.

File and data-base specifications are particularly important. The analyst must be aware of the physical layout of data in a file. The storage media and keys used to access data in the files need to be determined (see Chapter 7 for details on file design). The analyst should also determine the potential size of each file, the number of accesses and updates that may take place during a particular time period, and the length of time for which users may wish to retain each file. Since each of these specifications requires the use of computer facilities, the estimates help the analyst determine the potential cost of each design alternative.

The analyst must carefully examine each clerical procedure required in a particular system alternative. In a sense, the analyst must imagine himself or herself actually performing the steps required. From the receipt of data through the processing steps to the final output, the analyst must determine the most efficient methods for users to perform their required tasks.

Process-control measures were easier in the days of batch processing. With online systems, however, changes made to files and data bases are instantaneous. If the changes are made on the basis of incorrect data, incorrect values will be stored, accessed, and reported. The analyst must institute controls from initial data capture and entry through processing and storage to final reporting. Methods to restore data bases when errors in data entry occur should be developed. Security procedures should be instituted to prevent unauthorized access to stored data. Since the advent of privacy legislation (discussed in Chapter 17), the development of control procedures has become increasingly important.

Performing Feasibility Analysis

While developing each alternative system, the analyst must keep asking the question, "Is this feasible?" A design may require certain procedures that the organization is not staffed to handle; the design, therefore, must be discarded, or the appropriate staff acquired. The analyst may discover an alternative with great potential for reducing processing costs, but may find that the company does not own the hardware required to implement it. The analyst may choose to present this alternative to management rather than disregard it. The analyst must use personal judgment and experience to eliminate unfeasible alternatives.

In some cases, the question of a system's feasibility may also center around organizational constraints. Even though the proposed system may be technically feasible, questions such as, "Is the system practical?" and "Is the system cost-effective or necessary as a competitive response?" also need to be considered.

The users' educational backgrounds and organizational positions must be taken into consideration. The lack of familiarity of some employees with computer-based information systems may prohibit the use of a complex system. Highly educated

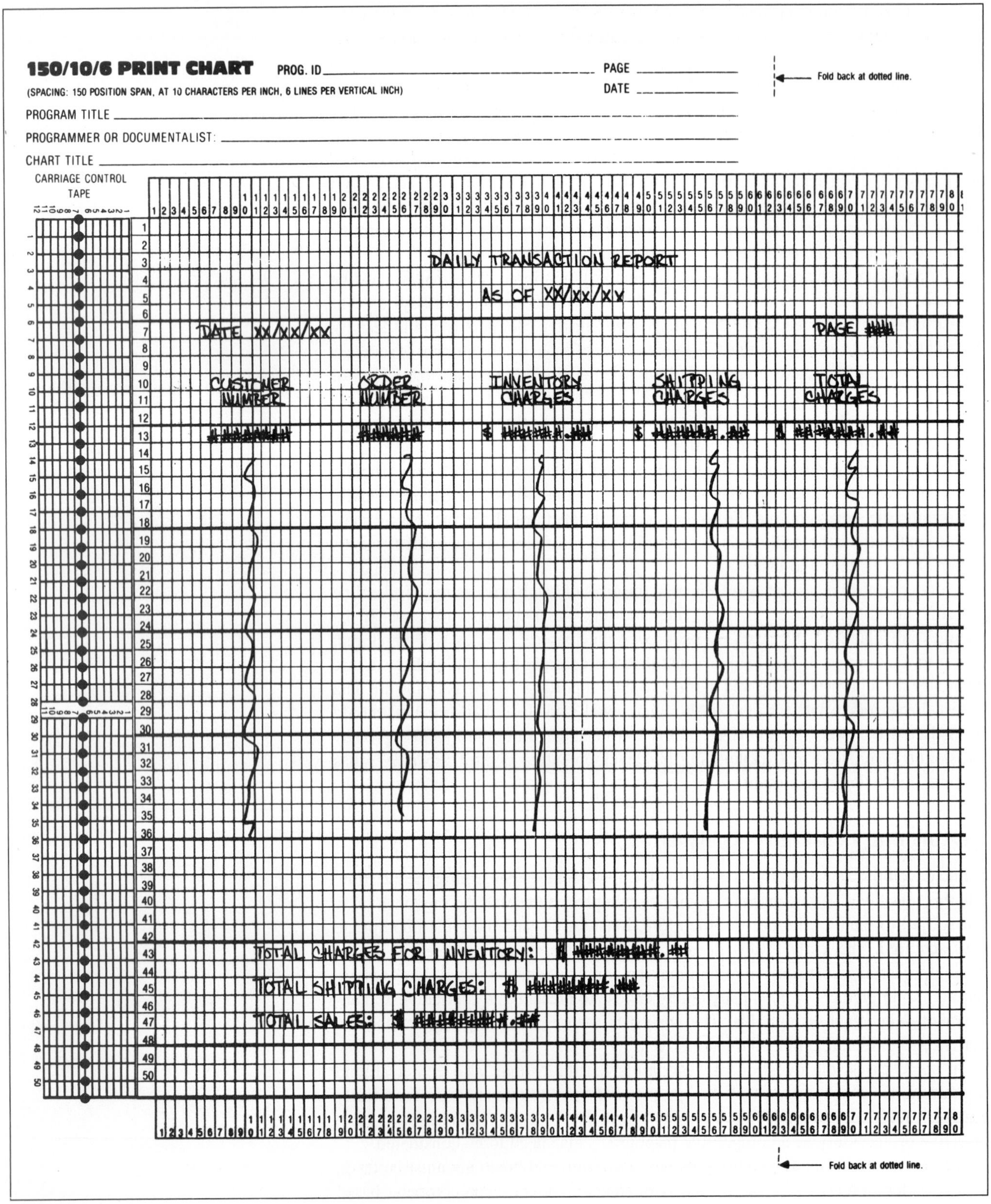

150/10/6 PRINT CHART   PROG. ID _____   PAGE _____

(SPACING: 150 POSITION SPAN, AT 10 CHARACTERS PER INCH, 6 LINES PER VERTICAL INCH)   DATE _____

◄— Fold back at dotted line.

PROGRAM TITLE _____

PROGRAMMER OR DOCUMENTALIST: _____

CHART TITLE _____

DAILY TRANSACTION REPORT

AS OF XX/XX/XX

DATE XX/XX/XX   PAGE ###

CUSTOMER   ORDER   INVENTORY   SHIPPING   TOTAL
NUMBER   NUMBER   CHARGES   CHARGES   CHARGES

#########   ####### $ ######.## $ ######.## $ #######.##

TOTAL CHARGES FOR INVENTORY: $ #######.##

TOTAL SHIPPING CHARGES: $ #######.##

TOTAL SALES: $ ########.##

◄— Fold back at dotted line.

FIGURE 14–14

Output Report Format

managers may resist a simple information system because they feel uneasy working with it. Companies in rural locations may be unable to properly staff data-processing departments.

Analysts must also determine whether there are legal constraints that affect the design of the system. For example, several presidents have proposed to Congress that a massive, integrated data base be created containing data about citizens receiving benefits from the government. The objective is to reduce fraud, inefficiency, and multiple payments. It is possible, however, that such a data base might violate privacy laws (see Chapter 17). Although the system is feasible from a technical standpoint, the controls that would have to be incorporated to conform with legal constraints have hindered its development.

When performing a feasibility analysis, time is frequently a limiting factor. A time constraint may appear before system development begins, during the development process, or during implementation. The required completion date may preclude the selection of a complex alternative, necessitate changing the selected design to one less complex, or require that the system be developed in stages different from those suggested by the analyst.

The economic feasibility of a project is paramount. Many systems have fallen by the wayside because of budgetary constraints. The system's economic feasibility is determined by cost/benefit analysis, which is discussed in the next section. In performing this analysis, the analyst must be extremely careful. Costs that at first appear to exceed the budget may in fact give rise to greater benefits. The expression ''you have to spend money to make money'' is often applicable here. It is up to the analyst to foresee such possibilities.

Performing Cost/Benefit Analysis

Cost/benefit analysis is a procedure commonly used in business decision making. A firm has limited financial resources. They must be allocated to projects that appear to offer the greatest return on the costs of initial development. In order for cost/benefit analysis to be performed, both costs and benefits must be quantified. Costs are easier to determine than benefits. Some benefits are tangible (or realizable as cash savings). Others are intangible (not necessarily obvious reductions in costs). Naturally, intangible benefits are especially difficult to determine. How does one estimate the benefit from an improved information system that provides better customer service?

An analyst might approach the cost/benefit analysis of an accounts-receivable system in the following fashion. A company is unable to respond to 20 percent of customer orders because of inefficiencies in its current information system. A proposed new system will reduce lost sales by increasing the customer service level so that only 5 percent of orders remain unprocessed. By observing the current sales level and predicting how much sales will increase if the new system is implemented, the analyst can approximate the cash benefits of the alternative.

The costs of an alternative include direct costs like the initial investment required for materials and equipment; setup costs required to create computer files from old manual systems, install data-processing equipment, and hire personnel; and educational costs to train the users of the new system. Ongoing expenses resulting from employees' salaries, computer operations, insurance, taxes, and rent must also be identified.

It is not always necessary for positive economic benefits to exist for an alternative to be considered feasible. For example, environmental impact statements are required by law from some companies. Design alternatives for a system that must produce these reports need to provide accurate and timely information in spite of the cost/benefit relationship involved. Careful planning, however, will minimize the resources required to develop such a system.

The analyst can also use statistics in determining costs and benefits of large system designs. Sampling and modeling enable the analyst to provide cost/benefit figures not readily apparent from available information. By modeling the complex interactions of accounts-receivable, inventory, and service levels, the analyst may be able to determine how savings in one area affect costs in another. Other techniques, ranging from judgment to common sense to experience, are useful to the analyst attempting to choose the best alternative.

The design alternative that management selects often depends on the conclusions of the cost/benefit analysis. The analyst must ensure that a comprehensive cost/benefit study has been performed on all alternatives.

Preparing the Design Report

Once the analyst has completed all of the steps described earlier, a report is prepared to communicate findings to management. The **system design report** should explain in general terms how the various designs will satisfy the information requirements determined in the analysis phase. The report should also review the information requirements uncovered in the system analysis, explain in both flowchart and narrative form the proposed designs, detail the corporate resources required to implement each alternative, and make a recommendation.

Since many organizational personnel may not have participated actively in the analysis stage of system development, the analyst restates information requirements in the design report to tell these decision makers the constraints considered in creating alternative designs. The restatement also shows that the analyst understands what information the new system should provide.

Each of the proposed alternatives should be explained in easy-to-understand narrative form. Technical jargon should be avoided. The purpose of the design report is to communicate; using words unfamiliar to the reader will hinder this communication process. Flowcharts for each alternative should be provided as well.

From the detailed design work performed on each alternative, the analyst should glean the important costs, benefits, and resources required for its implementation. This, more than any other portion of the report, will be analyzed carefully by those empowered to make a design selection. Their decisions will be based on the projected benefits of each design versus the corporate resources required to implement it.

Finally, the analyst should make a design recommendation. Due to familiarity with both the current system and each of the alternative designs, the analyst is in the best position to make a recommendation for implementing a successful alternative design. If the analyst has been thorough in analyzing resource costs and potential benefits, as well as objective in viewing corporate goals, this recommendation is apt to be adopted by management.

After evaluating the system design report, management can do one of three things: (a) approve the recommendation; (b) approve the recommendation with changes (this may include selecting another alternative); or (c) select none of the alternatives. The "do nothing" alternative is always feasible but will not solve any of the problems that led to the system analysis in the first place. If the design of the system is approved, the analyst proceeds with implementation.

Programming

A computerized information system depends on computer programs for converting data into information. Programs may be produced in-house or purchased in the form of commercially prepared software packages. If the programs are written in-house, the system analyst should help decide which language should be used. To make the system easier to maintain and change, programs should be developed in independent modules (see Chapter 11).

The analyst, in conjunction with the programming department, may wish to evaluate commercial software packages designed to perform tasks similar to those required of the selected design as an alternative to in-house programming. These software evaluations should be made on the basis of system compatibility and adaptability.

Testing

Before a system becomes operational, it must be tested and debugged. Testing should take place at all levels of operation. Programs are tested by dividing them into logical modules. Each module should be tested to ensure that input is accounted for, files are updated, and reports are correctly printed. Once all program testing is complete, system testing takes place. System testing involves checking all application programs that support the system. All clerical procedures used in data collection, data processing, and data storage and retrieval are included in system testing.

Documentation

Creating documentation involves taking an overview of the entire system including subsystems and their functions. Generally, documentation falls into one of three classifications: system documentation, program documentation, and procedure documentation. System documentation usually includes system flowcharts, forms and files input to the system's subsystems, and reports and files output from the subsystems. Program documentation includes program flowcharts, explanations of the program's logic patterns, and explanations of the data elements on computer files. Procedure documentation instructs users on how to perform particular functions in each subsystem. These instructions are designed to help users obtain the information they need quickly and easily.

Special Considerations

In designing solutions to business problems, analysts and programmers must be aware of other considerations besides developing the programs required to help solve a particular problem. Since system analysis and design concentrates on inputs, processing, and outputs, the following issues must be considered: (a) The form of input to the program determines how the program should ask for data. (b) Processing steps should verify the accuracy of data and identify potential errors. (c) The program may be required to produce output that is not in hard-copy form.

Today's computer systems give users a variety of ways to communicate with programs. The programmer must know in advance which input devices will be used to put data into the program. Different input devices require different input considerations. The input devices and forms of data input must be precisely defined before solution design begins, or considerable time may be required to rework programs designed to accept input in an inappropriate format.

Businesses are naturally concerned with the accuracy of data used by information managers to make decisions. Programmers must do their part to help keep data error free; merely designing a program with logically correct processing statements providing the required output may not be enough. Most programmers are required to include extensive edit checks on the data before storing it in data files. **Edit checks** are processing statements designed to identify potential errors in the input data.

Several broad types of edit checks can be incorporated into the solution design. In some situations, combinations of these edit checks are required. The determination of how many and what kinds of edit checks should be performed on input data is usually made by all personnel involved in the design solution. Users, management, system analysts, and programmers should all be involved in ensuring the integrity of the data input into the system.

In modern systems, not all data is entered directly into a program by users nor is all output fed directly to hard-copy reports. Many systems require the use of interdependent programs in which the output from one program is used as input to another. Programmers need to ensure that output from one program is in a form acceptable as input to another.

◼ SYSTEM IMPLEMENTATION

In the implementation stage of the system methodology, the analyst is able to see the transformation of ideas, flowcharts, and narratives into actual processes, flows, and information. This transition is not performed easily, however. Personnel must be trained to use the new system procedures, and a conversion must be made from the old system to the new one.

Personnel Training

Two groups of people interface with a system. The first group includes the people who develop, operate, and maintain the system. The second group includes the people who use the information generated by the system to support their decision making. Both groups must be aware of their responsibilities regarding the system's operation and of what they can and cannot expect from it. One of the primary responsibilities of the system analyst is to see that education and training are provided to both groups.

The user group includes general management, staff personnel, line managers, and other operating personnel. It may also include the organization's customers and suppliers. These users must be educated as to what functions they are to perform and what, in turn, the system will do for them. Procedure documentation (mentioned above) provides information to the users of the system on what functions they should perform.

The personnel who operate the system must be trained to prepare input data, load and unload files on storage devices, handle problems that occur during processing, and so on.

Education and training can be provided in large group seminars or in smaller tutorial sessions. The latter approach, though fairly costly, is more personal and more

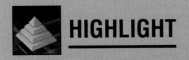
The Future of CASE

Computer-Aided Software Engineering (CASE) has become, and will continue to be, an increasingly important computer software development tool. To develop a new application, a designer must work through the necessary steps of analysis, design, programming, testing, documenting, and evaluating. All of these steps can be automated to some degree through the use of CASE tools.

An ideal CASE system would allow a designer to completely represent the design in picture (or diagram) form. Once the designer had specified how the desired application should work, the CASE system would be instructed to automatically create the required pieces to the application. This would include the required program source code, documentation, and a data-base design (if necessary). Ideally, this is what experts would like to see CASE systems do.

However, this ideal system reflects a futuristic view of CASE technology more than a realistic one. Although CASE systems have come a long way over the past few years, they still have a long way to go to realize that ideal. Many software developers believe that the future of software development rests with CASE systems. Software development time continues to be a bottleneck in the overall process of preparing products for market. Thus it is felt that some day CASE systems will greatly reduce the time required to develop new application software. Even though CASE has not yet reached its ideal form, there are many CASE tools available today that already help reduce software development time. Certain CASE tools are capable of automating some—if not all—of the required programming while others are capable of automating the design and documentation phases. Without a doubt CASE tools and entire CASE systems will play a major role in the development of many future applications.

---

appropriate for complex tasks. Another approach, used almost universally, is on-the-job training. As the name implies, the employee learns while actually performing the tasks required.

Personnel training and education are expensive, but they are essential to successful system implementation.

Conversion

The switch from an old system to a new one is referred to as a conversion. Conversion involves not only changes in the mode of processing data but also changes in equipment and clerical procedures.

Several approaches can be used to accomplish the conversion process. Those most often used are explained below:

■ *Parallel conversion.* When **parallel conversion** is used, the new system is operated side by side with the old one for some period of time. An advantage of this approach is that no data is lost if the new system fails. Also, it gives the user an opportunity to compare and reconcile the outputs from both systems. However, this method can be costly.

■ *Pilot conversion.* **Pilot conversion** involves converting only a small portion of the organization to the new system. For example, a new system may be implemented on one production line. This approach minimizes the risk to the organization as a whole in case unforeseen problems occur, and enables the organization to identify problems and correct them before implementing the system throughout the entire organization. A disadvantage of this method is that the total conversion process usually takes a long time.

■ *Phased conversion.* With **phased conversion,** the old system is gradually replaced by portions of the new one over a period of time. The difference between this method and pilot conversion is that in phased conversion the new system is segmented and only one segment is implemented at a time. Thus, the organization can adapt to the new system gradually over an extended period while the old system is gradually being phased out. One drawback is that an interface between the new system and the old system must be developed for use during the conversion process.

■ *Direct conversion.* **Direct** (or **crash**) **conversion** takes place all at once. This approach can be used to advantage if the old system is not operational or if the new system is completely different in structure and design. Since the old system is discontinued immediately upon implementation of the new one, the organization has nothing to fall back on if problems arise. Because of the high risk involved, this approach requires extreme care in planning and extensive testing of all system components.

◘ SYSTEM AUDIT AND REVIEW

Evaluating System Performance

After the conversion process is complete, the analyst must obtain feedback on the system's performance. This can be done by conducting an audit to evaluate the system's performance in terms of the initial objectives established for it. The evaluation should address the following questions:

1. Does the system perform as planned and deliver the anticipated benefits? How do the operating results compare with the initial objectives? If the benefits are below expectation, what can be done to improve the cost/benefit tradeoff?
2. Was the system completed on schedule and with the resources estimated?
3. Is all output from the system used?
4. Have old system procedures been eliminated and new ones implemented?
5. What controls have been established for input, processing, and output of data? Are these controls adequate?
6. Have users been educated about the new system? Is the system accepted by users? Do they have confidence in the reports generated?
7. Is the processing turnaround time satisfactory, or are delays frequent?

All persons involved in developing the system should be aware that a thorough audit will be performed. The anticipated audit acts as a strong incentive; it helps to ensure that a good system is designed and delivered on schedule. As a result of the audit or of user requests, some modification or improvements of the new system may be required.

Making Modifications and Improvements

A common belief among system users is that after a system has been installed, nothing more needs to be done. On the contrary, all systems must be continually maintained.

System maintenance detects and corrects errors, meets new information needs of management, and responds to changes in the environment.

One of the important tasks of the analyst during the system audit is to ensure that all system controls are working correctly. All procedures and programs related to the old system should have been eliminated. Many of the problems that the system analyst deals with during system maintenance and follow-up are problems that were identified during the system audit. A well-planned approach to system maintenance and follow-up is essential to the continued effectiveness of an information system.

Responding to Change

A well-designed information system is flexible and adaptable. Minor changes should be easily accommodated without large amounts of reprogramming. This is one of the reasons why structured programming was emphasized in Chapter 12; if each program module is independent, a minor change in one module will not snowball into other changes.

No matter how flexible or adaptable a system is, however, major changes become necessary over time. When the system has to be redesigned, the entire system cycle—analysis, design, programming, implementation, and audit and review—must be performed again. Keeping information systems responsive to information needs is a never-ending process.

CONCEPT SUMMARY 14–2

The Purposes and Steps of System Development Stage

Stage	Purpose	Steps
Analysis	To formulate overall objectives To determine focus of analysis	Gather data from internal and external sources Analyze data Prepare system analysis report
Design	To determine how a system can meet information requirements	Review goals and objectives Develop system model Evaluate organizational constraints Develop alternative designs Perform feasibility analysis Perform cost/benefit analysis Prepare system design report
Programming	To write programs that perform tasks according to system requirements	Test system programs Document all parts of system
Implementation	To bring the new system into use	Train personnel Switch from old system to new
Audit and review	To obtain feedback on system's performance	Compare actual performance with objectives Direct and correct errors Make changes as necessary

◘ PROTOTYPING

In the traditional method of system analysis and design, the system design phase involves developing a system model. The system model that is developed is based on data that has been gathered and analyzed by the system analyst. The model that is developed is typically diagrammed on paper so that the end user of the system can review it. Prototyping, however, differs from the traditional approach to system analysis by developing a working model, or *prototype,* of the system the analyst is proposing to the end user. The prototype is developed prior to the final design and is used as a tool to solicit feedback from the end user. The creation of a working prototype and the solicitation of the end user's feedback allows for the design of the system to be an evolutionary process. As the prototype is modified and adjusted, the design of the system is continually being refined to meet the user's specific needs. In the traditional approach to system analysis and design, the user would have to wait until the new system was implemented to have any hands-on experience with the system. As a result, any modifications or refinements to the system would have to be made at the end of the project. With prototyping, the user can gain hands-on experience with the system during the design phase rather than after the implementation phase. By incorporating this level of user input into the system being developed, the final system should have a much higher probability of being accepted by the user as well as meeting his or her needs much more closely.

It has been found that when prototyping is used during the design phase the overall time required to produce a system is reduced, thereby reducing the cost of the system. In addition, building a system that incorporates all of the features required by the end user is much more difficult without prototyping. Models that are diagrammed on paper are much more difficult to conceptualize than a working model. Prototyping also greatly aids the design of the user interface of a system. Once the prototype design is complete, it can also be used by the programmers assigned to develop the actual system. This too should reduce the amount of time and cost required to complete the development of the system.

Prototyping therefore serves as an alternative to a portion of the traditional approach to the system design phase of system analysis and design. Rather than developing and diagramming a system model and possible alternatives, the system analyst would develop a working model that the user could interact with. This interaction would lead to feedback which would then result in revisions and enhancements to the prototype and the design. By soliciting the user's feedback at this stage of the process, overall time requirements and costs should be reduced. The following is a list of positive and negative aspects of prototyping.

Positive Aspects

■ Increased user involvement in the design of the system.
■ Potentially reduces development time and costs.
■ Increased user involvement should lead to increased user satisfaction.

Negative Aspects

■ Not all proposed systems will lend themselves to prototyping.
■ When prototyping is used, the analyst must be careful not to neglect other phases of the system analysis and design.
■ The prototype may not be used in the final working version of the system.

◼ SUMMARY POINTS

◼ System analysis is conducted for any of four reasons: to solve a problem, to respond to a new requirement, to implement new technology, or to make broad system improvements.

◼ Problem solving is an attempt to correct or adjust a currently malfunctioning information system. The analyst must balance the desire to solve just the problem at hand with an attempt to get at the most fundamental causes of the problem. The latter could snowball into a major project.

◼ A new requirement is caused by either internal or external change. A typical example is a new law or a change in government regulations.

◼ New technology can force system analysis by making formerly infeasible alternatives feasible.

◼ The most comprehensive system analysis is conducted for a broad system improvement, which can be necessitated by rapid sales or rapid internal growth or by a desire to redesign the present system.

◼ Data is gathered during system analysis from internal and external sources. Interviews are an excellent way of collecting data and often lead to unexpected discoveries. A system analyst's observation of an existing information system can also reveal its inner workings. System flowcharts help the analyst get a better understanding of how the components in a system interrelate. Questionnaires can be helpful, but they are sometimes difficult to design, administer, and interpret. Formal reports tell the analyst much about the present workings of the system.

◼ An analyst should also collect data from external sources such as customers, suppliers, software vendors, hardware manufacturers, books, and periodicals.

◼ Data should be analyzed in any manner that helps the analyst understand the system. Grid charts, system flowcharts, and decision logic tables are three of the tools analysts use to accomplish this task.

◼ The final result of the system analysis stage is the system analysis report, a report to management reviewing the results of the analysis and the feasibility of proceeding with system design and implementation.

◼ If the system analysis report is approved, the analyst begins the design stage. Goals and objectives of the new or revised system are reviewed. A system model is developed and organizational constraints are evaluated.

◼ Alternative designs should always be generated in the design phase. There is always more than one way to design a system, and management likes to have alternatives from which to choose.

◼ When developing the various alternatives, the analyst must include tentative input forms or screens, output report formats, program specifications, file or data-base designs, clerical procedures, and process-control measures for each alternative.

◼ Each alternative should undergo a feasibility analysis. This involves looking at constraints such as those imposed by hardware, software, human resources, legal matters, time, and economics.

◼ A cost/benefit analysis should be conducted to determine which alternative is most viable economically. While tangible costs and benefits are easy to determine, intangible benefits are difficult to quantify.

◼ The final step in system design is preparing a design report to present to management. This report should explain the various alternatives and the costs, benefits, and resources associated with each. The report includes the analyst's recommendation.

■ The next stage of the system methodology is system programming. Programming is one of the most time-consuming parts of the system methodology and begins almost immediately after management has approved a design.

■ Testing is performed when each program module is completed. When all program testing is done, system testing commences.

■ Documentation is a necessary part of system and program development. System documentation provides an overview of the entire system and its subsystems and includes system flowcharts and narratives describing the input forms, output reports, and computer files.

■ During implementation, converting to the new system can be done in several ways. In parallel conversion, the old and the new system operate together for a period of time. In pilot conversion, the new system is first implemented in only a part of the organization to determine its adequacies and inadequacies; the latter are corrected before full-scale implementation. In phased conversion, the old system is gradually replaced with the new system one portion at a time. In direct conversion, the new system is implemented all at once.

■ Once a new system is operational, it must be audited to ascertain that the initial objectives of the system are being met and to find any problems occurring in the new system. System maintenance is the continued surveillance of system operations to determine what modifications are needed to meet the changing needs of management and to respond to changes in the environment.

■ Prototyping involves the creation of a working model of a system that can be used to solicit user feedback during the design phase of system analysis and design.

■ Prototyping creates a situation where the model goes through an evolutionary process that ultimately results in the design of the system.

■ Using prototyping should result in a system that more closely meets the needs of the user.

■ TERMS FOR REVIEW

action entries, p. 366

action stub, p. 366

condition entries, p. 366

condition stub, p. 366

decision logic table (DLT), p. 366

direct (crash) conversion, p. 380

edit check, p. 378

grid chart (tabular chart), p. 363

menu-driven system design, p. 371

online storage, p. 365

parallel conversion, p. 379

phased conversion, p. 380

pilot conversion, p. 379

system analysis, p. 357

system analysis report, p. 358

system design report, p. 376

system flowchart, p. 363

user-friendly, p. 371

■ REVIEW QUESTIONS

1. What is the first step of system analysis? Why is this step important? What is the second step? Who needs to agree with the system analyst on the information provided by the second step of the analysis?

2. List three reasons for conducting a system analysis.

3. List three ways in which data may be gathered from internal sources for the purpose of system analysis. Briefly describe some of the advantages and disadvantages related to each of these ways of gathering data.

4. How does the focus of data gathering differ from that of data analysis?

5. What information should be included in the system analysis report? Who is the report presented to and why?

6. What steps are included in the system design phase of system development? Give a brief description of each step.

7. Why is the development of a system model important to the system design phase?

8. Explain why the documentation of a system and its programs are important to the long-term success of the system.

9. List and briefly explain the types of system conversion available when implementing a new system. Given a situation where a new computer-based information system is replacing a manual system, what method of conversion might be best? Why?

10. What is prototyping? How does it differ from the traditional approach to system design? Is it better than the traditional approach? Why or why not?

American Airlines

The first regularly scheduled flight of what was to become American Airlines was made on April 15, 1926, when Charles Lindbergh flew the mail in a biplane from St. Louis to Chicago as chief pilot for the Robertson Company. Between 1929 and 1930, 85 small airline companies, including Robertson, were consolidated into an airline called American Airways, forerunner of today's American Airlines. In 1933, American introduced the first U.S. sleeper plane, the 18-passenger Curtice Condor, marking the debut of flight attendants on board. In 1934, the company formally reorganized as the current American Airlines and rapidly expanded air travel throughout the United States.

In the forties, American entered the airline catering business through a subsidiary called Sky Chefs and became the first airline to modernize with an all postwar fleet. In the fifties, American pioneered nonstop transcontinental service and built the world's first special facility for flight attendants in Dallas-Fort Worth. In the sixties, teaming with IBM, American introduced SABRE, the largest electronic data-processing system designed for business use. Throughout the seventies and eighties, American introduced revolutionary marketing programs and thoroughly upgraded its fleet with major acquisitions of new model Boeing 757 and 767 aircraft.

Today American Airlines is an international air carrier. With over 90,000 employees, American has been rapidly expanding its base of operations through merger agreements domestically and increased route service overseas. In 1991, it acquired three U.S.-to-London routes from TWA. With yearly passenger revenue in excess of $10 billion, American has established itself as a major participant in the future of airline transportation.

SABRE

American's first step at automating the reservation process came in 1952 with a device known as The Magnetronic Reservisor . . . in essence a computerized blackboard. By 1962, American and IBM had linked the electronic blackboard to the telephone with a computer system called

"Semi-Automated Business Research Environment"—SABRE. In 1976 American introduced a version of SABRE tailored specifically for travel agents. In the late 1970s, SABRE was used to develop American's sophisticated yield management system that predicts booking trends on specific flights and maximizes airline passenger revenue. SABRE also handles the reservations functions of many other airlines as well as other operational functions for American.

SABRE is the world's largest privately owned real time computer network. It is driven by eight large IBM mainframe computers running at the same time (TANDEM) at American's central processing site in Tulsa, Oklahoma. Today, nearly half of all U.S. air travel is booked through SABRE and more than 95 percent of U.S. travel agencies are automated.

SABRE, the world's largest privately owned real time computer network, books nearly half of all U.S. air travel, and does much more than that.

Professional SABRE, used by the travel agent, is the most comprehensive system. It can be linked electronically to Agency Data Systems (ADS), which is a powerful accounting and office management system. Another software service available is CAPTURE, which gives a company positive control of its travel and entertainment expenses and greatly simplifies its expense accounting.

Companies that want to manage their own travel arrangements but do not need all of SABRE's features can use a subset, manual Commercial SABRE. With this program, a company can use an ordinary personal computer or terminal to make arrangements for air travel, hotels, and rental cars. Finally, a smaller subset yet is available for individuals called EAASY SABRE and may be accessed through several different services.

SABRE FACTS

Subscribers: More than 17,000 locations with more than 80,000 terminals.

Peak Hour Usage: 2,187 messages per second

Peak Day Usage: 82.1 million messages

Fares in Data Base: 45 million

Fare Changes Entered Monthly: Up to 70 million

Airlines with Schedules in Data Base: 650

Hotel Properties: More than 20,000

Rental Car Companies: 50

SABRE also plays a major role in American Airlines operations. The system maintains inventory control on more than 920 million spare parts. The computer calculates flight plans, weight and balance, fuel requirements, and takeoff power settings for more than 2,300 flights per day. The system also handles all aircraft and crew scheduling, while tracking baggage and freight.

THE SABRE DATA BASES

The data bases required to support such wide-scale operations are extremely large. SABRE has divided its data structures into six physical environments. The Passenger Service System (PSS) is the heart of the operation and provides the booking services. It utilizes 370 IBM 3380s (each with four volumes of data, 630 megabytes per volume). This data is stored in a complete backup mode, thereby allocating half the drive for duplicate data.

The Flight Operating System (FOS) maintains flight plan generation and scheduled maintenance. This subsystem uses 48 IBM 3380 E-series (each capable of storing 5 gigabytes) providing over 200 gigabytes of online storage. The Commercial System providing airline accounting, payroll, and parts tracking utilizes a continuation of storage devices permitting 889 gigabytes. The remaining three environments are for software development, decision support, and communication and require around 300 gigabytes.

The responsibility of maintaining such a large online data base requires extensive hardware and operational support. American Airlines has designed and implemented one of the largest communication networks in the world. Massive data storage with redundant backup is essential to maintain the performance expected and required by the users.

DISCUSSION POINTS

1. Explain how SABRE operates as a management information system rather than merely a reservation system.

2. What special concerns must be addressed for SABRE to support independent travel agents and other airline bookings?

Management Information Systems and Decision Support Systems

ARTICLE

How Software Is Making Food Sales a Piece of Cake

Jeffrey Rothfeder, Jim Bartino, Lois Therrien, and Richard Brandt,
Business Week

Early this year, Frito-Lay Inc. had a problem in San Antonio and Houston. Sales were slumping in that area's supermarkets. So CEO Robert H. Beeby turned to his computer, called up the data for south Texas, and quickly isolated the cause. A regional competitor had just introduced El Galindo, a white-corn tortilla chip. The chip, it turned out, was getting good word of mouth—and as a result, more supermarket shelf space than Frito's traditional Tostitos tortilla chips. Within three months, Beeby had Frito-Lay producing a white-corn version of Tostitos that matched the competition and won back lost market share.

Two years ago, it might have taken Frito-Lay three months just to pinpoint the problem. Only in the past six months has the $4.5 billion snack-food division of PepsiCo Inc. finished installing a sophisticated "decision-support" system that gathers sales data daily from supermarkets, scans it for important clues about local trends, and flags executives about problems and opportunities in all of Frito-Lay's markets.

DATA OVERLOAD
Frito-Lay now has probably the most powerful knowledge-gathering machine in the business, although apparently not for long. Such consumer giants as Kraft USA, Procter & Gamble, and RJR Nabisco are already installing massive systems to track sales blips as current as yesterday and never older than a month

ago. These systems allow executives to take advantage of the mountains of sales data from electronic scanners.

For over a decade, scanners at supermarket checkout counters have been collecting data about what products are being bought at what price. But at first software didn't exist to present the information in a form marketing managers could easily use. Consequently, says John D. Little, professor of management at Massachusetts Institute of Technology and a director at Information Resources Inc., "the first scanner reports were delivered by forklift trucks." And, he adds, they were mostly ignored.

By the mid-1980s, A. C. Nielsen Co. and others had developed systems to sort out data by brand. Since then, though, "the amount of scanner information has increased something like five hundred-fold," says Danny L. Moore, Nielsen vice-president for product development. Weekly, rather than monthly, data are available, providing such specific details as how many cans of 32-ounce Prego tomato sauce with mushrooms were sold in a given store in a particular week.

To manage this rising tide of data, Nielsen and software makers, Information Resources and Metaphor Computer Systems, have recently developed "quasi-expert systems" (table). These automatically break down brand performance within re-

gions and detail how competing products are doing, which promotions work, and whether specific store displays are attracting customers. They also generate summary reports with graphs that highlight unusual product performance.

Marketers welcome these systems. Kathleen Mocniak, research and analysis director at Planters LifeSavers Co., recalls how executives had to wade through lists of numbers for relevant figures on regional performance. It was, she says, like "trying to get a drink of water from a fire hydrant."

Frito-Lay's experience shows how useful these systems can be. Updated daily on handheld terminals by 10,000 Frito-Lay salespeople, information on 100 Frito product lines in 400,000 stores appears on company computer screens in easy-to-read charts. Red means a sales drop, while yellow is a slowdown, and green is an uptick.

These daily snapshots have accelerated the information flow. Two years ago, says Michael H. Jordan, president of PepsiCo Worldwide Foods, "if I asked how we did in Kansas City on July 4th weekend, I'd get five partial responses three weeks later." It's still too early to know the system's impact on the bottom line, but Jordan says it eliminates a day of paperwork from each salesperson's weekly schedule.

Local Frito-Lay brand managers have persuaded Beeby and Jordan to

Software for Marketers

To interpret the flood of sales data now available from supermarket scanners, marketing companies are installing powerful software systems. Here are the most prominent programs.

Executive Information System

Frito-Lay developed this software with Comshare to track its own products' performance day-by-day. Frito-Lay salespeople gather the data from stores. Executives track the data on PCs.

Marketing Advisor

A. C. Nielsen is testing this software with RJR Nabisco's LifeSavers division. It tracks sales by region and highlights important changes. The data are gathered monthly from 3,000 supermarkets.

Cover Story

Information Resources Inc. is selling this program to companies such as lotion maker Jergens. Cover Story summarizes important trends in sales data collected monthly from 2,400 supermarkets.

Data: company reports

tighten relations with parent Pepsico to make even better use of the new information. About 7,000 Pepsi salespeople are scheduled to use the same handheld input system as Frito-Lay within the next two years. Then, the data from the two decision-support systems could be combined so managers at both companies can cooperate—possibly on promotions, discounts, and coupon campaigns.

BAD PRACTICES

Food companies hope these systems will further strengthen their influence with the supermarkets. Kraft, for instance, has been using data from its software system to help such chains as Kroger Co. and Pathmark decide how to stock their refrigerated section most effectively. Michael L. Blyth, Kraft's vice-president for trade marketing, wants to increase Kraft's leverage even more by supplying his sales people with a decision-support system that will generate even more details faster on Kraft products and the competition.

The systems also help giant companies compete better regionally. Tri-Sum Potato Chip Co. in Leominster, Mass., sells snack foods in central Massachusetts. But since Frito-Lay has been using its decision-support system to improve local promotions and expand its share of shelf space, Tri-Sum Presi-

dent Dick Duchesneau has found it much tougher to compete. "We don't have the resources that they do to shove products down people's throats," he adds.

But some marketing consultants argue that the new systems could end up hurting their users as well as the competition. They say the systems aggravate bad practices—especially the tendency to focus on short-term gains at the expense of building long-term brand loyalty. The software systems, by providing narrow windows of data, "reinforce this quick-fix orientation," says Jonathan R. Copulsky, a principal in Booz, Allen & Hamilton's Marketing Intensive Group.

And marketing systems still can't replace human decision-making. Even if the sales data are only one day old, relying on them is akin to "driving a car while looking through the rearview mirror," says MIT's Little. Also, computer systems may not pick up certain factors that affect sales, such as a region's economic health. But even though the systems have their glitches, they are very powerful weapons. Superior technology wins wars—even tortilla chip wars.

◻ INTRODUCTION

For many years computers have been used to perform routine and repetitive operations formerly done manually. When functions such as payroll preparation and order writing are computerized, many hours of human labor are saved. Each organization has specific needs that must be met by its computer system. The types of information that can be provided by a system are as diverse as the organization and the information. Since no two organizations are exactly alike, their computer systems are also different. Large hospitals, corporations, universities, or research laboratories usually need mainframe computers to handle their information needs, while a microcomputer and peripherals might easily handle the data processing requirements for a small retail store or restaurant. Once the information is processed, it may or may not be helpful to management. This chapter explains how a management information system (MIS) ensures that the information that has been processed is useful to a company by focusing on the information needs of the organization.

◼ DEFINITION OF A MANAGEMENT INFORMATION SYSTEM (MIS)

Information is data that has been processed and is useful in decision making. It helps decision makers by increasing knowledge and reducing uncertainty. Modern businesses cannot be run without information; it is the lifeblood of an organization. An information system can supply many types of information. Originally, information systems provided standard reports such as accounting statements, sales summaries, payroll reports, and personnel reports. More recently, information systems have been designed to provide information to support decision making. This application is called a **management information system (MIS).**

In Chapter 1, you learned how data processing takes raw facts called data and organizes them into information. Data processing is concerned with the immediate task of data organization. The emphasis in data processing is on the short-term or daily operations of an organization; it provides detailed information. An MIS is a formal information network using computers to provide management information for decision making. The emphasis in an MIS is on intermediate and long-range planning; therefore, less detailed and more summarized information is necessary. The goal of an MIS is to get the correct information to the appropriate manager at the right time and in a useful form. This is not always an easy task. See Concept Summary 15–1 for a review of the characteristics of data processing and management information systems.

CONCEPT SUMMARY 15–1	
Data Processing vs. Management Information Systems	
Characteristics of DP	**Characteristics of MIS**
Changes data into information	Provides correct and timely information to appropriate manager
Emphasis on short-term daily operations	Emphasis on intermediate and long-range operations
Provides detailed information	Provides summarized information

◼ LEVELS OF MANAGEMENT

In order for an MIS to be successful, it is important to determine the kinds of information each manager needs. To do this, one must understand the various levels of management that exist and the kinds of decisions that are made at each level of an organization. Three levels of management generally exist within an organization,

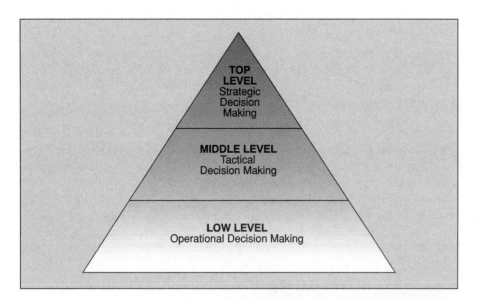

FIGURE 15–1

Levels of Management and the Decisions Made at Each Level

and managers at each of these levels make different types of decisions that require different types of information. Figure 15–1 depicts the three management levels.

Top-Level Management

Top-level managers are concerned with strategic decision-making. Activities at this level are future-oriented and involve a great deal of uncertainty. Examples include establishing goals and determining strategies to achieve the goals. These strategies may involve introducing new product lines, determining new markets, acquiring physical facilities, setting facilities policies, generating capital, and so forth.

Middle-Level Management

Middle-level managers are concerned with tactical decision making. The emphasis in middle-level management is on activities required to implement the strategies determined at the top level; thus, most middle-management decision making is tactical. Activities include planning working capital, scheduling production, formulating budgets, making short-term forecasts, and administering personnel. Much of the decision making at this level pertains to control and short-run planning.

Lower-Level Management

Members of the lowest level in the management hierarchy (first-line supervisors and foremen) make operating decisions to ensure that specific jobs are done. Activities at this level include maintaining inventory records, preparing sales invoices, determining raw material requirements, shipping orders, and assigning jobs to workers. Most of these operations are structured and the decisions are deterministic—they follow specific rules and patterns established at higher levels of management. The major function of lower-level management is controlling company results—keeping the results in line with plans and taking corrective actions if necessary.

FIGURE 15–2

Problems and Differences

Managers at all levels must be provided with decision-oriented information. The fact that the nature of decisions differs at the three levels creates a major difficulty for those attempting to develop an MIS: the information must be tailored to provide appropriate information to all levels (see Figure 15–2).

Decisions made at the lower level are generally routine and well defined. The needs of first-level supervisors can be met by normal administrative data-processing activities such as preparation of financial statements and routine record keeping. Although this level of decision making is fairly basic, it provides the data-processing foundation for the entire organization. If the information system is faulty at this level, the organization faces an immediate crisis.

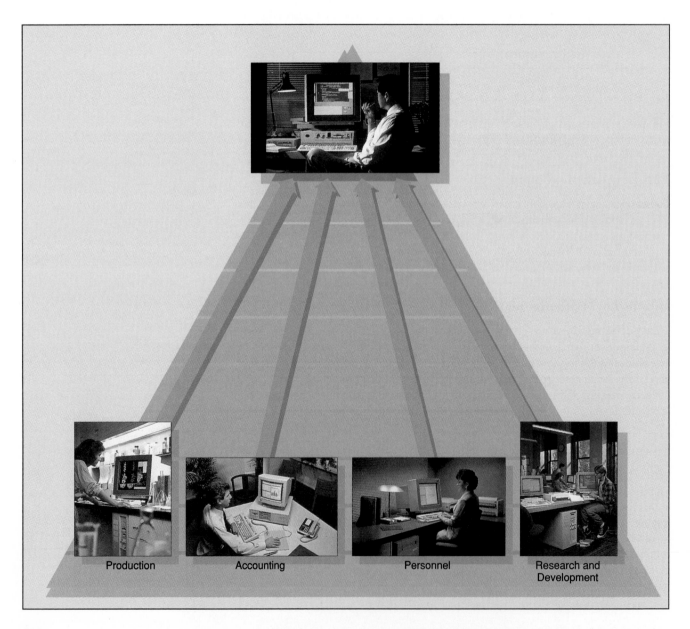

Production   Accounting   Personnel   Research and Development

Tactical decision making is characterized by an intermediate time horizon, a high use of internal information, and significant dependence on rapid processing and retrieval of data. The major focus of tactical decisions is how to make efficient use of organizational resources.

The main problems in MIS design arise when planners attempt to define and meet information requirements of top-level management. Delineating these information needs clearly is extremely difficult, if not impossible. Most problems are nonrepetitive, have great impact on the organization, and involve a great deal of uncertainty. Most information systems serve the needs of the two lower levels but are not adequately designed to cope with the variety of problems encountered by top management.

Since the information needs at the three levels differ, data has to be structured differently at each level. For routine operating decisions such as payroll preparation and inventory stocking, separate employee and inventory files are adequate. To serve the middle and top levels, the data should be organized to provide inquiry capabilities across functional lines and to handle routine information reports. Concept Summary 15–2 summarizes the differences among the decision-making levels.

CONCEPT SUMMARY 15–2

Differences among Decision-Making Levels

| Characteristics | Levels of Decision Making | | |
	Operational	Tactical	Strategic
Time horizon	Daily	Weekly/monthly	Yearly
Degree of structure	High	Moderate	Low
Use of external information	Low	Moderate	Very high
Use of internal information	Very high	High	Moderate
Degree of judgment	Low	Moderate	Very high
Information online	Very high	High	Moderate
Level of complexity	Low	Moderate	Very high
Information in real time	High	High	High

◻ TYPES OF REPORTS

Management information systems typically generate several types of reports containing information that may be used in decision making. Reports generated include scheduled listings, exception reports, predictive reports, and demand reports.

Scheduled Listings

Scheduled listings are produced at regular intervals and provide routine information to a wide variety of users. Since they are designed to provide information to many users, they tend to contain an overabundance of data. Much of the data may not be relevant to a particular user. Such listings constitute most of the output of current computer-based information systems.

Exception Reports

Exception reports are action-oriented management reports. The performance of business systems is monitored, and any deviation from expected results triggers the generation of a report. These reports can also be produced during processing, when items are collected and forwarded to the computer in a group. Exception reports are useful because they ignore all normal events and focus management's attention on abnormal situations that require special handling.

Predictive Reports

Predictive reports are used for planning. Future results are projected on the basis of decision models that can be either simple or highly complex. The usefulness of these reports depends on how well they can predict future events. Management can manipulate the variables included in a model to get responses to ''what if'' kinds of queries. Predictive reports are especially suited to the tactical and strategic decision making performed in the middle and upper levels of management.

Demand Reports

As the name implies, demand reports are produced only on request. Since these reports are not required on a continuing basis, they are often requested and displayed on a computer terminal. The MIS must have an extensive and appropriately structured data base to provide responses to unanticipated queries. No single data base can meet all the needs of the user, but a data base in a well-designed MIS should include data that may be needed to respond to possible user queries. Because it requires a sophisticated data base, demand reporting can be expensive, but it allows decision makers to obtain relevant and specific information at the moment it is needed.

◘ MANAGEMENT AND MIS

Although an MIS can help management make decisions, it cannot guarantee that the decisions will be successful. One problem that frequently arises is determining what information is needed by management. To many, decision making is an individual art. Experience, intuition, and chance affect the decision-making process. These inputs are all but impossible to quantify. In designing a system, the analyst relies on the user to determine information requirements. Frequently lacking precise ideas of what they need, managers request everything the computer can provide. The result is an overload of information. Instead of helping the manager, this information overload creates another problem: how to distinguish what is relevant from what is irrelevant.

After the MIS has been installed, management does not always consider the change beneficial. In some cases, however, the people who must use the system were not involved in the analysis and design; therefore their expectations are unrealistic. Managers frequently expect that decision making will be totally automatic after implementation of an MIS. They fail to recognize that unstructured tasks are difficult to program. Even though routine decisions (such as ordering materials when inventory stock goes below a certain point) can be programmed easily, decisions that depend on more than quantitative data require human evaluation, because the computer system has no intuitive capability.

Other problems may arise. As the computer takes over routine decisions, managers may resist further changes. They may fear that their responsibility for decision making will be reduced or that the computer will make their positions obsolete. They may fail to realize that the availability of good information can enhance their managerial performance.

The success of an MIS depends largely on the attitude and involvement of management. An MIS is most apt to be successful when it is implemented in an organization already operating on a sound basis, rather than in an organization seeking a miracle.

▣ DESIGN METHODOLOGY

When designing and implementing management information systems, the system analyst serves as the intermediary between the user (management) and the technology used to create the system. Therefore, part of a system analyst's responsibility includes keeping pace with computer and information processing technologies. As the pace of technological innovation accelerates, system analysts and data-processing departments must try to keep current with the changes. Since software development is extremely labor-intensive, it often lags behind existing hardware technology. As a result, data-processing departments today face a productivity problem; they must obtain greater software development for each dollar invested. The basic ways of increasing productivity are: (a) to automate the software development process; (b) to require employees to work harder, or longer, or both; or (c) to change the way things are done. Structured design attempts to achieve greater productivity by focusing on the third method.

Top-Down Design

Top-down design is a structured approach to designing an MIS. The approach attempts to simplify a system by breaking it down into logical functions, or modules. These, in turn, are further divided. The system is first defined in terms of the functions it must perform. Each of these functions is then translated into a module. The correct system design may require several of these modules to perform all the required tasks.

In top-down design, the most general level of organization is the main module; this overall view of the organization is most critical to the success of the system design. Modules at this level contain only broad descriptions of functions in the system. These functions are further broken down into lower-level modules that contain more detail about the specific steps to be performed. Depending on the complexity of the system, several levels of modules may be required, with the lowest-level modules containing the greatest amount of detail.

The modules of the system design are related to each other in a hierarchical manner. These relationships can be depicted graphically in a structure chart. Figure 15–3 shows a portion of such a chart for the application process at a university. Using top-down design, the application process is broken down into its main modules: reviewing the applications, notifying applicants, and considering applicants for financial aid. Each of these functions can be broken down into more specific tasks. For example, the review process consists of checking the application form, obtaining transcripts

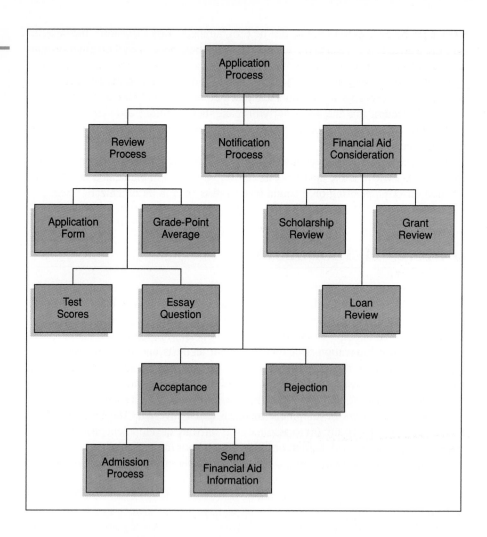

to verify the grade-point average, obtaining official SAT or ACT scores, and reading the essays submitted by the applicant. These tasks may be broken down even further, if necessary.

Design Alternatives

The development of an MIS is an integrated approach to organizing a company's activities. The company's MIS must be structured in a way that will allow it to realize the full benefits of integration. When considering alternative organizational structures, the analyst faces virtually unlimited possibilities. This section describes four basic design structures: centralized, hierarchical, distributed, and decentralized. These structures should be viewed as checkpoints along a continuous range of design alternatives rather than as separate, mutually exclusive options. For example, a system design may incorporate characteristics from both the distributed system and the decentralized system.

The **centralized design** is the most traditional approach. It involves the centralization of computer power. A separate electronic data-processing (EDP) or information systems (IS) department is set up to provide data-processing facilities for the organization. This department's personnel, like other staff personnel, support the operating units of the organization. All program development, as well as all equipment acquisition, is controlled by the EDP or IS group. Standard regulations and procedures are employed. Distant units use the centralized equipment by a remote access communication network. A common data base exists, permitting authorized users to access information (see Figure 15–4a).

When **hierarchical design** is used, the organization consists of multiple levels with varying degrees of responsibility and decision-making authority. In hierarchical design, each management level is given the computer power necessary to support its task objectives. At the lowest level, limited support is required, because the work is considered technical in nature. Middle-level support is more extensive, because managerial decisions at this level require more complicated analysis (hence, more information processing). Finally, top-level executives require little detailed information since they work with general issues requiring information that can be obtained only with greater processing and storage capabilities. An example of this design approach is shown in Figure 15–4b.

The **distributed design** approach identifies the existence of independent operating units but recognizes the benefits of central coordination and control. The organization is broken into the smallest activity centers requiring computer support. These centers may be based on organizational structure, geographical location, functions, operations, or a combination of these factors. Hardware (and often people) are placed within these activity centers to support their tasks. Total organizationwide control is often evidenced by the existence of standardized classes of hardware, common data bases, and coordinated system development. The distributed computer sites may or may not share data elements, workloads, and resources, depending on whether they are in communication with each other. An example of the distributed design approach is given in Figure 15–4c.

In a **decentralized design,** authority and responsibility for computer support are placed in relatively autonomous organizational operating units. These units usually parallel the management decision-making structure. Normally, no central control point exists; the authority for computer operations goes directly to the managers in charge of the operating units. Since there is no central control, each unit is free to acquire hardware, develop software, and make personnel decisions independently. Responsiveness to user needs is normally high because close working relationships are reinforced by the proximity of the system to its users. Communication among units is limited or nonexistent, thereby ruling out the possibility of common or shared applications. This design approach can only be used where an existing organizational structure supports decentralized management. Furthermore, it is not highly compatible with the MIS concept. An example of the decentralized design approach is shown in Figure 15–4d.

◾ DECISION SUPPORT SYSTEMS

Closely related to the MIS is the decision support system. Whereas an MIS supplies managers with information to support structured decisions, a **decision support system (DSS)** provides managers with information to support relatively unstructured decisions. For example, an MIS may provide information about sales trends, changes in productivity from one quarter to the next, or fluctuation in inventory levels. Information such as this tells the manager what has already happened. A DSS, on the

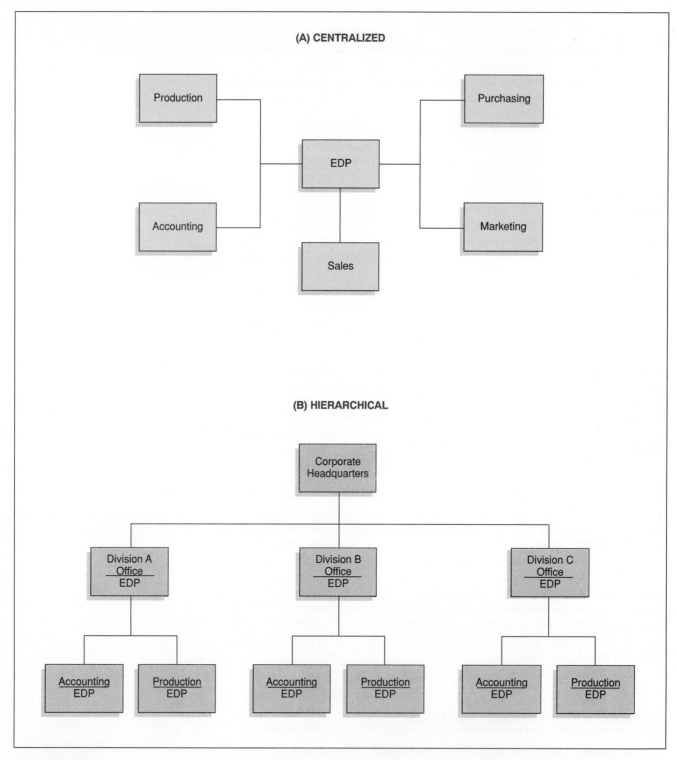

(A) CENTRALIZED

Production

Purchasing

EDP

Accounting

Marketing

Sales

(B) HIERARCHICAL

Corporate
Headquarters

Division A
Office
EDP

Division B
Office
EDP

Division C
Office
EDP

Accounting
EDP

Production
EDP

Accounting
EDP

Production
EDP

Accounting
EDP

Production
EDP

FIGURE 15–4

Sample Design Structures
Continued

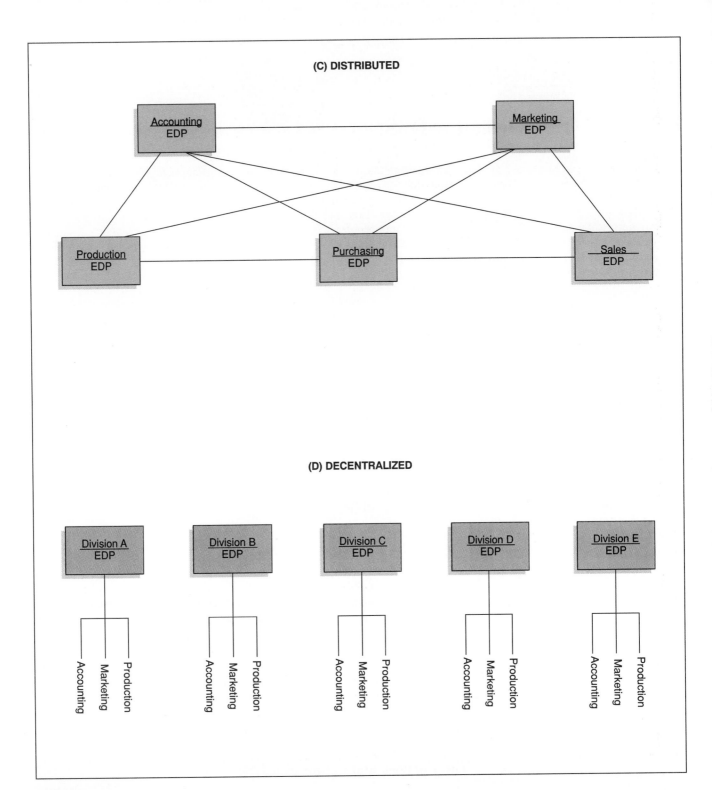

FIGURE 15–4

Continued

HIGHLIGHT

Who Best to Design a DSS?

A long-standing debate in MIS circles has been waged over who can best design an information system: the eventual user or a systems analyst. This question becomes even more important in the case of decision support systems, where the system (or model) is based on the manager's perception of a real-world system. At Spencer Gifts, they're betting that the users of the system have the knowledge and experience required to make a decision support system a valuable tool. The Spencer Integrated Retail Information System (SIRIS) is intended to provide merchandising managers and buyers with up-to-date information on retail sales trends. Like other companies employing modern computer technologies, Spencer Gifts is hoping that SIRIS will give them a competitive advantage in the marketplace.

The design of SIRIS was the combined effort of John Hacala, Chief Executive Officer, and Eugene Murtha, Vice President of Informa-

tion Systems at Spencer Gifts. Between them, Hacala and Murtha have forty-five years experience in retail sales. It is this experience and overall knowledge of retailing that has produced for Spencer Gifts an extremely useful decision support system to use in a very competitive market.

However, the entire effort required to create a decision support system must be considered before the question we began with (of who is best to design such a system) can be answered. In the case of SIRIS, more tasks than just identifying what the system should do had to be completed in order for the proposed system to become reality. Decisions concerning computer hardware, programming languages, data-base systems, documentation, and training all had to be made. It is in these areas that a system analyst's knowledge and experience can be beneficial.

Questions such as, "What computer system(s) will be best suited

for our DSS?" or "What programming language should be used to create our DSS?" are often best answered by system analysts. Therefore, the answer to our original question generally is *a team* of knowledgeable users and system analysts. In many ways, the system analyst must function as a bridge between the eventual users of the system and the available data processing technologies. The user(s) should serve as the providers of knowledge for the system and should be actively involved with the design of the system. The system analyst should take on the role of advisor during the design phase. Once the design is complete, the system analyst should employ knowledge and expertise to implement the system. The old saying "Two heads are better than one" very well fits the case of designing and implementing a useful information system.

other hand, may provide financial planning models or optimal production schedules that managers can use to determine what *might* happen.

Essentially, a DSS and an MIS do the same thing—they process data to get information that is useful to managers. What, then, is the difference between them? Some professionals in the information field believe the difference is that an MIS supports only structured or operational decisions, while a DSS supports unstructured or strategic decisions. The distinction is based on the type of decision supported. Others believe DSSs are merely subsystems of a larger MIS, capable of processing different types of data as a result of technological advances in hardware and software.

The Purpose and Scope of a DSS

Decision support systems separate structured (or operational) decision making from unstructured (or strategic) decision making. For example, a purchase order for a certain product may be generated automatically if an inventory stock level falls below a certain amount. Such a structured decision can be handled easily by a computer.

A decision support system, on the other hand, places more emphasis on semi-structured or unstructured decisions. While the computer is used as an analytical aid to decision making, the DSS does not attempt to automate the manager's decision making or to impose solutions. For example, an investment manager must make recommendations to a client concerning the client's investments. The manager's decision is based on stock performance and requires a certain amount of judgment. The computer can be used to aid the decision but cannot make the actual recommendation to the client.

The primary use of computer technology within a DSS has been to speed the processing of the large amounts of data needed for the manager to consider the full effects of a possible decision. This permits managers to consider a greater number of alternatives—alternatives that otherwise might not have been considered, because of time constraints. But as previously stated, a DSS, and within it the use of computers, must be a normal and comfortable extension of the manager's overall method of problem solving and decision making.

Advocates of DSS, therefore, claim that its emphasis is toward improving the effectiveness and quality of decision making. The purpose of the DSS is not to replace management information systems but to enhance them. Because advances are being made in applying computer technology to the areas of tactical and strategic decision making, the rewards that can be realized are even greater than those that have occurred in the area of operational decision making. Computer applications in the areas of tactical and strategic decision making are a logical step forward in the application of computer technology to management science and a logical addition to and advancement in the area of management information systems.

A Model: The Heart of a DSS

As stated in the section on decision-oriented reports, predictive reports use decision models to project future results. Such models are suited to tactical and strategic decision making, which is the focus of a DSS.

A **model** is a mathematical representation of an actual system. The model contains independent variables that influence the value of a dependent variable. Think of the independent variables as the input and the dependent variable as the output.

In the real world, many relationships are based on the effect of an independent variable on a dependent variable. For example, the price of a sofa depends on the costs of the materials needed to make it. Sales of a new brand of toothpaste depend, in part, on the amount of money spent advertising it. The number of microwave ovens sold depends on, or is a function of, the price of the oven. This relationship between price and sales could be represented by the following mathematical model:

Microwave oven sales $= f$(Price of the oven)

The relationship could be expressed as a mathematical equation. Then a manager could plug different prices into the equation and get some idea of how many microwave ovens would be sold at each price.

The fact that each manager must have a decision model based on his or her perception of the system is what has made the implementation of DSSs so difficult. Managerial styles, as well as the environments in which people manage, are unique to each manager. In order for the DSS to be useful, it must be designed to aid a manager in his or her particular decision-making style.

Once the model for the DSS is developed, it must be incorporated into a decision support system that can be used by the manager. Some decision support systems are designed to be used to assist a manager in making specific types of decisions. For example, a DSS might be designed to assist an advertising manager in determining how much to spend for a particular advertising campaign. This type of DSS can be developed by a company for use by its managers or it could be purchased from a software vendor. An alternative to developing or purchasing a DSS to be used for a specific purpose would be to purchase packages that can be used to develop different types of decision support systems. These packages could possibly include both software and hardware and would be used by a company to develop a variety of decision support systems to be used for differing purposes. Electronic spreadsheets (discussed in Chapter 13) for example, have been used on microcomputer systems to create decision support systems that can be used for financial planning. Expert system shells (also discussed in Chapter 13) can also be used to develop decision support systems. The decision support systems used by a particular company's management will depend upon the type of decision that needs to be made as well as the computer hardware and software expertise that exists within the company.

The Future of DSS

One of the key factors, if not the key factor, in the acceptance of decision support systems within business is management. How the management of a company views modeling and decision support systems is the critical factor that determines whether or not they are successfully implemented and used. Although decision modeling is used in a large number of firms, if its full potential is to be realized, obstacles such as management resistance, a lack of management sophistication, and interdepartmental communication problems must be overcome.

Many people feel that the acceptance and use of decision modeling and decision support systems in business is being slowed by the resistance of top management, which often has a skeptical attitude toward scientific management techniques and an unwillingness to accept and have confidence in these techniques. In addition, management is also sensitive to a situation in which the promise of what can be done with computers is far different from that which is finally accomplished. Before management will fully accept the use of computers and decision support systems, promises of what can be accomplished must be realistic. Until these promises are realized, management's willingness to accept new decision-making aids will be hindered.

Until recently, decision support systems have been discussed in a functional context. Each functional area of an organization may have its own DSS. The current trend, however, is the use of **simultaneous decision support systems,** or **corporate planning models.** The primary goal of simultaneous decision support systems is to combine into one system the various functional areas of an organization that affect the performance and output of other functional areas. The marketing areas of a firm, for instance, must coordinate advertising and sales efforts with production to ensure that the demand generated for a product can be met.

Organizations realize that consistent, overall strategic planning is required if the organization is to survive in a dynamic environment. For this reason, firms are attempting to develop simultaneous decision support systems that can coordinate the functional areas of a corporation as well as aid the organization's strategic and tactical planners. Figure 15–5 illustrates a possible structure for a simultaneous decision support system.

The number of organizations using simultaneous decision support systems or corporate planning models is growing. There is little doubt that the future of decision

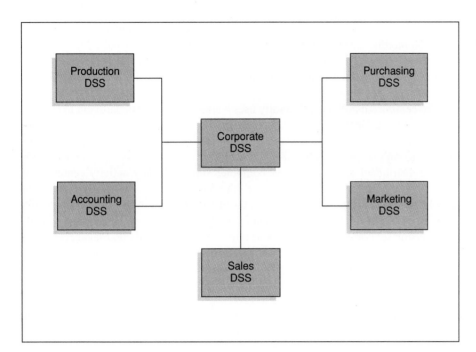

support systems lies in this direction. Advances in the areas of decision model development and applying computer technology to managerial decision making are helping simultaneous decision support systems gain widespread acceptance and use.

◘ SUMMARY POINTS

■ A management information system (MIS) is a formal information network that uses computer capabilities to provide management with the information necessary for decision making. The goal of an MIS is to get the correct information to the appropriate manager at the right time.

■ There are three levels of management: top-level management makes strategic and future-oriented decisions; middle-level management makes tactical decisions (implementing the strategies developed by top-level managers); and lower-level management makes the day-to-day decisions that keep the organization operating efficiently.

■ Managers at all levels must be provided with decision-oriented information. Since the information needs at the three management levels differ, data has to be structured differently at each level.

■ Decision-oriented reporting includes various types of reports required by management. Scheduled reports are produced at regular intervals and provide routine information. Exception reports are action-oriented and monitor performance—they indicate when a particular operation is not behaving as expected. Predictive reports use models to project possible outcomes of different decisions. Demand reports are usually one-time-only requests that cover unanticipated information needs.

■ Structured design is a method of breaking down a problem into logical segments, or modules. Each module performs a logical function. These modules, in turn, may be broken down further. Modules are related to one another in a hierarchical fashion, but each module is independent of the others.

■ The ways in which an MIS can be designed within the structure of an organization are virtually unlimited. Common approaches are centralized, hierarchical, distributed, and decentralized structures.

■ The centralized approach generally uses a single computer department to provide data processing for the entire organization.

■ The hierarchical approach gives each management level the computer power needed to support its task objectives.

■ The distributed approach places computer support in key activity centers, and information is shared among the various functions.

■ The decentralized approach places authority and responsibility for computer support in relatively autonomous organizational units.

■ Decision support systems emphasize effective decision making. Managers in strategic areas are provided with relevant information to help them make decisions. Support is provided for tasks that are not routine or structured. To be most useful, the decision support system should be compatible with the manager's decision-making processes.

■ The use of computers within decision support systems has primarily been to help speed the manager's analysis of decision alternatives.

■ A decision model acts as the heart of a decision support system. It is a mathematical representation of an actual system. The model should be developed by the manager who will use it so that it represents his or her perception of the actual system.

■ The future of DSS may lie in simultaneous decision support systems, or corporate planning models, which are decision support systems designed to coordinate decision making within an entire organization.

❑ TERMS FOR REVIEW

centralized design, p. 398

decentralized design, p. 399

decision support system (DSS), p. 399

distributed design, p. 399

hierarchical design, p. 399

management information system (MIS), p. 392

model, p. 403

simultaneous decision support system (corporate planning model), p. 404

■ REVIEW QUESTIONS

1. What is a management information system (MIS)? What is the emphasis of an MIS? What is its goal?

2. List each of the levels of management served by an MIS. Describe the types of information managers at these levels require.

3. What are the four types of listings or reports produced by an MIS? What are the characteristics of each of these types of reports?

4. Identify and describe some of the common problems when implementing an MIS.

5. Describe how a top-down design approach can lead to greater productivity within data-processing departments. Refer to Chapter 14 if necessary.

6. What are the four basic management information system design structures? Must designs fit into one of these structures exclusively, or can aspects from several structure types be combined to produce a design? Explain your answer.

7. Describe, in detail, how a distributed design is organized. Give an example of the type of organization that might require an MIS that incorporates a distributed design.

8. How does a decision support system (DSS) differ from an MIS?

9. Describe the advantages a DSS provides to managers. What are some of the key characteristics a DSS should exhibit if it is to be used effectively by a manager?

10. What is a model? Why is it important to a DSS?

Pepsi-Cola Company

The roots of Pepsi-Cola Company trace to 1893 and to Caleb Bradham, a young New Bern, North Carolina, pharmacist. Bradham formulated a drink combining carbonated water, sugar, vanilla, rare oils, and cola nuts for sale in his drug store. Called "Brad's Drink" initially, it was renamed Pepsi-Cola in 1896 and trademarked in 1903.

Over the next several years Bradham expanded the business by selling licenses to bottle the product, and in 1907, syrup sales exceeded 100,000 gallons for the first time. By the following year, there were 250 independent Pepsi bottling franchises in twenty-four states.

The business prospered for ten more years, but with the end of World War I came the collapse of the sugar market—and Pepsi-Cola Company—and the start of an almost thirteen year struggle back to solvency. But, in the 1930s, prosperity returned, thanks to innovations like twelve ounces of Pepsi for the price of six ounces of other colas and the first radio jingle ever to air nationally—"Pepsi-Cola hits the spot/Twelve full ounces, that's a lot . . ."

In 1948 the company moved its headquarters to New York City, and by the early 1950s, under the leadership of CEO Alfred Steele—whose wife was actress Joan Crawford—Pepsi was being advertised more as part of a modern lifestyle than as a bargain.

Pepsi's worldwide expansion led to the formation of a separate international division in 1954, and in 1959 when then-Vice President Nixon provided Soviet Premier Krushchev with a sample, Pepsi became the hit of the Moscow World's Fair—auguring Pepsi's becoming the first American product ever licensed for manufacture in the Soviet Union, fifteen years later.

"Pepsi Generation" in 1963 became both the name for the young people born during the post-war baby boom and an advertising theme still in use today. It was in the '60s too, that Diet Pepsi and Mountain Dew were added to the company's product line, and PepsiCo, Inc. was formed with the merger of Pepsi-Cola and Frito-Lay in 1965.

During the 1970s the initiation of a program of strategic acquisitions—Pizza Hut in 1977, Taco Bell in 1978, and Kentucky Fried Chicken in 1986—resulted in PepsiCo's becoming the world's largest restaurant company.

On the advertising front, the Pepsi Challenge became the most successful comparative campaign in soft drink history, and in 1977, Pepsi-Cola became the number-one-selling soft drink in food stores for the first time, as well as the number-one-selling branded product of any kind in American supermarkets—a rank it continues to hold.

The company's tradition of innovation carried into the '80s and '90s, with Pepsi's newest product, Slice, the first soft drink with real fruit juice. In advertising, stars like Michael Jackson, Michael J. Fox, and Ray Charles appeared in Pepsi commercials, while the company continued its long-established pattern of growth at a pace well ahead of its industry.

PEPSI-COLA COMPANY
Pepsi-Cola Company, like most major corporations, relies on computers for virtually all of the fundamental data accumulation and processing necessary for the conduct of the business. Therefore, accounting and record-keeping constitute one of the key missions of the MIS function.

Two of Pepsi's effective MIS applications, EIS for senior executives and DataServer for their lieutenants, provide timely information about key indicators and allow users to "drill down" into supporting data.

However, Pepsi information systems also play a key role in the overall decision-making and management of the business, the result of an MIS department philosophy of continually providing the improved systems and technology that help ease access to data and computing power for users throughout the company.

At the lowest operational level, Hewlett Packard and IBM mainframes are employed for transactional processing. General ledger functions—accounts receivable and payable—as well as other standard functions of the normal business cycle are processed and executed. Standardized reports of those transactions are provided for management review and action by twenty-eight day period, monthly, quarterly, or other desired formats.

Sales data is captured on these same transaction-processing systems and is categorized by product, channel of distribution, and customer. This information is accessed through INF*FACT on the IBM mainframe and can be integrated with the syndicated share data that is provided by Information Resources Inc. (IRI). The syndicated data, which is based on supermarket scanner data and covers Pepsi-Cola and competitor's products, is most often obtained through IRI's DataServer.

Finally, this same data is again reconfigured, this time into summary formats for management decision support. Sales trends, profitability trends, regional, demographic, or seasonal performance, or any of dozens of other key performance indicators are routinely available or can easily be created on request.

The technical tools for presenting the data allow the individual manager to determine the most practical format for evaluation, and in effect, to configure reporting to his or her own needs. That capability, in conjunction with the ability to access the mainframe from a personal computer, significantly expands executive decision support capabilities.

PEPSI-COLA COMPANY: SPECIALIZED COMPUTER APPLICATIONS

The increased capacities and sophistication of general purpose computer systems, the advent of user-friendly, easy-to-use computer hardware and software, plus the growing awareness of computer capabilities on the part of nontechnical managers and executives are contributing to the changing role of the computer in large organizations.

At Pepsi, as elsewhere, those characteristics are helping to expand utilization of the computer in diverse areas of the business. Below, two typical applications are described.

Executive Information System

One of the more exciting and innovative uses of information technology at Pepsi-Cola is the Executive Information System (EIS), which provides information about key busi-

ness indicators to senior level executives through the use of Comshare's Commander Software.

The system enables management to monitor overall performance, as well as category-specific performance, and to take appropriate managerial actions when indicated. Deviations from plan or other exception conditions, both positive and negative, are highlighted to enhance decision making.

EIS combines both the raw processing power and large data storage capabilities of the mainframe and the flexibility and ease of use of the personal computer. Data originates from a variety of sources—internal accounting systems, external tracking services, and online data bases, such as Dow Jones Newswire.

Along with its other capabilities, EIS is also designed to prevent data overload, since the data provided to the executive is highly compressed and customized into specific formats based on managerial needs.

As a result, one of the more attractive features of EIS is its ease of use. Instead of enduring an elaborate training program, executives access the system through a highly "intuitive" user interface. With the interface, most activity is controlled through a hand-held mouse instead of a keyboard. Companywide data is presented in previously formatted online reports, and when further levels of detail are desired, it is relatively simple to "drill down" into supporting data.

APPLICATION
Pepsi-Cola Company

DataServer

DataServer, a software product of IRI, is a relatively new technology to Pepsi. It is a comprehensive marketing decision support system used for developing effective marketing programs, analyzing competition, and enhancing research and analytical capabilities. It provides analytical flexibility through an easy-to-use personal computer interface with the mainframe computer. It integrates the strength of the mainframe data base and processor with the PC windowed recognition-based front-end to achieve timely data retrieval and analysis.

Unlike EIS, which is specifically targeted to senior executives and provides strategic information across both internal and syndicated data sources, DataServer is oriented toward tactical, short-term issues regarding IRI syndicated data. The DataServer is primarily targeted at analysts who are concerned with lower level details and specialty data, as well as the creation of specific output, such as customized report formats, graphs, spreadsheets, or documents. Therefore, when a senior manager's syndicated information needs exceed the scope of EIS, the information can usually be provided by more detailed DataServer inquiries. Since one of the strengths of DataServer is that it enables users to easily prepare complicated ad-hoc reports, it works as an information complement to EIS.

DISCUSSION POINTS

1. How does EIS support strategic decision making at Pepsi?
2. Why does Pepsi access external data bases?

The Impact of Computers on People and Organizations

With Complexity, a Threat of Chaos

Michael Alexander, *Computerworld*

Elaborate computer systems are increasingly being used to control everything from long-distance telephone calls to transcontinental flights. Now, some computer scientists worry that such complex computer systems are not as reliable as needed and, should they fail, they would set off mishaps that could result in the loss of life.

About 100 computer scientists convened to discuss their concerns about the reliability and safety of complex computer systems during a two-day summit meeting in Arlington, Va., sponsored by The Association for Computing Machinery (ACM). The scientists also discussed what some said is a disquieting trend toward the use of computer modeling to simulate human behavior.

Many of the scientists said they fear that as computer systems become more elaborate, they may be more prone to the sort of software glitches that triggered the shutdown of AT&T long-distance service for several hours early in 1990.

For example, the scientists pointed to such calamities as the two accidental downings of civilian aircraft and the radiation therapy machines that run amok, exposing four patients to fatal overdoses of of radiation. Those incidents were caused by software that did not perform as expected, they said.

"Commercial pilots are getting more and more information from radar and computer systems on board and not from their own senses," said Frederic Withington, a computer consultant and member of the ACM program committee. "If the information is wrong, the results can be disastrous, as in the case when the Soviets shot down a Korean airliner that had strayed into its territory. The flight was shot down basically because of a misprogrammed computer."

The nanosecond suddenness with which some events occur using computer-controlled systems means that we must also depend more on the systems and not on common sense when coping with emergencies, Withington said.

"We need to do our jobs [as software engineers] better, exercise software more thoroughly and anticipate problems, perhaps with a fail/safe mode so the system can sense when things are not right," Withington said.

In some instances, software engineers simply lack the intellectual capacity to develop nearly foolproof complex computer systems, said Anthony Wasserman, a software engineer and president of Interactive Development Environments, Inc. Systems such as multinational air traffic control may be beyond our grasp, but that is not stopping engineers from attempting to build such systems, he said.

"The fact is, whether it is a system for home shopping or electronic funds transfer, there is a level of complexity, and we need to better manage it," Wasserman said. He advocated a more structured approach to software design, which traditionally has been treated as a "programming mystique."

Complex systems are not necessarily less reliable, but more can go wrong, he said. For that reason, software engineers must do a more careful job of analyzing the risks associated with a complex system, even if it means stretching out the design process, Wasserman said.

Some scientists at the summit meeting also fretted that the growing reliance on computer modeling may lead some to use the technology to support conflicting points of view. For example, the scientists pointed to the use of computer simulations supporting conflicting theories of such hotly debated issues as global warming and the possibility of a nuclear winter.

The most useful models are typically those that have been applied to the physical world, where there are small numbers of known variables, said Stuart Dreyfus, a professor at the University of California at Berkeley, whose expertise is in examining the limits of modeling. Applying modeling to socio-economic situations or trying to predict human behavior "can lead to making inferior decisions," Dreyfus said.

For example, studies show that managers do not do a lot of detached meditation before making a decision, Dreyfus said. "They circulate, gossip and use intuition, not methodologies." Even the best of expert systems fail to come close to turning this sort of experience into rules that a computer can follow, he said.

"As long as we see models as untrustworthy but interesting, or as a new tool with error correction, they are not totally irrelevant,'' Dreyfus said.

When applied to limited variables with known interaction between those variables, computer modeling can be a ''fabulous tool,'' agreed Eleanor Wynn, an anthropologist and publisher of *Information Technology and People*. It is when computer modeling is used to simulate human behavior that problems can arise, she said. ''What happens so often is that they begin assuming that model is a reflection of the real world and not a hypothesis.''

One reason that computer systems fail is that their designers did not ad-equately consider the human element in their planning, said Rod Leddy, systems training consultant at Mobil Oil Corp. Computer-supported systems have to be designed with communication between users and technicians rather than from a distance or a set of abstractions, he said.

One solution may be to require computer scientists to study sociology, philosophy and other areas. European computer scientists have a broader education and are more comfortable incorporating those areas in computer systems design, Wynn said.

Despite fears that computer sys-tem failures will become more frequent, the scientists said they see cause for optimism: Computer users are more knowledgeable and are co-operating more closely with computer manufacturers to develop better systems; integrated sets of software tools are making software cheaper and more reliable; and new methods known as software quality metrics are helping to make software of complex computer systems more foolproof.

◘ INTRODUCTION

Computers, although incapable of conventional thought and feeling, greatly affect our personal lives and the world in which we live. Because of computer technology, the way in which we live has changed drastically in recent history. The computer revolution has had an impact on individuals and organizations alike. While most people agree that computers benefit our society, the computer revolution has had some negative effects on people and organizations.

This chapter discusses the impact the computer has had on both our individual lives and on organizations and their struggle to survive in an ever-changing environment. The behavioral aspects of the impact of computers is discussed, as is the nature of their impact on organizations in business, industry, and government. The chapter also reviews some of the effects the computer has had on the office environment by exploring office automation.

◘ BEHAVIORAL ASPECTS OF COMPUTER USE

Computer Anxiety

The rapid pace at which computers have been integrated into our society has created a group of people who fear the effects computers have on their lives and society in general. People who have this fear are said to be suffering from **computer anxiety** or **computerphobia.** In many cases these individuals are intimidated by computers. Some people not familiar with computers are afraid that if they make a mistake and press the wrong button, valuable information will be destroyed. Another common fear experienced by many people is the threat of job loss due to computerization. The overwhelming use of jargon associated with computers also leads to computer anxiety. Terms such as bits, bytes, Ks, ROM, CPU, disk drives, emulators, and networks can be confusing and intimidating to the computer novice.

CHAPTER 16

Age, too, is a factor that contributes to computerphobia. People who grew up in an environment largely unaffected by computer technology tend to resist using the machines, while young people are much quicker to accept the new technology. The fear of the continuing advancement of computers into our lives—a fear of the unfamiliar—is often referred to as *high-tech anxiety*. High-tech anxiety is predominant among older people, who have had limited contact with the computer in general.

Another type of computer anxiety is thought to be gender related. Recent studies involving women in computer fields, however, have shown that women in computer-related jobs perform their duties with a skill and confidence equal to that of males. Genevieve Cerf, an instructor in electrical engineering at Columbia University, feels that women make better programmers than men. Many studies have found that women are more organized, more verbal, and more likely to consider the end user when writing computer programs. Studies by biologists and psychologists suggest that women are better than men at skills that depend on the left hemisphere of the brain—communication and logic skills. Logic skills, in particular, are essential to computer programming.

One benefit for women who obtain a computer science degree and enter the field is pay. According to a National Science Foundation study, women with computer science degrees earn nearly 100 percent of the salary that men holding a similar position earn. This fact may seem trivial; however, in some occupations women earn as little as 59 cents for every dollar earned by a man in a similar position. The equal pay issue draws much attention and may be one reason why women account for 26 percent of computer professionals.

Still another type of computer anxiety stems from a fear of depersonalization. To many people, the use of a computer for things such as record keeping and billing often leads to a feeling of being treated as a number rather than as a person. This factor of impersonalization has led many people to develop negative attitudes concerning computers.

Computer Literacy

Computer literacy is a general knowledge about computers. This includes some technical knowledge about computer hardware and software and especially the ability to use computers to solve problems and an awareness of how computers affect our society.

Today, most people feel that being comfortable using computers to solve problems of both an academic and a personal nature is important. This implies that students need some knowledge of basic computer use and the functions of various hardware components. Computer literacy courses have been designed to teach these subjects. As more and more children and adults take computer literacy courses, computer anxiety will also be reduced within the overall population.

One goal of high school computer literacy courses is to give students an understanding of how computers work. Students learn to identify the parts of a computer; they also learn to follow the path that electricity takes and see firsthand the practical need for and use of the binary number system. Computer literacy courses also examine the effect of computers on society. Knowing the history of computers, examples of current uses, and projected future trends is important to understanding how computers are changing our lives.

The importance of computer literacy was evidenced by the proposal introduced by the Federal Commission on Excellence in Education in May 1983 to implement new guidelines to stem the "rising tide of mediocrity" in our society. Among these guidelines was a suggestion that all students be required to take a half-year of computer science in high school. Despite all the controversial opinions generated by the report, that particular suggestion was questioned by very few people. Why? The most likely answer is that parents and other adults realize there is no way to stop the growing use of computers. Schools cannot be allowed the option of ignoring computers, because these machines alter jobs, entertainment, and home life so radically. It is becoming evident that people who learn about computers are advancing in their jobs, while people who avoid the use of computers may be forfeiting promotions and even job security. Although computer literacy is vital in the education of younger generations, members of the adult work force should also take steps to gain computer literacy.

Job Displacement and Retraining

Ever since the Industrial Revolution, automation has been a source of concern to people. Technology has automated processes leading to greater efficiency and lower costs but it has also eliminated many jobs. The growing use of computers has led to the growing fear of unemployment and depersonalization. Whether or not this fear is justified is yet to be seen. Evidence of the past three decades does not indicate that increased automation leads to increased unemployment. To be sure, workers have been displaced; but each new technology has created new employment opportunities that more than compensate for the jobs eliminated. For example, the invention of the automatic weaving machine eliminated many jobs in the garment industry; but this effect was offset by the creation of a whole new industry involved in the manufacture and marketing of the new equipment.

Several studies have been conducted to determine the effects of computer automation on jobs. While the results have not been conclusive, in general they indicate that a certain amount of job displacement can be expected because the computers take over many routine clerical jobs. The extent to which such displacement occurs depends on several factors, including the following:

■ The goals that are sought from the use of the computer. Is the objective to be able to handle an increasing workload with the same personnel, or is it to reduce costs by eliminating jobs?

■ The growth rate of the organization. If the organization is expanding, it can more easily absorb workers whose jobs are being eliminated, since many new jobs are created to cope with the increasing business.

■ The planning that has gone into the acquisition and use of the computer. With careful preparation, an organization can anticipate the personnel changes a computer system will bring about and make plans either to reassign the affected people or to help them to find new jobs with other organizations. First-time use of a computer-based system will definitely create new jobs in the areas of computer operations, data entry, programming, and system analysis and design. Usually, though, the skills and education required for these jobs differ from those required for the eliminated jobs. Displaced employees can be trained, however, to handle jobs such as operating computer equipment and keying the data. Employees can also be sent to schools for more formal training.

The current task of retraining displaced and unemployed workers has been assumed by groups such as businesses (which provide internal retraining), colleges, vocational schools, private training centers, and the federal government (through aid to states). Some of the more popular programs for retraining include robotics maintenance,

FIGURE 16–1

Retraining can help workers whose jobs are eliminated by the introduction of computers into the workplace.

computer programming, numerical-control machinery programming and operation, word processing, computer maintenance, and electronics (see Figure 16–1).

Changes in the Workplace

Computers have made changes in the workplace common. Farmers, secretaries, and business managers alike have experienced the effects computers can have on their jobs. The office is one area that offers great potential for automation. Office automation is discussed in the following section, while the impact the computer has had on workers and workstations will be discussed here.

Worker interaction with computers has led to new concerns. Perhaps the concerns that have received the most publicity have been those regarding worker health. The biggest complaint of office workers in automated offices is that of eyestrain, followed by complaints of backstrain. It is recognized that with prolonged contact VDTs cause eyestrain, loss of visual acuity, changes in color perception, back and neck pain, stomachaches, and nausea.

To help alleviate some of the health concerns associated with the automated workplace, the science of ergonomics has emerged. **Ergonomics,** the method of researching and designing computer hardware and software to enhance employee productivity and comfort, promises a better, more productive workplace. Major areas of research include the different elements of the workstation and software.

To reduce such physical problems as eyestrain and backstrain, it is recommended that the time spent at a VDT be reduced to a maximum of two hours per day of continuous screen work, that periodic rest breaks be granted, and that pregnant women be permitted to transfer to a different working environment upon request. Recommendations have also been made regarding the design of the VDT and of the keyboard. Suggestions have been made regarding their slope, layout, adjustability, and the use of numeric keypads and function keys (see Figure 16–2).

Other problems with the workstation include poor lighting and noise generated by printers. Sound-dampening covers and internal sound dampening are recommended but still do not reduce the noise sufficiently. The best solution to date is to put the printers in a separate room or at least away from the workers' area. Along with these suggestions, recommendations have been made regarding the tables and chairs used for data-processing work.

The application of ergonomics to workstations has resulted in a 10 to 15 percent improvement in performance in some offices (see Figure 16–3).

FIGURE 16–3

An ergonomically designed workstation can help improve worker health and productivity.

Computer Related Health Problems and Ergonomics

It looks like a small TV screen—a rather harmless piece of equipment—yet the possible health problems caused by using a VDT (visual display terminal) have been debated for years. Employees have stated that working on VDTs has caused headaches, eyestrain, and backaches. Supporters of VDT use have shown that it is often not the VDT but the work environment that causes these problems. The eyestrain (a possible cause of headaches) is often caused by a glare produced by overhead fluorescent lighting. The backaches are often caused by inappropriate chairs and desks. A keyboard placed on a regular desk is often too high for workers. Adjustable desks and chairs can ease the strain on an employee's neck, back, and shoulders.

The Levi Strauss company, which has several hundred employees that work on microcomputers and computer terminals in its information services area, is taking steps to address these matters. The Video Display Terminal Task Force was established to determine what measures may be appropriate in providing its employ-

ees in the information services area with a more ergonomic work environment. The primary goal of the task force is to educate the employees on the value of ergonomics. The task force is designing educational materials for distribution to the employees as well as providing input into the design of ergonomic work areas.

The company, currently in the process of remodeling its work areas, has hired an architect to design adjustable and comfortable work areas. Since employees come in all shapes and sizes, a flexible work area design would allow individual employees to adjust their work areas to meet their own personal needs. In some cases, it is believed that computer-related health problems are due to the fact that work surfaces may be too high for some employees while too low for others. The company is also providing glare reduction screens to those employees who request them for use with their VDTs. Another area of concern is the electromagnetic field created by VDTs and its effect on the employee using the

VDT for long periods of time. The company is using flat panel display screens wherever possible because these display devices do not produce an electromagnetic field.

Although all possible causes of health problems are not yet recognized or understood, managers and company officials need to be sensitive to the possible health problems related to long-term use of computers and VDTs. Work areas should be designed in a flexible way so that they can be adjusted to meet the employees' particular needs. VDT usage should be limited so that working on a VDT is not the employee's only responsibility, and the general health of the employees should be monitored so that possible problems can be identified and resolved quickly. The role of ergonomics in our workplaces has become an important one. As more and more computer technology is used to automate the office, the study and understanding of computer-related health problems will become more and more vital.

■ OFFICE AUTOMATION

As computer technology enters the workplace, the office environment is experiencing changes. Businesses are realizing that automating office procedures is efficient, cost-effective, and, in fact, necessary to deal with the exploding information revolution. **Office automation,** the comprehensive term applied to this transition, refers to all processes that integrate computer and communication technology with the traditional manual processes. Virtually every office function—typing, filing, and communications—can be automated.

This section will discuss the characteristics of the elements that comprise office automation: word processing, communications, and local area networks.

Word Processing

Word processing is often considered the first building block in automating the workplace. It is the most widely adopted office automation technology; an estimated 75 percent of U.S. companies employ some type of word processing. Word processing, the manipulation of written text to achieve a desired output, bypasses the difficulties and shortcomings associated with traditional writing and typing. Word processors offer many functions to increase efficiency in the text-manipulation process.

A typical word-processing system consists of a keyboard for data input, a CRT or LED display screen for viewing text material, a secondary storage unit (disk or tape), and a printer for generating output (see Figure 16–4). Word processing is available in a variety of configurations, including electronic typewriters, dedicated word processors, dedicated data processors, and small business computers.

The major advantages of word processing over traditional text preparation are increased productivity and reduction in preparation time. Word processing, like data processing, relieves workers of time-consuming and routine tasks, thereby increasing standards of productivity and quality. It is estimated that a secretary's productivity can be increased 25 to 200 percent by using word processing. Because a document does not have to be retyped every time a change is made, the preparation time is reduced dramatically.

One disadvantage of word processing is the increase in the number of times a document is revised. Because it is so easy to change a document, personnel make changes more often than when documents are prepared manually. To a point this can be useful; however, there is a limit to the number of times a revision improves a document.

You may recall from Chapter 13 that standard features include automatic centering, pagination (page numbering), alphabetizing, justification of type, boldfacing, reformatting paragraphs, and the ability to search for, replace, and move text within a document. Additional features that have been added to word processors since their introduction include spelling checkers, thesauruses, and built-in dictionaries of definitions to provide the user with the meanings of unfamiliar words.

FIGURE 16–4

Word-Processing System

FIGURE 16–5

Facsimile System

In the future, word processors may include such features as making automatic and correct hyphenation of words (they only guess now), checking for the correctness of standard abbreviations, putting commas around dates, replacing numerals with written-out numbers, and checking for proper grammar. Many of these future word processor features are dependent upon the successful application of artificial intelligence to word processing tasks. In any case, the productivity of those that prepare documents has increased dramatically with the advent of word processors. This increase in productivity will undoubtedly increase well into the future as new capabilities are added to word processors.

Communications

An important benefit of office automation is the communication capabilities it makes possible. Such capabilities allow the electronic exchange of information between employees. Communications may be enhanced through forms such as electronic mail, teleconferencing, and telecomputing.

ELECTRONIC MAIL. **Electronic mail** is the transmission of messages at high speeds over telecommunication facilities. It is used primarily for internal, routine communications; however, with the development of new technology, it is beginning to replace the traditional postal service. The concept behind these computer-based mail systems involves the storage of messages in a special area until the recipient can access them. People using electronic mail systems can be in remote locations. Receivers are notified of waiting mail when they log on to their computer. They can then view the incoming mail items on a CRT screen or can have the items printed on their terminal. The mail can be revised, incorporated into other documents, passed along to new recipients, or filed like any other document in the system. Some electronic mail systems allow the sender to cancel the message if it has not yet been read by the recipient. The sender may also check to see if the messages he or she has sent have been read yet by the recipient by including a ''receipt required'' message with the document. Some systems also provide a delayed sending option, allowing the sender to create a message and have it sent at a set time in the future.

Facsimile systems, generally called **FAX systems,** are another form of electronic mail system that transmits across telephone lines (see Figure 16–5). Facsimile systems produce a picture of a page by scanning it, as a television camera scans a scene or a copier scans a printed page. The image is then transmitted to a receiver, where it is printed.

Another type of electronic message is the **voice message system (VMS),** or **voice mail.** In VMS, the sender records a message in the receiver's mail box. The spoken message is converted by the VMS into digital form and stored in the computer's memory. At the receiver's request, the message is reconverted into voice form. Unlike standard answering machines, with VMS recipients can fast-scan the messages. Voice mail also allows for longer messages than answering machines.

TELECONFERENCING. In an effort to reduce travel time and expenses associated with out-of-town travel, businesses are turning to teleconferencing. **Teleconferencing,** permitting two or more locations to communicate via electronic and image-producing facilities, offers businesses a viable alternative to long-distance, face-to-face communications.

Five forms of teleconferencing exist. The most basic form of conducting electronic meetings, **audio conferencing,** is simply a conference call linking three or more people. Ideal for impromptu conversations, audio conferencing requires no major equipment investments but is limited to voice only.

The next level, **augmented audio conferencing,** combines graphics with audio conferencing. In this situation, visual information accompanies the conversation in the form of facsimile, electronic blackboards, or freeze-frame slide shows. Augmented audio conferencing is frequently used for technical discussions that require supplemental graphics to explain concepts.

Computer conferencing is well suited for ongoing meetings among a number of people. Information is exchanged at the participants' convenience using computer terminals; participants need not attend at the same time. New material can be added or previously submitted ideas can be critiqued. This differs from electronic mail in that discrete messages are not transmitted; instead comments are input in reference to specific issues. Computer conferencing has been found to reduce decision-making time considerably.

Video seminars represent the next level of sophistication. They employ one-way, full-motion video with two-way audio. The most common application of video seminars is for formal presentations that involve a question-and-answer session such as a press conference. Individuals from the audience communicate with the presentation headquarters via a separate two-way phone link. The entire audience can hear the question and view the official response. Special facilities with television equipment are needed for this type of conferencing.

Finally, there is **videoconferencing**—the technology currently receiving the most attention. Videoconferencing, employing a two-way, full-motion video plus a two-way audio system, provides the most effective simulation of face-to-face communication (see Figure 16–6). It is the only form that meets the need for full interaction; the participants are able to see and hear each other's responses. Videoconferencing is best suited for planning groups, project teams, and other groups that want a full sense of participation. It is not suitable for all situations, however. It does not seem to be effective when a participant is trying to persuade an audience or to sell something.

FIGURE 16–6

Videoconferencing

The cost effectiveness of videoconferences depends upon the geographic dispersion of the company, the number of intracompany meetings, and the management structure of the company. If the company does not have major offices throughout the country, videoconferencing may not be cost-effective. Also, because different types of videoconferencing equipment are not compatible, it can only be used for conferences within the company, not with other companies.

TELECOMPUTING. Companies as well as individuals may subscribe to online information services—services that offer access to one or more data bases. This is often referred to as **telecomputing.** By accessing the online data bases, workers receive additional information and save considerable research time. There are many information services available that provide information on a wide variety of topics. Three of the more popular services are The Source, CompuServe, and Dow Jones News/Retrieval. Some of the services offered include news stories; potential news-making events; up-to-the-minute stock, bond, and commodity information; sports information; information on alcohol problems; and law libraries (see Figure 16–7).

Usually, a membership fee is charged to the user, and a password and account number are issued. The online service then usually charges the user for service time or connect time. The only equipment needed is a computer, a modem, and a communications software package to instruct the user's computer on how to talk to the computer at the other end. Employees can receive up-to-the-minute information with a minimal amount of effort and time.

FIGURE 16–7

Telecomputing offers us the ability to access an unlimited amount of information and services.

CONCEPT SUMMARY 16–1	
Forms of Electronic Communication	
Form	**Characteristics**
Electronic mail	Used primarily for internal communication
Teleconferencing	Used to reduce travel time and expenses
Telecomputing	Offers computer access to online data bases

▣ COMPUTERS IN BUSINESS AND INDUSTRY

As computers have entered American society, nowhere have they had more impact than in business and industry. Part of the reason is that using computers speeds operations, reduces mistakes in calculations, and gives companies efficient, cost-effective analyses that would be nearly impossible with manual operations. Another major reason for the great impact of computers is the domino effect. If Business A speeds up its operations through the use of computers, then Business B must also computerize to remain competitive. The same applies to the use of automation in industry. Once one factory incorporates automation, it sets a standard to be imitated and repeated.

These factors have caused a phenomenal increase in the number and types of computer applications in business and industry. Some experts even claim that these computer applications are helping to trigger a new type of industrial revolution.

Computers in Business

Because businesses are so varied in purpose and structure, it is nearly impossible to examine all business uses of computers. However, it is possible to look at how computers are used in many businesses. Businesses have special uses of computers. For example, a retail store might be interested in computerizing inventory, whereas a stock brokerage would be more interested in computerizing its customer files. In general, though, there are three areas in which computers are used in most businesses: accounting and finance, management, and marketing and sales.

ACCOUNTING AND FINANCE. In the past, financial transactions were tediously calculated, either by hand or by calculator, and recorded using pencil and paper. This method has rapidly become obsolete as computers have moved into virtually every area of accounting and finance. To illustrate this point, let us examine how computers are being used in the areas of general accounting, financial analysis, and information management.

General accounting software is a very popular type of business software. In fact, it was the first business software to be offered for personal computers. Some of the most common uses of general accounting software are for preparing checks, reports, and forms. Forms, because of their repetitive nature, are well suited to computer processing. General accounting packages that produce reports keep users informed of everything from inventory on hand to monthly credit account balances. Checks are a frequent form of output from general accounting software.

Today, the most common use of the computer in financial analysis is the electronic spreadsheet. Spreadsheets are used to design budgets, record sales, produce profit-and-loss statements, and aid in financial analysis. Refer to Chapter 13 for more information regarding spreadsheets.

Data management software for business computers gives them the capability of an electronic filing system. Data entered into selected categories can be retrieved by specifying, for example, files on employees receiving a certain salary or employees hired on a certain date. Systems like these make file retrieval faster and more flexible and decrease the amount of storage space required.

MANAGEMENT. Communication is an important part of business management, and computer graphics are becoming an essential part of business communication. In the average business, computers are used to produce graphs that keep management informed and up-to-date on company statistics, sales records, and the like.

It is well known in business that executives make 80 percent of their decisions based on 20 percent of the data—that 20 percent representing the core data necessary to run their businesses. Finding that data can be difficult for managers if they are presented with pages upon pages of data. Graphically displayed data makes the task much easier. It is widely agreed that such displays can help managers make better decisions. Also, comparisons, relationships and trends, and essential points can be clarified more easily with graphics (see Figure 16–8). Finally, computer graphics are the most cost-effective means of presenting the manager with that 20 percent of core data.

MARKETING AND SALES. Businesses use computers in a variety of ways to facilitate sales, record sales, update inventories after sales, and make projections based

FIGURE 16–8

Graphically displayed data helps make decision making easier for managers.

CHAPTER 16: THE IMPACT OF COMPUTERS ON PEOPLE AND ORGANIZATIONS

FIGURE 16–9

Salespeople use computers to keep track of sales data.

on expected sales (see Figure 16–9). In addition to these standard functions, some computers are also being used in customer contact.

The Helena Rubenstein cosmetic firm was instrumental in the movement of computers onto the sales floor. The cosmetic computer assisted customers in their decisions about perfumes, makeup, and colorings. The firm's effort was very successful and inspired similar applications by other companies.

Computers in Industry

The financial and bookkeeping uses of computers apply to both business and industry. However, industry also uses computers in designing and manufacturing products. In this chapter, we will discuss four of these ways: CAD/CAM, CIM, nondestructive testing, and robotics.

CAD/CAM. One of the fastest growing areas of computer use in industry is **computer-aided design (CAD). CAD** allows the engineer to design, draft, and analyze a prospective product using computer graphics on a video terminal (see Figure 16–10). The designer, working with full-color graphics, can easily make changes, and thus can test many versions of a product before the first prototype is ever built. CAD can also analyze designs for poor tolerance between parts and for stress points. This can save companies a great deal of money by eliminating defective designs before the money is spent to build a product.

Computer-aided design is often coupled with **computer-aided manufacturing (CAM).** The combination is referred to as **CAD/CAM.** Using CAD/CAM, the engineer can analyze not only the product but also the manufacturing process.

Once the rough design of the product has been entered into the computer, the engineer can have the computer simulate any manufacturing step (see Figure

FIGURE 16–10

Computer-aided design is used by engineers to design products.

16–11). For example, if the product must be drilled, the engineer can use a computerized drill that can be guided, either by the engineer or the computer, to simulate the drilling process. This simulation can be very helpful in two ways. First, it indicates any major problems that may be encountered on the assembly line—before it is even set up. Second, the computer will record exactly how the tool moved and will store that information on magnetic tape. If that factory uses robotics and **numerically controlled machinery,** those tapes can be used to drive the actual machines in manufacturing the product. In this way, CAD/CAM can take the engineer from idea to final product.

FIGURE 16–11

Computer-aided manufacturing is often coupled with computer-aided design in the manufacturing process.

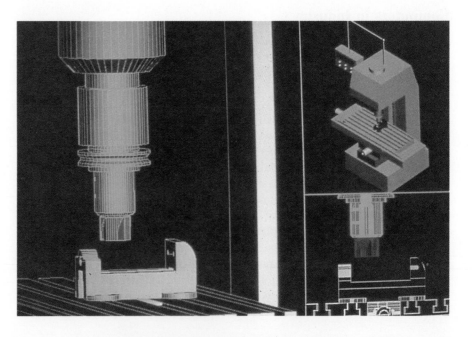

Desktop Manufacturing

You've heard of desktop publishing—now there's desktop manufacturing! What, you ask, is desktop manufacturing? Computer-aided design (CAD) and computer-aided engineering (CAE) have been used for a number of years to design parts or products made on machine tools. Even though the parts were designed using a computer, prototypes, or models, of the parts had to be produced by hand. This process often took weeks or even months to complete.

Enter a new technology called desktop manufacturing. Desktop manufacturing is changing the way three-dimensional prototypes and models are made. The desktop manufacturing systems currently in use or under development use such technologies as stereolithography, photochemical machining, laser sintering, and laminated-object manufacturing in order to—under computer control—construct a model of a part or product. Mercedes-Benz, for example, used such a system to create a prototype of an exhaust system for one of its cars. These models can be created in hours as compared to weeks or months if they were built by hand. The models are made using materials such as plastic, laminates, and paper.

One desktop manufacturing system currently available uses a computer, a laser, and liquid polymer plastic to create prototypes. The computer system divides the part into pieces, or slices, and then separately constructs each piece using the laser and plastic. The liquid polymer plastic used by this system is designed to harden when exposed to light. The plastic is shaped and then exposed to the light of the laser so that it will harden. Once all the pieces are completed, they are glued together to form the completed model.

The benefit realized from such systems as this is tremendous. The complex task of constructing models and prototypes can be dealt with efficiently and effectively through the use of the desktop manufacturing system. Tasks that used to take weeks and even months can now be almost magically accomplished in a few short hours.

COMPUTER INTEGRATED MANUFACTURING (CIM). For even greater savings and more efficient operation, manufacturers can tie CAD and CAM processes together with **computer-integrated manufacturing (CIM).** CIM is an attempt to link various departments of a company into a central data base. The CIM data base can help management run a more coordinated, efficient operation. The ideal CIM system would control the design and manufacture of a company's products without disruption. From raw materials to finished product, the operation would run smoothly. The CIM system would control scheduling and monitoring of operations.

In the United States no fully functional plants combine CAD/CAM and CIM. Some operations do employ the CIM concept in certain areas, though. Boeing, General Motors, and General Electric are experimenting with CIM. Boeing has saved $2.8 million annually by using CIM to link certain design and manufacturing operations.

To be successful, CIM requires a long-term commitment from management. General Electric found that CIM was most successful when implemented in a step-by-step plan. As the uses of CAD and CAM increase, CIM will become more common, too.

NONDESTRUCTIVE TESTING (NDT). Quality control has long been a problem for industry. Finding flaws or weaknesses in products is an important aspect of the successful operation of a company and is necessary for long-term growth. Until recently, most companies had to be content spotting flaws with a visual inspection or a physical stress test of their products. A visual inspection is effective only if the flaw is easily seen, and a stress test often destroys the object being tested.

Some manufacturers are relying on a new technology to test new and old products for flaws created during manufacturing or for weaknesses caused by wear and deterioration. The technology is called **nondestructive testing (NDT).** This process combines X rays, high-frequency sound waves, or laser beams with powerful microcomputers to inspect the interior of a product. Use of NDT locates the likely trouble while leaving the product intact. The process can detect the difference between dangerous flaws and harmless nicks.

Nondestructive testing is used to examine the interior of aircraft engines and to check welds in gas pipelines. Airplane mechanics may soon rely on NDT for early detection of metal deterioration. The growth in NDT is based on the increasing use of machines designed to operate near the limits of physical tolerance. Flaws that are not identified early could cause a disaster. Another reason for the growth of NDT is the increasing use of new, unpredictable materials. New construction materials may contain hard-to-discern flaws that could mean failure for a manufacturer.

Powerful new data-processing capabilities have made it possible for workers to determine the difference between serious and minor flaws. Being able to tell the difference between the two could save a company a great deal of money.

The use of computers in NDT to process data from radiology and ultrasound tests is growing in popularity. Radiology involves passing X rays or gamma rays through a product or structure. Flaws in the material appear as shadows on an X ray. Ultrasound testing uses high-frequency sound waves that are beamed into the test material. Flaws stop the sound beam, deflecting it to a source that collects and processes data about such things as the size and precise location of the defect.

CONCEPT SUMMARY 16–2

Computers in Industry

CAD	CAM	CIM	NDT
Computer-aided design	Computer-aided manufacturing	Computer-integrated manufacturing	Nondestructive testing
Using computers to design, draft and analyze prospective products	Using computers to simulate manufacturing steps	Using computers to link the departments of a company into a central data base	Using computers to identify hidden flaws in products

ROBOTICS. Almost everyone is familiar with the labels describing workers: those who perform management-level jobs are referred to as white-collar workers; those performing unskilled tasks or factory jobs are called blue-collar workers. However, the influx of computers into the working world of the factories has created another category: the steel-collar worker. The steel-collar workers are nonhuman—robots.

Science fiction writer Isaac Asimov popularized the term *robotics*. **Robotics** is the science that deals with robots, their construction, capabilities, and applications.

FIGURE 16–12

Robots are used on the assembly line to manufacture cars.

Currently, American factories have tens of thousands of robots hard at work (see Figure 16–12). By 1990 this figure is expected to reach nearly 150,000. General Motors, General Electric, and Westinghouse are the three leading users of industrial robots. These steel-collar workers perform standard jobs, such as spot welding and spray painting, as well as more complex jobs like fitting light bulbs into the dashboards of cars. The automobile industry is the leading user of robots in the United States.

Two generations of robots have appeared so far. The first generation possesses mechanical dexterity but no external sensory ability. These robots cannot see, hear, touch, or smell. Second-generation robots, however, possess more humanlike capabilities, including tactile sense or crude vision; they can "feel" how tightly they are gripping an object or "see" whether there are obstacles in their path.

◼ SUMMARY POINTS

◼ Computer anxiety is the fear people experience about computers and the effects computers may have on individual's lives and society.

◼ In order to prepare students for the future, computer literacy courses are being taught throughout elementary and secondary education systems.

◼ Studies conducted by Genevieve Cerf at Columbia University have found that, overall, women may make better programmers than men.

◼ Computer-related fields pay women and men equally for similar positions and work.

◼ Job displacement and retraining are issues that must be dealt with as computer technology continues to automate more and more jobs and processes.

◼ Ergonomics is the method of researching and designing computer hardware and software to enhance employee productivity and comfort. It has focused on recommendations for the workstation environment and for making software more user friendly.

◼ Office automation refers to all processes that integrate computer and communications technology with traditional manual office processes.

■ The manipulation of written text to achieve a desired output is referred to as word processing; word processing is the most widely adopted office automation technology.

■ Communication capabilities derived from office automation allow the exchange of information electronically between employees.

■ Electronic mail is the transmission of messages at high speeds over telecommunications facilities and can be in the form of an e-mail system, a facsimile system, or a voice message system.

■ The method of two or more remote locations communicating via electronic and image producing facilities is called teleconferencing. Five forms of teleconferencing exist: (1) audio conferencing, (2) augmented audio conferencing, (3) computer conferencing, (4) video seminars, and (5) videoconferencing.

■ Accessing online information services, called telecomputing, can provide a vast amount of information for minimal time and money.

■ Computerization in business has taken place primarily in three functional areas: (1) accounting and finance, (2) management, and (3) marketing and sales.

■ General accounting software, electronic spreadsheets, and data management software have been heavily used in the area of finance.

■ Computer graphics have become a very important factor in business communication and decision making.

■ Computer-aided design (CAD) allows an engineer to design, draft, and analyze a potential product without leaving the computer terminal.

■ The combination of computer-aided design and computer-aided manufacturing (CAD/CAM) allows the engineer to analyze both the design and manufacturing process.

■ Computer-integrated manufacturing (CIM) is an attempt to link various departments of a company into a central data base. The CIM data base can help management run a more coordinated, efficient operation.

■ Nondestructive testing (NDT) combines X rays, high-frequency sound waves, or laser beams with powerful microcomputers to inspect the interior of a product. Use of NDT locates the flaws while leaving the product intact.

■ Robots are being used in factories, primarily in the manufacture of automobiles, for tasks such as spot welding, spray painting, and fitting fixtures.

■ TERMS FOR REVIEW

◼ REVIEW QUESTIONS

1. What is computerphobia? Who does it affect the most? Who do you think will be least affected by it?

2. Do you consider yourself to be computer literate? Briefly explain why or why not.

3. What are some of the factors to consider when trying to determine if installing computers will result in job displacement and/or retraining?

4. What is ergonomics? Why has it been given a considerable amount of attention?

5. Briefly explain why you believe office automation has become almost essential if an office or company is to remain competitive in today's business world.

6. Describe some of the features of word processors that make their users productive.

7. Why has electronic mail become a popular form of communication both within companies and between companies?

8. What is teleconferencing? What are some of the advantages to teleconferencing? What are some of its disadvantages? List the five types of teleconferencing in use today.

9. Why have computer graphics become an important tool in business management?

10. What is NDT? Why is it considered a breakthrough in the area of quality control?

Ace Hardware Corporation

Ace Hardware—John Madden's hardware store—is a dealer-owned cooperative for hardware, home center, and lumber and building materials store owners. It has 5,200 stores in all 50 states and several foreign countries including Iceland, Yugoslavia, and Saudi Arabia. It aims to serve the independent Ace dealer by providing low-cost high-quality products, programs, and services.

COMPANY HISTORY

In 1924, a small group of Chicago area hardware retailers decided to pool their buying and promotional efforts, establishing the roots of Ace Hardware Corporation. The company incorporated in 1928 and bought its first warehouse in Chicago in 1929. As Ace expanded, it added distribution centers outside Chicago. Benicia, California, became the site of the first of these centers in 1969. In 1974, during its 50th anniversary, Ace began operating as a cooperative. In 1984, Ace began manufacturing its own paint. A state-of-the-art paint facility located in Matteson, Illinois, produces a variety of solvent-based and latex paints, including waterproofing sealer. The plant was constructed to reduce costs and improve paint quality. Ace paint continues to be one of the most successful private label products.

Today, all of the company's capital stock is owned by its dealers. From headquarters in Oak Brook, Illinois, Ace operates 14 retail support centers with another being planned in the southwestern United States. In 1989, wholesale sales were $1.547 billion, which was an 11.9 percent increase over 1988 sales. A board of directors, consisting of the chairman and nine dealer-members, establishes guidelines for the professional staff of 2,800.

Ace provides a variety of services to the dealer, including retail services and training and store development. It runs company-wide television, radio, and print advertising campaigns. The concept of regionalization provides more regional programs to address differences in needs, size, and location of dealers. It gives direct assistance from Ace personnel through in-store consultations to increase sales and profits, advertising, pricing, retail services, marketing, and special regional requests. It also develops regional forums that help develop a closer relationship and improve communications between dealers and their corporation.

ELECTRONIC ORDERING

Ace dealers sell many national brand products as well as more than 3,000 Ace label products. Over 95 percent of Ace dealers order merchandise electronically. A hand-held electronic ordering terminal is used to scan the bar-coded bin tag of items that need to be reordered. In addition, the dealer can review a warehouse reorder list (WRL), which is a computer-generated report that recommends purchases based upon past ordering history. All desired orders are entered at the store and electronically transmitted to the order entry computer in the data center at Ace's corporate offices. This computer edits and saves the store's order until the mainframe computer is ready to process it. Orders are processed using batch processing and order-fill documents, and reports are generated and transmitted for printing at the dealer's retail support center. The orders are checked for accuracy and placed on an Ace truck for delivery to the individual store the next day. The dealer's invoice, generated by the mainframe's invoice system, is sent with the order.

The 95% of Ace dealers who order electronically find their orders checked for accuracy and placed on an Ace truck for delivery the next day.

ADDITIONAL COMPUTER SERVICES

The Ace Management Information Systems (MIS) department offers a variety of additional services for the independent dealer. The system provides timely and accurate information, reduces costs through automation, and helps keep Ace on the competitive edge. Price tickets and bin tags can be produced electronically. Each dealer receives a computer-generated book listing all items stocked in the retail support center serving that dealer. Through electronic publishing, the text and graphics of over 44,000 items can be produced and updated quickly in this book.

A few years ago, Ace introduced an electronic communications program called ACENET. This program allows dealers to receive the latest information on products and pricing at their retail support center through an inventory inquiry option, keep track of their bulletins through a bulletin commitment report, send messages to the corporate offices through ACEMAIL, and tap into the Lumber and Building Materials Bulletin Board for special lumber mill offerings and daily price changes. Transactions through ACENET have soared to well over one million per month.

Recent enhancements to ACENET have provided Ace dealers with the ability to reserve order items through this process and receive their invoices electronically in advance of an order being received. Ace dealers can make inquiries about the status of their invoices and receive current information about dealer services. Claims processing is easier by computer, also. There is access to pertinent information on several bulletin reports, easier access of multiple store information, and identification of items "on allocation" on the Inventory Inquiry application. A complete listing of vendor information is available. In addition, Ace introduced a UPC (universal product code) bar code option that can be selected and used by Ace dealers whose in-store computer systems have scanning capabilities. Over three hundred PACE in-store computers permit access to company data and provide point-of-sale capabilities. This means a great number of functions are automated across the corporation, including the cashier area, accounting, and inventory control. The benefits of Ace's computerized operations have provided dealers with a better margin on costs and customer service.

DUSCUSSION POINTS

1. What features are available to simplify electronic ordering for the Ace dealer?

2. How does ACENET help dealers be competitive in the marketplace?

Computer Security, Crime, Ethics, and the Law

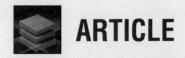

ARTICLE

Preventing the Dreaded 'Call' to Virus Busters

Michael Alexander, *Computerworld*

Personal computer viruses are better designed, more destructive, harder to get rid of once they hit and spreading more rapidly than ever before. Should you be worried? That depends on which virus buster you talk to.

"It is the single biggest security exposure outside of users making errors," said William Hugh Murray, an information systems security consultant in Wilton, Conn.

The Jerusalem virus, named after the city where it was first spotted in early 1987, and its variants have reached a critical mass of sorts. "The Jerusalem B virus probably doubles every two months or so," Murray said. "At some point, we are going to be inundated."

There is no cause for alarm, said David Stang, director of research at the National Computer Security Association in Washington, D.C. While there are a huge number of viruses, "the probability of getting one in a business setting is very low."

Most damage is caused not by viruses but by naive computer users trying to rid their PCs of viruses after being hit, he added.

The latest count of PC viruses is about 240, according to John McAfee, president of Interpath Corp. and the Computer Virus Industry Association in Santa Clara, Calif. . . .

Viruses that attack Apple Computer, Inc. Macintoshes number about 10 and are beginning to multiply rapidly, according to the virus busters.

Expert virus watchers agreed that viruses are more widespread than ever. What they disagreed on is how much of a threat they pose. Policies that restrict employees from running their own software on corporate machines and the judicious use of anti-virus software should be enough to ward off viruses.

"It is a realistic concern—one that people should be aware of but not panic about," said Ken Van Wyk, coordinator of the Computer Emergency Response Team at Carnegie Mellon University. "As with any risk, people should be aware of the facts and how these things work and take intelligent and educated steps to avoid them."

"The advice we have had so far is to wait until you see it and then purge it," Murray said. "That is no longer the conservative approach. We ought to immunize every machine."

Purchasing antivirus software is cheap in comparison to the cost of removing a virus, Murray said. The two most popular programs—Software Concepts Design's Flu Shot and Interpath's Viruscan—cost $10

to $15 per machine with site licenses, he said. "Compare that to what you would have to pay to purge a virus from an environment, and that is trivial."

Katie Hogue, president of Media Markets, Inc. in Alexandria, Va., agreed. She has yet to recover from having two PCs at her firm hit with the 4096 virus. . . .

The virus, which appeared after the computers were upgraded at a local computer store, infected some 220 files on floppy and hard disks. "All of my disks were infected, and because I never made backup copies of my masters, we lost all of our programs," Hogue said.

The cost of replacing programs and disks and hiring technicians to eradicate the virus amounted to $4,000. It may be impossible to calculate the cost of not being able to use the two computers for a month.

"It would have been cheaper to buy new PCs," Hogue said.

The 4096 is one of a new generation of highly destructive "Stealth" viruses, first spotted in the U.S. nearly a year ago, that appear to be spreading faster than previous generations of the techno-diseases. They are called Stealth viruses because they have been designed by their authors to avoid detection by antivirus software, much as a Stealth bomber avoids radar. They are difficult to remove even when found. The Stealth viruses, which include the 4096, Fish, 512, V800, V2000 and Joshi, are highly prolific and will often change like chameleons to avoid detection or latch onto files as they are being scanned by antivirus software.

"The Joshi and 4096 appear to be doubling every month and are moving faster than the Jerusalem," McAfee said.

Stealth viruses are better designed than their predecessors but so is antivirus software, Stang said. "Virus detection software runs faster and catches more."

◘ INTRODUCTION

There is no doubt that computers have had a very significant impact on our lives and our society. By the same token, extensive use of computers has created new problems that must be dealt with. Just as the computer's success is attributed to people's imagination, many of the problematic situations that must be dealt with result from human nature. Computer crime and security, for example, are two issues that have created considerable concern among individuals who use computers for personal and business purposes. With computers being used as the main means of storage of personal information on credit, employment, taxes, and other aspects of a person's life, privacy is becoming a growing concern.

This chapter reviews some of the human issues associated with the use of computers. Computer crime and security as well as ethics and privacy are discussed. The chapter concludes with a discussion of warranties and copyright law.

◘ COMPUTER CRIME AND SECURITY

Computer crime is a greater problem than most people realize. Americans are losing billions of dollars to high-technology criminals whose crimes go undetected and unpunished; estimates of losses range from at least $2 billion to more than $40 billion a year. While no one really knows how much is being stolen, the total appears to be growing fast.

The earliest known instance of electronic embezzlement occurred in 1958, just a few years after IBM began marketing its first line of business computers. By the mid-1970s, scores of such crimes were being reported every year, and yearly losses were estimated to be as high as $300 million.

Many more problems appear to be ahead. Home computers and electronic funds transfer (EFT) systems pose a new threat to the billions of dollars in data bases accessible through telephone lines (see Figure 17–1). Already, criminals have made illegal switches of money over the phone, and more cases can be expected as EFT systems become widespread. Furthermore, the trend to distributed systems presents many opportunities for security and privacy violations.

Computer Crime Defined

What is meant by the term *computer crime?* The legal community has been focusing on answering this question through legislation and court opinions. Taking a broad

FIGURE 17–1

Electronic funds transfer made possible with a home computer and telephone lines poses a threat to billions of dollars in data bases.

but practical view, computer crime can be defined as a criminal act that poses a greater threat to a computer user than it would to a non–computer user, or a criminal act that is accomplished through the use of a computer.

Computer crime, therefore, consists of two kinds of activity: (a) the use of a computer to perpetrate acts of deceit, theft, or concealment that are intended to provide financial, business-related, property, or service advantages; and (b) threats to the computer itself, such as theft of hardware or software, sabotage, and demands for ransom. Because computer crimes seldom involve acts of physical violence, they are generally classified as white-collar crimes. While there is no single type of person that commits computer crimes, computer criminals are often young and ambitious with impressive educational credentials. They tend to be technically competent and come from all employee levels, including technicians, programmers, managers, and high-ranking executives.

Types of Computer Crime

Computer crimes can be classified into four broad categories: sabotage, theft of services, property crimes, and financial crimes. This section examines each of these categories and gives examples drawn from actual crimes.

SABOTAGE. Sabotage of computers results in destruction or damage of computer hardware. This type of computer crime often resembles traditional sabotage because the computer itself is not used to carry out the destruction. Sabotage may require some sophistication if computer-assisted security systems must be thwarted or if the system is manipulated to do harm to itself.

Computers are targets of sabotage and vandalism especially during times of political activism. Dissident political groups during the 1960s, for instance, conducted assaults on computer installations, often causing extensive damage. Other forms of physical violence have included flooding the computer room, shooting a computer with a revolver, and waving an electromagnet through the data storage area.

Obviously, these acts of violence do not require any special expertise on the part of the criminal. Sabotage may, however, be conducted by dissatisfied former employees who put to use some of their knowledge of company operations to gain access to and destroy hardware and software.

Another form of sabotage that has been used on microcomputers is a troublesome program that not only disrupts computer service, but also can destroy the contents of a hard disk or a floppy disk. Such a program is a **virus,** so called because it can infect computer systems by replicating itself and attaching itself to other programs. Viruses can infect other systems from floppy disks or through networks. Once a virus is in a system and has replicated itself a predetermined number of times, it may attempt to erase or change the data on the hard disk or diskette. This can be extremely damaging to the unsuspecting user. Although viruses are very difficult to guard against, there are programs that can detect and counteract them. Floppy disks can be protected by engaging the write protect feature found on either type of disk (see Chapter 6).

One of the most publicized acts of computer sabotage occurred on November 2, 1988, when a virus traveled through Internet, an unclassified network used by government, business, and university researchers to exchange data and findings. Within hours, this particular virus—actually a self-contained program called a worm—had infected approximately 6,000 military, corporate, and university computers. In January of 1990, Robert Tappan Morris, Jr., a Cornell University graduate student, was convicted of unleashing the worm.

THEFT OF SERVICES. Computer services may be abused in a variety of ways. Some examples of theft of computer services have involved politicians using a city's computer to conduct campaign mailings and employees conducting unauthorized free-lance services on a company computer after working hours.

Time-sharing systems have been exposed to abuse due to inadequate or nonexistent security precautions. It is much easier to gain unauthorized access to a time-sharing system than to a closed system. Though most systems require the user to have a password to gain access, a system is only as good as the common sense and caution of its users. A time-sharing system that does not require regular changing of access codes is inviting the theft of valuable computer time. The amazing lack of care exercised by supposedly sophisticated users made national headlines when a group of high school computer buffs in Milwaukee were discovered accessing numerous information systems, including banks, hospitals, and the defense research center in Los Alamos, New Mexico. The students reportedly gained access by using each system's password. Some of the passwords had not been changed for years, while others were obtained from public sources.

Wiretapping is another technique used to gain unauthorized access to a time-sharing system. By tapping into a legitimate user's line, one can have free access to the system whenever the line is not being used by the authorized party.

One of the prime examples of computer services theft took place at the University of Alberta. In 1976, a student at the university began an independent study under the supervision of a professor. The purpose of the study was to investigate the security of the university's computer system, a time-sharing system with more than 5,000 users, some as far away as England. After discovering several gaps in the system's security, the student was able to develop a program that reduced the possibility of unauthorized use and tampering. The student brought this program to the attention of the computer center, which took no action on the student's recommendations. It was assumed that planned changes in the system would remove security shortcomings. However, the changes were not implemented for another nine months. During that period, the program, which was capable of displaying passwords, was leaked to several students on campus. "Code Green," as the program was nicknamed, was eventually run several thousand times.

The university attempted to crack down on the unauthorized users and revoked several students' access privileges. Two of the students involved could get the computer to display the complete listing of all user passwords, including those at the highest privilege levels. In essence, this gave them unlimited access to the computer's files and programs. These students retaliated against the university administration by occasionally rendering the system inoperable or periodically inserting an obscenity into the payroll file. With an unlimited supply of IDs, they were able to escape detection, compiling a library of the computer's programs and monitoring the implementation of the new security system. The desperate university computer personnel focused exclusively on this situation, keeping a detailed log of all terminal dialogues. This effort led them to a terminal in the geology department one evening, and the students were apprehended.

THEFT OF PROPERTY. The most obvious computer crime that comes to mind concerning crimes of property is the theft of computer equipment itself. Thefts have become more common with the increasing miniaturization of computer components and the advent of home computers. These crimes are easily absorbed into traditional concepts of crime and present no unique legal problems. More intriguing is the issue of what actually constitutes property in the context of computer crimes. Different courts have come to very different conclusions on this issue.

Computer crimes of property theft frequently involve merchandise from a company whose orders are processed by computers. These crimes are usually committed by internal personnel who have a thorough knowledge of the operation. By record manipulation, dummy accounts can be created, directing a product order to be shipped to an accomplice outside the organization. Similarly, one can cause checks to be paid out for receipt of nonexistent merchandise.

Theft of property need not be limited to actual merchandise but may also extend to software. People with access to a system's program library can easily obtain copies for personal use or, more frequently, for resale to a competitor. Technical security measures in a computer installation are of little use when dishonest personnel take advantage of their positions of responsibility.

This kind of theft is by no means limited to those within the company structure, however. A computer service having specialized programs but poor security may open itself up to unauthorized access by a competitor. All that is necessary is that the outsider gain access to proper codes. This is accomplished in a number of ways, including clandestine observation of a legitimate user logging on from a remote terminal or use of a remote minicomputer to test for possible access codes.

FINANCIAL CRIMES. Although not the most common type, financial computer crimes are perhaps the most serious in terms of monetary loss. With the projected increasing dependence on electronic fund transfers, implications for the future are serious.

A common method of committing this kind of crime involves checks. Mass-produced, negotiable instruments can be manipulated in a number of ways. An employee familiar with a firm's operations can direct the computer to make out multiple checks to the same person. Checks can also be rerouted to a false address. These crimes do not seem so incredible when one realizes the scope of *unintentional* mistakes that have been made with computerized checks. For example, the Social Security Administration once accidentally sent out 100,000 checks to the wrong addresses while the system's files were being consolidated.

Another form of a financial computer crime is known as the "round-off fraud." In this crime, the thief, perhaps a bank employee, collects the fractions of cents in customers' accounts that are created when the applicable interest rates are applied. These fractions are then stored in an account created by the thief. The theory is that fractions of cents collected from thousands of accounts on a regular basis will yield a substantial amount of money.

Still another crime involves juggling confidential information, both personal and corporate, within a computer. Once appropriate access is gained to records, the ability to alter them can be highly marketable. One group operating in California engaged in the business of creating favorable credit histories to clients seeking loans.

These cases exemplify the types of electronic crime being committed: manipulating input to the computer; changing computer programs; and stealing data, computer time, and computer programs. The possibilities for computer crime seem endless. It has been suggested that computers are used extensively by organized crime and that a computer-aided murder may already have taken place.

The unique threat of computer crime is that criminals often use computers to conceal not only their own identities but also the existence of the crimes. Law officers worry because solving computer crimes seems to depend on luck. Many such crimes are never discovered because company executives do not know enough about computers to detect them. Others go unreported to avoid scaring customers and stockholders. Many reported crimes do not result in convictions and jail terms because the complexities of data processing mystify most police officials, prosecutors, judges, and jurors. For a summary of the types of computer crimes, see Concept Summary 17–1.

CONCEPT SUMMARY 17–1	
Types of Computer Crime	
Type of Crime	**Description of Crime**
Sabotage	Destruction or damage of computer hardware and software
Theft of service	Unauthorized use of computer time
Theft of property	Stealing computer equipment
Financial crime	Using a computer to steal money from an individual or organization

Crime Prevention and Detection

The computer's ability to make statistical analyses is used in New York City to help authorities pinpoint buildings that are likely targets for arson. Several agencies contribute information to the computer about fires. Further data is available on fires that have occurred in the recent past. The computer constructs profiles of the most probable targets of arsonists. The city can keep a watch on the likely buildings and tell their owners how to lessen the risk of fires. The program is also intended to decrease the owners' incentive to burn the buildings to collect the insurance proceeds. Part of the data mix fed into the computer is the names of landlords who are behind in their taxes or who have been cited for safety or occupancy violations.

Another computerized crime predictor maintained by the FBI has drawn a good deal of criticism—some of it from members of Congress. No complaints are heard about the system as it pertains to tracking known criminals. But people are worried that the Justice Department may use the system to monitor people who are considered a threat to officials but who have never been convicted of a crime. Under the plan, the Secret Service can place in the FBI's National Crime Information Center computer the names of persons considered to be threats to the president, vice president, presidential candidates, visiting heads of state, or anyone else the Secret Service must protect. Among the most elaborate communication systems in the world, the National Crime Information Center is linked to 64,000 federal, state, and local justice agencies (see Figure 17–2).

The Secret Service receives about 9,000 reports a year about people who might constitute a danger to public figures. Of these, 300 to 400 are considered dangerous. By putting these names in the bureau's massive computer, the Secret Service is able to learn immediately if any of its suspects are arrested and can keep track of their movements. In addition, any local law enforcement agency can quickly determine if a person they are considering arresting or have arrested is a Secret Service suspect. Those concerned about civil liberties express fears that through this system anyone's name might find its way into the computer, possibly causing damage to an innocent person.

Not only have computers aided in crime prevention, they have also made some headlines in crime detection (see Figure 17–3). A far-ranging computer system helped put an end to the string of child killings in Atlanta. Using two IBM computers and several data bases, the Atlanta police department was able to pinpoint Wayne Williams as the prime suspect in the twenty-eight killings and ultimately convict him for the murder of two.

Because ten different law enforcement agencies were involved in the Atlanta cases, officials agreed early in the investigation that a system was needed for handling and

FIGURE 17–2

The FBI's National Crime Information Center (NCIC) computer is linked to state and local law enforcement agencies.

FIGURE 17–3

Computer technology has become an important tool in police work.

cross-checking the great volume of investigative data and tips that poured in. The computer system was designed so that key words could be fed into it to generate a printout of all other data that contained those words. For example, if someone reported seeing a blue van in the area where a body was discovered, operators could ask the computer to bring up all other references to ''blue'' and ''van.'' Through such repeated uses of the computer, Williams was finally apprehended. When Williams went to trial, the computer system was used to check defense testimony against prior statements, and the results were factored into the cross-examination.

Computer Security

Computer security involves the technical and administrative safeguards required to protect a computer-based system (hardware, personnel, and data) against the major hazards to which most computer systems are exposed and to control access to information (see Figure 17–4).

PHYSICAL THREATS TO SECURITY. Physical computer systems and data on storage devices are vulnerable to several hazards: fire, natural disaster, environmental problems, and sabotage.

Fire. Fire is a problem because most computer installations use combustible materials—magnetic tape, paper, and so on. If a fire starts, water cannot be used to extinguish it, because water can damage magnetic storage media and hardware.

FIGURE 17–4

Access to computer facilities is restricted at many installations by lock or entry equipment that requires special badges. Only people whose services are required to operate computer equipment are admitted.

COMPUTER CRIME AND SECURITY

Carbon-dioxide fire-extinguisher systems are hazardous because they would endanger employees, if any were trapped in the computer room. Halon, a nonpoisonous chemical gas, can be used in fire extinguishers, but such extinguishers are costly.

Natural Disasters. Many computer centers have been damaged or destroyed by floods, cyclones, hurricanes, and earthquakes. Floods pose a serious threat to the computer hardware and wiring. However, water in the absence of heat will not destroy magnetic tapes unless the tapes are allowed to retain moisture over an extended period of time. Protection against natural disasters should be a consideration when the location for the computer center is chosen; for example, the center should not be located in an area prone to flooding.

Environmental Problems. Usually, computers are installed in buildings that were not originally planned to accommodate them. This practice may lead to environmental problems. For example, water and steam pipes may run through a computer room; bursting pipes could result in extensive damage. Pipes on floors above the computer room are also potentially hazardous, so all ceiling holes should be sealed. Data on magnetic media can be destroyed by magnetic fields created by electric motors in the vicinity of the computer room. Other environmental problems include power failures, temporary surges or drops in power, and external radiation.

Sabotage. Sabotage represents the greatest physical risk to computer installations, Saboteurs can do great damage to computer centers with little risk of apprehension. For example, magnets can be used to scramble code on tapes, bombs can be planted, and communication lines can be cut. Providing adequate security against such acts of sabotage is extremely difficult and expensive.

DATA SECURITY MEASURES. In addition to safeguarding their computer systems from these physical difficulties, companies must protect stored data against illegitimate use by controlling access to it. There is no simple solution to these security problems. Organizations such as government agencies and businesses have instituted various security measures—most to restrict access to computerized records, others to provide for reconstruction of destroyed data. Some examples follow:

■ Backup copies of data are stored outside the organization's location, and recovery procedures are established.

■ Authorized users are given special passwords. Users are only given access to areas or levels of the system warranted by their job responsibilities. Codes and passwords should be changed frequently.

■ The scope of access to the computer system is proportionate to the user's security clearance and job responsibility. Access to specific portions of the data base can be gained only by those whose jobs necessitate it.

■ Installations are guarded by internal security forces. For example, access to the data-processing department may be restricted to personnel with special badges and keys (see Figure 17–5).

■ Computer professionals are hired to test security. They try to break into a computer system in order to point out weak spots in the system's security.

■ Data is **encrypted,** or translated into a secret code, by complex coding devices that scramble information before it is transmitted or stored. When data is transmitted to or from remote terminals, it is encrypted at one end and **decrypted,** or translated back into plain text, at the other. Files can also be protected by the data's being

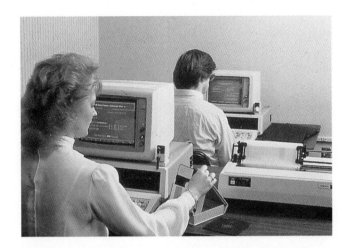

FIGURE 17–5

Devices such as data keys (left) and identification cards (right) help protect stored data by limiting access to the data.

encrypted before it is stored and decrypted after it has been retrieved. Data is principally encrypted on its way out of the computer and decrypted on its way back in.

■ Computer installations use detectors that identify legitimate individual computer users by fingerprints or voice patterns. For example, computer makers have developed attachments that grant access only to operators who put proper thumbprints on glass plates. Adoption of these expensive devices is slow, however, because they deter the main objectives of using computers: economy and convenience.

■ Call-back modems are used that restrict usage to authorized terminals only. The user calls in to connect to the system, and then the system hangs up and calls back on a predetermined number allocated only to the location of the user's terminal.

ESTABLISHING COMPUTER SECURITY. While these security measures help protect data, they are not complete. They may not prevent internal sabotage, fraud, or embezzlement. For example, an employee with a special access code may steal classified information. Banks and insurance companies are especially susceptible. Often, these companies do not wish to report the incidents because of the resulting bad publicity and the difficulty in solving such crimes.

How, then, can organizations establish computer security? First, computer users must recognize their role in security. If a high-level priority is assigned to security in the company, employees must be made aware of it and of the security measures that are being taken.

Second, many organizations recognize the need to have a well-trained security force—a department of security guards who specialize in maintaining data security, conducting system audits, and asking the right kinds of questions on a daily basis. Computerized records should be scrutinized regularly to see that everything is in order.

Third, a company should exercise a great deal of care in the selection and screening of the people who will have access to computers, terminals, and computer-stored data. Companies should choose programmers as carefully as they select attorneys or accountants.

Last, companies must discharge employees who stray beyond legal and ethical boundaries. Whenever these incidents occur, it is imperative that it be shown that they will not be tolerated and that, however hard the necessary course of action, those responsible for security and protection have the integrity to follow through.

Are Our Secrets Safe?

With computer use by the United States military on the increase, computer crime has become a very real threat to those assigned the task of keeping our military secrets safe. The only branch of the military that currently has agents trained specifically in the area of computer crime, however, is the Air Force Office of Special Investigations (AFOSI).

Attacks on military computer systems by hackers is on the rise. Military experts have reported that experienced hackers are organizing into groups, producing manuals, and providing their information to others so that they may break into government computer systems.

A number of recent cases illustrate the critical nature of computer crimes committed against military computers. The AFOSI recently aided other authorities in arresting a 14-year old boy who had downloaded files from a minicomputer at the Pentagon to another computer. Although the information in the files was not vitally important, the fact that the youth could gain access and download files is alarming.

In another case, a member of the U.S. Army used a stolen laptop computer and diskettes to provide information to the enemy on tank and helicopter deployment on the border of East and West Germany. Al-

though the Army believed that the individual had committed espionage, they could not prove it because the investigators could not find any evidence. Finally, an AFOSI investigator was sent to examine the computer and diskettes. He found the sensitive information stored in hidden files on both the laptop and diskettes.

As the level of both computer technology and expertise increase, the military must be prepared to defend itself against computer crime. The battles of the future may not be over land or sea as much as over information stored in the enemy's computer systems.

CONCEPT SUMMARY 17–2	
Computer Security	
Physical Threats to Security	
Fire	Environment problems
Natural disaster	Sabotage
Security Measures	
Make backup copies	
Issue passwords to authorized users	
Encrypt data	
Post security guards and identification detectors	

■ COMPUTER ETHICS

Another issue facing both organizations and individuals in relation to computer use is computer ethics. Questions of computer ethics also arise because of our all too human nature.

The term **computer ethics** refers to the standard of moral conduct in computer use. Although some specific laws have been enacted in problem areas such as privacy invasion and crime, ethics are a way in which the "spirit" of some laws can be carried to other computer-related activities. Some of the topics currently being addressed under the ethics issue include hacking, the security and privacy of data, employee loyalty, and the copying of computer software. Security and privacy of data are discussed in other sections of the chapter, while discussions of hacking, employee loyalty, and software copying follow.

Hacking

Hacking is a computer term used to describe the activity of computer enthusiasts who are challenged by the practice of breaking computer security measures. Hackers break in for a number of reasons including to gain access to confidential data or illegal computer time, or simply for the challenge. Computer users should be aware that seemingly innocent activities such as hacking are actually criminal acts. Regardless of the reason, hacking is the same as intentionally committing a crime. Gaining unauthorized access to another computer can be as serious as breaking into someone's home.

The case discussed earlier in which a group of Milwaukee high school students gained access to the defense research center's computer in Los Alamos, New Mexico is a prime example of hacking. The youths, after being caught, stated that they did not see any classified information, but that they did accidentally erase some files. The same group of students accessed another computer in a New York cancer center. The computer, which was used to monitor 250 cancer patients, failed for a short time due to the activity of these youths. When questioned about why they behaved this way, the group said they did not know it was a crime, and it gave them something to do in the evenings!

Employee Loyalty

Employee loyalty is another ethical issue that has surfaced in the area of data processing. Because the field of data processing is a dynamic environment with a shortage of qualified personnel, there are many job opportunities. There is also a great deal of job changing among data-processing personnel. Because an employee has some obligations to his or her current employer, there have been a number of court cases that address the issue of employee loyalty to employers.

In one particular case, a data-processing consultant employed by Firm A was seeking a similar job with Firm B. Firm B was in competition for consulting contracts with Firm A. Prior to being offered a position with Firm B, the consultant was asked to attend an interview with a potential client on behalf of the firm. Unbeknownst to either the consultant or Firm B, Firm A was also seeking a contract from the client.

When Firm A became aware of the situation they sued the consultant, who at that time worked for Firm B. The suit alleged that the consultant breached his duty of loyalty to Firm A. The day the consultant attended the interview, he had called in sick to Firm A. The court criticized the consultant, finding that the illness excuse not only permitted him to aid himself but also aid the competitor on the employer's time. An appellate court disagreed. The court ruled that since neither Firm B nor the consultant knew Firm A was also competing for the contract, the employee had the right to seek alternate employment. The court believed that employees have the right to change jobs as long as they are not under contract for a definite term. The court felt that the right should be exercisable without the necessity of revealing the plans to the current employer.

Although the court opinions differed, it should be noted that the courts do recognize some degree of duty of loyalty to the employer on the part of the employee. For this reason, all employees in the area of data processing should be aware of their obligations and rights as employees and as potential employees. Actions taken in the process of changing positions should be conducted in an ethical fashion.

Software Copying

Another area of ethical concern is **software copying,** or **piracy.** Software piracy is the unauthorized copying of a computer program that has been written by someone else. Many software manufacturers write security measures into their programs so that they cannot be copied without authorization. However, some computer enthusiasts are challenged by trying to break this form of security as well. Whether done for personal use or to sell for profit, software piracy is a crime.

Computer ethics cannot be emphasized enough. It is the responsibility of each computer user to evaluate his or her own actions and determine the standard of morals to be followed. Only through ethical behavior will the ultimate security and privacy of computers and computer data be assured. Public-domain software and shareware are discussed later in the chapter. Both of these topics also deal with the copying of computer software.

▣ PRIVACY

The widespread use of computers, information systems, and telecommunications systems has created a major concern in recent years—the invasion of individual privacy. **Privacy** involves an individual's ability to determine what, how, and when personal information is communicated to others. With computers becoming the main means of storing personal information relating to credit, employment, taxes, and other aspects of a person's life, the issue of privacy assumes great importance.

Issues

Before computerized record keeping became widespread, most business and government decisions about such benefits as credit, educational grants, and Medicare health insurance benefits were based on personal knowledge of the individuals involved and the limited data obtained from a decentralized system of public records. Privacy was protected to some extent by the inefficiency of the sources and methods of collecting data. The details of people's lives were maintained in widely dispersed, manually maintained files and in the memories of people who knew them. It was difficult to compile from these sources a detailed dossier on any individual.

Because computers have made data both easier to obtain and easier to store, more data is collected and stored (see Figure 17–6). Often an individual's data stored in one main file can be accessed easily by entering his or her social security number. The increased ease of obtaining data tempts organizations to collect more data than necessary. People have less control over who has access to personal data when it becomes part of a huge data base. They are unaware of whether their personal data files are complete and accurate. People may not even be aware that certain information is being kept.

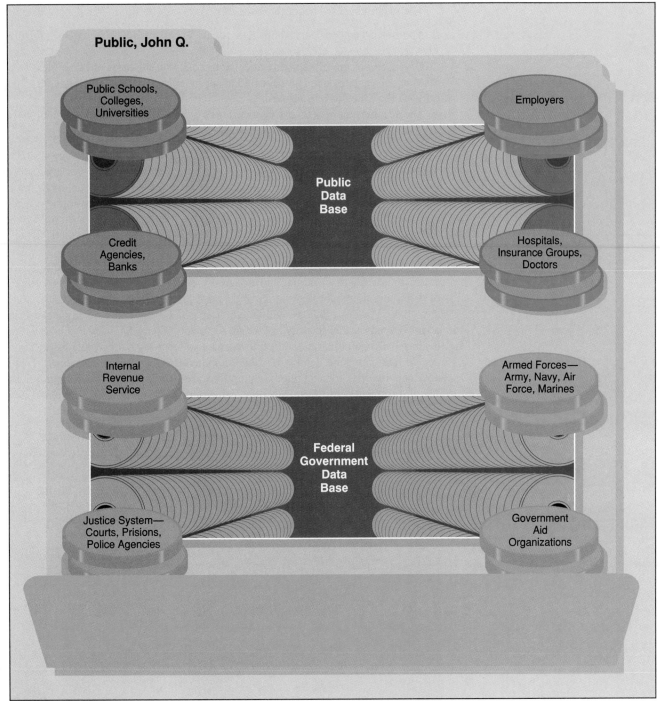

FIGURE 17–6

The stacks and rows of magnetic tapes show how easily just one corporation can accumulate and store huge amounts of data using computer systems. Multiply one corporation's data base by the many data bases kept by other organizations including the federal government, and you can see how John Q. Public could be completely unaware of what data is recorded about him. The ease with which organizations can record, store, and access data has led to concerns about data privacy and correct use of data.

The major concerns about the issue of privacy can be summarized as follows:

■ Too much personal data about individuals is collected and stored in computer files. This data is too easy to access and share.
■ Organizations are often making decisions solely on the basis of these files.
■ Much of the personal data collected about individuals may not be relevant to the purpose for which it is to be used.
■ The accuracy, completeness, and currency of the data may be unacceptably low.
■ The security of stored data is a problem.

Of course, the same computer systems that erode individual privacy are also allowing private and public institutions to operate more efficiently. For example, a firm must control its risks when issuing credit and, therefore, needs enough information about individuals to make responsible decisions. The solution to the privacy issue must be an appropriate balance between the legitimate needs of organizations for information about people and the rights of individuals to maintain their privacy.

The data bases that are responsible for the privacy concerns are most prevalent within the federal government (see Figure 17–7). Much of the data is acquired from census returns filed each decade and income tax returns filed annually. The Department of Transportation records owners of boats and aircraft. This department also notes any drivers' licenses that are withdrawn, suspended, or revoked by any state. Data about veterans, social security or welfare recipients, aliens, minority businesses, and dealers in alcohol, firearms, and explosives are stored away in huge data bases. Some people fear that using debit cards and computers for making purchases will create new opportunities for compiled assumptions about their habits and personal lives. The government could glean statistics concerning everything from where and how often a family dines out to what kinds of magazines and books they read.

Legislation

Since the early 1970s several laws have been enacted to protect privacy by controlling the collection, dissemination, and transmission of personal data. By far the most

FIGURE 17–7

Huge data bases such as the one maintained by the IRS lead many people to fear abuse of their privacy.

CHAPTER 17: COMPUTER SECURITY, CRIME, ETHICS AND THE LAW

numerous have been passed by the federal government to protect against abuse of the government's own record-keeping agencies. But state legislatures are also beginning to recognize the widespread abuses that computer technology has created, and numerous states are taking action to stop the abuse.

FEDERAL LEGISLATION. One of the first federal laws to address the problem of abuse was passed in 1970, while a second was passed in 1973. The Freedom of Information Act of 1970 allows individuals access to data about themselves in files collected by federal agencies. The law was passed because of the potential for the government to conceal its proceedings from the public. The Crime Control Act of 1973 protects the privacy of data collected for state criminal systems that are developed with federal funds.

Perhaps the most sweeping federal legislation was the Privacy Act of 1974. Signed on January 1, 1975, this act is designed to protect the privacy of individuals about whom the federal government maintains data. Although the act was a step in the right direction, it was criticized for its failure to reach beyond the federal government to state and private institutions. The act contains these provisions:

■ Individuals must be able to determine what information about themselves is being recorded and how it will be used.

■ Individuals must be provided with a way to correct inaccurate information that is collected about themselves.

■ Information collected for one purpose cannot be used for another purpose without the consent of the individual involved.

■ Organizations creating, manipulating, using, or divulging personal information must ensure that the information is reliable and must take precautions to prevent misuse of the information.

Several other laws have been passed by the federal government in an attempt to control data-base misuse and protect the privacy of individuals. The Family Educational Rights and Privacy Act of 1974 is designed to protect privacy by regulating access to computer-stored records of grades and behavior evaluations in both private and public schools. The act provides that no federal funds will be made available to an educational agency that has a policy of denying parents and students access to the student's relevant educational records. The Tax Reform Act of 1976 was passed to safeguard the confidentiality of personal tax information. The Right to Financial Privacy Act of 1978 provides further protection by limiting government access to the customer records of financial institutions, protecting to some degree the confidentiality of personal financial data.

As computer use has continued to grow during the 1980s and 1990s, the federal government has continued to enact legislation directed toward protecting the privacy of individuals. The increased use of electronic funds transfer led to the passage of the Electronic Funds Transfer Act of 1980. This law requires financial institutions to notify customers whenever a third party accesses a customer's account. The Computer Fraud and Abuse Act of 1986 is the result of many tortuous years of producing draft bills in both houses of Congress. In the final adopted version, only a few limited categories of privacy abuse are defined. One provision of the law prohibits individuals without authorization from knowingly accessing a computer to obtain financial or consumer credit records from financial or credit-reporting institutions.

Another provision prohibits individuals from knowingly and intentionally accessing a government computer or the computer of a financial institution and using, modifying, destroying, or disclosing information stored in the computer or preventing the use of the computer and causing more than $1,000 loss or loss in personal medical care. More recently, concern has focused on abuses of privacy during the actual transmission of data. This concern led to the drafting of the Electronic Communication Privacy Act of 1986 which prohibits the interception of data communications, for example, of electronic mail. The act also makes it illegal for a provider of electronic communications service to divulge knowingly the contents of a communication except to the intended parties.

STATE LEGISLATION. Many state laws regarding government record-keeping practices are patterned after the Privacy Act of 1974. Most states have enacted some controls on such practices in the public sector. Most of the laws have been passed since 1978. The majority of state legislatures have passed laws regarding computer crime, and most states address the privacy issue in one form or another. Computer crime laws on the state level are generally quite similar to each other. Differences lie mainly in how each state defines a particular term or violation. Some state laws address the unlawful access to data bases in more detail than the federal Comprehensive Crime Control Act of 1984.

Relatively few information-privacy violation cases have been litigated, whether on the state or federal level. Since one problem of privacy violation is that data is transferred and disclosed without the knowledge or consent of the subjects, people are not likely to know how their personal data is used and probably will not realize they may have a claim to take to court. Furthermore, privacy litigation is something of a contradiction in terms: by taking claims to court, litigants may expose private aspects of their lives to a far greater extent than the initial intrusion did.

■ WARRANTIES, COPYRIGHT LAW, PUBLIC-DOMAIN SOFTWARE, AND SHAREWARE

This portion of the chapter discusses two of the legal issues associated with owning a computer system—the warranties for hardware and software and the copyright law as it applies to computer software. A discussion of express and implied warranties will be followed by a review of copyright law and its application to the writing of computer programs. The section concludes with a brief discussion on public-domain software and shareware.

Warranties

The **Uniform Commercial Code (UCC)** is a set of provisions proposed by legal experts to promote uniformity among the state courts in their legal treatment of commercial transactions. By using Article Two of the UCC, the courts have a common basis for rendering decisions concerning the sale of computer hardware and software by vendors.

Common law, on the other hand, is based on customs and past judicial decisions in similar cases. If Article Two of the UCC does not apply to a transaction, then the common law of contracts will apply. The UCC is a far better system since it is more modern and basically abolishes the concept of *caveat emptor* (a Latin legal maxim meaning ''let the buyer beware''). Under Article Two of the UCC, for example, the computer user is given implied warranty protection, whereas under common law, buyer protection is not presumed or implied and must be negotiated and agreed upon in the final contract. Most computer vendors are reluctant to agree to such negotiations.

Two main conditions must be satisfied for the UCC to apply to computer acquisitions. First, the contract must be one for goods, not services. As a general rule, the UCC is not applicable to contracts for services. Second, the contract should be for the *sale* of goods. Article Two of the UCC does not normally apply to leases or licenses.

EXPRESS WARRANTIES. Under Article Two of the UCC, **express warranties** are created when the seller makes any promise or statement of fact concerning the goods being sold which the purchaser uses as a basis for purchasing the goods. By doing so, the seller warrants, or guarantees, that the goods are those that will meet the purchaser's needs. An express warranty may be created by the supplier's use of a description, sample, or model in attempting to sell the goods, although the seller's contract terms will often attempt to limit or disclaim all such warranties. Express warranties are also found in the written contract, such as statements that defective equipment will be replaced or repaired for up to one year after delivery. A **breach of contract** occurs if the goods fail to conform to the express warranty, in which case the buyer is entitled to a reduction in the price of the goods as compensatory damages. One drawback of express warranties is that the purchaser must keep the defective equipment. Therefore, unless expressly stated in the contract, the computer hardware or software would not have to be replaced, only reduced in price.

IMPLIED WARRANTIES. Implied warranties were also recognized under Article Two of the Uniform Commercial Code. **Implied warranties** suggest that a contract for the sale of goods automatically contains certain warranties that exist by law. An implied warranty need not be verbally made nor included in the written warranties of a contract to be effective. Two major types of implied warranties include implied warranty of merchantability and implied warranty of fitness for a particular purpose.

The **implied warranty of merchantability** only exists if the seller is considered a merchant. Computer and software vendors are classified as merchants because they are in the business of selling computer-related products on a repetitive basis. In the case of a purchased computer system, an implied warranty of merchantability guarantees the user that the system will function properly for a reasonable period of time. As in the case of express warranties, however, the purchaser must keep the defective equipment.

To create an **implied warranty of fitness** for a particular purpose, the purchaser must communicate to the supplier the specific purpose for which the product will be used. The purchaser must then rely upon the supplier's judgment, skill, and expertise to select suitable computer hardware and software. If the computer hardware or software later fails to meet those needs, the supplier has breached this implied warranty and is liable for damages. The violation of this warranty permits the purchaser to recover only a certain amount of the sales price.

Copyright Law

Acting under authority granted in the Constitution, since 1790 Congress has passed intellectual property legislation protecting the rights of authors. These copyright laws do not protect the idea behind the words, but merely the specific expression of the idea itself. Since 1964, the Copyright Office and courts have determined that computer programs are the "writing of an author" within the meaning of the Constitution. The federal Copyright Act of 1976 reinforced this protection for computer programs. Thus the actual language expression (instructions) adopted by a programmer is the copyright element in a computer program; the actual processes or methods embodied in the program are not within the scope of copyright law.

The creator of an original work possesses a copyright from the moment the work is fixed in some tangible medium, such as hard copy or disk storage. Since March 1, 1989, when the United States became a member of the International Berne Copyright Convention, most formal requirements of registration and identification have become optional. However because of numerous legal advantages and the relatively minor cost, authors should register their works with the Copyright Office and place a copyright notice on all copies of their works.

Two of the most important rights granted exclusively to authors under copyright law are the right to reproduce their works and the right to create a derivative work. Except for minor exceptions, only the holder of a copyright has the right to authorize copying of the protected material. The two most notable exceptions permit the legal owner of a work to make one archival copy for backup purposes as well as permitting the fair use of selected portions of copyrighted material in an extremely limited manner for educational purposes. Only the copyright holder has the right to develop derivative works, such as translations, based upon the original copyrighted material.

In applying laws that were created before electricity came into general use to computer technology, the courts have had to grapple with many novel issues. Computer programs in all forms—source, object, microcode—have been accepted as material protected by copyright. Electronic storage has been determined to be a fixed tangible medium for expression. Video screen displays warrant protection as long as they are not merely blank forms. Operating systems, but not programming languages themselves, are proper subject matter even though they control a machine or process rather than provide the expression of an idea. Reverse engineering through decompilation and analysis is a legal means for evaluating the idea rather than expression. Legal users may make a temporary copy of the program in the memory of the computer for execution purposes. Programs which have only a singular purpose (to break copy protection locks) are not illegal because they fulfill a legitimate need for backup.

Whether the user buys or leases computer software, it is important to remember that only one physical copy of the program has been legally acquired and that no copyright interest in the program has been transferred. The only right that the legal user has obtained is to run the program. A subsidiary right to create one additional copy of the work is strictly limited to personal backup and may not be viewed as a legitimate second copy. Many copyright holders of microcomputer operating system programs permit users to copy command or supervisor modules onto application disks, thereby permitting autobooting.

If a program is placed on a local area network, only the one copy may be executed at one time. Therefore, if the program is copied into the memory of the local user computer before execution, there must be a lock preventing a second user from accessing the program. An alternative solution would be the acquisition of a ''site license'' from the copyright holder that permits multiple users of the program on the network.

Licensing agreements for the right to use mainframe software may be even more restrictive. It is not uncommon to find a requirement for the use of a program limited to one machine with the serial number listed in the agreement. The right to modify the software may also be tightly controlled, requiring a continued maintenance agreement with the copyright holder.

Even though unauthorized copying of software is illegal and subjects the individual or corporation to both substantial civil and criminal penalties, it is obvious that many ignore the law. The proliferation of microcomputers accompanied by the ease of

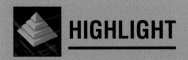
Apple vs. Microsoft

Since its introduction in 1984, the Apple Macintosh microcomputer has been one of the top selling personal computers. One of the primary reasons for its success has been its user-friendly graphic user interface (or GUI). Until recently, IBM PC and IBM PC compatible computers relied on a command-line user interface which is more difficult to use.

Recognizing the value of a GUI, Microsoft developed the Windows program to provide users of IBM PCs and PC-compatibles a user interface similar to that used on the Macintosh. Since the introduction of the Microsoft Windows v3.0 program, it has become one of the top selling programs for the IBM PC and PC-compatibles. However, because of its similarity in appearance to the user interface of the Macintosh, Apple is suing Microsoft for copyright infringement.

This court case has brought to light a significant question in relation to copyright law—whether the screen designs of software packages are included under copyright law. Apple is contending that, although the Microsoft Windows screens are not identical to theirs, the general design of the screens is a copy of those used on the Macintosh. The ultimate decision on this screen design issue rests with the courts and probably will not be settled for years. However, the fact that the issue has been brought to court will undoubtedly influence future software designs. An interesting question that arises is whether a company such as Apple should be able to control the development of similar user interface software through its copyright. Again, this is the very issue that the courts will address.

copying and difficulty of detection has made this segment of the computer industry extremely vulnerable. However, recently there have been numerous successful enforcement actions directed at both corporations and universities. Education and ethical persuasion are the most potent weapons being used against illegal copying by individuals.

Software that falls outside of copyright protection is termed *public-domain software*. This normally occurs when the author decides not to protect the copyright interest and publishes the software with that stipulation. Software developed with public or grant funds may also be contractually transferred into the public domain. Such software is frequently found in electronic bulletin boards, magazines, or through user groups.

Certain aspects of the application of copyright law to computer software are still unsettled. The 11th Amendment to the Constitution prohibits federal law from impacting state rights, thereby granting an immunity, subject to Congressional action, to state universities from infringement of federal copyright. There is a great deal of legal pressure to make the "look and feel"—or structure, sequence, and organization—of computer programs the true test of copyright infringement, rather than a literal copying of the expression.

One of the most confusing issues in computer law is determining who is the author of a program for copyright purposes. If an employee of a company develops a program during work time or on company computers, the author of the program is the company. However, if the creator of the program is merely an independent contractor hired by the company for software development, then the creator is also the author for copyright purposes. In the latter case, the company has most likely acquired only a license to use the program, unless the contract provides the transfer of other rights.

Copyright law does not provide an exclusive monopoly for protected work. If a second author creates an identical work without copying the protected work, there is no infringement. Thus, if a student were to develop a spreadsheet system that was identical to Lotus 1-2-3, but had never seen or heard about Lotus 1-2-3, the student would have created a program that itself would be protected by copyright and would not be in violation of copyright law. It is for this reason that there is a great deal of interest in applying patent protection to computer programs. A patent affords an exclusive monopoly and protects novel ideas or processes. However, as of today, the primary legal protection worldwide for computer programs is provided by well-established copyright law.

Public-Domain Software and Shareware

Software that is increasingly used in the computer field is **public-domain software.** Public-domain software is software that is unprotected by copyright law and, therefore, falls into the "public domain" of unrestricted use. Public-domain software, frequently obtained from electronic bulletin boards, is free to all users. The only cost associated with a public-domain program is the cost of the phone service needed to reach the bulletin board on which the program appears or the cost of the disk to which the program is copied.

Public-domain programs were originally written by computer hobbyists and amateurs to fill the void of commercial software available for microcomputers. The programs, which appeared on bulletin boards or were passed among members of user groups, were often undocumented and full of "bugs." Today there are fewer bugs in the programs, and many come with sophisticated documentation. Besides bulletin boards and user groups, public-domain software now can be obtained from online services such as CompuServ and The Source. Most public-domain programs include the source code for user convenience.

Closely related to public-domain software is **shareware.** Authors of shareware retain the copyright to their work. They make their programs available to the public with the idea that, if a user likes the program, he or she will make a donation to the author. Generally the source code is not distributed with a shareware program. Users of shareware are encouraged to copy and distribute the programs freely. The basic philosophy behind shareware is that users are in the best position to judge the value of a program and that authors, if they know their fees depend upon it, will produce a quality product. For this reason, the quality of shareware programs tends to surpass that of public-domain programs.

◘ SUMMARY POINTS

■ Taking a broad view, computer crime can be defined as any criminal act that poses a greater threat to a computer user than it would to a non–computer user, or a criminal act that is accomplished through the use of a computer.

■ Computer crimes can be classified in four categories: sabotage, theft of services, theft of property, and financial crimes.

■ Uses of computers in the prevention and detection of crimes include pinpointing likely arson targets, monitoring people who are potential threats to public officials, and handling and cross-checking data and tips in murder investigations.

■ Physical threats to computer security exist in the forms of fire, natural disasters, environmental problems (such as power failures, brownouts, and external radiation), and sabotage.

■ Data security is an issue that must also be addressed by organizations that store sensitive data on computers. Illegitimate use of data must be controlled through access-security measures.

■ Computer ethics refers to the standard of moral conduct for computer use. Lapses in computer ethics are largely the result of human nature.

■ Hacking is the practice of breaking computer security measures to gain unauthorized access to a computer system. Hacking is a criminal act.

■ Employee duty or loyalty is an ethical issue that can pose a serious problem to companies in competition for both business and employees.

■ Unauthorized software copying, or piracy, is a crime whether done for personal use or for profit.

■ The Freedom of Information Act of 1970 allows individuals access to data about themselves in files collected by federal agencies. The Crime Control Act of 1973 protects the privacy of data collected for state criminal systems.

■ The Privacy Act of 1974 is designed to protect the privacy of individuals about whom the federal government maintains data.

■ The Family Educational Rights and Privacy Act of 1974 is designed to protect privacy by regulating access to computer-stored records of grades and behavior evaluations in both private and public schools. The Tax Reform Act of 1976 was passed to safeguard the confidentiality of personal tax information, while the Right to Financial Privacy Act of 1978 limits government access to customer records in financial institutions.

■ The Fair Credit Reporting Act of 1970 attempts to regulate the information practices of private organizations and is intended to deter privacy violations by lending institutions that use computers to store and manipulate data.

■ As computer use has continued to grow during the 1980s and 1990s, the federal government has continued to enact legislation directed toward protecting the privacy of individuals. The increased use of electronic funds transfer led to the passage of the Electronic Funds Transfer Act of 1980. The Computer Fraud and Abuse Act of 1986 provides for protection from computer abuse in some areas that were overlooked in earlier legislation. The Electronic Communication Privacy Act of 1986 prohibits the interception of data communications, for example, electronic mail.

■ The majority of states have passed legislation regarding computer crime; most of these laws address the privacy issue in one form or another. Computer-crime laws on the state level are generally quite similar to each other, the differences being in the way terms or violations are defined.

■ The Uniform Commercial Code (UCC) is a set of provisions established by legal experts to act as a uniform guide to state courts for resolving contract disputes.

■ For the UCC to be applicable, the contract must be one for goods rather than services, and the contract should be for the sale of goods, not for leases or licenses.

■ Under Article Two of the UCC, express warranties and implied warranties can be created on behalf of the purchaser.

■ Copyright laws do not protect the idea behind the work, but merely the work itself. Therefore, a computer program itself is protected while the ideas and methods for creating the program are not protected.

■ The creator of a computer program possesses a copyright from the moment the work is saved, or stored, in a tangible medium. This medium can include hard copy (paper) or magnetic media such as disk or tape. Because of legal advantages and low cost, authors should register their works with the Copyright Office.

■ Public-domain software is software that is unprotected by copyright law and thus falls into the "public domain" of unrestricted use.

■ Authors of shareware retain the copyright to their work. Programs are made available to the public with the idea that a user will make a donation to the author.

❑ TERMS FOR REVIEW

breach of contract, p. 453

common law, p. 452

computer crime, p. 438

computer ethics, p. 447

computer security, p. 443

decrypted data, p. 444

encrypted data, p. 444

express warranty, p. 453

hacking, p. 447

implied warranty, p. 453

implied warranty of fitness, p. 453

implied warranty of merchantability, p. 453

privacy, p. 448

public-domain software, p. 456

shareware, p. 456

software copying (piracy), p. 448

Uniform Commercial Code (UCC), p. 452

virus, p. 439

❑ REVIEW QUESTIONS

1. What is computer crime? What types of individuals are most likely to commit computer crimes?

2. What are some of the more common types of computer crimes? Give a brief description of each.

3. What parts of a computer system must be protected by computer security measures? What are some of the physical threats to the security of computer systems?

4. What are some of the ways that data stored on computer systems can be protected?

5. What is meant by the term *computer ethics?* Are there specific laws that pertain to or govern the ethics of computer use?

6. What is hacking? Why is it an important issue?

7. Explain how you think our personal privacy has been affected by the widespread use of computers by businesses and government agencies. Do you believe computers pose a serious threat to our personal privacy? Why or why not?

8. What are the key privacy provisions contained in the Privacy Act of 1974?

9. How do express warranties and implied warranties differ? What are the two types of implied warranties? Give a brief description of each.

10. Why is the copyright law important to computer software vendors? What are the rights granted to the copyright holder under the law?

ALCOA

COMPANY HISTORY

Aluminum, which is the most plentiful metallic element in the earth's crust, occurs naturally only as a chemical compound. For many years, the difficulty of reducing it to metallic aluminum made the metal too expensive for commercial use. In 1886, two young men—independently but simultaneously—unlocked the secret of a lost-cost, electrolytic process for separating aluminum from its oxide. One of the men, Charles Martin Hall, a graduate of Oberlin College in Ohio, was able to bring his discovery to commercialization, and in 1888, six Pittsburgh industrialists financed the formation of the Pittsburgh Reduction Company, which later was renamed Aluminum Company of America (ALCOA).

Once aluminum was available at low cost, uses for the metal grew steadily. An early successful application was cooking utensils. The steel industry was also an early customer. Aluminum alloys became useful in the making of automobile parts after the turn of the century. As the uses for aluminum grew, so did ALCOA. World War II was a major turning point for the company. Wartime needs required vast amounts of additional aluminum, and ALCOA built many plants for the government. After the war, antitrust regulations required ALCOA to sell all but one of its wartime plants. Despite this setback, post-World War II growth was strong, and ALCOA prospered. Today, ALCOA and affiliated companies sell aluminum throughout the world. The past decade has brought major changes in the worldwide environment for aluminum producers, and ALCOA is becoming a broader-based company with a research thrust toward chemicals, ceramics, polymers, laminates, and advanced manufacturing systems.

DATA SECURITY

As ALCOA has become a more complex organization with an emphasis on research and development, data security has become an important aspect of the company's success. At ALCOA, the focus of data security is on support and acceptance by the user community. To ensure the support of the thousands of computer users at many remote locations, ALCOA has decentralized the responsibility for data security administration to several middle-level managers throughout the company.

ALCOA's security policy, security software, and positive user attitudes are all equally important to the effectiveness of the program. Of these, positive user attitudes are undoubtedly the most difficult to achieve. This is due partly to the logistics of creating security awareness among large numbers of users and partly to the inclination of people to adopt convenient data access practices rather than those intended to safeguard the corporation's data resources. Since people are more easily influenced by individuals whom they know well, local administrators are obviously in a better position to promote security than an unknown central administrator whose office may be three time zones away.

A decentralized security system at ALCOA has increased productivity, improved security, and decreased costs.

At ALCOA, the belief in positive user attitudes and local data security administrators is strong. According to national surveys, the odds that a computer criminal is a company insider are an astonishing 9 to 1. Central administrators are at a disadvantage in preventing crimes and abuses because they neither know nor are known by more than a few of the individuals who interface with the computer. ALCOA's local administrators, on the other hand, are likely to have job responsibilities that keep them in relatively close contact with the groups of computer users they control, either functionally or geographically. These administrators are more likely to know which users are high security risks. Traditionally, high security risks include employees who are disgruntled, are having money or drug problems, or are being transferred or terminated.

Local administrators can respond quickly to such situations by making direct online adjustments via security software. They are not deterred by the notion that security is someone else's problem, and they are not impeded by the phone calls and paperwork that are the bane of central administration. Also, potential violators are less likely to misuse the computer or commit a crime if they know and respect their local data security administrator.

One of the benefits of the decentralized security system at ALCOA has been increased productivity, as well as improved security and a decrease in costs. Decentralization has increased productivity by eliminating the need for central support personnel to process requests and the staff of central administrators to review and approve the requests. The task of processing requests for user IDs and file accesses has been automated by a combination of purchased security software and programs written in-house.

Decentralization has also increased user productivity by reducing the time users wait for computer change requests to be processed. Before decentralization, users had to fill out more specialized change request forms, have them approved and signed by an authorized individual, and mail them to the home office. At the home office, the signatures were validated, and the forms were reviewed, processed, and returned by mail to the individual who authorized them. This procedure took one to two weeks. Today, ALCOA's local security administrator makes these changes online with immediate confirmation of accuracy.

The success of a decentralized program depends upon a central individual to give direction to the overall program and ensure that all local administrators are observing certain standard rules. This may be one of the reasons that relatively few corporations (less than 20 percent) have adopted the decentralized approach to data security and accessing mainframe computers that has successfully been implemented at ALCOA. Also important to the success of a decentralized program are good naming conventions for data security programs, user-friendly security packages that spare local administrators from having to master a great deal of technical jargon, the coordinating of necessary changes to various data sets when user IDs are added or deleted, and the reporting of unauthorized access attempts to the administrators responsible for both the user and the data.

All of these measures and many more have helped make decentralization successful. From corporate headquarters to the grass roots level, decentralization has won the approval of the Aluminum Company of America.

DISCUSSION POINTS
1. Discuss how decentralization has improved data security at ALCOA.
2. Why is positive user attitude the most difficult aspect of data security to achieve?

Computers in Our Lives: Today and Tomorrow

Can Home Computers Predict Earthquakes?

Mel Mandell, *Computerworld*

If seismologist Edward Cranswick has his druthers, a network of home computers will provide valuable information on earthquakes in the San Francisco Bay area and perhaps even warn of the next big one.

Cranswick and his collaborator, Robert Banfill, have proposed that inexpensive seismic data acquisition units (SDAU) be attached to only a fraction of the many home computers in and around San Francisco. Having as few as 1% of the estimated 100,000 home computers in the area equipped with the SDAUs could provide important data on how different terrain responds to even the slightest of earthquakes, Cranswick said.

Cranswick, 39, a 10-year veteran of the U.S. Geological Survey in Golden, Colo., has been programming in Fortran since he was in high school in Nyack, N.Y. Banfill, 29, has been working with personal computers for 10 years. He operates a one-person business called Small Systems Support in Big Water, Utah. It was Banfill who convinced Cranswick that PCs could be substituted for large computers in the analysis of seismic data.

The owners of the home computers would be asked to buy the SDAUs, which, the proponents hope, could be made in volume for only $500 each. Each SDAU would consist of an accelerometer connected by cables to a box containing a small microprocessor, at least 1 M byte of memory and an internal clock. The accelerometer, which would measure motion in three directions, would be buried in the backyard. Any motion picked up by the accelerometer would be transmitted to the box, which would be loaded with "trigger" algorithms to eliminate unwanted information, such as earth movements caused by passing vehicles. Movements caused by quakes would be stored in random-access memory.

Once a day, the central computers at the Geological Survey offices in Menlo Park, Calif., would poll each SDAU via modem. Only the starting times and amplitude of each movement would be forwarded, Cranswick said, so each transmission should "last no longer than 30 seconds and not interfere with other uses." A light on the SDAU would inform the homeowner that seismic data has been collected. The homeowner could then call the data up on the screen of the home computer, study and compare it with data from prior quakes stored in the computer. Cranswick said he believes the amateur seismologists in this proposed network could eventually make contributions to seismic research.

The idea for a vast network of SDAUs first came to Cranswick more than 10 years ago after a great earthquake centered in Haicheng, China. Local peasants reported odd behavior by animals and changing water levels in wells just before the earthquake. At the time, some seismologists proposed the creation of low-cost, electronic "seismic animals" to warn of impending earthquakes.

Cranswick and Banfill proposed their concept at a meeting of the American Geophysical Union held in San Francisco on Dec. 6.

Reaction to the proposal was mostly positive. For instance, the head of the Geological Survey in Menlo Park said his office has long operated a network of sophisticated SDAUs, but they number only 84. They are tied to Digital Equipment Corp. PDP-1170, VAX 750 and VAX 780 computers.

Cranswick's network of home SDAUs is still at least a year away. First, he must locate manufacturers who will supply the accelerometer—the most costly component—at a reasonable price. Next, he and Banfill must create more sophisticated trigger algorithms to eliminate irrelevant data generated, for example, by the homeowner's dog unearthing a bone next to the buried accelerometer. Seismic analysis software for each kind of home computer must then be written "most likely in a mixture of languages including C and Fortran," Cranswick said.

The collaborators must then recruit and train amateur seismologists to install and test the SDAUs in the homes of volunteers who join the network.

◾ INTRODUCTION

Nearly fifty years ago, vacuum tubes controlled the electrical circuits in computers. Today, scientists dream of "growing" electronic circuits from protein material. In the 1930s and 1940s, robots played important roles in science fiction. Today robots are no longer visions of the future. They are working in our factories and helping our young people learn in school. A February 1964 *U.S. News and World Report* article, "Is the Computer Running Wild?" announced that the first computers run by integrated circuits would make their debut that year. Since then, computer technology has advanced so rapidly that computer scientists who grew up on vacuum tubes, transistors, and science fiction are performing research in areas that were technologically inconceivable only two or three decades ago.

The gains in technology have benefited many areas: artificial intelligence, robotics, medicine and science, home use, and education. This chapter discusses some of the current directions and concerns in these fields as well as some trends in hardware technology.

◾ TRENDS IN HARDWARE TECHNOLOGY

In 1958, Jack S. Kilby of Texas Instruments introduced the first integrated circuit. It was a crude little piece of metal with several fine wires and other components sandwiched with solder. Later, Robert N. Noyce of Fairchild Semiconductor designed another type of integrated circuit that better protected the circuits on the chip. Soon a single chip less than one-eighth of an inch square contained sixty-four complete circuits. The number of circuits etched on a single chip has continued to increase. Many companies are currently trying to develop technology that will allow for the creation of **dynamic random-access memory (DRAM)** chips capable of storing up to 64 million bits of data. Circuits have become so miniaturized that writers describe them in terms of angels dancing on the head of a pin and house-by-house maps of large cities etched on postage stamps (see Figure 18–1).

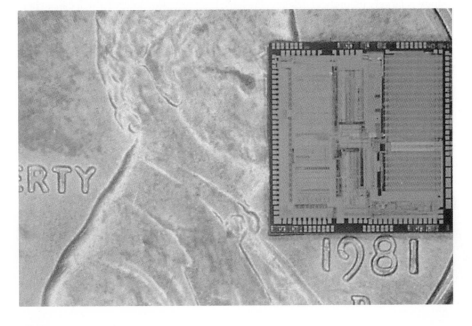

FIGURE 18–1

Computer chips (microprocessors) today provide as much computing power as yesterday's room-sized computers, yet would just cover the head of Lincoln on a penny.

Still scientists explore the building of even higher speed, ultralarge-scale integrated circuits. Technology being explored may allow for a single chip to contain the equivalent of four billion transistors. Packing many components in such a small space reduces the distance that electricity travels and achieves extremely fast computer speeds.

When electronic components are crowded closer together to decrease these distances, however, two problems arise. The first problem (as first mentioned in Chapter 2) is one that plagued the users of early computers: the generation of heat. The densely packed circuits in ultralarge-scale integrated circuits create enough heat and use enough power to burn out the chips. The second problem is an offshoot of the first. As circuits are crowded closer together, the chance increases that one circuit will receive unwanted signals from nearby circuits in what is often termed *cross talk*. (Cross talk resembles the problem you may experience when you make a long-distance telephone call and hear another conversation in the background.) The following sections discuss several ways in which scientists are solving these problems: the raw materials for making chips, laser technology, and parallel processing. Many people feel the development of technologies that solve these problems is signaling a movement into the fifth computer generation.

Chip Technology

As scientists address these problems, they try different materials to make chips. For example, integrated circuits made with gallium arsenide achieve speeds five to seven times those of the fastest silicon chips. Although expensive, gallium arsenide chips require lower voltages to operate, generate less heat, and create less cross talk than silicon chips. Their speed makes them suitable for use in supercomputers. They could also be used for memory chips and communications chips that are now too slow to keep up with the fastest microprocessors made of silicon. Because the chips resist radiation, they can be used in missile guidance and surveillance satellites.

Some scientists studying molecular electronics believe that tiny computer circuits (sometimes called biochips) can be grown from living material. Although the technology is largely theoretical, researchers have built organic molecules that can switch from conducting to nonconducting, just as silicon does. Most efforts to merge organic materials and computers are based on the principles of biosensors, which can reveal the presence of certain biological agents. In an organic computer, light would take the place of electrical currents in the computer switches that handle information.

Other researchers trying to build computer chips at the atomic level already are using special microscopes that can move atoms one by one. On a less theoretical level, scientists are building multichip modules in which several chips are placed in one package rather than mounted separately on the printed circuit board. This technology reduces heat and cross talk. Scientists are also developing read-write random-access memory chips that retain data even after the power source is turned off.

Laser Technology

Lasers aid computer technology in an important way: they carry digital signals through hair-thin fibers of the purest glass in a technology known as **fiber optics** (see Chapter 9). The tiny staccato pulses of light can turn on and off ninety million times per second. Fiber-optic cables are being used for linking computer terminals and mainframes in large industrial complexes and for connecting workstations in local-area

FIGURE 18–2

Optical Computer
AT&T Bell Labs engineer Alan Huang is developing an optical computer that uses light for its operations.

networks (LANs). They are also rapidly replacing conventional telephone lines; thus, they may soon carry high-definition television, interactive education, dial-up encyclopedias, and other information services into our homes.

Manufacturers of computer chips may also benefit from the use of laser beams. An ultraprecise laser beam could be used as a tiny blowtorch in correcting defective chips, sometimes 50 to 65 percent of the total production. Eventually, researchers hope to use lasers, computers, and robots for complete automation of the chip-building process. Some scientists, however, are working on computer chips that actually move tiny light beams through a maze of microscopic mirrors and lenses. Since photons—particles of light—are the fastest things in the universe, an optical computer would be many times faster than any computer currently available (see Figure 18–2). Its uses would include communications, robot vision, voice recognition, and remote sensing.

Parallel Processing

Traditional processing occurs serially. A single channel carries all the data bit by bit, one by one, between memory and the control unit. The concepts of multiprogramming and virtual memory give the illusion to multiple users that a computer is performing many tasks at once. The computer is really processing several programs during the same period of time by rotating segments of the programs in quick succession.

The human brain, on the other hand, processes information in parallel sequence. It deals with large amounts of data and handles many different cognitive tasks effortlessly and *simultaneously*. Innovative forms of hardware architecture facilitate **parallel processing** by computer. Parallel processing imitates the brain's behavior by dividing a problem into several portions and processing the portions simultaneously. The architecture involves two or more CPUs or microprocessors. Massively parallel machines contain thousands of microprocessors.

Parallel processing increases computer speed without further miniaturizing the circuitry and encountering the problems associated with densely packed electronic components. Applications using parallel processing include speech understanding, simulations, climate prediction, and artificial intelligence.

◾ ARTIFICIAL INTELLIGENCE

The term *number crunching* was born in the vacuum tube era of computing when mathematicians, scientists, and engineers used the machines for manipulating huge amounts of numerical data. Even today number crunching is what most computers do best. As programmers and developers of computer languages become more proficient at designing advanced software, however, number crunching will give way to more conceptual applications, which include voice recognition and robotics.

The new computers and languages only begin to imitate human intelligence at higher levels of abstraction. Humanlike thinking, common sense, self-teaching, and decision-making skills performed by machines are termed **artificial intelligence (AI).** Since human intelligence is not clearly understood, current AI programs incorporate just a few aspects of it. The most common AI applications are **expert systems** as described in Chapter 13. These systems imitate an expert in a field, drawing conclusions and making recommendations based on huge data bases of information and on *heuristics,* guidelines that help reduce options or uncertainty.

Some of today's expert systems are real-time systems, which respond to incoming data at a rate faster than the data is arriving. Real-time expert systems gather data by automatic sensors. They can help ease the problem of cognitive overload, which occurs when humans try to deal with too much data coming in too quickly. Real-time expert systems can be used in financial markets, air-traffic control towers, environmental systems, satellite control modules, and factories.

Many experts in AI contend that expert systems do not qualify as true AI. Intelligence involves coping with change and incorporating new information for improving performance, and expert systems do neither. The country's top researchers have taken different approaches to the way the wealth of human knowledge must be organized inside the computer. One approach is to build computer knowledge through **nonmonotonic logic,** a method developed by John McCarthy, who, in 1956 at the Massachusetts Institute of Technology (MIT), coined the term artificial intelligence.

Monotonic logic allows conclusions to be drawn from assumptions, and if more assumptions are added, the new conclusions will not make the previous conclusions wrong. For example, "If X is a bird and birds can fly, then X can fly" is monotonic logic. But what if X is a dead bird or a penguin? As you can see, monotonic logic doesn't always hold true. Nonmonotonic logic adapts to this by saying "X can fly unless something prevents it." In other words, it allows for unusual situations.

Another approach has been taken by other researchers, primarily Marvin Minsky at MIT and Roger Schank at the Institute for Learning Studies, Evanston (Ill.). It is based on the **script theory,** which says that in any particular situation, humans have an idea of how the thinking or dialogue would go. For instance, we each have a dentist's office script, a classroom script, and a restaurant script. Memories of past events are filed in our minds under keys associated with the structure of these scripts.

What these researchers want is to give the computer a way to use common sense and make inferences based on the situation at hand. Their approaches are symbolic. Recently, more attention has been given to **neural networks,** which are nonsymbolic methods of dealing with AI. Neural network models are interconnected nodes, or units, that include some functional features of neurons in the brain. A neural network has no explicit set of rules, but makes up its own rules that match the data as it comes in. It can learn from experience—that is, it can be trained through thousands of samples to pick out the chilies from the leaves, to read handwritten zip codes, to screen luggage and other airline cargo for plastic explosives, and to evaluate mortgage-loan risks. Current neural networks are computer programs, but some companies are developing new hardware, including analog chips, for neural networks. (Analog chips store information as a continuous range of values, which would help in better voice recognition devices, for example.)

If AI is to be developed further, experts need more accurate descriptions of human thought processes, improved programming for imitating those processes, large data bases, and improved hardware architecture.

Voice Recognition

Although the simplest way to input data into a computer is to speak, voice recognition technology is still primitive. ''Speaker-independent'' systems—those that accept a variety of voices—are expensive and have a vocabulary limited to a few dozen words. More versatile systems must be trained by the user to understand a particular vocabulary and recognize the user's voice pitch, accent, and inflection (see Figure 18–3). Each word must be enunciated and spoken discretely, that is, not run together with other words in a phrase.

Because of these limitations, voice recognition is best used with short-answer data and vocabularies limited to a particular subject, such as stocks or airline reservations. Research in voice recognition now focuses on the ability to accept larger vocabularies, different voices, and continuous, or flowing, speech.

FIGURE 18–3

Voice Recognition System
Despite his cerebral palsy this attorney can write briefs and documents himself using the DragonDictate system from Dragon Systems, Inc.

Some experts believe that keyboardless systems based on voice recognition and AI will become popular in the future. Users could hook the systems to their telephone lines to access just about any data base, leave messages on electronic bulletin boards, and conduct transactions—all without a single keystroke. Such systems would need to recognize natural language and overcome the problems associated with syntax and ambiguity. Users would not need to type specific codes or speak according to a standard question format but could simply request information in the same way they might ask another person. They could also direct computers to write application programs from general descriptions of need. Natural language would provide a simple yet precise way of stating these descriptions. (See Chapter 12 for a discussion of natural languages).

Robotics

Robotics will change as AI develops, too. Scientists are working hard to develop robots that are more mobile and sophisticated. Existing robots are deficient in four areas: vision, touch, mobility, and methods of instruction.

Perhaps the most crucial problem to overcome is that of vision. Robots see in only two dimensions, length and width; unlike humans they do not judge depth. Some scientists are designing robots that use fiber-optic ''eyes'' as tiny cameras for relaying images to their computers. As AI becomes more sophisticated, engineers can program robots to ''see'' objects and rotate them until recognition is possible. Robots with this capability work as bin-pickers, sorting different parts from huge baskets of parts used in building machinery or other products. When special chips designed for processing and analyzing images are perfected, the robots can recognize objects much faster through parallel processing. With these advances, robots would be able to navigate throughout a person's home without bumping into objects. A robot could travel to the next room through a door, rather than being stopped by the wall. In addition, when confronted with an object in its path, the robot could decide whether to roll over it, move it out of the way, travel around it, or call for help.

A second difficulty, robot touch, has improved greatly with the development of sophisticated sensors. Some robots are equipped with several kinds of hands—after all, a robot does not really care what it looks like! Ichiro Kato has developed a robot hand dexterous enough to play a Schumann melody on the piano. Karen Hensley, a robot researcher, designed a hand with a janitor's light bulb gripper that enables a robot to turn a doorknob. Other robot hands can pick up a raw egg as easily as a paperweight. Computer-driven robot arms can feed a bedridden patient and assist in nursing care.

Although most sensors are used to give robots skills in handling objects, scientists are experimenting with sensors that enable a robot to maintain balance while walking. Most of today's mobile robots travel on wheels, with the front two wheels providing the power to move and the back one or two wheels acting as balancers. Walking robots must maintain their own balance, and how do you program balance? Research in designing walking robots has been aided by a desk-high robot that bounces around on one leg, as if riding a pogo stick. The longer the robot can keep its balance, the more successful the engineers have been.

Finally, a robot is useless without an adequate way to receive instructions, learn new tasks, and even make rudimentary decisions. Most industrial robots are just one or two steps more advanced than human-operated machines. The features that distinguish them are their typical crane, or arm, and their ability to operate by themselves once the instructions are completed. Although current software can guide a robot to weld, drill holes, trim vinyl dashboards, paint fenders, sort parts, and assemble minute electronic components, robots cannot use a bank of programs in learning a new job or making decisions. In order to pass rigorous tests for home or hospital use, a mobile robot or robot arm must be able to distinguish between a glass of water and a cup of soup. It must recognize its master's voice and respond to natural language commands. It must recognize objects in its path and determine whether to proceed or stop. It must be able to sense how fast it is moving and how tightly it is clutching. And it must be able to synthesize existing programs so that the user can program it by simple English statements to do new tasks. All these abilities stem from research into human learning behavior and AI (see Figure 18–4).

Many robotics researchers try to solve these four problems with traditional methods of AI. Rodney Brooks at MIT, however, believes that robots do not need as much brain power as thought. He is designing small robots that look like insects and, in fact, are patterned after the way insects respond to the environment. The insectoid robots do not store information about having just completed a job, but act according to each new condition encountered. In the appropriate sizes, these robots could be used for exploring the surface of Mars, scouring barnacles off the hulls of ships, cleaning plaque from arteries, and checking under collapsed bridges for victims of earthquakes. With each new development in robotics, scientists predict that robots will even help quadriplegics the way seeing-eye dogs help the blind.

CONCEPT SUMMARY 18–1

Improvements in Technology

Idea	Improvement
Gallium arsenide chips	These chips are five to seven times faster than silicon chips, and help avoid the problem of cross talk
Organic Circuits	In theory, organic circuits would be much smaller and more powerful than today's chips and would use light instead of electrical current
Parallel processing	This concept allows computers to use two or more CPUs to process data simultaneously rather than in sequence
Lasers	Lasers in fiber optics improve telecommunications, and lasers can be used in the manufacture of chips and, eventually, may be placed on the chips
Voice recognition	New voice-recognition systems would be able to accept larger vocabularies, different voices, and continuous or flowing speech
Robotics	Research in robotics is geared toward improving robot vision, touch, mobility, and methods of receiving instruction

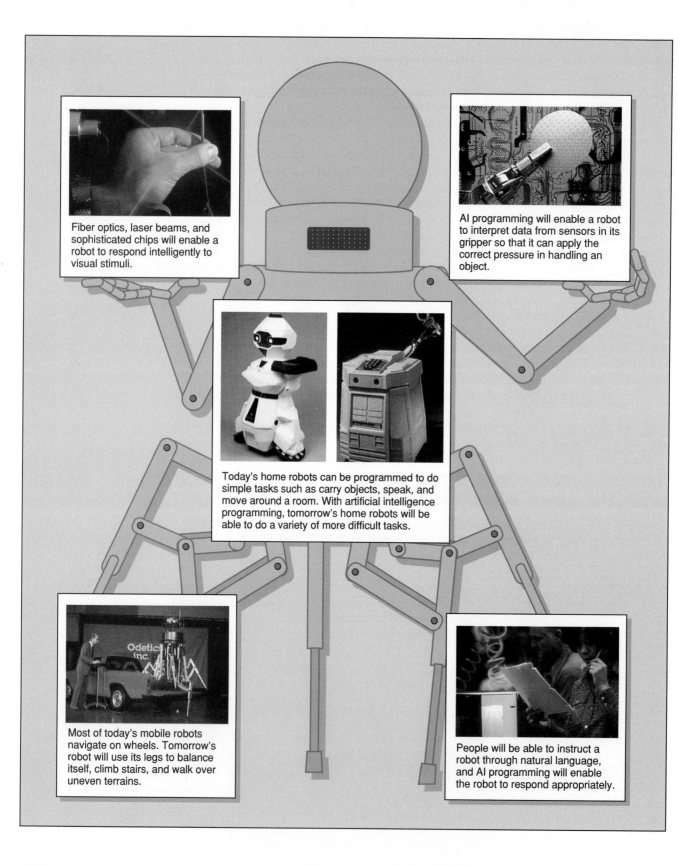

Fiber optics, laser beams, and sophisticated chips will enable a robot to respond intelligently to visual stimuli.

AI programming will enable a robot to interpret data from sensors in its gripper so that it can apply the correct pressure in handling an object.

Today's home robots can be programmed to do simple tasks such as carry objects, speak, and move around a room. With artificial intelligence programming, tomorrow's home robots will be able to do a variety of more difficult tasks.

Most of today's mobile robots navigate on wheels. Tomorrow's robot will use its legs to balance itself, climb stairs, and walk over uneven terrains.

People will be able to instruct a robot through natural language, and AI programming will enable the robot to respond appropriately.

▪ COMPUTERS IN MEDICINE

FIGURE 18–4

(Opposite Page) Synthesizing
Concepts of AI into a Robot

Medical personnel diagnose illnesses, provide treatments, and monitor patients. Computer technology is used in facilitating the timeliness and accuracy of these jobs, which in turn affects the quality of life.

Computer-Assisted Diagnosis

Computers are increasingly combined with testing equipment to provide diagnostic tools in hospitals and clinics (see Figure 18–5). Four common forms—multiphasic health testing, expert systems, computerized axial tomography, and nuclear magnetic resonance scanning—help with preventive health care and offer nonsurgical testing techniques. In **multiphasic health testing,** computer equipment aids in performing a series of tests, stores the results of the tests, and reports the results to doctors. Physical examinations are performed by trained technicians and paramedics using the computer equipment. Procedures include electrocardiograms, X-ray tests, blood tests, vision and hearing tests, blood pressure tests, and height and weight measurement. The computer system compares the results of the tests to predetermined standards of normal health. The patient's physician receives a report of the test results and meets with the patient. Multiphasic testing permits the doctor to spend more time on diagnosis and treatment, and can be valuable in preventive health care.

Expert systems also help physicians in making diagnoses. Among the early expert systems are MYCIN, developed at Stanford University for diagnosing diseases, and Chest Pain, developed by Dr. Evlin Kinney, a research cardiologist in Miami Beach, Florida, for analyzing chest pain. A newer system designed as a neural network is PAPNET, by Neuromedical Systems, Inc. It is used to spot suspect cells in pap smears. Medical expert systems provide only one factor for consideration in making a diagnosis. The physician or lab technician may want to reason through his or her conclusions again if they differ from the diagnosis offered by the expert system.

FIGURE 18–5

Computers in Diagnosis

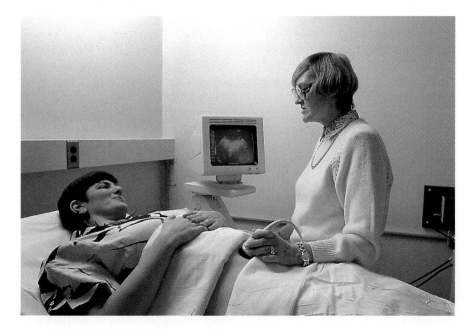

FIGURE 18–6

CAT Scan

A technician studies the image produced by a CAT scan that will help diagnose a medical problem.

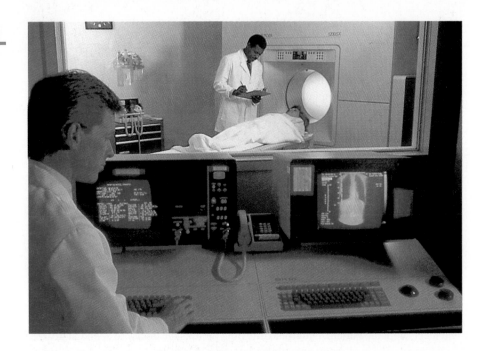

Computerized axial tomography, commonly known as CAT scanning, is a diagnostic aid that joins two tools—X-rays and computerized evaluations of X-ray pictures. A CAT scan can do something that ordinary X-ray tests cannot: it can provide clear pictures of cross-sections of the body. Using many cross-sections together provides a three-dimensional composite of an organ or bone (see Figure 18–6). Some CAT scan systems can construct a three-dimensional image of a human organ on a video monitor and re-create the actual movement of the organ in the simulated organ on the screen. Doctors are thus able to identify parts of the organ that are not functioning normally.

Nuclear magnetic resonance (NMR) scanning may soon replace the CAT scan in hospitals. In fact, many smaller hospitals are now purchasing the NMR machines. Unlike X-ray tests or CAT scans, NMR can "see" through thick bones. Moreover, NMR works without radiation. Magnetic pulses react differently when they come into contact with different parts of the body. A computer is used for collecting the results and creating a detailed picture of the inside of the body. Often NMR scanning is more successful in detecting problems than CAT scanning. Since the procedure does not use radiation, it can be used for testing children and pregnant women. There are some drawbacks to NMR scanning, however. For example, it does not produce clear images of bones or spot breast cancer. A more advanced level of magnetic resonance scanning can detect biochemical changes in the body and monitor the effects of heart medications and cancer drugs.

Both CAT scans and NMR scans allow doctors to conduct tests without invading the body through surgery. This prevents the infections, blood clots, and fatigue associated with surgery.

Computers also help ensure the success of reconstructive surgery. Computer-generated pictures can predict the results of reconstructive surgery. In the case of a patient with a deformed skull, CAT scan cross-sections are used to produce three-dimensional pictures of the skull. The computer studies the results of the CAT scan

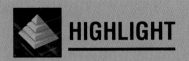
Practice Makes Perfect

Computer technology is making its mark in the area of surgery, just as it has in so many other areas of expertise. Dr. Richard Robb of the Mayo Clinic/Foundation has developed a program that allows doctors to practice surgical procedures before performing the actual surgery on patients. The program is capable of taking information about a patient from X rays and producing three- and four-dimensional images that the surgeon can practice ''operating'' on.

The program, called Analyze, was started by Dr. Robb and a team of five developers in 1975. Currently, there are more than eighty physicians, scientists, and researchers using Analyze to practice surgery and conduct medical research. One area where the program is of particular benefit is brain surgery. The program is capable of accurately displaying to within 1 mm the actual spot in the brain being operated on.

With a program such as Analyze, the risk to the patient can be reduced significantly. By being able to practice before going into the operating room, all possible circumstances can be recognized and dealt with before the operation begins.

In addition to real world situations, a program such as Analyze is extremely valuable in training new surgeons. In the past, a surgeon's knowledge was limited to personal experience or knowledge passed on from other doctors. With Analyze, a surgeon's base of knowledge and experience can be increased by employing the computer as a patient.

and presents a picture of the skull after reconstruction. Models based on the computer picture help the doctor plan the proper surgical techniques. They also help the patient visualize the outcome of the surgery.

The applications of computers in medicine are almost limitless. In the future computers could be used for testing the skills and efficiency of doctors. Computers may also be combined with robots for performing delicate surgery, sometimes from another location across the country. In addition, computers are used increasingly in hospitals and doctors' offices in everyday record-keeping and accounting procedures.

Computer-Assisted Treatment

New uses for computers in treatment are emerging daily, while other uses are being improved. For example, due to microprocessors, today's pacemakers are lighter in weight than earlier models. In addition, they can simulate the beating of a healthy heart: doctors can enter up to thirty separate functions, such as delay between pulses, pulse width, and energy output per pulse. In this way, a pacemaker can deal with each patient's particular heart problems.

Microprocessors also control the movements of artificial limbs. Electrical signals from muscles in an amputee's upper arms, for instance, can generate natural movements in an artificial arm and hand. These new artificial limbs are so sophisticated that they are powerful enough to open jars or crack walnuts, yet deft enough to pick up a tomato or a styrofoam cup full of coffee.

A person who must wear an artificial leg can now look forward to a light-weight leg with a comfortable socket. The leg, made at the Sabolich Prosthetic & Research Center in Oklahoma City, contains an electronic system that enables its wearer to

FIGURE 18–7

The Oklahoma City Running Leg
Wearing an Oklahoma City running leg, this teenager is able to run normally, step over step.

feel the ground (see Figure 18–7). Sensors in the foot send signals to the wearer's skin through wires, electrodes, and a small transmitter. The brain interprets these tingling sensations as pressure from the foot. The harder the wearer presses, the more signal he or she gets. This helps the wearer maintain balance. The center has also developed a prototype sense-of-feel hand with sensors in the thumb and index finger. Other researchers are working on chips that can bridge active nerve tissue with limbs that no longer operate due to stroke or injury.

Microprocessors are also being used for the controlled release of medications. One experimental device being tested by diabetic patients dispenses a forty-day supply of insulin from a refillable reservoir using a miniature pump. The reservoir is refilled with a hypodermic needle. Radio telemetry and a desktop computer console allow doctors to monitor a diabetic's blood sugar level and reprogram the rate at which the pump dispenses medicine. The device has the potential of eliminating some of the life-threatening side effects of diabetes.

Another use of computers in the treatment of patients involves using computer-controlled lasers. During surgery, lasers are used to destroy tiny, hard-to-reach tumors once considered inoperable. X-ray films taken before surgery pinpoint the tumor's location. The surgeon uses a powerful microscope with a laser attached to it to locate the tumor. After correctly positioning a dot of light that indicates where the laser will strike when activated, the surgeon presses a foot pedal that fires the laser and destroys the tumor. Computer-controlled lasers are also being used in the treatment of kidney stones. A patient being treated for kidney stones is submerged in a tank of water and a computer-controlled laser is aimed at the stone, already located by use of X-rays and dye injections. When the laser strikes the kidney stone, it is dissolved into minute harmless particles. Conventional treatment of kidney stones involves major surgery. The laser technique does not require cutting into the body cavity, thereby eliminating the complications of surgery and reducing the recovery period for the patient.

Scientists perform calculations, simulate real situations, and observe equipment and conditions while doing their research. Because of the enormous volumes of data that must be stored and processed for some scientific tasks, scientists use large computers for handling the data and producing output in a form that is easy to read and interpret. Often the tasks that require large amounts of data involve monitoring the environment, chemical industries, nuclear power plants, and the weather (see Figure 18–8). Immediate alert to problems in these areas is crucial. For example, the crisis that occurred at the Three Mile Island nuclear power plant when the temperature of the nuclear reactor exceeded safe limits and threatened to melt down the core may be avoided in the future with emergency management systems. The fatal gas leak at the Union Carbide plant in Bhopal, India, might have been prevented with advanced computerized warning systems.

San Francisco Bay residents will be glad when they can receive accurate and timely predictions of earthquakes. In the last decade, scientists have begun to estimate the long-term probability of major earthquakes along the San Andreas fault, using careful analysis of past earthquakes and new geologic data gathered from an extensive array of state-of-the-art instruments. These instruments include strain meters, which measure changes in the deformation of rock at a single point; the two-color laser geodimeter, which shoots a laser beam between hilltops to detect changes in the distance between them as small as 1 millimeter; and seismometers, which measure the motions of the earth. Data from these and other instruments are sent to computers that monitor and analyze the data and automatically contact geologists of any significant changes. Scientists are trying to analyze which of the instruments work best.

Computer models of earthquakes can help with predictions. The model considers an area's history of earthquakes, the locations of small quakes, the character of the rocks in the area, and other factors. Techniques are also available for analyzing disturbances in sediments and soil structures that indicate a history of earthquakes

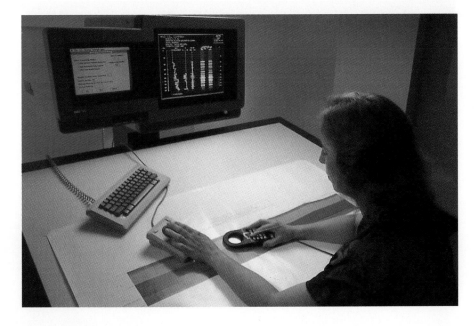

FIGURE 18–8

Computers in Science
This petroleum engineer searches for oil using an Explorations Systems workstation.

in a given area. Using the model and the data from the instruments, scientists can begin to estimate when earthquakes will happen in a given region.

Another application of scientific monitoring involves volcano watching. The May 1980 prediction of the eruption of Mount St. Helens in the state of Washington was predicted by scientists with the help of data analyzed by computers. Devices such as tiltmeters, which show trends in the tilt of the crater floor, and seismometers, which measure harmonic tremors around the volcano, sent data to a laboratory in Vancouver, Washington, every ten minutes. In the laboratory, computers analyzed that data, helping scientists predict volcanic activity. Because instruments like these are located inside the volcano, volcanic eruptions can be predicted within thirty minutes; this allows time for scientists working near and on the volcano to be quickly evacuated by helicopter. One thing that cannot be predicted, however, is the fury of the eruption and the extent of the mudflow it creates. Mount St. Helens, one of the most heavily monitored volcanoes in the world, surprised the scientists monitoring it with the heavy mudflow that followed its eruption.

The forecasting of weather is one of the most interesting applications of computers. The world's weather information, which includes variables such as air pressure, wind velocity, humidity, and temperature, is collected by the National Weather Service in Maryland from a variety of locations: hundreds of data-collecting programs (DCPs) placed on buoys, ships, weather balloons, and airplanes; about seventy weather stations; and four satellites. Computers housed at the meteorological center use incoming data from the DCPs to construct a mathematical description of the atmosphere. Forecasters use the results to prepare weather reports that are sent to local weather offices.

Even with the computing power of a new Cray Y-MP supercomputer, the weather forecast is only reliable up to six or six and a half days and cannot show how and when thunder clouds spawn tornadoes. This was readily shown when the weather service did not predict a tornado in Plainfield, Illinois, that left 28 people dead. In addition, a part that could have helped predict the dangerous storm had been sent to Atlanta weeks earlier for repair. To deal with similar problems, the U.S. government is planning a nationwide modernization of the weather service that includes five new

FIGURE 18–9

Numerically Modeled Storm
Numerical models of thunderstorms can help scientists understand the development of severe weather. The separation of updraft, represented by orange particles, and downdraft, represented by blue particles, is crucial for understanding storms.

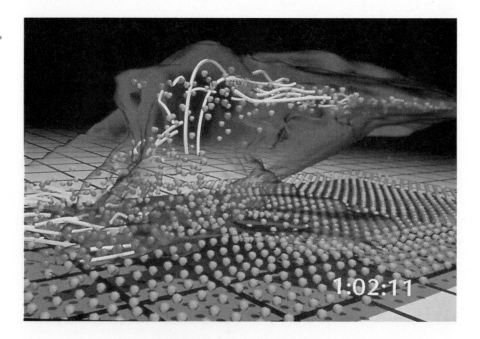

satellites, advanced storm-detection radars with easily replaceable parts, special radars designed to measure upper air winds, automated systems for recording surface weather conditions, and computer workstations for interpreting and displaying data. Weather forecasters will use a new algorithm for condensing data into graphic forms that are easy to read and monitor for changes (see Figure 18–9).

CONCEPT SUMMARY 18–2	
Computers in Medicine and Science	
Diagnosis	Multiphasic health testing Expert systems Computerized axial tomography (CAT) scanning Nuclear magnetic resonance (NMR)
Monitoring	Monitoring systems (for chemical plants and nuclear plants) Volcanic and earthquake activity Weather
Procedures	Pacemakers Artificial limbs Microprocessor-controlled release of medications Laser surgery

◘ COMPUTERS FOR ALL OF US

Much of our discussion has centered on computer technology that benefits research and industry. Eventually, the technology will trickle down into our everyday lives. In the meantime, what can we expect in the near future in the areas of personal computing, laser technology, and education? The following sections discuss ways in which we might use the new technologies at home and at school.

Computers at Home

Most of us are already dependent upon computers in ways that we may not notice. We conduct most of our transactions through computers at stores and banks. We send our automobiles to service centers that use computers to diagnose problems with timing, fuel mix, and emissions (see Figure 18–10). The weather reports, animated movies, and special effects that we see on television are computer-generated. Now, many analysts are predicting that home computer use will increase as fast, easy-to-use computers are available. In addition, they believe that more people will get used to making transactions from home computers and having fun with home-control and robotic devices linked to the computers. Some of these applications will become routine as people seek to avoid the costs and irritations of driving to run small errands. Homes of the future will not only be labor- and energy-saving for the homeowner, but also will help handicapped people to achieve independence.

FIGURE 18–10

Computerized Automobile Diagnosis
and Repair

The microcomputers that will be used at home in the future will have powerful graphics and computational capabilities. They will use less power than a 150-watt lightbulb. Screen displays will be larger and have a higher degree of resolution. The amount of memory will increase to handle many types of applications including artificial intelligence and intelligent tutors. Some computers will come in unexpected shapes, such as pens. And the prices will be affordable for most families.

Families will use their computers and telephones to conduct some banking and purchasing transactions and keep up with the status of their bank accounts, credit ratings, and store charges. They will receive video versions of major newspapers, stock market reports, restaurant listings, computer graphic art, music, and movie reviews. They will be able to finish high school or take college courses for credit through their microcomputers. They will learn to program their computers for customized tasks by inputting commands in English (or whatever language they speak naturally). Finally, they will use microcomputers increasingly in controlling the home environment and security. The center of the home may even move from the kitchen and fireplace to a new center, the electronic hearth where all these activities will take place, occurring primarily through a voice recognition interface.

Today, there are many showcase homes, including spectacular examples in the United States, Holland, and Japan, that are governed by state-of-the-art electronic devices. One such home has sensors in the floor that control lighting as a person walks through the rooms. A tracking system with infrared and microwave detectors monitors everyone's location. Drapes in the bedroom open automatically at daybreak, upon which the bathroom floor and towels warm up and the shower turns on at just the right temperature. A computer voice delivers voice mail and reminders of chores that need to be done. In one room, a retractable roof opens, but if it starts to rain, sensors will detect the moisture and direct the closing of the roof.

Computers are everywhere in the form of pen-based pads for recording appointments and other important information. Television, sound systems, and other entertainment components are computer-controlled. Heating, cooling, ventilation, and air

proach, and rooms greet everyone by name. The security system includes cameras, password-controlled entry doors, and fire alarms.

Less elaborate systems are available for new and existing homes. These systems govern appliance use and regulate energy consumption and ventilation (see Figure 18–11). In addition, most of us will be using appliances that incorporate chips with **fuzzy logic.** Fuzzy logic simulates human thinking and tolerates imprecision. It quantifies concepts such as pretty close, quite far, hot, cold, very unlikely, somewhat heavy, almost full, and so forth. Almost all new Japanese appliances use it. Washing machines use it to detect the amount of detergent and the water temperature needed to wash a tub of clothes. Toasters use it to determine when the bread is toasted. Cameras use it to adjust the picture if the photographer's hand trembles. As you can see, computers will soon be ubiquitous.

Interactive Video

The combination of optical disks and computer programming has created a promising tool called **interactive video.** Some educators believe it will replace the computer, the instructional film, and perhaps even textbooks in many fields. Interactive video merges graphics and sound with computer-generated text by linking an optical disk (videodisk), a videodisk player, a microcomputer with a color monitor and disk drive, and computer software. Using this equipment, a person can watch news footage of historical events, learn about the most current advances in science, and listen to the music of great composers or the speeches of famous people. The interactive process begins when the user responds to computer-generated questions and forms inquiries to input into the system (see Figure 18–12). The videodisk can be accessed at a chosen point, and motion sequences can be shown in slow motion or still frame for observing critical details.

Videodisk technology will change the way we share information. As a student, you may receive a homework package consisting of software on a floppy disk and graphics on a videodisk to play on your equipment at home. As an employee, you could use the technology for learning how to show new cars, trade shares on a stock exchange, or maintain and repair large earth-moving equipment. As a consumer, you will buy huge data bases of information on any topic ranging from medical subjects to career guidance or browse through videodisk catalogs of the latest merchandise.

FIGURE 18–11

Home Control System
Unity Systems Inc. markets a home control system that is activated from a wall-mounted touchscreen.

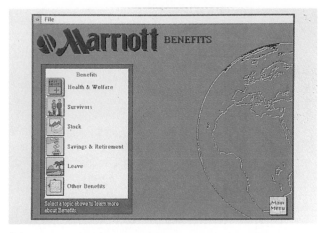

(a)

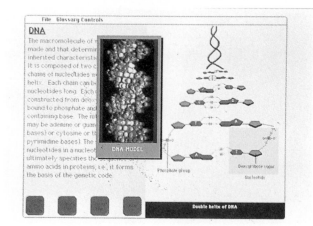

(b)

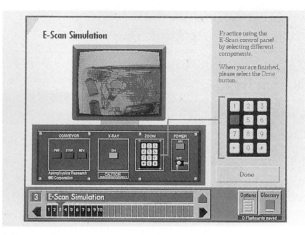

(c)

(d)

FIGURE 18–12

Authorware® Interactive Video Applications

a) University students can view employment information about Marriott Corporation through an interactive recruiting kiosk called The World of Marriott.

b) Encounters with Biology *is a reference application on biological reproduction used by general biology students at Ohio State University.*

c) Part of the American Airlines International Security Course requires students to use interactive lessons on the operation of the luggage X-ray machine.

d) The Emergency Response Simulator *is a prototype application to teach oil refinery employees safety procedures and disaster prevention.*

Interactive video has become so attractive that some people believe the videodisk player will become the most important peripheral device of this decade. The technology will become even more appealing when disks are developed that can be erased and reused. It will become one more technology to add to our electronic hearth.

Interactive video is currently being swallowed by the term **multimedia,** which covers the entire range of multisensory, interactive experiences now reaching consumers (see Figure 18–13). Multimedia includes sound, vision, and interactive components and may be accessed from CD-ROMs or through networks. Users can employ a special kind of data base system, called hypertext, to see all objects related to a particular object they are studying. For example, while reading information about the Civil War, a user might choose songs, upon which a score might appear or a song might be played. Icons used to view associated items are called hypertext links, or buttons. Eventually, multimedia will be capable of synthesizing speech and enabling musical improvisation.

To write hypertext or multimedia applications, a person would use an authoring tool. An authoring tool enables a person to create a final application by linking together objects, such as written text, a graph, a drawing, and music or sound effects. Some teachers believe that students should use multimedia and authoring tools to create

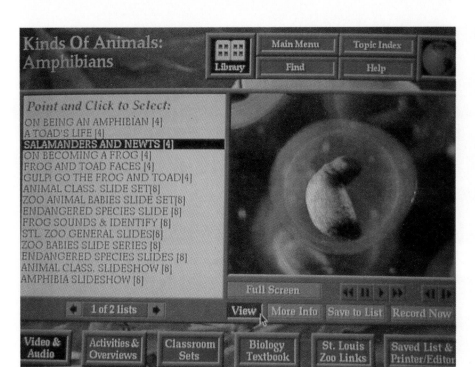

FIGURE 18–13

Multimedia

their own productions rather than using commercial programs. In fact, in the future, multimedia may replace standardized tests and teacher-made tests as a method of assessing student progress.

Virtual Reality

The ultimate in multimedia technology is **virtual reality,** in which three-dimensional images are delivered through blacked-out goggles and gloves bristling with wires, creating the illusion of being inside and moving through a scene. Inside the goggles, two slightly different views of a scene are projected on tiny liquid crystal screens. Because neither eye perceives the scene from exactly the same perspective, a three-dimensional effect is produced (see Figure 18–14). Moving the head changes the view, just as in real life. The Lycra glove, a data glove loaded with sensors and optical fibers, enables the user to manipulate the virtual objects.

Virtual reality has been used by pilots-in-training to learn how to fly and land airplanes. Caterpillar is testing virtual reality models of its earthmovers to improve performance and visibility. Writers who use computers could use virtual reality to flip through a manuscript as if it were a stack of papers. A homeowner could "walk through" a virtual model of the new kitchen and family room being planned. Already, Nintendo users can pull on a Mattel Power Glove and play virtual handball on a virtual court with a virtual opponent.

Virtual reality can be used to test the convenience and location of instruments in an airplane, appliances in a kitchen, and buttons on a factory control panel before the products are ever built. It could be used to teach new surgical techniques to surgeons. It could be used to teach mathematical concepts to students. Since students

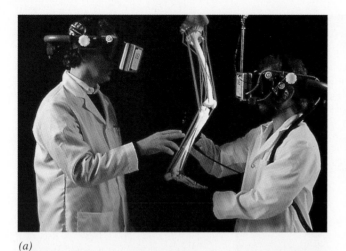
(a)

(b)

(c)

(d)

FIGURE 18–14

Virtual Reality

a) Using data gloves, doctors can manipulate the anatomy of a virtual leg.

b) A Ninendo power glove enables this boy to interact with Super Mario Brothers.

c) A grad student programs house plans into a virtual reality system that will enable 3-D tours of the facility before it is built.

d) Air-traffic controllers in the next decade may be using virtual reality equipment to guide planes.

comprehend images much faster than columns of numbers, they could use virtual reality programs to study algebra and physics. Literature could come alive, and history be experienced.

Education and Employees of the Future

Some futurists believe that one day almost every type of job will require employees to use computers. Education will certainly change through computer use and access to data bases. Most transactions will take place via computers and telecommunications. People with little computer experience will be profoundly affected. They will not be able to access a data base, read the material on the screen, or hold a job that requires a great deal of computer use. Therefore, some educators are pressing for extensive computer education in schools.

Computer education includes computer literacy and computer programming. Computer literacy courses teach technical knowledge about computers, the ability to use computers in solving problems, and awareness of how computers affect society. Programming classes often involve learning to program a computer in popular programming languages.

Toward a Cashless Society

Are we moving closer and closer to a cashless society? Many experts feel that the move to such a society will occur in two phases. In the first phase, debit cards—currently popular in Europe—will be used for payment of common services such as public telephones, public parking, vending machines, and public transportation. As these debit cards gain popularity, movement toward a truly cashless society will continue as banks and other companies develop and market smart cards that are actually capable of accessing an individual's bank account.

Companies such as Visa and Mastercard believe that smart cards will be vital to our society in the future. For smart cards to work, however, establishments accepting the cards must be connected to a network that can access the necessary accounts—so as to be able to verify purchases. This requirement has led Visa and Mastercard to take steps to improve their telecommunications networks. They will have to stand ready to handle a potential landslide of transactions. Visa and Mastercard believe that smart cards will ultimately replace cash and checks for making purchases. Taking into consideration such innovations as direct deposit of payroll checks and electronic funds transfer, both of which we already see, it is conceivable that our children or grandchildren might never need to even touch cash.

On the other hand, other researchers believe that computer education as a prerequisite for jobs is largely a myth. They say that only a small percentage of jobs will require actual knowledge of technical areas involving electronic circuits, computer programming, and hardware. Rather, they believe that reading and thinking skills and general knowledge will distinguish the haves from the have-nots (see Figure 18–15). If computers are to be used, they must become tools for learning these skills. Educators group software packages meant for teaching into an all-encompassing category: **computer-assisted instruction (CAI).** Through CAI, students encounter a patient "teacher" that allows them to learn at their own rates, receive immediate feedback, and feel comfortable with both successes and mistakes (see Figure 18–16). Included in CAI is a wide selection of software:

FIGURE 18–15

Computers in Higher Education

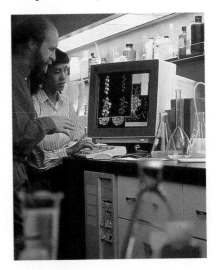

- Drills for quizzing the student.
- Tutorials for introducing students to new material and skills and quizzing them on their understanding of the material.
- Simulations that imitate real-world situations, allowing students to learn through experience and induction without having to take actual risks.
- Games for learning new concepts and practicing new skills.
- Problem-solving software that encourages exploration and application of previous knowledge.
- Multimedia experiences and productions.

The trend toward accountability in measuring how much a student learns may make the drills and tutorial attractive to teachers. But more than this, educators increasingly realize the importance of computer use in developing thinking skills.

Regardless of which computer skills are learned, people are realizing the many ways in which computers can help them learn, conduct business, take care of their

FIGURE 18–16

Microcomputers in Elementary School

health, and achieve competency at work. Although not everyone may learn how to write a computer program or how a computer works, most people can learn to use computers in meeting challenges of the future and enriching their lives.

❑ SUMMARY POINTS

■ Scientists are working on strategies to overcome two major problems with miniaturizing integrated circuits: heat generation and cross talk.

■ Gallium arsenide can be used to make chips that are faster, require less power, generate less heat, and are more resistant to radiation than silicon chips.

■ Scientists are trying to merge organic materials and computers to develop organic chips. The technology is largely theoretical, although biosensors and organic switches have been developed.

■ Research in fiber optics aids telecommunication development because digital pulses can be sent through the glass fibers. Fiber optics will be instrumental in bringing wide variety of information services into our homes. Some scientists are trying to build computers based on light rather than electrical circuits.

■ Parallel processing facilitates development of applications using forms of artificial intelligence because processing occurs simultaneously rather than serially.

■ Today's artificial intelligence applications are called expert systems. These systems imitate an expert in a field, drawing conclusions and making recommendations based on a huge data base. Some scientists believe expert systems are not true artificial intelligence. Neural networks learn from experience.

■ Principles of AI can improve voice recognition systems. Research focuses on the ability to accept larger vocabularies, different voices, and continuous or flowing speech.

■ Artificial intelligence will increase robot powers of sight and touch, help robots walk, and give them the ability to make decisions.

■ Computers are increasingly combined with testing equipment to provide diagnostic tools in hospitals and clinics. In multiphasic health testing (MPHT), computer equipment aids in performing a series of tests, stores the results of the tests, and reports the results to doctors. Doctors also use expert systems that help diagnose various conditions, including blood diseases and chest pain, for example.

■ Two noninvasive diagnostic aids used in hospitals and clinics are computerized axial tomography (CAT or CT), commonly known as a CAT scan, and nuclear magnetic resonance (NMR) scanning.

■ Microprocessors help in treatments, for example, in pacemakers, artificial limbs, and medication delivery systems.

■ Laser surgery for such conditions as kidney stones allows a surgeon to destroy the stones without cutting into a person.

■ Scientists use computers for solving many problems including monitoring chemical plants, nuclear plants, earthquakes, volcanoes, and the weather.

■ People will begin to use microcomputers for many tasks at home: monitoring energy consumption and security, accessing commercial data bases, performing business transactions, taking high school or college courses, and entertaining themselves.

■ Home appliances will increasingly be controlled by fuzzy logic chips.

■ Because of the potential for interactive video (learning in an interactive way using a computer system), some experts believe the videodisk player will become the most important peripheral device for microcomputer systems in this decade.

■ Multimedia is an all-encompassing term for the multisensory and interactive qualities of computer use. The ultimate in multimedia is virtual reality, in which a user experiences a virtual scene in three dimensions.

■ Some experts believe people who cannot use computers will be the newly disadvantaged. Others believe reading and thinking skills and general knowledge will determine the haves and have-nots of the future. Students can use computers for computer-assisted instruction (CAI) to learn such skills. CAI software includes drills, tutorials, simulations, games, and problem-solving software.

■ TERMS FOR REVIEW

◾ REVIEW QUESTIONS

1. What problems arise when scientists try to place more and more electronic components in a fixed amount of space?

2. Discuss two ways that scientists are trying to solve the problems indicated in question 1.

3. What do parallel processing and the human brain have in common? What are some applications where parallel processing might be used?

4. Describe what is meant by the term *artificial intelligence.* In what ways can you imagine artificial intelligence being used in the future?

5. Explain two ways in which researchers believe human knowledge can be incorporated into a computer.

6. How might voice recognition be used in the future? Outline some of your own thoughts, not necessarily those cited in the text.

7. What role do you think robots will play in our future? Will we eventually just sit back after programming the robots and not do any work at all?

8. Describe three ways in which microprocessors are being used to treat patients.

9. How would modernization of the Weather Service increase the reliability of the forecast?

10. What are some uses of interactive video and multimedia? Can you think of any that were not discussed in the text?

Mount Sinai Medical Center

Mount Sinai Medical Center, with over 1,120 beds, is one of the ten largest hospitals in the United States. It is spread over eight square city blocks and has a staff of nearly 7,000 clerical and professional employees. The annual operating budget is over $300 million.

The hospital was incorporated in 1852. In 1963, it added the Mount Sinai School of Medicine, affiliated with the City University of New York. Through making medical staff and facilities available to U.S. military personnel, the hospital has supported U.S. military operations from the Civil War to the Desert Storm operation. It is a major research hospital, specializing in cancer and inflammatory bowel disease.

CREATING AN INTEGRATED SYSTEM

As is the case with most large hospitals, Mount Sinai's data-processing operations evolved on a departmental basis with little central control or thought to the possibility of developing an institutional integration or much interaction between departments. Adding to this difficulty, the departmental approach left the medical center with a variety of hardware and software from different vendors to be pulled together to establish the desired integrated environment. Therefore, when it was decided to create an integrated system, serious problems had to be overcome.

The data-processing department identified over thirty areas of application which they believed essential if the medical center were to maintain the highest level of strategic management control and patient care efficiency. Financial applications represented some of the most obvious requirements. Therefore, a number of financial support systems were implemented. An online general ledger, budget, and cost accounting system provided instant access to a central data base. An integrated accounts payable, purchasing, and inventory system allowed departmental requests to be electronically transmitted and all information to be available for processing by each department concerned. An integrated payroll and human resources system kept track of deductions, advances to union dues, vacation and sick leave accrual and created ad hoc reports for human resources management as required. In addition, an integrated inpatient/outpatient management data base handled patient scheduling preadmission, admission, communications, and billing functions. Point-of-service terminals provided easy access to data bases.

MEETING FUTURE NEEDS

In March of 1989, the hospital received approval from the state of New York for the implementation of a family of new computer information systems. State approval led to the infusion of nearly $25 million in capital for the systems. The new systems will replace existing ones with state-of-the-art systems to automate large portions of the patient medical record, bringing computerized medical information to the patient bedside. They will provide enhanced operational and financial-management capabilities and establish a base of information to further the hospital's research mission.

LabCare at Mount Sinai analyzes blood and tissue samples and inputs the results into a data base accessible to authorized users hospital-wide.

The first components of the new system were installed in late 1989. They consisted of new systems for admissions, discharge and transfer, inventory, payroll, and accounts payable. Systems for pharmacy and radiology information management are currently being implemented. The

APPLICATION
Mount Sinai Medical Center

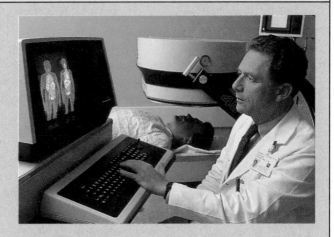

hospital information department is evaluating replacements for patient billing systems. It is also looking at a computerized system for keeping up-to-date on physician credentials information and is examining internal computerized mechanisms for ensuring the quality of patient care.

Mount Sinai acquired a state-of-the-art Amdahl mainframe computer to replace existing mainframes, bringing the current processing power to some 30 times the computing power it had in 1989. A new IBM minicomputer was also purchased for handling the operating room scheduling and management system.

The hospital has expanded its laboratory information system with a new computer and a new version of LabCare. LabCare is a proprietary system from Community Health Computing in Houston, Texas. It is used for recording clinical laboratory data from blood and tissue samples. The samples are submitted to equipment for analysis, whereupon the results are recorded in the data base. Once the data is in the system, authorized users can access the information as needed for evaluation and treatment of the respective patients' medical problems. The new system dramatically extends capabilities for providing access to laboratory data throughout the hospital.

In order to connect the computers to other computers around the hospital, Mount Sinai installed a hospital-wide local area network. It provides the capability to plug personnel computers and larger computers into sockets in the wall in order to link them to any of the other computers within the hospital's system. Hospital employees in nursing stations and offices thus can access the hospital's data bases and, in some areas, use electronic mail capabilities. The LAN provides the capacity for improving immediate patient care and making sure information about patients and treatments is current and accurate.

To make room for hospital expansion, the computers and other equipment were moved to a new data center location. As the conversion to the new system is spread over five years, Mount Sinai continues to study ways to maintain state-of-the-art information systems to serve patients and facilitate research. The new systems will establish a firm base for the hospital's operations well into the year 2000.

DISCUSSION POINTS
1. What were some of the problems that had to be overcome when developing Mount Sinai's integrated system?
2. What is the advantage of the local area network used by Mount Sinai?

■ INTRODUCTION

As was discussed in Chapter 8, each computer operating system has certain conventions that must be followed by the users and programs that interact with the files stored on the computer system. If you have not read the section entitled "IBM PC and MS-DOS Conventions" in Chapter 8, please do so before continuing on with the remainder of this appendix. The material presented in Chapter 8 provides an important foundation for the discussion of the commands that follow. In fact, even if you have previously read the material in Chapter 8, a review of the information regarding files, directories, and paths prior to reading about operating system commands here would be helpful.

■ DISK OPERATING SYSTEM COMMANDS

An operating system consists of a number of programs that control the functions of the computer system. In addition, an operating system provides commands that allow a user of the system to direct the computer in performing certain operations. For example, the user may want to initialize, or format, a disk so that it can be used to store programs and data. The operating system, therefore, must provide the user with some way of formatting a disk. In the case of the IBM PC DOS and MS-DOS operating systems, the FORMAT command is used to initialize or format a disk. The FORMAT command is provided as part of the operating system that is purchased for your personal computer. The remaining sections of this appendix will discuss some of the commonly used IBM PC DOS and MS-DOS commands.

Initializing a Disk

Before a blank disk can be used for storing programs and data, you must **format** or **initialize** it. Formatting prepares the disk so that data and programs can be stored on it according to the specifications of the DOS. When a used disk is reformatted, everything on the disk is erased so that the disk can be used for new data and programs. Never format a disk with data stored on it unless you are sure you no longer need the data.

Each type of computer uses a DOS to format the disks that will be used with it. A disk formatted with a DOS other than one of the MS-DOS versions may not work on an IBM PC DOS or MS-DOS compatible computer. To format a disk for use on an IBM PC DOS or MS-DOS computer, you need the DOS disk that came with the computer and a blank diskette or a disk you would like reformatted.

Directory Commands

The IBM PC DOS and MS-DOS directory commands can be used to create a new subdirectory, remove (delete) an existing subdirectory, change your working directory, and display the list of files in a directory.

MKDIR. The MKDIR command is used to create a subdirectory. The MKDIR command can be shortened to just the letters MD.

IBM PC and MS-DOS Operating System Commands

RMDIR. The command RMDIR is used to remove an existing subdirectory. The RDMIR command can also be shortened to just the letters RD. For example, the commands RMDIR DOS or RD DOS would delete the DOS subdirectory.

CHDIR. The command CHDIR is used to change from one working directory to another. The CHDIR command can also be shortened to just two letters—CD.

Movement from one directory to another can be easy if you understand how to tell the operating system where you want to go. Please refer to Figure A–1 and consider the following example. The user is currently in the directory A:\LEVEL_1\XYZ and would like to go to the directory A:\LEVEL_1\ABC. As you can see in Figure A–1, if the user were to move to this directory one step at a time, he or she would have to move up one directory level and then down into the ABC directory. However, the move from the first directory to the second directory can also be done with just one command. The command would be as follows:

CD A:\LEVEL_1\ABC

Besides explicitly telling the operating system what directory you would like to go to, there are a number of shorthand identifiers that can also be used. The command CD .., for example, changes the working directory to the directory immediately above the directory you are currently in. The command CD \ changes the working directory to the root directory of the current disk drive. In addition, if the directory is on the current disk drive, there is no need to specify the disk drive letter as part of the path name. In the example above, using the command CD\LEVEL_1\ABC would have been the same as using the command CD A:\LEVEL_1\ABC.

FIGURE A–1

Moving from One Directory to Another

DIR. The DIR command is used to display the list of files in a subdirectory. The command DIR DOS would be used to list the files contained in the DOS subdirectory. The command DIR B:\ would display a list of files in the root directory of Drive B.

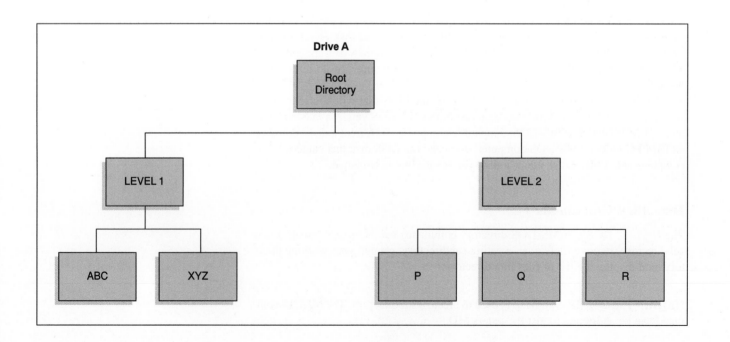

File Commands

IBM PC DOS and MS-DOS file commands allow a user to perform operations on files that are stored on disk or hard disk drives. With the file commands, a user can copy a file from one place to another, change the file's name, delete (or erase) a file, display a file's contents on the screen, or print a file. These commands can be used to operate on a single file or on multiple files with a single command. For example if a user wants to copy five files with similar names from a hard disk to a floppy disk, it is possible to accomplish this with a single command.

COPY. The COPY command is used to copy one or more files from one place to another. For example, the COPY command can be used to copy a file from one floppy disk to another, from a floppy disk to a hard disk, from a hard disk to a floppy disk, from one file on top of another file, from multiple files into one file, and from the display screen into a file.

The COPY command can be used in many different ways to accomplish many different tasks. For example, the command COPY A:FILE1.DAT C: will copy the file FILE1.DAT from the working directory on floppy disk Drive A to the working directory on hard disk Drive C. The command COPY A:FILE1.DAT D:\TEST will copy the file FILE1.DAT from the working directory on floppy disk Drive A to hard disk Drive D and the directory named TEST.

The command COPY C:\FILE2.DAT A: will copy the file FILE2.DAT from the root directory on hard disk Drive C to the working directory on Drive A. The command COPY C:FILE2.DAT A:\XYZ will copy the file FILE2.DAT from the working directory on hard disk Drive C to the XYZ directory on floppy disk Drive A.

The command COPY FILE1.DAT FILE2.DAT will copy the contents of the file FILE1.DAT into another file of the name FILE2.DAT. A word of caution should be noted, however. If the file FILE2.DAT already exists, the contents of FILE1.DAT will be written over top of FILE2.DAT destroying its original contents. If the file FILE2.DAT does not exist, the operating system will create a new file by that name.

The command COPY FILE1.DAT + FILE2.DAT + FILE3.DAT FILES123.DAT will copy the contents of FILE1.DAT, FILE2.DAT, and FILE3.DAT into one file named FILES123.DAT. The three files will be concatenated together in the order specified in the COPY command. Again, note that if the file FILES123.DAT existed prior to issuing the command shown, its contents will be destroyed when the new contents are written to the file.

The command COPY CON TESTFILE will copy everything typed on the display screen after the command is issued into a file named TESTFILE. In order to stop entry to the file and save its contents, press the F6 key and then press the Enter key. The source file name CON is an MS-DOS reserved name that indicates input is coming from the display screen (or console) rather than from another file.

DEL. The DEL command is used to delete (or erase) a file from a disk. For example, the command DEL FILE1.DAT would delete the file FILE1.DAT from the working directory. The command DEL C:\DATA\EMPLOYEE.DAT would delete the file EMPLOYEE.DAT from the directory DATA on DRIVE C.

REN. The REN (rename) command is used to change a file's name from one name to another. For example, the command REN FILE1.DAT FILE100.DAT would change the name of FILE1.DAT to FILE100.DAT. The command REN

A:\XYZ\TESTFILE TEST would rename the file TESTFILE on Drive A in the directory XYZ to TEST.

TYPE. The command TYPE can be used to display a file's contents on the display screen. For example, the command TYPE FILE1.DAT will display the contents of the file FILE1.DAT on the display screen. If the file exceeds a screenful in length, the MORE option can be used to display the file's contents one screen at a time. The command TYPE FILE1.DAT |MORE would cause the display of the file to pause after each screenful of information is displayed. The display will continue when you press any key on the keyboard.

PRINT. The command PRINT is used to send the contents of a file to a printer. The command PRINT FILE1.DAT will send the contents of FILE1.DAT to the printer, where a hard copy of the file will be created.

Using Wildcard Characters

The IBM PC DOS and MS-DOS operating systems also allow you to use what are known as wildcard characters when issuing commands that require file names. These wildcard characters allow one character or a number of characters of a filename to be treated in a generic fashion. The two wildcard characters used in IBM PC DOS and MS-DOS are the question mark (?) and the asterisk (*). When a question mark is used in a file name or file name extension, it means that any valid file name character can occupy that position within a file name. The asterisk, on the other hand, when used in a file name or file name extension means that any valid file name character can occupy that position or any of the remaining positions within a file name.

For example, the command DIR FILE?.DAT will list those files that begin with the letters, F, I, L, E and then have any other character in the position following the E. In the example given, the files listed must also have a file name extension of DAT. The command DIR *.DAT, however, will list all files with a file name extension of DAT.

Wildcard characters can also be used in any of the other file commands discussed above. For example, if we wanted to copy all files with a WKS file name extension from disk Drive A to hard disk Drive D, we could issue the command COPY A:* .WKS D:. This command would copy all the files in Drive A's working directory with a file name extension of WKS to the working directory on Drive D. The wildcard feature can be very powerful; however, caution should be exercised when using wildcards. You must be certain of the result of a command issued with wildcards. The command DEL *.*, for example, would most likely produce very undesirable results. It will delete all the files in the working directory. Therefore, exercise extreme caution when issuing commands with wildcard characters in the file names.

Other Useful DOS Commands

There are many DOS commands that can be very useful to both the novice and expert user. Because of the number of these commands and the many different ways to use these commands, all of the DOS commands cannot be covered in this text. We recommend, however, that you review your DOS manuals so that you can have a basic understanding of the types of commands available and their capabilities. The remainder of this appendix will discuss the IBM PC DOS and MS-DOS commands to copy the DOS system files onto a disk, check the version number of DOS your computer system is using, check for errors on a disk, and copy the entire contents of one diskette to another.

SYS. The SYS command is used to copy the DOS system files to a disk. Once these files are copied to a disk along with the COMMAND.COM file, it becomes a bootable disk. If the /S FORMAT command option was not used when the disk was originally formatted, the SYS command can be used to copy the three DOS operating system files to the disk.

VER. The VER command can be used to determine what version of IBM PC DOS or MS-DOS is currently being used by your computer.

CHKDSK. The CHKDSK command will check a disk to see if there are any errors that exist on the hard disk or floppy disk. If you use the /F switch with the CHKDSK command, the operating system will fix errors it finds on the disk after asking you for a Yes/No confirmation.

The information displayed includes information on the total number of bytes available on the disk, the total size and number of hidden files, the total size and number of directories, the total size and number of files you have created on your disk, and the total number of bytes still available for use on the disk. The last two lines of information printed by the CHKDSK command indicate the total size (in bytes) of your computer's memory and the total amount of memory that is available for use by programs that you run.

DISKCOPY. The DISKCOPY command is used to copy the entire contents of one disk to another. You should make copies of the disks that hold your files and programs as a precaution in case the originals are damaged or lost. Keep these backup disks in a place where they will not be damaged, and update them each time you update the original files or programs.

Macintosh Conventions and Commands

OUTLINE

□ INTRODUCTION

As described in Chapter 8, each operating system has certain conventions that must be followed. If you have not read the section entitled ''Apple Macintosh Conventions'' in Chapter 8, please do so now. The Chapter 8 material provides important foundational knowledge for the present discussion of Macintosh commands. Therefore please review the information in Chapter 8 regarding the system file, finder, and desktop prior to reading further about Macintosh commands.

□ ADDITIONAL MACINTOSH CONVENTIONS

In addition to the system file, finder, and desktop, if we are to have a complete understanding of the conventions used by the Macintosh icons, pointing, clicking, double-clicking, dragging, windows, and dialog boxes must also be discussed. The following sections will give detailed information regarding each of these topics.

Icons

The icons that appear on the Macintosh desktop represent either an application, a document, a folder, or a disk. An **application** is a program. Programs like MacWrite, MacPaint, MacDraw, Microsoft Word, Aldus PageMaker, and Microsoft Works are all applications. A **document** is where data is stored on a Macintosh. A document may contain the data entered into a spreadsheet or it may contain the text of a business letter. For example, one chapter of a novel created using Microsoft Word would be considered a document. A folder is a place where applications, documents, and other folders can be stored. Just as paper file folders are used to organize paper documents, folders on a Macintosh are used to organize the data and information stored on disks. A disk can be either a floppy disk or a hard disk.

Pointing

To position the pointer at a particular location on the desktop, simply hold the mouse in one hand and push it across the top of the desk or table the computer is sitting on. If you want the pointer to move to the left, push the mouse to the left. If you want the pointer to move up, push the mouse up. The movement of the pointer on the display screen will follow the movement of the mouse on the desk or tabletop.

If you run out of room on the desk or tabletop, you may pick the mouse up and move it to a new location without moving the pointer on the Macintosh's desktop. The pointer on the desktop moves only when the ball on the bottom of the mouse is rolling.) For example, let's say you are moving the pointer toward the far right-hand side of the desktop, but halfway across you run out of room for moving the mouse. Simply pick the mouse up, move it back to the left, and set it back down. Once you have done this, you may then begin to move the mouse to the right again to position the pointer where you want it.

Clicking

In order to use the items represented by icons, you must first select the desired icon. The process of selecting an icon involves positioning the pointer on the icon and then pressing the button on the mouse once, or clicking. To select a disk, for example,

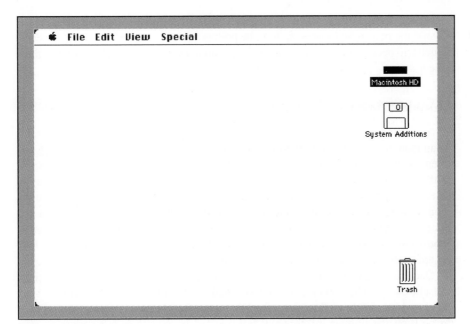

position the pointer on the disk's icon and then press the button on the mouse once. Notice that the disk icon changes from an outline to a solid color, or becomes highlighted, when you select it (see Figure B–1). Choosing a command from one of the pull-down menus is similar to selecting an icon. To choose a command from one of the menus, simply position the pointer on the Apple icon or one of the menu names on the top line of the Macintosh screen, called the menu bar (see Figure B–2). Once the pointer is positioned properly, press and hold down the mouse button. The menu

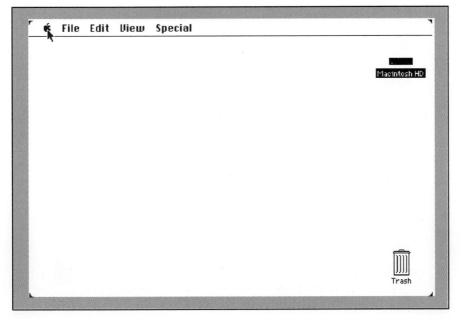

ADDITIONAL MACINTOSH CONVENTIONS

that corresponds to the Apple icon or menu name will be pulled down. As you continue to hold the mouse button down, drag the pointer to the command you want to select, which will become highlighted. When the command you want to choose is highlighted (see Figure B–3), release the mouse button.

Double-Clicking

In order to load an application into the computer's memory or to view the contents of an icon, the icon must be both selected and opened. This process of selecting and opening an icon can be done in two ways. The icon can first be selected, then opened with the Open command from the File menu. However, the most common way to select and open an icon is to use the technique called double-clicking. To select an icon, remember, you position the pointer on the icon and press the mouse button once. To both select and open an icon, position the pointer on the icon and press the mouse button two times quickly. This is known as double-clicking; it will either load an application into memory or open a window displaying the contents of the icon.

Once the application is loaded or the window opened, it, at some point in time, must be closed. This too may be accomplished in one of two ways. The window may be closed by selecting Close from the File menu. Another way to close a window is to position the pointer in the small box located in the upper left corner of open windows, called the close box, and pressing the mouse button once. In order to unload an application from memory, the Quit command in the File menu must be used.

Dragging

Dragging allows you to move an icon from one location on the desktop to another location. For example, we can move a disk icon from the upper right-hand corner of the screen to the lower left-hand corner of the screen. The icons that appear on the desktop can be moved to suit your own needs. In order to cancel the dragging of an

FIGURE B–3

The Apple Menu Options

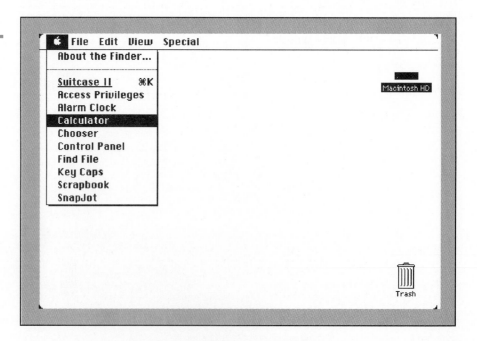

APPENDIX B: MACINTOSH CONVENTIONS AND COMMANDS

icon and put it back at its original location on the desktop, simply drag the icon's outline to the menu bar and release the mouse button. This will return the icon to its original position on the desktop. Documents can be copied by dragging them from one disk to another. If, for example, you would like to copy a document from your hard disk to a floppy disk you would drag the document's icon from its location on the hard disk to the appropriate location on the floppy disk. In this case, the hard disk would be considered the source disk while the floppy disk would be the destination disk.

Windows

The Macintosh uses windows in a variety of ways. **Windows** are used to present information to the user, carry on a dialog with the user, and allow the user to enter information into an application. Windows can be small or large, and the size of most windows can be changed by the user. Like icons, windows can be moved around on the desktop to suit the user's needs. Windows are used by the operating system to display the contents of an icon when it is opened. Windows are also used by applications to allow the user to view some portion of a document. See Figure B–4 for an example of a typical window and the terms used to describe its parts.

Multiple windows can be opened by the user at one time. These windows can physically overlap on the desktop, but they cannot be moved off the desktop. When multiple windows are open, the window in the forefront, with the horizontal lines in the title bar, is the active window. Any other open window on the desktop can be made active by positioning the pointer inside it and pressing the mouse button once.

FIGURE B–4

A Typical Macintosh Window and Its Parts

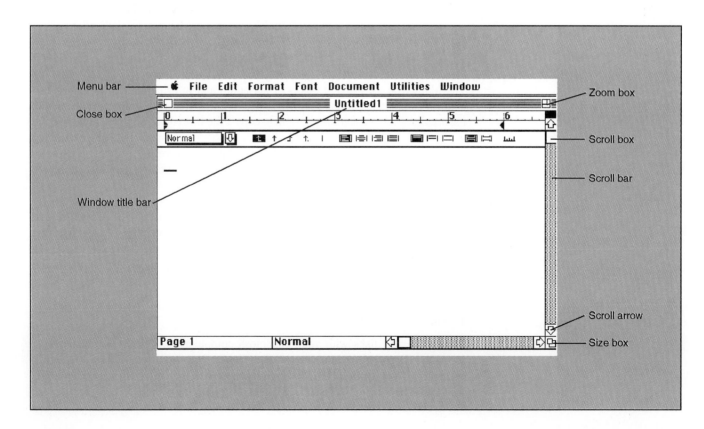

Several important operations can be performed with windows. A window can be moved from one location to another on the desktop, the size of the window can be changed, and the contents of a document too large to fit in a single screen can be repositioned in a window to allow viewing of the entire document. In order to move a window from one location to another, position the pointer anywhere in the title bar displayed at the top of the window and press the mouse button. The title bar normally includes the name of the window. Once the pointer is on the title bar and the mouse button is pressed, you may drag the window from one location on the desktop to another location. The size of the window can be changed using the size box in the lower right-hand corner of the open window (see Figure B–4). Position the pointer on the size box, press the mouse button, and then drag the window's borders until the window is the size you want. The zoom box can also be used to change a window's size. The zoom box, located in the upper right-hand corner of a window, can be used to switch between an enlarged window size and the size you have chosen. The contents of a document larger than a single screen can be repositioned in relation to the window in one of two ways. The first way to change what is displayed in the window is to use the scroll boxes in the scroll bars at the right and bottom sides of the window. The scroll boxes can be moved by positioning the pointer in the scroll box you would like to move, pressing the mouse button, and dragging the scroll box to the desired location on the scroll bar (see Figure B–4). The scroll boxes represent the vertical and horizontal positions of the window in relation to the entire document. For example, if the part of the document you want to view is about halfway through it, move the scroll box to the middle of the scroll bar. The second way to reposition the window is to use the scroll arrows at the ends of the vertical and horizontal scroll bars (see Figure B–4). For example, positioning the pointer on the down arrow on the vertical scroll bar and clicking once will move the document up one line. This method of repositioning a window's contents may vary from application to application.

Dialog Boxes

The Macintosh uses dialog boxes to get additional information from users and to confirm commands that the user has issued to the operating system. If, for example, the user has told the operating system to copy a file from one disk onto another where a file of the same name already exists, the operating system will ask the user to confirm that he or she would really like to do this. This gives the user an opportunity to cancel the operation if the file on the second disk should not be overwritten with the file on the first disk (see Figure B–5).

When a dialog box is presented to the user, the most likely response is normally enclosed in a bold outline. This response can be selected in one of two ways. The user can position the pointer on the appropriate response and click to select it, or the user can press the Return key to accept the response in the bold outline. Any response not outlined in bold must be selected using the mouse to move the pointer to the appropriate location on the screen and clicking once.

Initializing Disks

Before you use disks with your Macintosh computer, they must be initialized, or formatted. There are several ways a disk can be initialized for use in a Macintosh computer. If you would like to use a brand-new disk that is not formatted, you may insert it into a Macintosh disk drive. When the operating system detects that the disk has not been initialized, it will display a dialog box on the screen and ask you if you

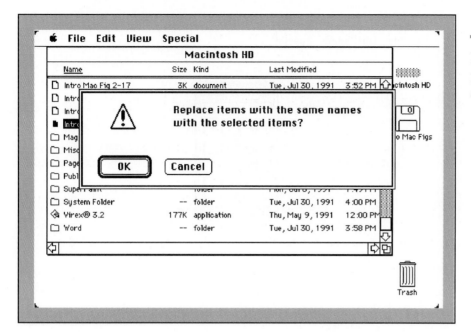

FIGURE B–5

A Dialog Box Asking for Confirmation to Replace the Contents of One File with Another File of the Same Name

would like to initialize the disk. Some disk manufacturers also sell disks that are formatted for Macintosh computers. Preformatted disks normally cost slightly more than unformatted disks, so you should be sure that the formatted disks you are buying have been formatted for use in a Macintosh computer. If a disk already has information on it and you would like to erase the contents of the disk (which effectively reinitializes the disk), you may use the Erase Disk option from the Special menu.

Alarm Clock

The Alarm Clock option in the Apple menu displays the system time in a small window. The system time is maintained by a battery in the Macintosh computer. By pressing the lever icon on the right-hand side of the window, you can enlarge the window so that it displays the date and alarm clock setting as well. When this enlarged window is open, you can set the date, system time, or alarm time. The alarm clock portion of this option allows you to set an alarm that will be sounded when the system time is equal to the time you have selected.

Calculator

The Calculator selection in the Apple menu allows you to perform calculations just like you would on a normal calculator. Once the calculator is displayed (see Figure B–6), you can use either the pointer, the number keys on the keyboard, or the numeric keypad to perform addition, multiplication, subtraction, and division.

Chooser

The Chooser is a desk accessory that allows you to select devices for use with your Macintosh. For instance, the Chooser is where you would select the printer or the modem you would like to use with your Macintosh. Therefore, the Chooser is very

FIGURE B–6

The Calculator

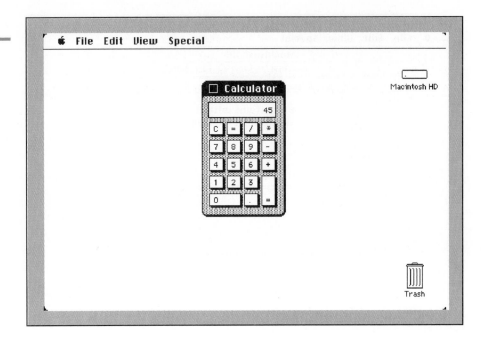

important because you cannot use these devices without first selecting them using the Chooser. Figure B–7 illustrates how you would use the Chooser to select a printer.

◼ THE APPLE MENU

The desk accessories are accessed by positioning the pointer on the Apple icon located in the upper left-hand corner of the display screen and pressing and holding down

FIGURE B–7

Using The Chooser to Select a Printer

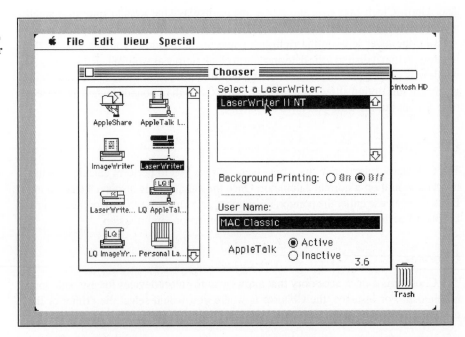

the mouse button. The Apple menu is available when the desktop is displayed as well as at any time you are using an application such as a word processor or a spreadsheet. The type and number of desk accessories may change from Macintosh to Macintosh, but nearly all Macintosh computers have desk accessories that include information about the Finder, Alarm Clock, Calculator, Chooser, Control Panel, Find File, Key Caps, and Scrapbook.

About the Finder

Choosing About the Finder from the Apple menu causes a window that gives information about the version of the Finder currently being used to be displayed. This information includes the Finder's version number as well as information about when the Finder program was created. Information about the Finder is available when the Finder is the current application. If another application is in use, the first selection in the Apple menu will provide similar information about that application. If, for example, MacWrite is the application currently being used, information about MacWrite will be displayed in the window.

The Apple menu contains the list of desk accessories available to the user. A **desk accessory** is an application designed to perform a very specific task, such as finding a file stored on a disk.

Control Panel

The Control Panel (see Figure B–8) is used to adjust a number of settings for your Macintosh computer. The Control Panel settings include the speaker volume, the pattern for the desktop, the rate at which the insertion point blinks, the double-click speed of the mouse, and the rate at which keys will repeat if they are held down.

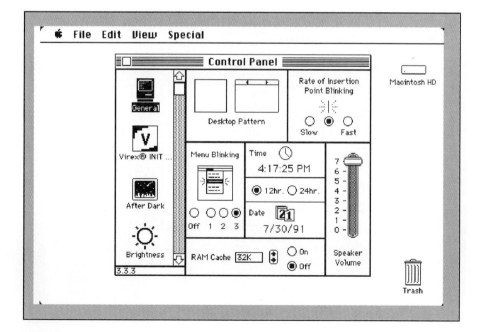

FIGURE B–8

The Control Panel

Find File

The Find File desk accessory allows you to search for lost files including applications or documents. Find File will allow you to search disks and folders for the file you are looking for. Find File is flexible enough that it will allow you to enter only a portion of the file name you wish to search for. If Find File locates any files that match the partial name, it will display those file names to you. Once a file name is displayed, you may highlight it and Find File will display the file's location to you.

Key Caps

The Key Caps desk accessory is used to display the many characters contained in the fonts that can be used on a Macintosh. A **font** is a set of characters that can be displayed on the Macintosh screen or printed on a printer connected to the Macintosh. The Key Caps desk accessory, therefore, gives you the ability to see or search for characters that you would like to use in a document. Fonts will be discussed in greater detail in the application portion of the text. Some of the commonly used fonts include Courier, Helvetica, Times, New York, and Chicago, just to mention a few.

When you choose the Key Caps desk accessory from the Apple menu, a window appears showing a diagram of the keyboard (see Figure B–9). You then choose the name of the font you would like to display characters from using the Key Caps menu that appears in the menu bar. Once the font has been chosen, you can use either the pointer or the keyboard to identify the characters you would like displayed. If you press the Shift key, one set of the font's special characters is displayed. Pressing the Option key will display another set of the font's special characters, and pressing the Option and Shift keys together will display yet another set. As characters are selected or typed, they are displayed in the top portion of the Key Caps window (see Figure B–10). The Key Caps desk accessory can be extremely valuable in helping you to locate characters such as ® or © that you would like included in a document or to determine which keys to use to insert an accent in a foreign word.

FIGURE B–9

The Key Caps Window and Font Menu

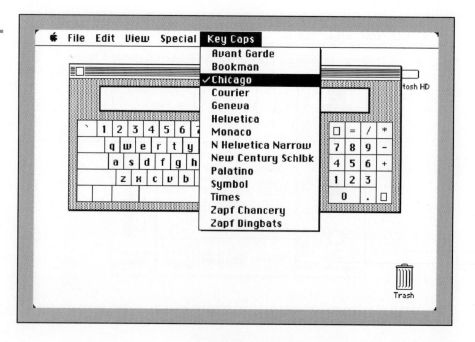

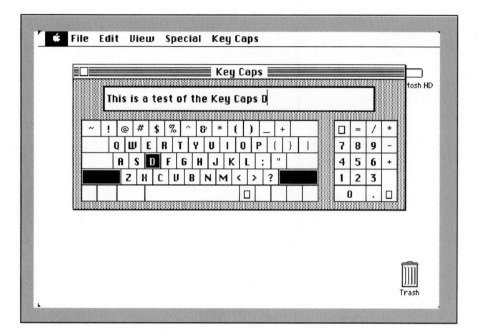

Scrapbook

The Scrapbook selection in the Apple menu allows you to insert a block of text or a picture from the Scrapbook into a document without having to retype or redraw it each time. For example, if you had a paragraph that you wanted to use in many documents, you could place the paragraph in the Scrapbook and use it as often as you want without having to retype it. The editing commands, Cut, Copy, and Paste, are used to move information in and out of the Scrapbook.

❑ THE FILE MENU

The commands in the Finder application's File menu (see Figure B–11) are accessed by positioning the pointer over the word *File* in the menu bar and pressing and holding down the mouse button. The File menu commands allow you to do such things as create a new file folder, open a file, print a file, close a file, get information about a file, duplicate a file, put away a file, and eject a disk from its disk drive.

The commands listed in the File menu may not always be available to the user. When a command is not available, it is dimmed in the menu listing and cannot be highlighted (see Figure B–11). The commands that are available when the menu is pulled down depend on the current status of the icons on the desktop. If, for example, there are no icons selected, the Open, Duplicate, and Get Info commands will not be available for use. If there is not a disk selected, the Eject command will not be available for use. This is also true of commands in the other menus that will be described in this appendix. If a command is not available based on the status of the desktop, it will be dimmed in the menu and will not be offered to the user as a valid selection.

Commands that are available in the Finder application's menu are unique to the Finder. Commands on menus in other applications are also unique and therefore the

The Finder Application's File Menu

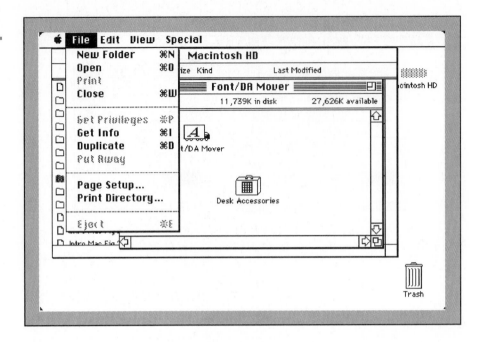

types of operations that can be performed will depend on the particular application being used. However, the majority of Macintosh applications adhere to a consistent user interface, which means that commands are arranged on menus in a fairly standard way from one application to another.

New Folder

The New Folder option in the File menu allows you to create a new folder. This folder is empty when it is first created. The folder is created with the name "Empty Folder". You may change the name of the folder by simply typing a new name for the folder and then pressing the Return key when the name of the new folder is still highlighted.

Open

The Open command in the File menu is used to open an icon into a window. To use the Open command, you must first select the icon to be opened. Once the icon is selected, it can be opened by choosing the Open option in the File menu. Opening an icon in this manner is the same as opening the icon by double-clicking. If the icon being opened belongs to a particular application, that application will also be opened. For example, if the icon being opened is a MacWrite document, the MacWrite application will be loaded, and the window that is opened will contain the document you selected. There is also a shortcut method for executing many of the commands that appear in the pull-down menus. This shortcut method involves the use of the keyboard rather than the mouse. The Command (or Apple) key is used in combination with other keys to execute commands that appear in menus. The key combinations for commands that have keyboard equivalents are shown on the right side of the pull-down menus. (You should note that not all commands have keyboard equivalents.) Notice that in the File menu, the Command key along with the *O* key (shown on the right side of the menu as ⌘ 0) can be used to execute the Open command. Using this shortcut method of executing a command eliminates the need to pull down a menu and choose a command. When you use the keyboard equivalent to execute a command, the name of the menu blinks to give visual reinforcement that a command from the menu has been executed. For example, when the Open command is executed using the keyboard equivalent, the word File on the menu bar blinks. In many cases, this method of executing commands is easier and quicker. Although you must memorize the letter key used in combination with the Command key to execute the desired command, Apple's specifications to Macintosh software developers have resulted in fairly consistent use of these keyboard equivalents, so commands you learn in one application are usually the same in other software that uses keyboard equivalents.

Print

The Print command in the File menu allows you to print a document from the desktop. The application that created the document must be accessible by the Finder, however, for the document to print successfully.

Close

The Close command in the File menu allows you to close a selected icon. Closing an icon in this manner is the same as using the close box in the upper left-hand corner of the open window.

Get Info

The Get Info command in the File menu opens a window that displays information about the selected icon. The information displayed includes the kind of file the icon represents, the size of the file, where the file is located (on floppy disk or hard disk), when the file was created, and when the file was last modified. The Get Info command also allows you to indicate if the file should be locked. A locked file cannot be removed from the disk, and its name cannot be changed. The contents of a locked file, however, can be modified.

In addition, the Get Info command allows you to enter text that provides information about the file. This text can be typed in while the Get Info window for the file is displayed on the desktop (see Figure B–12).

Duplicate

The Duplicate command in the File menu allows you to make a copy of any of the icons on a disk. When the duplicate is created, it will be given the same name as the icon being duplicated, but will be preceded with the words *Copy of.* You may change the name of the duplicate icon by simply typing a new name for the icon and then pressing the Return key when the name of the new icon is still highlighted.

Put Away

The Put Away command is used to put a particular icon back into the folder or disk it came from. Simply choose the Put Away option from the File menu after selecting the icon.

FIGURE B–12

Highlighted Text in the Information Window

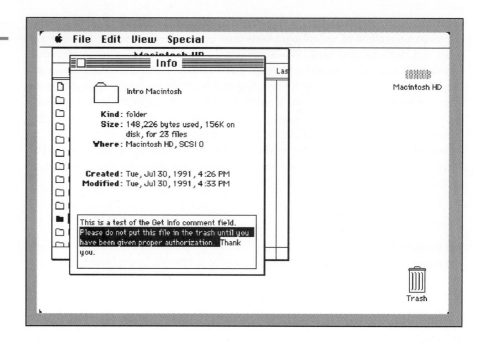

Eject

The Eject command in the File menu ejects the selected disk from the disk drive. Once the disk is ejected, its icon is no longer selected but stays on the desktop. You may continue to use the disk's icon after the disk has been ejected. However, if you perform some operation that requires the Finder to access the disk, you will be asked to put the disk back into the disk drive.

■ THE EDIT MENU

The commands in the Finder application's Edit menu (see Figure B–13) allow you to edit icon names, the text that is entered for an icon in the information window, and the text that is entered using the desk accessories. The Edit menu commands allow you to perform operations such as undoing the last editing command, cutting text, copying text, pasting text, selecting all icons in an active window, and looking at the contents of the Clipboard.

The Clipboard is where text that is cut or copied is placed on a temporary basis. If, for example, you cut a block of text, it will be stored on the Clipboard until another block of text is copied or cut. In other words, each time text is cut or copied it replaces the previous contents of the Clipboard.

Undo

The Undo command in the Edit menu undoes the last text editing command that was executed. This command is very useful in circumstances where, for whatever reason, you decide you would like to take back the last text editing command you executed.

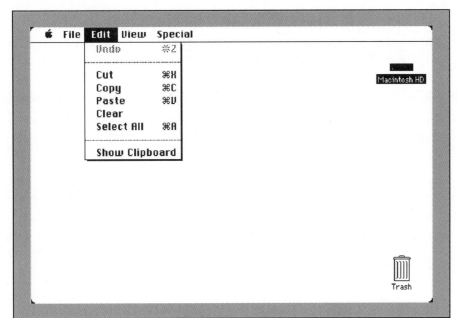

The Finder Application's Edit Menu

Cut

The Cut command in the Edit menu removes a selected block of text. The block of text that is cut is placed on the Clipboard. Remember however, that cutting a block of text onto the Clipboard will destroy the previous contents of the Clipboard.

The I-beam pointer is used to select a block of text. To select a block of text, you must move the pointer to the point in the text where you would like to begin marking the block and press and hold down the mouse button. Then drag the pointer to the place in the text where you would like the block to end. Once at the end of the block of text, release the mouse button. The text you have selected will be highlighted on the screen. A block of text can be as small as one character or as large as an entire document.

Copy

The Copy command in the Edit menu is used to copy a selected block of text onto the Clipboard. The selected block of text is not removed from the document but is simply duplicated on the Clipboard. Remember however, that copying a block of text onto the Clipboard will destroy the previous contents of the Clipboard.

Paste

The Paste command in the Edit menu inserts the text currently on the Clipboard at the current location of the insertion point.

Clear

The Clear command in the Edit menu removes a selected block of text. However, the block of text that is cut is not placed on the Clipboard.

Select All

The Select All command in the Edit menu allows you to select all icons in the currently active window.

Show Clipboard

The Show Clipboard command in the Edit menu opens a window that displays the current contents of the Clipboard.

◾ THE VIEW MENU

The commands in the Finder application's View menu (see Figure B–14) allow you to look at a directory of the documents and applications stored in folders, on disk, or in the Trash in different ways. The ways in which you can look at the directory include by small icon, icon, name, date, size, and kind.

By Small Icon

The By Small Icon selection in the View menu displays a list of files with a small icon to the left of the file name. This view may be preferable to the By Icon view in cases where you have a large number of files. The small icon and name will take less space on the screen and therefore more files can be displayed in the window.

By Icon

The By Icon selection in the View menu allows you to view a list of files by their icon. When viewing a directory in this way, you can edit the file name and drag the file icon to another location on the desktop using the pointer (see Figure B–15). This

FIGURE B–14

The Finder Application's View Menu

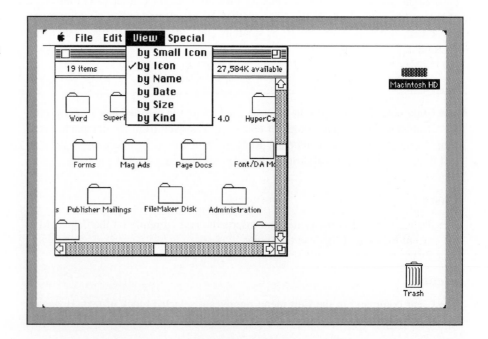

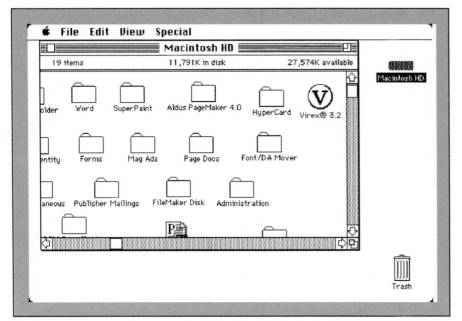

is the way that files are viewed by default. When a disk is initialized, the view is set to By Icon by default. The By Icon view may be the most pleasing. However, the By Name view is the most common view used by those that work on a Macintosh on a daily basis.

By Name

The By Name selection in the View menu allows you to view a list of files in alphabetical ascending order (see Figure B–16). Files whose names begin with the

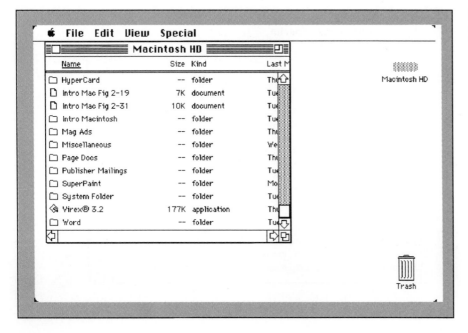

FIGURE B–16

The By Name View

letter *A* are listed first. If file names begin with numbers, the names will be listed in ascending numerical order. If a list of files includes names that begin with both numbers and letters, those file names beginning with numbers will appear before those beginning with letters.

By Date

The By Date selection in the View menu allows you to view a list of files in chronological order by each file's modification date. The most recently changed file is listed first.

By Size

The By Size selection in the View menu allows you to view a list of files according to their size. The list is ordered such that the largest file is first and the smallest file is last.

By Kind

The By Kind selection in the View menu allows you to view a list of files according to the type of file. The list is ordered by application, folder, or document. If a file is a document, the application used to create it is also listed (see Figure B–17).

■ THE SPECIAL MENU

The Finder application's Special menu (see Figure B–18) includes commands that allow you to organize (or clean up) a particular file folder, empty the Trash, erase and initialize a disk, or make a disk start up using a particular application.

FIGURE B–17

The By Kind View

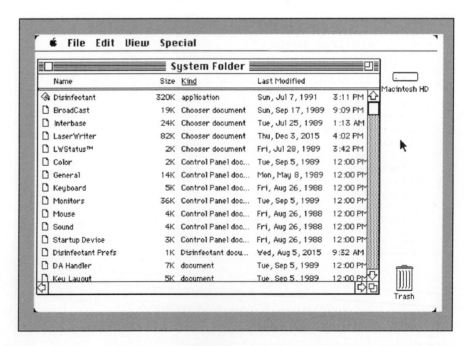

APPENDIX B: MACINTOSH CONVENTIONS AND COMMANDS

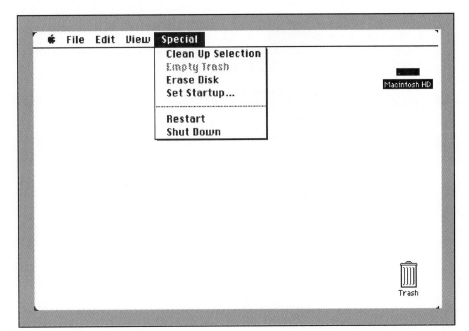

Clean Up Selection

The Clean Up command in the Special menu will arrange the file icons on the desktop or within a folder in neat rows and columns. However, this command will work only on files that are being viewed by their icons.

Empty Trash

The Empty Trash command in the Special menu will erase the contents of the Trash. If you move an icon from the desktop or a folder into the Trash, it will not be removed permanently until you select the Empty Trash command (see Figure B–19) or shut the computer off. Therefore, if an icon is moved into the Trash, but the Trash has not been emptied, the icon can be recovered and moved back onto the desktop or into a folder.

Erase Disk

The Erase Disk command in the Special menu will erase the entire contents of as well as initialize a disk. This selection should be used with extreme caution.

Set Startup

The Set Startup command in the Special menu allows you to configure a disk so that when the computer is started with that disk it will go immediately into a particular application.

Restart

The Restart command in the Special menu allows you to restart the computer. This

FIGURE B–19

Choosing the Empty Trash Command

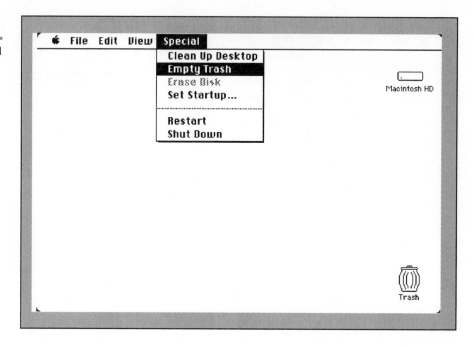

is helpful in situations where you would like to restart the computer with a different startup configuration. For example, if you would like to switch from Finder to MultiFinder, one method would be to use the Set Startup command and choose MultiFinder in the Set Startup window. You would then choose Restart from the Special menu, and when the computer starts up again MultiFinder would be active. The Restart command automatically ejects any disks in the disk drive, empties the Trash, and restarts the computer. Using the Restart command is preferable to performing each of these steps manually.

Shut Down

The Shut Down command is used to turn the computer off when you have finished using it. Like Restart, Shut Down also ejects all disks from the disk drives and empties the Trash. On some Macintosh computers, Shut Down will automatically turn the power off and on others it will inform the user that it is safe to turn the power off.

Application Software Supplement

Word Processors

◻ INTRODUCTION

Of all the application software available, word processors meet the largest variety of users' needs. The number of programs that have been developed to serve this incredibly wide range of needs has made word processing the most competitive market in application software. Word processors not only are a useful tool for more users than any other application program, they are the easiest application software programs to learn. These two facts combine to make word processors huge sellers.

Word processors have not only improved, but enhanced the writing process. In the first generation of word processors, users were satisfied with simply being able to edit text before it appeared on paper. Word processors enable users to change, move, or erase words, sentences, and paragraphs without retyping the whole document. The final version is printed after the writer is completely satisfied with it. Today, such standard features are old hat. Many word processors now enhance the writing process by checking spelling, offering a better word choice with a thesaurus, and automatically compiling an index or a table of contents. Not only that, more and more word-processing packages are incorporating features that used to be found only in desktop publishing programs. These features include the ability to import graphics into a document, to print text in columns, and to create tables.

This section introduces you to word processing. It explains word processing and its uses, and details some of the common features of word-processing packages. In addition, it discusses current trends in word-processing software, including the move toward desktop publishing.

◻ UNDERSTANDING WORD PROCESSORS

A word processor is a program that lets you write, edit, format, and print text. Basically, the purpose of all word processors is the same: to help the user create a good-looking and well-written document. To familiarize you with word-processing concepts, Table I–1 provides a quick reference to terms frequently encountered when using this type of program.

Many word processors divide the computer screen into two areas. One area gives information about the status of the program and the format of the document. The other area contains the text of the document being edited.

The part of the screen that gives information about the status of the program often contains a menu, a list of commands or prompts on the display screen. For example, an editing menu in a word processor might include commands such as copy, move, delete, print, format, insert, and undo. A user could perform any of these commands on the document being created. A **status line,** also found in this part of the screen, supplies format information about the document, such as the line and column number where the cursor is located, the page number of the text on the screen, and the number of words or characters in the document (Figure I–1).

The remainder of the screen, which contains the words as they are typed, is often called the **editing window.** All editing of a document takes place in the editing window. When a mistake is made, it can easily be corrected in the editing window. Words, sentences, and even entire paragraphs can be moved, modified, or deleted by special commands.

TABLE I–1

Frequently Encountered Word-Processing Terms

Term	Definition
Automatic page numbering	A feature that enables a word processor to automatically number the pages of the printed copy.
Block	A group of characters, such as a sentence or paragraph.
Block operation	A feature that allows the user to define a block of text and then perform a specific operation on the entire block. Common block operations include block move, block copy, block save, and block delete.
Boldface	Heavy type, for example, this is **boldface.**
Buffer	An area set aside in memory to temporarily hold text.
Character	A letter, number, or symbol.
Character enhancement	Underlining, boldfacing, italicizing, subscripting, and superscripting.
Control character	A coded character that does not print but is part of the command sequence in a word processor.
Cursor	The marker on the display screen indicating where the next character can be displayed.
Default setting	A value used by the word processor when not instructed to use any other.
Deletion	A feature in which a character, word, sentence, or larger block of text may be removed from the existing text.
Document-oriented word processor	A word processor that treats a document as a single, continuous file.
Editing	The act of changing or reformatting text.
Footer	A piece of text that is printed at the bottom of each page, such as a page number.
Format	The layout of a page; for example, the number of lines, the margin settings, and so on.
Global	An instruction that will be carried out throughout an entire document, for example, global search and replace.
Header	A piece of text that is stored separately from the text and printed at the top of each page.
Insertion	A feature in which a character, word, sentence, or larger block of text is added to the existing text.
Justification	A feature for making lines of text even at the margins.

TABLE I-1 Word-Processing Terms, *Continued*

Term	Definition
Line editor	The type of editor that allows the user to edit only one line at a time.
Memory-based word processor	A word processor that can only accommodate documents that fit into available memory; longer documents must be placed in two or more separate files.
Menu	A list of commands or prompts on the display screen.
Page-oriented word processor	A word processor that treats a document as a series of pages.
Print formatting	The function of a word processor that communicates with the printer to tell it how to print the text on paper.
Print preview	A feature that allows the user to view a general representation on the screen of how the document will look when printed.
Proportional spacing	A method in which the printer inserts very small spaces between words and letters to produce a more professional appearance; also called *microspacing*.
Screen editor	The type of editor that allows the user to edit an entire screen at a time.
Screen formatting	A function of a word processor that controls how the text will appear on the screen.
Scrolling	Moving a line of text onto or off the screen.
Search and find	A routine that searches for, and places the cursor at, a specified string of characters.
Search and replace	A routine that searches for a specified character string and replaces it with the specified replacement string.
Status line	A message line above or below the text area on a display screen that gives format and system information.
Subscript	A character that prints below the usual text baseline.
Superscript	A character that prints above the usual text baseline.
Text editing	The function of a word processor that enables the user to enter and edit text.
Text file	A file that contains text, as opposed to a program.
Virtual representation	An approach to screen formatting that allows the user to see on the screen exactly how the printed output will look.
Word wrap	The feature by which a word is automatically moved to the beginning of the next line if it goes past the right margin.

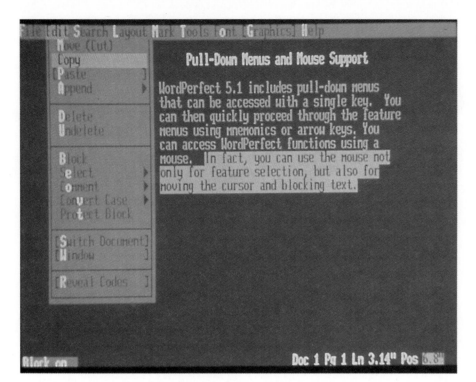

FIGURE I–1

Screen Display from WordPerfect 5.1
*WordPerfect 5.1 includes pull-down
menus. The pull-down menu shown here
is the Edit menu. The status line is in
the lower right corner of the screen.*

When text is first entered, the computer's RAM (random-access memory) stores the text. For short documents, entire contents are kept in RAM. The storage method used for long documents depends on whether the word processor is memory based or disk based. In a **memory-based word processor,** the entire document must fit into memory. Documents larger than available memory are divided into two or more documents and saved in separate files. AppleWriter II and PFS:WRITE are examples of memory-based word processors. Creating and editing a large document with a memory-based word processor is difficult if text must be moved between separate files frequently.

Creating and editing a large document with a **disk-based word processor** is much easier. A disk-based word processor loads into memory only the part of the document that is being edited, storing the remainder in temporary disk files. When you edit a different part of the document, text is automatically transferred between temporary disk files and RAM, usually without a significant delay. Some operations, such as jumping from the first page to the last page of a large document, can cause noticeable delays of a minute or more. However, a current trend in word processors is for them to work with greater speed. Most word processors try to minimize any kind of delay. With a disk-based word processor, the size of a document is limited only by the amount of disk space that is available. Microsoft Word, WordStar, and Multimate are examples of disk-based word processors.

To save a document, a text file must first be created on a disk. There are different ways to create a file on disk. Some word processors treat a text file as a series of pages, much like a typewriter. This type of word processor is referred to as a **page-oriented word processor.** Display Write and Multimate are page-oriented word processors. A page-oriented word processor is geared to work page by page. Text is automatically segmented into pages and only one page of a document can be created or saved on disk at a time. Also, only one page of a document can be edited at a time. For example, in Display Write it is impossible to see the bottom of one page and the top of the next page at the same time on the screen.

A **document-oriented word processor** treats a document as a single continuous file, and the entire document can be saved with one command. WordPerfect, WordStar, and Microsoft Word are document-oriented word processors. Document-oriented word processors make editing a long document easier because pages do not have to be worked on separately. The bottom portion of one page and the top portion of the next page can appear on the screen at the same time.

Once a document is saved, it can be retrieved at any time either for printing or further editing. A document can be put in perfect order before one word is committed to paper.

In the 90s, an entirely new class of word processors emerged. This new class is comprised of the graphics-based programs, which are designed mostly for the Microsoft Windows environment. The main difference between character-based word processors and graphics-based word processors is that the latter allow you to create and edit text on a screen that exactly represents the printed page. These word processors will be covered in Section VI, which deals with the Windows environment. The focus of this section is on character-based word processors.

◼ USES OF WORD PROCESSORS

Word processors are used in many places, including homes, businesses, and schools. In 1986, *PC Magazine* identified three categories of word processors: personal, professional, and corporate. In 1988, *PC Magazine* reported that the breadth of suitable uses for word processors had grown to such an extent that grouping word processors by distinct categories is no longer appropriate. As the quality of word processors has improved, the difference between personal, corporate, and professional programs has become less distinct. Still, some word processors obviously are better suited for certain applications than others. Looking at the *uses* of word processors, *PC Magazine* added two groups to the list: personal, professional, corporate, legal, and desktop publishing.

At home, word processors can be used to write school reports, personal letters, or minutes from a meeting. Most word processors for home use are easier to operate than those designed for business use because they usually have fewer features than business word processors. For example, print-formatting capabilities, which control page breaks, page numbering, and character enhancements are limited in a word-processing package for home use.

Schools are increasing their use of word processors. Students can write essays or reports on the computers in their classroom or computer lab. Often, teachers can format tests and worksheets on a computer much faster than on a typewriter. Of course, school secretaries can use word processors to prepare school reports and letters.

In offices, word processors are used to produce reports, formal correspondence, brochures, and other important documents. They merge names and addresses into form letters to personalize the letters. They check the spelling of documents. Today, standard features of a business-oriented word processing package include mail-merge, a spelling checker, a thesaurus, and an outlining facility.

When word processors were first introduced, analysts predicted they would usher in the era of the paperless office. These analysts reasoned that documents could be stored in memory instead of being printed on paper. If someone needed to read a document, he or she could simply retrieve it and read it from the computer screen. Documents could be sent from one computer to another via a modem.

Not only has this prediction not come to pass, the exact opposite has happened. Because of their power and flexibility, word processors are capable of printing documents that achieve the quality that used to be attainable only by professional printers. Word processors are capable of printing a document as short as a memo or as long as a full-length book. So instead of leading to a paperless office, the proliferation of word processors found in homes, schools, and offices has lead to the greatest increase in the use of paper since the early days of the first printing presses!

Obviously the legal profession is an area that handles a great deal of written material; therefore, some word processing programs have taken into account the unique needs of lawyers. These packages include such features as a style checker for legal citations, the inclusion of legal terminology in the spelling checker, the ability to create a table of authorities, automatic line numbering, and red-lining—a function that makes it possible to compare additions and deletions in successive versions of a document.

More and more word-processing programs are encroaching on the low end of desktop publishing. Desktop publishing enables professional-quality documents to be created and printed using a microcomputer and a laser printer. Desktop publishing features found on some word processors include the ability to integrate graphics into text documents, manipulate the placement of text and graphics on a page, and mix type sizes and fonts within a document.

Newsletters are one of the most popular uses for desktop publishing within a business. Desktop publishing simplifies the process of creating professional-looking newsletters. Companies also use desktop publishing to create instructional materials or training materials. Desktop publishing is also useful for creating marketing materials such as brochures, pamphlets, or catalogs.

CHECKPOINT I–1

1. Explain how a word processor makes it easy to correct mistakes made when you type a document.

2. Where is text stored when it is first entered on the computer?

3. Describe how a word processor can be used in a home.

4. Describe how a word processor can be used in an office.

5. Describe how a word processor might be used for desktop publishing.

◘ FEATURES OF WORD PROCESSORS

All word processors perform the same basic tasks of entering, editing, and formatting text, moving blocks of text, and searching for and replacing strings of text. In the past, the number of features—and consequently the price—distinguished one word processor from another. This is not as true today. Previously, features such as mail-merge and a spelling checker came separately and had to be purchased as an extra addition to a word processing package. Today, these are standard features that come as part of many word-processing packages. In addition, competition in the word-processing software market has kept prices down.

Currently, style seems to be what distinguishes one word processor from another. The "style" of a word-processing package involves how the program works. No two word-processing packages perform a task in exactly the same way. Sometimes the phrase "look and feel" is used to describe the style of a word processor: what the program looks like on the computer screen and the feel a person gets from using it. A common term that is used when discussing word processors is **WYSIWYG,** pronounced *wizeewig*. The letters stand for "what you see is what you get." This means that what the user sees on the screen matches as closely as possible what actually appears on the paper when the document is printed. For example, if a word is going to be underlined when it is printed, does the underline appear on the computer screen? How closely a word processor comes to WYSIWYG is another factor that determines its style, or its look and feel (Figure I–2).

Another factor that separates word processors is the set of conveniences each program offers. Some word processors allow you to display and work with more than one document at a time. Some programs remember up to the last five deletions that were made so that any of them can be restored if necessary. Some programs allow you to create a detailed summary description of each file. The conveniences a word processing package should include is a matter of user preference.

The remainder of this section discusses the writing and editing, screen formatting, and print formatting features that are available in most word processors. In addition, it will discuss some of the more current features, including desktop publishing features, that are found mostly in the newer word processors.

Writing and Editing Features

Writing and editing features make typing and changing text fast and easy. They make

FIGURE I–2

WYSIWYG
WordStar's 6.0 Advanced Page Preview displays pages exactly how they will appear when printed.

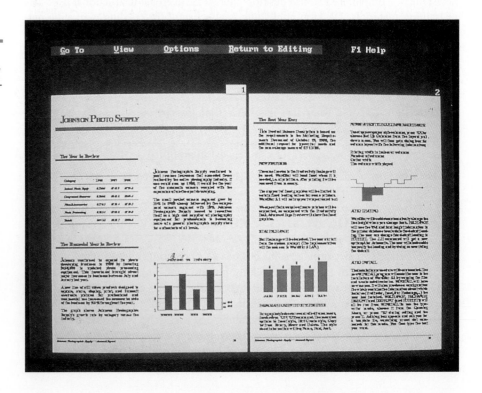

many of the mechanics typically associated with the manual writing of documents—such as cutting, pasting, and retyping—obsolete.

CURSOR MOVEMENT. The **cursor** is the line or box on the screen that shows the point where text can be entered on the screen. Most word-processing packages allow cursor movement anywhere on the screen, which speeds up typing and editing.

Keys used to move the cursor are programmed in the software package. Many computers use arrow keys to move the cursor. Today the mouse is gaining popularity as a hardware device. Some word-processing packages rely on a mouse to control the cursor.

Most systems offer many of the following possibilities for moving the cursor. By pressing one or two designated keys, the cursor will move to the location indicated.

- *Home:* Moves the cursor to the top left corner of the screen.
- *Top of page:* Moves the cursor to the first character on the screen.
- *End of page:* Moves the cursor to the last character on the screen.
- *Tab:* Moves the cursor to the right a set number of spaces.
- *Page up:* Displays the previous screen of text.
- *Page down:* Displays the following screen of text.
- *Next word:* Moves the cursor to the first character of the next word.
- *Previous word:* Moves the cursor to the first character of the word before it.
- *Beginning of line:* Moves the cursor to the first character of the first word in a line.
- *End of line:* Moves the cursor to the first character of the last word in a line.
- *Next page:* Shows the following page of the document and places the cursor at the first character on that page.
- *Previous page:* Shows the previous page of the document and places the cursor at the first character on that page.
- *Goto:* Moves the cursor to a specified location.

SCROLLING. If a document has twenty-five or more lines, all of the lines cannot be seen on the screen at once. **Scrolling** moves the lines of text on and off the screen. New lines move onto the screen as other lines scroll off. Scrolling can be visualized by imagining that the document is contained on a scroll and that the computer screen is a stationary window placed over the scroll. If we were to wind the scroll up, lines of text would disappear off the top of the screen and new lines would appear on the bottom. Word processors also allow you to scroll down. In this case, lines of text disappear off the bottom of the screen and new lines appear on the top.

Word processors also allow horizontal scrolling. Most monitors display up to 80 characters across the screen. If a line has more than 80 characters in it, characters will scroll off the left side of the screen as the cursor is moved to the right.

INSERT AND REPLACE. The **insert and replace** features allow new characters to be entered into a document, replacing old characters. They are commonly used functions in any word processor. Insert lets you add characters, words, sentences or larger blocks of text to the existing document. A new character or characters can be inserted in the middle of existing text. The characters that follow the inserted text move to the right to make room for it. The replace feature, sometimes called typeover, lets you make changes to a document by typing over existing text. As you enter text, the old text is replaced by the new text you key in.

Most programs give you a choice of being in the insert mode, where new characters are added to the existing text without deleting anything, or in the typeover or replacement mode, where new characters take the place of existing characters. Users commonly do most of their work in the insert mode, since it is easy to unintentionally lose text while working in the typeover mode. To switch between the two modes, programs use a command that acts as a toggle switch to put the program in one mode or the other. When the command is executed again, it switches to the other mode. The command used to toggle between the two modes varies from word processor to word processor, although many programs use the Insert key.

WORD WRAP. When you have reached the end of a line using a typewriter, you press the Return key to go to the beginning of the next line. Word processors have a feature called **word wrap** which eliminates the need for pressing Return to move on to the next line while entering text. At the end of a line, if a word goes past the margin, it automatically moves to the next line. This allows you to type faster since you do not have to know where each line must stop.

DELETE. Word processors allow for **deletion** of a character, word, or larger block of text from the document. There are typically two forms of character deletion in word processors. The first, backward deletion, deletes the character to the left of the cursor, moves the cursor back to that blank position, and then shifts the rest of the line over to fill in the space left blank. Most delete features automatically adjust the rest of the text to fill in the space. Typically the backspace key is used for reverse deletion. For example, each time the backspace key is pressed, it moves the cursor back one space, erases the character in that space, and closes up any remaining text.

Forward deletion is the second form of character deletion. The cursor is placed under or on the character to be deleted, and a delete command is executed, which erases the deleted character from the text. The remaining text shifts to the left filling the gap. This command is typically performed by pressing a single key, such as the Delete key. Continually executing this command, for example holding down the Delete key, continues the deleting and shifting. Entire words or phrases can be deleted using this method. Which of the two methods is more useful depends on the situation. Backward deletion is often used to correct typographical errors immediately after they are made. Forward deletion is commonly used to edit an existing document for meaning or style. Methods of deleting large sections of text are discussed in the next section on block operations.

BLOCK OPERATIONS. **Block operations,** which allow manipulation of large numbers of characters at the same time, are much more efficient than single-character operations. To begin block operations, mark the beginning and end of the block of characters you wish to manipulate. This is followed by the command to manipulate the block.

Marking a block of text typically requires that the cursor be moved to the beginning of the block, where a command is issued marking the beginning of the block. The cursor is then moved to the end of the block, and a similar command is issued marking the end of the block. The actual method for marking a block of text varies. Some programs have separate commands to mark the beginning and end of the block, whereas others use the same command for both. Some programs provide shortcuts for marking a word, sentence, paragraph, or even the entire document.

Word processing programs often display marked text differently from the rest of the text. Two common ways are inverse video and highlighting. Inverse video reverses the screen colors of the marked area of the text. Highlighting increases the intensity of the characters in the marked area.

Typical block operations include the following:

- Block-delete
- Block-move
- Block-copy
- Block-save
- Block-merge

Block delete marks a block of text and then issues a single command to delete the entire block of text. In some programs, once you delete a block of text it is irretrievably lost. Other, more "friendly" programs place the deleted block of text into a **buffer** (also called a clipboard). A buffer is a separate area of memory in which characters can be stored and retrieved. Typically, only one block of text can be stored in a buffer at a time. Newer word processors, however, can accommodate more than one block of text in the buffer. On older models, however, when another block of text is placed in the buffer, the previously stored block is erased. Some word processors allow you to view the contents of the buffer.

Block-move marks a block of text and then moves it from one location to another. (See Figure I–3.) This procedure is usually performed in one of two ways. The first way marks the block and places the cursor at the point to which you want to move the block. A command is issued to move the block of text. The second way, the cut and paste method, marks the block of text. Next, a command to cut the block is made. The text moves into the buffer and disappears from the display screen. Other operations that do not use the buffer may be performed next, or you can place the cursor where you want the text to be inserted and issue a paste command to place the block from the buffer back into the text.

Block-copy marks a block of text and duplicates it at a new location. Block-copies are accomplished in a similar fashion as block-moves, except the blocked text remains

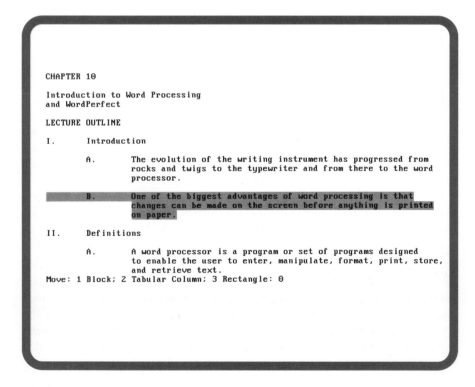

FIGURE I–3

The Block-Move Command from WordPerfect
WordPerfect uses the cut and paste method for moving blocks of text. The highlighted text will be cut from the document. The user can then move the cursor to the new location and press the Enter key to retrieve the block at the cursor's location.

in its original location since it is copied rather than deleted. Typically, once a block of text has been copied it can be retrieved an unlimited number of times. Only the most current block of text that has been copied, however, can be retrieved.

Block-save marks a block of text and saves it as a new file on a disk. **Block-merge** reads a file from disk and merges it with the document currently in memory.

UNDO. An **undo** feature cancels a command, allowing you to undo what you have done. The text returns to the form in which it existed before the command. For example, if you delete a page when you only meant to delete a word, the undo feature retrieves the page. In most word processors, however, the undo feature will only work for the last action taken. If you delete a page by mistake and then type even one new character, you may not be able to retrieve the page.

SEARCH. A **search** feature lets you look for a word or phrase in the document. This is helpful when you find a misspelled word in a long report. You can search for each occurrence of the word and then correct it.

Most word processors have a **search and replace** feature. This feature not only finds a certain word or phrase but also lets you replace it with another word or phrase. **Global search and replace** finds all occurrences of a word or words and automatically replaces the word with another word or words. For example, if a report uses the pronoun *he,* with one command you could find each *he* and change it to *she.*

Some word processors allow you only to search forward from the point of the cursor. Others are more flexible and allow you to search backward or to request a global search no matter where the cursor is presently located. Several options for beginning a match, that is, what the beginning characters must be in order for the program to consider that word a match, may also be available. Typical options are the following:

■ *Upper/lower case match:* The case of the strings must match exactly. For example, the string ''pizza'' would not match the string ''Pizza''.

■ *Whole word only match:* The string search must be for a separate word. For example, the string ''good'' would not be found in ''goodness''.

■ *Wildcard match:* Finds any words containing the specified characters in the specified location. For example if ''*'' were a wildcard character, ''re*'' would find *report, retread, rehire,* and so on.

SAVE. This feature saves the text stored in RAM onto a secondary storage device such as a floppy disk. When typing a long document, you should issue the save command often. Then, if the power goes off or you accidentally erase a large block of text, most of it will be saved on disk.

With some word processors, you can save a document and continue typing. Others assume you are finished when you save a document. If you want to continue, you have to load the document into memory again.

Screen-Formatting Features

Screen-formatting features control how the text appears on the screen and include displays that give on-screen information about the document. A small area on the screen displays status information, menu/command selections, and help/error messages. The larger portion shows the text being edited. The number of lines allocated to each section depends on the individual program. Users with less experience generally want more information displayed, whereas more experienced users generally prefer to have less information and more of the text displayed. Many programs avoid this conflict by allowing users to decide how much information to display. The following are some of the more common screen-formatting features.

SCREEN-ORIENTED WORD PROCESSING. In any word processor, the relationship between what is on the screen and what is printed on paper is important. Ideally, what you see on the screen should exactly match what is printed on the paper. As was mentioned earlier, this is generally referred to as "what you see is what you get." It is also known as **screen-oriented word processing.** Actually, most word processors will not match exactly. For example, you might choose to have the title of a paper centered on the page. With some word processors, the title may appear on the screen at the left margin, but when the paper is printed, the title will be centered. A more screen-oriented word processor centers the title on the screen. Some word processors may not show certain character enhancements on the screen, such as boldface or italics, but these character enhancements appear when the document is printed (Figure I–4). The closer a particular software package comes to screen-oriented word processing, the easier it is to format a document correctly the first time it is printed. An alternative to screen-oriented word processing is off-screen print formatting, which is discussed in the section on print-formatting features.

STATUS DISPLAYS. Some word processors show a status line on the screen. This line gives format information about the document. Examples of items in the status line are the following:

- Line number where the cursor is located
- Column where the cursor is located
- Page number of the page in the document where the cursor is currently located
- Amount of available memory
- Number of words or characters in the document
- Ruler line showing margins, tab stops, and indents

TABS/INDENTS. The **tab** feature of most word processors works the same as the tab key on a typewriter. Set tabs in any column and activate them by pressing the Tab key. Options include tabs that place columns of words to the left, center, or right of the tab setting. With some word processors, you set tabs so that columns of numbers line up along their decimal points.

The **indent** feature is used to indent all lines of a paragraph the same number of spaces in from the left margin. This feature is often used for lists and long quotations (Figure I–5).

PAGE BREAKS. Some word processors display a mark indicating the end of one page and the beginning of another. This feature helps avoid bad breaks in the text. For example, you would not want the last word of a paragraph on a new page. Page breaks can be set to occur automatically after a certain number of lines, or they can be manually placed at any position in the document. Inserting manual page breaks can be tedious; however, relying on automatic page breaks can create such problems as orphan and widow lines. An orphan line occurs when the first line of a paragraph is the bottom line of a page. The remainder of the paragraph follows at the top of the next page. A widow line occurs when the last line of a paragraph falls at the top of a page. The preceding lines of the paragraph are located on the bottom of the page preceding the widow line.

FIGURE I-4

Screen-Oriented Word Processing
Many word processors include a page preview feature that displays the text exactly as it will print. WordPerfect's page viewing feature, shown here, displays both text and graphics exactly as they will print on the page.

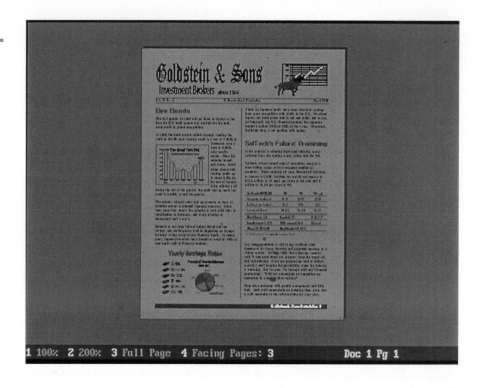

FIGURE I-5

The Indent Feature
Microsoft Word for Windows allows the user to easily indent and add bullets to any list.

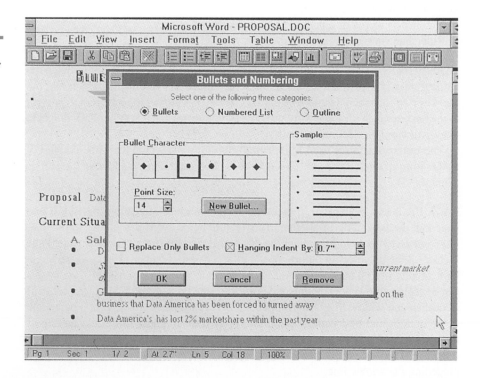

Print-Formatting Features

Print-formatting features determine how a document will look, such as the width of the margins and the amount of space between lines. Some word processors embed codes or print formatting commands within the text that direct the printer as to how to print the document. The exact commands may vary based on the particular word-processing program or the type of printer being used. Printer commands are usually surrounded by a special character such as a period or backslash that identifies them as printer commands. The special character print-formatting commands in a document are not printed. A print-formatting program interprets these commands and sends the results to the printer. This makes it difficult to tell how a document will look when it is printed by looking at what is on the screen. Some programs offer a print-preview feature that allows you to see on the display screen what the document will look like when it is printed. Most new programs use the screen-oriented formatting approach, which is easier to use and understand.

Print-formatting can be divided into three processes: page design, paragraph layout, and character attributes. Page design is the process of fitting the text on a page. Margins, headers and footers, and page numbering are all a part of a page design (Figure I–6).

MARGIN SETTINGS. Some word processors allow margins to be set on all four sides. Others allow only the left and right margins to be set. When the margins can be set by the user, many word processors have **default settings.** Default settings are preset margins that are activated when the user does not state any others.

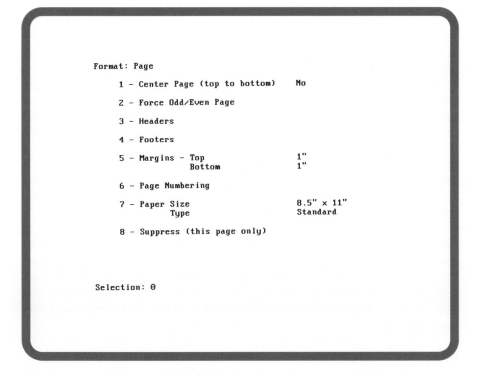

```
Format: Page

        1 - Center Page (top to bottom)     No

        2 - Force Odd/Even Page

        3 - Headers

        4 - Footers

        5 - Margins - Top                    1"
                      Bottom                 1"

        6 - Page Numbering

        7 - Paper Size                       8.5" x 11"
                     Type                    Standard

        8 - Suppress (this page only)



        Selection: 0
```

FIGURE I–6

The Page Format menu from WordPerfect

The selections made from the Page Format menu will determine the design of the page.

HEADERS AND FOOTERS. A **header** is a piece of text printed at the top of the page, such as a title for each page of text. A **footer** is a piece of text that is printed at the bottom of a page, such as a page number. Headers and footers are stored separately from the text. They are automatically printed at the appropriate place on every page in the document. There are usually options to place them left, right, or centered on a page.

PAGE LENGTH. Page length is typically stated in terms of the number of lines per page. The standard page is 8½-by-11 inches. One of the most common settings for this size of page is 6 lines per inch or 66 lines per an 11-inch page.

AUTOMATIC PAGE NUMBERING. A word processor that has **automatic page numbering** produces pages with printed page numbers. Some word processors let you choose where the page numbers appear. Others can print them only in one place, such as in the top right corner.

PARAGRAPH LAYOUT. On most word processors the Enter or Return key ends a string of characters forming a paragraph. Paragraph length could be one word or many sentences long. Typical areas of concern when designing a paragraph layout include paragraph margins and justification of text.

PARAGRAPH MARGINS. Most word processors allow control of margin settings for individual paragraphs, thereby overriding the page margins. This allows you to set off certain portions of the text.

CENTERED, LEFT, RIGHT, AND FULLY JUSTIFIED TEXT. Most word processors allow for centered, left, right, or fully justified text (Figure I–7 shows an example of each).

When you use a typewriter and **center** a line, you must count the characters in the line, divide this number by two, and then backspace that many times from the center of the page. Most word processors let you center a word or line by simply pressing one or two keys.

Left justified text is placed flush against the left margin with the right margin allowed to be ragged or uneven. Right justified text is placed flush against the right margin with the left margin allowed to be ragged. Fully justified text (usually referred to simply as justified text) is placed flush against both the left and right margins. One way to accomplish this is by adding spaces between words. However, this method can give the document an awkward appearance when the spacing between words varies widely. Another, more precise method is to use microspacing or proportional spacing. This method automatically inserts very small spaces between letters and words to give the document a more professional appearance.

LINE SPACING. A **line-spacing** feature lets the user choose the amount of space between lines. A document that is single spaced has no blank lines between printed lines. A double-spaced document has one blank line between printed lines. Many word processors allow for triple spacing. With some word processors, the line spacing appears only in the printed document and not on the screen. The screen shows only single spacing.

CHARACTER ATTRIBUTES. The appearance of an individual character is determined by its attributes. The attributes include character size, design, and enhancement.

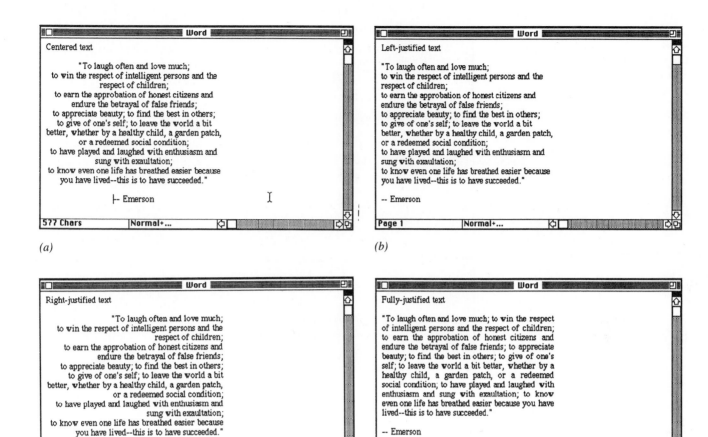

(a)

(b)

(c)

(d)

Character enhancements change the normal appearance of a character. They include such modifications as boldface, underline, italics, subscript, and superscript words. Boldface is type that is darker **(boldface).** Underlined words have a line printed under them (underline). Italic words slant to the right *(italic).* Subscript lowers the selected characters below the baseline of the text (sub$_{script}$). Superscript raises the selected characters above the baseline of the text (super^{script}). If the word processor has these features, the printer must have the capability to print them (Figure I–8).

Other Features

HELP FACILITIES. On-line help screens are tips called up on the display screen that give information about a command or function. Help screens are presented through a menu or context-sensitive system. With a menu system, whenever the help function is activated, a menu of all the available help topics is displayed. The user chooses the topic about which information is needed. With a context-sensitive system the program monitors the command or function being performed. When help is activated, the user immediately receives help information about the command or function being used.

FIGURE I–7

Examples of Text Justification from Microsoft Word

a. *Centered Text*
b. *Left Justified Text*
c. *Right Justified Text*
d. *Fully Justified Text*

FIGURE I-8

Character Enhancements

Examples of bold, underline, and italic text are shown in this sample newsletter

WINDOWS. In word processing, a window is an area of the screen that allows you to view a document or portions of a document. Early word processors had only one window. With one window, only one portion of a document can be seen at a time. The trend today is toward multiple windows. With multiple windows, several portions of one document or portions of several documents can all be seen at the same time. There are advantages to using more than one document window. You can edit several documents at once to maintain consistency. While writing a document, you can go to other documents or to other places in the current document for information. You can easily copy and move text between documents or within the current document.

DICTIONARIES AND THESAURUSES. Two valuable tools for any writer are a dictionary and a thesaurus. Many programs incorporate one or both of these on disk. A dictionary program allows a user to check spelling quickly and efficiently. Most dictionaries on disk include between 20,000 and 80,000 words. Some dictionaries on disk, however, include more than 100,000 words. Words spelled incorrectly or words not included in the dictionary are highlighted in some manner so the user can check them and make appropriate corrections. Many dictionaries allow you to add words to them. The electronic thesaurus allows you to request the synonyms of any word on the screen that is contained in the thesaurus (Figure I–9). If the word is not in the thesaurus, a message stating so is usually displayed. Some programs may let you add a new word with the appropriate synonyms.

PRINT MERGE. Many programs have a print merge option that allows you to print multiple versions of a document or personalize a form letter (Figure I–10). The option typically consists of two documents. The main document contains standard text that remains constant, with instructions and special fields that are used to receive the text

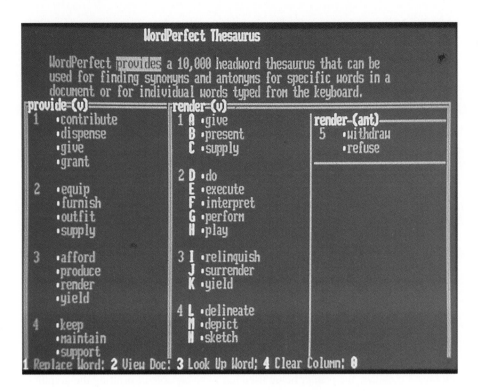

FIGURE I–9

Thesaurus
WordPerfect's thesaurus displays both synonyms and antonyms for specific words.

that varies from letter to letter. The merge document contains pieces of text that vary from letter to letter, such as names and addresses.

OUTLINING. Some of the more business-oriented word processors include an outline feature. A word processor with an integrated outline processor lets you set up an

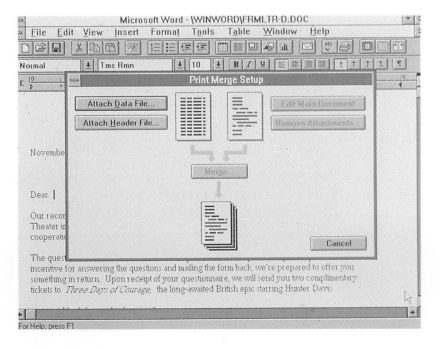

FIGURE I–10

Print Merge
Microsoft Word for Windows includes a Print Merge Helper feature that simplifies the process of generating form letters.

outline structure with different levels of headings and subheadings. Subheadings can be moved to other parts of the outline and the value of subheading can be increased or decreased within the outline hierarchy (Figure I–11).

HYPHENATION. The hyphenation feature of some word processors scans a document and prompts you as to where a hyphen can be inserted. Manual hyphenation enables the user to select exactly where the hyphen should be inserted in the word. With automatic hyphenation, hyphens are automatically inserted according to the program's rules and dictionary.

SORTING. The sorting feature enables the user to sort a list in ascending (a–z, 0–9) or descending (z–a, 9–0) order. Some word processing packages can sort on more than one variable.

MATH. Some word processors are capable of performing simple calculations such as adding, subtracting, dividing, and multiplying. The result of the calculation is inserted in the document.

DRAWING. The ability to set apart a portion of a document or report with lines and boxes is a useful feature that can add a professional touch to business and organizational documents. The title of a report, for example, could be highlighted by drawing a box around it. Some word processors offer a range of options and characters for drawing. Of course, the printer being used has to be capable of printing the graphics.

COLUMNS. The ability to put text into columns is also an important feature included in some word-processing packages. Some packages allow both parallel and

FIGURE I–11

Outlining
Ami Pro 2.0 includes an outline feature shown here in the window labeled OUTLINE.SAM. Ami Pro 2.0 also includes a revision marking feature and a scientific and equation editor feature.

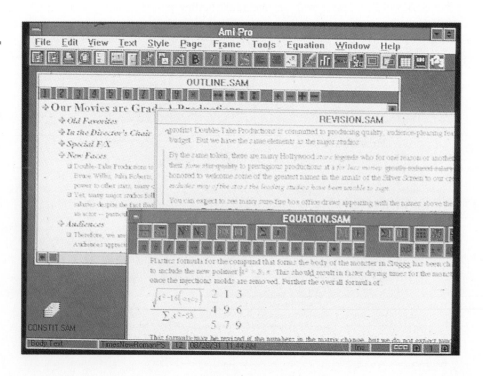

newspaper-style columns. Newspaper-style columns are columns where a single story or article runs to the bottom of one column and then continues at the top of the next column (Figure I–12). Depending on the word processing package, anywhere from 2 to 24 columns can be defined on a single page.

INDEXING/TABLE OF CONTENTS. The indexing feature included on some word processors enables you to generate an alphabetized index of key words or phrases with their corresponding page numbers. The table of contents feature generates a table of contents page that includes all the headings indicated by the user with their corresponding page number.

MACROS. A macro is a string of text that has been created and saved in a special macro file. The entire string of text can then be retrieved by pressing a key or a certain key combination. For example, if a lengthy title of a company is used throughout a report, you could enter that company's name once as a macro and then whenever you came to that name while entering the report, you would just type the key combination needed to retrieve the macro and the entire company name would appear on the screen (Figure I–13).

◻ HARDWARE REQUIREMENTS

Certain minimum hardware requirements must be met before a word-processing system is functional. The exact hardware needed to run a package depends on the word processor.

The most fundamental piece of hardware needed to run a word processor is a computer with sufficient memory to run the program. With the increased sophistication of even basic word-processing programs, the RAM requirements to run these programs have increased. Whereas in the early days of word processing a simple

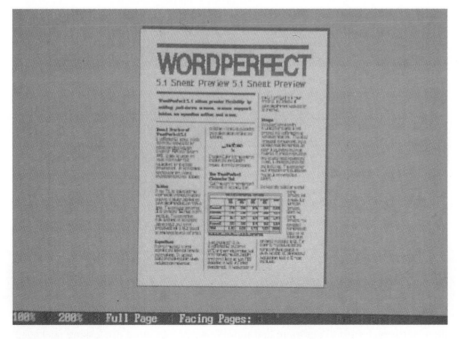

FIGURE I–12

Newspaper Style Columns Created with WordPerfect 5.1

FIGURE I-13

Macros

Lotus Manuscript 2.0's Tools option includes a macro feature.

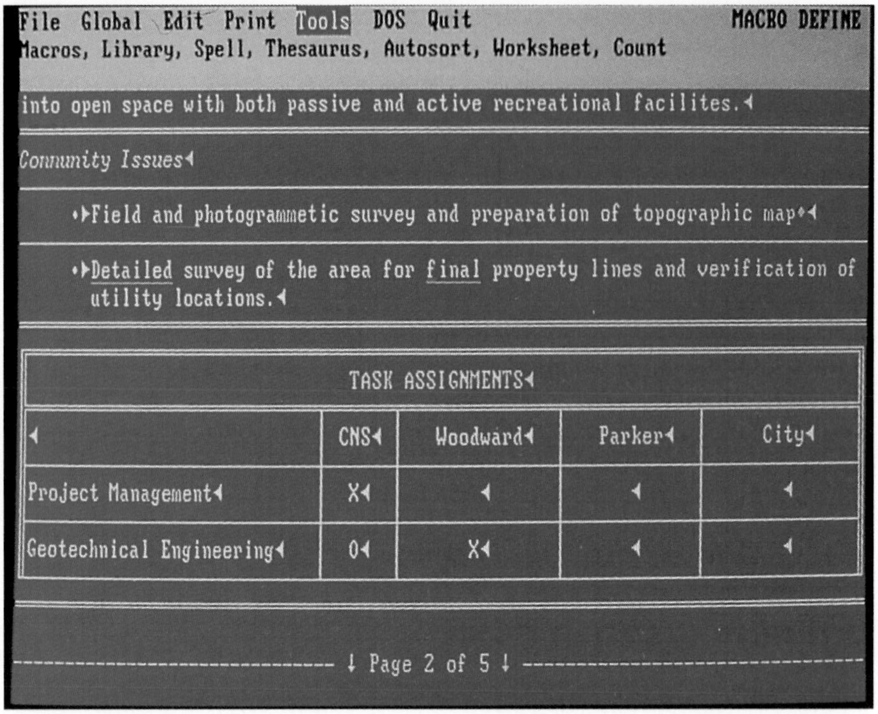

```
 File  Global  Edit  Print  Tools  DOS  Quit          MACRO DEFINE
Macros, Library, Spell, Thesaurus, Autosort, Worksheet, Count

into open space with both passive and active recreational facilites.◄

Community Issues◄

    ◆►Field and photogrammetic survey and preparation of topographic map◆◄

    ◆►Detailed survey of the area for final property lines and verification of
      utility locations.◄


    ┌─────────────────────────────────────────────────────────────────┐
    │                      TASK ASSIGNMENTS◄                            │
    ├───────────────────┬────────┬──────────┬──────────┬───────────────┤
    │ ◄                 │ CNS◄   │ Woodward◄ │ Parker◄  │    City◄      │
    ├───────────────────┼────────┼──────────┼──────────┼───────────────┤
    │ Project Management◄│ X◄    │   ◄      │   ◄      │      ◄        │
    ├───────────────────┼────────┼──────────┼──────────┼───────────────┤
    │ Geotechnical Engineering◄│ O◄ │ X◄   │   ◄      │      ◄        │
    └───────────────────┴────────┴──────────┴──────────┴───────────────┘


─────────────────────────── ↓ Page 2 of 5 ↓ ───────────────────────────
```

program might only require 64K RAM, today's simple word-processing programs generally require 384K. The more sophisticated programs require 512K. Some word-processing programs require as much as 640K to run properly.

The increased sophistication of word-processing programs has also made it necessary to have at least two floppy disk drives to run most of them. Even running some of the sophisticated word-processing programs on two floppy disk drives can be tedious. These programs really are best suited to running on a hard disk drive. For example, in order to run WordPerfect 5.1 from two floppy disk drives, each drive must be at least 720K or larger.

A monitor on which to view the text being entered is needed. The higher the resolution of the monitor, the sharper and clearer the characters will appear. High-resolution color monitors can be particularly helpful as some of the word processing programs display various functions in different colors. For example on some monitors WordPerfect displays italicized text in yellow and text that is superscript in pink.

Finally, a printer is needed. There are many types of printers on the market. Generally, a printer is selected based on how the word processor will be used. For example, an inexpensive, dot-matrix printer is adequate if the word processor is mostly being used for writing short letters and school reports. However, if the word processor is being used for desktop publishing, a laser printer is usually required.

❑ CURRENT TRENDS

Since word processing is the most competitive market in personal computer software, there has been a rush to get more and more features into word processing packages. If one word processor can claim to have a feature that none of the others have, that

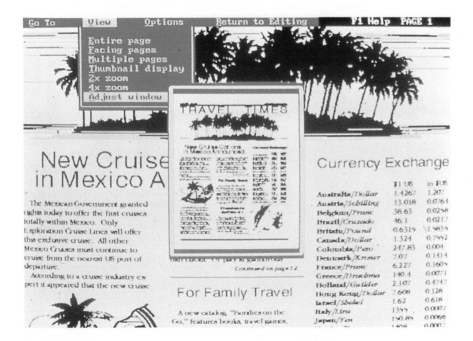

Continued on page 12

FIGURE I–14

Combining Graphics with Text
WordStar 6.0 allows the user to combine text and graphics.

might provide a significant marketing advantage. Most word processors on the market today have a plethora of features, many of which the average user will never need.

Some companies are trying to address the competition in the word-processing market by creating word processors that are specialized. For example, word processors have been developed that are specifically designed for the legal, insurance, and publishing environments. Of course, the problem with specialization is that if the word processor becomes too specialized, its potential market also becomes too limited.

Combining word processing with desktop publishing is certainly a current trend. This combination is sometimes called document processing. The newer word processors are trying to inject more and more desktop publishing features into their packages. Such desktop publishing features include the ability to merge graphics (Figure I–14), the ability to use a wide variety of type styles and sizes (Figure I–15) and the ability to control the positioning of texts or graphics on the page (Figure I–16).

In business-oriented word processors, another trend is the combination of word processors with other applications, such as spreadsheets and data managers, in an integrated environment. For example, the ability to combine word processing with a spreadsheet is useful if you need to incorporate spreadsheet tables or charts into a business report (Figure I–17).

---

1. Name the three general groups of word-processing features.

2. Describe word wrap.

3. Why is the undo feature useful?

4. Describe what type of information is included in the status line on the screen.

5. Name three print-formatting features.

CHECKPOINT I–2

FIGURE I–15

Fonts
Publisher's Type Foundry from ZSoft Corporation allows the user to build an entire type font library of sizes and styles from a single typeface.

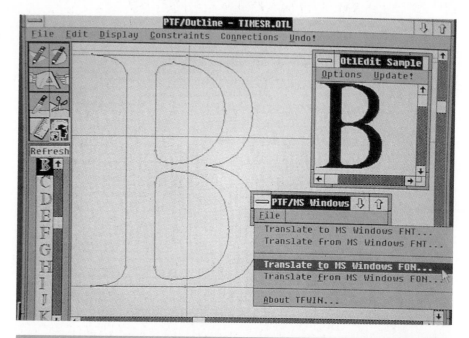

FIGURE I–16

Placing Graphics in a Document
With WordPerfect 5.0, graphics can be placed anywhere on the page.

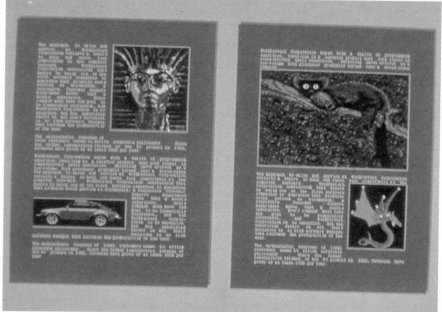

❑ SUMMARY POINTS

■ Word processors are used in homes, businesses, schools, and many other settings.

■ A word processor lets the user write, edit, format, and print text.

■ Text entered on a word processor is stored in RAM. Text that is stored using a secondary storage device, such as a floppy disk, can be retrieved later.

■ The features of a word processor depend on the purpose for which it will be used.

■ Common writing and editing features are cursor moving, word wrap, scrolling, insert and replace, delete, search, undo, and save.

■ Common screen-formatting features include tabs, page breaks, and status displays.

FIGURE I-17

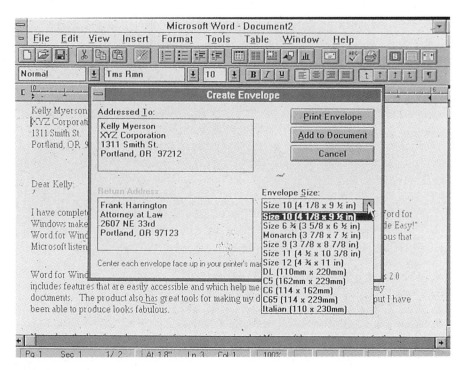

■ Common print-formatting features are margin settings, line spacing, centering, automatic page numbering, and special characters.

■ The basic hardware needed to run a word processor includes the computer, disk drive, monitor, printer, and printer interface card. More and more memory is being required by modern systems.

■ Some current trends in word-processing software include greater specialization, increasing connectivity with other programs such as spreadsheet programs and data managers, and a move toward document processing, which is the combination of word processing and desktop publishing.

◘ TERMS FOR REVIEW

automatic page numbering, p. A-16

block-copy, p. A-12

block-delete, p. A-11

block-merge, p. A-12

block-move, p. A-11

block operations, p. A-10

block-save, p. A-12

buffer, p. A-11

centered text, p. A-16

cursor, p. A-9

default settings, p. A-15

deletion, p. A-10

disk-based word processor, p. A-5

document-oriented word processor, p. A-6

editing window, p. A-2

footer, p. A-16

global search and replace, p. A-12

header, p. A-16

indent, p. A-13

insert and replace, p. A-9

line-spacing, p. A-16

memory-based word processor, p. A-5

◼ REVIEW QUESTIONS

1. What information does the status line of a word processor supply?

2. Describe the difference between a page-oriented word processor and a document-oriented word processor.

3. List five uses for a word processor.

4. What is the purpose of the scrolling feature?

5. Describe three block operations.

6. What is meant by "search and replace"?

7. What is a window in word processing? Why would it be useful to be able to work with multiple windows?

8. List the basic hardware devices needed for a computer to run a word-processing program.

9. Describe two of the current trends in word processing.

10. Describe three jobs you can do with a word-processor program that you could not do with a typewriter.

SECTION II

Spreadsheets

OUTLINE

INTRODUCTION

Like most computer programs, a **spreadsheet** takes care of simple, commonly encountered manual tasks. Basically, a spreadsheet program is a calculator that uses a computer's memory capability to solve mathematically oriented problems. With a spreadsheet program, you can set up columns of numbers to keep track of money or objects.

Typically, a pencil, a piece of paper, and a calculator are the tools used to solve mathematical problems. With a spreadsheet program, computers can calculate at the speed of electricity. This capability is useful with more complicated formulas. Imagine doing your tax returns and realizing after finishing that you forgot to include income from a part-time job as part of your yearly income. Every calculation following that part of the form would be incorrect. With a spreadsheet program, however, you simply insert the forgotten number and instantly recalculate all the totals. This is only one example of what a spreadsheet can do. With the ability to recalculate, as well as store, print, merge, and sort numeric information, a spreadsheet is an extremely useful tool.

This chapter describes what a spreadsheet is and how it is used, and covers features common to most spreadsheet programs. In addition, it discusses current trends in spreadsheet programs.

WHAT IS A SPREADSHEET?

Ledger sheets are primarily used in the business environment by accountants and managers for financial calculations and the recording of transactions. A spreadsheet is actually a ledger sheet like the one shown in Figure II–1. To keep the numbers in line, ledger sheets have columns in which the numbers are written.

An **electronic spreadsheet** is a grid of columns and rows used to store and manipulate numeric information. The grid appears on the display screen, and data is stored in the computer's memory. Probably the most significant advantage of an electronic spreadsheet over the traditional spreadsheet is the ability to store not only numbers but also formulas for calculating numbers. One number in a formula can easily be changed without reentering the entire formula. Table II–1 is a quick reference to terms frequently encountered when using an electronic spreadsheet.

A spreadsheet program enables a computer to perform complex mathematical calculations. Numbers, or **values,** are entered into the **cells** formed by the columns

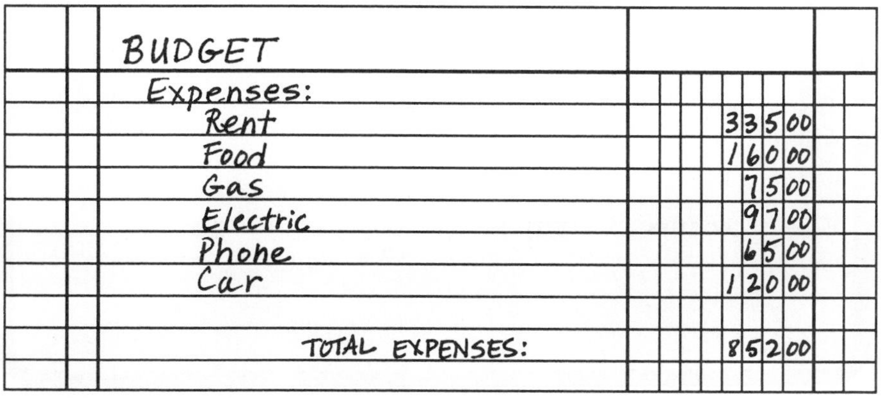
BUDGET
Expenses:
Rent 335 00
Food 160 00
Gas 75 00
Electric 97 00
Phone 65 00
Car 120 00
TOTAL EXPENSES: 852 00

FIGURE II–1

Traditional Paper Spreadsheet

TABLE II–1

Terms Associated with Electronic Spreadsheets

Term	Definition
Cell	A storage location within a spreadsheet used to store a single piece of information relevant to the spreadsheet.
Coordinate	The location of a cell within a spreadsheet; a combination of the column letter and row number that intersect at a specific cell.
Formula	A mathematical equation used in a spreadsheet.
Label	Information used for describing some aspect of a spreadsheet. A label can be made up of alphabetic or numeric information, but no arithmetic may be performed on a label.
Value	A single piece of numeric information used in the calculations of a spreadsheet.
Window	The portion of a worksheet that can be seen on the computer display screen.

and rows. Each cell relates to a certain storage location in the computer's memory. **Labels** can be entered to identify what the numbers mean (see Figure II–2).

Formulas as well as values can be entered into cells. A formula is a mathematical expression that can contain numbers from other cells. If a number in a formula is changed, the program automatically recalculates, using the new number.

FIGURE II–2

Labels and Values
Columns A, B, D, and F contain labels.
Columns C, E, and G contain values.

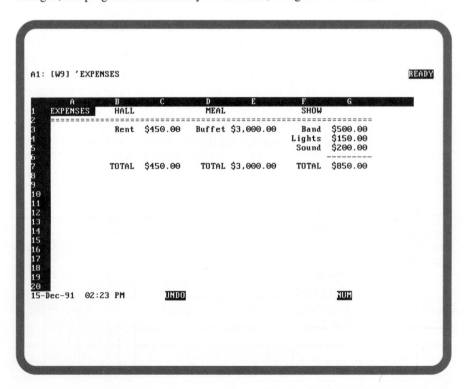

Since electronic spreadsheets can instantaneously recalculate a formula, they can be used to ask "what if" questions. These are questions seeking to find out what will happen to certain numbers in a spreadsheet if other numbers change. The following are examples of "what if" questions:

■ What if I spend $50 more at the grocery store each month?
■ What if the interest earned by my savings account goes up 0.5 percent?
■ What if I take a job working on commission rather than salary?

With a spreadsheet program, the computer instantly adjusts the numbers affected by the changed number. If a person calculated the numbers by hand or with a calculator, all the numbers would have to be recopied on a new paper spreadsheet. A spreadsheet program calculates in seconds what it would take a person several hours to do by hand. The new spreadsheet appears almost immediately on the screen.

■ How a Spreadsheet Works

When a new spreadsheet is loaded into the computer, a screen similar to the one shown in Figure II–3 appears. An electronic spreadsheet is comprised of numbers listed down the left side of the grid, which represent the rows, and the letters listed across the top of the grid, which represent the columns. Each cell in the spreadsheet has a name, or **coordinate.** The coordinate of a cell consists of a letter for its column and a number for its row. For example, if the cursor was at the cell in the upper left corner of the spreadsheet it would be in cell A1 since the first column is column A and the first row is row 1. Cell position C4 is in column C and row 4. Cell position D16 is in column D, row 16.

Data is entered into a spreadsheet by typing on the keyboard. The data enters the cell where the cursor is located. Figure II–4 is a very simple example of data entered into a spreadsheet. In this figure, the formula B2 + B3 + B4 + B5 + B6 + B7 enters cell B9. The "C2" that appears in parentheses in front of the formula signifies

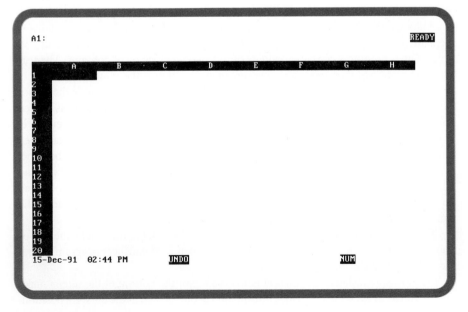

FIGURE II–3

A New Spreadsheet When First Loaded

FIGURE II–4

Electronic Spreadsheet for a Home
Budget

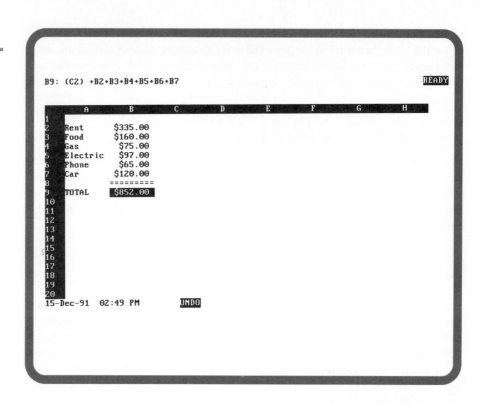

that the number should appear as currency with two decimal places. Notice that the number $632.00 appears on the screen in cell B9. That number is the sum of the numbers in cells B2 through B7 formatted as currency carried out to two decimal places. If a number in any one of the six cells in the formula changes, the entire spreadsheet will be recalculated.

In Figure II–4 the cells in column A contain labels. Each label tells what the number in the same row in column B represents. For example, the label FOOD in cell A3 indicates that the number in cell B3 stands for the amount of money spent on food.

Although the size of the spreadsheet—how many rows and columns it contains—depends on the program, most spreadsheets contain at least 64 columns and 256 rows. Other programs contain hundreds of rows and thousands of columns. The part of the spreadsheet that appears on the screen at one time is the **window.**

On most spreadsheet programs, the arrow keys on the keyboard move the cursor so that other parts of the spreadsheet can be seen on the screen. If the cursor is moved outside the window, the spreadsheet scrolls to reveal that part of the spreadsheet where the cursor is currently located. If you try to scroll past a border of a spreadsheet, most programs will beep or provide a message telling you that this cannot be done.

Another way to move the cursor is with a GOTO command. A GOTO command jumps the cursor to a specified cell coordinate. For example, if the cursor is located in cell A1, you can command it to go to cell R130. The GOTO command allows the cursor to move quickly to another location in the spreadsheet.

The cell identified by the cursor is the active cell available for immediate use or modification. Cell A1 is always the active cell when a spreadsheet program is first started. Moving the cursor changes the active cell.

On most spreadsheets, the lines at either the top or the bottom of the screen make up the **status area,** which provides information about the cell at the cursor's position.

In Figure II–4, the first item at the top of the screen, B9, indicates that the cursor is currently located in cell B9. After the (C2), already discussed, the next item displayed in the status area shows what was actually entered into the cell. In this example, the formula B2 + B3 + B4 + B5 + B6 + B7 was entered in cell B9.

There are several modes of operation in a spreadsheet. These modes may have slightly different names among different programs, but the functions are similar. We will refer to these modes as the ready mode, the entry mode, and the command mode.

When a spreadsheet program starts, it is always in the ready mode. This is the mode that enables the cursor to be moved around the spreadsheet. Notice in Figure II–4 the word "READY" in the upper right corner of the screen. In this ready mode, typing any valid character or command will activate one of the other modes. For example, typing a slash (/) in Lotus 1-2-3 puts you into the command mode. When the command mode is activated, the **command area,** a menu of the available commands, appears on the screen. Many spreadsheets have more than one command level; that is, by selecting one command, a menu showing additional available commands appears.

New information is entered into the active cell when the program is in the entry mode. The entry mode is activated by typing a letter, number, or symbol (for example, a plus, minus, left parenthesis, @ sign, or quotation mark). While in the entry mode, the cursor cannot be moved. The entry mode is typically terminated by pressing the Enter key. This causes whatever was in the cell before to be erased and replaced with the contents just entered. Pressing the Escape key also terminates the entry mode but leaves the old contents of the cell intact.

◼ Uses of Spreadsheets

Managers in decision-making positions frequently use spreadsheets. These individuals are responsible for making sure their companies run smoothly. Since an important part of running any business is managing money, goods, and employees, a spreadsheet program can be invaluable.

Business data, such as sales figures, expenses, payroll amounts, prices, and other numbers, are stored in the spreadsheet (Figure II–5). A manager can enter formulas to calculate profits and losses. Other formulas compute the percentage of profits paid in taxes. An increase in the cost of a material used in manufacturing can be entered into a spreadsheet to show how the increase affects profits. By using a spreadsheet to quickly answer "what if" questions, a manager can, in short, spend more time thinking about how to run the business.

Because these programs simplify any task that requires calculating numbers, owners of home computers can also benefit from using spreadsheets. One common home use of a spreadsheet program is to keep track of household expenses. The program can figure the percentage of each paycheck that goes to rent, electricity, and food. You can then see which expenses increase and decrease each month. You can also find out how much should be saved each month for a family vacation or a new appliance.

A spreadsheet program can keep track of a team's weekly bowling scores. It can record and calculate charitable contributions. It can keep track of your grades at school and determine the marks you need to get the grades you want.

Complex spreadsheets are used in science and engineering. Scientists can use spreadsheets to calculate the outcomes of their experiments under different conditions. Engineers can use them to estimate the cost of a job when preparing bids on a contract.

FIGURE II–5

Microsoft® Excel Spreadsheet Used to
Store Payroll Amounts

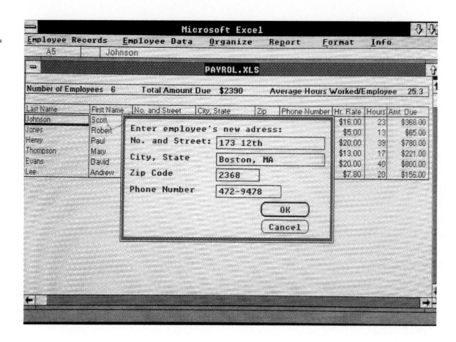

Once they have the contract, they can use spreadsheets to keep track of the quantities
of materials ordered. When the job is completed, the spreadsheet can go to the
accounting department to help in billing the customer.

CHECKPOINT II–1

1. How is a spreadsheet used?

2. What is the purpose of labels in a spreadsheet?

3. How is each cell in a spreadsheet named?

4. Suppose cell B4 contains the value 56. If the formula B4/2 is entered into cell
B9, what value will be shown in cell B9? What would the spreadsheet program do
if the value in cell B4 were changed to 70?

5. How are spreadsheets used in businesses? How are they used in homes?

■ FEATURES OF SPREADSHEETS

More than two hundred spreadsheet programs are on the market today. Lotus 1-2-3
is the most commonly used spreadsheet program, although some other spreadsheet
programs are giving Lotus stiff competition, such as Borland's Quattro Pro and
Microsoft's Excel. Spreadsheet programs have features to fit certain needs. Many are
easy to use. Others help the user solve a specific type of problem. Still others have
features to give them speed during processing.

The purpose of most spreadsheet features is to make the program flexible. This
means that the user can adapt the spreadsheet to individual needs. The following
common features are found in most spreadsheets.

Variable Column Width

Variable column width is a feature that allows the user to set the width of columns. This feature is particularly useful when entering long descriptive labels.

For example, if names of people are used as labels in a column with a width of twelve characters, some names might not fit in a cell. Shortening the names might be confusing. With the variable column width feature, you can set the column to hold as many characters as needed. That way each name fits in the cells, avoiding confusion (Figure II–6).

Automatic Spillover

The **automatic spillover** feature allows labels that are too long for one cell to spill over into the next cell. This feature solves the same problem as variable column width does, but only for labels, not for values. For example, if you have a label with 16 characters in cell B3 and column B has a column width of 12, the first 12 characters will be placed in cell B3. The last 4 characters will run over into cell B4. If, however, you had a value with 16 numbers in it in cell B3, the cell would be filled with asterisks or some other character symbol. In order for the actual number to be displayed in the cell, the column width would have to be changed to 16. The automatic spillover feature only works with labels (Figure II–7).

Titles

A **title** feature shows the labels in a spreadsheet on the screen at all times. This feature is useful when the spreadsheet has data in many columns and rows. If labels are

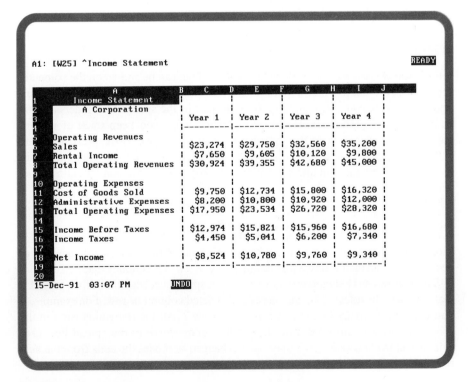

FIGURE II–6

Variable Column Width on Lotus 1-2-3
Column A has 25 characters, columns B, D, F, H, and J have only 1 character, and columns C, E, G, and I have 9 characters.

FIGURE II-7

Automatic Spillover from Lotus 1-2-3
*The title "Income Statement" spills
over from column A to column B.*

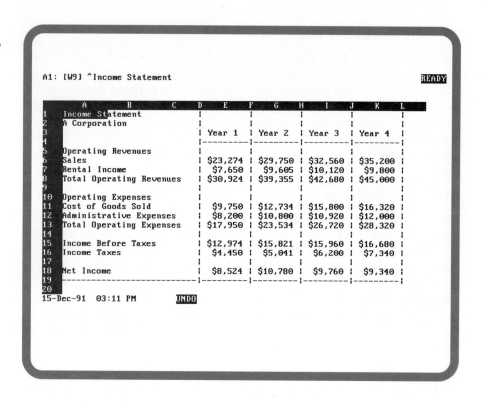

entered in the first column, they cannot be seen if the cursor is positioned in column 30. The title feature freezes labels on the screen so they can be seen at all times, regardless of which columns or rows appear on the screen. Titles can be frozen in rows only, in columns only, or in both rows and columns.

Windows

Since a spreadsheet has more columns and rows than can be shown on the computer screen at one time, a window feature lets you divide the screen into miniscreens. Each window thus created shows a different part of the spreadsheet independently of the others (Figure II-8). The window feature helps you keep track of what is happening in other parts of the spreadsheet or in other files. Most spreadsheets are capable of displaying only two windows at the same time; however some programs, in particular those that run under the Windows program (see Section VI), allow more (Figure II-9).

Inserting and Deleting Rows and Columns

Most spreadsheets allow you to add new columns or rows to the spreadsheet as needed. You can also remove a column or row, even if it contains data.

This feature can be dangerous, however, if the spreadsheet does not adjust formulas that contain cells affected by the inserted or deleted column or row. For example, if you add a new row 6, the old row 6 becomes row 7. All the remaining rows in the spreadsheet are renumbered, too. If a formula somewhere in the spreadsheet uses cells from the old row 6, it will have to be changed so it uses the cells from the new row 7. If the formula is not changed, it will be wrong.

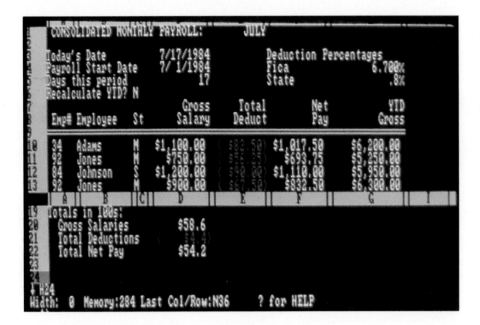

FIGURE II–8

Windows
Two windows are displayed on this spreadsheet. The first window displays cells A1 through G13. The second window displays cells A19 through G23.

Some spreadsheets automatically adjust the formulas. If a row or column is added that affects cells used in formulas, the program changes the cells in the formulas to correspond to their new location in the spreadsheet.

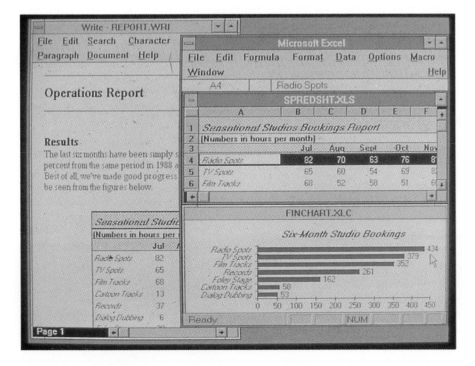

FIGURE II–9

Displaying more than Two Windows
A spreadsheet file, a chart, and a word processing file are all displayed on the screen at one time using the Microsoft Windows Program.

FIGURE II–10

Spreadsheet Graphics

This 3-dimensional bargraph was generated from the spreadsheet at the left using the Microsoft Excel program for Windows.

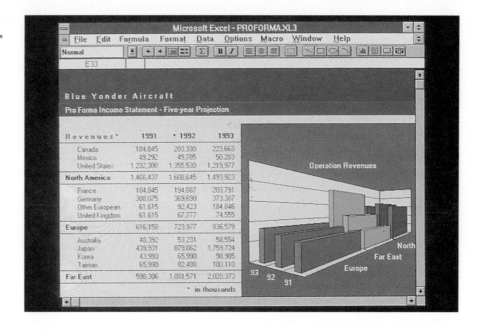

Graphics

Many spreadsheets can create graphs using data from the spreadsheet. These may be bar or line graphs or pie charts (Figure II–10).

Predefined Formulas

Most spreadsheet programs allow a user to save frequently used formulas. If a spreadsheet is used frequently for the same purpose, you may want to set up a **template.** A template saves time by using a set of predefined formulas already entered into a spreadsheet. For example, a template could be prepared for weekly bowling scores. Then each week the new figures could be entered without having to reenter the formulas. Templates are time savers.

Some spreadsheets come with predefined formulas already stored in the program. These ready-to-use templates are for specific purposes such as real estate management or investment tracking.

Locking Cells

To prevent a user from altering or destroying a template, cells containing formulas can be **locked.** Once a cell is locked, no one (without the correct password) can change it. Cells are locked by using a special command supplied by the spreadsheet program.

Hiding Cells

Some spreadsheets can hide the contents of a cell, so they are not shown on the screen. This feature is useful when a company enters data that employees are not supposed to see. When a person uses the spreadsheet, the contents of **hidden cells** are not displayed on the screen.

Formatting Cells

Formatting commands control how the contents of a cell are displayed. Both values and labels can be formatted. Options for formatting the contents of a cell containing a value include embedded commas, leading dollar signs, trailing percent signs, and the number of places included after the decimal point. In many programs, cells containing either values or labels can be formatted so that the contents are right justified, left justified, or centered within the cell. Once you decide how you want a cell formatted, you issue the appropriate formatting command and the format rule for that cell is created. The format rule is stored for each cell along with the cell's value. Most programs display the formatting rule for the active cell in the status area (Figure II–11).

Format rules can be assigned to an individual cell, a group of cells, or globally for the entire spreadsheet. In many spreadsheets, issuing a global format command does not override individual or previously given group format commands.

Ranges

A range of cells is a rectangular group of cells that is treated as a unit for some operation. A range may be a single cell, part of a column, part of a row, or a larger rectangle of cells from several rows and columns (Figure II–12). Methods used to identify a cell range vary from program to program. Some programs use cursor movement keys, some use a mouse, and others have the user specify the coordinates of the upper-left and lower-right corners of the range.

Once a range of cells has been marked, several different operations can be performed. For example, a specific range of calls can be printed, copied, moved, or deleted.

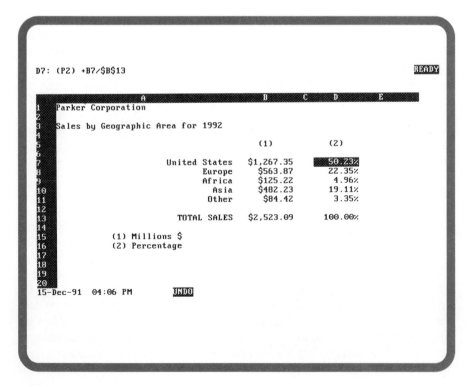

FIGURE II–11

Formatting Rule for Cell D7 in Lotus 1-2-3
The status line displays the current format of cell D7. P2 means percentage with two decimal places.

FIGURE II–12

A Range of Cells on Lotus 1-2-3
The range of cells B5 through D18 have been marked on this worksheet.

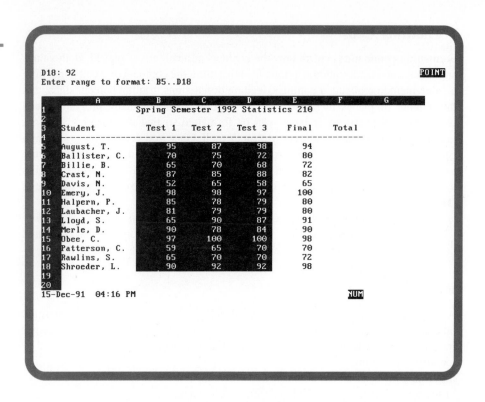

Copy

The **copy** feature is a frequently used spreadsheet feature. This function allows the user to copy a cell or group of cells to another part of the spreadsheet. For example, if you use the same data several times in one spreadsheet, you can continually copy the cell containing that data throughout the spreadsheet. With the copy feature, the same data only has to be entered once.

Most spreadsheets allow you to copy cells from one spreadsheet to another. Some spreadsheet programs use windows and a temporary storage area (often called a buffer or clipboard) to copy from one spreadsheet to another. Other spreadsheet programs allow the user to specify a range of cells in another spreadsheet stored on disk and then directly read that information from the disk into the active spreadsheet.

Recalculation

The **recalculation** feature automatically adjusts the result of a formula when a cell used in the formula changes. In some programs, you can turn the recalculation feature on and off. You might want to turn it off if you are changing several cells. When the recalculation feature is off, only the value for the cell just entered is recalculated. The computer will not process changes in any formula that result from changing the contents of the cell until you request them. To bring the entire spreadsheet up to date, the user has to tell the spreadsheet program to recalculate the formulas. When the user tells the program to recalculate all the formulas (rather than having the program automatically recalculate formulas as soon as a cell is changed), it is called manual recalculation. In the manual recalculation mode, the program waits until given the appropriate command before recalculating the spreadsheet. When the automatic re-calculation mode is in effect, the computer recalculates all formulas after each entry, which can waste a lot of time in a large spreadsheet.

Sorting

Some spreadsheet programs sort data within the spreadsheet. **Sorting** can be done alphabetically if the cells contain labels. Sorting can also be done numerically if the cells contain numbers or formulas.

Functions

Most spreadsheets provide functions as a shortcut to accomplish certain tasks. The most common categories of functions are statistical, mathematical, financial, string, and logical. Statistical functions accept a list of items and automatically calculate the statistics. Some common statistical functions include computing the average and the standard deviation of a list of items. Mathematical functions accept a single value and perform a mathematical transformation on that value. Other mathematical functions include trigonometric functions and an exponential function. Financial functions calculate the compounding of interest rates on sums of money over time. Other common financial functions compute internal rate of return and net present value. String functions perform operations on text in the spreadsheet. Common string functions calculate the number of characters in a string, convert a string from a label format to a value format, and truncate a string after a certain number of characters. Logical functions test the condition of cells or compare the values between two cells.

Macros

More sophisticated spreadsheet programs that are used primarily in the business environment include a **macro** feature. Macros enable you to automate and customize a spreadsheet to meet your particular needs. Put simply, a macro is a sequence of keystrokes entered into one or more cells that can be activated with a single command that often involves only two keystrokes. This sequence of keystrokes can include labels, values, any of the spreadsheet commands, and special macro commands. The sequence of keystrokes, written in the macro command language of the spreadsheet being used, becomes a simple program.

A simple example of a macro would be a lengthy label that is used throughout a spreadsheet. A user could create a macro for that label. Then, wherever the label appeared in the spreadsheet, the user would simply evoke the macro by pressing two keys. The actual label would appear in that cell, saving the user a lot of time and lessening the likelihood of a typographical error. A sophisticated example of a macro would be a full-fledged program used for developing custom business applications.

Macros can be used to automate almost any spreadsheet task. Macros are used most often to perform the following:

■ Automating frequently used spreadsheet commands. For example, a macro that formatted a cell to appear with a trailing percent sign might be useful in a spreadsheet that contained a lot of percentages.

■ Typing the same label in a spreadsheet. For example, if a spreadsheet repeatedly contained the first six months of the year as labels, a macro of those months would save the user a lot of typing.

■ Performing a repetitive procedure that requires a series of sequential commands. For example, the printing of a spreadsheet involves a series of sequential commands. A macro that printed a worksheet would be useful to those who needed hard copies of all their work.

■ Developing a customized worksheet for someone who is not familiar with spreadsheet programs.

File Linking

A feature that many of the newer spreadsheets are including is called file linking. Lotus introduced file linking with Lotus 1-2-3 Release 2.2. A cell in a Release 2.2. worksheet can contain a link to a cell in another file. If the contents of that cell are changed, the cell in the worksheet to which it is linked will be updated the next time that worksheet is loaded or when the user issues a command to update the link.

Lotus 1-2-3 Release 3.0 and the latest versions of Quattro Pro and Excel all offer more sophisticated file-linking capabilities. Instead of only linking a cell in one worksheet to a cell in another file, these programs allow the user to link formulas to cells and to ranges in files on a disk.

Multiple Pages

The multiple page feature is sometimes referred to as a "3-D" spreadsheet. This feature is found in the newer spreadsheet programs. All spreadsheets have two dimensions, length and width, formed by the columns and rows. Spreadsheets can also have "depth." For example, if a company stored monthly sales figures in separate spreadsheet files and those files were stacked on top of one another like pages (in twelve sales files from January through December) the spreadsheets could be seen as having "depth." One cell, for example one region's sales figures for a particular product, could be tracked throughout the year, from January to February, and so on. This data can then all be consolidated on a separate worksheet. A spreadsheet that has multiple page capabilities enables a user to layer consecutive worksheet pages within a file (Figure II–13).

Different programs take a different approach to the multiple page function. Lotus 1-2-3 Release 3.0 works with the multiple pages as one file. A file can hold up to 256 worksheet pages stacked behind one another. Quattro Pro treats each page as a separate file. The pages are placed in variable-size windows. The windows can be positioned anywhere on the screen.

■ Hardware Requirements

Minimum hardware requirements must be met to make a spreadsheet functional, the exact hardware depending on the particular package. The following are basic hardware requirements for any spreadsheet program.

■ *Internal memory.* All software packages require that the computer have a minimum amount of internal RAM memory. With a spreadsheet program, memory is used to store program instructions and the data entered into the spreadsheet. The more internal memory the computer has, the more data can be stored in a spreadsheet.

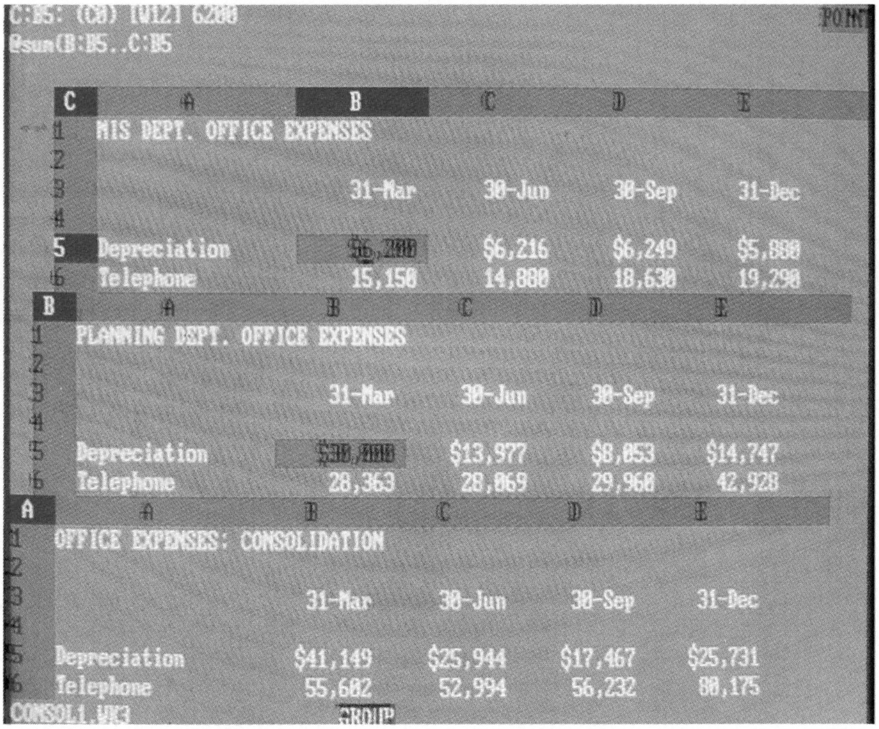

FIGURE II–13

3-D Worksheet from Lotus 1-2-3 Release 3.0
This 3-D worksheet illustrates how a user would perform consolidation of office expenses from several departments. Three consecutive worksheets are displayed. As the formula in the upper-left portion of the screen indicates, the user is adding the depreciation expenses for the various departments. The pointer is located in the same cells on both sheets B and C.

■ *Secondary storage.* Floppy disks are a common type of secondary storage used with spreadsheets. If floppy disks are your secondary storage, two disk drives are needed. Although business-oriented spreadsheet programs may be capable of running on two floppy disk drives, it usually is far more efficient to run these programs on a computer with a hard disk drive and at least one floppy disk drive.

■ *Printers.* The type of printer needed depends on how the spreadsheets will be used. If spreadsheets are mostly for your personal use, a dot-matrix printer is adequate. But if the spreadsheets are to be used for business purposes, a letter-quality printer is more appropriate. Since most spreadsheets are too large to fit on $8\frac{1}{2} \times 11''$ paper, a printer that will hold oversize paper and print in condensed type is also desirable. If the spreadsheet program is being used to create graphs, the printer should be capable of producing graphs.

■ *Monitor display.* If the spreadsheet program is being used to create graphs, the monitor also should be capable of displaying graphs. A special graphics board can be installed in the computer that enables the graphs to be displayed. If the computer does not have a graphics board, most spreadsheet programs with graphics capabilities allow the user to create a graph and print it even though it cannot be seen on the screen.

As spreadsheet programs become more sophisticated, the hardware needed to run them also has to be more sophisticated. For example, Lotus 1-2-3 Release 3.0 requires a computer with at least a 286 processor and 1 MB of available memory in order to run.

◼ CURRENT TRENDS

Just as desktop publishing is moving into the area of word processing, so is user-definable graphics moving into the area of spreadsheets. With the advent of laser printers and more sophisticated spreadsheet programs, businesses are now using spreadsheet programs to create some of their forms. For example, the spreadsheet program Excel is capable of producing a legal 1040 tax form.

Another parallel can be drawn between the current trends in word processing and in spreadsheets. Word processing programs are including more and more desktop publishing features, eliminating the need to acquire a separate desktop publishing program. Similarly, spreadsheet programs are beginning to include presentation graphics features, eliminating the need to acquire a separate presentation graphics program, such as Harvard Graphics. Quattro Pro, for example has built-in presentation graphics capabilities such as a draw program, clip art, and a slide show facility. Lotus 1-2-3 Release 3.1 includes the ability to use many different fonts, colors, lines, and borders. Important data can be highlighted, text and graphics can be combined on one page and graphs can be annotated (Figure II–14).

Another trend in spreadsheets is a move towards simplifying data consolidation, that is, taking data from several worksheets and consolidating it into a new worksheet. The latest version of Excel, for example, includes a new feature called Data Consolidate. Data Consolidate allows the user to point and click to summarize as many as 256 worksheets. The user first loads a set of worksheets and then highlights the areas in each that are to be consolidated. Excel creates a summary worksheet based on the labels in the detail worksheets. For example, all the cells under the label 1991 and in the row labeled ''Commissions'' would be added together in a summary sheet.

FIGURE II–14

Presentation Graphics Features in Spreadsheet Programs
This spreadsheet from Microsoft Excel for Windows use a draw program and boxed text to highlight certain data.

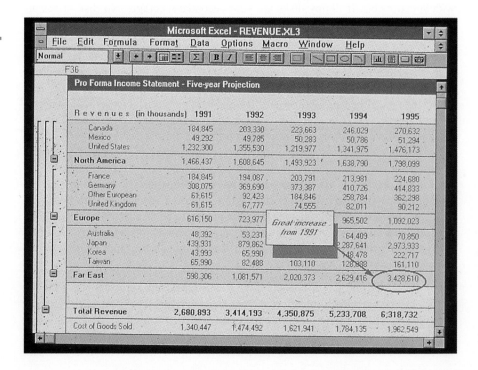

One of the fastest growing trends in spreadsheet programs is what is known as ''add-in products.'' Add-in products work in conjunction with an existing spreadsheet program to enhance it. Today there are over forty add-in products available for many of the popular spreadsheet programs.

Word processing is a popular add-in product for many spreadsheet users. Word processing is the most popular application in personal computing. Spreadsheets are the second most popular application. Being able to combine the top two applications results in an enormous productivity gain. With a word-processing add-in product, a user could, while working in a spreadsheet, access a word-processing document simply by pressing one or two keys. Data could then be taken from the spreadsheet and placed into the word-processing document. Add-in word processors can greatly simplify the process of writing business reports.

Some add-in word processors are capable of dynamic linking. Dynamic linking links an area in the spreadsheet with an area in the word-processing document. If any changes are made to the spreadsheet, the word-processing document automatically adjusts to reflect those changes.

Some of the more sophisticated spreadsheet programs are including simple word-processing features right in the spreadsheet program. The TEXT command in Lotus 1-2-3- Release 3.1, for example, allows the user to specify a worksheet range that can be used as a word-processing window. The font, color, and attribute of the text in the word-processing window can easily be changed. Text entered into this window automatically wraps around at the end of each line.

Another popular add-in product is a sideways printing program. Nearly all spreadsheets created for business purposes are too long to fit across a piece of paper that is only 8½ inches wide. A sideways add-in program prints a spreadsheet vertically down the paper rather than horizontally across paper. Lotus 1-2-3 Release 2.2 includes a printing utility called Allways. In addition to printing much more attractive output, the Allways printing utility allows spreadsheets to be printed vertically down the paper.

Add-in graphics, add-in data base managers, and add-in communications are also popular. This current trend of developing add-in products for spreadsheet programs indicates a move toward a truly integrated environment. An integrated environment is one in which, for example, the user can easily move from a spreadsheet to a word processor to a data base. In the ideal integrated environment, all the applications would be dynamically linked. That is, a change made in one application would automatically be reflected in all the other applications. It would not matter which application was used to make the change. The most current information would be found at once in the spreadsheet, the word processor, and the data base.

CHECKPOINT II–2

1. What problem is solved by a variable column width feature?

2. Explain the danger of adding or removing a column from a spreadsheet when the column contains data.

3. What is a template?

4. Why would you want to hide the contents of a cell?

5. Explain how a recalculation feature works.

■ SUMMARY POINTS

■ Spreadsheet programs help solve math problems. They let you set up columns of numbers to keep track of numeric data.

■ An electronic spreadsheet is a program that displays data on a grid of columns and rows.

■ Values (numbers) are entered into cells formed by the columns and rows. Labels can be entered to tell you what the numbers mean.

■ Formulas are mathematical expressions that can also be entered into the cells of a spreadsheet.

■ Spreadsheets help answer ''what if'' questions. ''What if'' questions are formed when you want to know what will happen to certain numbers in a spreadsheet if other numbers change.

■ A cell's coordinate tells the cell's location in the spreadsheet. It is made up of a letter or letters for its column and a number for its row.

■ The part of a spreadsheet that you can see on the screen at one time is called the window. The status area shows information about the cell at the cursor's position. The command area displays usable commands.

■ Spreadsheets are used by people in business to help them make decisions about running their companies. In homes, spreadsheets are used to simplify any task that requires calculating numbers.

■ Spreadsheet programs have different features to fit different needs.

■ The variable column width feature lets you set the width of columns.

■ The automatic spillover feature allows labels that are too long for one cell to spill over into the next cell.

■ An insert feature lets you add new columns or rows to the spreadsheet after data has been entered. A delete feature lets you remove a column or row.

■ A template is a set of predefined formulas already entered into a spreadsheet.

■ A locking cell feature lets you lock a cell so data cannot be changed or erased unless you use a special command. Another feature lets you hide the contents of a cell.

■ A title feature shows spreadsheet labels on the screen at all times.

■ A copy feature lets you copy a cell or group of cells to another part of the spreadsheet.

■ The recalculation feature automatically adjusts the result of a formula when one of the cells used in it is changed.

■ The hardware requirements to consider with a spreadsheet program are internal memory size, and the type of secondary storage, printer, and monitor display needed.

■ One growing trend in spreadsheet programs is the development of add-in products. Add-in products are used in conjunction with a spreadsheet program to enhance it. Some examples of add-in products are word processing, graphics, and data-base management.

■ TERMS FOR REVIEW

cell, p. A-27

command area, p. A-31

coordinate, p. A-29

copy, p. A-38

electronic spreadsheet, p. A-27

formula, p. A-28

hidden cells, p. A-36

lables, p. A-28

locked cells, p. A-36

macro, p. A-39

recalculation, p. A-38

sorting, p. A-39

spreadsheet, p. A-27

status area, p. A-30

template, p. A-36

value, p. A-27

variable column width, p. A-33

window, p. A-30

■ REVIEW QUESTIONS

1. Define the following terms: *value, cell, label,* and *formula.*

2. When are "what if" questions used?

3. Where would cell E10 be located in a spreadsheet? Where would cell H7 be located?

4. What is the window of a spreadsheet?

5. What type of information is found in the status area of a spreadsheet?

6. Think of two ways you personally could use a spreadsheet program. Explain these uses.

7. Why is an automatic spillover feature helpful when you enter labels in a spreadsheet?

8. Why would you want to store predefined formulas in a spreadsheet?

9. What is the purpose of locking cells?

10. How does a title feature help you in a spreadsheet program?

11. What does the term *dynamic linking* mean?

Data Managers

◼ INTRODUCTION

Schools, hospitals, restaurants, and in fact all types of businesses store data. The ability to retrieve, sort, and analyze data quickly and efficiently could make the difference between a company's success and failure. No other business application has more strategic importance to a company than a data-base management system. The types of data collected include employee records, customer records, inventory, invoice information, and insurance information. Before microcomputers became standard business equipment, the most common way to organize data was to store the records in folders in file cabinets. File cabinets, however, use a lot of space, and sometimes several departments may keep the same data. This duplication of data is a waste of time, effort, and space and can lead to confusion or errors when data has to be updated.

Data managers are software packages that computerize record-keeping tasks. This section explains what a data manager is and how it works. It also describes how data managers are used and summarizes their most common features.

◼ WHAT IS A DATA MANAGER?

A data-manager software package is used to organize files. Data managers let you store and access data with your computer. All the data previously kept in folders and envelopes in a manual filing system can be stored on secondary storage devices such as floppy disks.

Understanding how data is stored in a filing cabinet is easy. Folders with related data are kept in the drawers of the cabinet. Each folder has a label that identifies the contents. The contents of each drawer may be related to a certain topic. To find one data item, you would have to select the appropriate drawer and then search through the folders in that drawer to find the one with the data you needed.

With a data manager, data is recorded electronically on a secondary storage device. Instead of people looking through drawers and folders for a certain item, the computer searches the disk or tape for it.

Each data item, such as a student name, an insurance policy number, or the amount of a bill, is called a **field** (Figure III–1).

A group of related fields form a **record.** Your school may keep a record about each student. A student record might contain fields such as the student name, home address, parents' names, class standing, courses taken, and grade-point average.

A **file** is a group of related records. For example, all the student records in a school make up one file. The school may have other files, such as one for teacher records, another for financial records, and yet another for school board records. Data managers are useful because they perform the tasks of data storage and retrieval faster and more easily than a manual filing system. Most data managers can perform the following tasks:

- Add or delete data within a file
- Search a file for certain data
- Update or change data in a file
- Sort data into some order
- Print all or part of the data in a file

Tasks such as adding, deleting, or changing data are completed quickly and easily with a computer and data-management software. A user can search a file for the

```
  Layout   Organize   Append   Go To   Exit                    5:39:03 pm

                                                    Bytes remaining:    3916
  ┌─────┬──────────────┬─────────────┬───────┬──────┬─────────┐
  │ Num │  Field Name  │  Field Type │ Width │ Dec  │  Index  │
  ├─────┼──────────────┼─────────────┼───────┼──────┼─────────┤
  │  1  │ SS_NUMBER    │ Character   │   9   │      │    Y    │
  │  2  │ LAST_NAME    │ Character   │  10   │      │    N    │
  │  3  │ FIRST_NAME   │ Character   │  10   │      │    N    │
  │  4  │ ADDRESS      │ Character   │  16   │      │    N    │
  │  5  │ CITY         │ Character   │  15   │      │    N    │
  │  6  │ STATE        │ Character   │   2   │      │    N    │
  │  7  │ MAJOR        │ Character   │  10   │      │    N    │
  │  8  │ PROGRAM      │ Character   │   8   │      │    N    │
  │  9  │ GPA          │ Numeric     │   4   │   2  │    N    │
  │     │              │             │       │      │         │


  Database C:\dbase\<NEW>          Field 1/9                     Num
              Enter the field name.  Insert/Delete field:Ctrl-N/Ctrl-U
  Field names begin with a letter and may contain letters, digits and underscores
```

records with the same field or fields. A file can be sorted alphabetically or numerically by field. Any field can be used to sort a file. Some packages allow a file to be sorted by more than one field at a time.

There are two distinct types of data managers: file data bases and relational data bases. They differ mainly in the way they organize and access data. File managers and relational data bases are discussed in the following sections.

File Managers

File managers, or flat-file managers as they are sometimes called, were originally developed to replace traditional filing systems. With traditional filing systems, each office had records needed for that office. At a college or university, the admissions office might have kept records of student names, addresses, parent names, and standard test scores. The health center might have kept student names, addresses, parent names, and medical histories on file. Each file was used only by the office in which it was kept.

With the advent of computers and computerized record keeping, the procedures and methods of recording and filing data were converted from paper, file folders, and file cabinets to computer software and storage devices. Each office or department still had access only to its own independent files.

Flat-file data managers store data in a two dimensional table similar to a spreadsheet. Columns represent fields while rows represent records. Flat-file data bases can access only one file at a time. There is only one two-way path that data can take between the data files and the flat-file data-base software program (Figure III–2). Because file managers work with only one file at a time, only one file can be open at a time. If a user wants to see records from a second file, the current file must first be closed. Data cannot be pulled from two files into one report.

FIGURE III–2

A File Manager's Data Organization

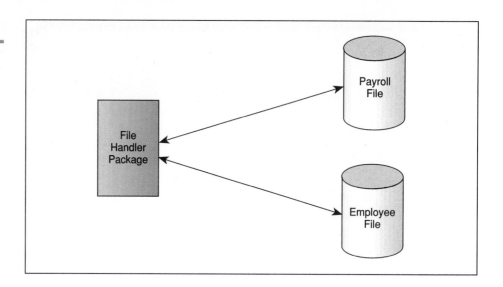

In recent years, however, the lines between flat-file data managers and relational managers have become blurred as flat-file programs have become more sophisticated. Today, some flat-file programs offer varying degrees of relational skills. For example, a lookup feature in some flat-file programs allows the user to view more than one file at a time. Some flat-file programs even allow the user to link one file to several others.

Flat files do have a tendency to have problems with **data redundancy.** Data redundancy is the repeating of data in different files. Usually, different files contain the same information. In the university example, students' names and addresses and parents' names are repeated in each file. When the same data items are kept in many files, quickly updating or changing them in all the files is difficult. If an address has to be changed, for example, it has to be individually changed in each record where it appears. The user cannot make the change once and have that change reflected in every place the address appears.

The best file-management programs are easy to use and, at the same time, powerful enough to handle the data-management needs of a majority of users. File managers are most useful in small organizations where some data redundancy is not a problem. They can be used effectively when information is not often shared among offices or departments.

Relational Data Bases

File-management software has some drawbacks for companies with enormous amounts of data. Because of the duplication of data and the difficulty of keeping one piece of information—such as an employee address—current in several files, large companies often use **relational data bases.** The main difference between a flat-file manager and a relational data base is that the latter can draw from more than one file at a time. A user can open and use data from several files at once. Unlike file managers that can only manage one file at a time, relational data bases can manipulate multiple files (Figure III–3).

The exact definition of *relational* in reference to relational data bases is currently under debate. For microcomputer users, a relational data base is simply a data base

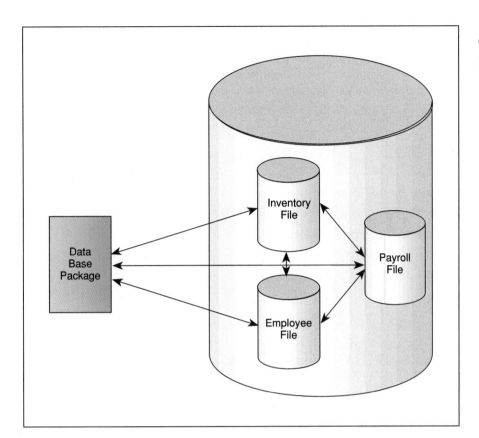

FIGURE III–3

A Relational Data Base's Organization

that can draw information from more than one file at a time. For minicomputers and mainframes, however, the term *relational* means a lot more than merely accessing data in multiple files. Dr. Edgar F. Codd, previously a scientist at IBM, published a paper in 1970 which outlined the concept of a "Relational Model." This pioneering work brought about a revolution in how we think about storing data on computers. Codd's concept of a Relational Model is much more complex than simply being able to access more than one file at a time. In 1986, Codd published another paper that detailed twelve rules a program must follow to qualify as being truly relational. According to Codd, most of the "relational" data-base software on the market today falls short of meeting his conditions. Even though some experts consider the current use of the word *relational* as it applies to relational data bases sloppy, it is commonly accepted in the microcomputer software market that a program is indeed relational if it allows the user to pull data from multiple files.

Relational data bases separate data into several files. Those files are then linked through one or more shared relations. A shared relation would be data that is common to all the files, that is, a common field or fields. One example of a common field might be employee name. Relational data bases, therefore, allow access to multiple files as long as those files are related through common fields. Using a relational data base, the user sets up files with a manageable number of fields. Data can then be pulled from certain fields in selected files for viewing, editing, calculation, or reporting.

Data can be accessed from a relational data base in many ways. A university data base might be accessed by the admissions office, the registrar's office, the financial aid office, and the deans' offices. A college dean might request the names of students who will graduate with academic honors, whereas the financial aid director might need a listing of all students participating in a work-study program.

Relational data bases reduce data redundancy and make updating a file easier. New data has to be entered only once. Using the university data base as an example, if a student's address changed, that change would only have to be entered once. All files containing the student's address would automatically adjust to reflect the change.

CHECKPOINT III–1

1. Define the term *data manager.*
2. Explain the difference between a field, a record, and a file.
3. Name the five tasks most data managers can perform.
4. What is the main difference between a file manager and a relational data base?
5. What forms the link or the relation between files in a relational data base?

■ USES OF DATA MANAGERS

Data managers are used in the home, in business, and for specialized purposes. The next sections describe how data managers are used in each of these areas.

Home Uses

Data managers are popular software packages for home use. They can be used to create and organize a computerized address book, holiday card list, or recipe file. A data manager can be used for just about any type of record keeping. Collectors of coins, stamps, baseball cards or any other items can keep an up-to-date file of their collections.

By computerizing recording and filing tasks in the home, you can keep records in a compact form. Instead of having numerous notebooks and folders that must be maintained manually, you enter new data into the computer. You can store files on several floppy disks.

Besides storing files in a compact form, data managers can find the data much faster than an individual looking through folders and notebooks. For example, they can be used to prepare reports for the filing of taxes. You could keep a record of financial transactions throughout the year and place a field labeled ''Tax Deductible'' in the data record to indicate whether a transaction was tax related. At tax time, the data manager could be used to pick out the tax-related transactions and print a report.

Other home uses of data managers include keeping personal records, creating mailing lists, keeping appointment calendars, and indexing books in a personal library.

Business Uses

Data bases lie at the heart of most businesses' use of computers. Data bases are used to maintain employee records, control inventory, and list suppliers and customers. Data bases can generate payroll checks, invoices, and balance sheets. Most of the

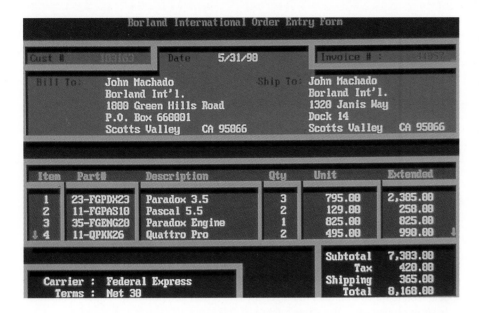

FIGURE III–4

A Computerized Order Entry Form in Borland's Paradox 3.5
A mathematical feature computes a subtotal for each order then adds the tax and shipping to compute the total.

critical elements of running a business can be performed on a data base. Today, microcomputer data-base packages are providing services which previously could only be performed on minicomputers and mainframes.

With the increasing sophistication of low-end data managers, even owners of small businesses can now have the kind of timely and accurate information they need to manage their business well. For example, a small sporting goods retail store could computerize its inventory to improve sales through more efficient and timely record keeping. By recording daily sales, managers can easily see when the stock levels are low and what they must reorder. The store can have an ample supply of items at all times.

Some data managers perform mathematical tasks (Figure III–4). They can total the values of the same field in each record, or find the average, or find records with the lowest or highest value in the field. A data manager with mathematical capabilities can determine dollar sales of an item for a certain period. The mathematical features of a data manager can also be used for inventory control. Employees need not count the items in the store. The data manager can display subtotal and total inventory for tax reporting at the end of the year.

A major benefit of computerized record keeping is the savings in time in both updating data and searching for information. Data managers free employees to concentrate on tasks that can only be done by humans, such as talking to customers or planning new displays.

Specialized Uses

Some data managers are designed for use in special or unique situations. Data managers can be designed to meet the unique need of a specific business.

Pharmacies, for example, use data bases to store drug and patient information to help pharmacists avoid giving patients medicines that may be harmful. With a data base, a pharmacist could determine if a particular drug would react adversely with another drug the patient was taking, or if the patent was allergic to a drug.

Creating mailing lists is another popular specialized application. A data manager can store data about people, such as names, addresses, interests, hobbies, and purchases. People's interests and hobbies can be determined from studying the products they order or magazines they receive. For example, the data manager can sort and print a list of people who order sewing or craft items or who receive craft catalogs. The data manager can then print mailing labels for these people.

Data managers can be used with word processors to produce personalized form letters for individuals or organizations found on the mailing lists. They can supply the names and addresses to be inserted in the letter (Figure III–5).

◻ FEATURES OF DATA MANAGERS

Most data managers offer standard features that are selected from a main menu and submenus by typing the number or letter of the option or by moving the cursor to it. The features include adding and deleting records, searching for and updating records, sorting the data file, indexing the data file, and printing (Figure III–6). More specialized features of a data manager include report generation and query facilities. A brief overview of each of these features follows.

Add and Delete

The **add** feature allows you to add another record to an existing file. The **delete** feature allows you to remove or erase a record you no longer want.

Search and Update

The **search** feature searches for the record or records that contain specified data. You

FIGURE III–5

Specialized Applications
Symantec's Q&A 3.0 combines file management and word processing. This screen illustrates Q&A's sophisticated mail merge function.

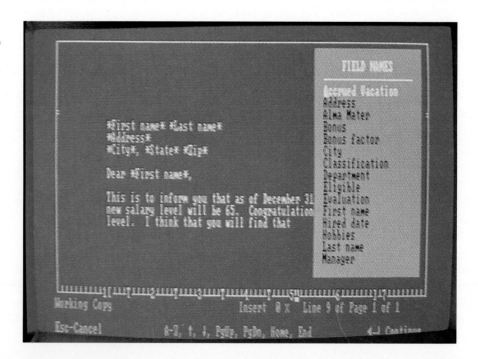

FIGURE III–6

```
 Catalog   Tools   Exit                                        6:21:28 pm
                           dBASE IV CONTROL CENTER
                        CATALOG: C:\DBASE\UNTITLED.CAT

        Data        Queries       Forms       Reports      Labels      Applications
   ┌─────────────┬─────────────┬─────────────┬─────────────┬─────────────┬─────────────┐
   │  <create>   │  <create>   │  <create>   │  <create>   │  <create>   │  <create>   │
   │             │             │             │             │             │             │
   │             │             │             │             │             │             │
   │             │             │             │             │             │             │
   │             │             │             │             │             │             │
   └─────────────┴─────────────┴─────────────┴─────────────┴─────────────┴─────────────┘

   File:        New file
   Description: Press ENTER on <create> to create a new file

     Help:F1  Use:◄─┘  Data:F2  Design:Shift-F2  Quick Report:Shift-F9  Menus:F10
```

The Control Center in dBASE IV
From the Control Center a user can create database files, display and edit data, create queries, design data entry forms, and prepare and print reports and mailing labels.

may want to know which of your friends and relatives have birthdays in March. With a data manager, you can search the file for the records with March in the birthday field.

The **update** feature lets you change data contained in a record. If your aunt moves to a new city, you would want to change her address in your file. First, you could search the file for your aunt's record. Then you could change the data in the address field.

Data Verification

Data verification is a feature that helps to ensure that the correct data is entered into each field. There are two methods used to verify that the data entered into a field is correct. One method allows the user to define fields as required fields. Required fields are fields that must be completed before the record can be saved. For example, if a field that held Social Security numbers was defined as a required field, every record in the file would have to have an entry in the SOCIAL SECURITY NUMBER field. If that field were blank in a record, the program would not move on to the next record until data was entered into that field. Defining fields as numeric or character is also a method of data verification. If a letter is entered into a field defined as numeric, the program will beep, letting the user know a mistake has been entered.

Some programs let the user define the format of a field. For example, if a file contained a PHONE filed, that field could be formatted to appear as three digits, a hyphen, and then four digits. The hyphen would be entered automatically; the user would not have to key it in each time.

FIGURE III-7

The Sort Feature

This screen shows the Paradox program from Borland International, Inc. sorting on four fields—state, city, last name, and first name.

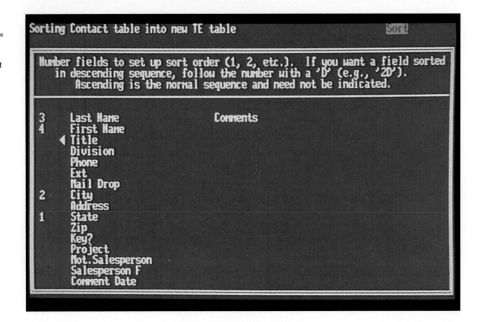

Sorting Contact table into new TE table   Sort

Number fields to set up sort order (1, 2, etc.). If you want a field sorted
in descending sequence, follow the number with a 'D' (e.g., '2D').
Ascending is the normal sequence and need not be indicated.

```
3    Last Name              Comments
4    First Name
   ◄ Title
     Division
     Phone
     Ext
     Mail Drop
2    City
     Address
1    State
     Zip
     Key?
     Project
     Not.Salesperson
     Salesperson F
     Comment Date
```

Sort

The **sort** feature is used to arrange the records in a file. Records are usually stored in the order they are entered, but the computer can sort the records in any order according to one data field. Some programs can sort records on more than one field at a time (Figure III–7). The most common ways to sort records are alphabetically and numerically.

You might want to sort your friends and relatives file in alphabetical order according to last name. The computer looks at the name field. Then it arranges the records in alphabetical order. You could also sort the records in order according to the years in which people were born, starting with the earliest year.

Before sorting records in a certain order, you must see whether the data fields are organized in a way that makes the sort possible. It is always a good idea to spend some time planning the organization of a data-base file before you actually create the file so that you will be able to manipulate the file in the ways you wish. For example, you could not sort records according to last name if you had only created one name field and then entered names into that field as first name, last name. In this case the computer could sort only according to first name. It is a good practice to always create at least two name fields, a last name field and a first name field. With a separate last name field, the computer could sort records according to last name. You can see from this example that it is important to know what you want to be able to do with your data before you create your data-base file.

Indexing

An **index** is used to maintain ascending or descending order among a list of entries. An advantage to indexing over sorting is that with indexing, a list can be ordered by more than one **key** without holding redundant data. This is accomplished by creating separate indices for each order desired. With indices, a master list contains all information, with each entry assigned a number. For example,

Master List			
No.	Name	Position	Salary
1	Smith	Programmer	22,000
2	Wills	Plumber	50,000
3	Jones	Painter	18,000
4	Taylor	Writer	20,000

When an index is created, it consists of only a list of keys in order and a pointer to the master list. For example,

Name Index		Salary Index	
Key	Master No.	Key	Master No.
Jones	3	18,000	3
Smith	1	20,000	4
Taylor	4	22,000	1
Wills	2	50,000	2

The name index is used to look up a name and the salary index used to look up a salary.

Print

The print feature lets you print a hard copy of your files. Some data managers can even print reports. Others print simple lists of the records in a file. To print mailing lists or mailing labels, the data manager must have the print feature.

The most basic print feature allows records to be sorted and printed in the sorted order. Some data managers allow users to state which data fields from each record they want printed. Others can only print the entire record.

Report Generator

A report generator produces printed reports from lists stored in one or multiple files. The purpose of report writing is to get answers out of the data base. The power and flexibility of report writers vary greatly from program to program. Some simply print lists in column format, while others print in column and row formats and may perform mathematical operations. Other options include selecting only a portion of a list, selecting where columns or rows will be printed on a page, and selecting which columns or rows should be totaled, averaged, or converted to percentages.

Band-oriented report writers are easier to use. A band-oriented report writer provides separate sections of the screen for the top of the page, the beginning of the summary, records, the end of the summary, and so on. This approach makes it easier to lay out headers, footers, titles, and detail sections in a report (Figure III–8).

Query Facilities

In a data base management system, data can be requested by using a query facility. No matter how a data base is designed, its purpose is to answer users' questions, or "queries." Questions such as "How many," "What," and "Find" are common

FIGURE III-8

The Band-Oriented Report Writer
dBASE IV's Advanced Relational Report Writer uses a ''band'' concept to assist users in visually designing their reports. The report writer supports styling options such as bold, italics, underline, super- and subscript, as well as five user-defined fonts.

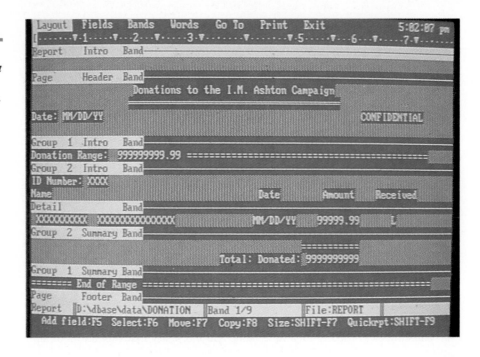

queries (Figure III–9). Some query facilities are complicated to use. However, many are easy enough to allow a nonprogrammer to process and update information stored in a data base. Some programs require a specific query language, whereas others allow use of natural language commands.

Many data base management programs include a query-by-example (QBE) facility. QBE allows the user to ask questions by filling out a table. The user fills in the table

FIGURE III-9

Query Facilities
This screen from Borland's Paradox 3.5 shows a query asking for all the customers living in California who are over 20 years old.

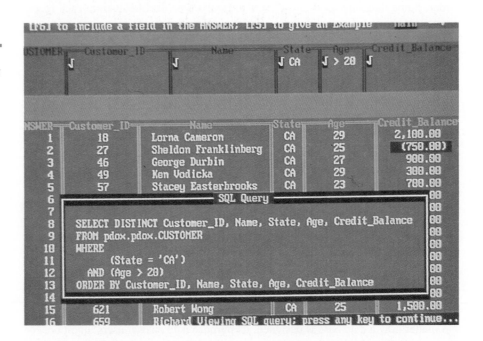

by selecting the desired fields and entering the criteria for the search. For example, if the user wanted to find all customers living in Ohio, he or she might fill out the table by entering OH in the STATE field. The query would return only those records with OH entered in the STATE field. A sophisticated relational data base program can use QBE to draw fields from as many as eight files for a single report or form.

Programming Languages

Many of the sophisticated relational data bases include a programming language that enables the user to construct complex systems that link many steps. These systems can then be run by menus, also created using the programming language. The menus make it possible for a person with little computer skill to use the data base.

Relational data bases that include programming languages are capable of far more complex and sophisticated procedures than data bases without programming languages. The languages included in relational data bases are classified as either procedural or nonprocedural. A nonprocedural language allows you to tell the program *what* you want done. A procedural language requires you to tell the computer *how* to do it. Nonprocedural languages are easier to use.

◼ HARDWARE REQUIREMENTS

Hardware requirements for data managers vary from package to package, depending largely on the capabilities of the particular package. However, some basic hardware requirements need to be considered for any data-manager package. Following is a brief discussion of each of these requirements.

Most data managers require a certain amount of internal memory, or RAM. File managers and less sophisticated relational data bases typically require from 256K to 640K. The more sophisticated relational data bases, however, require at least 512K. The relational data bases usually require a hard drive as well. These packages can require anywhere from 698K to 6.8MB of disk space for installation.

A secondary storage device is needed to store the files created with a data manager. Hard disks, floppy disks, and magnetic tape all can be used as secondary storage devices with data bases. The type of storage device used depends on the amount and type of data being stored.

A printer is necessary for printing mailing labels or for hard copies of reports. The type of printer needed depends on how you want to use the data manager. If the data manager is used mostly for printing files for personal use, a dot-matrix printer will work well. But if it is used to generate presentation-quality reports, or used with a word processor to print letters and mailing labels, a letter-quality printer might be needed.

A monochrome monitor should work well for most data-management purposes. If the data manager is going to be used with graphics software, a color monitor with graphics power might be needed.

These hardware requirements are only the basic requirements common to most data-management packages. Other requirements not listed here depend on the package chosen. Before using any data-management package, it is a good idea to review the hardware requirements listed on the software package and in the documentation.

FIGURE III–10

Ease of Use

Some programs allow the user to set up data base information in a standard form to make it easier to use.

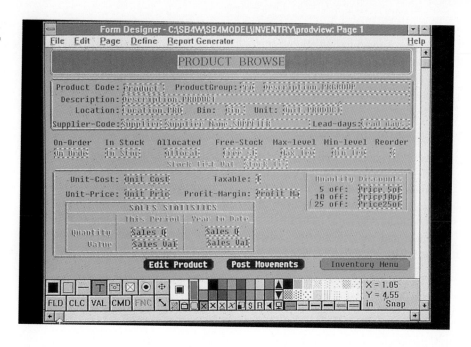

◻ CURRENT TRENDS

Over the past several years, both flat-file and relational data base software have added many more features. In addition, most programs are relatively easy to use. As was mentioned earlier, flat-file data bases have improved to the point where they are, in their own way, as sophisticated as relational data bases. These flat-file managers remain very easy to use. Even powerful and sophisticated relational data bases, which originally could only be understood by programmers, have been simplified—without sacrificing any of their features—to the point where nonprogrammers can begin using them quickly and easily. The addition of menus and online help to many of these programs is one way that they have been made easier for novices to use (Figure III–10).

In addition to adding more features, data base programs have become more productivity-enhancing and powerful in the past several years. Another clear trend is in the attitude many more organizations are taking toward data base management software. More organizations are running data base systems on microcomputers in addition to mainframes and minicomputers. This has led to an increased implementation of LAN-based information systems (Figure III–11).

This high-level sharing of data and processing power on a network of microcomputers, minicomputers, and mainframes, is called **distributed processing.** It has been predicted that distributed processing will become the new corporate computing standard. This emphasis on multiuser capabilities has meant that the data base management software has had to either improve or add features such as file and record locking. File locking places restrictions on a file in order to prevent loss of data. Record locking allows only one user to change a particular record at a time. Even though only one person at a time can edit a record, other users might be able to browse, query, or report on the same data at the same time.

In summary, data managers have added more features and have become more powerful. There has also been a shift in attitude towards this software. LAN-based information systems are supplementing minicomputer and mainframe systems. In-

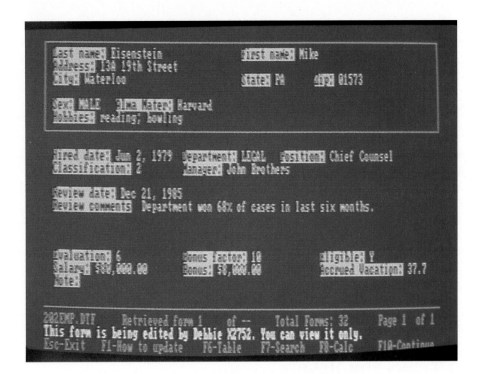

FIGURE III–11

This screen shows Symantec's Q&A set up in a network environment. The bottom of the screen indicates the record is being edited by someone in the network. When one person makes changes and exits the form, everyone else's screen will be automatically updated.

creasingly, organizations are using data managers in a distributed processing environment. Enhanced personal computers that are faster and have more memory and better operating systems are making these trends possible.

CHECKPOINT III–2

1. Describe three ways a data manager can be used by a home computer user.

2. Explain how a data manager is used to create mailing lists.

3. Which data-management features are used to find and change the address in one record in a file? Which feature is to be used to put the records in a file in a certain order according to one data field?

4. What kinds of math tasks can some data managers perform?

5. Name three hardware requirements to consider before using a data manager.

❏ SUMMARY POINTS

■ Data managers are software packages used to create, store, and manipulate data files. Data stored by a data manager is recorded electronically on storage media such as floppy disks.

■ Each data item stored by a data manager is called a field. A group of related fields forms a record. The related records make up a file.

■ Most data managers perform five basic tasks: add or delete data within a file, search a file for certain data, update or change data, sort data into some order, and print all or part of the data in a file.

■ File managers and relational data bases are two types of data managers.

■ File managers, or flat-file managers, access only one data file at a time. Data redundancy sometimes occurs with file managers.

■ Relational data bases can access more than one file at a time. Data from multiple files can be accessed for viewing, editing, calculating, or reporting. In order to access multiple files, those files have to be linked through common fields.

■ Data managers are used in homes to create and organize computerized address books, holiday and birthday card lists, and recipe files. They are used by collectors to keep track of coin and stamp collections, as another example.

■ In business, data managers replace the traditional filing system of papers, folders, and filing cabinets that store employee records, inventory records, and customer files.

■ One special use of data managers is to create mailing lists and labels.

■ The hardware requirements to consider for a data manager are amount of internal memory, a hard disk drive, secondary storage, type of printer, and type of monitor.

■ Two important current trends in data-management software are the increased features and power and the move towards using data managers in a distributed processing environment.

❑ TERMS FOR REVIEW

add, p. A-52	index, p. A-54
data manager, p. A-46	key, p. A-54
data redundancy, p. A-48	record, p. A-46
delete, p. A-52	relational data base, p. A-48
field, p. A-46	search, p. A-52
file, p. A-46	sort, p. A-54
file manager, p. A-47	update, p. A-53

❑ REVIEW QUESTIONS

1. Explain how fields, records, and files differ.
2. Define *file manager*. Define *relational data base*.
3. Explain the difference between a file manager and a relational data base.
4. What is data redundancy? Which type of data manager reduces data redundancy?
5. What type of organization might use a file manager? What type of organization might use a relational data base?
6. How are data managers used in offices?
7. List three uses of a data manager not mentioned in the chapter. Describe each of these uses.
8. Name common features of data managers. Explain the use of each feature.
9. What should you consider before choosing a printer to use with a data manager?
10. What are the current trends in data-base software development? Why are these trends occurring? What is making them possible?

◻ INTRODUCTION

By the 1980s, microcomputers had become a standard piece of office equipment. Managers' jobs had become more productive and efficient through the use of application software such as word processors, data managers, and spreadsheets. Application software had become so fundamental to their work that managers looked for ways to use more than one application at a time. A company's comptroller, for example, might use a spreadsheet to compute a monthly profit and loss statement, and a graphics program to translate some of the figures in the statement into a pie chart. With an individual software package for each application, the comptroller would have to save the current file, shut down the current program, change disks, load a new program, and open a new file each time applications were switched. This process was frustrating and contributed to the development of single programs that could perform more than one function. The result of this effort was integrated software.

In a conventional sense, integration suggests blending two or more parts into a unified whole. Integrated software makes several applications available to a user at one time and makes it possible to move data between applications. Users generally expect that integrated software will conform to these three standards:

1. The software consists of application programs that are usually separate.
2. The software provides easy movement of data among the separate applications.
3. A common group of commands is used for all the applications in the software package.

This section introduces you to integrated software. It explains what integrated software is, how it is used, and some different types of integrated software on the market today.

◻ UNDERSTANDING INTEGRATED SOFTWARE

When working with individual application packages, sometimes referred to as stand-alone software, the user finds that each program has its own way of presenting itself. For example, pressing the keys Ctrl-Q and S is the command to save a document in WordStar 2000, but in WordPerfect, the F10 key is pressed. This difference in commands is frustrating. If you want to run several different programs, you have to have the time and patience to master each program's commands, menus, and other conventions.

Not only is there command incompatibility among stand-alone software, but there is data incompatibility as well. A word-processing program can write a financial report, but it may not be able to generate a graph to be included in the report. A spreadsheet program may be able to analyze an incredible amount of financial data, but it may not be able to incorporate that same data into a graph.

Integrated software attempts to maximize both command and data compatibility. Basically, integrated software is two or more application programs that work together allowing easy movement of data between the applications. In addition, integrated software uses a common group of commands among all the applications. For example, the command used to block off a section of text in a word processor is the same command used to block off a section of rows and columns in a spreadsheet.

For data to be compatible, programs must use the same data format. A data format determines how a program reads information. For example, data items in one program

FIGURE IV–1

Integrated Software Package Structure

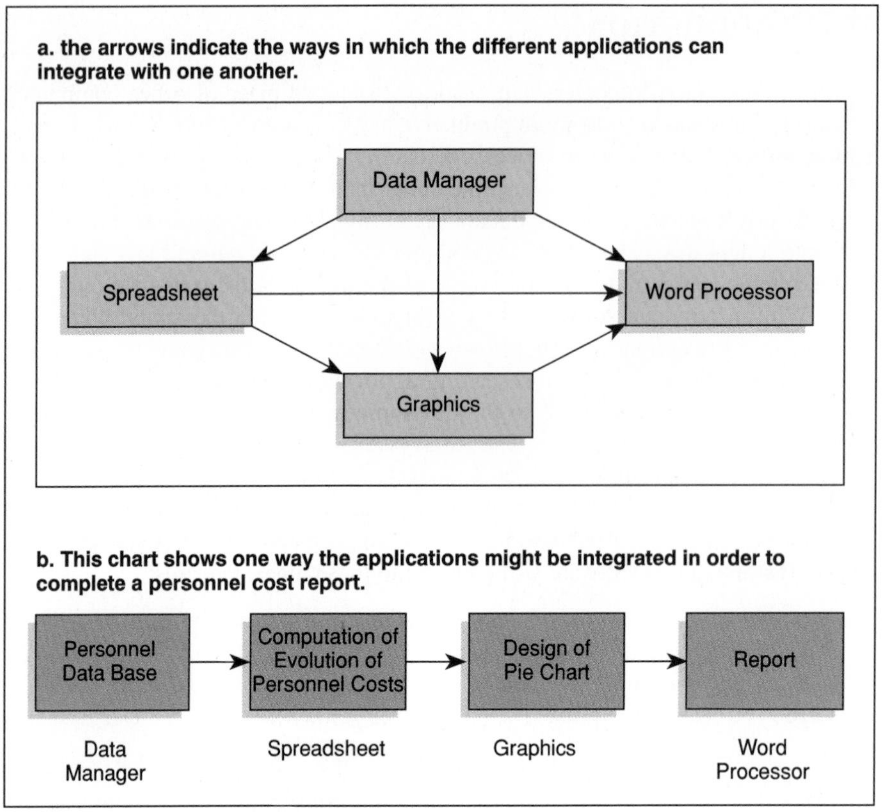

a. the arrows indicate the ways in which the different applications can integrate with one another.

b. This chart shows one way the applications might be integrated in order to complete a personnel cost report.

may be separated by a comma; in another program, data items may be separated by a space. If data formats match, the same data can be used in different programs. For example, a mailing list in a data manager can be used by a word processor. Financial data in a spreadsheet can be turned into a graph by a graphics program, and the graph can be embedded into a report produced on a word processor.

Applications often included in an integrated software package are data managers, spreadsheet analysis, word processing, and graphics (Figure IV–1). Another application found in some integrated packages is communications. Even though an integrated software package includes several applications, it is generally based on one predominant application. The other applications in the package usually support the predominant one. For example, the word processor is predominant in Jack 2; Symphony is based on a spreadsheet (Figure IV–2); and Metafile is based on a data base. In general, the abilities of the leading application are greater than those of the other applications in the package.

■ USES OF INTEGRATED SOFTWARE

The cost of integrated software and the hardware required to run it are two reasons why integrated software is rarely used in homes. Prices for integrated software packages range from $300 to $1,500, but most packages cost over $400. Few people are willing to invest that much money in software that will just be used in the home, and few need the sophistication of an integrated package for their personal computing needs.

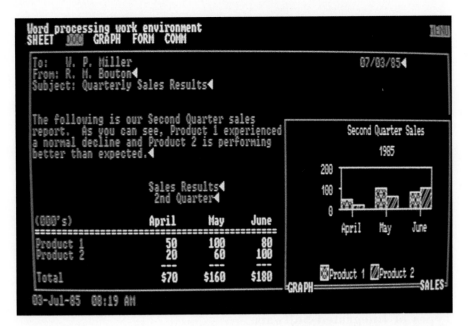

FIGURE IV–2

Spreadsheet, Graphics, and Text Integrated on a Screen from Symphony by Lotus Development Corporation

There are lower-end integrated packages that may not perform all the functions of their high-end sisters, but that are less expensive and will run on microcomputers with less memory. AppleWorks, by Claris, and Microsoft Works, by Microsoft Corporation, are two examples of lower-end integrated software packages that are used in homes and schools. These lower-end packages cost between $150 and $200 (Figure IV–3). One use for an integrated software package found in the home might be to combine addresses stored in a database module with an invitation stored in a

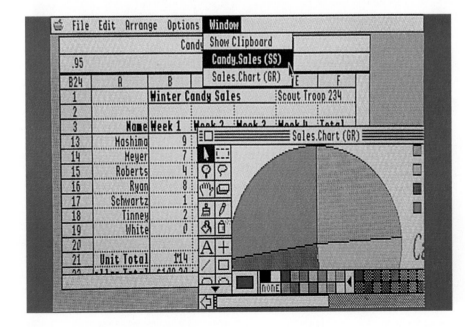

FIGURE IV–3

Integrated Software for Home Use
AppleWorks by Claris is a popular integrated program used in many homes and schools.

word-processing module to create a mass mailing for a party. In schools, integrated software packages are used to teach students how to run application software programs.

In business, however, integrated software is extremely useful. Any business already using **stand-alone** word processing, spreadsheet analysis, data management, or graphics packages probably could benefit from an integrated package. For example, a securities analyst may primarily use an electronic spreadsheet to keep track of financial records. Periodically, however, the analyst may want to use a modem to retrieve data from Dow Jones News/Retrieval service. Or she may want the use of a data base for client information. Occasionally, she may need to write a report with a word processor, and in that report she may want to include a pie chart representing percentages from spreadsheet figures. With stand-alone software, the securities analyst would have to learn how to completely run four to five different programs. Every time she wanted to switch applications, she would have to go through the process of quitting one program and loading another. An integrated software package would certainly make this securities analyst's work a lot easier by eliminating the complexities of moving from one application to another. (Figure IV–4).

Types of Integrated Software

There are four types of integrated software. The first is the all-in-one package. This is perhaps the most widely known and used integrated software. The all-in-one package combines several common applications to make a single program. Symphony by Lotus Development and Framework by Ashton-Tate are two of the more popular all-in-one packages. Symphony combines a spreadsheet with graphics, word-processing, and data-base functions (Figure IV–5). Framework contains these same four applications along with outlining and communications capabilities. These packages make moving from one application to another very convenient for the user because each application is really a component of a single program.

FIGURE IV–4

Integrating Applications
Graphics from Enable Software, an integrated program, can be created from the spreadsheet or data base module and moved into a word processing file.

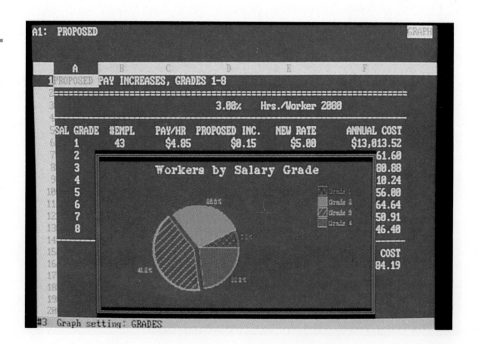

(a)

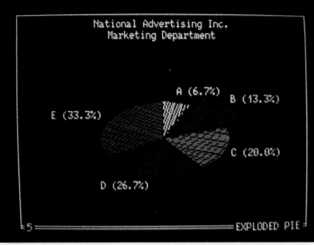

(b)

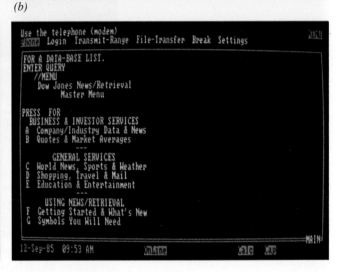

(c)

(d)

All-in-one packages also offer the user the benefit of a common command set. For example, the delete command would be the same whether the user was deleting from the spreadsheet or the word processor. Consistency of commands is especially valuable to a person who may use some applications on a limited basis. The user does not have to memorize a lot of seldom-used commands.

There are some drawbacks to all-in-one packages. The functions represented in all-in-one packages are generally not as complete as the functions offered in single application programs. An all-in-one package with complex word-processing capabilities may be weak in the spreadsheet or graphics area. Therefore, a user with highly sophisticated graphics requirements may find such a package lacking in graphics capabilities and would want to use a stand-alone package for graphics needs.

Memory requirements are another drawback of all-in-one packages. Some all-in-one integrated packages require as much as 640K to run.

The second type of integrated software is called the integrated series. These programs are actually separate application programs that share a common command set. The command set allows data to be transferred from one application to another quickly

FIGURE IV–5

Four Screens from Symphony by Lotus Development Corporation
a. Spreadsheet.
b. Graphics.
c. Word Processing.
d. Data-base communications.

FIGURE IV-6

Systems Integrator

Topview from IBM is a systems integrator that uses windows to display several programs at the same time.

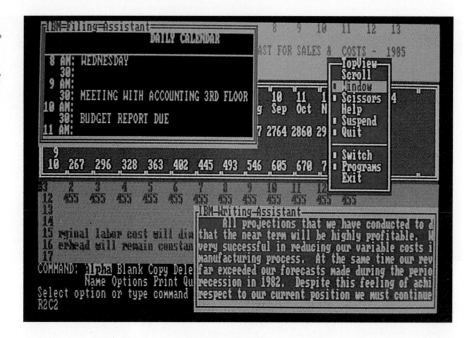

and easily. Smart Software by Innovative Software is one example of an integrated series. Programs in an integrated series offer the varied functions and ease of transfer of stand-alone programs without using the memory requirements of all-in-one packages.

The **systems integrator** is the third type of integrated software. The systems integrator makes it possible to move data residing in memory from one stand-alone package to another. The integrator also permits simultaneous operation of stand-alone packages. IBM produces a systems integrator called Topview (Figure IV-6). One advantage of this type of integration is that it allows the user to select the stand-alone application that is best suited for the user's needs. A drawback, however, is that the stand-alone packages do not usually offer common command sets, so the user must memorize dissimilar commands. Systems integrators also use large amounts of RAM, which makes them unsuitable for use with small microcomputers.

The last type of software integration, the background utility approach, offers limited integration capabilities. This method permits the user to load a type of **utility software** commonly called "desk accessories" into RAM. Calculators, calendars, telephone dialers, and notepads are all types of desk accessories. Once the utility software is loaded, a stand-alone application program is also loaded into RAM. The user can then select the desk accessory needed to accompany the application program (Figure IV-7). Many microcomputer users feel that background utilities more than meet their software needs. A background utility is useful with stand-alone programs, but the utility programs use so much RAM that some application programs will not load.

Needs of the individual user vary greatly. Each user must evaluate his or her software needs before selecting an integrated package. Determining whether each application has enough features to produce the quality of output desired is an important consideration when selecting an integrated software package.

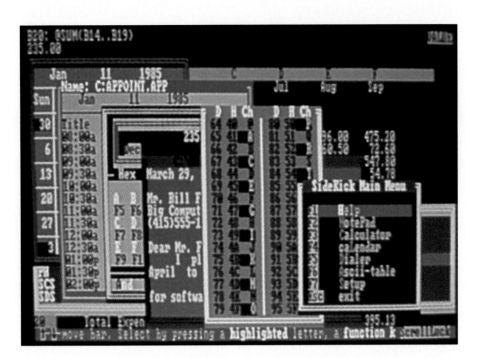

FIGURE IV–7

SideKick Desk Accessories on Top of
Lotus 1-2-3

◼ FEATURES OF INTEGRATED SOFTWARE

Many types of integrated software packages are on the market today. As was mentioned in the previous section, high-end integrated packages are extremely sophisticated and include many more features than the low-end packages. In addition, each of the modules in a high-end package has more features than the modules in a low-end package. For example, some of the word processors in the lower-end packages cannot create columns or footnotes. The spreadsheets in lower-end packages might be limited in their numbers of rows and columns. The features discussed in the section are not common to all integrated packages, but they are found in many of the higher-end packages.

Help Option

Many integrated packages have a context-sensitive help option. The help screen that appears is related to the activity being performed when the help command was issued. A help screen is a window that appears over the file on the screen. In the help screen is an explanation of the current activity being performed.

Getting context-sensitive help is like having a reference book that is always open to the right page. No matter what function is being performed, when the user activates the help command, the help screen that appears provides assistance on that function.

Windows

With an integrated package that supports windows, the user can display several modules on the screen at the same time (Figure IV–8). Some programs can only

FIGURE IV–8

Displaying Modules in Windows

A word-processing file, spreadsheet, and data base report are displayed here in three different windows using Enable Software.

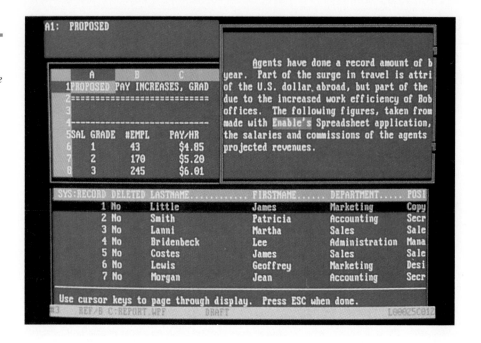

display two windows at once. Other programs can display up to thirty windows. Some programs limit the number of windows that can be open according to the RAM capacity of the computer being used. Other packages claim that an unlimited number of windows can be open. However, a user can easily become confused if too many windows are open at the same time. Generally, a computer screen becomes too cluttered if more than six windows are open at a time.

Even though several windows are open, only one window can be the current window, or the window currently being accessed by the user. In some integrated programs, only the current window can be active or can actually be in use. The other windows are frozen on the screen. They can be seen, but no activity can be performed in them. In order to access an application appearing in another window, the user has to make that window be the current window. In other integrated programs, more than one window can be in use at the same time. For example, in one window a data base file can be sorting while in another window the user is updating figures in a spreadsheet. In this example, even though the window with the data base file is active, since the file is being sorted, there is still only one current window. The current window is the window with the spreadsheet because this is the window the user is actually working in. The data base file is being sorted in the background without any user intervention. In order to update figures in the spreadsheet, however, the user has to access that window.

Zoom

If too many windows are open at the same time, they have to become very small in order for them all to fit. This can make working in the current window difficult; it may be too small. The zoom feature allows the user to zoom in on the current window, enlarging it to fill up the entire screen while the other windows temporarily disappear.

◘ HARDWARE REQUIREMENTS

Generally, the hardware requirements for an integrated software package are far greater than the hardware requirements for stand-alone software. To be more specific, the exact hardware needed to run a package depends on that particular integrated software package.

Most integrated software packages require a computer with a lot of internal memory. Some packages may only require 256K of RAM, but most require 512K or more.

A minimum of two disk drives is necessary for most integrated software packages. Some packages even require a hard disk.

Since one primary purpose of integrated software is to be able to integrate graphics with spreadsheets and word processors, having an integrated package without a graphics monitor does not make much sense. Some integrated packages even require a monitor with a color graphics board.

The final hardware consideration is a printer. Letter-quality printers are generally used with integrated software since the software is most often used in business. Another consideration is the graphics capability of the printer. The printer should be able to print a quality reproduction of whatever graph the integrated package is capable of generating.

◘ CURRENT TRENDS

Integrated packages were predicted to become enormously popular in the business and corporate office environment. Several packages, such as Symphony by Lotus, Framework by Ashton-Tate and Enable by the Software Group, are very popular. These are all excellent integrated packages that have certainly found a market in the business world.

Integrated packages did not, however, become as popular as originally predicted. There are several reasons for this. First, no application offered in an integrated package is quite as good as the best available stand-alone of that application. As was mentioned earlier, usually one application in an integrated package is predominant, while the other applications simply support it.

The second problem with integrated software is that not all users want or need all the functions that come in an integrated package. For example, a user might want an integrated word processor, spreadsheet, and data manager, but have no use for a graphics program.

As was mentioned in Section II on spreadsheets, it seems as if the current trend for those who want to work in an integrated environment is to purchase add-in products. The major difference between add-in products and an integrated package is that users can choose exactly what they want rather than just having to take everything that comes in an integrated package.

The current trend in software development towards compatibility also may be affecting the sales of integrated software. Previously there was very little compatibility between software programs. Importing a spreadsheet file into a word-processing document was virtually impossible, for example. Currently, however, software developers are making more of an effort to develop programs capable of working with other programs on the market. It is now very easy, for example, to import a Lotus 1-2-3 worksheet into a WordPerfect document. As software programs become compatible with one another, the need for integrated software may not be as great.

This is not to say that the concept of integration is a dead one in the computer industry. But the push in integration is no longer in integrating various applications programs. The current trend in integration is towards what is called multimedia computing. Multimedia computing will integrate color video images, sound, and computer applications. For example, a laser-disk encyclopedia could include voices, video, and sound to expand upon the text and drawings. Multimedia systems are just in the beginning stages of development. Currently they are being used for industrial training, education, and public information kiosks. Cornell University medical students, for example, use a multimedia system to help them learn physiology. The system works on Macintosh computers connected to optical disks containing text, detailed drawings, and animated sequences. It is still far too early to tell the direction that multimedia computing will take.

In the meantime, integrated application programs are still quite popular and definitely fill a need in business, education, and personal use software.

◘ SUMMARY POINTS

■ An integrated software package consists of separate application programs.

■ The major characteristics of an integrated software package are the ability to move data easily among the separate applications and the use of a common group of commands.

■ Data management, word processing, spreadsheet analysis, and graphics are the applications usually incorporated in an integrated software package.

■ Integrated software packages are usually based on a major application, with the other applications supporting the major one.

■ Integrated software packages were developed as microcomputers began to be used for powerful and complex computing applications.

■ There are four types of integrated software packages. They are all-in-one packages, integrated series packages, systems integration packages, and background utility approach packages.

■ The availability of add-in products combined with a move towards software compatibility has affected the popularity of integrated software.

◘ TERMS FOR REVIEW

integrated software, p. A-61   systems integrator, p. A-66
stand-alone program, p. A-64   utility program, p. A-66

◘ REVIEW QUESTIONS

1. Define *integration* as it is used in conjunction with software.
2. What applications are commonly used in integrated software?
3. What is an all-in-one package?
4. What are the drawbacks to all-in-one packages?
5. What is a systems integrator?
6. What is the background utility approach?
7. What are some of the reasons for integrated packages not becoming as popular as originally predicted?

INTRODUCTION

Expert systems technology is a subfield of research in the area of **artificial intelligence.** Artificial intelligence efforts seek to develop techniques whereby computers can be used to solve problems that appear to require imagination, intuition, or intelligence. Artificial intelligence is a very broad concept encompassing a number of applications, one of which is expert systems technology.

Expert systems technology is the development of computer software that simulates human problem-solving abilities. An expert system uses human knowledge that has been collected and stored in a computer to solve problems that ordinarily can be solved only by a human expert. Expert systems imitate the reasoning process experts go through to solve a specific problem.

The purpose of this section is to introduce you to expert systems. It includes an explanation of these systems, how they work, how they are being used, and some of their common features.

UNDERSTANDING EXPERT SYSTEMS

Expert systems technology is one outcome of research in artificial intelligence. In 1957 Allen Newell of the RAND Corporation and Herbert Simon from Carnegie-Mellon University began work on a machine that could reason. They wanted to create a machine capable of incorporating problem-solving techniques applicable to a broad range of problems. They called their machine the General Problem Solver.

In order to identify the problem-solving techniques they wanted their machine to emulate, Newell and Simon gathered together human subjects and gave them problems to solve. They asked their subjects to do all their thinking aloud. By closely analyzing how humans solve problems, they began to identify specific problem-solving techniques. This method of learning how people reason by asking human experts to reason aloud while they are solving a problem is still used today by developers of expert systems.

The object of an expert system is to transfer the expertise of a human expert from that person to a computer and then from the computer to other humans who may not be experts in the field. When an end user accesses information from an expert system, it is called a **consultation.**

The first step in developing such a system is to gather as much information about the specific **domain** as possible. The domain is the field or area of activity. Examples of various domains would be medicine, law, tax analysis, geology, and engineering. The **domain knowledge,** or the knowledge pertaining to a specific domain, could be gathered from books, manuals, human experts, data bases, special research reports, or a combination of all these sources.

The domain knowledge comprises part of the **knowledge base.** The knowledge base contains everything necessary for understanding, formulating, and solving the problem (Figure V–1). In addition to the domain knowledge, the knowledge base contains special **heuristics,** or rules of thumb and trial-and-error methods that experts use to solve problems.

Most expert systems are rule based. That is, the knowledge is stored mainly in the form of rules. Rules are generally stated as IF/THEN propositions. The following is an example of such a rule:

OUTLINE

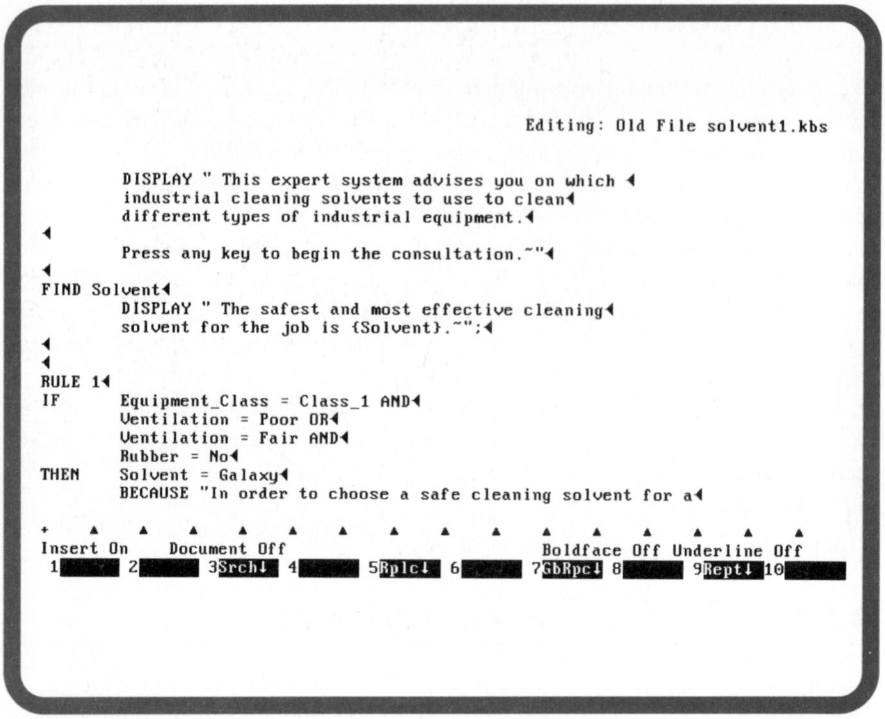

FIGURE V–1

The Knowledge Base

This screen from WordTech's VP-Expert shows a portion of a knowledge base.

```
                                                  Editing: Old File solvent1.kbs


         DISPLAY " This expert system advises you on which ◄
         industrial cleaning solvents to use to clean◄
         different types of industrial equipment.◄
    ◄
         Press any key to begin the consultation.~"◄
    ◄
FIND Solvent◄
         DISPLAY " The safest and most effective cleaning◄
         solvent for the job is {Solvent}.~";◄
    ◄
    ◄
RULE 1◄
IF       Equipment_Class = Class_1 AND◄
         Ventilation = Poor OR◄
         Ventilation = Fair AND◄
         Rubber = No◄
THEN     Solvent = Galaxy◄
         BECAUSE "In order to choose a safe cleaning solvent for a◄

+      ▲   ▲   ▲    ▲   ▲    ▲    ▲    ▲    ▲    ▲    ▲    ▲    ▲    ▲
Insert On   Document Off                   Boldface Off Underline Off
     1      2      3Srch↓ 4      5Rplc↓ 6       7SbRpc↓ 8      9Rept↓ 10
```

IF temperature > 98.6 AND
    Temperature < = 102
THEN fever = moderate

Such a rule could be used to help diagnose an illness. Basically this rule says if the body temperature is greater than 98.6 but not more than 102, then the person has a moderate fever.

The unique feature of an expert system is its ability to reason. The computer is programmed so that it can make inferences from data stored in the knowledge base. The "brain" of an expert system is the **inference engine,** the component where the reasoning is performed. The inference engine includes procedures regarding problem solving.

Obviously, developing and programming an expert system from scratch is the work of professionals. The designers of expert systems typically are artificial intelligence specialists. Usually, the designers are not the people who will perform consultations on the system. The people who will use the system, the end users, generally have little or no knowledge of artificial intelligence. Expert systems have to be designed with the end user in mind. Therefore, the user interface is an important consideration in designing such systems. The user interface in an expert system has to enable an end user to easily perform a consultation regardless of previous computer experience (Figure V–2).

Today, expert systems are available to people who do not have access to designers capable of programming a system from scratch. Programs called expert system shells or expert system development tools can be purchased as an application software package. These programs provide the inference engine, the user interface, and the

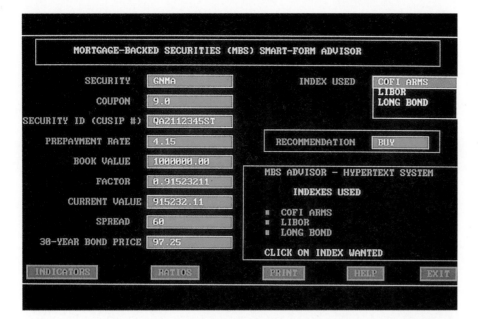

FIGURE V–2

The User Interface
Using WordTech's VP-Expert, expert systems that display screens resembling regular paper forms can be created. These forms, called "SmartForms" can adapt themselves to the user, displaying fields that are appropriate and dispensing with inappropriate fields. This figure shows an application created using VP-Expert's SmartForm capability.

commands of an expert system. In fact, the only thing that has to be provided is the domain knowledge. Providing the domain knowledge is no small order. But expert system development tools have increased the availability of expert systems to the general public.

In addition to expert system shells, there are expert system toolkits. Whereas an expert system shell is a ready made interpreter that follows a particular style, a toolkit offers various features of many different styles, together with sophisticated graphics and modeling facilities so that different parts of a computer expert system can be developed by using the most appropriate style (Figure V–3). The advantage of toolkits

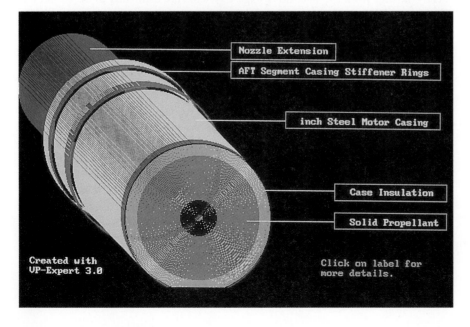

FIGURE V–3

Using Graphics with Expert Systems
This picture shows a graphics file that has been imported into WordTech's VP-Expert. Graphics are used to enhance consultations or to make an expert application visually more appealing.

is that they are more flexible than shells. The disadvantages of toolkits are that they take longer to learn how to use and they are more expensive than shells.

Parts of the business sector have high hopes for expert systems. Some developers predict that expert systems will soon become an essential part of office decision making. Expert systems are seen as a possible solution to the productivity problem in American manufacturing. Tasks such as ordering supplies, designing products, and monitoring quality control now account for more than 70 percent of the cost of manufacturing a product. Expert systems could take over many of these tasks.

■ USES OF EXPERT SYSTEMS

Expert systems are used in the fields of law, medicine, engineering, business, geology, financial analysis, and tax analysis, among others. Expert systems have the potential of functioning better than any single human expert in making judgments within these expertise areas. These systems perform such functions as recommending strategies, diagnosing illness, analyzing structures, and training personnel. When used in these areas, expert systems can cut costs, boost quality and improve productivity.

Some specific examples of expert systems that have been developed will help to demonstrate how they are used. The ACE system, developed by Bell Laboratories, identifies trouble spots in telephone networks and recommends appropriate repair and preventive maintenance. The DART system, developed by Stanford University, assists in diagnosing faults in computer hardware systems using information about the design of the device under study. The MYCIN system, also developed at Stanford, identifies bacterial diseases of the blood and prescribes antibiotic treatments. The CATS-1 system diagnoses malfunctions and prescribes repairs for General Electric's diesel electric locomotive engines. STEAMER is a system used to train inexperienced workers to operate complex ship engines. PROSPECTOR is an expert mineral-exploration system that has been used to discover mineral deposits in Washington valued at $100 million.

IBM has 100 expert systems that, among other things, test computer disk drives. Yearly savings from the disk-drive expert systems are estimated to be $8 million. The Internal Revenue Service will soon be using an expert system to detect suspicious deductions and errors on tax returns. American Express uses an expert system to authorize questionable charges. Previously, charges that were not authorized by a computer program were passed on to human authorizers. These authorizers had a 4-inch-thick rule book, several computer screens filled with account information, and 70 seconds to make a decision. Now, an expert system analyzes questionable transactions.

DEC uses several expert systems in various parts of its operation. XCON is an expert system that was developed cooperatively with Carnegie Mellon in 1979. It is used to configure VAX and PDP-11 computers for production. The National Dispatcher Router (NDR) is used to minimize truck-transportation costs. The system saves DEC approximately $1 million a year. DEC also uses the Electronic Computer-Aided Process Planning (ECAPP) system to plan the manufacturing process for assembling electronic components on printed circuit boards.

In addition to highly specialized expert systems such as these, more and more expert systems are being developed that have broader purposes. One school system developed a trouble-shooting expert system for its teachers. Many of the teachers had little computer experience and were having problems using the computers. As a result, far too many repair calls were being made, incurring a great expense both in terms of lost computer time as well as in repair bills. Many, if not most, of the problems could be solved by the teachers themselves. The expert system, by asking a series of simple questions, helped teachers identify and fix their problems. This expert system ended up saving the school system an enormous amount of money in needless computer repairs.

Some expert systems have even been designed for home use. One example of an expert system sold for home use is a system by Paperback Software. It helps the user choose from over 600 top-rated American wines the appropriate wine to serve for any meal or occasion.

■ FEATURES OF EXPERT SYSTEMS

There is a wide variety of expert systems on the market today. Prices for expert systems can range from $500 to $30,000. The features found in expert systems vary greatly from program to program. The functions described in this section are a part of most expert systems, however.

Explanation Capacity

An explanation capacity is the ability of the system to explain its advice or recommendations. Systems with an explanation capacity can trace the conclusion drawn back to the sources—the reasons why, that is, the rules that were applied—determining how the conclusion was reached.

Many expert systems have the ability to express relative degrees of certainty. That is, the system can determine just how certain a specific conclusion is. The following might, for example, draw a 75% confidence level from an expert system:

```
    IF  Weather = Hot
THEN  Season = Summer
```

Expert systems can also ask the user to identify the certainty level of answers input to the system. For example, if an expert system asked for input to the following question:

In what year will plant relocation occur?

the user could attach a degree of certainty to the response, such as there is 90% certainty the relocation will occur in 1994.

User Friendly

A user interface that is friendly and easy to follow is another feature the more recent expert systems are trying to include (Figure V–4). Online help and menus are two features found in most expert system shells.

Some expert systems are capable of accessing spreadsheet and data-base files. Data contained in the spreadsheet or data base is moved into the system's knowledge base and becomes part of the domain knowledge.

Explanation Subsystem

Most expert systems include an explanation subsystem. The explanation subsystem can trace a conclusion back to its source. That is, the explanation subsystem can

FIGURE V–4

User Friendly Expert Systems
The GUI version of the expert system EXSYS Professional can run in the major windowed environments such as Microsoft Windows. With EXSYS Pro, the end user interface can be completely customized, making the expert system easier to use. The custom screen shown here was created with EXSYS Pro and is running under Microsoft Windows.

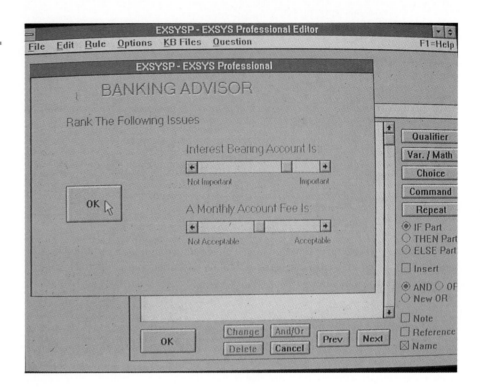

indicate to the end user how a certain conclusion was reached or why a certain alternative was rejected.

Forward Chaining

Forward chaining is a search technique that applies user-specific knowledge to the knowledge-base rules. The expert system then reasons forward to reach its conclusions. Forward chaining is most useful when the user wants to know everything about the domain that is being examined.

Backward Chaining

Backward chaining applies a user-specific goal to the appropriate rules in the expert system in order to determine if a solution exists. Backward chaining is most useful when the user is trying to satisfy a specific goal. The expert system reasons backward from the goal to determine what is needed to reach the goal.

Fuzzy Sets

Expert systems can define, display and edit fuzzy sets. Fuzzy sets are used in expert systems to provide probalistic definitions to knowledge. For example, a member of the middle class might earn between $25,000 and $60,000 a year or earn between $18,000 and $65,000 a year. The concept of middle class is "Fuzzy." Expert systems can use fuzzy sets in rules for forward or backward chaining.

■ HARDWARE REQUIREMENTS

Most early expert systems required special-purpose computing hardware such as Lisp machines. A Lisp machine is a specially designed artificial intelligence workstation. Today, all expert system microprograms can run on regular computers, but many of the major commercial expert systems require mainframes or large minicomputers.

Expert system shells, on the other hand, can run on microcomputers. A lot of memory space is needed, however. To be able to build a serious expert system, a hard disk and at least 512K RAM are desirable. Some expert system development tools, such as VP-Expert, can run on 384K and two disk drives.

Some expert systems and expert system shells enable the user to display the results of a consultation trace graphically. A consultation trace helps to detect logic errors that may be occurring in the knowledge base. In order to be able to display this graphic representation, the computer system being used has to be equipped with a graphics card.

The only other hardware consideration is a printer. Expert systems and expert system shells can print the results of a consultation. The type of printer needed depends on how the hard copy is to be used. If the hard copy is going to be used for presentation purposes, then a letter-quality printer would be needed. In other cases, a dot-matrix printer would suffice.

■ CURRENT TRENDS

Expert systems have developed greatly since their inception. Many expert systems are now in use functioning as "assistant" programs to guide new or unskilled workers. With an expert system in place, a new employee has the potential of performing at the level of an expert. Expert systems have fundamentally changed the amount of knowledge that is distributed and retained in the workplace.

The recent growth in expert systems technology has led to the development of a new discipline called knowledge engineering. Knowledge engineering is the art and science of building an expert system. People who pursue this discipline are known as knowledge engineers.

Two relatively recent trends in expert systems are to apply expert systems to real-time problems and to combine expert systems with neural networks. Real time is generally considered to mean "fast" or "faster than a human can do it." Real time computer systems are found in every thing from a household thermostat to a space satellite. The complex real-time computer systems control a large number of functions at a very fast rate. In addition, they are able to consider many constantly changing factors before a decision can be reached.

Most expert systems currently in use are not concerned with time. Time is not a major issue with diagnostics systems such as MYCIN, training systems such as STEAMER, or systems that aid manufacturing such as ECAPP, for example. With these systems, a human provides the input and the data does not change during the problem-solving session. A real-time expert system has to handle data that is rapidly changing. The input for a real-time expert system comes from automatic sensors that are monitoring a process rather than from people. The Hubble Space Telescope, for

FIGURE V–5

VP-Expert's Dynamic Images
This figure illustrates some of the dynamic images, like gauges and meters, which are included with VP-Expert. A Dynamic Image is a graphic object that is linked to the value of a specified variable. When the value of the variable changes, the graphic object is updated to reflect the new value.

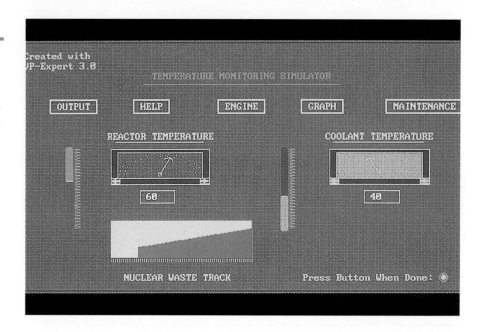

example, uses a real-time expert system to help control its complex computer system. Other areas where real-time expert systems could be used to monitor complex computer systems include military operations, nuclear and electrical power plants, air traffic control, and hospitals. During the 1990s, expert systems will increasingly be used for monitoring and controlling complex computer systems (Figure V–5).

Business, academic, and scientific applications that combine expert systems with neural networks have been developed. Neural networks are another area of artificial intelligence. They use the physical structure of the brain as a basic model. A neural network is comprised of many simple processing units called neurons. Neurons are arranged in layers. Each layer is connected to the layer above and the layer below. The network is trained to associate certain inputs with certain outputs. That is, they are trained to recognize patterns rather than discrete symbols. Expert systems do well handling problems where there are hard and fast rules. Neural networks, on the other hand, do well handling problems related to diagnosis, for example, where understanding a pattern of relationships is needed.

Currently, there are four methods for connecting expert systems with neural networks. Expert systems can be used to train neural networks; neural networks can formulate sensor data into a form that can be used by an expert system; expert systems can control the flow of information through neural networks; and expert systems can analyze responses provided by neural networks.

▣ SUMMARY POINTS

■ Expert systems are the result of years of research in the area of artificial intelligence.
■ Expert system technology is the development of software that imitates the problem-solving process of human experts. The object of such systems is to transfer the expertise of a human expert to others who may not be leaders in the field.

■ The domain is the specific field of knowledge that an expert system addresses. The domain knowledge is the factual information pertaining to a domain.

■ The domain knowledge and special heuristics—the rules pertaining to problem solving within a domain—together form the knowledge base of a system.

■ The designer of an expert system typically is not the end user. The designer is often an artificial intelligence specialist. The end user is the person who accesses the expert system for a consultation; that is, to obtain information regarding a specific domain.

■ The unique feature of an expert system is its ability to reason and explain. The inference engine is the component where the reasoning takes place.

■ Expert systems are used to recommend strategies, diagnose illness, analyze structures, and train personnel in such fields as law, medicine, engineering, business, geology, financial analysis, and tax analysis.

■ With the increasing development of small expert systems shells that run on microcomputers, many more practical applications are being found for expert systems.

■ Knowledge engineering is the art and science of building an expert system.

■ Real-time expert systems handle data that is changing rapidly. Automatic sensors that are monitoring a process provide the input for real-time expert systems.

■ Expert systems are being combined with neural networks, which are another area of artificial intelligence.

■ TERMS FOR REVIEW

artificial intelligence, p. A-71	expert systems technology, p. A-71
consultation, p. A-71	heuristics, p. A-71
domain, p. A-71	inference engine, p. A-72
domain knowledge, p. A-71	knowledge base, p. A-71

■ REVIEW QUESTIONS

1. Explain the meaning of *domain, domain knowledge, knowledge base,* and *heuristics,* as these terms relate to expert systems.

2. What is the difference between an expert system and an expert system shell?

3. Name some expert systems that have been developed, and tell how are they used.

4. Explain what an expert system's explanation capacity is.

5. Identify and explain two features of an expert system.

Graphical User Interface and Windows 3.0

OUTLINE

■ INTRODUCTION

Graphical User Interface, or GUI, is a term that has become increasingly popular. Before the advent of Windows 3.0, GUI was primarily used to refer to Macintosh computers. Generally, GUI incorporates four elements. These are sometimes referred to by the rather inglorious acronym WIMP, which stands for **windows, icons,** menus, and pointing device. A GUI uses a mouse to point to icons representing documents and programs. The command menus are pull-down (or pop-up), and separate windows can be displayed on the screen at the same time.

The Apple Macintosh was the first computer to utilize GUI. A GUI for an IBM or IBM clone never seemed like a practical possibility until the release of Windows 3.0. The first two versions of Windows were mostly suited for graphics presentations. In addition, the memory constraints and poor performance of earlier versions of Windows prevented them from becoming very popular. Windows 3.0, however, took the computing world by storm. It is suitable for anything from word processing to spreadsheets to presentation graphics. It has been predicted that Windows 3.0 will radically change the way people use PCs. Whether or not this is true remains to be seen. It is true, however, that Windows 3.0 is a very popular program that is likely to become even more popular in the years to come.

■ UNDERSTANDING GUI AND WINDOWS 3.0

Computers either have a GUI, graphical user interface, or a CLI, **command line interface.** Macintosh computers all use GUI. When you buy a Macintosh computer, the GUI is bundled with it. IBM PCs and IBM clones that do not use Windows or another GUI program, use CLI. With CLI, commands are mostly typed at the keyboard, a mouse is not needed, there are no icons, and applications do not run in a window (see Figure VI–1).

Macintosh computers and Windows for PC compatibles are not the only GUIs available. Other GUI's include Ensemble, which is a PC-compatible GUI, and Amiga's Workbench. GUI's for Unix systems include Open Look and Motif. NextStep, which is the user interface for the Next computer, is another GUI.

FIGURE VI–1

Displayed on the Monitors are a Graphical User Interface (left) and a Command Line Interface (right)

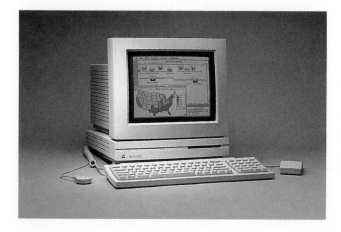

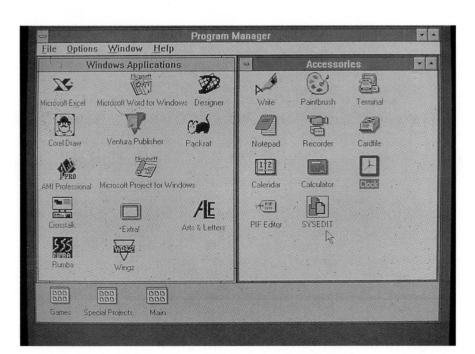

FIGURE VI–2

The Program Manager

Windows 3.0 is currently the most popular PC-compatible GUI. Nearly 1200 Windows programs have been written since Windows was first released. One of the reasons why Windows is so popular is because applications running under Windows all have a standard user interface. That is, the basics of how to use every Windows application is the same. How to open files, how to copy data, how to cut and paste data, how to print, is the same in all Windows applications. This makes it easier for people to learn how to use application programs.

The central part of Windows is the Program Manager (see Figure VI–2). Any installed DOS or Windows-based program can be started from the Program Manager by double-clicking on an icon that represents it. Once an application has been started and is running, it can be reduced to an icon on the screen and put aside to be used later.

Another part of Windows is the File Manager. The File Manager shows a tree-oriented view of disks in multiple windows. Many file management operations can be performed simply by clicking and dragging using the mouse. For example, you can move all the files from one subdirectory to another by dragging the file listing of the source directory to the target directory listing. There is also a search command that allows you to find files no matter where they may be on the disk.

The Control Panel is another part of Windows that allows you to set the options for screen colors, fonts, printers, keyboard and mouse action, and so on (see Figure VI–3). The Control Panel allows you to modify Windows to suit your personal tastes.

Windows comes with several useful accessories. There is a Notepad that can edit files up to 50K, a clock that can show time in either an analog or digital format, a calendar that combines a month-at-glance calendar and a daily appointment book, a cardfile that can be used to keep track of names, addresses, phone numbers, and so on, and a calculator that includes statistical and scientific functions. Paintbrush is another desktop accessory that is based on ZSoft's PC Paintbrush program. Paintbrush allows you to create simple or complex color drawings. Write is a word processing

FIGURE VI–3

The Control Panel

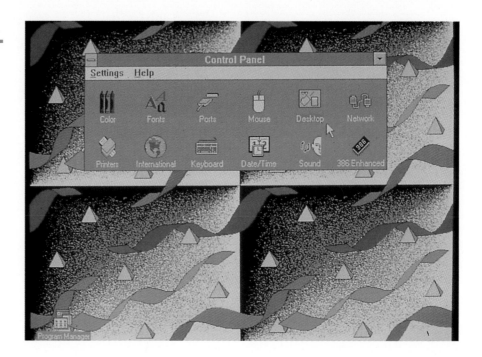

application that can be used to create and print documents. Terminal is a communications application that offers both XModem and Kermit transfers. Recorder is a macro recorder that allows you to record and store keystrokes and mouse actions as macros in order to automate any routine task. Finally, Windows includes the classic card game Solitaire.

◼ USES OF WINDOWS 3.0

Just about any application you can think of has a program that will run under Windows (see Figure VI–4). In word processing there is Ami Professional by Samma Corporation, Word for Windows by Microsoft, WordPerfect for Windows by WordPerfect Corporation, Legacy by NBI Inc., and JetForm by Indigo Software. In desktop publishing, there is PageMaker by Aldus and Ventura Publisher 3.0 by Xerox Desktop Software. In database software there is Superbase 4 by Precision Software Inc., Omnis 5 by Blyth Software Inc. SQL Windows by Gupta Technologies, and dBFast/Windows by Bumblebee Software. In spreadsheet software there is Excel by Microsoft and Lotus 1-2-3 Release 3.1 by Lotus Development Corp.

These are only some of the more popular application programs available for Windows. In addition there are graphics and presentation software, utility software, and communication software.

Although Windows is mostly found in business settings, it is also used in the home and educational environments. People use applications running under Windows in the same way they use DOS-based applications; Windows simply helps people to work faster and most efficiently.

One example of how Windows could be used for a financial planner serves to illustrate how Windows might function in the business environment. A financial planner could use a communications program running under Windows to connect to the Dow Jones News Retrieval Service to obtain stock prices. The financial planner

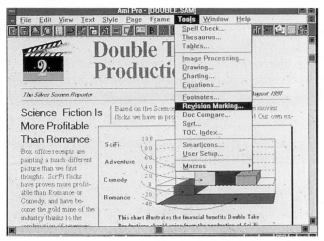

(a)

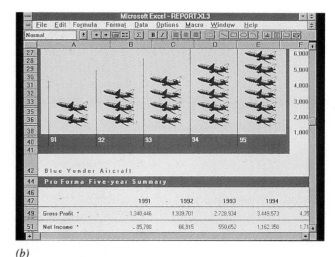

(b)

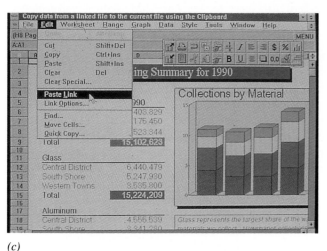

(c)

(d)

could then copy the stock prices to the Windows **clipboard.** The prices could then be pasted from the clipboard into a spreadsheet. From the spreadsheet, the financial planner could create a bar chart. The planner could then write a report in a word processor and copy the bar chart from the spreadsheet into the report.

■ FEATURES OF WINDOWS 3.0

Windows 3.0 includes many features that have helped to make it the popular program it is today. These features include the Standard Mode memory management scheme, the 386 Enhanced Mode, multi-tasking, Dynamic Data Exchange, and extensive context-sensitive, online help.

Standard Mode Memory Management

One of the reasons why Windows 3.0 became so popular is that it eliminates the 640K barrier for DOS. That is, Windows can make full use of the extended memory

FIGURE VI–4

Just a Few of the Application Software Programs Available for Windows

a) Ami Professional (word processing software)

b) Microsoft Excel and

c) Lotus 1-2-3 (spreadsheet software)

d) Superbase 4 (data base software)

in 286- and 386-based PCs. In order to use standard mode memory management, the computer must have an 80286 or 80386 microprocessor and at least 1MB of RAM. If it does, Windows 3.0 and all Windows-based applications will run in the microprocessor's protected mode which means that the computer can use all the RAM between 640K and 1MB. DOS normally ignores any RAM over 640K. Plus, Windows will use any additional RAM over 1MB. This memory management scheme is called *standard mode*.

Running Windows in standard mode leads to a significant improvement in the amount of RAM available to Windows applications. As a result, there is a significant improvement in the performance of Windows applications.

386 Enhanced Mode and Multi-tasking

The 386 enhanced mode is available on 80386- and 80486-based PCs with more than 2MB of RAM. Essentially, the 386 enhanced mode adds two more capabilities to the standard mode. First, it adds the ability to run non-Windows-based, DOS applications in a window rather than in a full screen. Second, it adds virtual memory, which is a way of using hard-disk space to simulate RAM. With virtual memory, Windows 3.0 can perform as if it had access to many times as much RAM as is actually available.

What the 386 enhanced mode does is take advantage of the Virtual 86 mode of the 386 and 486 processors. This feature creates what is called a protected "virtual machine" which assigns a 1MB address space for each DOS application. That is, each DOS application in effect gets its own 1MB virtual machine, controlled by the 386 or 486 processor. Each program, then, thinks it owns the machine. Since each program acts as if it owns the machine, DOS applications in Windows can be run alongside Windows applications. Text and graphics can be cut and pasted between them. It does not matter if the DOS applications are in text-mode or graphics based.

The 386 enhanced mode, then, allows you to multitask operations. Basically, **multitasking** simply means the ability to run more than one application at the same time (see Figure VI–5). With Windows 3.0 in the 386 enhanced mode, you can open six or more applications at the same time, with each application running in its own window. You can easily move from one application to another and you can easily cut data from one application and paste it into another.

Dynamic Data Exchange

Dynamic Data Exchange, or DDE, is a method by which programs operating under Windows can exchange various types of data. Any Windows-based program that supports DDE can exchange data with any other Windows-based program supporting DDE. The data can be either text or graphics.

To create a DDE link, you open the source document containing the data you want to link with another file and copy the data to be linked to the clipboard. Open the destination file, place the cursor where the data to be linked should appear, and select PAST LINK. If the linked data ever changes in the source document, it is automatically changed in the destination file. More than one DDE link can be set up in a file.

The Help Feature

Windows 3.0 includes a very extensive online, context-sensitive Help feature that includes graphics. Topics can be selected from a Master Index. You can browse

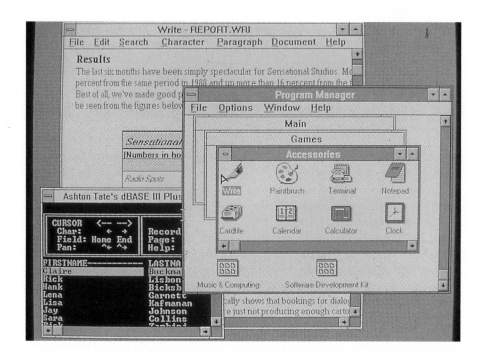

FIGURE VI–5

Multitasking
Both a data base and a word processor are being used at the same time.

through a series of related topics to find a particular topic or you can search for a topic using the Search command. It is also possible to retrace your path through help topics you have covered. If a word is marked with a dotted underline, you can click on that word to get its definition. If a phrase is marked with a solid underline, you can jump to a more detailed explanation of it. If you want to be able to quickly return to a certain item in the help system, you can mark that item with a bookmark. Help text can also be supplemented with your own notes, and you can print a hard copy of any help text, as well.

❑ HARDWARE REQUIREMENTS

Windows 3.0 will run on a PC with 640K of memory. A CGA or better color screen, or a Hercules monochrome screen is needed. Windows will run with or without a mouse.

These are the minimum requirements. For the standard mode, an 80286 processor (or higher) and 1MB or more of memory is needed. For the 386 enhanced mode, an 80386 (or higher) processor and 2MB or more of memory is needed. A minimum of 12MHz, a mouse, an EGA or VGA color display, a hard disk with 6 to 8 MB of free disk space, and at least one floppy disk drive are also needed for the program to run efficiently.

❑ CURRENT TRENDS

When Windows 3.0 was first released it received a lot of positive publicity. Orders for the program came in so fast that it was back-ordered for months. Reviewers for the various computer magazines didn't have enough good things to say about Windows 3.0. From all the hype the program initially received, people were convinced Windows 3.0 would revolutionize computing on a PC (see Figure VI–6).

Now that some of the initial hype has died down, a more conservative perspective of Windows 3.0 is being voiced. For the novice computer user, a GUI makes the computer easier to use. Because GUI provides interface consistency, once you have mastered one application you have basically mastered them all. But people who are already comfortable using a CLI may have little nuisances that clutter up the computer screen. So, unlike the first predictions, not *everyone* has a need for GUI. Many people prefer operating with a CLI.

Whether or not Windows 3.0 continues to be as popular as it is now depends somewhat on what happens to OS/2 Presentation Manager. Presentation Manager is the GUI developed to run with the OS/2 operating system. Windows 3.0 and Presentation Manager share many common elements. They both include universal pull-down menus and context-sensitive help. All the programs that run under Windows 3.0, as do all the programs for Presentation Manager, share conventions for file and editing commands. Several programs can be run at the same time, each in its own window, and you can easily move from one program to another in either Windows 3.0 or Presentation Manager.

Right now Windows 3.0 is more popular than Presentation Manager. A lot of that has to do with the fact that there are far more applications available for Windows 3.0 than there are for Presentation Manager. But as Presentation Manager develops and more applications become available for it, that may change.

There is no doubt that Windows 3.0 will continue to be very popular and that more applications will be developed to run under Windows. Whether or not it will become the PC standard remains to be seen.

❑ SUMMARY POINTS

- GUI incorporates four elements: windows, icons, menus, and a pointing device.
- All Macintosh computers come bundled with GUI.
- Windows 3.0 is currently the most popular PC-compatible GUI.
- The central part of Windows is the Program Manager, from which any installed DOS or Windows-based program can be started by double-clicking on an icon.
- The File Manager in Windows 3.0 performs many file management operations.
- Accessories that come with Windows 3.0 include a notepad, clock, calculator, calendar, cardfile, and a macro recorder. In addition Windows 3.0 comes with a paint application called Paintbrush, a word processor called Write and a communications application called Terminal.
- The standard mode in Windows 3.0 lets you use all the memory in your system to run programs and load data.
- The 386 enhanced mode in Windows 3.0 allows you to run non-Windows-based applications in their own windows. In addition, it takes advantage of the Virtual 86 mode of the 386 and 486 processor to allow multi-tasking of both Windows applications and DOS programs.
- Dynamic Data Exchange is a method for linking data between two programs. With a DDE link, if the linked data in the source document is changed, that change is automatically reflected in the destination file.

■ The minimum hardware requirements for Windows 3.0 are a PC with 640K of memory and a CGA or better color screen or a Hercules monochrome screen.

■ The future of Windows 3.0 depends partially on the development of OS/2's Presentations Manager.

❏ TERMS FOR REVIEW

clipboard, p. A-83

command-line interface, p. A-80

graphical-user interface, p. A-80

icon, p. A-80

multitasking, p. A-84

window, p. A-80

❏ REVIEW QUESTIONS

1. Name some GUIs other than Windows 3.0.
2. What are the four elements of GUI?
3. What is the difference between GUI and CLI?
4. What is the purpose of the Control Panel in Windows 3.0?
5. Explain the concept of a "virtual machine" and how that concept applies to Windows 3.0.
6. Explain the concept of multi-tasking and how that concept applies to Windows 3.0.
7. What is DDE? How do you create a DDE link in Windows 3.0?

Glossary

Abacus An early device used for mathematical calculations; it consists of a rectangular frame with beads strung on wires.

Access To get or retrieve data from a computer system.

Access mechanism The device that positions the read/write head of a direct-access storage device over a particular track.

Accounting machine A mechanically operated forerunner of the computer; could read data from punched cards, perform calculations, rearrange data, and print results in varied formats.

Acoustic-coupler modem A device used in telecommunications that is attached to a computer by a cable and that connects to a standard telephone handset.

Action entries One of four sections of a decision logic table; specifies what actions should be taken.

Action stub One of four sections of a decision logic table; describes possible actions applicable to the decision being made.

Activity The proportion of records processed during an update run.

Ada A high-level programming language developed for use by the Department of Defense. Named for Augusta Ada Byron, Countess of Lovelace and daughter of the poet Lord Byron, Ada is a sophisticated structured language that supports concurrent processing.

Add A feature that allows you to add another record to an existing file.

Address A unique identifier assigned to each memory location within primary storage.

American Standard Code for Information Interchange (ASCII) A seven-bit standard code used for information interchange among data-processing systems, communication systems, and associated equipment.

Amount field The field where a clerk manually inserts the amount of the check; used in the processing of bank checks.

Analog computer A computer that measures the change in continuous electrical or physical conditions rather than counting data; contrast with digital computer.

Analog transmission Transmission of data over communication channels in a continuous wave form.

Analytical engine A machine (designed by Charles Babbage) capable of addition, subtraction, multiplication, division, and storage of intermediate results in a memory unit. Too advanced for its time, the analytical engine was forgotten for nearly a hundred years.

Application *See* Application program.

Application program A sequence of instructions written to solve a specific user problem.

Application programmer The person who converts a design for a system into instructions for the computer; they are responsible for testing, debugging, documenting, and implementing programs.

Arithmetic Logic Unit (ALU) The section of the processor or CPU that handles arithmetic computations and logical operations.

Artificial intelligence (AI) Field of research currently developing techniques whereby computers can be used to solve problems that appear to require imagination, intuition, or intelligence.

ASCII-8 An eight-bit version of ASCII developed for computers that require eight-bit rather than seven-bit codes.

Assembler program The translator program for an assembly language program; produces a machine-language program (object program) which can then be executed.

Assembly language A low-level programming language that uses convenient abbreviations called mnemonics rather than the groupings of 0s and 1s used in machine language. Because instructions in assembly language generally have a one-to-one correspondence with machine-language instructions, assembly language is easier to translate into machine language than are high-level language statements.

Attribute A characteristic field within a record in a computer file.

Audio conferencing A conference call that links three or more people.

Audit trail A means of verifying the accuracy of information; a description of the path that leads to the original data upon which the information is based.

Augmented audio conferencing A form of teleconferencing that combines graphics and audio conferencing.

Automatic page numbering A feature that enables a word processor to automatically number the pages of the printed copy.

Automatic teller machine (ATM) Remote terminal that allows bank customers to make transactions with the bank's central computer; user can check account balances, transfer funds, make deposits and withdrawals, and so forth.

Back-end processor A small CPU serving as an interface between a large CPU and a large data base stored on a direct-access storage device.

Background partition In a multiprogramming system, a partition handling a lower-priority program that is executed only when high-priority programs are not using the system.

Background program In a multiprogramming system, a program that can be executed whenever the facilities of the system are not needed by a high-priority program.

Backup copies Second copies of original magnetic storage tapes made to prevent data loss.

Bandwidth Also known as grade; the range of width of the frequencies available for transmission of a given channel.

Bar-code reader A device used to read a bar code by means of reflected light, such as a scanner that reads the Universal Product Code on supermarket products.

BASIC (Beginners' All-purpose Symbolic Instruction Code) A high-level programming language commonly used for interactive problem solving by users; it is widely implemented on microcomputers and is often taught to beginning programmers.

Batch file access A method of processing transactions in which transactions are gathered (collected) for a period of time and then processed all at once.

Binary number system Number system used in computer operations that uses the digits 0 and 1 and has a base of 2; corresponds to the two possible states in machine circuitry, "on" and "off."

Binary representation Use of a two-state, or binary, system to represent data, as in setting and resetting the electrical state of semiconductor memory to either 0 or 1.

Binary system *See* Binary number system.

Biochip In theory, a chip whose circuits will be built from the proteins and enzymes of living matter such as *E. coli* bacteria.

Bit Short for BInary digiT; the smallest unit of data that the computer can handle and that can be represented in the digits (0 and 1) of binary notation.

Bit cells The name for storage locations in semiconductors.

Bletchley Park A computer built by two Englishmen, Dilwyn Knox and Alan Turing, that was used successfully during World War II to decipher German codes.

Block-copy A feature that marks a block of text and duplicates it at a new location.

Block-delete A feature that marks a block of text and then issues a single command to delete the entire block of text.

Block-merge A feature that reads a file from disk and merges it with the document currently in memory.

Block-move A feature that marks a block of text and then moves it from one location to another.

Block operation A feature that allows the user to define a block of text and then perform a specific operation on the entire block. Common block operations include block move, block copy, block save, and block delete.

Block-save A feature that makes a block of text and saves it as a new file on disk.

Blocked record Records grouped together on magnetic tape or magnetic disk to reduce the number of interrecord gaps and more fully utilize the storage medium.

Boot To load the start-up instructions into the computer's memory.

Branch A statement used to alter the normal flow of program execution.

Breach of contract The instance when goods fail to meet the terms of either an express warranty or implied warranty.

Broad-band channel A communication channel that can transmit data at rates of up to 120,000 bits per second; for example, microwaves.

Bubble memory A memory medium in which data is represented by magnetized spots (magnetic domains) resting on a thin film of semiconductor material.

Buffer A separate area of memory in which characters can be stored and retrieved; used when transmitting data from one device to another.

Bug A program error.

Bus configuration A configuration often used with local-area networks in which multiple stations connected to a communication cable can communicate directly with any other station on the line.

Byte A fixed number of adjacent bits operated on as a unit.

C A high-level structured programming language that includes low-level language instructions, C is popular because it is portable and is implemented on a wide variety of computer systems.

Cache memory Also known as a high-speed buffer; a working buffer or temporary area used to help speed the execution of a program.

CAD/CAM The combination of computer-aided design and computer-aided manufacturing with which an engineer can analyze not only a product but also the manufacturing process.

Cell The unique location in an electronic spreadsheet where a row and a column intersect.

Centered text A feature of most word-processing programs that allows you to center a word or line by simply pressing one or two keys.

Central processing unit (CPU) Acts as the "brain" of the computer; composed of three sections—arithmetic/logic unit (ALU), control unit, and memory unit.

Centralized design An information structure in which a separate data-processing department is used to provide data-processing facilities for the entire organization.

Chain printer An output device that has the character set engraved in type and assembled in a chain that revolves horizontally past all print position; prints when a print hammer (one for each column of the paper) presses the paper against an inked ribbon that presses against the characters on the print chain.

Channel A limited-capacity computer that takes over the tasks of input and output in order to free the CPU to handle internal processing operations.

Character A single letter, digit, or special sign (like $, #, or *). Characters are represented by bytes in computer storage.

Charge-coupled device (CCD) A storage device made of silicon that is nearly 100 times faster than magnetic bubble storage.

Chief Programmer Team (CPT) A method of organization used in developing software systems in industry in which a chief programmer supervises the development and testing of software; programmer productivity and software reliability are increased.

Clipboard The intermediary place where data from one file is temporarily placed before it is integrated into another file.

Clock speed The number of electronic pulses a microprocessor can produce each second.

COBOL (COmmon Business-Oriented Language) A high-level programming language generally used for business applications; it is well suited to manipulating large data files.

Coding The processing of writing a problem solution in a computer programming language.

Command area The part of the screen that shows a menu of the available commands.

Command-line user interface A user interface that, by design, requires the user to type in commands that are then executed by the computer's operating system.

Common law Law that is based on customs and past judicial decisions in similar cases.

Communication channel A medium for carrying data from one location to another.

Compact disk (CD) A nonerasable 4¾ inch disk used as a storage medium for microcomputers; it can store about 1,000 times more bytes than a single-sided floppy disk.

Compatibility The ability to use equipment or software produced by one manufacturer on a computer produced by another manufacturer.

Compiler program The translator program for a high-level language such as FORTRAN or COBOL; translates the entire source program into machine language, creating an object program that can be executed.

Composite color monitor A computer monitor offering composite color and resolution slightly better than a TV.

Computer A general-purpose electronic machine with applications limited only by the creativity of the people who use it; its power is derived from its speed, accuracy, and memory.

Computer-aided design (CAD) Process of designing, drafting, and analyzing a prospective product using computer graphics on a video terminal.

Computer-aided engineering (CAE) A system, used in the design of electronic products, that allows engineers to interact with the computer during simulation runs as errors are identified.

Computer-aided manufacturing (CAM) Use of a computer to simulate or monitor the steps of a manufacturing process.

Computer-assisted instruction (CAI) Use of a computer to instruct or drill a student on an individual or small-group basis.

Computer anxiety A fear individuals have of the effects computers have on their lives and society in general.

Computer conferencing A form of teleconferencing that uses computer terminals for the transmission of messages; participants need not be using the terminal in order to receive the message—it will be waiting the next time they use the terminal.

Computer crime A criminal act that poses a greater threat to a computer user than to a non-computer user, or a criminal act that is accomplished through the use of a computer.

Computer ethics A term used to refer to the standard of moral conduct in computer use; a way in which the "spirit" of some laws are applied to computer-related activities.

Computer-integrated manufacturing (CIM) An arrangement that links various departments within an organization to a central data base for the purpose of improving the efficiency of the manufacturing process.

Computer operator The person responsible for setting up equipment; mounting and removing tapes, disks, and diskettes; and monitoring the operation of the computer.

Computer security Instituting the technical and administrative safeguards necessary to protect a computer-based system against the hazards to which computer systems are exposed and to control access to information.

Computerized axial tomography (CT or CAT) scanning Form of noninvasive physical testing that combines x-ray techniques and computers to aid diagnosis.

Concentrator A device that systematically allocates the use of communication channels among several terminals.

Concurrent Taking place within the same time interval. In multiprogramming, concurrency occurs when processing alternates between different programs.

Condition entries One of four sections of a decision logic table; answers questions in the condition stub.

Condition stub One of four sections of a decision logic table; describes all options to be considered in making a decision.

Consultation When a user accesses information from an expert system.

Continuous form A data-entry form, such as cash register tape, utilized by OCR devices.

Control program A routine, usually part of an operating system, that aids in controlling the operations and management of a computer system.

Control unit The section of the CPU that directs the sequence of operations by electrical signals and governs the actions of the various units that make up the computer.

Coordinate The location of a cell within a spreadsheet; a combination of the column letter and row number that intersect at a specific cell.

Copy A function that allows the user to copy a cell or group of cells to another part of the spreadsheet.

Corporate planning model *See* Simultaneous decision support system.

Crash conversion *See* Direct conversion

Cursor The marker on the display screen indicating where the next character can be displayed.

Cut form Data-entry form such as a phone or utility bill; used by OCR devices.

Cylinder The tracks on all disk surfaces that may be read without repositioning the read/write arm.

Daisy-wheel printer An output device resembling an office typewriter; it employs a flat disk with petal-like projections, each having a character at its tip; printing occurs one character at a time.

Data Facts; the raw material of information.

Data base Collection of data that is commonly defined and consistently organized to fit the information needs of a wide variety of users in an organization.

Data-base administrator (DBA) The person who oversees the implementation and administration of an organization's data base(s).

Data-base analyst The person responsible for the analysis, design and implementation of the data base.

Data-base management system (DBMS) A set of programs that serves as the interface between the data base and the programmer, operating system, and users; also programs used to design and maintain data bases.

Data buffering Reading data into a separate storage unit normally contained in the control unit of the input/output system.

Data communication The electronic transmission of data from one site to another, usually over communication channels such as telephone or microwave.

Data definition language (DDL) The language in which the schema, which states how records within a data base are related, is written. This language differs depending on the type of data-base management system being used.

Data-entry operator The person who transcribes data into a form suitable for computer processing.

Data manager A software package used to organize files that lets you store and access data with your computer.

Data manipulation language (DML) The language used to access a hierarchical or a relational data base to provide a way for users to access the data base. The data manipulation language is different for each type of data-base management system.

Data processing The steps involved in collecting, manipulating, and distributing data.

Data redundancy The repeating of data in different files so that if data changes, it must be updated in all the files in which it occurs.

Data structure A particular relationship between the data elements in a computer file.

Datacom handler Another name for multiplexer and concentrator.

Debug *See* Debugging.

Debugging The process of locating, isolating, and correcting errors in a program.

Decentralized design An information structure in which the authority and responsibility for computer support are placed in relatively autonomous organization operating units.

Decimal number system A number system based on the powers of ten.

Decision logic table (DLT) A table that organizes relevant facts in a clear and concise manner to aid a decision-making process.

Decision support system (DSS) An integrated system that draws on data from a wide variety of sources such as data bases to provide a supportive tool for managerial decision-making. Generally, managers use fourth-generation programming languages to access decision support systems.

Decrypted Data Data that is translated back into regular text after being encrypted for security reasons.

Default setting A value used by the word processor when not instructed to use any other.

Delete A feature that allows you to remove or erase a record you no longer want.

Deletion A feature in which a character, word, sentence, or larger block of text may be removed from the existing text.

Demodulation The process of retrieving data from a modulated carrier wave.

Desired output The portion of the software development process where the system's output is defined.

Desk checking A method used in both system and application program debugging in which the sequence of operations is mentally traced to verify the correctness of program logic.

Desktop A metaphor for the user's working environment in the Macintosh user interface or in any graphical user interface, such as Microsoft Windows.

Detail diagram Used in HIPO packages to describe the specific functions performed and data items used in a given module.

Digital computer Type of computer commonly used in business applications; operates on distinct data (for example, digits) by performing arithmetic and logic processes on specific data units.

Digital transmission The transmission of data as distinct on and off pulses.

Direct-access storage device (DASD) Auxiliary storage device that allows data to be stored and accessed either randomly or sequentially.

Direct-connect modem A device used in telecommunications that is attached to a computer by a cable and that connects directly to a telephone line by plugging into a standard phone jack.

Direct conversion A method of system implementation in which the old system is abandoned and the new one implemented all at once.

Directory Contains record keys and their corresponding addresses; used to obtain the address of a record with a direct-access file design.

Disk address The method used to identify a data record on a magnetic disk; consists of the disk surface number, track number, and record number.

Disk-based word processor A word processor that loads into memory only the part of the document that is being edited, storing the remainder in temporary disk files.

Disk drive The mechanical device used to rotate a disk pack during the data transmission.

Disk pack A stack of magnetic disks.

Diskette. *See* Floppy disk.

Distributed computing A system in which processing is done at a site other than that of the central computer.

Distributed data processing (DDP) *See* Distributed computing.

Distributed design An information structure in which independent operating units have some data-processing facilities but there is still central control and coordination of computer resources.

Domain In expert systems technology, the domain is the area of activity or specialty that the system includes, such as medicine, law, or tax analysis.

Domain knowledge The knowledge pertaining to a specific domain that is gathered from outside sources.

Document A file that contains information entered into the computer by the user.

Document-oriented word processor A word processor that treats a document as a single, continuous file.

Dot-matrix printer A type of impact printer that creates characters through the use of dot-matrix patterns.

Drum printer An impact printer that consists of a metal cylinder with rows of characters engraved on its surface; one line of print is produced with each drum rotation.

Dump A hard-copy printout of the contents of computer memory; valuable in debugging programs.

Dynamic random-access memory (DRAM) chip Pronounced dee-ram, the type of memory chip used in most personal computers; it must be constantly refreshed.

E-mail *See* Electronic mail.

Edit checks Processing statements designed to identify potential errors in the input data.

Editing window The text area of the screen which contains the words as they are typed.

EDVAC (Electronic Discrete Variable Automatic Computer) A stored-program computer developed at the University of Pennsylvania.

Electronic data processing (EDP) Data processing performed largely by electronic equipment, such as computers, rather than by manual means.

Electronic funds transfer (EFT) A cashless method of managing money; accounts involved in a transaction are adjusted by electronic communications between computers.

Electronic mail Transmission of messages at high speeds over telecommunication facilities.

Electronic spreadsheet An electronic ledger sheet used to store and manipulate any type of numeric data.

Electrostatic printer A nonimpact printer in which electromagnetic impulses and heat are used to affix characters to paper.

Electrothermal printer A nonimpact printer that uses a special heat-sensitive paper; characters are formed when heated rods in a matrix touch the paper.

Encrypted data A term describing data that is translated into a secret code for security reasons.

End-user development tools Tools that allow the end-user to develop an application package, usually through the use of a fourth-generation programming language. Examples of end-user development tools are simulation software, statistical packages, and database management systems.

ENIAC (Electronic Numerical Integrator and Calculator) The first general-purpose electronic digital computer; it was developed by John W. Mauchly and J. Presper Eckert at the University of Pennsylvania.

Erasable programmable read-only memory (EPROM) A form of read-only memory that can be erased and reprogrammed, but only by being submitted to a special process such as exposure to ultraviolet light.

Ergonomics The method of researching and designing computer hardware and software to enhance employee productivity and comfort.

Even parity A method of coding in which an even number of 1 bits represent each character; used to enhance the detection of errors.

Expert system Form of artificial intelligence software designed to imitate the same decision-making and evaluation processes of experts in a specific field.

Expert systems technology The development of computer software that simulates human problem-solving abilities. An expert system uses human knowledge that has been collected and stored in a computer to solve problems that ordinarily can be solved only by a human expert.

Express warranty Created when the seller makes any promise or statement of fact concerning the goods being sold, which the purchaser uses as a basis for purchasing the goods.

Extended Binary Coded Decimal Interchange Code (EBCDIC) An eight-bit code for character representation.

Facsimile system Produces a picture of a page by scanning it.

FAX system *See* Facsimile system.

Feedback A check within a system to see whether predetermined goals are being met; the return of information about the effectiveness of the system.

Fiber optics A data transmission concept using laser pulses and cables made of tiny threads of glass that can transmit huge amounts of data at the speed of light.

Field A meaningful collection of characters, such as a social security number or a person's name.

File A grouping of related records, such as student records; sometimes referred to as a data set.

File manager An application package designed to duplicate the traditional manual methods of filing records.

File server The portion of a local-area network (LAN) that allows for the sharing of peripheral devices and information.

Finder The portion of the Macintosh operating system that displays the desktop and manages the data and information stored on disk.

First-generation computer Computer that used vacuum tubes; developed in the 1950s; much faster than earlier mechanical devices, but very slow in comparison to today's computer.

Flat panel display Output devices most commonly used on portable microcomputers. Three common types includes liquid crystal display (LCD), gas plasma, and electroluminescence.

Flexible disk *See* Floppy disk.

Floppy disk A low-cost direct-access form of data storage made of plastic and coated with a magnetizable substance upon which data are stored; disks come in varying sizes.

Floppy diskette *See* Floppy disk.

Flowchart Of two kinds: the program flowchart, which is a graphic representation of the types and sequences of operations in a program; and the system flowchart, which shows the flow of data through an entire system.

Folder A device on the desktop that can hold documents, applications, and other folders; a tool used to help organize the desktop.

Footer A piece of text that is printed at the bottom of each page, such as a page number.

Formal design review Also called a structured walk-through; an evaluation of the design of a software system by a group of managers, analysts, and programmers to determine completeness, accuracy, and quality of the design.

Formula A mathematical equation used in a spreadsheet.

FORTRAN (FORmula TRANslator) The oldest high-level programming language, it is used primarily in performing mathematical or scientific operations.

Four-bit binary coded decimal (BCD) A four-bit computer code that uses four-bit groupings to represent digits in decimal numbers.

Fourth-generation computer Computer that uses chips made by large-scale integration and offers significant price and performance improvements over earlier computers.

Front-end processor A small CPU serving as an interface between a large CPU and peripheral devices.

Fully distributed configuration A network design in which every set of nodes in the network can communicate directly with every other set of nodes through a single communication link.

Functional tools A category of application software packages that perform specific tasks or functions, such as inventory control.

Fuzzy logic Logic that allows for imprecision based on rules that set ranges for characteristics.

Garbage in-garbage out (GIGO) A phrase illustrating the fact that the meaningfulness of computer output relies on the accuracy or relevancy of the data fed into the processor.

Global Search and replace A feature that finds all occurrences of a word or words and automatically replaces the word with another word or words.

Grade *See* Bandwidth.

Graphic display device A visual-display device that projects output in the form of graphs and line drawings and accepts input from a keyboard or light pen.

Graphical user interfaces (GUI) A user interface to the computer's operating system that uses graphics, or pictures, and menus to simplify the user's task of working with the computer.

Graphics package An application software package designed to allow the user to display images on the display screen or a printer.

Graphics tablet A flat board-like object that, when drawn on, transfers the image to a computer screen.

Grid chart (tabular chart) A chart used in system analysis and design to summarize the relationships between functions of an organization.

Hacking A term used to describe the activity of computer enthusiasts who are challenged by the practice of breaking computer security measures designed to prevent unauthorized access to a particular computer system.

Hard copy Printed output.

Hardware Physical components that make up a computer system.

Hard-wired Memory instructions that cannot be changed or deleted by other stored-program instructions.

Hashing *See* Randomizing.

Header A piece of text that is stored separately from the text and printed at the top of each page.

Heuristics The rules and trial-and-error methods that expert systems programs use to solve problems.

Hexadecimal number system A base 16 number system commonly used when printing the contents of memory to aid programmers in detecting errors.

Hidden cells A feature that allows the user to hide data in a cell so that the contents are not displayed on the screen.

Hierarchical configuration A network design for multiple CPUs in which an organization's needs are divided into multiple levels that receive different levels of computer support.

Hierarchical design An information structure in which each level within an organization has necessary computer power; responsibility for control and coordination goes to the top level.

Hierarchical structure Also called tree structure; the data structure in which one primary element may have numerous secondary elements linked to it at lower levels.

High-level language A computer programming language that is oriented toward the human programmer rather than the computer itself.

HIPO (Hierarchy plus Input-Process-Output) A method of diagramming a solution to a problem; highlights the inputs, processing, and outputs of program modules.

Icon A graphic, or picture, used to represent such things as an application, document, folder, or disk on the Macintosh desktop and other graphical user interfaces.

Impact printer A printer that forms characters by physically striking a ribbon against a paper.

Implied warranty A warranty that provides for the automatic inclusion of certain warranties in a contract for the sale of goods.

Implied warranty of fitness A situation in which the purchaser relies on a seller's expertise to recommend a good that will meet his or her needs; if the good later fails to meet the purchaser's needs the seller has breached the warranty.

Implied warranty of merchantability Guarantees the purchaser that the good purchased will function properly for a reasonable period of time.

Indent A feature used to indent all lines of a paragraph the same

number of spaces from the left margin. This feature is often used for long quotations.

Index A feature used to maintain ascending or descending order among a list of entries.

Inference engine The "brain" of an expert system that allows the computer to make inferences from data stored in its knowledge base.

Informal design review An attempt to detect problems early in the software development process.

Information Data that has been organized and processed so that it is meaningful.

In-house An organization's use of its own personnel or resources to develop programs or other problem-solving systems.

Ink-jet printer A nonimpact printer that uses a stream of charged ink to form dot-matrix characters.

Input Data submitted to the computer for processing.

Input/output bound A situation in which the CPU is slowed down because of I/O operations, which are extremely slow in comparison to CPU internal processing speeds.

Input/output control unit A device located between one or more I/O devices that performs code conversion.

Input/output management system A subsystem of the operating system that controls and coordinates the CPU while receiving input from channels, executing instructions of programs in memory, and regulating output.

Insert and replace A feature that allows new characters to be entered into a document, replacing old characters.

Instruction set The fundamental logical and arithmetic procedures that the computer can perform, such as addition, subtraction, and comparison.

Integrated circuit An electronic circuit etched on a small silicon chip less than⅛-inch square, permitting much faster processing than with transistors and at a greatly reduced price.

Integrated software Two or more application programs that work together, allowing easy movement of data between the applications; the applications also use a common group of commands.

Interactive video A multimedia learning concept that merges computer text, sound, and graphics by using a videodisk, videodisk player, microcomputer with monitor and disk drive, and computer software.

Interblock gap (IBG) A space on magnetic tape that facilitates processing; separates records grouped together as a block on the tape.

Internal modem A modem that plugs into the internal circuitry of a computer; no external cables or connections are needed.

Interpreter A high-level language translator that evaluates and translates a program one statement at a time; used extensively on microcomputer systems because it takes up less memory than a compiler.

Interrecord gap (IRG) A space that separates records stored on magnetic tape; allows the tape drive to regain speed during processing.

Interrupt A condition or event that temporarily suspends normal processing operations.

Inverted structure A structure that indexes a simple file by specific record attributes.

Job-control language (JCL) A language that serves as the communication link between the programmer and the operating system.

Job-control program A control program that translates the job-control statements written by a programmer into machine-language instructions that can be executed by the computer.

K (kilobyte) A symbol used to denote 1,024 (2^{10}) memory units (1,024 bytes) when referring to a computer's memory capacity; often rounded to 1,000 bytes.

Key The unique identifier or field of a record; used to sort records for processing or to locate specific records within a file.

Keypunch operator Person who uses a keypunch machine to transfer data from source documents to computer storage.

Key value A value used to arrange records within a data file or data base.

Knowledge base In expert systems technology, the knowledge base contains everything necessary for understanding, formulating, and solving problems.

Label A name written beside a programming instruction that acts as an identifier for that instruction; also, in spreadsheets, information used to describe some aspect of the spreadsheet.

Laptop portable A small microcomputer that is powered by a rechargeable battery, weighs between eight and twelve pounds, and normally has a hard disk and a 3½″ floppy disk drive.

Large-scale Integration (LSI) Method by which circuits containing thousands of electronic components are densely packed on a single silicon chip.

Laser printer A type of nonimpact printer that combines laser beams and electrophotographic technology to form images on paper.

Laser storage system A storage device using laser technology to encode data onto a metallic surface; usually used for mass storage.

Librarian The person responsible for classifying, cataloging, and maintaining the files and programs stored on cards, tapes, disks and diskettes, and all other storage media in a computer library.

Librarian program Software that manages the storage and use of library programs by maintaining a directory of programs in the system library and appropriate procedures for additions and deletions.

Light pen A pen-shaped object with a photoelectric cell at its end; used to draw lines on a visual display screen.

Linear structure A data structure in which the records in a computer file are arranged sequentially in a specified order.

Line-spacing A feature that legs the user choose the amount of space between lines.

Link A transmission channel that connects nodes.

Linkage editor A subprogram of the operating system that links the object program from the system residence device to application program object modules.

Local system Peripherals connected directly to the CPU.

Local-area network (LAN) A way of connecting microcomputers together to allow for the sharing of peripheral devices and information and for communication between the members of the network.

Locked cells A feature that prevents a user from altering or destroying a template by locking the cell with a special command.

Logical file The combination of data needed to meet a user's needs.

Logo An education-oriented procedure-oriented, interactive programming language designed to allow anyone to begin programming and communicating with computers quickly.

Loop A structure that allows a specified sequence of instructions to be executed repeatedly as long as stated conditions remain true.

Low-level language A computer programming language that is oriented toward the computer rather than a programmer.

Machine language The only set of instructions that a computer can execute directly; a code that designates the proper electrical states in the computer as combinations of zeros and ones.

Macro A sequence of keystrokes entered into one or more cells that can be activated with a single command that often involves only two keystrokes.

Magnetic core Iron-alloy, doughnut-shaped ring about the size of a pinhead of which memory can be composed; individual cores can store one binary digit (its state is determined by the direction of an electrical current); the cores are strung on a grid of fine wires that carry the current.

Magnetic disk A direct-access storage medium consisting of a metal platter coated on both sides with a magnetic recording material upon which data are stored in the form of magnetized spots.

Magnetic domain A magnetized spot representing data in bubble memory.

Magnetic drum Cylinder with a magnetic outer surface on which data can be stored by magnetizing specific positions on the surface.

Magnetic-ink character reader A device used to perform magnetic-ink character recognition (MICR).

Magnetic-ink character recognition (MICR) A process that involves reading characters composed of magnetized particles; often used to sort checks for subsequent processing.

Magnetic tape A sequential storage medium consisting of a narrow strip of plastic upon which spots of iron-oxide are magnetized to represent data.

Mainframe A type of large, full-scale computer capable of supporting many peripheral devices.

Maintenance programmer The person who maintains programs by making needed changes and improvements.

Management information system (MIS) A system designed to provide information used to support structured managerial decision making; its goal is to get the correct information to the appropriate manager at the right time.

Management Information System (MIS) manager The person responsible for planning and tying together all the information resources of a firm.

Mark I First automatic calculator.

Mark sensing *See* Optical-mark recognition.

Master file A file that contains all existing records organized according to the key field; updated by records in a transaction file.

Materials requirement planning (MRP) A manufacturing system that ties together different manufacturing needs such as raw materials planning and inventory control into interacting systems. The interacting systems allow a manufacturer to plan and control operations efficiently.

Megahertz (MHz) One million times per second; the unit of measurement for the speed of a computer's clock.

Memory The section of the CPU that holds instructions, data, and intermediate and final results during processing; also referred to as primary memory, internal memory, and main memory.

Memory-based word processor A word processor that can only accommodate documents that fit into available memory; longer documents must be placed in two or more separate files.

Memory management In a multiprogramming environment, the process of keeping the programs in memory separate.

Menu driven system design An application program is said to be menu-driven when it provides the user with "menus" displaying available choices or selections to help guide the user through the process of using the software.

Message switching The task of a communications processor of receiving messages and routing them to appropriate destinations.

Microcomputer A small, low-priced computer used in homes, schools, and businesses; also called a personal computer.

Microprocessor A programmable processing unit (placed on a silicon chip) containing arithmetic, logic, and control circuitry; used in microcomputers, calculators, and microwave ovens and in many other applications.

Microprogram A sequence of instructions wired into read-only memory; used to tailor a system to meet the user's specific processing requirements.

Minicomputer A type of computer with the components of a full-sized system but with smaller memory capacity.

Mnemonics A symbolic name (memory aid); used in symbolic languages (for example, assembly language) and high-level programming languages.

Model A mathematical representation of an actual system, containing independent variables that influence the value of a dependent variable.

Modem Also called a data set; a device that modulates and demodulates signals transmitted over communication facilities.

Modular approach A method of simplifying a programming project by breaking it into segments or subunits referred to as modules.

Modulation A technology used in modems to make data processing signals compatible with communication facilities.

Module Part of a whole; a program segment or subsystem; a set of logically related program statements that perform one specified task in a program.

Monochrome monitor A computer monitor that displays amber, green, or white characters on a black background.

Mouse A hardware device used to move the pointer on the Macintosh desktop and other graphical user interfaces; movement of the pointer on the display screen corresponds to the movement of the mouse on the desk or tabletop.

MS-DOS The disk operating system used on IBM PCs and compatible computers.

Multimedia Computer applications that combine audio and video components with interactive applications.

Multiphasic health testing (MPHT) Computer-assisted testing plan that compiles data on patients and their test results, which are compared with norms or means to aid the physician in making a diagnosis.

Multiplexer A device that permits more than one I/O device to transmit data over the same communication channel.

Multiprocessing A multiple CPU configuration in which jobs are processed simultaneously.

Multiprogramming The process of executing multiple programs concurrently; the CPU switches from one program to another so quickly that program execution seems to be simultaneous.

Multitasking Running two or more programs on a computer at once.

Napier's Bones A portable multiplication tool (described by John Napier) consisting of ivory rods that slide up and down against each other; forerunner of the slide rule.

Narrow bandwidth channel A communication channel that can transmit data only at a rate between 45 and 90 bits per second; for example, telegraph lines.

Natural language Designed primarily for novice computer users; uses English-like statements usually for the purpose of accessing data in a data base.

Needed input The portion of the software development process where the input required to produce the desired output is determined.

Network The linking together of multiple CPUs.

Network interface card (NIC) An integrated circuit board that is plugged into the circuitry of each microcomputer on a local-area network (LAN); allows the members of the network to communicate with each other.

Network operating system (NOS) The computer software that controls the use of a local-area network (LAN) by its members.

Network structure The data structure in which a primary data element may have many secondary elements linked to it and any given secondary element may be linked to numerous primary elements.

Neural network A type of software or hardware that attempts to imitate the way the brain works by creating connections for the nodes and units in the system.

Next-sequential-instruction feature The ability of a computer to execute program steps in the order in which they are stored in memory unless branching takes place.

Node The endpoint of a network; consists of CPUs, printers, CRTs, or any other physical devices.

Nondestructive read/destructive write The feature of computer memory that permits data to be read and retained in its original state, allowing it to be referenced repeatedly during processing.

Nondestructive testing (NDT) Testing done electronically to avoid breaking, cutting, or tearing apart a product to find a problem.

Nonimpact printer The use of heat, laser technology, or photographic techniques to print output.

Nonmonotonic logic A type of logic that adapts to exceptions to ordinary monotonic logical statements and allows conclusions to be drawn from assumptions.

Notebook portable The smallest microcomputer available; typically weighs less than eight pounds, has one 3½″ floppy disk drive, and operates on rechargeable batteries.

Nuclear magnetic resonance (NMR) A computerized, noninvasive diagnostic tool that involves sending magnetic pulses through the body to identify medical problems.

Numeric bits The four rightmost bit positions of six-bit BCD used to encode numeric data.

Numerically controlled machinery Manufacturing machinery that is driven by a magnetic punched tape created by a tape punch that is driven by computer software.

Object program A sequence of machine-executable instructions derived from source-program statements by a language-translator program.

Octal number system Number system in which each position represents a power of eight.

Odd parity A method of coding in which an odd number of 1 bits is used to represent each character; facilitates error checking.

Office automation Integration of computer and communication technology with traditional office procedures to increase productivity and efficiency.

Online file access Provides the ability to retrieve current information at any time; when a transaction is created, related information is updated simultaneously.

Online storage In direct communication with the computer.

On-us field The section of a check that contains the customer's checking-account number.

Op code The part of a machine or assembly language instruction that tells the computer what function to perform.

Operand The part of an instruction that tells where to find the data or equipment on which to operate.

Operating system A collection of programs designed to permit a computer system to manage itself and to avoid idle CPU time while increasing utilization of computer resources.

Operation code (op code) The part of an instruction that indicates what operation is to be performed.

Optical character A special type of character that can be read by an optical-character reader.

Optical-character recognition (OCR) A method of electronic scanning that reads numbers, letters, and other characters and then converts the optical images into appropriate electrical signals.

Optical disk A storage device that stores data as the presence or absence of a pit burned into the surface of the disk by a laser beam.

Optical-mark page reader A device that senses marks on an OMR document as the document passes under a light source.

Optical-mark recognition (OMR) Mark sensing; a method of electronic scanning that reads marks on a page and converts the optical images into appropriate electrical signals.

Output Information that comes from the computer, as a result of processing, into a form that can be used by people.

Overview diagram Used in an HIPO package to describe in greater detail a module shown in the visual table of contents.

Packaged software A set of standardized computer programs, procedures, and related documentation necessary for solving specific problems.

Page Material that fits in one page frame of memory.

Page frame In a virtual memory environment, one of the fixed-sized physical areas into which memory is divided.

Page-oriented word processor A word processor that treats a document as a series of pages.

Paging A method of implementing virtual memory: data and programs are broken into fixed-sized blocks, or pages, and loaded into memory when needed during processing.

Parallel conversion A system implementation approach in which the new system is operated side by side with the old one until all differences are reconciled.

Parallel processing A type of processing in which instructions and data are handled simultaneously.

Parity bit A bit added to detect incorrect transmission of data; it conducts internal checks to determine whether the correct number of bits is present.

Pascal A high-level structured programming language that was originally developed for instructional purposes and that is now commonly used in a wide variety of applications.

Pascaline A device invented by Blaise Pascal used to add and subtract; a series of rotating gears performed the calculations.

Path A path is a way in which the user can indicate to the MS-DOS (or PC DOS) operating system where a file or files are located on a disk. The path may include directory names as well as file names.

PC-DOS The disk operating system used on IBM personal computers.

Peripheral device Device that attaches to the central processing unit, such as a storage device or an input or output device.

Phased conversed A method of system implementation in which the old system is gradually replaced by the new one.

Physical file The way data is stored by the computer.

Pilot conversion The implementation of a new system into an organization on a piecemeal basis.

Plotter An output device that prepares graphic, hard copy of information; it can produce lines, curves, and complex shapes.

Point-of-sale (POS) system A computerized system that records information required for such things as inventory control and accounting at the point where a good is sold; see also source-data automation.

Point-of-sale (POS) terminal An input device that records information at the point where a good is sold.

Poll The process used by a concentrator to determine if an input/output device is ready to send a message to the CPU.

Portable The characteristic of a program that can be run on many different computers with minimal changes.

Portable computer A small computer (microcomputer) weighing between twelve and seventeen pounds. Does not use an external power source and normally includes a hard disk and 3½″ floppy disk drive.

Primary key A unique field for a record; used to sort records for processing or to locate a particular record within a file.

Print-formatting The function of a word processor that communicates with the printer to tell it how to print the text on paper.

Print-wheel printer An impact printer with 120 wheels each containing 48 characters. To produce characters on paper, the wheels rotate into position, forming an entire line of characters, then a hammer presses paper against the wheels.

Privacy An individual's right regarding the collection, processing, storage, dissemination, and use of data about his or her personal attributes and activities.

Problem definition The portion of the software development process where the problem to be solved is defined including desired output, needed input and processing requirements.

Problem-oriented language A programming language where the problem and solution can be described without requiring a high level of programming skills.

Procedure-oriented language A programming language where the emphasis is placed on the computational and logical procedures required to solve a problem.

Process To transform data into useful information by classifying, sorting, calculating, summarizing, or storing.

Process-bound A condition that occurs when a program monopolizes the processing facilities of the computer, making it impossible for other programs to be executed.

Processing The portion of the data processing flow that occurs in a computer's CPU.

Processing program A routine, usually part of the operating system, that is used to simplify program preparation and execution.

Processing requirements The portion of the software development process that turns needed input into desired output.

Processor The term used collectively to refer to the ALU and control unit.

Productivity tools Application software packages that can increase the productivity of the user. Examples are text processors and graphics packages.

Program The instructions issued to the computer so that specific tasks may be completed; also referred to as software.

Program specifications The documentation for a programming problem definition; it includes the desired output, needed input, and the processing requirements.

Programmable communications processor A device that relieves the CPU of the task of monitoring data transmission.

Programmable read-only memory (PROM) Read-only memory that can be programmed by the manufacturer or by the user for special functions to meet the unique needs of the user.

Programming language A communication system people can use to communicate with computers.

Prompt A message or cue that guides a user—it indicates to the user what type of input is required or what might be wrong in the case of an error.

Proper program A structured program in which each individual segment or module has only one entrance and one exit.

Protocol The description of the rules of communication when transmitting and receiving data on a network.

Pseudocode An informal design language used to represent the logic of a programming problem solution.

Public domain software Programs unprotected by copyright law for free, unrestricted public use.

Punched card A heavy paper storage medium on which data is represented by holes punched according to a coding scheme much like that used on Hollerith's cards.

Random-access memory (RAM) A form of memory into which instructions and data can be read, written, and erased; directly accessed by the computer; temporary memory that is erased when the computer is turned off.

Random-access memory (RAM) disk A portion of RAM memory that is temporarily treated as a storage device.

Randomizing A mathematical process applied to the record key that produces the storage address of the record.

Reading The process of accessing the same instructions or data over and over.

Read-only memory (ROM) The part of computer hardware containing items (circuitry patterns) that cannot be deleted or changed by stored-program instructions because they are wired into the computer.

Read/write head An electromagnet used as a component of a tape or disk drive; in reading data, it detects magnetized areas and translates them into electrical pulses; writing data, it magnetizes appropriate areas and erases data stored there previously.

Read/write notch The oblong or rectangular opening in the jacket of a floppy disk through which the read/write head accesses the disk.

Real memory *See* Memory.

Recalculation A feature that automatically adjusts the result of a formula when a cell used in the formal changes.

Record A collection of data items, or fields, that relates to a single unit, such as a student.

Region In multiprogramming, with a variable number of tasks, a term often used to mean the internal space allocated for a particular program; a variable-sized partition.

Register An internal computer component used for temporary storage of an instruction or data; capable of accepting, holding, and transferring that instruction or data very rapidly.

Relational data base A data base that allows the user to open and use data from several files at one time.

Relational structure The data structure that places the data elements in a table with rows representing records and columns containing fields.

Reliability The ability of a program to consistently obtain correct results.

Remote system A system in which terminals are connected to the central computer by a communication channel.

Remote terminal A terminal that is placed at a location distant from the central computer.

Remote-terminal operator A person involved with the preparation of input data at a location at some distance from the computer itself.

Resident routine A frequently used component of the supervisor that is initially loaded into memory.

Retrieve To access previously stored data.

RGB (red-green-blue) monitors A computer monitor that displays in three colors with high resolution.

Ring configuration A network design in which a number of computers are connected by a single transmission line in a ring formation.

Robotics The science that deals with robots, their construction, capabilities, and applications.

Root directory In the MS- and PC-DOS operating systems, the root directory is the directory created by default when a floppy disk or hard disk is formatted. There can be only one root directory per disk.

Scanner A device that reads printed material so that it can be put in a computer-readable form without having to retype, redraw, reprint, or rephotograph the material.

Schema A program that describes how records and files within a database are related to one another.

Screen-formatting A function of a word processor that controls how the text will appear on the screen.

Screen-oriented word processing A word processor that ideally matches what is seen on the screen with what is printed on paper. See also WYSIWYG.

Script theory A theory used in the research of artificial intelligence which is based on the concept that any circumstance can be described by a script. For example, each person may have a dentist office script, a classroom script, and a restaurant script. These scripts shape a person's behavior and influence how he or she may react in similar situations. Script theory attempts to apply this logic to computers so that they may "think" like humans.

Scrolling Moving a line of text onto or off the screen.

Search A feature that lets you look for a word or phrase in a document.

Search and replace A feature that finds a certain word or phrase but also lets you replace it with another word or phrase.

Secondary key Fields that are used to gain access to records on a file; may not be unique identifiers.

Second-generation computer A computer that used transistors; it was smaller, faster, and had larger storage capacity than the first-generation computers.

Segment A variable-sized block or portion of a program used in a virtual memory system.

Segmentation A method of implementing virtual memory; involves dividing a program into variable-sized blocks, called segments, depending on the program logic.

Selection A logic pattern that requires the computer to make a comparison; the result of the comparison determines which execution path will be taken next.

Selector channel A channel that can accept input from only one device at a time; generally used with high-speed I/O devices such as a magnetic tape or magnetic-disk unit.

Semiconductor memory Memory composed of circuitry on silicon chips; smaller than magnetic cores and allows for faster processing; more expensive than core memory and requires a constant power source.

Sequential file design Records are organized in a file in a specific order based on the value of the key field.

Sequential processing The process of creating a new master file each time transactions are processed; requires batch file access.

Serial processing A method of processing in which programs are executed one at a time; usually found in simple operating systems such as those used on the earliest computer systems.

Shareware Programs that are distributed to the public; the author retains the copyright to the programs with the expectation that users will make donations to the author based upon the value of the program to the users.

Silicon chip Solid-logic circuitry on a small piece of silicon used to form the memory of third- and fourth-generation computers.

Simple sequence A logic pattern in which one statement is executed after another, in the order in which they occur in the program.

Simple structure A data structure in which the records in a computer file are arranged sequentially.

Simulation The use of a model to project the outcome of a particular real-world situation.

Simultaneous decision support system A decision support system that attempts to incorporate into one system the decision making of various functional areas of an organization so that consistent, overall decisions can be made by management.

Six-bit Binary Coded Decimal (BCD) A data representation scheme that is used to represent the decimal digits 0 through 9, the letters A through Z, and twenty-eight special characters.

Soft copy A temporary, or nonpermanent, record of machine output; for example, a CRT display.

Software Program or programs used to direct the computer in solving problems and overseeing operations.

Software copying (piracy) The unauthorized copying of a computer program.

Software development process A sequence of four steps used to develop the solution to a programming problem in a structured manner. The steps are: (1) Define and document the problem. (2) Design and document a solution. (3) Write and document the program. (4) Debug and test the program and revise the documentation, if necessary.

Sort A feature used to arrange the records in a file.

Sort/merge program A type of operating system utility program; used to sort records to facilitate updating and subsequent combining of files to form a single, updated file.

Source-data automation The use of special equipment to collect data at its source.

Special-purpose language A computer programming language that has been designed for a specific purpose.

Spelling checker Application software that checks words in a document against a dictionary file. Any words in the document that are not in the file are flagged. Spelling checkers are often included in word processing packages.

Spreadsheet A spreadsheet is a grid of columns and rows used to store and manipulate numeric information. The electronic spreadsheet takes the place of ledger sheets used by accountants.

Stand-alone program A single, self-contained application program that serves one purpose.

Star configuration A network design in which all transactions must go through a central computer before being routed to the appropriate network computer.

Statistical package A software package that performs statistical analysis of data. Examples are SAS, SPSS, and Minitab.

Status area Lines at either the top or the bottom of the screen make up the status area and provide information about the cell at the cursor's position.

Status line A message line above or below the text area on a display screen that gives format and system information.

Stepped Reckoner Machine designed by von Liebniz that could add, subtract, multiply, divide, and calculate square roots.

Storage Also referred to as secondary, external, or auxiliary storage; supplements memory and is external to the CPU; data is accessed at slower speeds.

Stored program Instructions stored in the computer's memory in electronic form; can be executed repeatedly during processing.

Stored-program concept The idea that program instructions can be stored in memory in electrical form so that no human intervention is required during processing; allows the computer to process the instructions at its own speed.

Structure chart A graphic representation of the results of the top-down design process, displaying the modules of the solution and their relationships to one another; of two types, system and process.

Structured language A computer programming language that is used to develop programs that are modular, logical, and easy to modify and maintain.

Structured programming A collection of techniques that encourages the development of well-designed, less error-prone programs with easy-to-follow logic. Structured programming techniques can be divided into two categories: (1) structured design techniques, such as top-down design, that are used in designing a problem solution, and (2) structure coding techniques, which state the rules that are followed when a program is actually coded.

Structured walkthrough *See* Formal design review.

Subdirectory In the MS- and PC-DOS operating systems, a subdirectory is an extension of the root directory.

Subroutine A sequence of statements not within the main line of the program; saves the programmer time by not having to write the same instructions over again in different parts of the program.

Supercomputer The largest, fastest, most expensive type of computer in existence, capable of performing millions of calculations per second and processing enormous amounts of data.

Superconductors Metals that are capable of transmitting high levels of current.

Supermicrocomputer A microcomputer built around a 32-bit microprocessor that is powerful enough to compete with low-end minicomputers.

Supervisor program Also known as a monitor or executive; the major component of the operating system; coordinates the activities of all other parts of the operating system.

Swapping In a virtual memory environment, the process of transferring a program section from virtual memory to memory, and vice versa.

Symbolic language The use of mnemonic symbols to represent instructions; must be translated into machine language before being executed by the computer.

Synergism A situation where the combined efforts of all parts of an information system achieve a greater effect than the sum of the individual parts.

Syntax The grammatical rules of a language.

System A group of related elements that work toward a common goal.

System analysis The process of determining the requirements for implementing and maintaining an information system.

System analysis report A report given to top management after the system analysis phase has been completed to report the findings of the system study; includes a statement of objectives, constraints, and possible alternatives.

System analyst The person who is responsible for system analysis, design, and implementation of computer-based information systems and who is the communication link or interface between users and technical persons.

System design report The phase of the system life cycle in which information system design alternatives are developed and presented to management. These alternatives should contain information on system inputs, processing, and outputs.

System flowchart The group of symbols that represents the general information flow; focuses on inputs and outputs rather than on internal computer operations.

System library A collection of files in which various parts of an operating system are stored.

System program Programs that coordinate the operation of computer circuitry and assist in the development of application programs. System programs are designed to facilitate the efficient use of the computer's resources.

System programmer The person responsible for creating and maintaining system software.

System residence device A storage device (disk, tape, or drum) on which operating-system programs are stored and from which they are loaded into memory.

Systems integrator An operating environment that makes it possible to move data from one stand-alone program to another. A systems integrator uses windows to allow the simultaneous operation of stand-alone programs.

Tab A feature that works the same as the tab key on a typewriter. Options include tabs that place columns of words and numbers to the left, center, or right of the tab sitting.

Tape drive A device that moves magnetic tape past a read/write head.

Telecommunication The combined use of communication facilities, such as telephone systems and data-processing equipment.

Telecommuting Method of working at home by communicating via telecommunication facilities.

Telecomputing A term referring to the use of online information services that offer access to one or more data bases; for example, CompuServe, The Source, Prodigy and Dow Jones News/Retrieval.

Teleconferencing The method of two or more remote locations communicating via electronic and image-producing facilities.

Telecopier system *See* Facsimile system.

Template In a spreadsheet program, a template is a set of predefined formulas already entered into the spreadsheet so that new figures can be entered without having to reenter the formulas.

Testing The process of executing a program with input data that is either a representative sample of actual data or a facsimile of it to determine if it will always obtain correct results.

Third-generation computer A computer characterized by the use of integrated circuits, reduced size, lower costs, and increased speed and reliability.

Thrashing Programs in which little actual processing occurs in comparison to the amount of swapping.

Time-sharing system An arrangement in which two or more users can access the same central computer resources and receive what seem to be simultaneous results.

Time slicing A technique used in a time-sharing system that allocates a small portion of processing time to each user.

Top-down design A method of defining a solution in terms of major functions to be performed, and further breaking down the major functions into subfunctions; the further the breakdown, the greater the detail.

Touch-tone device A terminal used with ordinary telephone lines to transmit data.

Track A horizontal row following the length of a magnetic tape on which data can be recorded; one of a series of concentric circles on the surface of a magnetic disk.

Transaction file A file containing changes to be made to the master file.

Transient routine A supervisor routine that remains in memory with the remainder of the operating system.

Transistor A type of circuitry characteristic of second-generation computers; smaller, faster, and more reliable than vacuum tubes but inferior to third-generation, large-scale integration.

Transit field The section of a check, preprinted with magnetic ink, that includes the bank number.

Transparent user interface An operating system that reduces the amount of knowledge required by a user.

Transportable computer A computer that weighs more than seventeen pounds, but is still small enough to be carried; requires an external power source. It contains a hard disk drive and is normally comparable in power to a desktop microcomputer.

Turnkey system An integrated system including hardware, software, training, and support developed for particular businesses.

Undo A feature that cancels a command, allowing you to undo what you have done.

Uniform Commercial Code (UCC) A set of provisions proposed by legal experts to promote consistency among state courts in the legal treatment of commercial transactions between sellers and purchasers.

UNIVAC I (UNIVersal Automatic Computer) One of the first commercial electronic computers; became available in 1951.

Universal Product Code (UPC) A machine-readable code consisting of thirty dark bars and twenty-nine spaces that identifies a product and its manufacturer; commonly used on most grocery items.

Update A feature that allows you to change data contained in a record.

Unstructured language A computer programming language that results in programs that are poorly organized and difficult to modify and maintain.

Users group An informal group of owners of a particular microcomputer or software package who meet to exchange information about hardware, software, service, and support.

User friendly An easy-to-use, understandable software design that makes it easy for noncomputer personnel to use an application software package.

Utility program A program within an operating system that performs a specialized function.

Vacuum tube A device (resembling the light bulb) from which almost all air has been removed and through which electricity can pass; often found in old radios and televisions; used in first-generation computers to control internal operations.

Variable A meaningful name assigned by the programmer to memory locations of which the values can change.

Variable column width A software feature that allows the user to set the width of columns.

Verification Mathematically proving that a program or a program module is correctly designed.

Very-Large-Scale Integration (VLSI) A type of circuitry replacing large-scale integration in fourth-generation computers; smaller, faster, and less costly than large-scale integration.

Videoconferencing A technology that employs a two-way, full-motion video plus a two-way audio system for the purpose of conducting conferences between two remote locations through communication facilities.

Video seminar A form of teleconferencing that employs a one-way, full-motion video with two-way radio.

Virtual memory An extension of multiprogramming in which portions of programs not being used are kept in storage until needed, giving the impression that memory is unlimited; contrast with memory.

Virtual reality A computer system including hardware and software that enables a person to experience and manipulate a three-dimensional world that exists only in projected images.

Virtual storage *See* Virtual memory.

Virus A form of sabotage; a program that acts as a time bomb that can destroy the contents of a hard or floppy disk.

Visual table of contents Used in HIPO packages; includes blocks with identification numbers that are used as a reference in other HIPO diagrams.

Voice mail *See* Voice message system.

Voice message system (VMS) The sender activates a special ''message'' key on the telephone, dials the receiver's number, and records the message. A button lights on the receiver's phone, and when it is convenient, the receiver can activate the phone and listen to the message.

Voice recognition A method of data entry that involves speaking into a microphone attached to a computer system.

Voice synthesizer A method of computer output that provides information to users in the form of sequences of sound that resemble the human voice.

Voice-grade channel A communication channel that has a wider frequency range and can transmit data at rates between 300 and 9,600 bits per second; for example, a telephone line.

Volatility The frequency of changes made to a file during a certain period of time.

Wand reader A device used in reading source-data represented in optical bar-code form.

Window The portion of a document that can be seen on the computer display screen.

Word processor An application software package designed for the preparation of text; involves writing, editing, and printing.

Word size The number of bits that can be manipulated at one time.

Words Storage locations within memory.

Word wrap The feature by which a word is automatically moved to the beginning of the next line if it goes past the right margin.

Working directory The directory where the user is located on either a floppy disk or a hard disk in the MS- or PC-DOS operating system.

Workstations The members of a local-area network (LAN) where work on applications takes place.

Writing The process of storing new instructions or data in computer memory.

WYSIWYG A common term that is used when discussing word processors, pronounced *wizeewig*. The letters stand for ''what you see is what you get.'' This means that what you see on the screen matches as closely as possible what actually appears when the document is printed.

Xerographic printer A type of nonimpact printer that uses printing methods similar to those used in common xerographic copying machines.

Zone bit A bit used in different combinations with numeric bits to represent numbers, letters, and special characters.

Index

educational uses, 20–21, 152
ergonomics and, 416–418
evolution of, 27–54
"father" of, 31
fire threats, 443–444
first generation of, 34–36
fishing implementation, 194
food company uses, 390–391
fourth generation of, 39–41
functions of, 9
future of, 41
generations of, 34–41
  chart, 41
  components, 40
government uses, 22
health problems and, 416–418
history of, 27–54
impact of, 411–433
industrial uses, 425–429
information processing and, 3
insurance uses, 18
job-displacement problems, 415–416
journalism and, 194
law enforcement uses, 2, 22, 149, 442–443
library uses, 160
mainframe, 14–15
manufacturing uses, 18, 67, 352–353, 427
management uses, 424
medical implementations, 21–22, 152, 471–474
  computerized axial tomography, 472
  diagnosis, 471–473
  multiphasic health testing, 471
  rehabilitation uses, 473–474
menu-driven, 371
micro, 12, 187–220
military uses, 237
mini, 13–14
miniaturization of, 39–41, 190
monitoring uses, 21
movies/special effects and, 20
next generation of, 41
office automation, 19
parking violation uses, 2
photography uses, 20
portable, 193–194
purchase of, 207
  chart, 16
restaurant implementations, 108
retraining and, 415–416
sales and marketing uses, 18, 116–117, 194, 424–425
science uses, 462, 475
second generation of, 36–38
size of, 11
speed of, 9, 42, 149, 464
  factors influencing, 9
  in parallel processing, 466
  source-data automation and, 112
  units of measure, 9
standardization of, 38

storage in, 10
super, 15–16
surgery implementations, 472–473
third generation of, 38–39
travel reservation systems, 151
types of, 11
theft in, 440–441
uses, 16–22
voice recognition, 111, 213
volcano research and, 476
weather forecasting uses, 476–477
women and, 414
workplace implementations, 416–417
computer security, 443–446
  and ALCOA, 459–460
  and computer viruses, 436–437, 439
  and encryption of data, 444–445
  and voice recognition, 445
  in the military, 446
  company policies, 445
  threats to, 443–444
computer scanners, 111
computer software, see software
  accounting, 337
  CASE packages, 340
  choosing, 347–349
  commercial, 333–334
  data-base management systems, 346–347
  decision support systems, 343–344
  definition of, 3
  desktop publishing, 337
  electronic spreadsheets, 335–336
  end-user software development tools, 346
    in marketing, 391
  expert systems, 345–346, A-71–A-79
  file managers, 336
  functional tools, 336–341
  graphics, 335
  in business, 336–341
  in manufacturing, 337–339
  mail-merge, 335
  productivity tools, 334–336
  sales analysis, 340
  simulation, 342–343
  statistical, 346
  turnkey systems, 340–341
  word processing, 334–335
computer speed, see computers
computer storage, 135
  see storage
computer support services, 43
  see customer services
computer system
  components of, 83
  crash conversion, 380
  data communication in, 223
  direct conversion, 380
  evaluation of, 380
  local, 233
  parallel conversion, 379

parts of, 83
phased conversion, 380
pilot conversion, 379–380
remote, 233
storage in, 136
testing of, 377
time-sharing, 233–234
top-down design, 397–398
user friendly, 371
computer training, 209
computer trends, 463–466
computer viruses, 436–437
  containment of, 436
  definition of, 439
computer warranties, 452–453
Computing-Tabulating-Recording Company
  (CTR), 31, 104
concentrators, 231–232
concurrent processing, 261
condition entries, 366
condition stub, 366
conditional programming logic, 279
construction, computers in, 18
consultation and expert systems, A-71
Consultative Committee on International Telephone & Telegraph, 239
context-sensitive help option
  in integrated software, A-67
  in Windows 3.0, A-84
continuous form, 117
control panel
  Macintosh, 501–502
  Windows 3.0, A-81
Control Program for Microprocessors, 197
control programs, 256–258
control structures, 306–315
  see logic patterns
control unit, 83
conversion, in system implementation, 379–380
coordinate, in electronic spreadsheets, A-29
coprocessor, 206
COPY command in MS-DOS, 491
copy protection, 211
copyright
  Apple and Microsoft, 455
  law, 453–456
  unsettled issues, 455–456
Copyright Act of 1976, 453
core memory, 87, 93
corporate planning models, 404
Corporation for Open Systems (COS), 239
cost/benefit analysis, 375–376
Countess of Lovelace, see Byron, Augusta Ada
CP/M, see Control Program for Microprocessors
CPU, see central processing unit
CPT, see chief programmer team
crash conversion, 380
Crime Control Act of 1973, 451
crime control, computers in, 22, 149, 442–443
crime prevention, 441–446

electrothermal printer, 123
e-mail, see electronic mail
emergency 9-1-1 systems, 22
employees
  computer security and, 444–445, 447–448
  education and, 482–483
  telecommuting and, 241
encryption technology, 444–445
Enigma, 32
end-user development tools, 341–345
engineering, computer-aided, 68
ENIAC, see Electronic Numerical Integrator and
  Calculator
entry mode in electronic spreadsheets, A-31
environment, systems, 59–61
EPROM, see erasable programmable read-only
  memory
erasable optical (E-O) drive, 152
erasable programmable read-only memory, 90
ergonomics, 416–418
error handling
  assembler programs and, 309
  input and, 109
  language translators and, 296, 307
  software and, 210, 281–282
  system programming and, 377
errors
  C and, 320
  desk checking and, 297
  structured programming techniques and, 283
  structured review and, 293
Ethernet, 238
ethics, 446–448
even parity, 100
evolution of computers, 27–54
exception reports, 396
Exchange Carrier Standards Association, 239
executive program, see supervisor program
executable files (MS-DOS), 201
expansion boards, see add-ons
expert system, 466, 345–347
  decision support systems and, 404
  food processing and, 356
  medical, 471
  real-time, 466, A-78
  space shuttle cargo and, 348
expert system shell, 346, A-72–A-73
expert system (supplement), A-71–A-79
  backward chaining, A-76
  definition, A-71–A-74
  explanation capacity, A-75
  explanation subsystem, A-75–A-76
  features of, A-75–A-76
  forward chaining in, A-76
  fuzzy sets in, A-76
  hardware requirements, A-77
  trends, A-77–A-78
  user friendly, A-75
  uses of, A-74–A-75
expert system toolkit, A-73

express warranties, 453
Extended Binary Coded Decimal Interchange
  Code, 99, 136
  representation chart, 99
external storage, see storage

F

facsimile system, 420
fail/safe, 412
Fairchild Semiconductor, 38
families of computers, 38
  and IBM, 104
Family Educational Rights and Privacy Act of
  1974, 451
"father" backup copies, 165
"father of computers," 31
FAX, see facsimile system
feasibility analysis in system design, 373
Federal Bureau of Investigation, 22, 442
Federal Express, 130–132
Federal Reserve System, 241
feedback, 8
  in information systems, 59
fiber optics, 224, 225, 464–465
  and local-area networks, 238
field, 4, 162
  in data managers, A-46, A-47
  in relational data bases, 178
  shared relation in, A-49
fifth-generation computers, 41
file, 161
  activity in, 166
  and data managers, A-46, A-47
  definition of, 6
  inverted, 176
  organization of, 159–173
  physical and logical, 175
  volatility of, 167
file access, 163
file arrangement, 161
file commands (MS-DOS), 491–492
file design, 163–173
file handler, 204
file locking in data managers, A-58
file manager, 336, A-47–A-48
  in Windows 3.0, A-81
File menu (Macintosh), 503–506
  Close, 505
  Duplicate, 505
  Eject, 506
  Get Info, 505
  New Folder, 504
  Open, 504–505
  Print, 505
  Put Away, 505
file name extensions in MS-DOS, 202
file names in MS-DOS, 202
file organization, 159–173

file processing, 161
  and programming languages, 325
files and MS-DOS operating system conventions,
  201–203
  batch, 201–202
  data, 201, 202
  executable, 201
  program, 201
file server, 236
file specifications in system design, 373
financial crimes, 440–441
financing, computers in, 65
Finder, Macintosh, 199, 501
Find file (Macintosh), 502
fingerprint scanners, 69
firmware, 89
first-generation computers, 34–36
  and machine language, 36
first-generation robots, 429
First Information Processing Co, Inc., 329–330
fishing by computer, 194
fixed scanner, 116
flat-file managers, see file managers
flat panel display screens, 127
  and portables, 194
flexible disk, see floppy disk
flight simulator, 271
flight trainer, 36
floppy disk, 145
  background, 145
  mass storage and, 148
  microcomputers and, 212
  parts of, 146
flowchart symbols, 289
flowcharts, 288
FOCUS programming language, 323
folder icon (Macintosh), 199, 494
fonts, 121, 123, 213
  data managers and, A-56
  Macintosh, 199
  spreadsheets and, A-42
  word processors and, A-24
Ford Motor Company, 352–353
formal design review, 293
formal reports in system analysis, 361, 362
formatting
  cells in electronic spreadsheets, A-37
  documents in word processors, 204, 334,
    419–420, A-12–A-17
formatting a disk, see initializing
formulas, in electronic spreadsheets, 204, 336,
  A-28, A-36
FORTRAN, 310–311, 325
  example, 312–313
  origin of, 305
FORTRAN 8X, 310
four-bit binary coded decimal, 98
fourth-generation computers, 39, 41
fourth-generation programming languages
  (4GL), 322, 323

law enforcement, 2, 149, 442–443
LCD, see liquid-crystal display
letter-quality printers, 213
Lewinski, Richard, and Enigma, 32
LEXIS network, 244
librarian, computer, 69
  and chief programmer team, 292
library/librarian program, 259, 307
Library of Congress, 22, 134, 151
light pen, 111, 213
linear structure, 176
line-at-a-time printers, 120, 121
link, in multiple CPU networks, 234
linkage editor, 259, 307
liquid crystal display, 127
load module, 307
local-area network, 236–238
  copyright and, 454
  crime data bases and, 149
  data managers and, A-58
  fiber optics and, 464–465
  in the military, 237
  Mount Sinai Medical Center and, 488
  scheduling communication satellites and, 240
local system, 233
logical comparisons, 9, 83, 296
logical file, 175
logical relationships and data base structure, 180
logic patterns for programs, 278–280
  action diagrams and, 291
  flowcharts and, 290
  pseudocode and, 288
Logo programming language, 321–322
  example, 322
loop logic pattern, 279, 281
loop programming statement, 296
low-level programming language, 306, 307–310
LSI, see large-scale integration

M

machine-dependent languages, 310
machine-independent languages, 316
machine language, 305, 307
  advantages of, 308
  definition of, 36
  job-control language and, 257
Macintosh, see Apple Computer, Inc.
Macintosh, background, 46
Macintosh conventions/commands, 494–512
  alarm clock, 499
  Apple menu, 500–503
  calculator, 499, 500
  chooser, 499–500
  clicking, 494, 496
  dialog boxes, 498, 499
  double clicking, 496
  dragging, 496–497
  Edit menu, 506–508
  File menu, 503–506

icons, 494
initializing disks, 498–499
pointing, 494
Special menu, 510–512
View menu, 508–510
windows, 497–499
Macintosh Finder, 195, 196, 197, 198
Macintosh user interface, 262
macros, 211
  electronic spreadsheets and, A-39–A-40
  software package, 336
  word processing and, A-21, A-22
magnetic bubble memory, 149
magnetic cores, 36, 37, 87
  data representation in, 93
magnetic disk, 10, 109, 135, 141
  advantages and disadvantages of, 145–146
  beginning of, 37
  characteristics of, 147
  floppy, 145
  selectors and, 233
magnetic disk drive, 168
magnetic domains, 89
magnetic drums, 36, 256
magnetic-ink character reader, 112
magnetic-ink character recognition, 112–113, 114, 359
magnetic-ink characters, 113
magnetic-ink character set, 114
magnetic tape, 10, 37, 109, 135
  advantages and disadvantages of, 140–141
  cartridges, 140
  characteristics of, 135, 141
  definition of, 35
  interblock gaps, 138, 139
  interrecord gaps on, 138–139
  sequential file processing and, 166
  selectors and, 233
magnetic tape drive, 137
mail-merge, 335
mail-order, microcomputers, 208
main control module, and structured programing, 284
main memory/storage, see memory
main module, MIS, 397
main system board, 191, 192
mainframe, origin of, 83
mainframe computers, 14–15
  cost of, 14
  installation, 14
  manufacturers of, 15, 104–106
  multiprocessing and, 266
  vendors, 14–15
maintenance programmer, 70–71
management
  computers and, 424
  decision-making levels, 392–395
  functional information flow to, 394
management information system, 389–410
  Ace Hardware and, 432–433

compared with data processing, 392
  design methodology, 397–399
  Pepsi-Cola Company and, 408–410
  problems of, 394, 396–397
  reports for, 395–396
management information system manager, 73
management system design, 400–401
manual data entry methods, 109–111
manufacturing, 18
  and materials requirement planning, 67
manufacturing application packages, 337
manufacturing resource planning, 338
maps, computerized and customized, 341
marketing, and information systems, 66, 424–425
mark-sensing, see optical-mark recognition
Mark I, 32
mass storage, 135, 147–148
  General Dynamics and, 157
  lasers and minicomputers, 150
  optical disks and crime data bases, 149
master file
  direct-access file design and, 168
  sequential processing and, 164, 168
materials requirement planning, 67
math coprocessor, 206
math, in word processing, A-20
matrices
  and bit cells, 87–88
  printers and, 120–121, 123
Mauchly, John, 32, 34
McCarthy, John, 466
medicine, computers in, 21–22
  hypermedia in, 152
  monitoring in, 21–22
megahertz, 92
membrane keyboards, 212
memory, 84, 86–91, 135
  bubble, 89
  cache, 91
  chips, 38, 87
  CPU and, 83
  definition of, 6
  erasable programmable read-only, 90
  locations, 86
    and dumps, 298
    and machine language, 306–308
    in virtual memory, 263
  operating systems and, 257
  primary, 87
  programmable read-only, 90
  random-access, 89
  read-only, 89–90
  registers, 91
  semiconductor, 87, 93
  size of, 10
  words and, 95
memory-based word processor, A-5
memory management/protection, 262
memory segmentation, 84
menu bars, 200, 201

menu-driven computer system, in system design, 371

menus
  data managers and, A-58
  graphic user interfaces, 198
  information services and, 242, 243, 244
  pull-down, 199
  transparent user interfaces and, 197

message switching, 233

MHz, see megahertz

mice, see mouse

MICR, see magnetic-ink character recognition

microcomputer
  add-ons, 213
  monitors, 211–212
  peripherals, 212–213
  ports, 191–192
  printers, 212–213

microcomputers, 12, 187–220
  advertising and, 71
  buyer's checklist, 214–215
  characteristics of, 189–190
  choosing, 207–213
  compact disks and, 151
  competition in, 195
  copyright law and, 454–455
  cost of, 12, 190
  development, 39, 45–48
  diskettes and, 145
  earthquake prediction and, 462
  guide to purchase, 207–213
  home use, 478
  input devices, 109–111
  insurance business and, 18
  kit form, 46
  laptop, 19
  mail-order purchase of, 208
  manufacturers of, 46–48
  market for, 12
  operating systems for, 195–203
  pioneers in, 46–48
  popularity of, 12, 39, 189
  portables, 193–194
  power of, 12
  processors in, 83
  programming languages for, 325
  sizes of, 195
  software for, 12
  tape storage for, 135
  text retrieval and, 56
  uses of, 194, 204

microfloppy disk, 145

microphones, 111

microprocessors, 12, 40, 83
  bits and, 45
  choosing, 211
  compared to mainframes, 190
  definition of, 12
  development of, 28, 39, 45
  medical uses, 473–474

microcomputers and, 190
  parallel processing and, 465–466
  patent, 28
  manufacturing of, 45
  multiple, 194
  operating systems and, 197
  speed of, 92
  supermicrocomputers and, 194
  uses of, 45–46

microprograms, 90

Microsoft, 188, 271–272
  copyright and Apple, 455
  MS-DOS and PC DOS, 197
  Windows 3.0, 195, 196, 197, 198, 272

microwave communication channels, 224, 225–226

middle-level programming language, 319

military, computers in, 237, 446

minicomputers, 13–14, 38, 39
  compared with microcomputer networks, 195
  communication and, 13
  installation, 13
  manufacturers of, 14
  market for, 13–14
  mass storage and, 148, 150
  modular implementation of, 13
  software for, 13
  text retrieval and, 56
  uses of, 13

mini supercomputers, 16

Minsky, Marvin, 466

MIPS (millions of instructions per second), 9

MIS, see management information system

MITS, 46

MKDIR (or MD) command (MS-DOS), 489

mnemonic symbols
  in assembly language, 308
  in symbolic languages, 36

modems, 213, 228–229
  and portables, 194
  and telecommuting, 241

modes, of channels, 226

models
  decision support systems and, 403–404
  earthquake prediction and, 475–476
  medical use, 473
  reliability of, 412–413
  simulation software, 342
  system model, 370
    versus prototyping, 382
  weather forecasting and, 476–477

modular approach to software design, 283–284

modular programs, 283

modulation, 228

modules, 283
  chief programmer team and, 292
  Oberon and, 274
  Pascal and, 315
  structured programming and, 294–295
  testing and, 296–297

top-down design (MIS) and, 397

molecular electronics, 464

monitor program, see supervisor program

monitor resolution, 126–127

monitors, see visual display devices
  choosing, 211, 214
  composite color, 126
  monochrome, 126
  multimedia and, 151
  RGB, 126–127

monochrome monitors, 126

MOS Technology, 47

motherboard, see main system board

Mount Sinai Medical Center, 487–488

mouse, 109, 213

MRP, see materials requirement planning

MS-DOS, see Microsoft
  conventions, 200–203
  graphic user interface for, 198
  operating system commands, 489–493

multichip modules, 464

multimedia, 21, 480–481
  compact disks and, 151
  programming and, 283
  software integration and, A-70
  transparent user interfaces and, 197, 198, 199

multiphasic health testing, 471

multiple CPU networks, 234–236

multiplexers, 231–232

multiprocessing, 265
  definition of, 265
  diagram of, 266–267

multiprogramming, 260–262
  and Ada, 319
  virtual storage and, 262–263

multitasking, A-84
  see multiprogramming

N

nanoseconds, 9

Napier's Bones/rods, 29

Napier, John, 29

narrow bandwidth channels, 226

National Bureau of Standards, 239

National Crime Information Center, 442

natural programming languages, 323–325
  robots and, 469
  telephone computing and, 468, 478
  voice recognition and, 468

NBS, see National Bureau of Standards

NCIC, see National Crime Information Center

NDT, see nondestructive testing

near-letter-quality characters, 121, 213

near-typeset quality, 337

needed input, 277

network data structure, 178, 179, 347

network configuration, 234–236

network interface card (NIC), 237

CREDITS

Articles

Chapter 1:	Reprinted from *Computerworld,* August 27, 1990. © 1990 by CW Publishing, Inc., Framingham, MA 01701.
Chapter 2:	Reprinted from *Computerworld,* September 3, 1990. © 1990 by CW Publishing, Inc., Framingham, MA 01701.
Chapter 3:	Reprinted from *Business Week,* June 18, 1990, by special permission. © 1990 by McGraw-Hill, Inc.
Chapter 4:	Reprinted from *Business Week,* June 15, 1990. © 1990 by McGraw-Hill, Inc.
Chapter 5:	Reprinted from *Computerworld,* April 30, 1990. © 1990 by C.W. Publishing, Inc. Framingham, MA 01701.
Chapter 6:	Reprinted from *Computerworld,* September 10, 1990. © 1990 by C.W. Publishing, Inc., Framingham, MA 01701.
Chapter 7:	Reprinted from *Computerworld,* November 19, 1990. © 1990 by C.W. Publishing, Inc., Framingham, MA 01701.
Chapter 8:	Reprinted from *InfoWorld,* July 8, 1991. © 1991 by *Info World* Publishing Corp., a subsidiary of IDG Communications, Inc., 155 Bovet Road, San Mateo, CA 94402. Further reproduction is prohibited.
Chapter 9:	Reprinted from *Computerworld,* January 14, 1991. © 1991 by C.W. Publishing, Inc., Framingham, MA 01701.
Chapter 10:	Reprinted from *Computerworld,* October 8, 1990. © 1990 by C.W. Publishing, Inc., Framingham, MA 01701.
Chapter 11:	Reprinted from *Business Week,* Innovation 1990, by special permission. © 1990 by McGraw Hill, Inc.
Chapter 12:	Reprinted from *Computerworld,* June 24, 1991. © 1991 by C.W. Publishing, Inc., Framingham, MA 01701.
Chapter 13:	Reprinted from *Computerworld,* December 17, 1990. © 1990 by C.W. Publishing, Inc., Framingham, MA 01701.
Chapter 14:	Reprinted from *Computerworld,* September 17, 1990. © 1990 by C.W. Publishing, Inc., Framingham, MA 01701.
Chapter 15:	Reprinted from *Business Week,* July 2, 1990, by special permission. © 1990 by McGraw-Hill, Inc.
Chapter 16:	Reprinted from *Computerworld,* November 5, 1990. © 1990 by C.W. Publishing, Inc., Framingham, MA 01701.
Chapter 17:	Reprinted from *Computerworld,* September 10, 1990. © 1990 by C.W. Publishing, Inc., Framingham, MA 01701.
Chapter 18:	Reprinted from *Computerworld,* January 7, 1991. © 1991 by C.W. Publishing, Inc., Framingham, MA 01701.

Photo Credits

Chapter 1: **1** © Lou Jones, the Image Bank; **10** Bill Gallery, Stock Boston; **12** Mosgrove, courtesy Apple Computer, Inc.; **13** courtesy Unisys Corporation; **14** courtesy Unisys Corporation; **17** courtesy Unisys Corporation; **18** (top) courtesy Hewlett-Packard Corporation; **18** (bottom) courtesy Cincinnati Milacron; **19** (top) courtesy Compaq Corporation; **19** (bottom) courtesy Roland Corporation; **21** (top) courtesy Kurzweil Applied Intelligence, Inc.; **21** (bottom) © Chris Jones, the Stock Market; **22** © Kent Dufault, courtesy AT&T; **26** courtesy Texas Instruments.

Chapter 2: **27** courtesy International Business Machines, Corporation; **29, 30** (both photos) **31** (all three photos), **32** courtesy International Business Machines Corporation; **33** courtesy Unisys Corporation; **34** The Institute for Advanced Study, Princeton, New Jersey; **35** (top) courtesy Unisys Corporation; **35** (bottom) courtesy of the National Museum of American History; **36, 37** (top & bottom) courtesy International Business Machines Corporation; **38** courtesy Digital Equipment Corporation; **40** (top) courtesy International Business Machines Corporation; **40** (bottom) courtesy Motorola, Inc.; **43** courtesy International Business Machines Corporation; **44** courtesy Hewlett-Packard Company; **47** (top three photos) courtesy Apple Computer, Inc.; **47** (bottom) courtesy Commodore Business Machines, Inc.; **48** (top left